DISCARD

Broadcasting in Asia and the Pacific

International and Comparative Broadcasting
A Series Edited by Sydney W. Head

Broadcasting in Asia and the Pacific

A Continental Survey of
Radio and Television

Edited by
John A. Lent

Temple University Press
Philadelphia

Temple University Press, Philadelphia 19122

Published 1978 jointly with Heinemann Educational Books (Asia) Ltd.,
Kowloon, Hong Kong

International Standard Book Number: 0 - 87722 - 068 - 9
Library of Congress Catalog Card Number: 75 - 44708

Support for this publication was provided by a generous grant from the
Press Foundation of Asia.

Contents

Bibliography

Preface

As is so often the case with ventures of this type, *Broadcasting in Asia and the Pacific* was prepared to fill a gap. For, although books have been written on individual national systems of the region (especially those of Japan, Australia, and India) and still others mentioned Asia and the Pacific as parts of world-wide surveys (notably UNESCO works and *World Radio & TV Handbook*), there has not been a systematic, descriptive treatment of all broadcasting services of the area within the covers of one volume. This book, then, is a first. It complements the regional works carried out by Sydney Head and Burton Paulu on broadcasting in Africa and Eastern Europe, respectively, as well as adding to the growing list of literature on Asian and Pacific mass media.

The last point is significant. For example, just in the five years since *Broadcasting in Asia and the Pacific* was conceived, numerous journals and newsletters *(e.g., Media Asia, Indian Press, Philippine Journal of Communications Studies, Leader: Malaysian Journalism Review, Pacific Islands Communication Newsletter, Media for Asia's Communications Industry, CEPTA Circuit)* have emerged to add to this store of knowledge. Actually, it has only been a little more than a decade in which most of the periodical literature on Asian mass media has appeared, usually following on the heels of the development of national or regional professional media organizations. Since 1964, the major regional organizations that have been created to deal with mass media training, production, and documentation include the Asian Broadcasting Union, Press Foundation of Asia, University of Philippines Institute of Mass Communications, National (Asian) Broadcasting Training Centre, Asian Mass Communication Research and Information Center, and CEPTA TV Association. In nearly every case, a plethora of research reports and periodicals resulted. By 1974, at least 140 mass-media training, educational, or research organizations functioned in Asia.

With the development of mass-media education and research of such magnitude, this book should prove useful to the increasing numbers of Asians who are pursuing studies in mass communications, as well to scholars throughout the world.

Broadcasting in this survey is meant to include radio and television, as well as wired systems, such as in China and in former British colonies which still have rediffusion services. Forty-four countries, territories, and dependencies, ranging from Afghanistan on the periphery of West Asia to the islands of the central South Pacific, form Asia and the Pacific as defined here. Asian countries are divided by the regional confines normally utilized by Asian scholars — East Asia, Southeast Asia, and South Asia. Full descriptions of seven East Asian countries are provided, plus some data on Mongolia. Ten Southeast Asian nations are portrayed in individual chapters, Brunei in a shorter section; and chapters on six South Asian countries, plus brief descriptions of Bhutan and Sikkim, are presented. Finally, 17 islands of Oceania complete the national systems portion of the volume. Not included are the Asian portion of the Soviet Union or the countries of the Middle East, often called West Asia.

In addition to national systems of broadcasting, ten cross-system functions of radio and television in the region are analyzed, including specialized program services such as international broadcasting, religious broadcasting, and instructional television, and international, regional, and national assistance programs in broadcasting provided by ABU, BBC, UNESCO, CEDO, etc.

The time period covered in most chapters was originally from the development of broadcasting — usually in the 1920s and 1930s — to 1972-73, when most of the volume was written. The Indonesia, Philippine, both Indochina, and religious broadcasting chapters, however were completely rewritten in 1975, and I updated all chapters to mid-1975, when fresh data were available. Because of many difficulties involved with my making a transition from Penang to Philadelphia (during which time the airlines "permanently misplaced" part of my luggage which included some of these manuscripts), and because of the financial situation in the book-publishing industry, the appearance of this book has been delayed. Despite these drawbacks, attempts have been made to make the time frame, as well as style and format, as even as possible, which is always a problem in a symposium of this sort.

All of the chapters, except one, were written exclusively for this book and represent original efforts on the part of the contributing authors. The first chapter, by Sir Charles Moses, is a reprint from *The 1974 Asian Press and Media Directory*, published by the Press Foundation of Asia, Manila.

Chapter authors represent a mixture of Asian and Pacific national broadcasting personnel and international communication scholars, trainers, and practitioners. Of the contributing authors writing on national systems, 13 are citizens of the countries they describe, two others are Asians writing about a country other than their own but with which they are familiar, and ten are international scholars and educators who have had extensive experience in Asia and the Pacific. The ten cross-system authors are nationals of the Philippines, Great Britain, Germany, United States, and the Pacific Islands who have worked in broadcasting education and development in the region.

Although the writers were given specific guidelines from the outset, some took different paths to arrive, in most cases, at similar destinations — i.e., at the structural and functional foundations of broadcasting. The guidelines included content and form suggestions, point of view desired, and checklists of national systems analysis topics and program and production analysis. The following criteria were suggested for evaluation of national broadcasting systems: special requirements imposed on broadcasting (by geographic, linguistic, social, political, economic, and military factors, and infrastructure); facilities (number of stations and receivers, types of emission, and reception employed); governance (supervising or licensing bodies, administrative and legal features, insulation from political control); finance (set-use fees, advertising revenue, other revenue, capital, and recurrent budgets); advertising practices (method of sales, salience, sponsorship, subject matter rules, rates, and business terms); programming (amounts by language and type, foreign and indigenous, network and local, types of services, specialized services, unusual features); program production organization; educational broadcasting; foreign influences; training facilities; relations with other media; pressures (government-political, economic, cultural-religious); and equipment.

For the most part, topics covered are oriented to historical development, control, ownership and pressures, programming and performance, facilities, financing and advertising, external services, audiences, training, and research. Examples of some approaches taken include territorial breakdown, as used by the authors of the Pacific Islands (dealing with 14 islands) and North Vietnam, Khmer, and Laos chapters; broadcasting subsystem analysis, as used in the Indonesian chapter to describe examples of Christian, rural, amateur, and schools broadcasting; the broadcasting organization technique, utilized especially in the Mácau chapter to explain Emissora de Radiodifusão de Mácau and Radio Vila Verde; or the ideological approach, used frequently in the chapters on China, North Korea, and Burma.

Topical emphasis varies from chapter to chapter as would be expected when describing nations of different ideological and developmental objectives. The same applies to chapter size: certainly broadcasting in China, Japan, or Australia merits more attention that that in Nepal, Mácau, or Fiji, primarily because the countries themselves are more prominently represented on a global sphere, but also because their broadcasting services are more highly developed. On the other hand, Afghanistan, which is hardly a major world power, receives considerable attention because it is used as an example of the problems broadcasters face in a multilingual, highly bureaucratic, and technically deficient society. In other cases, the size of the chapter depended on the amount of data available; thus the brevity of information on North Korea, Nepal, and Mácau.

Another difference in style that should be noted concerns the use of documentation. Although contributing authors were encouraged to use full documentation, this did not always occur. Often, this resulted from the lack of available written materials (for example, virtually nothing has been written on mass media in the Himalayan states of Nepal, Bhutan, and Sikkim), or because of the inaccessibility of government documents pertaining to broadcasting; many of these bureaucratic governments are extremely secretive. At other times, authors avoided citing sources because most of their information came from personal experiences, from work in broadcasting, or from personal contacts either through interviews or correspondence. Finally, the European and Asian academic disciplines, under which many of the contributing authors were educated, do not place as great an emphasis on citing sources as in the United States. For the convenience of the reader, citations have been incorporated briefly and parenthetically at the appropriate places in the text. These citations refer to a single composite bibliography for the entire work, which is alphabetized letter by letter.

Broadcasting in Asia and the Pacific is organized into three parts. Part 1 is an overview of broadcasting in Asia and the Pacific; Part 2, a description of the individual national systems; and Part 3, cross-system functions. Part 2 is further divided regionally (East Asia, Southeast Asia, South Asia, and Oceania), and Part 3 by specialized program services and assistance and cooperation programs. Each national system chapter is prefaced with historical and demographic data on the country. The order of countries within any region results partly from historical perspective and geopolitical considerations. For example, Taiwan precedes China under East Asia only because the author on Taiwan describes the earliest history of Chinese broadcasting. In the South Asia section, the first three countries discussed are India, Pakistan, and Bangladesh, placed in that order because of the nature of their evolution into nationhood — i.e., Pakistan was partitioned from India and Bangladesh was split from Pakistan. At other times, the placement within a region was based on the importance or size of the broadcasting system itself.

John A. Lent

Philadelphia and Penang

Acknowledgements

First of all, some of the individual authors in this volume wish to make acknowledgments. For example, the treatment of broadcasting in Hong Kong was possible only through the courteous cooperation of top management personnel in government and broadcasting. Special thanks are expressed to D. E. Brooks, Director of Broadcasting, Radio Hong Kong; George Ho, General Manager, T. P. Kwong, Director of Programming, and Nick Demuth, Director of English Programs, all of Hong Kong Commercial Broadcasting Company; Don Gale, General Manager of Broadcasting, Rediffusion; Lincoln W. Miller, Assistant to the Managing Director, Television Broadcasts Ltd.; D. J. Duncan-Smith, Secretary, Television Authority; John Berry, Manager, Overseas Services, Cable and Wireless Ltd.

Information on Indochina broadcasting was collected during field trips to Vietnam by the authors — Lichty in 1968 and Hoffer in 1969. Also, Lichty collected data in Hong Kong, Japan, and Thailand in 1975. They wish to thank the following agencies for primary data: Offices of East Asian and Pacific Area, USIA, Department of State; Federal Records Center, Suitland, Md.; USIA Archives; Department of Air Force Research and Analysis Division Archives, Pentagon; Douglas Pike Collection, Center for Research Library, Chicago; and JUSPAO. Information through correspondence, for which they are thankful, was received from Voice of Vietnam, Hanoi; broadcast officials in Phnom Penh: Ministère de l'Information de la Propagande et du Tourisme, Vientiane, Laos. Tapes of Voice of Vietnam were provided by Forrest Edwards, Bureau Chief, Associated Press, Hong Kong. Part of Hoffer's research was supported by a grant from the Graduate School, University of Wisconsin—Madison. Data for the authors' 1975 section of their South Vietnam chapter came from radio monitor reports and interviews by Lichty with the following in Hong Kong and Bangkok during the summer of 1975: Ken Englais, Paul Oakley, and Paul Vogel of United Press International; Vu Van Yen of Associated Press; Don Ronk of ABC; Jerry Liles of CBS; James McGinley of USIS; Richard Comford of Bergen Community College doing research in Laos.

For the chapter on Thailand, interviews were conducted in 1972 by Scandlen with: Chamnon Rangsikul, Director of News, Public Relations Department; Fred Ayers, Director of Business Research Ltd.; Lt. Col. Jiam Yodpetch, Army Signal Corps; Col. Tawon Chuayprasidt, Director of Programming, Army Television; Pichai Wasanasong, Thai broadcasting pioneer; Rod Douglas, HSA Radio announcer; Lou Polichetti, USIS; Ananda Sharuprapai; Peter Couling, Director, Diethelm Advertising Ltd.; David Knapp, Diethelm Advertising Ltd.; Jack Evans, Director, Cathay Advertising; Prasong La-Orpaksin, Advertising Director, Channel 3; Chamnong Kumalvisai, Chief of Knowledge Department, Public Relations Department; Dhani Manyati, Regular Broadcasting Services, Public Relations Department; Col. Sanong Boonyanit, Director of Engineering, Army Television Channel 7; and Bruce Gaston. Their help is gratefully acknowledged.

A number of Afghan broadcasters interviewed by Mehria in 1972 remain anonymous to protect them from political retaliation. The information obtained, however, from Klaus Kaegeler, Chief of the West German Technical Advisory Team in Kabul, and Said Waseeq, Radio Kabul, can be acknowledged.

When Gunaratne returned to his homeland, Sri Lanka, to carry out media fieldwork in 1972, he interviewed, among others, M. A. de Silva, dissenting member of the Jayasuriya Broadcasting Commission, and Susil Moonesinghe, Chairman and Director-General of Ceylon Broadcasting Corporation.

Much of the material for the chapters on Australia and New Zealand came from Toogood's personal experiences in the two countries, especially as a producer-director at New Zealand Broadcasting Corporation, as well as from a research trip in 1971, when he had formal interviews with: R. T. Peacock, Chairman, New Zealand Broadcasting Authority (NZBA); J. F. D'Ath, Secretary, NZBA; L. R. Skeats, Director-General; K. Donaldson, Program Director, R. Melford, Chief Producer, B. Broadhead, Director of Public Affairs, P. A. Fabian, Public Relations Manager, all of New Zealand Broadcasting Corporation; D. Gapes, General Manager, Radio Hauraki; G. Dryden, Associated Network Group TV; Sir R. Madgwick, Chairman, P. Lucas, Head of Information Services, both of Australian Broadcasting Commission; J. H. Oswin, General Manager, ATN Channel 7; I. Simpson, Federation of Australian Commercial Television Stations; D. Foster, Federation of Australian Commercial Broadcasters. He also made informal contacts with many additional public and private broadcasters who were very helpful.

Among Pacific Island broadcasters interviewed in 1970 by Barney were: Raymond Paull, News Director, Fiji Broadcasting Corporation; Leavea Lefi, Program Supervisor and News Editor, Radio ZAP, Western Samoa; F. E. Betham, Acting Government Statistician, Western Samoa; Mike Monti, Program Organizer, Radio ZCO, Tonga; Vern Williams, Manager, Radio WVUV, American Samoa; Dennis Falk, Director of Media, Education Department, American Samoa; Edwin Engledow, Director, Office of Information, Government of American Samoa.

Concerning international broadcasting to Asia, Browne interviewed in 1969-70 the following: Edith Coliver and L. Z. Yuan, Asia Foundation; Peter

Homfray, Jack Duncan, and Colin Johnston, Radio Australia; Hiroshi Takano and T. Ozasa Radio Japan; Pen-Pao Chen, Voice of Free China; Liu Ding-yih, Central Broadcasting Station, Taiwan; Lee Lien, Cheng Sheng Broadcasting Corporation, Taiwan; Donald Brooks, Radio Hong Kong; L. LaDany, China News Analysis, Hong Kong; William Hsu, Union Research Institute, Hong Kong; James Bradshaw, American Consulate, Hong Kong; Carl Lawrence, Far East Broadcasting Company, Manila; Sir Charles Moses, Asian Broadcasting Union, Sydney; Ahmed Taher and M. F. Faki, United Arab Republic Broadcasting Corporation, Cairo; Vitali Ziminl, Sergei Rudin, and Sergei Grib, Radio Moscow; Hugh Howse and Asher Lee, BBC External Services, London; Fritz Littlejohn and Grant Worrell, Voice of America, Washington D.C.; Peter Janecki and Wendell Thompson, Office of Research, USIA, Washington D.C. In addition, the author received information on international broadcasts from extensive monitoring and questionnaires.

The following provided information on Asian religious broadcasting, primarily through returns to Bernardez' 1972 questionnaire: A. O. Robson, Australian Broadcasting Commission; E. H. Tolentino, Far East Broadcasting Company, Fr. James Reuter, Philippine Federation of Catholic Broadcasters, Roland C. Kauth, Lutheran Church in the Philippines, James O. Terry, Jr., Southern Baptist Mission, all in Manila; Fr. Raymond Parent, Kuangchi Program Service, Rev. David Chao, Lutheran Voice and Joint Lutheran Television Center, both in Taipei; Rev. Thomas W. Lung, AVEC, Hong Kong; James Metcalfe, Far East Broadcasting Company, Bangkok; Nguyen Quang Trung, Alexandre de Rhodes Educational Television Center, Pastor Nguyen van Van, Evangelical Church of Vietnam, both in Saigon; Karel S. Lasut, Evangelical Church of Minahassa, Indonesia; Far East Broadcasting Associates, Singapore; Kenneth M. de Lanerolle, National Christian Council of Ceylon, Eddie Ranasinghe, Christian Literature Society of Ceylon, Fr. S. M. Selvaratnam, Social Communications Center, all of Colombo; Fr. Jan Slijkerman, Beschi College, Fr. Tomy Luiz, St. Xavier's College, both in India; E. Otto DeCamp, Christian Broadcasting System, Seoul; and Futoshi Ota, AVACO, Tokyo.

Finally, personal observation by Sherman during a field trip to ABU member countries in 1968 provided much of the background data for his chapter. He wishes to thank officials at the ABU Secretariats in Sydney and Tokyo, as well as those at stations in Western Samoa, Indonesia, Malaysia, Hong Kong, and Taiwan, who generously consented to being interviewed.

The list of people who helped me personally in getting this project together seems endless. The following, however, should be acknowledged:

Numerous broadcast management personnel in the Philippines, Japan, Malaysia, Laos, and Korea who, over the years, granted me interviews which lent insights into the status and problems of Asian broadcasting. Because I have authored the Philippine chapter in this book, only those personnel I interviewed in the Philippines in 1964-65, and 1973, will be mentioned; the data they gave set the background for this chapter: most helpful were Francisco Trinidad,

General Manager, Philippine Broadcasting Service; Jose Tierro, Program Director, CBN; Aurelio Javellana, Manager, Mindanao Broadcasting; Reuben Canoy, Radio Mindanao; Raul Ortega, Manila Broadcasting; Nitoy Escano, Sales Director, CBN-ABS-MBS; Antonio Suarez, Provincial Sales Manager, CBN-ABS-MBS; Oscar Lopez, General Manager, CBN-ABS-MBS; Phil Delfino, ABS; Juan Mercado, Philippine Press Institute; the late O. Abad Santos, Philippine News Service; and Eddie Sanchez, Philippine Press Institute.

Alan Hancock, UNESCO; Sydney Head, Temple University; Michael Wilson, UNESCO Afghanistan; Lester Goodman, UNESCO Indonesia; William 'Ted' Haney, FEBC San Francisco; and Chong Seck Chim, Ministry of Education in Malaysia, read and commented on all, or parts of, the manuscript. Goodman, in fact, rewrote the ETV section of the Indonesian chapter, and Haney updated the religious broadcasting section.

I am appreciative of the efforts of a number of others who helped me find knowledgeable contributing authors, among them being Fr. Leo Larkin, Center for Educational Television, Manila; Alan Hancock; Roger Domyahn, formerly of University of Iowa; Hugh Cordier, University of Iowa; Y. V. L. Rao, AMIC, Singapore; Bumrongsook Siha-Umphai, Chulalongkorn University, Bangkok; Ichiro Matsui, ABU; and Art Hungerford, formerly of Pennsylvania State University.

B. B. Denney, formerly of Lao National Radio, and Victor Anant, formerly of AMIC, who for sensitive reasons could not write chapters, did contribute useful information on Laos and Singapore.

I owe thanks and apologies to Josie Patron, National Media Production Center, Manila, and Florangel Rosario, formerly of University of Hawaii. They contributed a great deal of data for the Philippine chapter which, unfortunately, was lost with my luggage in transit from Penang. In fact, Patron and Rosario were originally to be coauthors of the Philippine chapter.

Gratitude is extended to all of the contributing authors, many of whom sacrificed long hours gathering data on broadcasting systems, some of which had never been studied systematically heretofore. Some authors have written two and three revisions in an attempt to keep the data current. Others allowed me to edit their chapters freely in my effort to bring some consistency of style and format to the manuscript. Whiting and Everest made special trips to Afghanistan and Mácau, respectively, for the sole purpose of gathering information for this book; Lichty returned to Southeast Asia in 1975 to update his chapters; Bernardez did a questionnaire survey; and others, such as Scandlen in Thailand, carried out research field trips.

I would like to thank the Press Foundation of Asia in Manila for its generous monetary contribution toward the publication of this book.

And, as always, my wife, Martha, and our five children are to be thanked, for in the long run, they are the ones who sacrifice the most when a project of this magnitude is attempted.

Part 1   Introduction

1. Asian Broadcasting: Problems, Challenges, and Prospects

Sir Charles Moses

Asia contains nearly two-thirds of the earth's human inhabitants. Two of its countries each have more people than the whole of the neighboring continent of Africa. While there are great cities in Asia which make full use of modern technology, many of its people live in a traditional manner and are often isolated, sometimes lacking even the old and simple means of communication such as roads. There are also the barriers created by a great diversity of languages and cultures: in some cases hundreds of different languages and dialects exist within the boundaries of one country. These are a few of the basic facts that make up the Asian environment in which the broadcasting media must operate.

Clearly, broadcasting — radio and television — has a major role in this vast continent. Radio can reach millions immediately and relatively cheaply, including audiences in remote areas. In some countries, radio is the only available means of making rapid contact with all populated areas: indeed, a few broadcasting services transmit what are the equivalent of telegrams for conveying official and urgent personal messages to locations where conventional communications services — postal, telegraph, telephone — are not available or are very slow. Television also has these qualities of immediacy and wide coverage. If augmented by a satellite, as in the projected Indian experiment known as SITE, it could provide spoken and visual contact with the whole population in those Asian countries which are vast in area and where the installation of relay links and transmitters on the ground is therefore a very costly and necessarily slow process.

Broadcasting has also the obvious advantage that it by-passes illiteracy — an important drag on progress in many developing countries where the spread of education, even when strenuously pursued, is barely able to keep up with the increase in population.

Sir Charles Moses was Secretary-General of the Asian Broadcasting Union. Sir Charles, who read this book manuscript, agreed to write the foreword, but because of other responsibilities, was unable to do so. He and the Press Foundation of Asia have given permission for this paper to be reprinted from the *1974 Asian Press and Media Directory*.

But the potential of broadcasting to cover the great distances of Asia is of little value unless the audience has the means of receiving its messages. At this physical level of the availability of equipment to send and receive, there are great contrasts in different parts of the continent. In Japan and a few other places nearly everyone can have his or her transistor radio and most households have a TV set: over 24 million Japanese households, in a population of a little over 100 million, are licensed as having at least one TV receiver. In some other countries, radio receivers are spread thinly and, if there is a TV service, TV sets are a luxury for the very few. In India, for example, there are now about 60,000 TV receivers among over 560 million people, although it is hoped that this situation will be changed when the plans based on SITE, using community receivers, can be put into effect.

The transistor radio, battery operated, has certainly had a revolutionary effect on the size of Asian radio audiences. Where governments in developing countries have encouraged the local manufacture, assembly, or importation of such receivers and have refrained from imposing special taxes on them as convenient sources of revenue, transistor sets are within the financial means of large sections of the community.

But there is as yet no equivalent of the cheap transistor in television or a generally available battery-operated television receiver that could conveniently be used where electric power is not available. It is possible to envisage a relatively cheap single channel TV set, powered by some source other than the electric mains and not requiring frequent maintenance, which might be used as a community receiver in the developing countries. But this type of receiver does not yet exist.

Thus radio remains the main broadcasting medium in many Asian countries and it has a very important job to do. This point is often overlooked by people from the industrialized areas of the world who now think of broadcasting mainly in terms of TV — in fact, of color TV. TV in color — the expensive medium — is being introduced in an increasing number of Asian nations but it would be unrealistic to expect that in most of them it will reach any but the privileged few for many years to come.

The sophisticated minority, the leaders, are important but economic progress in the developing countries depends on involving the whole community in the processes of change and growth. The broadcasting media are an excellent tool for this purpose, offering not only the means of distributing information and creating a climate for development, but also providing a genuine national forum for feedback from the community to the planners. But this function of broadcasting in Asia depends on coverage — on the ability to reach most of the potential audience. Big Asian cities may give the impression that transistors are everywhere, but there is a pressing need in many areas for much more to be done in providing access to receivers — radios and, where possible, simple black and white televisions — for the ordinary people of the developing countries.

As to what comes out of the receiver, there is such diversity in the Asian continent in cultures and attitudes, and in the way the broadcasting media are used, that any general comments inevitably misrepresent the situation in some nations.

It can be said that broadcasting in Asia is mainly national, controlled by government departments or, in some countries whose number is gradually increasing, by public corporations. This does not mean that it is noncommercial; with only a few exceptions, national broadcasting in Asia derives a substantial part of its revenue from advertising. National control presupposes a determination to use the broadcasting media for developmental purposes. It also has problems such as, in some cases, requirements to observe budgetary and staffing procedures unsuited to the media or reluctance to explore new ways of using broadcasting to meet the particular needs of the target audience.

In the developing countries where there are privately owned broadcasting organizations, many of these have shown a strong sense of responsibility toward community service. There are many examples of educational and developmental work undertaken by commercial stations which had no obligatory national responsibilities.

In its early years, broadcasting was regarded in many countries in the region as primarily an entertainment service and therefore did not rate very highly in the allocation of limited funds at the disposal of governments. Radio and television must of course be entertaining; it is very easy to switch off a boring program. But it gradually came to be understood by the broadcasters and their governments that the media were the means of doing many things — of arousing interest in developmental projects, of guiding farmers to more efficient methods, of explaining hygiene and child care to women, of providing extra resources for classroom teachers and of training teachers, of teaching technical skills, and so on. This effort was often seen as a one-way channel — the broadcasters to the audience — with not very much coming back in the opposite direction. More recently, experience has shown the need for a two-way channel, for the audience to be directly involved in a dialogue wherever this is possible, which requires much more effort on the part of the broadcasters.

In most Asian countries, there has been, and still is, a very great shortage of trained broadcasting staff to undertake this complex task of presenting education, using that word in its broadest sense, in an entertaining way. Staff often had to learn on the job, by trial and error, or were sometimes sent away to other parts of the world for training in a context irrelevant to that in their own countries. The broadcasting media were often accused of being ineffective when campaigns organized by untrained or inexperienced staff were not successful.

Although this problem is still pressing in many of the developing nations of Asia, it is gradually being overcome. The larger broadcasting organizations now have their own training centers which are being strengthened and improved and most of which are open, under various aid programs, to trainees from other countries. UNESCO and the Asian Broadcasting Union, with the help of numerous other international bodies, have been working for some years on a regional broadcasting training project aimed particularly at the training of instructors, assistance to existing training centers in the region, and meeting the needs of the smaller broadcasting organizations which do not have the resources to mount their own training courses. The number still requiring training is great, both among existing broadcasters and to provide for expansion of services, but the standard of professionalism in broadcasting is approaching that in the older field of Asian journalism.

There is also among governments and planners a growing realization of the full potential of broadcasting in development. The extent to which this is so varies considerably at present from country to country. In some nations, broadcasting is being drawn into the planning effort and is responding with imagination and professional skill in supporting developmental projects; in others, broadcasting is still something of a "poor relation," whose potential is not fully understood.

With improvement in the staff-training situation, broadcasters in the developing countries of Asia have a much greater capacity for the production of radio and TV programs designed to meet the needs of their own countries, whether in entertainment or in more serious fields. Like the press, radio and TV are demanding media; there is a long spread of hours to be filled every day. For TV in particular, where production is expensive in its requirements for staff and equipment, there is consequently a temptation to use a high percentage of imported programs, even if they come from another culture with a completely different set of values. In a number of Asian countries, there is a strong positive movement away from this situation, and the broadcasting organizations are taking a leading role in encouraging the work of local writers, musicians, and performers, with the aim of building up their own sources of program material.

In the past nine or ten years, the Asian Broadcasting Union (ABU) has taken a useful part in these developments and has provided the means through which the broadcasters of Asia and the Pacific may work together in professional fields of common interest. The ABU's region covers the whole of Asia and the western half of the Pacific, stretching from Turkey on the edge of Europe to the island groups in the middle of the Pacific, such as Tonga, Fiji, and Western Samoa. When the ABU was officially established on 1 July 1964, after a series of conferences initiated by Nippon Hoso Kyokai (NHK), the national broadcasting service in Japan, it had 11 members in this vast area. Today, membership in the region comprises 40 organizations, representing most of the countries of the area, as well as 14 associate members in other parts of the world, including the major broadcasters of Europe and North America.

The ABU's members in its own region are, like the region itself, very diverse. They range in size from NHK in Japan, the largest broadcasting organization in the world and a world leader in advancing technology, to organizations with a total staff of about 20, using simply-equipped radio studios. They come from many different cultural backgrounds, with a wide variety of languages, religions, and political views. But the ABU has proved that this diversity is not divisive, provided there is good will.

In response to the interests of its members, the ABU has become involved in its short history in numerous aspects of broadcasting in Asia, from organizing program exchanges to studies of engineering problems. Two areas that have recently claimed special attention are broadcast news, a vitally important element in every radio and TV service in the region, and the development of special programs for the youth of Asia.

The ABU is not, however, concerned only with its own region. Broadcasters throughout the world have common professional interests and problems, and satellites will increasingly bring the rest of the world into Asian homes. From the first of its annual general assemblies in 1964, the ABU's members have emphasized their interest in establishing close contacts with sister broadcasting unions in other regions, and the ABU has in recent years played a leading role in the rapidly developing collaboration among these international bodies.

Part 2   National Systems

2. East Asia

What Asian scholars have come to term "East Asia" represents the bulk of the population, land, and resources of the continent of Asia. Over half of all Asians (1.08 billion) live in the eight nations of East Asia. The region's long history of conflict is attested to by the fact that there are two governments claiming to be China and two representing Korea. East Asia also includes two of the few remaining colonies in the world — British Hong Kong and Portuguese Mácau.

This section on East Asia begins with the Republic of China (Taiwan) because the author of that chapter has dealt with Chinese broadcasting history from its inception on the mainland in 1922.

Although detailed information on broadcasting in another East Asian nation, the Mongolian People's Republic, is limited, some data are included here for background purposes.

The Mongol princes, long feudatories of China, declared their independence under Soviet protection in 1911. A revolutionary government was set up in 1921, and the People's Republic of Mongolia came into existence in 1924, becoming the world's second Communist state. The nation is made up of 1.4 million people spread over 18 provinces. The capital city, Ulan Bator, has the largest population, 326,400.

According to *Asia 1975 Yearbook,* Mongolia has one national and 20 city and provincial radio stations, all government owned and controlled, and one government television channel, supplied by the Soviet Union with two programs via Molniya/orbita satellite system. The number of radio receivers in 1974 was estimated at 148,000; the number of television sets a year earlier, 34,000. Broadcasting is expected to promote and propagate the Mongolian communist ideology.

2.1 Republic of China (Taiwan), *by Chia-shih Hsu*

Taiwan, formerly known as Formosa, became the first republic in Asia when the Chinese inhabitants objected to the island being ceded to Japan after the Sino-Japanese War in 1894. After Japan's defeat in 1945, Taiwan was returned to China as a province. When the Communists took over the mainland, the Republic of China, under Chiang Kai-shek, moved to Taiwan in 1949. In November 1971, the United Nations General Assembly voted to expel Taiwan and seat the People's Republic of China. Shortly after, a number of nations ceased diplomatic relations with the island nation.

Taiwan is made up of 78 islands with 15.7 million people and has five cities of at least a half-million population — Taipei (the capital), Kaohsiung, Taichung, Tainan, and Keelung. Most mass media are concentrated in Taipei. Besides the broadcasting stations, there are 31 dailies with an estimated 1.5 million circulation in the Republic of China.

Educational levels are quite high on the island: more than 98% of elementary school-age children are in classrooms, and 85% of those completing sixth grade go on to junior high school. The country has nearly 100 universities, colleges, and advanced technical institutes. About 85% of the people speak a second language after Mandarin, usually either Hakka, an aboriginal dialect, or Japanese. Economically, Taiwan has been well off in recent years; in 1975, the income per capita was $697.*

2.1.1 Introduction

A Chinese peasant in Taiwan is quite possibly a newspaper reader or radio listener, but more likely he is a television viewer. A 1972 audience study conducted in two central Taiwan villages found, for example, that among 200 subjects interviewed, 90 watched television, 45 read newspapers, and 36 listened to radio every day (Shih 1972).

Without doing any interviewing, an observer on a southbound train from Taipei can ascertain the degree of penetration of TV into rural areas simply by noticing the forest of antennas rising from the one-storied brick houses and clay huts. If unregistered sets were taken into account, there must have been a million television receivers in Taiwan in 1972, or one per 15 people. By 1975, the number of TV receivers was estimated at 2.5 million, one-third of which were in color. The audience was estimated at 14 million (*Free China Weekly*, 29 June 1975, p. 2).

No one anticipated such a phenomenal growth of the medium on the island when in 1962 the first commercial TV station was established. In 1956, when

Chia-shih Hsu is Dean of the Graduate School of Journalism, National Chengchi University, Taipei; Manchurian correspondent and deputy managing editor of *Central Daily News* for 20 years; news commentator, China Television Service; Secretary-General of the Taipei Press Council until 1971; and author of *The Trap of Symbols* and *Theories of Mass Communications* plus numerous articles.

*Unless indicated otherwise, all mentions of currency are in United States dollars.

the Ministry of Education proposed a TV station to the Executive Yuan (cabinet), the request was turned down because of the huge expenditure involved, the effects of the medium on the public, and the burden such a luxury would cause to the government and the citizens (Chang 1973, p. 76). But the accelerated growth of the island's economy, which scored an average annual rate of 9.9% during 1961-70 (compared to 7.2% during 1951-60), certainly played a major role in television's success. The economic record for 1971 was even more impressive with the GNP moving ahead almost 11.5% to reach $6.2 million and income per capita increasing to $329.

There are other reasons for TV's success as well. For example, the rapid development of Taiwan's power industry during the 1960s made electricity available even to lone homesteads on remote mountaintops and seashores. Foreign investment, coupled with inexpensive labor, turned Taiwan into a chief Asian manufacturer and exporter of electronic products. In 1972, Taiwan produced more than 3.5 million TV receivers, a 100% increase over 1971. This accounted for 19% of the world's production. But Taiwan also imported over 16,000 United States and Japanese color TV sets in 1973-74. The government, in an effort to combat Taiwan's trade deficit of $153 million, banned the importation of TV sets, among other items, after May 1974 (*Data for Decision*, 20-26 May 1974, p. 1901).

Advantages of this new industry accrued to Taiwan residents in the form of lower prices for television sets. For instance, the cost of producing a 19-inch color TV set is only $187. Finally, there is no yearly license on television and radio sets; once-only registration fees of $2 and $1 are required, respectively.

2.1.2 Development

Mainland Chinese came to know radio broadcasting for the first time in December 1922, when an American businessman, P. Osborn, and his friend, Mr. Tseng, set up a 50-w. station in Shanghai's Tai Lai department store. A month later, Osborn's second station commenced operations from his own Shanghai department store. This station, in cooperation with a Shanghai newspaper, initiated the first local newscasts to be heard in China (see Wang 1971).

Not until 1927 did the government build its own radio stations, at Tientsin and Peking. Both were under direct control of the Ministry of Communications. Shortly after, several provincial governments also established stations.

During the precommunist period, the most important development in Chinese broadcasting was the setting up, by the ruling Kuomintang party, of Nanking's Central Broadcasting Station on 1 August 1928. In 1932, when Central Broadcasting Station installed a 75-kw. short-wave transmitter, the whole of China and most of Southeast Asia was brought into its coverage area (Peng 1971, p. 11). Central Broadcasting Station continued its expansion with the result that by the end of World War II, it was the center of a national network of ten affiliated stations.

Eighty-one stations operated in China immediately before and during World

War II. According to the Ministry of Education in Taipei, 11 of these stations were part of the Kuomintang-operated network, with Central Broadcasting Station as its nucleus; 3 were operated by the Ministry of Communications of the central government; 18 by provincial or other local governments; 2 by the military; and 47 by private enterprises. Most of the private stations broadcast from large cities such as Shanghai, Tientsin, Peking, Hanchow, and Canton. The military stations were developed by the Ministry of War during World War II.

Radio communication played a significant role in solidifying China during the war. It was only through the use of radio that the government and people of the free zones could communicate with their countrymen in Japanese-held areas. Clandestine newspapers in captive provinces relied upon Central Broadcasting Station for news; underground fighters depended upon the station for action guidance. The station at Chungking (wartime capital) was also an indispensable tool of the government's overseas information campaigns.

After V-J Day, the Central Broadcasting Network expanded into China's newly recovered territories, increasing its number of affiliated stations to 39 with 72 medium-wave transmitters of a combined power of 392 kw. At this time, the network was renamed Broadcasting Corporation of China (BCC). When the Communist takeover occurred in 1949, BCC lost all its mainland stations and retreated with the Republic of China government to the island province of Taiwan. There, BCC maintained a network of five small stations in Taipei, Taichung, Tainan, Chiayi, and Hwalien, left behind by the Japanese after the war. The stations still showed the damaging effects of American heavy air attacks during the final stages of the conflict.

Actually, the first radio station on Taiwan had been developed 17 June 1925 at Taipei. Known as Taiwan Radio, it was a creation of the Japanese colonial government. Initially operating on 50w., the transmitter power was upped to 1 kw. in 1927, and then to 10 kw. in 1931. In that year, an island-wide network was completed with four additional stations at Taichung, Tainan, Kaohsiung, and Hwalien. All of these stations were under the control of the governor's office.

When the Chinese took over Taiwan in 1945, they inherited a shaky economy overtaxed by the long war. Thus economic strangulation, as well as the political uncertainty on the mainland, severely handicapped the development of broadcasting on Taiwan. For example, in 1947, the number of radio sets on the island and the adjacent Penghu Islands was 9,740, or fewer than 1.5 sets for every 1,000 people. Advertising as a source of revenue was almost unknown to both private and public radio stations because the local business circles had not begun to realize the marketing function of radio. Hard times for Taiwan broadcasting, however, as for all aspects of national life, did not last long. With the coming of political stabilization, resumption of American aid, and the launching of land reform in 1951, Taiwan's economy began to recover. Correspondingly, broadcasting showed growth signs, and by the end of 1955 the number of registered radio sets increased tenfold since 1945 (to 104,307), the number of stations to 11.

The most spectacular expansion of radio broadcasting came, however, during the decade beginning with 1956, the period when government stepped up its developmental efforts considerably. The result was that by 1966, 33 radio companies operating 77 stations and using 197 transmitters were in use, with a combined power of 1,367.45 kw. (*China Yearbook 1966*, p. 213). Registered radio receivers totalled 1,362,366, with an equal number estimated unregistered. Availability of cheap transistor radios was given as the main reason for the inability of the government to enforce the registration law.

As television became more popular on Taiwan after 1967, radio's expansion was slowed somewhat. In early 1974, about three million radio sets, excluding those in the armed services, were in use on Taiwan and the other islands of the Republic of China. Therefore, according to Ministry of Communications figures, Taiwan ranked among the world leaders in proportion of sets per population, with about 260 for every 1,000 persons. At the same time, the number of transmitters used by 110 different radio stations was 224 with a combined transmission power of 3,158.7 kw. (*China Yearbook 1974*, p. 332).

Even more impressive is the story of the younger electronic medium, television. Government-controlled National Education TV (NETV), established in February 1962, was Taiwan's first television station. NETV, using a 100-w. transmitter, initially ran for three hours daily, with an effective receiving radius of 50 kilometers from downtown Taipei. NETV was discontinued to avoid overlapping of efforts when the government, in the 1970s, initiated a more extensive instructional TV program in cooperation with the China Television Service.

The real television age dawned upon Taiwan on the Double-Tenth (10 October) 1962, when one-third of the nation watched the spectacular National Day celebrations on what they called "electric viewing machines." The program was telecast from the scene in Taipei by Taiwan Television Enterprise (TTV) to formally inaugurate its services, initially to northern Taiwan. TTV's island-wide relay system was completed three years later.

Television became keenly competitive with the births of China Television Company (CTV) in 1969 and China Television Service (CTS) in 1971. All three stations, despite maintaining different forms of ownership, operate on a self-supporting basis, depending on advertising revenue. The result has been a squeeze on the national advertising budget which is too small to keep three stations functioning well.

In 1971, according to the Taipei Business Association of Advertising, television accounted for $15.5 million, or 29.5% of the nation's total advertising expenditure, tailing newspapers (35.8%), but leading all other media, including radio (7.2%). After a 15% commission was deducted by agencies, the television industry received $13.2 million. Considering that Taiwan TV stations have annual recurrent expenditures of about $4 million each, it becomes obvious that each station's share of total advertising revenue is barely enough to break even.

By the summer of 1972, the stations felt it necessary to cut expenditures by first curtailing daytime telecast time, from about five to two hours at noon, and then releasing "unnecessary" employees. TTV laid off 35 employees in June 1972; CTS, 44 the following month. Also, in early 1974, Taiwan's three commercial TV networks reduced their airtime by nearly two hours each — to six hours daily — in an effort to conserve energy (Bernama News Service, 5 January 1974). Despite the financial stress, Taiwan TV stations still produce more hours of color programming than black and white. Color programs since 1973 have increased to 95% of telecasting on the three all-island TV networks. TTV was using only color transmission in 1975; CTV, 99%, and CTS, 85% color programming that year. Competition for advertising was so keen and the volume in prime time rose so high that the government intervened. A mass communications law stipulating that advertising take up no more than 10% of program time was implemented (*Asia 1974 Yearbook*, p. 304).

The youngest member of the broadcasting industry of Taiwan is FM radio, begun 1 August 1968 by BCC to celebrate its fortieth anniversary. In 1972, each of BCC's four FM stations, located in Taipei, Taichung, Kaohsiung, and Hwalien, broadcast 12 hours, chiefly music, on weekdays and 16 hours on Sundays. FM receivers in use on Taiwan in early 1972 totaled 6,443.

2.1.3 Control

Ownership. The Republic of China had adopted multiownership of its mass media during precommunist days on the mainland. This characteristic prevails yet on Taiwan. For example, radio stations on Taiwan are now owned either by the Kuomintang, private enterprises, or government agencies. The Kuomintang stations make up the largest radio network (BCC), divided into three systems: overseas service known as Voice of Free China, the mainland service known as Central Broadcasting Station, and the domestic service. They are on the air 550 hours daily in 17 languages and dialects; most of BCC's output is for mainland and overseas audiences. The four BCC island-wide domestic networks broadcast in Mandarin and the Amoy dialect. One network is primarily educational; another is FM. BCC domestic stations are located at Taipei, Hsinchu, Miaoli, Taichung, Chiayi, Tainan, Kaohsiung, Hwalien, and Taitung (*China Yearbook 1974*, p. 332). There are 28 privately owned broadcast companies with 59 medium-wave transmitters of a combined power of 80 kw. Various government agencies, such as the Police Bureau, Armed Forces, Youth Corps, Ministry of Education, and Taipei Municipal Government, own 80 medium-wave and 8 shortwave transmitters with a combined power of 438 kw. (See Table 1.)

Mixed ownership patterns predominate in the television industry; not one station is entirely owned by government, Kuomintang, or private citizens. The Taiwan Provincial Government invested 49% of Taiwan Television Enterprise's capital; 11% was invested by local private sources and 40% from Japanese private firms (manufacturers Nippon Electric Corporation, Hitachi, and Toshiba, and broadcaster Fuji Television). China Television Company was established by BCC,

Table 1.   Radio Stations, Republic of China, 1972

Ownership Type	No. of Companies	No. of Stations	No. of Transmitters				Aggregate kw.			
			MW	SW	FM	Total	MW	SW	FM	Total
Party	1	21	52	21	4	77	1609.6	541.5	10.5	2161.6
Government	9	39	80	8		88	414.5	24		438.5
Private	28	51	59			59	80			80
Total	38	111	191	29	4	224	2104.1	565.5	10.5	2680.1

which contributed 50% of the capital; 28% came from a financing group formed by 28 private radio companies, and 22% came from a group of private citizens who had applied for a TV station license. The triadic ownership of CTV resulted from a government decision saying that the nation could have only one more TV station in addition to the existing two – at that time TTV and ETV. BCC, other radio stations, and a group of private individuals were all interested in investing in a station. In order not to disappoint any of them, the government urged these groups to merge as the grantee of the third TV station license. The China Television Service (CTS), which took over ETV's function and prompted it to fold, was originally a joint venture of the Ministries of Education and Defense. In an effort to expand its capital in 1972, the station added large amounts of private investment, and in the process decreased the government's investment to 49%.

Despite their heavy dependence on public agencies for financing, all three TV stations are technically defined as "private," operating entirely on sales of advertising time. The only exception is CTS, which in addition to selling advertising time receives a relatively small amount of tuition for its instructional programs. TTV, in its early years, drew a small part of its income from selling receivers but dropped the operation when it was no longer profitable.

Government regulation. Routine regulatory powers over broadcasting are vested in the Ministry of Communications and, until 1973, the Bureau of Cultural Affairs (BOCA) of the Ministry of Education. In mid-1973, the functions of BOCA were assumed by the Government Information Office (GIO). The Ministry of Communications is concerned with technical aspects, such as issuing broadcasting licenses, allocating frequencies and channels, and registering individual receiver licenses. GIO (and BOCA before it) is responsible for electronic media contents. In the absence of a statutory broadcasting law, basic policies, as well as more detailed rules, had been specified in an administrative code used by BOCA as its working guideline. In May 1972, however, a broadcasting law was finally drafted by the cabinet and sent to the Legislative Yuan for deliberation. It had not been approved by mid-1973 (see Chang 1973, pp. 41-52).

Largely a restatement of policies spelled out in the administrative code, the proposed broadcasting law was expected to be a more effective regulator, capable of succeeding where the code had failed – in the "purification" of broadcast content. Basic programming guidelines in the administrative code, and to a large extent in the future law, stipulate: upholding and publicizing national goals and government policies; encouraging anticommunist morals and beliefs; strengthening China's traditional moral standard and healthy social norms; protecting public interests and social safety; promoting entertainment of good taste; and assisting efforts for economic betterment.

In addition, the administrative code regulates the maximum commercial time a station may sell (20%), the proportion of programs in dialects (no more than 50%) and the minimum time for nonentertainment programs (50%).

Restrictive as the code sounds, except for articles on national goals and policies, it has never been effectively enforced, either on radio or television. This has resulted from the lack of a thorough monitoring system, as well as the heavy investment in large stations by the public sector, a factor that may have made some of the big stations too powerful for a subcabinet agency such as BOCA.

Other forms of control. Of course, government and party ownership, either total or partial, gives ruling authorities a voice in programming policy. But these influences are greatly offset by the fact that all stations, whether government or private, must rely on advertising revenue for survival. This has been especially true in the highly competitive 1970s when advertising growth lagged behind the development of new broadcasting stations. To attract time buyers, broadcasting media had to lower their programming standards, hoping to gain larger audiences by giving the people what they wanted rather than what the government felt they needed. Thus, on television, particularly during prime time, violence, popular songs, and emotion-packed soap operas were the daily fare. Taiwan's three commercial TV stations agreed in early 1974 to clean up their programs of "violence, myths, and absurdities" after threats that the networks would be nationalized. In negotiations with the Government Information Office, the networks agreed to devote more time to newscasts, to limit the amount of commercials to 5 minutes for every 30 minutes of programming, to allow GIO to censor all commercials, to set up a screening committee for song festival shows, to omit program hosts from advertisements and to drop patent medicines as prizes in guessing games (*Media for Asia's Communications Industry* 1974e, p. 20).

The formal, self-disciplinary organization for electronic media is the Taipei Press Council, originally a watchdog of newspapers. But in April 1971 the council expanded its functions to include radio and television as well. By 1973, no effective action had been taken by the council concerning radio and TV programming. Actually, the council does not have enforcing power; it can only give warnings or advice.

Because of TV's low-taste entertainment fare, disappointed intellectuals in 1972 demanded more government involvement in broadcasting and urged changing the whole system into a public-controlled institution, similar to those of British Broadcasting Corporation or Nippon Hoso Kyokai. The three TV stations responded to the mounting pressure by signing a self-policing covenant in May 1972. The covenant, applicable to all TV programs except newscasts, restricted the use of programs negating the principle of racial, religious, and sexual equality; containing superstitution, absurdities, and abnormalities; encouraging greediness, depravity, carnality, gambling, fighting, cruelty, larceny, dope addiction, fraud, and vulgarity; and containing overexposure of the human body.

The sincerity of television broadcasters in carrying out these pledges remains to be seen, since the covenant does not delineate how the rules will be enforced or punishment meted out.

2.1.4 Performance

Programming. As in many countries, Taiwan's radio and television are chiefly entertainment media. Independent research has shown that city dwellers and rural peasants alike obtain their daily news more often from newspapers than from either radio or TV (Shih 1972; Chu and Chi 1965, pp. 19–20).

Using 1972 schedules of BCC's two domestic services as examples, one can determine the content of a typical radio station in Taiwan. On the Mandarin network, entertainment occupied 35% of the time; public service, 31%; education, 21%; news, 12%; and commercials, 1%. On the second network, which uses the local dialects of Amoy and Hakka, the percentages were: entertainment, 48%; service, 26%; education, 15%; news, 6%; and commercials, 5% (BBC *Challenge Statement* 1972). The most popular radio entertainment includes Taiwan opera, Mandarin popular music, and "broadcasting dramas," sentiment-packed soap operas in Mandarin or Amoy.

With the inroads made by television, some radio stations tried to retain their audiences by enriching news and music programs, others by developing specialized services. For example, a Taipei station in 1969 started a "Drivers' Club" program, aimed at the city's more than 10,000 taxi drivers, while another station launched a daily two-hour show designed for barbers and beauticians in Taipei's 1,500 barber shops and beauty salons. The 1970 inauguration of "Traffic Service," an island-wide, around-the-clock, daily broadcast by the Police Broadcasting Network served a similar purpose (Ho 1971). The Police Broadcasting Network, 21 years old in 1975, had grown from one station to four in Taipei, Hsinchu, Changhwa, and Kaohsiung, plus short-wave to service the east coast. It broadcasts on AM and FM and includes two stations broadcasting traffic information programs. The network is unique in that it was established to train policemen but converted to public service when, after a year, it was found that only 4% of its listeners were policemen. Police Broadcasting Network emphasizes legal counseling to the public and broadcasts information on lost property and missing persons ten times daily (*Free China Review* 1975, p. 51).

Television in Taiwan is even more entertainment-oriented than radio. A content analysis of TTV in 1973 reported that 78% of the total telecast time was allocated to entertainment, 10% to news, 7% to education, and 5% to public service (Chang 1973, p. 79).

In the early 1970s, the total weekly telecast time rose from 63.5 to about 80 hours. According to 1972 BOCA figures, the program composition of the three Taiwan TV services was 44.1% entertainment, 24.5% education, 13.4% advertising, 9.5% news, and 8.5% public service. Still a third survey, published in 1975, gave these combined figures for the three services: news, 14.5%; public service, 11.6%; culture and education, 18.9%; entertainment, 47.3%; and advertisements, 7.2% ("Quick TV Facts" 1975). Mandarin was the most frequently used TV broadcast language (67.9% of the total weekly program hours), followed by English (21.1%), chiefly in imported U.S. TV shows, and Amoy (11%). All Amoy-dialect programs are entertainment. They are highly valued by advertisers who feel that Amoy shows can carry their messages to rural people more readily than other TV fare. As a result, Amoy shows, regardless of their quality, dominate the prime time of all three stations. Serious concern has been expressed by those who think the "Speak Mandarin" movement, a national policy, could be fatally hindered if this new trend is not checked. (It is argued that the "Speak Mandarin" [the national language] movement is essential for national unity formation on the island where Amoy and Hakka are spoken by most people over 50 years old.) People preferring more diversified TV during prime time are also opposed to this total submission of the medium to the advertisers' will.

Educational broadcasting. Systemic efforts have been made on Taiwan to supplement school instruction with electronic media. Educational Radio, with an island-wide service of instructional programs, has existed since 1950. Broadcasting eight hours daily, the station offers courses on both the high school and college levels, in languages, history, geography, and government. In addition, a number of social education programs on cooking, tailoring, and do-it-yourself topics are provided. In 1966, the government-owned station opened its second, more deliberate educational service, "School on the Air," offering a complete vocational program in commerce. Nearly every radio or TV station carries "Learn English" programs, catering to listeners who wish to learn the most popular foreign language in Taiwan.

Upon its establishment in October 1971, China Television Service took over government-sponsored TV instruction by absorbing the Ministry of Education service, Educational TV. Authorized by the ministry, CTS airs 25½ hours of educational broadcasts per week, including a complete senior high-school program, vocational commerce courses, and a program consisting of nine courses that may be recognized as formal college electives. A teacher-college program was added in 1972. Four state-operated universities, 19 public senior high schools, and ten public commerce schools and junior colleges are the sources of software for CTS's instructional broadcasts. CTS instructional fare is telecast 6-8 A.M. on weekdays and 6-10 A.M. on Sundays; a part of the morning program is rebroadcast from 1:30-2:30 P.M. daily. Vocal portions of all shows are taped and rebroadcast later on Education Radio and military radio stations, mainly for those who do not own TV sets.

A registered student who wishes to complete the senior high-school or commerce-school program with a diploma, must study at least three years. Diplomas are awarded to those who have gained the minimum number of credits and passed a graduation test. Credit certificates are issued by the cooperating university to students who successfully complete any college elective courses. The tuition fee for the high-school or commerce-school programs is $25 a year; the fee for college courses is $1.25 a semester credit. Enrollment figures for May 1972 were 3,353, high school; 5,376, commerce school; and 8,504, college. By 1975, over 45,000 students had registered for the courses (*Free China Weekly*, 29 June 1975, p. 2).

2.1.5 Conclusion

International communication through electronic media is far from being a one-way street in Taiwan. Thousands of words from radio stations on mainland China and other overseas stations can be received anywhere on the island (see §§6.1.3 and 6.1.4).

Not until 1969, however, when a satellite ground station was set up by the Ministry of Communications, was the feeling of a McLuhanian "global village" sensed by the man in the street. By communication satellite millions of TV viewers on Taiwan watched the Apollo XII's moon trip in November 1969, the Osaka World Fair in 1970, and Munich Olympics in 1972. Also, excited Chinese in 1970, 1971, and 1972 watched their school boys win, lose, and recapture the Little League World Series championship on the other side of the earth. In fact, between 1969 and 1972, CTV had made 20 transmissions by satellite; TTV, 17; and CTS, 5 (Hsu 1974, p. 37). The first earth station, developed at Yangmingshan, a suburb of Taipei, handles messages with the United States, Japan, and other nations via Intelsat VI over the Pacific. A second earth station was put into service 29 January 1974. Also located at Yangmingshan, it handles communications with European and African countries (*Data for Decision*, 4-10 February 1974, p. 1562).

"Retribalization" might be too dramatic and exaggerative a term, but there is little doubt that Taiwan has begun to be integrated into the closely knit, instant global communication system, despite the present economic difficulties faced by the nation's electronic media and the fact that the printed media are not dying as quickly as predicted by McLuhan.

2.2 People's Republic of China, *by James C. Y. Chu*

After many centuries, China's dynastic rule came to an end in 1911, overthrown

James C.Y. Chu is Associate Professor of Mass Communication at California State University in Chico. He is a former Government Information Office employee, World College of Journalism instructor, and BCC news editor, all in Taipei. He is the author of a study on reading habits of the rural population of Taiwan, and he received his Ph.D. from Southern Illinois University.

by the forces of Sun Yat-sen. The next four decades were marked by confusion as the Kuomintang Party tried to reunite the country, Manchuria was seized by the Japanese in 1931, and China entered the Pacific war in full force. The Kuomintang government lost tremendous ground during World War II as the Communists, under Mao Tse-tung, moved toward total control. Finally, the People's Republic of China was proclaimed 1 October 1949.

Made up of 21 provinces, 5 autonomous regions, and two special municipalities (Peking and Shanghai), China has a land area of 9.56 million square kilometers, the largest in Asia. The total population, largest of any nation in the world, was estimated at 899 million in 1973. At least ten cities have populations of two million or more, the largest being Peking (the capital) with eight million, and Shanghai with six million. The national media apparatus are located in these two key cities.

School enrollments and literacy rates are high in China, although opportunities for higher education continued to be fewer since the Cultural Revolution of the 1960s. Rural educational opportunities have improved considerably so that almost all school-age children are able to get some schooling. Interest in foreign languages continues, although, as the *Asia Yearbook 1975* reported, the fanfare about radio lessons in English, so conspicuous in the recent past, disappeared.

The rapid extension in rural wired broadcasting in recent years peaked in 1974, with the announcements by some provincial authorities that between 70% and 100% of the production brigades in Hupeh and Hunan received these broadcasts. The *Asia Yearbook 1975* reported:

Over 90 per cent of the production brigades and teams hear broadcasts and 63 per cent of the rural households are equipped with loudspeakers, many of which also possess small medium-wave radio receivers. The radio network was overriding some of the problems of illiteracy and semi-literacy and minimising the effectiveness of newspapers, posters and other written instructions.

2.2.1 Ideology and Structure

The structure and functions of broadcasting in today's China are determined by the Chinese Communist Party's philosophy of mass media, which flows directly from Marxist-Leninist doctrine. It emphasizes the effective manipulation of coercive and persuasive mass media as an instrument of power and control. Marxism-Leninism holds that the media are tools of class struggle and, as such, must assume such militant roles as "collective propagandist," "collective agitator," and "collective organizer."

This doctrine is rigidly followed and stressed by Mao Tse-tung. According to Mao, the functions of mass media are to publicize party decisions, educate the masses, and form a link between the party and masses. Through the mass media, the party strives to develop in the masses the proletarian characteristics that will make them loyal and useful citizens of the country. To achieve these missions, the mass media must become the party's "loyal eyes, ears, and tongue," and "an important bridge for daily contact between the Party and innumerable people, and a powerful tool for the Party to guide revolutionary struggle and construction" (*Jen-min Jih-pao*, 1960a).

It is "an art of Marxist-Leninist leadership" to be good at translating the party's policies into the actions of the masses (Mao 1967, p. 241). In the view of Mao Tse-tung, this is not merely journalistic work, but party work. Accordingly, the press, radio, and other mass media must be run by the whole party (*Jen-min Jih-pao*, 1960b). The mass media cannot rely, Mao says, "merely on a few persons working behind closed doors" (Mao 1967, p. 242), because some journalists, lacking experience, may not realize the wishes of the party and reflect fully its policies. Hence, he believes it necessary to subordinate mass media to the leadership of the party.

This party management of mass media consists of two characteristics: "walking on two legs" and "three-in-one combination," to put them in Chinese Communist jargon. "Walking on two legs" refers to the cooperation of the professional journalists with the nonprofessionals, while the "three-in-one combination" means the unity of party leadership, professional journalists and the masses in carrying out media missions. In short, the crux of Mao's philosophy of mass communications is the "mass line," referring to the "line of the masses under the leadership of the party." Within this philosophical framework, the People's Republic of China establishes the structure of its broadcasting system: Figure 1. Organizational Chart, Chinese Broadcasting

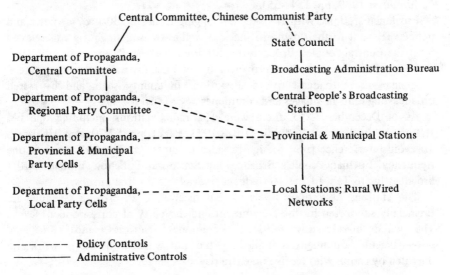

To fulfill the roles of propagandist, educator, and organizer, the broadcasting system is completely under the control of the Department of Propaganda of the Communist Party Central Committee. The department operates through

propaganda divisions in every regional, provincial, and local branch of the Communist Party and governmental agencies in charge of cultural and educational affairs. The Broadcasting Administration Bureau carries out party policies channeled through the State Council. This dual system of supervision operates all the way from the national Central People's Broadcasting Station in Peking to provincial stations in each capital, to municipal stations servicing the cities, and to local stations in counties, communes, factories, and mines.

The Central People's Broadcasting Station in Peking, nerve center of the network with 300-kw. transmitters, operates in domestic and overseas systems. The domestic system consists of five services. The first and second services are devoted to news, dissemination of policies formulated by the party and government, analysis of foreign news, drama, novel series, opera, life of the People's Liberation Army, sciences, technology of agricultural production, and special programs for youth and preschool children. The third service features Chinese opera, music, literature, and artistic activities; the fourth service is directed at the ethnic minorities; and the fifth service is used as a psychological warfare instrument against the Nationalist Chinese regime in Taiwan (see §6.1.4 for a fuller description). The fifth service uses both Mandarin and local dialects, such as Amoy and Hakka, to reach the audience 24 hours daily. According to one report, 51 medium-wave and 86 short-wave frequencies are used by the Central Station for domestic services; 149 medium-wave and short-wave frequencies in 31 languages for overseas services (*Yearbook on Chinese Communism* 1969, pp. 154–55).

Provincial stations, with transmitters ranging from 50-250 kw., air news and policies relevant to their own provinces, as well as transmitting programs relayed from the Central People's Broadcasting Station in Peking. Programs of municipal stations are similar to those of provincial outlets. Usually national and provincial programs are rebroadcast by local stations in county seats and by wired broadcasting units in villages and communes.

As of December 1970, there were 152 radio stations, including one FM station, in the People's Republic (FBIS 1971, Part I, pp. 52-70; Part III, p. 9). To avoid interference from foreign broadcasts, most stations use more than one frequency. Fuchien People's Broadcasting Station at Foochow, a major outlet broadcasting to Taiwan, has 16 frequencies available for that purpose.

The stations at various levels, which receive no advertising revenue, are financially supported by the government and the party at correspondent levels. The wired broadcasting units in communes, factories, and mines are self-sufficient. Equipment is funded by the unit which owns the network and operated by cadres who receive no extra pay.

2.2.2 Growth

On 5 September 1945, the Communists established their first broadcasting station in a temple about 19 miles from Yenan, the Communist stronghold in Northwest China. The station was part of an all-out offensive strategy against the

Nationalist Chinese government. Called Yenan Hsin Hua (New China) Broadcasting Station and equipped with a 300-w. transmitter, it was on the air only two hours a day. The programs, intended for audiences in Kuomintang territories, disseminated news and commentaries about Communist-controlled areas and party policies. On its third anniversary, the station's daily time was extended to three hours and later some English-language programs were added (Wen 1955, pp. 232-33).

A second station, Chang Kiakow (Kalgan) Hsin Hua Broadcasting Station, began functioning at about the same time as the Yenan station. By the end of 1948, 16 stations had been established in Manchuria, Sinkiang, eastern and northern China. The Communists claimed that broadcasting from these stations had a tremendous impact on the morale of Nationalist officers, many of whom joined the People's Liberation Army as a result. When the Communists took over the mainland in October 1949, 49 government-operated stations with a total of 89 transmitters existed. Of these, 17 were newly established, while the others were confiscated Kuomintang stations (Mei 1950).

Privately owned stations allowed to operate during the earliest stage of the Communist regime included 33 outlets with a total power capacity of 13,000 w. in 1950. Located in Shanghai (22), Canton (3), Chungking (3), Ningpo (2), Peking (1), Tientsin (1), and Tsingtao (1), these stations were ultimately taken over by the Bureau of Broadcasting Affairs. Their facilities were handed over to people's broadcasting stations throughout the country.

In 1950, the number of radio sets was estimated at 1-1.1 million, half of which were Japanese-made medium-wave receivers (Mei 1950). Metropolitan residents and those in industrial areas of Manchuria and eastern China were the usual owners, broadcasting being almost nonexistent in rural areas before 1950. To facilitate broadcasting at this lowest level of the administrative structure, Communist cadres in the countryside began using loudspeakers for collective listening.

With the establishment of the People's Republic of China on 1 October 1949, the Communists' first radio station near Yenan was officially renamed the Central People's Broadcasting Station. It broadcast 15½ hours daily, 50% of which was news, 25% public education, and another 25% culture and entertainment. As part of its education component, in late 1949, the station started a natural-sciences series featuring lectures by scientists and professors. In January 1950, a social-sciences series, with emphasis on Marxism and Leninism, was added. The entertainment program included revolutionary and folk songs, drama, and foreign music, mostly Russian. Choruses and opera troupes from schools, factories, and People's Liberation Army units were invited to present shows. The Central Station's news program covered the editorials of leading national newspapers, news stories provided by the New China News Agency (NCNA), and its own correspondents (Wen 1950).

At provincial, municipal, and local levels, stations are required to transmit news, commentaries, and other important political programs relayed from the

Central Station, as well as to produce shows to meet the needs of the people, government, and party units at various levels. In the 1950s, one of the most significant programs at many local stations was "Russian Forum," designed to teach Russian. Within six months of the establishment of the Communist regime, 14 people's stations at the local level presented this program with an estimated audience of 40,000 (Mei 1950).

Despite shortage of equipment and professional personnel, the development of provincial, municipal, and local stations made steady headway in the 1950s. The number of stations increased from 54 in 1951 to 73 in 1953 and 97 in 1958 (Liu 1971, p. 187). By June 1959, the deputy director of the Bureau of Broadcasting Affairs reported 107 stations in operation, with a combined radiating power nearly 33 times that of 1949 (Chou 1959, p. 5). By the end of 1959, 122 radio stations existed under the supervision of the bureau (Liu 1971, p. 187). Most of this growth occurred during campaigns of agricultural collectivization, the 1955-56 campaign of "agricultural producers' cooperatives," and the 1958-59 "people's communes." The broadcasting industry in the People's Republic continued to grow in the 1960s, and by 1967 there were 151 stations (*Yearbook on Chinese Communism* 1967, pp. 1321–25).

Little is known about the number of radio receivers in operation in today's China. In 1965, it was reported that there were over 11.5 million radio receivers, or 16 per 1,000 inhabitants (UNESCO, *Statistical Yearbook* 1972, p. 838). But organized efforts to promote collective listening have enlarged the audience substantially. It is reported that in the beginning of 1970, there were 1,021 radio broadcasting transmitters in China: 713 medium-wave, 307 short-wave, and one in the ultrahigh frequency (UHF) band. The single UHF transmitter was the only FM facility in China. The FM station was operated by the Ministry of Culture and Education as an outlet for educational programs for Peking audiences. Forty-six of the short-wave transmitters were assigned to the China Press Agency, a subsidiary of New China News Agency, for transmitting NCNA's daily news file to both domestic and foreign audiences (*Area Handbook for the People's Republic of China* 1972, p. 365).

Only a small number of radio sets were produced in the early post-1949 days. But by the end of the First Five-Year Plan (1953-57), during which time China received technical aid from the Soviet Union to produce transmitters, electronic tubes, and other broadcasting equipment, the country became self-sufficient in radio equipment. During this period, Peking, Shanghai, and Nanking became centers of China's electronics industry; the Nanking Radio Factory reportedly produced 400 radio sets a day. This factory manufactures a popular brand called *Hsiungmao* (Panda), a five-valve, short-wave and medium-wave radio set. Other popular brands include *Chunlei* (Spring Thunder), made in Shanghai, and *Moutan* (Peony) in Peking. Peking's Tungfeng No. 1 Radio Factory and Chung-chow's No. 3 Radio Factory used silicon transistors in making an inexpensive set for workers, peasants, and soldiers. Factories producing electronic equipment also have been set up in remote areas such as Chinghai, Ningsia, and Tibet. As of 26 June 1972, provinces and autonomous regions produced transistor radios (*Peking Review* 1972).

2.2.3 Monitoring and Wired Broadcasting

To solve the problems of insufficient radio facilities and limited number of radio receivers in the early 1950s, the Chinese began developing "radio-receiver networks." The Information Administration's "Decisions Regarding the Establishment of Radio-Receiving Networks," issued in April 1950, recognized the importance of radio as an instrument of mass education and propaganda which could bypass the limitations of illiteracy and newspaper shortage. The directive ordered government agencies at county and municipal levels, People's Liberation Army units, and all organizations, factories, and schools to appoint broadcasting monitors. The duties of monitors were to listen and take down news, political instructions, and other important contents broadcast by central and provincial stations; to announce the programs broadcast by stations in advance; to organize people within a unit to listen to the programs collectively; and to publish the contents of important programs in the form of small newspapers, *tatzepao* (big-character poster or wall newspaper), or mimeographed sheets for public meetings (Yu 1964, pp. 124-25; Liu 1964b, pp. 3-5).

Two similar directives were issued by the central administration. As a result, radio monitoring teams were organized at various units of the lowest level of political, military, economic, and educational structures in the country. The monitors worked under the dual leadership of the local government and the provincial and municipal information administration. In fact, they were supervised by local party cells or by mass organizations such as trade-union locals in factories. On 29 April 1950, the Central People's Broadcasting Station, in its "Regulations on the Work of Monitors," commanded monitors to place emphasis on speeches of Chinese Communist leaders, lectures by outstanding social-science scholars, news, and government decrees in order to raise the political consciousness of the audience. They were also instructed to report to their local broadcasting station which contents had been selected and distributed and the public reaction to them. Thus, monitors provided audience feedback which allowed the stations to adjust programs (Houn 1961, pp. 160-61; Liu 1964b, p. 7).

As part of this monitoring system, the Chinese Communists in the autumn of 1950 developed "wired broadcasting networks," patterned after the Soviet Union radio-diffusion exchange system. The wired broadcasting system in China employs a central receiver, with an amplifier and a switchboard housed in a studio. Station broadcasts are picked up by the powerful off-the-air receiver, amplified, and sent through the switchboard to loudspeakers connected to the wired broadcasting distribution point (Liu 1964a, pp. 573-74).

Wired broadcasting loudspeakers are installed everywhere — in village squares, school playgrounds, marketplaces, rice paddies, factories, mines, communal mess halls, dormitories, households, and even on treetops and telephone poles. As one observer said, "One can escape the sun and moon – but not the loudspeaker" (Chandra-Sekkar 1961, p. 8). Of course, under this system, listeners have no choice but to receive the official messages selected by the operators.

Although wired broadcasting networks started as early as 1950, until 1955 the government emphasized the monitoring system and collective listening. According to an incomplete report, the number of monitoring stations increased from 20,519 to 50,200 between 1952 and 1955, while the number of monitors jumped from 14,260 in 1951 to 42,722 in 1952 (Liu 1964b, p. 10).

In December 1955, the Third National Conference on Broadcasting Work held in Peking began to concentrate on the development of wired broadcasting networks. The conference decided to build more than 900 wired broadcasting distribution centers in the country in 1956, with a total of 450,000–500,000 wired loudspeakers; 80% of the units and loudspeakers were to be installed in rural areas. A report on the conference explained:

By the end of 1957, there will be more than 1,800 (wired) broadcasting stations [i.e., receiver-distribution units] in rural areas throughout the country, with 1,360,000 loudspeakers. In some provinces . . . broadcasts will reach every *tsun* (village) and every cooperative. By 1962 there will be more than 5,400 (wired) broadcasting stations in the rural areas of the whole country, with 6,700,000 loudspeakers. [New China News Agency, 24 December 1956]

To promote the campaign for "agricultural producers' cooperatives," the policy gave rural areas the top priority in setting up wired broadcasting units. It was decided that the networks must "first reach the villages and the cooperatives, and later the homes of the peasants" (Yu 1964, p. 127).

Acting as an instrument of party propaganda and agitation at the local level, the wired broadcasting system is used for "the political and cultural education of the peasants, the dissemination of advanced experiences in agricultural production, and the advancement of cultural life in rural areas" (*Jen-min Jih-pao*, 12 December 1955). In February 1959, the Sixth National Conference on Broadcasting Work further declared that the major functions of wired units in communes were "to guide production, and to relay programs of the central and provincial stations." The conference recommended wired broadcasting units "not to hurry in making their own programs" (*Hsin-wen Chan-hsien* 1959c, p. 2).

Peasants in communes have been encouraged by the party to bear the major burden of the construction cost, maintenance, and management of wired broadcasting units. The New China News Agency once described the "spirit of self-reliance" in developing wired broadcasting units as follows:

The setting up of a broadcasting station [i.e., units] by a commune, the installation of rediffusion lines by a production brigade or team depends mainly on collectively accumulated funds. Many areas use local materials to produce the facilities themselves. The poor and lower-middle peasants of the Kuanyintang production brigade of Mihsien county, Homan province, used indigenous methods to produce well over three hundred loudspeakers, and rediffusion reaches every household. [New China News Agency, 21 September 1971.]

Currently, wired units at the county level are financially supported by the government, while those in communes are expected to be operated on the basis of self-reliance, with annual government subsidies of 2,000–3,000 yuans ($1,304-$1,783) (Yung 1969, p. 74).

The agricultural collectivization period of 1955-59 marked a rapid growth of wired broadcasting in China. The number of wired broadcasting units increased from 835 in 1955 to 11,124 in 1959, the number of loudspeakers from 90,500 to 4,570,000 (Liu 1971, p. 120). Especially between 1958 and 1959, the number of wired broadcasting units almost doubled. For instance, by 1959 in the province of Shantung, the wired broadcasting system reached every hsien (county) and 66% of the communes in the province, with a total of 193,000 loudspeakers (*Hsin-wen Chan-hsien* 1959d, p. 10).

With the frustration of the Great Leap Forward movement in 1959, the development of wired broadcasting systems came to a standstill. In 1960, Liu Shao-chi, then president of the People's Republic, issued a decree called "expert-operated broadcasting" policy, which further hampered development of wired units in rural areas (Su 1969, p. 53). "As early as 1958, the year of the Great Leap Forward," the New China News Agency reported, "all 12 production brigades under the Wangwa People's Commune in Kuyuan county (in Ningsia province) were linked by radio rediffusion." The Mao-dominated news agency continued, "in 1963, the rediffusion system stopped operation, on orders from the 'capitalist roaders' in power," meaning Liu and his followers. They were accused of being opposed to "the masses' studying and applying of Mao Tse-tung's thoughts in a living way" and of doing "their utmost to prevent the masses from hearing Chairman Mao's voice" by disrupting the operation of rural radio networks (New China News Agency, 27 October 1969). As a result, by 1964 the number of wired broadcasting units in the nation declined to 1,975 (Liu 1971, p. 120).

Despite enormous efforts of pro-Mao revolutionary committees to bring wired broadcasting networks under their control, the system suffered some damage during the Cultural Revolution of 1966-68. Wires were cut and equipment destroyed by the rampage of rival Red Guards. Wired units in Inner Mongolia stopped operating for more than two years; many units in rural areas of Anhwei, Hupeh, Hunan, Chekian, Szechwan, Kweichow, Yunnan, Shantung, Honan, Kiangsi, Fukien, Shensi, and Heilungkiang ceased operations in this period (Su 1969, p. 54).

In 1968, the Ninth National Congress of the Chinese Communist Party decided to "strive to do broadcasting work well" in order to send the latest instructions from the central leadership down to the grassroots level. Since then, a mass movement of restoring and expanding rural wired broadcasting networks has been promoted. According to a New China News Agency release of 21

September 1971, radio rediffusion networks covered over 98% of the production brigades and over 87% of the production teams throughout the nation. In line with this movement, radio manufacturers in China have distributed large quantities of loudspeakers, transistor radio sets, and three-purpose transistorized sets (radio-phonograph-amplifier) to meet the increasing demand of rural wired units (Yung 1969, p. 78). In 1975, the Chinese reported a total of 106 million wired loudspeakers in the countryside (Butterfield 1975).

As for programs of wired broadcasting units, it was decided in 1956 that, "while it is necessary to relay certain programs of the Central People's Broadcasting Station at specified hours, a more important task should be to strive to improve locally-originated programs." Furthermore, local programs were to be designed "to publicize and promote agricultural producers' cooperatives, to constantly stimulate the enthusiasm for labor among the peasants; to agitate for high agricultural production, and to satisfy the peasants' demands for cultural life" (Yung 1969, p. 78).

The following are examples of programs distributed by a wired broadcasting unit in a commune at Chunan in Shantung (Yu Yu-hsiu 1963, pp. 11-13). The two- or three-hour program starts at 8:30 P.M. with the playing of the Chinese national anthem, followed by a 30-minute relay of Central Broadcasting Station's daily report of national and foreign news. Next, a talk on the background of the news is usually scheduled. A 20-minute program, "For Rural Commune Members," originated by the Shantung Provincial People's Broadcasting Station, is relayed, including farm news, policies concerning the people's communes, and stories of successful farm work and management. Technological items are coordinated with the seasons. In spring, they may deal with the most rational methods of close planting; in summer, field management and control of crop pests and insects; and in winter, the best ways of grain storage. Health talks follow the same pattern: how to prevent gastrointestinal ailments in summer and colds in winter. "Life in Chunan" reports on production experiences and news of local happenings. Local model farmers are frequent speakers on the program. A 1975 report on a county in Kwangtung Province said loudspeakers operate from 5:30 A.M. to 9:30 P.M., carrying editorials from *Jen-Min Jih-Pao* and *Hung Chi,* lectures on production, and criticism of local officials and peasants (Butterfield 1975).

Entertainment programs, or "cultural programs" in Chinese Communist jargon, account for more than 50% of the unit's program time. The performances of the Peking Opera, recorded by the Central and Shantung provincial stations, are relayed by the wired unit daily. Each Saturday, the local wired unit transmits live local theater performances staged by Chunan's Peking Opera Troupe. Revolutionary songs and storytelling are other favorite items of entertainment.

Although their programs are politically oriented, the wired stations certainly have widened the horizons and cultural lives of rural inhabitants. The wires stretch far and wide, connecting remote villages with the outside world.

2.2.4 Use of Radio during the Cultural Revolution

The objective of the Great Proletarian Cultural Revolution during 1966-68, as the theoretical magazine *Hung Chi* (Red Flag) observed, was "to topple the handful of Party persons in authority taking the capitalist road, destroy bourgeois ideology, establish the ascendancy of Mao Tse-tung's thought, change people's world outlook, and dig out the roots of revisionism, so as to consolidate and strengthen the dictatorship of the proletariat in our country and consolidate and develop the socialist system" (Yu 1970, p. 73).

During this mass campaign, the Maoists accused "China's Khrushchev," Liu Shao-chi, and his followers of advocating an "open door" press policy in contrast to the traditional Communist concept of the party controlling the press. They were also denounced for urging the press to serve all readers, not just the proletariat; favoring impartial reporting; and encouraging the press to cater to popular interest (*Juang-ming Jih-pao* 1968). This professionally oriented concept of the press is unacceptable to Mao Tse-tung. To him, professionalism is a deviation from Lenin's press concept and, therefore, is considered politically unhealthy and dangerous. What was most alarming to Mao was the appearance after 1961 of political criticism in the form of stories and plays in party-controlled newspapers and journals. This situation indicated that journalists tended to align themselves with professionally oriented, anti-Mao elements.

In the early stage of the Cultural Revolution, when most newspapers and journals were in the hands of the pro-Liu faction, the Maoists had to resort to the *tatzepao* or radio to rally support from the masses. It is said that the Cultural Revolution was formally inaugurated 1 June 1966 when the Central Station in Peking broadcast the text of the first big-character poster of the Great Proletarian Cultural Revolution (Elegant 1971, pp. 163-66), attacking the Liu-controlled school administration of Peking University, a key political battlefield in modern China.

Apparently the Maoists made extensive use of the radio during the Cultural Revolution. Every major decision of the Communist Party Central Committee was broadcast, usually reaching the masses a day ahead of the newspapers. In the process, radio messages served as authoritative instructions to Red Guards throughout China in their actions against the revisionists.

In January 1967, at least nine provincial stations suspended all local news programs for over ten days, because the power struggle between Maoists and anti-Maoists in the provincial party committees created confusion in local propaganda policies (Yeh 1967, p. 58). It was not until February 1967, when provincial power passed into the hands of the People's Liberation Army that provincial broadcasting stations resumed their normal programs. The PLA took over at least part of the local party committee's supervisory role in propaganda work (Neuhauser 1968, p. 467). PLA propaganda teams toured the countryside to interpret party decisions and to work with radio stations at the grassroots level in organizing propaganda programs. By November 1967, Mao himself could report, "The comrades of the broadcasting stations have won the power of control. It is a good thing that power is now in the hands of proletarian revolutionaries" (Chen 1970, p. 134).

Generally, radio stations functioned normally during the Cultural Revolution, despite the chaos and confusion that emerged in some provinces. When it was all over, broadcasting fared quite well, escaping severe Maoist criticism, partly because stations rarely broadcast their own political commentaries. Instead, they transmitted editorials and news stories originally written by party organs. When a station transmitted objectionable editorials or news reports, the newspapers originating the items were held responsible, not the station.

2.2.5 Style and Content

It is often difficult for Westerners, accustomed to the idea that programs in Communist countries are dull, to realize what brilliant and vivid styles are stressed in mass-communications messages in China (although often they are not achieved, just talked about). With its deep concern in communications, the Chinese Communist Party, from its birth, placed great emphasis on the style of expression. Mao, in one of his major statements concerning the style of literature and arts, said, "Our demands are the unity of politics and techniques, the unity of contents and form, and the unity of the political contents of the revolution and the most possible perfection of the forms of art" (Yang 1959b, p. 22). The literary style, as advocated by Mao, is the one which combines brilliancy with vividness.

Evidently many broadcasting programs in China do not measure up to these criteria. Discussing improvement of broadcasting style, one Chinese broadcaster commented, "In some (broadcasting) programs, not a few of the sentences are extraordinarily lengthy, unpolished and unintelligible, partly literary and partly vernacular, with foreign accents and alien intonation, poor vocabulary, inappropriate terminology, coinage of new terms, excessive use of abbreviations, incomprehensible literary style, poor punctuation, and the like phenomena." Popularization and oralization are the two basic requirements of broadcasting expression in China. To meet these goals, the party urges broadcasters "to collect the folkways of the people, to learn their simple, lively speech and to absorb the spirit of the folk songs" (Yang 1959b, p. 22).

Contents of broadcasting programs in China can be classified into eight types, each having a great deal of functional singificance. The first type may be called information programs, including policy decisions; national, local and foreign news; weather reports; and publication announcements of ideological journals. Because the People's Republic of China is an organized society, policy statements are continually handed down through mass media. Major policy statements, including speeches, directives, and explanatory articles relating to policy decisions, are published in leading national newspapers and journals and then relayed by radio stations if they are of broad significance. For example, in

August 1968, *People's Daily, Red Flag,* and *Liberation Army Daily* jointly published an editorial entitled "Carry the Great Revolution on the Front of Journalism through to the End," repudiating the counter-revolutionary, revisionist line on journalism upheld by Liu Shao-chi. Representing an official press guideline during the Cultural Revolution, the 6,000-word article was broadcast verbatim throughout the country in late August and early September. Following the publication of this article, newspapers throughout China acclaimed Mao's press instruction. Meanwhile radio stations at various levels immediately broadcast the newspapers' reactions, the Shanghai People's Broadcasting Station reporting the warm response of that city's press, the Yunan People's Broadcasting Station claiming the new press instructions spelled "the complete bankruptcy of the plot to restore capitalism perpetrated by China's Khrushchev and his agents in Yunnan" (*Daily Report, Communist China,* 9-10 September 1968).

Foreign news reports are usually twisted to fit ideological concepts, i.e., the evils of capitalism or virtues of socialism. The report of anti-war demonstrations at the 1968 Chicago Democratic Convention, for example, illustrates the manifestations of Chinese Communist propaganda. "These demonstrations dealt a powerful blow to the U.S. monopoly capitalist class which was 'choosing' a presidential candidate of the Democratic Party at its convention in Chicago," the Chinese Communists broadcast. "Fearing that the news of the mass struggle might leak out to the world, the reactionary police even beat up some bourgeois reporters at the scene of struggle," it added (*Daily Report, Communist China,* 28 August 1968).

The Chinese Communist regime regards weather forecasts as an "indispensable basis" for planning agricultural, herding, fishing, salt-making, and various industrial endeavors. The Central People's Broadcast Station and the Research Institute of Meteorological Science have jointly conducted weather forecasts since 1949. At frequent intervals during rainy seasons, the amount of rainfall of every water system and the flux, reservoir level, and state of dam floodgates are broadcast. No longer must the peasants in China rely upon their personal experience in predicting weather, as was the case before 1949.

Publication announcements of ideological journals are also important items of information. For example, the Central People's Broadcasting Station transmits the table of contents of *Red Flag* on the day of this journal's appearance. Publication of new books concerning important issues is also broadcast nationwide, partly to add special significance to these works. Such publications are usually required studies to be discussed by party members and cadres in study sessions.

A second type of program may be termed discussion and criticism, concentrating on concrete experience in policy implementation and criticism of failures, errors, and deviations. This program includes lengthy principles of party lines without leading to a specific decision; it is useful to the leadership in creating a climate of favorable opinion for a forthcoming decision. Such speeches, however, need not be followed by a policy announcement: circumstances may change and a new policy direction may be pursued.

Implementation of policies is important in a Communist society, and people are urged to exchange experiences in order to learn from one another and subsequently to attain the goal set by a party policy. Broadcasting stations at different levels frequently invite cadres directly involved in a major project to tell their experiences, usually the successful ones, on the air.

Airtime is also devoted, however, to the criticism of failures, errors, deviations, crimes, and shortcomings. Of course, much of the criticism will not be published, but, if it serves as an example, it will first appear in the newspapers and then be broadcast. Such criticism appears more frequently in mass media at the local level, providing a mechanism for the release of frustration and grievances.

Aid-to-production items make up a third type of broadcasting content, because radio stations are expected to promote industrial and agricultural production. Broadcasting programs in China must be designed to mobilize all workers and peasants for active and passionate participation in production, one provincial official emphasized (Yu Shiu 1959, p. 10).

Items of interest in this category would be agricultural innovations, technological developments, labor conditions, and working experiences in farms or factories. An example of an aid-to-production broadcasting program was aired in 1958 when the party chairman of Hopei province decided to promote an extensive manure-accumulating movement. To educate the people on the significance of this drive, the provincial committee ordered local party committees to help each radio station produce a special "marathon program," "conference on the air" in Chinese Communist jargon, to explain the importance of manure as a fertilizer and the use of tools and methods for collecting it. As a result, in Chun-lung Hsien, more than 50,000 kilograms of manure were collected in a single day. Within 15 days, the provincial people's station aired four "manure-accumulating" marathon programs and 49 special reports featuring this drive (*Hsin-wen Chan-hsien* 1959a, pp. 20-21).

A fourth type of program dealing with education consists of a wide variety of materials, including lectures on social and natural sciences, tales of loyalty and heroism, and foreign-language lessons.

Social-science lectures deal almost exclusively with Marxist-Leninist and Maoist thought, while most science programs are designed to answer technical problems confronting the country's industrial, agricultural, and transportation systems.

In the 1950s, when China maintained close ties with the Soviet Union, the foreign language taught on the air was Russian. As the relationship between China and the Soviet Union became openly hostile, the Russian learning program was cancelled. Recently, since President Nixon's visit to Peking in 1972, an English-language boom has swept China, and Shanghai has been made the site of a pilot program in English-language instruction by radio. Three 30-minute lessons, scheduled daily at breakfast, lunch, and supper times, have become most popular among middle-school students. The craze also has caught on with factory workers, hotel workers, and even pedicab drivers in the street, some of whom have equipped themselves with transistor radios to learn English. Like other radio shows, English lessons are dominated with revolutionary themes. For instance, the first lesson of the 84-page textbook offers such sentences as "Chairman Mao is our great leader. We must listen to Chairman Mao and follow the Party." Another lesson contains such passages as, "The sun is red. The sun is bright. The sun is Chairman Mao. The sun is the Communist Party of China. We love Chairman Mao. We love the Communist Party of China" (*Christian Science Monitor,* 1972b). On 5 March 1973, a year after the English lessons were inaugurated in Shanghai, the Shanghai People's Station began broadcasting lessons in Japanese twice daily "in order to meet the needs of workers, peasants and soldiers, as well as the broad revolutionary masses in the study of Japanese" (*New York Times,* 1 April 1973). The foreign-language broadcast lessons are seen as an indication of the deep-rooted China drive to broaden diplomatic and trade contacts.

To model oneself after heroes and learn from great people has always been the mainstay of Mao's teachings. Heroes in modern Chinese Communist literature are very carefully selected from among three major groups: great founding figures of the party, soldier-heroes from the lowest ranks of the People's Liberation Army, and model men of action. The emulation of heroes in China is not a Communist invention; it dominated Confucian education in the form of stories about great emperors, scholars, statesmen, generals, obedient children, and pure and undefiled widows. What is different under the Communist system is the careful ideological control of hero characterizations, the use of mass campaigns to publicize heroes' deeds, and the degree of intensity and active participation encouraged. Moreover, with intensive campaigns by mass media, people are encouraged to imitate heroic acts of the *same* hero at the *same* time. A nation-wide campaign usually starts with a stream of reports and editorials in the *People's Daily* on the acts of a specific hero. These stories are reprinted in provincial and local newspapers and transmitted by radio stations at all levels.

There have been times however, when broadcasting stations have taken the initiative in starting a nation-wide campaign of heroism. For example, in February 1966, Wang Chin-hsi's story was broadcast nationally. Wang, known as the "Man of Iron," was a drill-team captain who pioneered in the drive to open up the Taching oilfields. Through radio and television, Wang told how his team moved and installed heavy machinery by hand, improvised for lack of materials, and sacrificed personal comfort to save capital for the country (Sheridan 1968, pp. 51, 62).

The fifth type of program, entertainment, features musical selections, drama, Chinese opera, and comic monologue with political and revolutionary themes. While Western music is not excluded, selections are dominated by revolutionary songs and marches. The following songs appearing in Chinese Communist broadcasting schedules may illustrate the nature of musical programs: "The East Is Red," "Never Allow American Imperialists to Occupy Our Precious Island — Taiwan," "Firmly Determined to Liberate Taiwan," "Praise People's Communes," "Praise the First Socialist Train," "Sword," and the "Anti-Aggression" marching song (*Hsin-wen Chan-hsien* 1959b, p. 26). For lack of specialized radio performers, most dramatic programs are live or recorded broadcasts of actual theater performances. The comic monologue, a traditional Chinese entertainment, has been transformed into a vehicle for political slogans.

Children's shows, designed to cultivate Communist concepts of virtues, values, and social norms in the minds of children, arouse their interest in science, promote their physical health, and inspire them to follow examples of "good men and good deeds" typified by the party, form the sixth category (Cheng, 1959, pp. 13-16). Much of the material is prepared by child education specialists, but children are invited to present revolutionary drama and talent shows.

Two other types of programs deserve special attention, sports and ethnic minorities shows. Sports programs are meant to arouse public interest in, and provide basic knowledge of, athletics. Glorification of athletes is discouraged. As in Western countries, sports programs are dominated by live broadcasts of meets and games (Yang 1959a, pp. 8-11).

China is one of the world's great cultural mosaics, composed of the Han race and 54 minorities, each with a distinctive culture. Although the minorities account for only 6% of China's population of 899 million, they occupy nearly 60% of its total land. Since the Communists came to power, a sustained drive has been mounted to integrate the minorities into the national culture. As part of this drive, the Central People's Broadcasting Station and 16 local stations have introduced special programs aimed at minorities in languages such as Tibetan, Kazakh, Uighur, and Mongolian. Special emphasis is placed either on the oppression the minorities are said to have suffered in pre-Communist days or on their present happiness (Chu 1959, p. 25).

2.2.6 Television

In May 1958, the Central People's Broadcasting Station in Peking inaugurated television broadcasting in the People's Republic. By the mid-1960s, 12 stations served the densest urban areas, and, by 1970, 30 urban stations had been developed. Only Peking had two stations. In December 1972, there was at least one station in each of China's 29 provinces, except Tibet. In January 1975, 47 stations operated, serving every province and autonomous region except Tibet, which is apparently too remote and mountainous to be accessible to microwave and cable relays from Peking. Although scant information exists concerning the number of available TV sets, it was estimated in late 1973 that there were between 100,000 and 300,000. According to Wang Nan-sheng, chief of the Television Department of the Central People's Broadcasting Station in Peking, about 50% of the TV receivers were in party and government offices, workers' clubs, and commune halls; the others were privately owned (Hangen 1970, p. 9; *Christian Science Monitor*, 1972c; *San Francisco Chronicle*, 3 December 1973). The scarcity of sets is attributed to their high cost: a black and white, 12-inch receiver costs $250, while a skilled worker earns only about $40 monthly.

In January 1970, an NBC news team in Hong Kong monitored Canton's television output for three weeks and found Canton's schedule commenced at 7 P.M. with the appearance of Mao's portrait and the singing of "The East Is Red," China's unofficial national anthem. The opening program was a newscast consisting of several film stories on topics such as the commemoration of a hero, the work of an educated youth in a remote village, the reception of foreign visitors by the Chinese leadership, and the "heroic struggle" of the North Vietnamese (for coverage of the Vietnam War, see Yeh 1966, pp. 8-11). Next came revolutionary ballet and films, usually old Chinese movies about the anti-Japanese war or the war against the Nationalist Chinese. After the Sino-Soviet ideological rift in the early 1960s and the border dispute in 1969, all but a few Russian films, such as "Lenin in October" and "Lenin in 1918," were removed from the Chinese TV screen. Occasionally, North Korean, North Vietnamese, and Albanian movies with Chinese subtitles are shown. Sign-off on Canton TV came at 10:30 P.M. The entire program was completely devoid of any interruption for commercials. The audience, however, cannot escape the bombardment of Maoism — the Chinese substitute for commercials — at any moment of the telecasts (see Green 1972, pp. 247-49).

Television stations in China normally operate three or four hours a day, but some do not have a daily schedule. About 50% of the airtime is devoted to news and sports, the latter being the most popular programs in China. Peking television carries live coverage of all major sports tournaments in the capital and relays the programs through its microwave system to numerous other stations. "Social education" programs, accounting for 30% of total airtime, range from workers, peasants, or soldiers discussing their experiences in learning and applying Maoist thought, to a lecture on the need for hygiene. Other programs can be categorized as entertainment, featuring revolutionary ballet, "model drama," music, and acrobatics. Detective shows are nonexistent, the closest thing being films featuring the search for headquarters of Nationalist Chinese agents on the mainland (Smith 1972; *Christian Science Monitor* 1972c). Recently, there has been a lessening of emphasis on the cult of Mao Tse-tung in TV programming. Until the end of 1971, the daily sign-on consisted of a chorus of "The East Is Red," praising the greatness of Mao, accompanied by the screening of his portrait. That was replaced by quotes from Mao's works, and by 1975 even the quotes had been abandoned (Burns 1975).

Educational television in China started in March 1960 with the inauguration of Peking Television College under the joint auspices of the Peking City Department of Education, Peking University, Peking Normal University, Peking Normal College, Peking Television Station, and Peking People's Broadcasting

Station. College-level courses in Chinese literature, mathematics, physics, and chemistry, as well as one preparatory class, were offered. Stress is on applying theories to practical production. Suggestions in the improvement of teaching materials are solicited from scientists and workers in factories, mines and laboratories. In every district of Peking, the TV college has established tutoring centers where students may receive help from advisers, usually school teachers, experienced engineers, or advanced students. By August 1962, there were 3,400 enrolled at the college, which allocated 1,000 TV sets to the urban and suburban areas of Peking to form a television teaching network (Fan 1961, pp. 10-11; *Jen-min Jih-pao* 1962). In July 1975, the TV station in Shanghai introduced an "Educational Seminar" which included topics such as plant pathology and dental hygiene. Speakers for the programs are recruited from Shanghai universities, and from "experienced workers and peasants" in factories, communes, or production brigades (New China News Agency, 9 July 1975).

After nearly 17 years of development, television in China is finally leaving its infancy. In the early days, the Chinese imported television equipment from the Soviet Union; now, however, they buy monitor equipment from Great Britain and lenses from France and Japan. At the same time, they are endeavoring to improve their television on the basis of self-reliance. In May 1973, Channel 8 in Peking began its color telecast. While it is still in the preliminary stage, there are no color sets on the market. Those in use are made in Japan and used by organizations. The Chinese are looking toward the West for expertise needed to inaugurate a large-scale color transmission. In October 1972, a group of Chinese TV technicians visited France, West Germany, and other European nations to examine color-television services. In August 1973, RCA announced that it would propose to help the Chinese construct color-TV picture-tube plants in China (*Peking Review* 1971, p. 15; *New York Times*, 29 August 1973). By early 1974 China had begun producing a complete range of color-TV equipment, including receivers, fixed and mobile transmitters, and control consoles, and was purchasing a color-TV outside-broadcast vehicle from Pye TV Ltd. of England (*Data for Decision*, 11-17 February 1974, p. 1571; *Media for Asia Communications Industry* [hereafter *Media*] 1974f, p. 20).

2.2.7 Training

To meet the need for the development of broadcasting, China has, since the 1950s, placed great emphasis on the training of broadcasting personnel (see Ch and Fang 1972, pp. 489-97). Under party auspices and with the support of broadcasting stations throughout China, the Peking Broadcasting College was inaugurated in 1959. It consists of departments of radio-TV news, radio electronics, and foreign languages, as well as a vocational institute for radio technology. The emphasis of the five-year training program is on fundament technical training, Marxist-Leninist doctrine, current affairs, and party policies The college aims to provide students with a general theoretical basis of Marxism-Leninism and to enable them to understand correctly the policies the party; to help them acquire a stable proletarian stand and world view and develop Communist ways of thinking, of speaking out and doing "courageously," and of pursuing what is right and practical; to cultivate the habit and behavior of learning through hardship and the passionate love for labor, solidarity, friendship, and simplicity; to teach general productive and social knowledge and the standard style of writing; and to enable students to manage broadcast propaganda, acquire the basic knowledge and skill of broadcast techniques, and master one foreign language (Yung 1959, pp. 28-29).

The objectives of Peking Broadcasting College mirror the basic education policy in Communist China, i.e., the unity of education and productive labor and the subordination of education to political goals. The party has imposed rigid requirements for admission to the college, registering only those who are "politically reliable," usually party and Communist Youth Corps members and children of workers and peasants. At least ten other institutions were set up by 1960 to train broadcasting personnel.

The departments of propaganda of the party committees at various levels and provincial broadcasting stations also conduct short-term broadcasting classes to meet local needs of broadcasting personnel. For example, in 1970, Tibet Broadcasting Station offered a three-month broadcasting technology course, requesting each Tibetan *hsien* (county) to recommend at least one "politically reliable" student with some basic knowledge of radio for admission (*Yearbook on Chinese Communism* 1971, p. 190). To create more radio technicians for the future, the Communist regime has started developing children's talents in this field. In China's "Children's Palaces" (recreational centers), there is a special course in the assembly of transistor radios, designed to give students practical knowledge of radio (*Christian Science Monitor* 1972a).

Many of the reporters, editors, and announcers in wired broadcasting units are products of short-term training programs. They are in their early twenties and hold high-school diplomas. After completing the specialized training, they are assigned to work at a unit in their home county. Besides assuming regular duties at the unit, each young broadcaster has to participate in farm work and call on listeners, particularly old people. Each broadcaster has a circle of "listener-friends," whom he contacts every fortnight or month for suggestions. A usual way is to sit through a program together, or to discuss a prepared script. Feeling that they are a part of the wired unit, peasants often report interesting news — the achievements of a production team, outstanding deeds by members of the team, and anecdotes from daily life — by telephone, mail, or even on foot (Yu Yu-hsiu 1963, p. 13).

2.2.8 External Broadcasting

The purpose of China's external broadcasting has been primarily to articulate Chinese foreign policy, to tell the world of political, social, economic, and scientific achievements of the country, and ultimately to enhance her status in international communities. In trying to help a pro-Communist party overthrow the government in a foreign country, Peking's external broadcasting would disseminate information which set various segments of the society against each other and against the government.

The external broadcasting service, known as Radio Peking, started its broadcasting in 1950 in six foreign languages (English, Japanese, Vietnamese, Indonesian, Burmese, and Thai) for seven hours a day to the audiences in the neighboring countries, and in five Chinese dialects for 17½ hours a week for overseas Chinese in Southeast Asia. After the Korean War, Peking's direct interest in the cause of revolution outside China was reflected in its active participation in international conferences of nonalignment countries and in a sizeable expansion of the external broadcasting service. In 1956, broadcasting hours to overseas Chinese were increased to 45½ a week. Programs to Cambodia and Laos, English broadcasts to the Near and Middle East, and English and Spanish to Europe were added. Transmissions in Arabic, Persian, and Turkish, and French broadcasting to Africa were initiated in 1957 and 1958. By June 1958, Radio Peking aired programs in 15 foreign languages for 22 hours a day (Mei 1950; Houn 1961, p. 151).

Ten years later, Peking's programs were broadcast in 31 languages, ranging from Tagalog (the native tongue of the Philippines) to Swahili, and in five Chinese dialects with a total of 1,720 hours a week, including 60 hours to North America, 412 to Northeast Asia, 319 to South and Southeast Asia, 417 to Europe, 105 to Africa (sub-Sahara), 35 to the Arab World and North Africa, 70 to Latin America, and 302 to Russia. Apparently the single country receiving the most attention from Radio Peking is Russia. With the deterioration of relations between these two Communist giants, Radio Peking's Russian-language program increased from 98 hours a week in 1966 to 302 in 1968 (Kimberley 1969).

Any sudden increase in broadcasting time to a particular area usually indicates China's specific foreign-policy moves. For example, Peking's active diplomatic offensive in Europe in 1970 witnessed a corresponding increase in broadcast time to Italy and Turkey. China eventually established her diplomatic relations with Italy and Turkey in November 1970 and August 1971, respectively. An international crisis can result in a significant shift in Radio Peking's schedules. During the French student riots in May and June of 1968, for instance, Peking increased its French broadcasting to Europe from 14-56 hours a week to voice its firm support to the antigovernment elements. Following the Soviet invasion of Czechoslovakia in August 1968, Radio Peking initiated a program in Czech, lasting three hours a day, to denounce the "revisionist imperialism," meaning the Soviet Union's foreign policy.

At peak hours, Radio Peking puts into operation more than 40 different transmitters with power outputs of up to 240,000 w. While accurate information concerning the locations of Radio Peking's many powerful transmitters is not available, it is evident that they are scattered throughout the entire China mainland. At least two of the principal Radio Peking transmitters are operating from Canton. Others are located at Urumchi, Sinkiang, mainly for broadcasts in

Russian, and in Harbin, Manchuria. Some of Radio Peking's broadcasts to Europe, Africa, and North America are believed to be relayed from Chiak, capital of Albania (Kimberley 1969). Together with Radio Moscow, the Voice of America, and the British Broadcasting Corporation, Radio Peking is among the four international broadcasting giants in the world.

2.2.9 Conclusion

Radio played a small role in the lives of most people in China before the Communists came to power in 1949. Although the Nationalists had striven to build a nation-wide broadcasting system, radio stations in operation were predominantly in big cities and seaports such as Shanghai, Peking, and Canton. It was after the 1950s that the broadcasting network started spreading from the center to the provinces, and from the provincial capitals to the local level. But it is the wired broadcasting network that penetrates into every part of the nation. The radio diffusion system that connects villages and remote regions with the outside world has changed the lives of the people in these areas.

Of course, the Chinese Communists did not invent this system; it was initiated in the Soviet Union (Inkeles 1958, p. 239). The difference between the Soviet and Chinese wired broadcast networks lies not in purposes or natures of the systems, but in their intensity and scope. The New China News Agency reported in 1971 that the wired broadcast networks had covered more than 96% of the production brigades in the nation.

The Chinese Communist leadership has long realized the importance of television as a "propaganda medium," but the expense of setting up a vast TV network is considerable to China, because of the economic difficulties and strains she has suffered since 1958.

Both radio and television programs in China are predominantly political and revolution-oriented. It is true that under the Communist rule, broadcasting and other mass media are merely propaganda devices. Yet, at the great cost of freedom of the press and other political freedoms, the Chinese Communists have succeeded in controlling the country, despite grave divisions among the leadership, and in restoring to the Chinese their national pride.

2.3 Republic of Korea (South Korea), *by Sunwoo Nam*

Japan's 36-year rule over Korea ended with World War II, when the nation was divided into half — the Americans holding the South, the Russians the North. With the overthrow of the Syngman Rhee government in 1960, South Korea changed from a presidential to a cabinet system of government. The Republic of Korea has been in and out of emergency rule numerous times over the past three

Sunwoo Nam is Associate Professor at Norfolk State College and former Assistant Professor of Journalism at the University of Hawaii. He was a journalist with *Dong-A Daily News* for five years. He was a Fulbright and East Asian Studies Scholar and received his Ph.D. from the University of Wisconsin.

decades. In October 1972, President Park Chung Hee proclaimed the most recent emergency period. The North-South question, i.e., the perpetuation of the two-Koreas status or establishment of one Korea under confederation, remained deadlocked in 1975. Mass communications has played a key role in this struggle over reunification. For example, in November 1972 both governments agreed to desist from hostile propaganda. That agreement was broached two years later, however, when South Koreans were accused of sending propaganda balloons into the North and the northerners were blamed for operating a clandestine radio station near the demilitarized zone.

South Korea, consisting of 2,917 islands plus the peninsula, has a total population of 33.3 million; nearly a third of these people are concentrated in seven cities, the largest being the capital, Seoul. The income per capita in 1973 was $373.

Wracked by charges of corruption and general discontent among students, opposition politicians, and the clergy, the Park government in 1974-75 set down numerous repressive decrees, including many aimed at the mass media. Among South Korea's 14 dailies, *Dong-A Ilbo,* the largest with 500,000 circulation, and its sister broadcasting station, felt the harshest blows.

2.3.1   Introduction

It is axiomatic that a country's mass-media system is shaped by its environment, both internal and external, and is interdependent with other subsystems. Geopolitical factors that historically shaped the fate of South Korea have largely influenced present-day broadcasting conditions as well. For example, the impact of Japanese broadcasting is felt in South Korea not only because of the colonial legacy, but also because of the proximity. The Chinese influence, another traditional source, is held at a minimum in South Korea because of political and ideological considerations, since South Korea is in the Western camp. The 1945 division of Korea into two parts, traumatic experiences of the 1950-53 Korean War, and subsequent confrontation between the two Koreas, all took their toll in terms of what South Korean broadcasting can and cannot do.

Economic factors, such as growing GNP, income per capita, and rapid industrialization, also aid the growth of broadcasting media. Some researchers claim a spiraling relationship between media development and expansion in other sectors of society (Schramm 1960, pp. 131-40). To a certain extent, this has probably happened in South Korea, although with the advent of television, conspicuous consumption for the sake of national prestige may be a better explanation.

Television is still a very expensive medium for South Korea. The problem was compounded in late 1972 when the Commerce and Industry Ministry was supposed to decide whether color television was practicable for South Korea. The debate flared up after the ministry announced that test production was underway to turn out 300,000 color-TV sets, 10% of which would be destined for local buyers. *Dong-A Ilbo* carried a critical article saying that the sales of color-TV sets to South Korean citizens at that time was a "fringe operation of a new export venture which would amount to letting the tail wag the dog" (*The Asian* 1972). The ministry stated that the priority for some years would have to be given to spreading black and white sets among the less-privileged rural population. South Korea manufactured its first color-TV sets by early 1974 as a result of a joint venture between two Korean and two Japanese firms. By June of the same year, there were at least three other Korean produces of color-TV sets. All of the sets, expected to run into the tens of thousands by 1975, were for export, because South Korea does not have a color-TV station (*Data for Decision*, 10-16 June 1974, p. 1968). The government plans to develop its first color-TV station in 1977 (*FEER* 1974, p. 38).

One survey conducted by the Korean Broadcasting Association in 1970 claimed that even in metropolitan Seoul, only 20% of the households had TV sets — 218,679 out of 335,864 sets in South Korea — whereas there were 3,053,259 radio-receiving sets, out of which 7,286 were amplifiers and 512,884 were wired receivers (*Radio and Television Yearbook 1971*, pp. 306, 311). Another source reported that in 1972 there were about 900,000 TV sets in Korea, 91% of them in urban areas. To help make television practicable for rural audiences, the Commerce and Industry Ministry in 1973 planned to develop a receiver that costs about one-third that of standard models. Initially, 1,000 such sets were to be distributed to villages where new community-development projects were being undertaken (*AMC Bulletin* 1973b).

The 46 radio stations in Korea in 1970 included 17 owned by the government and 29 owned privately. The government radio network also had 14 transmission and 25 relay facilities. FM broadcasting, begun very recently, numbered four stations in October 1970 (*Radio and Television Yearbook* 1971, p. 373). A more recent source gave the number of radio transmitters as 123 (70 long and medium-wave, 6 short-wave, and 47 FM) (UNESCO 1975, p. 304). As for television, the Korean Broadcasting Corporation has stations in ten cities, plus 17 low-power repeaters; Tong-Yang Broadcasting (TBC), two stations; Hankuk Munhwa Broadcasting Corporation, seven stations; and the American forces Korea Network, 11 stations (*WRTH* 1974, p. 296).

The first use of satellites for communication in South Korea was achieved in 1969 when KBS-TV and Tong-Yang Broadcasting Company brought Korean viewers the Apollo moon-landing. During the moon-landing mission, more than 50,000 Seoul citizens watched on a giant screen in the city plaza. The Korean government joined the Intelsat system in 1969, and the following year, with the help from the United States, the Ministry of Telecommunication established an earth station in Keumsan, 30 miles from Seoul. Its use for television has been minimal; during a 15-month period in 1970-71, only 22 hours, 39 minutes of time was spent for television service. Most of the shows were received from the United States, a few from Japan (Hur 1974, pp. 42-45).

2.3.2 Historical Development

Korean broadcasting has come a long way since its meager beginning in 1927. Seoul Broadcasting Station as a legal corporation started 16 February 1927, with the call letters JODK and with 1 kw. of power. Because of an exorbitant listening fee, the majority of the sets were owned by the Japanese occupiers (6,881 out of 8,204 in 1929) who basked in the sudden-found prosperity in their colony. Korean and Japanese were used alternately as broadcast languages until 1934. Even under the constant surveillance and censorship of the Japanese, broadcasting did much to inspire local artists to express themselves in such a way as to preserve Korean culture as distinct from Japanese.

During the Korean War, the American Forces Korean Network (AFKN), initially an extension of Far East Network in Japan, started radio broadcasts in Seoul in September 1950. By 1958, AFKN had also developed a television station. On 12 May 1956, Korea had its first television station when, with the aid of an equipment contract with RCA in the United States, HLKZ-TV came on the air. A commercial setup operating in Seoul, HLKZ-TV was sold to the president of a Korean newspaper company in 1957, and the firm was rechristened Dae-Han Broadcasting Company. A fire in 1959 destroyed the station and it died. The then-government company, Korean Broadcasting System, started KBS-TV in December 1961. By 1963, set fees were levied to help make up the deficit the station incurred. Tong-Yang Broadcasting initiated its TV operations in 1964 (Suh 1968).

Quantitatively and qualitatively, Korean broadcasting expanded during the 1960s. Before then, broadcasting was government operated, except for a couple of Christian stations. The establishment of Munwha Broadcasting Company (MBC) in December 1961 marked the commencement of dual governance with government and privately owned networks and individual stations.

The publicly managed Korean Broadcasting Corporation (KBC), formerly known as Korean Broadcasting System and the largest electronic medium outfit in South Korea, has its key station in Seoul and a total of 51 stations throughout the nation, including two each of 500 kw. and 100 kw. KBC operates two domestic networks and an international broadcasting service consisting of three short-wave stations in Seoul, Suwon, and Taegu. International services include broadcasts designed for 11 areas of the world (*WRTH* 1974, p. 157). Before 1973, KBC had been a state-run enterprise for 46 years. During that time, it saw its role as "propagating the government policies of independence, self-sufficiency and self-help for the people" and claimed to devote itself to contribute to the modernization of South Korea and reunification of both Koreas (*Radio and Television Yearbook* 1971, p. 77). It also sought to engender a healthy and joyous livelihood for the people and to distribute and nurture national culture and arts.

Among important commercial radio networks are Hankuk Munhwa Broadcasting Company, with 15 different stations; Dong-A Broadcasting System; and Tong-Yang Broadcasting Company. A number of Christian organizations also broadcast in Korea, such as Christian Broadcasting System, with five stations; Evangelical Alliance Mission, with its TEAM Radio Far East station, and Far East Broadcasting Company. The American Forces Korean Network has 17 medium-wave and four FM stations in South Korea (*WRTH* 1974, p. 159). Additionally, 500,000 receivers are connected to a wired rediffusion service (UNESCO 1975, p. 306).

2.3.3 Governance

KBC radio in 1972 was supported solely by the government fund, whereas KBC television was financed jointly by collection of viewer fees and the government fund. Use of advertising by KBC-TV was halted when two commercial TV stations began slicing into the advertising pie. KBC radio and TV were under the supervision of the Ministry of Culture and Public Information, which is also the licensing body for privately owned, commercial outlets. Technical functions of KBC were controlled by the Ministry of Communication.

According to the Broadcasting Law, passed in 1963 and amended the following year, each South Korean station must have a deliberative body on programming, composed of more than five members with good educations and reputations and hopefully representing varied classes and professions. As for programming itself, a balance must be struck among news, cultural enlightenment, music, entertainment, and "others." A 1964 presidential decree on the Broadcasting Law specified the weekly content proportions as follows: news, more than 10%; education and cultural enlightenment, more than 30%; entertainment, more than 20%; advertising, "some"; and other broadcasts, "some."

Another feature of the South Korean Broadcasting Law is the provision of retraction contained in Section 12. Stations must investigate merits of complaints that individual rights have been infringed by its broadcasts. The complaint must be accompanied by a demand for retraction within seven days of the broadcast. If it is found that the broadcast was not factual, the station should broadcast a retraction of the same magnitude as the original broadcast.

Under Section 21 of the law, stations must report monthly to the Ministry of Culture and Public Information a summary of their broadcasting, based on a diary of daily broadcasts. The penalty for not complying with these and other sections of the law was relatively mild until the new Broadcasting Law went into effect in 1973; now, it is a fine of won 200,000 ($500).

No insulation from direct political control exists in South Korea, if the control is from government and the ruling party. Thus government-operated networks definitely are voices of the administration. But even private networks are not truly independent. For example, the largest, Munwha Broadcasting Company, is operated by a group having close relationships with the ruling party; another, Tong-Yang Broadcasting Company, is part of a media chain of newspapers and magazines owned by an extremely wealthy industrialist who seems bent on maintaining the status quo. Christian Broadcasting System is operated under the supervision of the Association of Korean Christian Denominations.

Governmental fear of the emergence of a real independent network is evidenced by the repeated rejections of applications for a network by Dong-A Broadcasting Station, owned by *Dong-A Ilbo,* the closest thing to an opposition paper in South Korea. Dong-A Broadcasting has a single station in Seoul whose news coverage is reputed to be the most comprehensive and authoritative among all stations. The station suffered the displeasure of government in 1964 when two of its staff were charged with seditious speech for their presentation of a mildly sarcastic radio program called "Parrot." After several months in jail, they were found innocent by the court.

In late 1974 and early 1975, Dong-A Broadcasting often found itself the victim of Park repression. On 12 February 1975, for example, a press conference of the president of the opposition New Democratic Party aired over Dong-A was jammed. Reporters calling in news stories for live broadcasts found their telephone lines were dead (Jameson 1975, p. 5-A). On 17 March, while the station and its sister, *Dong-A Ilbo,* the largest Korean daily, were striking because of government abuse, a group of 200 "thugs" aided by police broke into the building and harassed staff members. As one reporter wrote:

The producers, announcers and engineers (50 in all), who were on the 4th floor of the building in the broadcasting office, were dragged out by the thugs, who had entered by breaking the shutters. A producer . . . was beaten by several of the intruders, and fainted as a result of the pain. . . . The thugs kicked the female announcers, who left the building weeping [Kim 1975].

A look at 1970 advertising statistics of privately owned stations makes one suspect the possibility of indirect governmental help to favored stations. Munwha Broadcasting Company, which is supposed to be very sympathetic to government, had 80 major advertisers in its account, whereas Tong-Yang Broadcasting Company and Dong-A Broadcasting, both major stations, had 49 and 37 respectively (*Dong-A Yearbook* 1971 p. 717).

When one speaks about the control of broadcasting in a given country, he must concurrently talk about the nature of the political system itself. If the political system is characterized by what might be termed modernizing authoritarian or modernizing dictatorial features (and South Korea vacillates between the two), then broadcasting will certainly reflect overall lack of subsystem autonomy. In other words, not just media are under the control of the ruling elite, but all other subsystems, such as the judiciary, labor unions, and colleges.

According to the ruling elite of South Korea, the continued provocation and threat of invasion from North Korea necessitate restrictions on civil liberties, such as press freedom, so that the nation can defend itself. That being the case, restrictions on broadcasting and other media will continue as long as this definition of a crisis situation remains unchanged. Even the 4 July 1972 announcement by both Koreas that a dialogue should be initiated and that a military solution must be renounced did not immediately affect the scope of South Korean civil liberties.

2.3.4 Self-Regulation

In the early 1960s, the Korean government promoted the concept of self-regulation among broadcasting stations. On 14 June 1963, the Korean Broadcasting Ethics Commission was inaugurated under the supervision of the Ministry of Public Information. The commission originally consisted of one representative from each of the seven stations and six from fields other than broadcasting. One of the commission's first acts was to develop a rather inclusive code of ethics. Befitting a developing country, the Korean code stipulates, "Commercial broadcasting should especially endeavor to contribute to the economic development of Korea." One of the major subjects the code deals with is advertising. Before discussing code regulations on advertising, it might be wise to first cover broadcast advertising generally.

In South Korea, most advertising time is sold by the network and station advertising staffs, although there are a few program companies usually allied with the networks or individual stations. Most purchasers of broadcast time sponsor the popular serial soap operas and variety shows rather than buy spot announcements. Probably the largest advertisers in broadcasting are the pharmaceutical, food-manufacturing, and alcoholic and beverage companies.

Radio advertising fees in Seoul range from Won 5,600 ($14) for a ten-second spot announcement in prime time to Won 62,800 ($132) for sponsoring an hour program in prime time. Television rates are from the equivalent of $16 for a ten-second spot to $250 for sponsoring an hour show in prime time (*Radio and Television Yearbook* 1971, pp. 299, 304).

The Korean Broadcasting Code of Ethics regulates the volume of commercial messages on the air. For example, until 1973, less than a minute of advertisements could be allotted for five minutes of broadcasting time, less than three minutes for 30 minutes of airtime, and less than 10% for shows over 30 minutes.

Self-regulatory advertising codes of the private broadcasting industry also provide for professional and review committees. All commercial messages should clear the review committee before going on the air, except for messages that cannot wait because of the locale of the station or the time factor. The professional committee rules on cases that cannot be decided by the review committee. Occasionally, it also decides on acceptable expressions and language to be used in commercial messages.

The Code of Ethics also guards against broadcasting social taboos, ranging from drug abuse to explicit portrayal of sex relations on television. Although these taboos should be understood as an effort to preserve Korean culture and tradition in the inevitable clash between things Korean and Western, some of a political nature are difficult to justify. For example, because of the confrontation between the two Koreas, program content praising North Korea may be justifiably suppressed, but banning songs or novels written by individuals who went to North Korea may be a little too authoritarian.

During its first eight years, the Korean Broadcasting Ethics Commission dealt with violations of the code in the four major areas of news reporting and commentating, entertainment, popular music, and advertising (*Radio and Television Yearbook* 1971, p. 715). Under news reporting, cases ranged from revealing names and addresses of juvenile offenders to failure to obtain screening on national security matters. Vulgar expressions and obscenities in soap operas, variety, and comedy shows were noted by the commission, as were imitation, vulgarities, and Japanese tunes under the category of popular music. Advertising messages in violation of the code dealt with exaggeration to the extent of criticizing other products, stimulation of a gambling spirit, and undue praise for foreign items.

In mid-1975, the Broadcasting Ethics Commission cracked down on obscene and violent television commercials, banning 25 TV spots considered objectionable. The banned commercials were primarily for Korean products. According to one publication:

Familiar names among the 25 were Dial Soap, Melrose Vodka. . . . For exposing too much skin − on children as well as on shapely models − ads for one sun oil, one body lotion and Panda towels were killed. An ad for men's hair oil called Vister was considered too violent. An oil stove and a mayonnaise commercial were also objectionable. The judges must have had Linda Lovelace on their minds because the largest group considered obscene was eight advertisements for ice cream bars and cones. Although quite innocuous by western standards, they usually featured beautiful girls excitedly licking or sucking Popsicle-type bars. . . . Undoubtedly the worst offender was a new product called Venus Love Peanuts Cone; not bad until you learn that in Korean "peanuts" is always plural and the "t" is always silent [*Media,* August 1975, p. 21] .

2.3.5 Programming

Korean radio broadcasting, both government and private, is not predominantly entertainment oriented; rather, it serves to inform with large dosages of news, cultural enlightenment, and service information (see Table 2).

Cultural-enlightenment broadcasts are usually lectures by professors, writers, and other intellectuals, while service information refers to tips for daily living, e.g., programs for housewives, farmers, and taxicab drivers. Such programming must be acceptable to South Korean audiences; a 1972 study showed 30% of the urban and 60% of the rural populations listed radio as their main source of information (Mun 1972, pp. 25-26). Another study, based on stratified random sampling in the Seoul-Inchon-Suwon metropolitan areas, revealed that over 50% of the respondents listen to radio daily (*Dong-A Yearbook* 1971, p. 716).

Naturally, one would expect differences between the programming of KBC and that of other stations. For example, KBC newsreporting has taken the form

Table 2.   South Korean Radio Program Types, September 1970

Program Type	Percentage of Total Broadcast Fare
News	16.2
Cultural Enlightenment	9.7
Service Information	16.3
Music	26.9
Drama	15.7
Entertainment	8.7
Other	6.5
Total	100.0

Source: Dong-A Yearbook 1971, p. 715.

of government public relations. In addition, KBC handles special broadcast services, e.g., educational broadcasting, armed forces hours, and anti-Communist programs, none of which are very common to privately owned networks and stations.

External services are provided almost solely by KBC. What little privately owned stations broadcast externally usually goes to North Korea in the form of dramatizations of the good life of South Korea and letters to North Koreans. In 1970, this amounted to a total of 2 hours and 20 minutes per day. The external services of KBC broadcast in Korean, Japanese, Chinese, Vietnamese, English, French, Spanish, and Russian for a total of 19 hours daily (UNESCO, 1975, p. 306). Programs are based on packages for foreign syndication. Purposes behind such efforts are to gain world-wide support by propagating the picture of South Korean national development and condemning the "barbaric invasion of the Puppet Regime of North Korea" (Radio and Television Yearbook 1971, p. 211). The latter position was modified somewhat after the 4 July 1972 agreement between the two Koreas; no longer were broadcasts to refer to North Korea as the puppet regime, and name-calling generally was discontinued. But the agreement was broken by 1974.

Additionally, KBC's external service gives special stress to broadcasting to the Communist world, especially to North Korea. This particular role, as defined by the Korean Broadcasting Association, is: to criticize the contradictions of Communism; to stimulate the internal collapse of puppet North Korea; to show the superiority of liberal democracy; to encourage favorable disposition toward the Republic of Korea in the minds of North Koreans; and to cultivate the spirit of nationhood for the future democratic reunification. Total KBC programming of anti-Communist messages in 1972 came to a daily 33 hours: 26 by medium-wave, 7 by short-wave; 41% of this total was designed as psychological warfare, 51% as propaganda to favorably dispose North Koreans toward South Korea.

Korean Broadcasting Corporation is also the only provider of educational broadcasting. What KBC does in the way of schools broadcasting, however, is almost negligible in both effect and amount of time allocated. One of the networks of KBC radio has scheduled several hours of educational broadcasting, out of which 105 minutes per day are actually schools (in-class) broadcasting. KBC-TV spent 90 minutes daily on schools broadcasting until April 1973 when the programs were dropped completely for their ineffectiveness. Produced jointly by the Ministry of Education and KBC, the schools broadcasts generally suffer from a lack of receivers in the classrooms. A 1969 study revealed that although 80.4% of all elementary schools had radio sets, over two-thirds of these had only one set. [Not that low compared to other countries of the world — editor.] The same study pointed out the difficulties of relating the broadcasts to the classroom. For example, 55.4% of the elementary-school principals indicated the need to change the hours of broadcasts and 25% desired changes in content (*Radio and Television Yearbook* 1971, pp. 39—40).

Educational television in South Korea was no less a failure because of the same problems, complicated by premature attempts to reach secondary schools. A rumor circulated in mid-1973 that the Korean Educational Development Institute would develop full-scale ETV for classroom use to bridge the gap between rural and urban schools.

Thus far, schools broadcasting in South Korea has not been very encouraging, the main criticism being that it is not responsive to the needs of schools. In addition, it has been plagued by insufficient funds to purchase sets and the lack of evaluative research. As for other educational fare, some of which competes with prime-time shows on other stations, it is difficult to assess its effectiveness without audience research. One ambitious project initiated by the government in 1972 created the Korean Radio Correspondence College which will use KBC to provide college education to those who cannot obtain or afford admission into regular colleges. In less than a year, 12,000 students were enrolled.

South Korean television has a large news and cultural affairs schedule, larger, say, than in the United States. The Korean Broadcasting Association feels the nation's television programming is characterized by an equal ratio of entertainment and non-entertainment shows, by the relegation of foreign movies to a back seat, by an emphasis on cultural-enlightenment programs (at the same time there is a lack of development of documentaries), and by the major role soap operas play in the entertainment field (see Table 3). An unusual trait of TV programming in South Korea is that morning hours are filled with rebroadcasts of previous night programs (*Radio and Television Yearbook* 1971, p. 71).

Despite the importance placed on locally produced soap-opera drama, South Korean television still is saturated with foreign-produced programs, mainly from the United States: "Bonanza," "Marcus Welby," "Hawaii Five-O," "Robin Hood," "Gunsmoke," "Disneyland," and "Ironside," among others, are included in the prime-time schedules of all three TV stations. Voices of Korean actors are dubbed in. In addition, old Hollywood movies are offered as late shows. Criticism of TV content exists, as noted by one critic's remarks that the violence-laden and otherwise mediocre TV programs are apparently designed to dull the critical senses of people (Lee 1972, pp. 226—31).

Table 3. South Korean Television Program Types, 1970

Program Type	Percentage of Broadcast Fare		
	KBC	TBC	MBC
News	16	9.1	15.8
Cultural Enlightenment	25	23.4	25.9
Education	7	–	–
Sports	–	3.1	4.2
Drama		18.9	13.0
Shows and Entertainment	}51{	13.0	11.5
Foreign and Korean Movies		24.0	17.2
Other	1	8.5	12.4
Total	100	100.0	100.0

Source: Radio and Television Yearbook 1971, p. 71.

2.3.6 Problems

In addition to the problems already indicated, South Korean broadcasting is also afflicted by a dependence upon foreign programs and equipment, inadequate local training, and a very thorny press-freedom issue.

Foreign influences in South Korean broadcasting become obvious when one looks at the backgrounds of decision-making personnel at nearly all stations; most are products of Japanese or United States schools. The result has been that South Korean programs are modeled after those in Japan or the United States, without creating much of a Korean style. In addition, foreign material, especially from the United States, inundates large portions of the nation's broadcasting time. Of course, the presence of the United States Armed Forces Korea Network (radio and TV) is a contributing factor toward the Americanization of South Korean programming. There is a high interest in Japanese programs among South Koreans, partly because many older Koreans understand that language, and partly because in southern coastal regions Japanese TV signals are better received than those of South Korea. It is rumored that when TV stations contemplate program changes, they send their producers and directors to the southern port of Pusan to watch Japanese TV.

South Korean broadcasting is dependent on the United States and Japan for its more sophisticated equipment as well. Firms in both countries have been known to dispose of surplus black-and-white TV sets in South Korea, when their own countries entered the color-broadcast era. With some exceptions of locally made equipment, a large amount of the nation's broadcast machinery, especially for television, bears the names of RCA, Ampex, Toshiba, and NEC. Most of South Korea's radio receivers are manufactured more or less domestically, while TV sets are merely assembled from Japanese parts. When in late 1972 South Korea began test-producing color-TV sets, the venture was undertaken with technical support and parts imports from Japanese firms. Apparently repair of TV receivers has been a major problem in Korea. In 1974 the Korean Broadcasting System established a mobile TV-servicing team which was to visit cities and districts to repair receivers free of charge (*ABU Newsletter,* August 1974, p. 20).

Although South Korea has nine universities with journalism-broadcasting departments, not one is technically equipped to train broadcast-media personnel. Therefore, training tends to be on-the-job. Annually, stations recruit job applicants through a highly competitive examination. On-the-job training lasts from six months to a year. A few trainees are granted scholarships to study abroad.

Probably the most severe problem facing South Korean broadcasting is in the realm of freedom of the press. As it applies to broadcasting media, press freedom in South Korea is rather elusive. Of course, with government-operated radio and TV networks, very little freedom exists on programming and personnel decisions. KBC information programs publicize governmental successes to the extent that if one's only source of news were KBC, he would believe everything is going very well in South Korea, a very distorted picture indeed. Governmental use of broadcasting, however, for birth-control and development campaigns is bearing fruit, probably because the intensification of rural electrification and the wiring of villages with amplifiers and speakers have allowed radio to penetrate the hinterlands.

Although the privately owned broadcasting industry is supposedly self-regulated through its own code and commission, more fundamentally these stations are circumscribed by geopolitical factors facing the nation. The government's anti-Communist policy, plus provocation from the North, makes any objective reporting of Communist affairs, especially those of North Korea, nearly impossible. Even the terminology to be used by media in discussing Communist leaders and governments has been specified by the authorities or by standing custom. For example, not even the 4 July 1972 agreement was able to change the media custom of referring to Communist leaders without the prefix, "Mr.".

Naturally, broadcasters are extremely cautious in their reporting of national security and defense affairs. One generally expects freedom of press and speech to contract during wartime or crisis situations. If a situation is defined, however, as a crisis or national emergency by the ruling elite, despite objective facts to the contrary, the resulting restriction of freedom is difficult for some intellectuals to tolerate. This is especially so if the intellectuals suspect, as in South Korea, that the real reason for the proclamation of national emergency was a desire on the part of the present leadership to perpetuate itself.

In South Korea, exposés of governmental and societal corruption by broadcasting stations may be construed as criticism of the present state of affairs — be it national emergency or martial law — and as propaganda aids to North Koreans. Thus, broadcasters must be wary of investigative reporting.

Additionally, Korean broadcasters are not allowed to editorialize on the air, government authorities tending to view broadcast media as separate from the press, which does have the editorial function (Lee 1969, p. 71).

2.3.7   Emergency and Martial Law

Control over broadcasting content, even that of privately owned stations, tightened with the declaration of a national emergency in South Korea at the end of 1971. During this period the president was empowered to restrict the media as he saw fit, all in the name of national security. In line with "government directives emphasizing national security entertainment," privately owned stations reconstituted their programs, dropping broad news coverage and social-comment programs such as "30 minute news shows," "the opinions of citizens," "radio columns," and "accidental firing" segments. They were replaced with relatively innocuous shows such as "short news presentation and request music," "living economy," "echo of classics," and "foreign topics" (*Shin Dong-A,* February 1972, p. 347). Furthermore, at the behest of the Ministry of Culture and Public Information, entertainment programs, such as the daily serialization, began to deal with national-security materials — anti-Communist items emphasizing the importance of emergency measures in the name of national security.

On the heels of the national emergency period, President Park in October 1972 declared martial law in South Korea. Subsequent events changed the entire political system — from a purported Western-style democracy to a Korean-type democracy — but the martial-law rule itself was mainly an indication of what South Koreans would have to get used to, i.e., a strong president unencumbered by any limitation on the number of terms of office, a new constitution spelling out the "Korean democracy," a window-dress and ineffectual legislature, and a stringent policy forbidding any criticism of government in the name of national solidarity.

Such far-reaching and all-encompassing "revitalizing reforms" cannot fail to produce long-term repercussions on every subsystem of society, press and broadcasting media included. The stage was set for the two months of martial rule when outright censorship of all media occurred. Symbolic of the severity of the rule were the bayonet-wielding soldiers guarding the gate of the *Dong-A Ilbo* building, which also houses Dong-A Broadcasting.

In addition to such negative control of mass media, there is a trend among South Korean journalists to play activist roles in support of President Park's "save the nation" movement. They not only refrain from opposing the new framework of leadership, but also faithfully parrot slogans exhorting the people to join in the nation-building work. At least in 1972, there were many hortatory slogans promoted by journalists, possibly because of the forthcoming elections. In short, mass media have been mobilized to be active supporters of a government which finds President Park in the inviolable father-figure role. Thus, South Korea now has one of the most controlled media situations outside the

Communist world.

Another justification offered for these extraordinary measures is that South Korea will be made strong and prosperous under martial law and thereby better able to deal with North Korea in its quest for a peaceful unification. The surprise 4 July 1972 thaw between the two Koreas produced a major change in the long-standing practice of psychological warfare by both sides. Initially, the vilification campaigns generally heard in external broadcasts subsided considerably by mutual agreement. After a number of talks by high-level government and Red Cross personnel, in both Pyongyang and Seoul, all psychological-warfare broadcasts were dropped in November 1972, but resumed by 1974.

The thaw that brought such drastic changes in external broadcasting, however, failed to produce much reform in South Korean domestic broadcasting policy; if anything, control over broadcasting was stiffened during that period. In the face of such tight domestic regulation, the South Korean government's plan to make KBC a public corporation was not generally interpreted as a genuine effort to increase broadcasting freedom. The revised Broadcasting Law of February 1973, which made KBC a public corporation under the new name Korean Broadcasting Corporation, changed other aspects of electronic media as well. For one thing, it put sharp teeth into the Broadcasting Ethics Commission, which is now composed of 15 members – one each representing KBC and the privately owned stations, and 7-13 representing educational, religious, cultural, and other fields. A new extensive code of ethics was promulgated by the commission, any stipulations of which are violated results in the commission demanding an apology, correction, explanation, or retraction. Also, the commission can demand the discontinuation of the appearance or writing of the person responsible. A station must immediately broadcast the commission's review upon such a demand, and carry out what is demanded within seven days. Should the station not comply with the commission's demand, the Ministry of Culture and Public Information can order such compliance on the strength of its licensing powers.

The emergency cabinet, on 9 March 1973, also revised the presidential decree of the Broadcasting Law. The revised decree stipulates that a select, five to seven member committee of the ethics commission shall meet more than once weekly to review content of all stations. If a station should not agree with committee findings, it can appeal only once within three days.

The decree also increased the proportion of programming devoted to cultural enlightenment from 20-30% and placed a specific limit on the number and duration of advertisements. Overall, a program sponsor can utilize no more than 10% of a show's total time for commercials. As for spot commercials, TV stations can insert three breaks, each of which can contain four messages of 20-second duration, in any given hour. Radio stations can place four commercial periods, each of which can contain four messages of 20-second duration, in an hour. The total impact of these stipulations is likely to be a severe blow to private stations, which not only have to revamp their offerings but also must contend with the lessening of advertising revenue.

Trends in South Korea, as well as in most of Asia, raise a serious question about the compatibility of developmental efforts by government and freedom of press and speech. The governments point out that if press criticism of developmental projects is permitted, people lose faith in the ruling elite and the needed social mobilization for development is tampered with. Under this guise, ruling elites in developing nations control the press in the name of development and/or national security. Because the governments feel electronic media have some magic power in the mobilization of the masses, more stringent controls are usually placed on radio and television.

2.3.8 Conclusion

The logical question to ask at this point is: How does the broadcasting system of South Korea respond to the nation's particular needs? Of course, there can be no easy answer to such a broad question; the answer would be determined by the geopolitical area one is discussing. In South Korea, a fundamental problem of great magnitude is the gap between the urban and rural areas, a gap not just confined to mass media but to all socioeconomic phenomena. According to one sociologist, the distribution of mass communication in rural areas amounts to only 20%, whereas it is over 80% in Seoul (Ko 1972, p. 100). The problem, however, is much deeper. The content of broadcast media, especially that of television, is centered around urban, upper-middle-class values and norms, thus contributing to a serious sense of deprivation and frustration in the rural population.

2.4 Democratic People's Republic of Korea (North Korea), *by Sunwoo Nam and John A. Lent*

The Russian-backed Democratic People's Republic of Korea was a creation of World War II (see §2.3). Since September 1948, North Korea has been led by Kim Il Sung, a resistance leader thrust into a position of unprecedented adoration.

The 16-million North Koreans are not as urban-centered as are the people in numerous other Asian nations. The capital, Pyongyang, is the largest city with about 1.5 million; the next three largest cities barely reach 300,000 each.

John A. Lent is Professor of Communications at Temple University; he developed and headed the first university mass communications program in Malaysia at University Sains Malaysia, 1972–74. He was a Fulbright scholar, Philippines, 1964–65; author of *The Asian Newspapers' Reluctant Revolution; Third World Mass Media and Their Search for Modernity: The Case of Commonwealth Caribbean; Philippine Mass Communications: Before 1811, After 1966; Asian Mass Communications: A Comprehensive Bibliography;* and nearly 100 articles in journals in 16 nations. He received his Ph.D. from the University of Iowa.

Education is emphasized; in 1973, the government was pushing ahead with plans for universal ten-year compulsory higher education.

Besides the broadcasting operation described below, North Korea is served by ten dailies, which, along with the cinema, television, and theater, offer little but unabashed propaganda, most of it praising Kim Il Sung.

The income per capita was $330 in 1973, but this comparatively low figure is supplemented with many fringe benefits, such as low-cost housing and electricity and free medical treatment and education.

2.4.1 Ideology

Broadcasting in the Democratic People's Republic of Korea is characterized by the unstinting practice of Leninism-Stalinism. Party Secretary and Premier Kim Il Sung is often called a miniature Stalin because of the personality cult built around him, to a great extent by North Korean mass media.

True to the Leninist concept, broadcasting, as well as all North Korean media, is under direct government control. As such, it must play a "mobilizing, agitational, propagandistic and organizing role in equipping the popular masses with revolutionary ideas about the creation of a new society" (Union of Korean Journalists 1971, p. 12). North Korean Communists generally take pride in the role of media in mobilizing the masses under the control of the Communist Party. One publication boasted:

The mass media organs in our country, under the wise leadership of Comrade Kim, are working enthusiastically to organize and mobilize the working masses for carrying out of the political, economic and cultural development, as directed by the Party. [*Central Yearbook* 1968, p. 200]

In Kim's own words, the mass media play a vital role in revolutionary struggles as a "sharp and militant ideological weapon" (Union of Korean Journalists 1971, p. 12). Early in his regime, Kim emphasized the gradual introduction of *juche,* the single ideological system of independence and political line of the working class, into the party mass media with the goal of serving the revolution of North Korea.

North Korean broadcasting, as all mass media, is used constantly as an arm of the state to carry out party campaigns. In the post-Korean War construction period, media were used to imbue the masses with the importance of industrialization, to spread Kim's ideas on taking "ten, one hundred steps while others take only one, to make possible the rapid transition of our formerly backward country to the ranks of developed countries." Broadcasters and journalists struggled for the elimination of conservatism and backward ideas, "raised high the banner of Marxism-Leninism, of proletarian internationalism, the revolutionary banner of the anti-imperialist and anti-American struggle," and waged a battle to protect the unity of the socialist camp (Union of Korean Journalists 1971, p. 13). Kim, as would be expected, gave keen attention to the development of mass media, personally creating the "Order of Samil Volgan," the highest journalistic award, and fixing both a Day of Radio and a Day of the Press, with the aim of encouraging media personnel.

2.4.2 Organization

North Korean domestic broadcasting is structurally organized similar to that of other Communist countries, that is, along national, provincial, and municipal and county lines. At each stage, broadcasting stations are controlled by a committee. The Central Broadcasting Committee in Pyongyang, under the direct control of the cabinet of North Korea, is the key to the whole operation.

The Ministry of Communication is in charge of technical operations of the stations, while the cabinet, through the Central Broadcasting Committee, programs the domestic service. The Party Bureau for South of the Workers Party (North Korean Communist Party) is directly responsible for Pyongyang Broadcasting Committee which, in turn, controls foreign broadcasts. The Workers Party is also in charge of the Bureau of Agitprop. (see Figure 2).

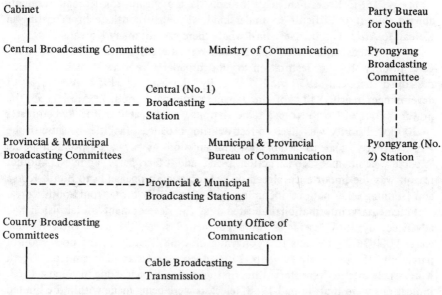

Source: North Korean Fact Book 1971, p. 488.

Figure 2. Broadcasting System of North Korea.

Domestically, the 20 local stations in cities and provincial municipalities are primarily relay stations for Central Broadcasting Station No. 1 in Pyongyang (*WRTH* 1974, p. 156). The home service's two programs on both medium- and short-wave are on the air 19 and 21 hours daily (UNESCO 1975, p. 308). Most domestic broadcasts are received by a wired distribution network which extends to most towns and villages, reaching about a million homes and community listening posts. The local stations also program some of their own materials dealing with the life and culture of their regions. Reporting from North Korea in 1974, one reporter wrote:

Loudspeakers broadcast the current transmissions from Radio Pyongyang. In the 200-metre deep Bongha (Torch) station, a reading of Comrade Kim's works was followed by a radio play about the Korean War. The station echoed disconcertingly to the sound of battle cries, artillery and machine guns. Nobody took the slightest notice. The rows of passive faces were switched right off. Perhaps that was the closest the visitor can get to the pulse of Pyongyang. [Spurr, 1974a, p. 28]

Broadcasts in the external service are beamed to Southeast Asia, Latin America, Near and Middle East, Far East, Europe, Japan, and of course South Korea. Languages of broadcast are Japanese, English, Chinese, French, Spanish, Russian, Arabic, and Korean (*North Korean Fact Book* 1971, p. 486; *WRTH* 1974, p. 156). Korean-language broadcasts are meant for Korean residents abroad, but it is difficult to understand why they continue broadcasting in Korean to Africa and the Near East where there are not many Koreans.

As indicated earlier, after the Korean War, the government of North Korea gave priority to the restoration of the broadcast services, which had been destroyed between 1950 and 1953. By the end of 1954, the level of development reached that of the Japanese colonial period. In April 1955, the power output of North Korean radio stations was increased to 150 kw. and later to 300 kw. Priority was given to restructuring broadcast facilities because of the Workers Party goal to attain fast transmission of messages promoting the "people's economic reconstruction plan" and other party policies. Another reason was the importance placed on broadcasting propaganda to South Korea and jamming other nations' incoming signals, especially those from South Korea.

Fragmentary information indicated that the development of television had advanced, by 1968, as far as the experimental stage. Estimates showed there were 2,000-3,000 TV sets in Pyongyang in 1968, mainly in the possession of party elite (Shinn et al, 1969, p. 272). According to another source, "North Koreans claimed to have started the first television broadcasting in August 1963. Indications were that, in mid-1968, telecasts were being made within the limited area of Pyongyang for a few hours one or two evenings each week" (*Central Yearbook* 1969, p. 193). In 1974, a reporter who had been in North Korea said Pyongyang Television broadcasts six hours nightly and all day Sunday. He also reported that 80% of the population owned TV sets (Spurr 1974a, p. 28).

2.4.3 Programming

The guiding theme of all North Korean radio programs is allegiance to the party and indoctrination of its tenets. News and analysis, weather, music, drama, reading of novels and poetry, comedy, and other programs never fail to mention one or more of these topics: "hero of the Korean people, Kim Il Sung," the achievements of workers, and the denigration of South Korea.

Two examples of program themes will suffice: a news account of "Comrade so and so, following the commands of Comrade Kim Il Sung, was so enthusiastic in his work that he accomplished 180% of his goal even before the deadline and further substituted for his sick comrade"; a dramatization on the theme, "North Korea is the best place to live in the world, and South Korea is the worst place, not fitting for habitation, being an inferno" (*North Korean Fact Book* 1971, p. 489). Vilification of the South Korean government leadership, however, lessened somewhat after the 4 July 1972 communique, but resumed by 1974-75. Entertainment programs also carry political messages, much as the Peking opera does in China.

In external broadcasts, North Korea places major emphasis on efforts to unify Korea through whatever means at its disposal. Broadcasting beamed to South Korea is meant to be a method of psychological warfare. For example, when in 1967, North Korean infiltrators engaged in various sabotage activities, ranging from property destruction to killing, North Korean broadcasting reported it as an antigovernment, anti-American uprising, indigenous to South Korea. Contents of the broadcasts to South Korea, on the air 21 hours daily, using medium-wave and short-wave, again consist of glorification of North Korea and castigation of the "free world." According to 1965 data, broadcasts to South Koreans occupied more time than internal broadcasts to North Koreans, the latter being 19 hours (*Central Yearbook* 1965, p. 193).

Additionally the North Korean government in 1962, established a "Marxist-Leninist Broadcasting University" to broadcast two hours daily of lectures on Communism, designed for South Korean students. More specific goals of that "university" were outlined by its president, who said:

Even after 17 years (in 1962) from Liberation, . . . (the country) is not unified yet. . . . (The university) is established to expedite the building of a socialist country in North Korea, and to encourage the struggle against Americans to save the nation in South Korea, . . . to open up avenues of learning for entire South Korean people including workers, peasants, youth and students, to insure systematic instruction of the Marxist-Leninist theory and of the policies of our party. [*North Korean Fact Book* 1971, p. 490]

In short, North Korean broadcasting is the voice of the party and government, reflecting the thinking, to the minutest detail, of a handful of leaders. In the wake of Nixon's 1972 China visit, this North Korean leadership began to relax its rigid stand on the unification issue, proposing a type of nonwar pact with South Korea in order to facilitate reunification. A major revision of its position came about in that the North Koreans were not requiring the total withdrawal of American forces from South Korea. Furthermore, the North Korean Communist Party, through its spokesman in Tokyo, hinted at a desire to permit "expanded relations and an end to our confrontation with the United States" (Washington Post Service 1972).

It was expected that this shift of policy line would be reflected in North Korean broadcasting — at least its foreign version word for word, somewhat like the sudden show of courtesy shown President Nixon, erstwhile archenemy of China, by the Chinese media during his visit. But, in 1975, the policy shifted again amid talk of growing unrest between North and South Korea and the possibility of the United States being drawn into another Korean war.

2.5   Japan, *by Izumi Tadokoro*

Many scholars trace Japan's modernization period to the Meiji Restoration of 1858. The trends to modernity, however, had been set into motion by the Tokugawa government years before. After about 80 years of contact with Westerners, mainly Portuguese and Dutch, in the sixteenth century, Japan closed its doors to the outside world until 1853. During the next century of exploration and exploitation, Japan conquered Korea, Manchuria, China, and finally, Southeast Asia. Since World War II, the country has kept a low profile globally, except in the economic arena where it has excelled. In 1974, Japan faced more frustration, instability, and lack of faith in government than at any time since World War II, mainly because of rising commodity prices and shortages of goods. Criticism mounted against the government because of the state of the economy, and especially after *Bungei Shunju,* a popular magazine, exposed Watergate-type tactics in the Tanaka administration. The prime minister was forced out of office shortly after.

Japan, made up of four main islands — Hokkaido, Honshu, Shikoku, and Kyushu — has the fourth largest population in Asia, approximately 105.5 million. The major cities are Tokyo, the capital, and Osaka. Japanese education and literacy rates are among the highest in the world, as are media availability and penetration. For example, the 123 dailies account for a readership of 39.8 million, and the big three of Japanese newspapers (*Asahi, Mainichi,* and *Yomiuri*) are the largest-circulated, commercially operated dailies in the world. Japanese broadcasting is even more impressive: the number of radio and television stations runs into the thousands; the number of radio receivers is 45 million and television sets, 25.2 million.

2.5.1   Scale and Volume

"Unique" is the word that best describes Japanese broadcasting. The system in Japan resembles neither those of most Asian and European countries, where broadcasting is solely government-operated, nor that of the United States, where commercial broadcasting dominates. Actually, two systems function in Japan: Nippon Hoso Kyokai (NHK) and commercial broadcasters. NHK a special public corporation, acquires its revenue entirely from receiver fees, while the

Izumi Tadokoro is Chief of the Broadcasting and Telecommunications Section, Nihon Shimbun Kyokai, Tokyo; Lecturer on broadcasting at Hosei University and Seikei University; and a member of the Japan Society of Journalism and Mass Communication.

102 commercial companies are financed by advertising revenue. The two systems are nearly equal in scale and strength as well as in their impact upon the Japanese people.

NHK is made up of two national TV networks (general and educational), two UHF high-power (100 kw.) experimental TV stations in Tokyo and Osaka, two medium-wave radio networks, one FM radio network, and Radio Japan, the overseas service offering general and regional broadcasts in 23 languages. Gross revenue for NHK in 1972 was about $450 million, most of which came from receiver fees of 24 million households possessing TV sets. Radio receiver fees were abolished in March 1968.

As for commercial broadcasting, 102 companies existed in June 1972, 36 having both TV and medium-wave radio stations, 50 TV stations (VHF or UHF), 11 medium-wave radio stations, 4 FM radio stations, and one short-wave radio station. All radio and TV enterprises, except for the one short-wave radio outlet, were originally licensed for regional or local broadcasting, but have since been linked into several quasi networks. Because Japan does not have network companies such as those in the United States, key stations have played the role of network organizations. Most TV programs are transmitted from Tokyo key stations, or from Osaka, Nagoya, and Fukuoka semikey stations, to their subscribing outlets in local cities, in the process accounting for the four or five quasi networks. Medium-wave radio stations are linked by two quasi networks. In 1971, the advertising revenue of commercial broadcasting was estimated at $840 million for TV, $129 million for radio. Gross revenues, however, must be discounted by the 20% commission paid to advertising agencies.

As a result of this proliferation of outlets, a Tokyo resident, for example, has a selection of eight TV channels (three NHK, five commercial), and ten radio services (two NHK medium-wave, four commercial medium-wave, two FM, one short-wave commercial, and one English-language station). This last is operated by the Far East Network for members of the U.S. Armed Forces stationed in Japan. A rural resident, for instance in Aomori prefecture at the northern end of Honshu, can select from four TV channels (two NHK, two commercial) and from five radio programs, with broadcasting hours as long as those in Tokyo. In large cities, such as Osaka, Nagoya, Kitakyushu, and Sapporo, the situation is nearly the same as in Tokyo; and in rural areas, the Aomori case would be considered a minimum level. Moreover, Tokyo TV programs are received by cable in some parts of Japan, in addition to local telecasts. All Japanese stations broadcast daily from early morning until midnight; some commercial radio stations are on the air for almost 24 hours.

Almost every Japanese family owns both radio and TV sets, millions of households having two or more television receivers. Manufacturer sources estimate about 40 million radio receivers and more than 30 million TV sets in use in the country. By the end of 1971, half of the TV sets were color models.

Undoubtedly, the Japanese are heavy TV viewers. According to a 1970 NHK survey, an average Japanese spends more than three hours a day viewing TV, about 30 minutes listening to radio, and less than 30 minutes reading newspapers (*Japanese Press* 1971).

This boom in broadcasting must be a consequence of the unique coexistence of NHK and commercial firms. Before the end of World War II, broadcasting in Japan had been monopolized by NHK and completely under government control. Then, after Japan's defeat, while NHK was permitted by the occupying forces to continue, SCAP (Supreme Commander of Allied Powers) added commercial broadcasting to provide competition. Later, when TV arrived, equal opportunity was given to both NHK and the commercial organizations. The ensuing competition drove both NHK and commercial broadcasters to expand their operations, diversify program contents, and modernize their facilities. The present administrator of broadcasting for the government, the Minister of Post, owes much to SCAP for setting up the competitive situation, because it allows him to control broadcasting on the principle of divide and rule.

2.5.2 History, Governance, Ownership

Japanese broadcasting has about half a century of history divided into three periods: from inauguration of services in 1925 to the end of World War II, the occupation period of the late 1940s, and from about 1950 to the present.

During the first era, wireless telecommunications, through the Wireless Telegraph Act of 1915, came under government control. Later, just before licensing of broadcasting stations began, debates were held as to what the nature of the medium should be − governmental or private. In 1924, the government decided to license three stations as public corporations, but not before persuading various license applicants, such as newspapers, press agencies, radio-equipment dealers and local influential people, to join in setting them up. Tokyo Broadcasting Station commenced broadcasting 22 March 1925, followed by the Osaka and Nagoya stations. Financing of these outlets was through receiver license fees, since commercial broadcasting had been prohibited. The stations did not operate long, however, before the Ministry of Communications forced them to merge, forming a nation-wide network. Thus, a corporate juridical person, Nippon Hoso Kyokai (Japan Broadcasting Corporation), was established in August 1926, initiating "the unified monopolistic operation period" (*History of Broadcasting in Japan* 1967, p. 360; see also, *Radio and TV of the World* 1972, p. 187).

Besides the usual radio fare, NHK during this period broadcast a number of spectacular events such as the accession ceremony of Emperor Hirohito in 1928 (first nation-wide broadcast), an appeal to insurgent soldiers to surrender at the so-called February 26 (1936) Incident, the Olympic Games of 1936, and the beginning and end of war in the Pacific.

During World War II, the militaristic government imposed strict regulations on all media. Broadcasting and other media were controlled by the Information Bureau, a military arm of the government. NHK broadcasting became the voice of the militarists, and an effective one because of the five million sets in the country. The audience was licensed to receive medium-wave broadcasts only and was forbidden to tune in overseas stations. The number of receivers increased to seven million by 1944, but war damage decreased this number considerably the following year. NHK's overseas short-wave radio had started in 1935. It was turned into "stratagem broadcasting" during the war, but stopped entirely by SCAP in 1945. Overseas services commenced again in 1952 as Radio Japan (*History of Broadcasting in Japan* 1967, p. 81).

From August 1945 to June 1950, broadcasting entered a new phase with the enactment of the Radio Wave Law, Broadcast Law, and Radio Regulatory Commission Establishment Law. In addition, SCAP issued a radio code in September 1945, similar to its press code, ordering Japanese broadcasters to adhere strictly to facts in newscasts, eliminate propaganda from programming, and inhibit "false or destructive" criticism of the Allied Powers. All broadcasting content was censored; by 1947, however, censorship receded to post factum and finally was abolished in late 1949. In December 1945, SCAP also issued a memorandum on the reorganization of NHK, intending to make broadcasting public. The memorandum suggested the establishment of an advisory committee of 15 to 20 members selected from the public. The committee was instructed to make a clear delineation between the responsibilities of the NHK president and the government, granting, in effect, autonomy to NHK. The committee was to allow NHK the right to discharge or transfer its officers who had relationships with the militaristic movement during the war.

The advisory committee, started in January 1946, included 17 members, several of whom were Socialists and Communists in compliance with a SCAP suggestion. The committee, however, did not function as well as expected. Candidates for the NHK presidency were nominated by the committee, but a draft of a broadcasting law did not materialize, partly through the fault of SCAP. Instead, SCAP had decided to control NHK through the Board of Communication (later, Ministry of Telecommunication). As the advisory committee became dysfunctional, it was scrapped in 1947 (Tadao 1967).

During the post-war interval, NHK radio programs did not change considerably, although serial drama, quiz shows, and audience participation programs came into existence, and election broadcasting was begun in March 1946.

A series of three laws in June 1950 inaugurated the present stage of Japanese broadcasting. The Radio Wave Law was designed to promote "public welfare through impartial and efficient utilization of radio wave." Article 7 of the law provides that a license be granted as long as an applicant fulfills the conditions (a) in accordance with the technical standard, (b) if spectrum space is available, (c) the applicant is in appropriate financial position, and (d) in accordance with an established standard set by the government. One person may not own or govern more than one broadcasting company in Japan, nor own or govern newspapers, radio, and TV stations in the same market, unless many broadcasters function in the market. The phrase "own or govern" was construed to mean a person having more than 10% of the stock, or the right to represent the company, or the post of managing director. In short, group ownership of broadcasting companies and local monopoly of mass media are forbidden by the administrative guideline. Because the rule allows for exceptions, local monopoly exists in some rural areas. But, on a nation-wide scale, mass-media giants or conglomerates are hindered. Conglomerate functions seem to be fulfilled by looser and more temporal alliances among various companies.

Broadcasting stations were to be regulated under the Radio Wave Law and Broadcast Law. The creation of the Radio Regulatory Commission, an independent administrative body similar to the FCC in the United States, was a proposal under the new Establishment Law. The commission was expected to administer broadcasting impartially; it did so, but was disbanded by the government after two years. All authority rendered to the commission was transferred to the Ministry of Telecommunication (later, Ministry of Post). Though short-lived, the commission accomplished two significant tasks: one was the licensing of commercial broadcasters in 1951; the other, licensing of television simultaneously to NHK and commercial stations in July 1952.

The Broadcast Law, besides regulating stations to meet the public welfare, also strives for the sound development of electronic media in accordance with these principles: to secure the maximum availability and benefits of broadcasting to the people; to assure freedom of expression through broadcasting by guaranteeing the impartiality, integrity, and autonomy of broadcasting; and to make broadcasting contribute to the development of healthy democracy by clarifying responsibility of those persons engaged in the profession. Based upon these principles, freedom of broadcast programming (Art. 3), impartiality of domestic programs (Art. 44), and "equal time" (Art. 45) were provided.

NHK was therefore reorganized to be a public corporation, its purpose, as described by Article 7 of the law, being "to conduct its broadcasting for the public welfare in such a manner that its broadcasting may be received all over Japan." The law designed that the NHK president should be appointed by the corporation's board of governors, who, in turn, should be appointed by the prime minister with the consent of both houses of the Diet. The Broadcast Law, for the first time, also provided for commercial broadcasters under the name "private broadcast enterprisers."

Immediately after the war, several newspaper companies and advertising agencies instituted commercial radio companies expecting SCAP to introduce the American broadcasting format. They were disappointed only for a few years, until SCAP issued the policy of two coexisting systems. Possibly the reason SCAP favored two systems was related to its fears that NHK, as Japan's sole radio organization, was infiltrated by communists. For example, in July 1950, SCAP ordered NHK to dismiss 119 "Communists and their sympathizers." Though the Japanese were not sure of the financial feasibility of commercial radio, SCAP preferred to take a risk with commercial broadcasting rather than chance the alternative possibility that the only existing system, NHK, might become an over-bureaucratic monopoly led by totalitarian principles.

Sixteen commercial stations were licensed in April 1951, immediately after which they jointly established the National Association of Commercial Broadcasters in Japan. By September of the same year, some of them began operations. The success of these commercial enterprises inspired the number of broadcasters to increase rapidly.

Then followed television. NHK started TV in Tokyo during February 1953, and NTV (Nihon Television), a Tokyo commercial company, followed in September. NHK, from the outset, instituted TV receiver license fees. Meanwhile, realizing a need to persuade the public that TV was important enough to be affordable, NTV worked out an idea of "street or plaza TV," placing sets at busy corners or in plazas to attract a potential audience. Commercial TV was not as profitable initially as commercial radio had been, but the interest aroused among the people for TV quietly paved the way for the expansion of broadcasting coverage throughout Japan. In 1957, more than 30 local TV companies were licensed; during the same year, the first allocation plan of TV, designed to allocate spectrum space for stations, was implemented. In 1959, NHK acquired a second TV channel for educational programs.

It was apparent by 1959 that Japanese television might hatch golden eggs. By 9 April, when the wedding parade of Crown Prince Akihito was televised, stocks of TV sets had been sold out. In fact, several million TV sets were sold as a result of this wedding. A year later, with ten million sets in use, both systems decided to launch color telecasting. Color TV stumbled for a few years, just as black and white had originally, but programming of the 1964 Tokyo Olympics in color spurred tremendous interest in polychrome sets. Although such programming was not justified by the 30,000 color sets in use at that time, it was another gamble that paid off for Japanese broadcasters.

The 1960s became the television era in Japan. In spite of a 1965 recession, TV advertising revenue increased rapidly until by 1972 it had equaled that of newspapers, the top advertising medium. Innovations and technical developments went forward and various approaches were made to develop new styles of programming. In 1967, channels in the UHF spectrum were opened for TV transmission, with the result that many regional and local UHF stations commenced operations. Because of this, television election campaign speeches were realized after an amendment of the election law in 1969. Previously, the large number of regional and local candidates could not be accommodated on the few local stations that existed. As TV progressed, the cinema and radio felt the shock waves. As the number of movie-goers decreased, some cinema firms went into bankruptcy, while others changed into production shops for TV films or became departments of a conglomerate leisure industry. For example, Toho movie industry moved its film department to an affiliated production firm which remained as a complex of bowling alleys, country clubs, etc. In short, the Japanese movie industry today is on the brink of extinction as a mass medium.

The radio industry, although seriously affected by TV in the mid-1960s, did not falter as movies had. Radio stations survived by changing the dimensions of programs to segmented audiences, such as automobile drivers, or students in late-night preparation for examinations.

Another aspect of radio's renaissance was the 1969 development of FM as a music medium on four commercial stations and NHK. FM radio had been introduced on an experimental basis to NHK in 1957 and to a private college in 1958, both of which lasted about ten years.

2.5.3 Organizational Changes

It may sound paradoxical that at the height of its expansion and prosperity, Japanese broadcasting, confronted with a series of difficult problems, is quite concerned about its future. One decision weighing on the minds of broadcasters is whether a revision of the broadcasting systems is necessary at this time. The Broadcasting Law under which stations operate was promulgated in 1950 and, since then, the broadcasting industry has gone through spectacular growth. Of course, several amendments have been made to the law, particularly in 1959 with the establishment of the Broadcast Programme Consultative Committees, both for NHK and commercial broadcasters; the creation of a set of standards for domestic broadcast programming; a provision calling for maintenance of harmony among cultural, educational news, and entertainment programs; and the prohibition of network programming for commercial stations.

Drastic revisions to the law were planned by the government again in 1962, when a research committee was appointed for that purpose. As a result of the committee's report, the government sent a draft law to the Diet in 1966, but it was rejected. In the 1970s, the necessity for revision of the law was haunting many concerned with broadcasting, various pressures coming from the ruling party, the bureaucratic officials of the Ministry of Post, interested citizens' groups, and opposition parties. Questions of concern included: Is the control over programs appropriate? Is it feasible to assess receiver fees? Are networks necessary to commercial broadcasters? Does the Minister of Post have too much power over broadcasting?

Possibly revision of the broadcasting system will occur in the mid-1970s, though the dimensions of such changes are not altogether clear. The critical point of such a revision will concern program standards. Japanese programs are usually locally produced and of a high level of expression; newscasts, however, especially have been criticized by government for being partial or coarse. One source explained these criticisms in this fashion:

In short, logics of the government and the ruling party may be rendered to a dual mechanism, levelling blames of partiality on those programs that are critical to the government while laying blames of coarseness on some of entertainment programs which may destroy the good morals and manners of the establishment. These two patterns of disparagement alter one after another just like a merry-go-round. [Okada 1970, p. 8]

While government oftentimes seems to abuse its power over the electronic media, broadcasters are obedient to government criticisms, wishes, and regulations, at least on the surface. For example, commercial broadcasters often classify programs arbitrarily as to categories, merely to meet governmental requirements on the percentage of broadcast hours devoted to, for instance, educational and cultural programs.

2.5.4 Programming

Several surveys show the viewing peaks for television to be 7-10 A.M. and 7-10:30 P.M., and the most popular genre to be drama, followed by "wide shows," which are variety programs of news, information, music, or interviews. The most popular morning show is NHK's "Serial TV Novel," a daily 15-minute serial drama whose story begins in April and concludes in March of the following year. A characteristic of the TV novel is that the audience can do something else while it is on the air and still not miss the plot; in other words, it lends itself to both viewing and listening or listening alone. "Wide shows" are transmitted by both NHK and the commercial outfits during morning peak hours, as well as in the afternoon and at midnight. Programs for children are on the air in the morning and early evening, the former being educational programs, and the latter animations and "monster" programs. Popular programs during evening peak hours are dramas of all kinds, professional baseball games, and studium shows, a form of variety program inviting hundreds of people to the studio.

On occasions of serious accidents or significant events, both NHK and commercial stations change their schedules to air special programs. As examples, airplane disasters, the 1970 hijack case by ultraleft students, the 1972 gunfights between leftists and police in Karuizawa, and the first moon walk in 1969, all consumed long, consecutive TV program hours. Often, for such important events, the commercial broadcasters produce special shows jointly.

The Apollo moon walk was significant in Japanese television history for it aroused special interest in satellite relay programs. One source, claiming the number of Japanese who saw the first moon walk at 58 million, said, "The tremendous number of special satellite relay programs broadcast before and after the moon landing by all of Japan's television stations aroused a great deal of interest throughout Japan" (*Japanese Press* 1970, p. 95).

Radio has no peak hours of listening. About half of radio's time is devoted to music, most of which is multihour disc-jockey shows, which also include many insertions of news, commercial messages, and talks. Music-request shows and consultation programs, where listeners call in their questions to be answered by a host, are also quite popular; on the other hand, radio drama has become scarce.

News plays a crucial role both on television and radio. Newsgathering is often a cooperative venture with broadcasting and print media working together. NHK has its own newsgathering organization but also obtains news material from various domestic and foreign news agencies. Commercial broadcasters are more dependent upon newspapers for their newscast data. Although all stations have newsgathering sections, these usually copy local news items from newspapers and national news from broadcasting's news agency. Each of the five key TV stations in Tokyo works as a partner with a national newspaper in the newsgathering field.

NHK has contributed the bulk of Japanese educational fare, both to television and radio. It has constructed TV and radio educational networks which are utilized by primary schools. Commercial stations have made some efforts in educational programming, but conscientious producers feel they are being driven into a corner by management's avarice for ever-increasing profits.

By the 1970s, the government, anticipating rising needs for technical knowledge and adult education, announced plans to establish a national open university. "University of the Air" students would not be required to attend classes (except for temporal schoolings) and would gain credits through broadcasting viewing or listening. Though the university was still far from reality in 1972, experimental broadcasting for the service had taken place in August 1971 on short-wave radio and in February 1972 on NHK UHF experimental stations in Tokyo and Osaka. The experiments were resumed in April 1972.

Needless to say, all broadcasting in Japan, except for that of Far East Network and the Far East Broadcasting Company station in Okinawa prefecture, is in the Japanese language. Since its birth, broadcasting has contributed to the pervasion of common Japanese accents throughout the country. Its merit, on the one hand, was that it helped promote primary education; a demerit, however, was that such a philosophy stifled feelings of localism, in the process destroying the cultures of local communities. In the 1970s, broadcasters were being asked to join in helping to restore local cultures.

2.5.5 Broadcasting Freedom

On the surface, it would seem that limitations on broadcasting freedom are few in Japan. Media freedom is secured to a significant degree, if one is talking about laws and rules alone. But self censorship, through fear of governmental reprisals, can be a major hindrance.

After the Japan-United States Security Treaty riots of 1960, the government and ruling Liberal Democratic Party, having been made aware of television's powerful impact upon the masses, tightened controls over the medium. Television had broadcast the Security Treaty debates in the Diet, revealing the ambiguity of the government's decision. Television news reported daily upon demonstrations that erupted over the treaty's adoption, oftentimes showing policemen overreacting to the demonstrators.

During the 1960s, several incidents of governmental interference with broadcasting caused political controversy. The center of some of these disputes over broadcasting rights related to the Vietnam War. For example, when Nihon TV Network (NTV) in 1965 attempted to broadcast a series of TV documentaries entitled, "A Chronicle of South Vietnam Marine Corps," a telephone call from a cabinet minister blocked the series after the first of the shows was aired.

The cabinet minister, whose combined functions are similar to those of a presidential press secretary and director of communications as existed in the Nixon administration in the United States, chided NTV for carrying a program "too cruel to be seen in the living rooms of the audience." This incident, as well as a few others, resulted in broadcasters setting up self-control guidelines.

Similar cases of a mixture of governmental pressure and self-control occur several times a year. For example, Hideo Den, a Tokyo Broadcasting Station (TBS) news commentator known and respected for his sharp criticisms, was suddenly removed from his program, "Newscope," in March 1968. The year before his removal, Den had visited North Vietnam, resulting in his broadcasting a special program, "Hanoi — The Testimony of Hideo Den." His report outraged members of the ruling elite. In 1967 and 1968, other cases involved TBS news programs. The "Narita Case" resulted when a TBS-TV news car was discovered carrying several farmers who had opposed the government's requisition of their land for a new international airport at Narita. A director and newsmen were accused of being partial, but controls were imposed upon Den who had nothing to do with the case. Later, Den described his last broadcast at TBS:

I cannot forget the certain days of March, when one top management member of TBS urged me to come to his chamber and ordered me to surrender my post in the "Newscope." And the last appearance on March 27 created such an emotion that I tried hard not to surface an impulse in my heart. I broadcast several items of news as was scheduled, as the director finally showed me a board with a script "10 seconds to the ending." The time has come to depart at length from my audience. Suppressing the drive of appealing loudly why I was obliged to vanish away from the Brown Tube, my tongue moved by itself saying, "Now, farewell to you all," instead of ordinary "Now see you tomorrow." [Den 1971, pp. 9-10]

As in a number of nations, particularly the United States, TV newsmen in Japan are being ordered to submit broadcast materials as evidence in courtrooms. For example, the Fukuoka District Court in 1969 demanded NHK and three Fukuoka commercial stations to submit news films as court evidence. All four stations refused, contending that to do so would impede their future newsgathering activities and result in limiting freedom of news reporting. The Supreme Court unanimously rejected the broadcasters' special appeal, upholding the lower court's decision. The Supreme Court ruled that the principle of fair trial superseded that of freedom of newsgathering, although warning at the same time against court abuse of news films used as evidence (*Japanese Press* 1970, p. 91). The court did not stipulate what would constitute "abuse of news films." Kozo Kawakami, NHK director general of broadcasting at the time, commented on the decision:

[When] we were forced to submit our news films, the freedom of news reporting was violated. It is my hope that the press world will tackle this problem most seriously, together with the problem of getting legislation passed that will recognize the right of reporters not to reveal their news sources. [*Japanese Press* 1970, p. 94]

2.5.6 Competition and Vulgarity

Corresponding to the freedom principle is that of responsibility; in a crowded broadcast field such as that of Japan, the keen sense of competition can, and often does, lead to irresponsible and vulgar programming.

Commercial broadcasters, especially key stations, are extremely anxious to obtain good ratings for their programs in the weekly listener surveys. Such ratings, of course, are indispensable to broadcasters for their acquisition of ample revenue and maintenance/expansion of broadcast territories. Although program steering committees of individual stations, as well as the Better Broadcast Programme Committee, are constantly scrutinizing broadcasting performances, their influences are minimal when pitted against the philosophy of competition.

NHK, whose programs are generally considered respectable and elegant, nonetheless must seek more popularity because of assessment of receiver fees. Article 32 of the Broadcast Law stipulates NHK must conclude contracts with viewers who own TV sets "capable of receiving the broadcasting provided by NHK." Because these viewers are obliged to pay about $1 a month for black-and-white and $1.50 a month for color-television licenses, NHK realizes it must provide more popular programs to its paying audience than commercial stations which survive through advertising. Consequently, commercial broadcasters, feeling their share of the audience is threatened, react by lowering their standards. Moreover, governmental "impartiality" checks (often conducted in a partial fashion) tend to make broadcasters uneasy, at which point they decide in favor of "safe" progovernmental popular programming. Accordingly, it is becoming increasingly difficult to voice criticism against the government. In the backs of broadcasters' minds is the reminder that the postal minister renews the station license every three years.

The stations' financial pressures are certainly reflected in their programming. Although they enjoyed a boom period in the 1960s, TV stations in Japan were tightening their budgets in the early 1970s. Commercial broadcasters, whose revenue consists of time and spot sales and charges for program production, found that, with the arrival of color TV, program-production charges paid by advertisers were no longer balancing with real production costs.

Further, growing payroll burdens (commercial broadcasting maintains about 25,000 employees; NHK, 16,000) and network maintenance costs have compelled key stations to minimize production functions to such an extent that they began subcontracting the production of TV dramas, movies, and animations to production affiliates. A key TV station in Tokyo, NET, even cut off its news-producing function in 1971. Thus, many programs made within stations in the 1970s were low-cost "wide shows," studio music types, and the like. To assure survival, key stations have extended business activities beyond mass communication, investing in golf courses, bowling alleys, construction companies, computer schools, sound and videotape companies, and CATV.

NHK's financial situation is also perilous. Prohibited by law from engaging in investments, NHK depends solely upon receiver fees; with the change to color, a new fee will be necessary within a few years. When that time comes, it is very likely a storm of protest will result with investigations and debates on the whole nature of the fees. At this stage of technical progress, there are very few other revenue possibilities for NHK. In large cities, where TV reception is increasingly disturbed by multistoried buildings, complaints from audiences have made it very difficult for NHK to collect the revenue fees. Thus, to a large degree, both commercial and NHK companies are at a loss as to what they can do next.

2.5.7 UHF and FM

UHF television stations, in existence since 1967, were nearly equal to the number of VHF outlets by the early 1970s. Originally the intent of adding the UHF system was to diversify local programs but, in reality, centralized national network programs via UHF have come to be as important in the local scene as shows produced by local VHF outlets.

In September 1967, the Minister of Post, Takeji Kobayashi, announced that all TV stations in Japan should convert to UHF within ten years on the grounds that emerging needs compelled the allocation of VHF channels for moving "important wireless communications." The announcement was a *deus ex machina* for UHF broadcasters; UHF counters and all-channel TV sets spread widely throughout Japan shortly after. Kobayashi's prophecy had not become a reality by 1973, though the government was still adhering to the policy behind it. Such a policy is unrealistic, requiring billions of yen without providing any important benefits. Thus not many Japanese broadcasters feel it will be implemented in that ten-year time period.

Kobayashi also declared that a major reorganization of the radio broadcasting system would be forthcoming within a decade. His suggestion was that all local radio stations should convert to FM, while medium-wave radio should be concentrated in several large cities to cover national or regional areas with increased wattage. Simultaneously, he would make it possible for NHK to operate a national FM network, as well as for a few music FM radio broadcasters to function in large cities. The reorganization of medium-wave radio was partly realized in 1971, in quite a different manner than originally conceived, namely, allocating slightly more wattage to large city stations.

2.5.8 Technology and the Future

Mass media in Japan entered the computerization age in the 1960s. Many broadcasters have installed computers, not only for administrative, but also for automatic program transmissions and spot commercial insertions. NHK undoubtedly leads the field in computer utilization, having purchased its first electronic data system in 1961. NHK uses computerization effectively in most areas of its operation; since late 1968, it has been employing a system of its own making, named "NHK-TOPICS" (Total On-Line Program and Information System). NHK-TOPICS is composed of two parts:

Scheduling Management and Allocating Resources Technique (SMART) — Use of computers for program scheduling, calculations and allocations of facilities, equipment and personnel. Automatic Broadcast Control System (ABCS) — Automation of connections to channels inside and outside the stations and operation of equipment during program recording or transmission and monitoring during trouble through computer control. [*This Is NHK* 1972, p. 9]

NHK's technical potential is enormous; besides the equipment mentioned above, NHK also has within its organization research components to experiment and innovate in broadcasting. These are the Technical Research Laboratory, Broadcasting Science Research Laboratory, Radio and Television Culture Research Institute, and Public Opinion Research Institute.

Not only NHK, but commercial broadcasters as well, are eagerly seeking the new media of the 1970s. One of their hopes is cable television. The history of CATV is almost as old as TV broadcasting in Japan. Although for years cable systems were limited to master antenna TV systems in rural areas, toward the end of the 1960s some ambitious enterprisers, watching successes in the United States and Canada, blueprinted CATV development for Japan.

In 1970, four public corporations, hoping to wire up metropolitan areas, were founded in Tokyo, Osaka, Nagoya, and Fukuoka, with participation from NHK, commercial broadcasters, newspaper companies, the telephone and telegraph company, equipment manufacturers, and bankers. By 1972, they found themselves in difficult circumstances, struggling to survive. Likewise, various plans of "wired cities," "wired new towns" or "wired farms" were by 1973 in full bloom, but only expending money and time. It is not likely that cable systems will plant themselves into the next generation of Japanese television. It is more likely that CATV in Japan will continue to supplement TV broadcasting for at least a decade; after that, it is not possible to predict what will happen.

Similarly, video cassettes, called video packages (VP) in Japan, do not seem bound for great success for the time being. Several VP companies have been established since 1970 but have not made much headway. VPs could be useful to the Japanese, but so far their benefits do not offset their very high prices.

Although CATV and VP will have supplementary roles in the telecommunications of the 1970s, they will not replace television, as predicted by some. First of all, CATV is a local medium in nature; thus, it would be very expensive to wire the whole nation for CATV, and fruitless too, because Japan is now a homogeneous society, not one made up of different communities.

Second, VP is intended to meet personal demands for specified information in the form of audio-visual media, but no matter how sophisticated Japanese become, they will not sacrifice general TV for such a specialized medium.

Third, local origination of CATV will be too expensive for CATV operators, while cable commercials will not become numerous as long as CATV systems have few subscribers. Subscriber numbers will be restricted because they must pay both a receiver's and subscription fee.

Fourth, all public telecommunication systems in Japan are monopolized by Nippon Telegraph and Telephone Public Corporation (NTT), which has long-term plans to build a two-way audio-visual network across Japan. If such a project were to materialize, it would be questionable as to whether any CATV system would hold together under the stress.

A more hopeful venture related to Japanese broadcasting is TV-facsimile. In March 1972 the Minister of Post asked his advisory committee on techniques of wireless telecommunications to report on the feasibility of TV-facsimile. It would appear that within a decade this medium will be in wide use in Japan, affording a new dimension to broadcasting.

Although of less importance, duplication of vocal information, or simulcasting, on TV will be put into practice within several years. This technique, which enables TV to broadcast foreign pictures in both the original language and Japanese, is gaining popularity in the country. Experiments in the development of SHF spectrums and of laser-beam utilization are also proceeding in Japan.

From the early stage of Intelsat, the Japanese government and broadcasters have taken an active part in satellite TV news transmission. Through satellite transmission, events such as Olympic Games and moon landings were provided the Japanese audience. The presentations were made possible by the aid of the Japan Satellite News Pool, consisting of NHK and commercial broadcasters.

2.5.9 Okinawa

Okinawa (Ryukyu) was returned to Japan by the United States on 15 May 1972. Before the end of World War II, radio broadcasting on Okinawa was conducted by NHK as an inherent part of the Japanese system. The station was forced to close as a result of American air raids.

In 1950, a radio station operated by the United States Ryukyu government commenced broadcasting in Japanese. It was changed to a public educational foundation in 1954, and then to a private company, Ryukyu Broadcasting Company (RBC), in 1959. The first telecast on Okinawa was in 1958 by a private company, Okinawa Television (OTV), first linked to NHK and later to a network on the Japanese mainland. RBC began telecasting in 1959 and was linked to a mainland network immediately.

Another commercial radio station went into operation in 1958; a decade later, a public TV corporation, Okinawa Hoso Kyokai (OHK), was developed, resulting from recommendations of a newly legislated Broadcast Law of Okinawa. OHK relayed NHK programs and, naturally, at the time of reversion in 1972 was absorbed into NHK.

Difficult broadcasting problems that arose from Okinawa's reversion related to the existence on the islands of a Voice of America relay station and Far East Broadcasting Company (FEBC), which has been broadcasting in Okinawa since 1958. After some complex deliberations between Japan and the United States, VOA and the English broadcast of FEBC were allowed to continue for at least five years after the day of reversion, while the Chinese segment of FEBC ceased.

2.6 Hong Kong, *by F. Alton Everest*

Hong Kong was acquired by Britain from China between 1842 and 1898. Most of the land area of Hong Kong (365 of the total 398 square miles) is scheduled to revert to China in 1997, under terms of a 99-year lease signed in 1898.

Today, Hong Kong may be a "pearl in your hand" to starry-eyed tourists, but it is more a "dollar in your pocket" to local businessmen. The exceedingly rapid growth in population is no more amazing than an even greater growth in industry and commerce. Other Asian nations, struggling for a foothold in their new-found freedom from the yoke of colonialism, look with awe as Hong Kong, a British crown colony, demonstrates an amazing ability to create wealth and to make progress in distributing it among the workers. The average income per capita is over $600 per year, one of the highest in Asia.

Hong Kong consists of 236 islands and islets, many of them waterless and uninhabited, and a portion of the Chinese mainland (Kowloon and New Territories) adjoining Kwangtung Province. Most of the terrain is steep and rugged; only 50 square miles are suitable for agriculture.

The population of Hong Kong is 4.23 million, a million of these having crossed the border from China since 1950. The Hong Kong government has almost kept pace with the influx with its spectacular public-housing projects. The population is 98.5% Chinese, most of whom speak Cantonese, but Mandarin, Hakka, Fukien, Swatowese, Chiu Chow, and other minority dialects are also represented.

Of the mass media, radio must be considered the most effective, at least in its penetration. Surveys conducted by three commercial firms operating in Hong Kong indicate a 91% penetration by radio. This is surprising until one learns that transistor radios are available for $1.75, and, in the crowded conditions prevailing, one radio reaches many people.

2.6.1 Radio Hong Kong

The pioneer of Hong Kong broadcasting is Radio Hong Kong (RHK), first on the air in 1928 with the call letters ZBW and a 250-w. transmitter, established and operated primarily in English by enthusiastic and dedicated amateurs. In 1935,

F. Alton Everest, until recently, was with the Radio-TV Division, Hong Kong Baptist College. He was formerly a consulting engineer with Moody Institute of Science for 25 years where he was responsible for production of Moody science documentaries. He worked with experimental TV as early as 1936 and is the author of four books and 50 papers on electronics, radio-TV, and acoustics. He has received numerous awards including an honorary doctorate and fellow status in two societies.

Hong Kong became known to listeners around the world as ZBW2, opened on the short-wave band. Broadcasts continued throughout the Japanese occupation of World War II but manned, of course, by Japanese. When the British resumed control of the colony, the station's equipment was found intact, though sadly run down. Amateurs took up their task once more and continued to operate the station until the first professional broadcaster arrived in 1947.

Government control of Radio Hong Kong, exercised in the very early years through a committee, was placed in the hands of the postmaster general in 1939. Three years later, the Japanese took over the station and operated it during the war. The postmaster general regained control after World War II. In 1951, the public relations officer was given the responsibility for Radio Hong Kong which was transferred to the Controller of Broadcasting in 1953. From that time on, the Broadcasting Department under the Director of Broadcasting has been charged with this responsibility.

There is no overall legislation covering radio broadcasting as there is with television. Radio Hong Kong, now the official government station, is not regulated by any legislation although commercial radio and television stations are controlled by licenses issued in accordance with regulations of the Telecommunications Ordinance.

After a 40-year history of outgrowing its premises and moving to other less-than-adequate facilities, in 1969 Radio Hong Kong moved into a $6 million facility housing 16 studios. There, separate 20-kw. transmitters are used for the Chinese and English services of Radio Hong Kong, the former on 640 kHz (18 hours per day) and the latter on 545 kHz (19 hours daily). The mountainous terrain requires higher AM transmitting power than would normally be necessary for the 400-square-mile coverage. For the VHF/FM services, separate 50-kw. transmitters carry the Chinese and English programs. Again, the mountainous character of the colony requires numerous repeater/translators, and these are being planned to improve the FM reception.

License fees were imposed on all radio receiving sets from the very beginning of Radio Hong Kong in 1928. There was a conscious effort to keep broadcasting expenditure in line with license fees collected from 1946 to the abandonment of the plan in 1967. The growth of collection of license fees, from 300 in 1928 to 4,371 in 1946, and finally 181,967 in 1967, gives a clue to the expansion of the radio audience in this presurvey era.

The abandonment of license fees in 1967 came about as enforcement of the law became very difficult with the proliferation of transistor radios. It was estimated that there were a million radios in use when the fee was eliminated.

Because of its governmental sponsorship, Radio Hong Kong carries no advertising and takes a view of programming quite different from commercial stations, as indicated by this government statement:

The aim of the Government broadcasting services is to provide balanced programmes, but with some emphasis being laid on information and public affairs. The Government wants people to be informed about what Government and public institutions are doing, and why; and for responsible public opinion on matters of public concern to be reflected back to it. Government broadcasting should be of assistance also in developing better mutual understanding of the problems and attitudes of different communities who make up the colony's society. [Brooks 1969-70, p. 3]

The 1971 census breaks down languages spoken in Hong Kong as Cantonese, 88.1%; all other Chinese dialects, 10.3%; English, 1.0%; and others, 0.6%. Although 98.5% of the people speak and understand some Chinese dialect, only Cantonese represents a major group. The remaining 10.3% is fragmented among dozens of dialects, only one of which (Hakka) represents as much as 2.6% of the population. The fact that Hong Kong is populated by a polyglot people makes the work of those responsible for radio and TV programming very difficult. The broadcasting director said the limited number of transmission channels does not allow for the provision of services to satisfy all racial, cultural, and lingual groups in Hong Kong (Brooks, 1968-69, p. 3). Not only are channels limited, but the lack of funds to program for fragmented minority groups is also a major concern. Therefore, although many Chinese dialects are spoken in Hong Kong, Radio Hong Kong uses only Cantonese on the Chinese channels, apart from two daily newscasts in Kuoyu.

Also, for a large part of the program day, Radio Hong Kong transmits the same Chinese and English programs over both AM and FM channels. During certain times of the day, principally the evening hours, the Chinese and English FM channels are split from the AM and carry their own specialized programs, usually news and music (see Table 4). During the typical week, the Chinese FM channel was programmed separately about 11% and the English FM about 26% of the total time.

Table 4.   Typical Program Week, Radio Hong Kong (Week of 19-25 March 1972)

Program Category	AM & FM (Duplicate Progs.)				FM (Split off from AM)			
	Chinese		English		Chinese		English	
	Hrs./wk.	%	Hrs./wk.	%	Hrs./wk.	%	Hrs./wk.	%
Children's	5.5	4.4	0.8	0.6	0.0	0.0	0.0	0.0
Drama	22.5	17.9	6.5	4.9	0.0	0.0	0.0	0.0
Education	1.2	1.0	0.0	0.0	0.0	0.0	2.0	4.1
General Entertainment	3.5	2.8	6.0	4.5	0.0	0.0	0.0	0.0
Music	52.6	41.7	88.5	66.7	11.4	72.6	31.2	64.7
News/Current Events	18.5	14.7	21.1	15.7	2.9	18.4	13.4	27.8
Religion	0.0	0.0	2.0	1.5	1.0	6.4	1.7	3.5
Sports	3.2	2.5	0.3	0.2	0.0	0.0	0.0	0.0
Talks	16.2	12.8	3.2	2.4	0.4	2.6	0.0	0.0
Unclassified	2.8	2.2	4.6	3.5	0.0	0.0	0.0	0.0
Total	126.0	100.0	133.0	100.0	15.7	100.0	48.3	100.0

Source: Radio Hong Kong.

Chinese and English program percentages follow similar trends in most instances. One exception is the much greater time devoted to drama on the Chinese channel, which reflects the immense popularity of serialized drama among the Chinese. Radio Hong Kong, freed from economic restraints, shows heavy emphasis on music – 41.7–72.6% – compared to Commercial Radio – 3.8–7.6% (see §2.6.2.).

About 25% of Radio Hong Kong's program material comes from foreign sources, including regular relays and rebroadcasts of BBC World Service and BBC Chinese Service, occasional ones of VOA, and syndicated material from Deutsche Welle, Radio Nederland, Radio Canada, Australian Broadcasting Commission, British Forces Broadcasting Network, and United Kingdom Central Office of Information.

Radio Hong Kong is doing its bit to maintain local cultural attributes. Cantonese opera, for example, is fast dying out, not from lack of interest, but because actors who have been well paid in radio, television, and motion pictures shun the low pay of traditional opera companies. Radio Hong Kong maintains the only permanent group in Hong Kong, The Radio Hong Kong Lung Cheung Opera Company, as well as a permanent Cantonese orchestra and other Cantonese drama groups. These services are greatly appreciated by the Chinese who attend public performances given several times monthly before audiences of 10,000–30,000.

In early 1968, the government decided that Radio Hong Kong should establish a television unit to produce public affairs programs for transmission by the two commercial television outlets already in operation, TVB and RTV. The unit is now established in Broadcasting House after extensive modifications to adapt recently constructed radio studios to the TV function. Broadcasting such material is in line with the general policy of requiring commercial broadcast licensees to transmit government educational and public affairs shows. Hong Kong authorities impose strict obligations on all commercial broadcasters; they must give free airtime for government-produced programs – most turned out by Radio Hong Kong TV Unit – and include talk and discussion shows and a Chinese drama schedule (*Variety* 1975h, p. 114).

2.6.2 Commercial Radio

The monopoly of Radio Hong Kong came to an end in 1959 when a commercial station commenced transmissions. A license had been awarded George Ho to form a company to transmit a commercial service in English and another in Chinese. The Hong Kong Commercial Broadcasting Co., Ltd., known as Commercial Radio, broadcast its first programs on 26 August 1959. This action followed the general pattern in the United Kingdom where the Independent Television Authority was licensed in 1954 to provide a commercial program in competition with the BBC.

Advertisers were happy to have this access to the large Chinese audience, and listeners benefitted as variety was added to their radio fare. Competition has undoubtedly had a good effect on all broadcasting efforts in Hong Kong. Programs broadcast by Commercial Radio greatly stimulated sales of radio receivers and the payment of receiver license fees. In the 25 months following the initiation of Commercial Radio programs and the simultaneous increase of Radio Hong Kong broadcast hours, the number of licenses jumped by 48,241, or over 58%. It had taken the previous ten years to add that many.

From the beginning, Commercial Radio offered both English and Chinese services. In 1963, a second Chinese radio service, known as Chinese-2, was opened to complement the first, offering quality fare and educational material to sophisticated listeners such as white-collar workers, students, and the more affluent.

After a history of temporary expedients in transmitting equipment, moving of both studio and transmitter locations, and frequency shifts, Commercial Radio settled down in August 1971 in excellent studio and administrative facilities on Broadcast Drive. This move brought the studio machinery up to the standard of transmitting equipment which had been installed in 1967 on Peng Chau Island, 12 miles southwest of the studios. The four 10 kw. AM transmitters (one a spare) operate on the following frequencies: English, 1050 kHz; Chinese-1, 850 kHz; Chinese-2, 610 kHz. They are fed by FM link from the studio. All services start at 6 A.M.; the Chinese services close at midnight and the English at 1 A.M.

Commercial Radio has been forced to apply for frequency shifts at least a half-dozen times because of serious interference from broadcasting stations in China and Taiwan. Shifting frequency is not necessarily a permanent solution as the interfering stations in China have been known to move frequency in a way that, in some cases, appears to be a deliberate attempt to jam the Commercial Radio signal.

As far as programming goes, practically all of Commercial Radio's shows are produced in their own studios, even though no quotas are imposed on imports. For example, the English service offers 127 hours per week of nationally produced programs to only 6 hours of imported shows; Chinese-1 and -2 services, 126 hours nationally to 5 locally produced. A relatively high number of live hours are clocked by all three services, about 84% on English and Chinese-2 and about 60% on Chinese-1.

Commercial Radio is the largest producer, outside of China at least, of Cantonese-language programs in the world, and employs on contract writers, producers, actors, and storytellers. Composers and musicians are employed as need arises. Not only do all programs originate in Hong Kong, some are actually exported to Radio Singapore, Radio Malaysia, The Voice of Chinatown in San Francisco, and elsewhere. Rights to several radio plays written for Commercial Radio have been purchased by film companies.

The most popular shows broadcast by the Chinese services are Mandarin song requests and dramas. On the English service, pop music is most popular. The live serial soap opera is a favorite of Chinese listeners, especially among the less educated. During a typical week, the English and Chinese-2 channels carried no dramas while Chinese-1 presented 19½ hours of them. Outside broadcasts are used extensively for both English and Chinese programming. All major soccer matches, Chinese operas, and talent shows provide attractive fare for the Chinese through outside broadcasts. The English service does not cover soccer but does air all major events in cricket, tennis, boxing, and auto racing (see Table 5).

Table 5. Typical Program Week, Commercial Radio (Hong Kong)
(Week of 5-11 March 1972)

Program Category	English Service		Chinese-1 Service		Chinese-2 Service	
	Hrs./wk.	%	Hrs./wk.	%	Hrs./wk.	%
Advertising/Promotion	4.5	3.4	12.0	9.2	5.0	3.8
Children's	0.0	0.0	1.5	1.1	0.0	0.0
Drama	0.0	0.0	19.5	14.9	0.0	0.0
Education	0.5	0.3	2.5	1.9	9.0	6.9
General Entertainment	108.5	81.6	65.0	49.6	90.0	68.7
Music	9.0	6.8	10.0	7.6	5.0	3.8
News/Current Events	9.7	7.3	17.5	13.4	15.0	11.4
Religion	0.0	0.0	0.0	0.0	0.0	0.0
Sports	0.5	0.4	2.0	1.5	4.0	3.1
Talks	0.3	0.2	1.0	0.8	1.0	0.8
Unclassified	0.0	0.0	0.0	0.0	2.0	1.5
Total Hours	133.0	100.0	131.0	100.0	131.0	100.0

Source: Commercial Radio Program Log.

Because radio broadcasts in Hong Kong can be readily picked up throughout a sizable portion of South China, news and talk shows can be considered as operating in a sensitive area. Under the terms of the original license under which Commercial Radio works, the only newscasts permitted are those from Government Information Services. This clause has been enforced with decreasing strictness because, no doubt, of increasing confidence on the part of government officials in the maturity and self-discipline of Commercial Radio management, producers, and news writers. The clause remains in the license agreement, however, and could be stringently enforced on a moment's notice if circumstances so required. Officials of Commercial Radio are inclined to believe that their news coverage of the Communist riots of 1967 did much to demonstrate their discretion and to strengthen their position in the eyes of government. In 1974, Commercial Radio started to compose its own news bulletins. Today, news editing and presentation are subject only to normal restraints — i.e., they should be fair, accurate, objective, balanced, free from commentary, in good taste, and free of advertising (Chang 1975, p. 15).

Until 1974, Government Information Services supplied ten-minute news bulletins, which were broadcast as received, news headlines, and news from government departments which were regarded as optional information sources, along with material from the UPI audio wire service and the station's own teams. Some news was obtained by monitoring overseas sources such as VOA, BBC, and occasionally NHK and Radio Australia. If the clause had been enforced to the letter, Commercial Radio could not have broadcast news from any source other than Government Information Services.

Important educational programs designed to assist primary school children to prepare for "school leaving" examinations in English, Chinese, and mathematics are also offered by the Commercial Radio. Tens of thousands of textbooks have been distributed at or below cost since the early 1960s. Five half-hour programs in Chinese literature are broadcast weekly for adults.

Commercial Radio's license agreement limits commercial announcements to 10% of daily program time. There is no limit for any given hours as in television. In the week's programming shown in Table 5, commercials account for 3.4% on the English service and 9.2% and 3.8% on Chinese-1 and Chinese-2 services, respectively. Commercial Radio would be allowed to cram their day's allowance of commercials into 1.8 hours of prime time on a single service, but the effect on the audience of such an extreme move provides adequate control. Content of commercials, aside from fraudulent claims, is left largely to the discretion of the station.

2.6.3 Cable Services

Strictly speaking, the wired audio and television service of Rediffusion (RTV) does not fall under broadcasting, since no signal is radiated. In a practical sense, however, it is very much a part of the Hong Kong electronic media scene and makes itself ' '+ in competition for audience, advertising revenue, and talent. In addition, Red fusion, which had been offering cable TV services, was re-equipped in 1973 for wireless TV transmission in English and Chinese (*Media* June 1974, p. 23).

Rediffusion (Hong Kong) Limited is a locally controlled subsidiary of the British company, Rediffusion International, and is similar to subsidiaries operating in Britain and other Commonwealth countries, including Singapore and Malaysia in Southeast Asia. Hong Kong's Rediffusion audio operation began in 1949, primarily because the government felt incapable of increasing financial support to public service broadcasting. Two wire audio services, one supplying Rediffusion's own programs and the other relaying Radio Hong Kong shows, were begun at that time. Rediffusion English TV service (405 lines) opened in 1957, and in 1963 a Chinese TV service was inaugurated.

Rediffusion operates under license agreement with the Hong Kong government and pays a royalty to the government based upon the number of subscribers, in addition to the normal company tax. The audio service had about 50,000 subscribers in 1972; the television service 110,000. These subscribers were largely Europeans and affluent, English-speaking Chinese, perhaps as much as 80% of the latter fast-growing component of Hong Kong society. Services of Rediffusion cover the densely populated urban areas and extend to the islands and many outlying villages in New Territories. Over 1,400 miles of trunk lines and another 4,000 miles of subscriber feed lines stretch throughout the colony.

Rediffusion now offers four separate audio services. The Silver Network's 119 hours of programs per week are entirely in Cantonese, while the Gold Network splits its 119 hours among the minorities, giving token programming in Mandarin, Chiu Chow, Hakka, and Fukien dialects. The All Music Network airs about 62 hours per week, all in English, and is interrupted by ETV transmissions. A fourth service is the Educational Network, transmitting to classrooms, 90% in Cantonese and 10% in Swatowese. Schools programs on the Educational Network during the second term of 1972 totalled about 15 hours weekly, an amount far exceeding the license obligation. It is generally conceded that in the early days the Rediffusion audio service stimulated the extension of the Radio Hong Kong service and the formation of commercial radio.

Rediffusion also has two cable television services, Channel 1 carrying a full Chinese service and Channel 2, a full English facility. The programming breakdown of a typical week in 1972 for both the Chinese and English channels showed educational programs, music shows, and feature films are all emphasized more on the Chinese than on the English channel (see Table 6). But drama on the Chinese channel actually is lower than on the English one. Whereas broadcasting outlets catering to the Chinese masses generally carry large quantities of the very popular soap operas, Rediffusion's cable TV service, being relatively expensive for the viewer, is selective toward the better-educated Chinese, whose tastes are more in line with those patronizing the English channel.

Table 6. Typical Program Week, Rediffusion Television (RTV)
(Period Analyzed: 20 February – 18 March 1972)

Program Category	Channel 1 (Chinese)		Channel 2 (English)	
	Hrs./wk.	%	Hrs./wk.	%
Advertising/Promotion	5.1	4.3	1.9	2.9
Children's	11.3	9.6	9.1	13.7
Drama	13.2	11.2	16.7	25.2
Education	7.7	6.5	0.9	1.4
Feature Films	29.0	24.5	8.0	12.0
General Entertainment	7.4	6.3	6.3	9.5
Music	5.3	4.5	0.6	0.9
News/Current Events	15.3	12.9	9.2	13.8
Religion	0.0	0.0	0.0	0.0
Sports	3.6	3.0	2.5	3.8
Talks	0.9	0.8	0.3	0.4
Government Programs	13.3	11.2	10.4	15.7
Unclassified	6.2	5.2	0.5	0.7
Total Hours	118.3	100.0	66.4	100.0

Source: Hong Kong Television Authority.

In a typical month — in this case, March 1972 — the Chinese channel carried 12% English shows, the English channel, 9% Cantonese programs. This was time devoted to educational schools programs in English, Chinese, and other subjects.

On the English channel, imported British and American shows are used in about equal proportions (33.4—32.8%). On the Chinese channel, however, a preponderance of American shows is used (7—14.7%). Action-oriented American shows are far more popular with Chinese than talk-type British programs. The use of Western material on the Chinese channel does, of course, necessitate a heavy involvement in language dubbing. The Chinese channel uses nearly four times as much live material as the English station (39—14.7%). Hong Kong government programs make up 16.1% of the English and 11.8% of the Chinese channels. Rediffusion is required to carry a small amount of government material free of charge, but carrying educational fare on the cable TV channels is voluntary.

2.6.4 Television

Although Rediffusion's English-language cable TV service started in 1957, wireless television in Hong Kong was delayed for another ten years (see Green 1972, p. 247). This resulted partly because cable TV was largely a luxury service for expatriate government servants and businessmen during a decade of preoccupation with housing the hundreds of thousands of refugees pouring into Hong Kong. In 1967, the government issued an exclusive five-year license to transmit a television service to Television Broadcasts, Ltd. (HKTVB), a locally controlled private company. This ended Rediffusion's ten-year monopoly via cable TV. More important, for the less-affluent Chinese — the vast majority — a free TV service was now available once they bought an inexpensive receiver. The government license fee on receiving sets was abandoned as HKTVB came on the air. TV sets appeared everywhere, even on the sampans and junks of Aberdeen where people ran power lines ashore to tap electric current.

Like the other Hong Kong broadcasting companies, HKTVB programs for two channels, the Jade (Chinese) and Pearl (English). Program emphasis of the Chinese channel is comparable, in most instances, to that of the English channel. They differ widely in the percentages of feature films and government information they present. The Chinese channel carries far more feature films than the English service. Government-supplied programs make up 17.1% of the English schedule and less than 1% of the Chinese channel (see Table 7).

For the week analyzed, use of American shows on HKTVB exceeded those from Britain and other Commonwealth countries by three to one on the English and nine to one on the Chinese channel, again reflecting the Chinese preference for action-packed American TV fare. The Chinese channel used 34.2% live programs to the English station's 18.2%. Both RTV and HKTVB are able to program 18 or 20 hours per week of Mandarin and Cantonese films from Hong Kong sources.

Language dubbing for the utilization of foreign films is one of HKTVB's

Table 7. Typical Program Week, Television Broadcasts Ltd. (HKTVB)
(Period Analyzed: 20 February–18 March 1972)

Program Category	TVB-Jade (Chinese)		TVB-Pearl (English)	
	Hrs./wk.	%	Hrs./wk.	%
Advertising/Promotion	5.3	5.5	2.2	3.0
Children's	10.0	10.3	7.6	10.3
Drama	17.3	17.9	12.9	17.5
Education	2.5	2.6	0.0	0.0
Feature Films	24.7	25.5	12.2	16.6
General Entertainment	15.7	16.2	8.8	12.0
Music	1.1	1.1	0.4	0.5
News/Current Events	13.0	13.4	10.2	13.8
Religion	0.0	0.0	0.0	0.0
Sports	4.7	4.9	5.0	6.8
Talks	0.05	0.05	0.9	1.2
Government Programs	0.75	0.75	12.6	17.1
Unclassified	1.7	1.8	0.9	1.2
Total Hours	96.8	100.00	73.7	100.0

Source: Hong Kong Television Authority.

heaviest activities. Two studios are engaged in this activity 16 hours daily, six and a half days weekly. The traditional system of language dubbing is to break the film down into short segments which are made into picture loops for lip-movement cues. The voice is recorded on synchronized magnetic loops which are eventually spliced together to form the finished sound track in the new language. Such a laborious process is too slow for HKTVB. Instead, they record the Chinese on pulse-synchronized quarter-inch tape on a stop-and-go basis. HKTVB also does it own film subtitling. Translated material is put on a scroll which is superimposed on the picture through a vidicon camera chain and hand-timed by an operator with a script.

Talent is being trained at the studios on a continuing basis in dance, drama, and script-writing. In addition, about 150 amateur and free-lance artists are employed on a fairly regular schedule. A staff orchestra provides both Chinese and Western music. HKTVB also has a direct link with Hong Kong's largest motion-picture company inasmuch as Run Run Shaw, chairman of Shaw Brothers, is a vice-chairman of HKTVB. The station is also affiliated with Capital Artists, leading Hong Kong live-entertainment agency (*Variety* 1975h, p. 114).

Another area of programming where HKTVB places emphasis is outside broadcasting. Two vans and a number of film camera teams are on the road five days a week collecting materials.

HKTVB is also deep in the changeover to the PAL color system. About 60% of the live Chinese programs and 10% of the English are released in color. Of the 600,000 wireless TV sets in the colony in 1972, only about 1% of them were color, although of the 9,000 sets sold per month that year, about 25% were polychrome. Another way of putting it is that in the first half of 1972, the number of color sets approximately doubled.

Both Rediffusion and HKTVB must limit their advertising to 10% of the day's program time. The terms of HKTVB's license follow the advertising standards of the Television Authority, in that no more than seven minutes of advertising may be included in any one hour. Rediffusion's older license contains the feature of 10% of total program time, but not the hourly limitation. Any renewal of RTV's 15-year license, however, which was to expire in 1973, will undoubtedly include the hourly limitation in the interest of uniformity and consistency.

The total advertising gross for Hong Kong in 1971 was about $40 million. Although the portion captured by television in the United States is approximately 43% and 30% in Britain, Japan, and Taiwan, in Hong Kong it was only about 16% due to a less-developed society and to the fact that there are some 60 newspapers in Hong Kong. Reducing this by 25% for commissions and royalties left only about $4.8 million to support TV operations in 1971. In 1974, TV advertising billings in Hong Kong were up 30% from the previous year, from $10.4 million to $13.6 million, probably because of the rapid growth of the new wireless TV. Radio, during the same period, was down 3% (from $1.27 million to $1.24 million). Commercial stations had reduced rates and reclassified airtime to meet increased TV competition (*Media* 1975c, p. 21).

2.6.5 Educational Television

Commercial television companies of Hong Kong are required by the government to transmit schools programs free of charge if requested. In September 1971 this became a reality as programs started to flow from the education department's Educational Television Centre to become an integral part of the curriculum.

Hong Kong Educational Television (ETV) occupies a compact two-storey building. Three image orthicon camera chains, two videotape recorders, telecine, and other machinery indicate the completeness of the operation. One studio, equipped with facilities for production of primary-school programs, is fully used, the other is designed to handle secondary schools shows when ETV expands to that level. Signals are fed by coaxial cable to RTV and HKTVB.

By 1972, about 1,000 TV receivers were used in the schools, serving 100,000 third-year primary pupils. In 1974, over 400,000 students in primary schools were covered by educational television programs. Each school receiver serves two groups of students because the schools operate on a two-session basis, one morning, one afternoon. The first subject areas to be treated are English, Chinese, mathematics, and social studies. Continuous evaluation indicates excellent results in all areas but English, Chinese children not being familiar with the modern situational and direct method of teaching English adopted by ETV. Instead, they are accustomed to the teaching of English by recitation in chorus, syllable by syllable, and often through the use of Cantonese. Recent evaluations indicate, however, that by slowing the pace this new approach to English instruction is achieving wider acceptance. Time donated by commercial television organizations for primary-schools transmissions in 1972 was 7½ hours per week on each of three channels, RTV Chinese and English and HKTVB English. Color television is planned by Educational Television by 1976. Also, an additional 250,000 students were expected to be served by ETV in the next few years. The service's goal is to cover at least the first three years of secondary education (*Media* 1974k, p. 26).

2.6.6 Future of Television

HKTVB's license was due to expire in 1972, Rediffusion's in 1973. In April 1972, the Television Authority put an end to speculation about the future of television by announcing that Hong Kong would have two additional TV stations making a total of three. Of course, the news was received with more enthusiasm by the general public and RTV (the latter wanting to get into broadcast television) than by HKTVB, which had enjoyed a monopoly on TV broadcasting for five years.

Rediffusion Television's English service was inaugurated 22 April 1974, amid much controversy. Before RTV began English telecasts, Hong Kong's English-speaking audience had only TVB-Pearl. The Chinese section of RTV went on the air in December 1973 (*Media,* June 1974, p. 23). Rediffusion Television showed large gains in audience figures during its first year. In June 1974, RTV's audience was 18% of the total; by October of the same year, the figure was 34% (*Media,* February 1975, p. 25).

The Television Authority further stated that one of the new TV stations would be required to operate separate services in both English and Chinese, whereas the second station would use Chinese only. The latter would offer "specialized services in the public interest" for purposes other than entertainment; actually, the station is obliged to broadcast two hours nightly of educational programs. All three stations were to share transmitter sites and a common antenna mast. Other probable requirements include a fixed royalty to the government of 25% of net profits, majority local ownership, and local programming control. Announcement was also made that HKTVB would be offered a renewal of its license, subject to certain changes in the Television Ordinance.

Radio Hong Kong's Television Unit survives as an important sector of the TV industry. In December 1973, RHKTV Unit started to produce color programs and was expected to achieve full-scale color production by the end of 1974. One of Radio Hong Kong's popular TV shows in 1974 was "Needle Point," a 30-minute forum and audience-participation telecast screened over TVB-Pearl and RTV-1 channels in Cantonese. Estimated to have an audience of 2 million, the show was meant to "prick enemies of the public," devoting some time to inflation and spiraling costs. After one show which called for an end to profiteering, a group of businessmen tried unsuccessfully to drive the program off the air. The colony's cabinet (Government Executive Council) decided not to cancel or change the show (*Media Asia* 1974, p. 8; *Media* 1974i, p. 23; *Media,* June 1974, p. 23). In mid-1975, however, "Needle Point" succumbed to the pressure and went off the air. It was replaced by a tamer show, "A Matter of Concern" (*Media,* September 1975, p. 25). Hong Kong's first live phone-in TV show went on the air in March 1974. Called "Confrontation," it was telecast in Chinese over Radio Hong Kong's Television Unit, as part of an effort to produce more and better current-affairs programs aimed at securing greater audience participation (*Media,* February 1974, p. 28).

A recent development pointed to the possibility of stricter censorship of sex and violence on television. An April 1974 report of the government's Television Authority called for curbs on portrayal of "the thoughtless use of violence" which is "likely to produce a distorted picture of life, particularly to young viewers." The views of the Television Authority were supported by community leaders who also called for controls on the portrayal of sex on TV programs and commercials. Simultaneously, the government's Film and Television Division conducted a precedent-setting survey to assess public opinion on TV censorship (*Media* 1974g, p. 23). By mid-1975, TV stations had cleaned up their children's shows, cutting out superhero programs such as the Japanese production, "The Masked Rider" (*Media,* July 1975, pp. 20-21; *Media,* September 1975, p. 25). Also, TV stations were asked by the government board to be more careful in presenting social-satire programs which "may be harmful to the community's best interests" (*Media,* August 1975, p. 22).

2.6.7 Broadcasting in Emergencies

Hong Kong broadcasting has had some of its finest and worst hours during emergencies created by both nature and man. A few examples will suffice. In June 1966, Radio Hong Kong, while in its old studios on Hong Kong Island, felt the full force of a cloudburst. With power gone and the emergency generator flooded, the controller of the English service swam through heavy debris to reach the studio where, with the aid of a microphone, a hand-driven turntable, and a set of batteries, he fed important news in both Chinese and English to the transmitters.

On 6 May 1967, a demonstration in Kowloon at San Po Kong touched off Communist disturbances that had Hong Kong reeling for months. The news crews of Radio Hong Kong, Commercial Radio, and Rediffusion (TVB did not open until November that year) swung into action. The hard-hitting editorials of Lum Bun of Commercial Radio's Chinese service resulted in his becoming the number one target of the Communists. His car was set afire while he and a junior staff member were in it and both men died in the holocaust.

In August 1971, Typhoon Rose made a direct hit on Hong Kong, and winds of 200 miles per hour put Commercial Radio transmitters off the air for seven days.

2.6.8 Satellite Communications

Broadcasting services in Hong Kong have the potential of live pickups from, and live program feed to, almost any spot in the world through Intelsat satellites and the Hong Kong earth station.

In late 1969, Cable & Wireless, a state corporation, put into service their first station, Hong Kong 1, to work with the Intelsat satellite over the Pacific Ocean. Two years later, Hong Kong 2 became operative with the Intelsat III satellite positioned over the Indian Ocean. Initially, Hong Kong 1 was to handle traffic with the United States, Australia, Japan, and Thailand, and Hong Kong 2, traffic with the United Kingdom, Germany, India, Indonesia, Malaysia, and Singapore. The two dish-shaped antennas, 90 and 97 feet in diameter, are designed to hold track in wind gusts of 60 miles per hour. Stowed for survival (pointed directly upward and securely battened down), they are designed to withstand winds of 210 miles per hour.

Most satellite usage is still too expensive for Hong Kong television, except for cases of very exceptional news. For example, the satellite image was used for the most newsworthy high spots of President Nixon's visit to China in February 1972, but film arriving one day after the event carried the major burden of coverage.

For the time being, most of the economic justification for communications via satellite in Hong Kong was in international telephony and telex. Because of the colony's being an international business hub, Hong Kong's need for international communication traffic is about the same as that of all of Australia.

2.7 Mácau, *by F. Alton Everest*

Fifteen years after Vasco da Gama founded a sea route to India, Jorge Alvares, in 1513, anchored his ship off the South China coast. Portuguese trade with the Chinese has, with many ups and downs, been going on ever since. Mácau became the center of this trade about 1557 and, as an overseas province of Portugal, flourishes to this day.

Mácau is perched precariously on a tiny peninsula at the mouth of the Pearl River (the Chu-Kiang), which carries the confluence of the three great rivers of South China. Canton is only 60 miles up the river and Hong Kong, 40 miles to the east. Mácau covers only 6 square miles, the city itself accounting for 2.1 and the two nearby islands, Taipa and Coloane, the remaining 3.9. The islands are connected with each other by a causeway road and will soon by joined to the mainland by a bridge.

The population of Mácau, according to the 1970 census, was 248,636, a rise of 46% in ten years because of the strong influx from neighboring countries. Of this population, 97% are Chinese.

Besides broadcasting, Mácau is served by eight dailies, three in Portuguese and five in Chinese. The largest is *Macanese Gazeta,* the victim of government economic sanctions in 1974, when it supported the sweeping reforms campaign of the Centro Democratico de Mácau (CDM). The government at the same time canceled in midbroadcast a weekly CDM program on Radio Mácau, explaining the program contained half-truths and the action was taken "to safeguard the best interest of the public."

2.7.1 Early Broadcasting

The first radio broadcasting in Mácau, under the sponsorship of the Mácau police, was established in 1936 with the call letters CQN. Five years later, the Radio Club of Mácau, a group of interested citizens rather than professional broadcasters, took over this responsibility, broadcasting on 900 kHz with a 250-w. transmitter under the call CR9AA. The Radio Club continued its broadcasting, with the blessing and some financial help of the Mácau government, through World War II, but financial problems forced the station to close 15 February 1954. At least 5,000 licensed radio sets were in Mácau at that time.

All of these transmissions were controlled by the Mácau government and financed partly through annual license fees of $4 per set. Until its discontinuance in 1966 the fee was divided between the Radio Club and Lisbon authorities.

In addition to activity on the medium-wave band, the Radio Club also broadcast sporadically on short-wave, the signals reaching as far as Europe, United States, Canada, and Brazil. The first short-wave broadcast was on 22 April 1941, from studios in the Post Office Building. This overseas service was officially inaugurated by Governor Gabriel Teixeira on 28 May 1941, using a 250-w. transmitter on the 49-meter band with the call CRY9 — later changed to CR9XM.

2.7.2 Emissora de Radiodiffusaõ de Mácau

Following the shutdown of CR9AA in 1954, there were eight years of silence in broadcasting in Mácau, until legislation was passed 17 February 1962, formally establishing Emissora de Radiodiffusaõ de Mácau (ERM). By 1963, ERM was on the air with two AM channels — one broadcasting in Portuguese on 900 kHz with 10 kw. of power, the other in Cantonese on 1,200 kHz with a 250-w. transmitter — and one FM channel, broadcasting in Portuguese and Cantonese on 98 mHz with 1 kw. of power.

By the early 1970s, the 900 kHz AM channel was served by two 10-kw. transmitters, each of which was put into use on alternate days as a maintenance procedure. The 250-w. transmitter, used as long ago as World War II, eventually will be replaced by one of the two 10-kw. transmitters now in use on the 900 kHz AM channel. Originally located in the Department of Postal, Telephonic, and Telegraphic Services, ERM moved in 1970 into its own building with excellent studio facilities. The original channels were retained.

Ground space is so scarce in Mácau that the present towers of the antenna system are on concrete bases rising out of the city's fresh-water reservoir. A copper ground system cannot be used because of danger of polluting the water supply through corrosion products, but experiments have been conducted with a new coating of American origin for the copper mesh and initial results have been encouraging.

The Portuguese-language program is adjusted to the habits of that segment of the community, with shows in the early morning (7:30–8:30 A.M.), at midday (1–2:30 P.M.) and in the evening (8–11 P.M.). The Cantonese service programs only from 4–8 P.M. daily. An FM channel carries the same Portuguese and Chinese programs as the AM stations, except between 9 and 11 P.M. on Tuesday, Thursday, and Sunday when FM splits to specialize in classical music.

Freed by government support from the rigors of competing for advertising revenue, ERM generally emphasizes cultural programs. On the Portuguese channel, music from Portugal and Brazil is popular. Although ERM has no news team of its own, newscasts are included in each of the three daily broadcasts on this channel, based on material garnered from Portuguese press agencies and short-wave relay from Lisbon. Radio plays, variety shows, a weekly children's program, and two sports events per week complete the Portuguese schedule. Other fare is received, both on tape and disk, from Radio Portugal, Radio Sweden, Radio Nederland, Office de Radiodiffusion-Télévision Francaise (ORTF), New Zealand Broadcasting Corporation, and Radio Nacional de España, some of which is in Portuguese.

On the Chinese channel, programs are made up primarily of Cantonese and Mandarin operas and popular songs. On Sundays, European music and pop songs are sometimes transmitted. Three times a week, a sports program covering local and foreign athletic events is presented. Soccer matches are relayed to ERM direct from the Overseas Service of Emissora Nacional in Lisbon. Radio plays and stories based on Chinese history are produced by the ERM staff. A taped program on science and general information is obtained from Germany, and French lessons, broadcast once a week, are supplied on tape by ORTF through the French Consulate in Hong Kong (see Table 8).

Table 8. Typical Program Week, Emissora de Radiodifusão de Mácau (ERM)

Program Category	Portuguese		Cantonese	
	Hrs./wk.	%	Hrs./wk.	%
Advertising/Promotion				
Children's	1.0	2.6		
Drama	2.0	5.1	1.0	3.6
Education	1.5	3.8	1.0	3.6
General Entertainment	10.5	27.0	14.5	51.8
Music	15.0	38.5	8.5	30.3
News/Current Affairs	5.0	12.8	1.0	3.6
Religion				
Sports	1.0	2.6	0.5	1.8
Talks	2.0	5.1	1.0	3.6
Unclassified	1.0	2.5	0.5	1.7
Total Hours	39.0	100.0	28.0	100.0

2.7.3 Radio Vila Verde

Radio Vila Verde became the first commercial station in Macau when it went on the air in April 1951. Using a 10-kw. transmitter, Vila Verde transmits on a frequency of 735 kHz. The station maintains studios and sales offices in both Mácau and Hong Kong, only 40 miles away; however, over 95% of its business transactions take place in Hong Kong. The station's existence depends largely on advertising revenue from Hong Kong.

Radio Vila Verde broadcasts seven days weekly from 7 A.M. to midnight, and all programming is in Cantonese. A strong emphasis is placed on entertainment with no news or educational fare provided. The heavy programming of Cantonese opera makes up the general entertainment category, whereas favorite Mandarin songs (60%) and Western pop music (40%) make up most of the station's musical material.

Because gambling is outlawed in Hong Kong, except for government-condoned horse racing, Mácau casinos are heavily patronized by Hong Kong residents and tourists. Radio Vila Verde reflects this interest in gambling—90% of the 13½ hours per week set aside for sports programs consists of live remote broadcasts of dog racing; the rest is horse racing. The large audience for dog-racing broadcasts is indicated by the fact that time charges are four times as high during the races as for comparable time in the evenings when races are not aired (see Table 9).

Table 9. Typical Program Week, Radio Vila Verde

Program Category	Hrs./wk.	Percentage
Advertising/Promotion	1.3	1.2
Children's	1.7	1.3
Drama	26.0	22.8
Education		
General Entertainment	20.7	18.2
Music	46.5	40.8
News/Current Affairs		
Religion	0.3	0.3
Sports	13.5	11.9
Talks	4.0	3.5
Unclassified		
Total Hours	114.0	100.0

2.7.4 Audience

Mácau residents receive good radio reception from four channels: ERM and Radio Vila Verde in Mácau, and Radio Hong Kong and Commercial Radio in Hong Kong. Radio signals of usable strength are also received from numerous stations in China, particularly Canton and Peking, but apparently the audience held by these stations is small because of the monotonous propagandistic programs.

Many potential radio listeners in Mácau are lost to the attraction of evening television. Although Mácau has no television station, channel TVB from Hong Kong comes in quite well. The TVB Cantonese variety show, "Enjoy Yourself Tonight," is very popular among Chinese and local-born, bilingual Portuguese. There are an estimated 12,000 television sets in Mácau, almost all of which are owned or rented by people connected with casinos who can afford such luxuries. In 1974, one publication reported that a Japanese firm, Kamai Shochiku Ltd., had submitted proposals to the Mácau government to build a TV station in Mácau to beam programs to Hong Kong. Such a station would cause Hong Kong authorities considerable problems of interference, censorship, and political rivalry. Because Portugal is not a member of the International Tele-communication Union, Mácau has no legal restrictions on directing programs to Hong Kong (*Media* 1974g, pp. 22–23). A year later, a group of Mácau and foreign investors submitted an application for a Mácau station.

But radio is still the chief medium in Mácau and, judging from the number of receivers, it is expanding. In 1958, 11,000 licensed radio sets existed in Mácau; by 1972, the estimated number was 50,000, about one set per five residents.

3. Southeast Asia

Southeast Asia has been newsworthy, at least for the past two decades, primarily because of the Indochina War, but also because of the unstable nature of many of the newly emergent nations of that region. Martial law and emergency decrees, often resulting in one-man rule, have existed in the Philippines, Thailand, Singapore, Indonesia, Burma, Malaysia, and, of course, Vietnam, Laos, and Khmer Republic. A result has been that mass media-government relationships have been left in an uneasy state.

This section begins with descriptions of the broadcasting systems of Indochina — South Vietnam, North Vietnam, Khmer Republic, and Laos, a region French-controlled until 1953, of 289,728 square miles with a population of nearly 50 million. The section proceeds to relate the story of radio and television in the Malay Peninsula states of Thailand, Malaysia, and Singapore, followed by the island-nations of Indonesia and the Philippines, and finally Burma. The colonial implants upon all of these systems, except that of Thailand, which escaped formal European colonization, are pointed out by the individual authors.

Although Brunei is not listed in this survey, because of the lack of a contributing author, we provide here the information available. Brunei, a British protectorate since 1888, occupies 2,226 square miles, divided into four districts, within the boundary of Sarawak, East Malaysia. Its 145,000 people are mainly Malay (65%) and Chinese (23%), who have, after Japan, the second highest income per capita in Asia. Most of the money comes from Brunei's rich oil deposits. The nation does not have a daily newspaper, although there is a government radio station. Brunei Broadcasting Service (BBS) operates a network with medium-wave transmitters at Tutong (10 and 20 kw.), Berakas (10 kw.), and Kuala Belait (0.6 kw.). BBS broadcasts mainly in Bahasa Malaysia (13 hours daily), English (½ hour), Chinese (5 hours), and Ghurkhali (1 hour). Of Radio Brunei's 180 hours of weekly programs, over 80% are of national origin, the main categories being light entertainment and news and information (UNESCO 1975, p. 261). The number of radio receivers is 22,000. No receiver license fee is required, and low-cost receivers are made available by the government on easy terms for poor families.

A major phenomenon is that Brunei, in March 1975, started color-television transmissions, using the most modern equipment in the area and doing it quite rapidly — the whole operation was designed and built in less than seven months.

Ironically, the best equipment will be catering to the smallest television audience in Asia; only 5,000 receivers are expected to be sold in the first two years. In 1975, there were 5,000 registered owners of black-and-white receivers who picked up less-than-adequate reception from neighboring Sabah. The equipment for the transmitter is British; also, only British-made color-TV receivers have been approved for import into Brunei. The television service is part of Brunei's Five-Year Plan for Economic Development (Solley 1975, p. 46; *Media* 1975b, p. 4).

3.1 Republic of Vietnam (South Vietnam), *by Thomas W. Hoffer and Lawrence W. Lichty*

The Republic of Vietnam (often referred to as the Government of Vietnam or South Vietnam) was created in 1954, after French forces surrendered at Dien Bien Phu. Agreements reached in Geneva in July of that year established a provisional military demarcation line (DMZ) at the 17th parallel.

Vietnam (North and South), a Chinese province until about the tenth century, was ruled from Hanoi (the capital) by its own people until 1883, when, under the Treaty of Protectorate, the French gained control, divided the region into three administrative zones, and named it Tonkin. After the Japanese occupation during World War II, the Viet Minh in August 1945 created a new republic with Hanoi as capital again. But French rule was reestablished in 1946 and fighting continued with the Viet Minh until 21 July 1954.

From 1954 to 1959, Premier Ngo Dinh Diem seemed to be leading South Vietnam out of chaos into statehood. By December 1960, however, the National Liberation Front — also called Viet Cong or Vietnamese Communists — was

Thomas W. Hoffer is Assistant Professor of Communications, Florida State University; he has TV and film experience on military, academic, and professional levels. He was advisor to the U.S. Navy in Vietnam (1969) where he investigated the use of mass media in national development and pacification. He received his Ph. D. at the University of Wisconsin.

Lawrence W. Lichty is Professor of Communication Arts at the University of Wisconsin, and Staff Director, Wisconsin Commission on Cable Communications. He conducted research in Asia in 1968 and 1975. He is consulting editor for three broadcasting and speech journals and the compiler of a broadcasting bibliography, as well as coauthor of two broadcasting books.

formed, and Diem declared a state of emergency. His control became more centralized, repressive, and brutal. After protests, the Diem regime was overthrown on 1 November 1963, with the complicity of United States agencies. During the next four years, until October 1967, the Republic of Vietnam underwent at least eleven formal changes in government leadership. During the entire period, and especially in the 1960s and 1970s, an internecine war raged, with the United States involved in ground, air, and naval operations. In January 1973, the Paris Peace Agreement put an end to direct involvement by United States armed forces and prescribed a cease-fire in South Vietnam. The cease-fire, however, was not observed, and finally in the spring of 1975 South Vietnam was conquered by Hanoi-supported troops.

South Vietnam stretches nearly 600 miles from the rugged Annam Cordillera Mountains in the North to the Mekong Delta. The population is 20.4 million, with 1.8 million in the capital of Saigon (since spring of 1975 renamed Ho Chi Minh City). The income per capita of these people in 1973-74 was estimated at $120.

Besides the broadcasting services, South Vietnam before 1975 was served by at least 26 major dailies in Vietnamese and Chinese. The press actively campaigned against the Thieu government and was punished accordingly — by high registration fees, suspension of papers, and arrests of journalists.

3.1.1 Introduction

The development of broadcasting in South Vietnam came mostly from the American military and United States aid in the country. By the early 1970s, the United States had established a fairly complete and sophisticated broadcasting system. But on 30 April 1975 the United States presence in what had been known as the Republic of Vietnam, or South Vietnam, ended.

Geographically, more than two-thirds of southern Vietnam is made up of rugged mountains and high plains running north and south. Nearly half the land area is jungle. Another third is deep bush or swamp. The jungle is often so dense that it may cut down the normally expected range of radio stations by as much as 70%. Signal propagation is also limited by atmospheric and magnetic variations. For example, it is easier to receive northern Vietnamese broadcasts in southern Vietnam than vice versa, given equal power and wave-length conditions.

Nearly 85% of the population of southern Vietnam is ethnically Vietnamese; the others are Chinese — concentrated near Saigon — and highland tribes called Montagnards and Khmers. Three dialects, broken down by north, central, and south sections of the southern area, are spoken by ethnic Vietnamese. They differ in vocabulary, tone pattern, and pronunciation, but there appears to be little difficulty among the three regions in understanding one another. Many urban Vietnamese also spoke French.

Before 1965, the several local and provincial broadcasting stations catered strongly to ethnic interests, particularly Chinese and Montagnard audiences. As political centralization increased, these stations were replaced by regional ones, broadcasting programs originated in Saigon. The number of broadcast services for French, Thai, Cambodian, English, and Montagnard audiences varied from 1962 to 1970, but increased emphasis was given to the largest minority highland tribe with Jarai-language broadcasting from Radio Pleiku. Most of the 17 remaining tribal groups spoke different languages and had little familiarity with radio.

After the occupation of South Vietnam by northern elements in May 1975, newspapers, cinema, and broadcast media promulgated the political line of the northern Lao Dong Party and the Saigon revolutionary government (the Military Administrative Committee), comprised of numerous subdivisions extending into family groups (*New York Times* 1975).

Because of the war, transportation and communication have been severely limited. In 1967, less than 4,000 miles of surfaced road was available. As the nation entered the 1970s, fewer than 200,000 households had electricity in a nation with an estimated 20 million people.

An agricultural economy based on rice typifies ethnic Vietnamese villages. Family loyalty is probably the most important force in Vientam, and before April 1975 some content of South Vietnamese broadcasting reflected strong appeals to the "fatherland" and the family, particularly stressing the value of harmony.

An important factor that influenced the development and utilization of broadcasting was the revolutionary movement led by the National Liberation Front (NLF), the Communist Party in South Vietnam and their armed forces. Finally, the United States military presence was largely responsible for the construction of southern Vietnamese television and the upgrading of radio service.

3.1.2 Origins of Radio

Vo Tuyen Viet Nam (VTVN), or Radio Vietnam, began operations 1 January 1950 under French control, which was relinquished in July 1954. By February 1955, the Vietnamese had assumed full control and all French broadcasting ceased. Broadcasting was a government monopoly patterned after the French bureaucracy. VTVN was a department of the Ministry of Information and was presided over by a five-member board of directors. During the existence of the Republic of Vietnam, this ministry also had a field arm, the Vietnamese Information Service (VIS) comprised of about 5,500 employees who conducted information activities at the province, district, and village levels. According to the United States Information Agency (USIA/USIS), the mission of the VIS was to:

Augment, through face-to-face meetings, study seminars and local publications and broadcasts, the electronic media in disseminating news and information on GVN programs. VIS workers are the transmission belt for publications, films and radio and television receivers and other material originating from the Saigon-based ministry. These workers are also expected to be the eyes and ears for the electronic media. [USIA 1970]

In 1961, there were six stations in the broadcasting network, and most programs originated from Saigon. VTVN Channel A was primarily the national voice. In the early 1960s, with NLF pressure on the Diem regime, the government decided that a single, high-power propaganda station in Saigon was best for the nation. Inaugurated in May 1964, that station was the predecessor of the Voice of Freedom.

USIA has estimated that from 1956–72 the United States invested about $12.5 million in the VTVN network; the South Vietnam counterpart funds amounted to about $2.5 million from 1965–72. In the first year of its aid, the United States agreed to help the South Vietnamese increase the power of the Saigon station from 5 to 10 kw., construct new 1 kw. facilities in Nha Trang, Quang Ngai, and Can Tho, and improve short-wave transmission facilities in Saigon and Hue. At that time, the government planned to establish an 11-station medium-wave network.

Table 10.   Stations in South Vietnam, 1970-74

Area	VTVN Ch A	Ch B	Ch C	AFVN AM	FM	Korean AM	THVN Ch	KW	AFVN TV Ch	KW
Saigon	100	20		50	100	5	(9)	225	(11)	240
Qui Nhon	50 (100 kw.)[a]			10	25	10	(9)	45	(11)	40
Nha Trang	50 (100 kw.)			10	25	5			(11)	40
Danang	50 (100 kw.)			10	25		(7)	1	(11)	40
Dalat	1 (1 kw.)									
Can Tho	10 (10 kw.)						(11)	200	(78)	1
Quang Ngai	10 (10 kw.)									
Hue	10 (20 kw.)						(9)	45		
Ban Me Thout	10 (50 kw.)									
Quang Tri				1					(11)	40
Pleiku				10	25				(11)	40
Phan Rang									(78)	1
Phu Tho			10							
Phy Yen	(.25)									
Hoi An						1				
Tuy Hao						1			(11)	40
Chu Lai				1	.3				(13)	40
Ninh Hao					.05					
Cam Ranh					.05					
Phu Cat					.4					
Camp Eagle				1					(78)	1

Note: Figures show the Vietnam, Korean, and U.S. stations operating in 1970 with a 1974 update. For AM and FM stations, the power is given in kilowatts; for television, the channel and kilowatts are given.

[a]These figures in parenthesis are the 1974 power descriptions from *Asian Press and Media Directory.*

When the Diem regime organized its "strategic hamlet" program, plans were initiated to erect a network of several 50-w. stations in the hamlets. This plan for decentralized broadcasting was significantly altered after 1965. Later a Voice of America (VOA) plan called for a 12-station network that would reach 95% of the Vietnamese population. During Tet 1968, it became apparent that this network structure needed revision again because of the number of attacks directed at VTVN stations. Saigon propagandists and USIA settled on a high-power, four-station network for Channel A with four additional regional stations (see Table 10).

Before 1972, internal political problems among the various ministries, aided by individuals closely guarding their own prerogatives, did much to inhibit a timely and consistent content input to the national radio network, even on subjects which had no apparent political overtones. For example, in 1963, coordination among the Ministry of Information, pacification, and health agencies was nearly impossible even to launch a campaign to stamp out malaria in the Delta. Yet by 1969, the major problem on intergovernmental cooperation was recognized as a principle pacification objective with several campaigns urging the cessation of bureaucratic infighting.

After Diem's downfall the USIS began a joint training program for VTVN personnel. Training conducted by the USIS and later VOA personnel included radio writing, production techniques, studio engineering, and technical subjects.

3.1.3 Radio Facilities and Programming

VTVN Channel A. Four medium-wave stations in Danang, Qui Nhon, Nha Trang, and Saigon make up the major outlets for the VTVN Channel A network. These stations broadcast 75% of the network-originated content from Saigon with the remainder programmed for regional audiences. Subsidiary stations were located in Hue, Quang Ngai, Ban Me Thout, and Can Tho, using low medium-wave frequencies with much lower power. Up to 1972, these stations were allowed to produce up to 75% of their own programming and were required to carry network offerings for the remaining time. All stations were required to carry network news broadcasts every hour on the hour for varying periods of 5, 10, and 15 minutes. Channel A was the largest network intended primarily for the civilian populations. In mid-1969, music and news accounted for nearly one-half of the VTVN offerings, while other programs included religious, "pacification," commentary, drama, and development fare. News programs made up about 15% of a sample week in mid-1969, often focusing on details of pacification. During that period, only 4% of the programs systematically presented educational or children's material. Several commentaries and editorials were used, amounting to about 4% of the Channel A schedule.

In Saigon, both Channel A and B transmitters broadcast 24 hours daily; in other cities, stations were usually on the air from 8-15 hours daily.

VTVN Channels B and C. Channel B was operated by VTVN but programmed by the Armed Forces Vietnam Network (ARVN) and its General

Political Warfare Department. Intended mainly for military audiences and their dependents, in 1969 it included music and poetry as on Channel A, but less drama. There were a number of programs aimed specifically at the military and dependents. Channel C services were intended primarily for minority audiences including the Chinese, French, Thai, Cambodian, and English.

1975. As the end of April 1975 approached, radio was increasingly used to relay the confusing and vascillating decisions of the outgoing RVN adminis- tration as it changed presidents, vice-presidents, premiers, and chiefs of staff and inched toward surrender. The competition for the attention of the southern Vietnamese was intense as Radio Saigon and Liberation Radio attempted to relay the latest directives and policy statements. At 9:30 A.M. on 29 April 1975, Radio Saigon announced that Nguyen Van Can had left Saigon the previous evening and that a new premier was appointed by President Duong Van Minh, who held the office for two days before the takeover by the Communists. By the next day, 30 April, a recording of Minh was played at 10:24 A.M. calling for a ceasefire, just about five hours after the last American evacuation helicoptor left the city. During the period 29-30 April, the Saigon home service broadcast light and popular music interrupted for official announcements. Health and welfare workers were asked to return to their posts; deserters and looters were warned. On 30 April at 12:15 P.M., the flag of the Vietnamese Liberation Army flew in front of Independence Palace in Saigon. Following various exhortations about the "victory," Radio Saigon broadcast several appeals by worker, student, musician, and journalist groups to support the new government. Later in the afternoon, live announcements or recordings were broadcast calling on Saigon forces to surrender, announcing complete dissolution of the administration from the center of the local level. At 4:08 P.M., the first communique of the "Saigon-Cholon-Gia Dinh People's Liberation Armed Forces" was broadcast, announcing full control of Saigon. Saigon radio later invited its audiences to listen to a program by Liberation Radio which turned out to be a demonstration of support for the new regime. Liberation Radio had abandoned its schedule and played patriotic songs, sometimes interrupting for news of the United States evacuation and other "successes." Short-wave broadcasts urging refugee Viet- namese to return to Vietnam were picked up by listeners just arriving in Guam.

After the surrender, Radio Saigon shortened its operating hours, broadcasting from about 5:30 A.M. to about 10:30 P.M. Apparently the external services were inoperative for a time, but by July 1975, both internal and external broadcasts appeared to be very similar in content (Interview, Paul Vogel, Summer 1975). Little is known about the status of the regional southern Vietnamese stations, although no evidence exists to suggest that the new political regime does not continue to use the apparatus set up by the Vietnamese and the United States government.

3.1.4   Television

As early as 1954, the Michigan State Advisory Group recommended that television be introduced into South Vietnam, mainly for political, literacy, and educational purposes. Vietnamese and Americans considered the idea totally inappropriate for a combat zone; others argued that television would enhance the prestige of South Vietnam, help unify, and perhaps create new wants as a basis for markets in electronic devices. South Vietnam may be the only country where television was introduced, in part, with the hope it would interest people in buying sets, thus inducing them to spend money and reduce inflation. The U.S. State Department, the Mission in Saigon, and the South Vietnamese government agreed that exclusive American television would lend credence to North Vietnam's charges of U.S. imperialism. Thus in 1964 a U.S. Mission Council's report recommended that two systems be built: one for South Vietnamese, the other for American servicemen.

On 7 February 1966, a U.S. Navy Super Constellation (C-121) rolled down the runway of the Saigon airport, climbed to 10,500 feet — reaching a spot about 20 miles southeast of Saigon — and banked into an oval pattern at the slowest possible speed of about 170 miles an hour. Inside, there were three 2-5 kw. transmitters, two videotape machines, audio control panels and sets of 16mm. telecine equipment, a studio about the size of a large clothes closet, a small studio camera, and radio receiving and transmitting equipment. Operating in the tail section was a 100-kw. diesel generator to supply power for the television equipment, as well as two air-conditioning systems. At 7:30 that evening, the first THVN program was broadcast on Channel 9, featuring a newscast, May Day parade film, comedy skit, short film showing prospective Vietnamese pilots in training, and a brief introduction by Prime Minister Nguyen Ky and U.S. Ambassador Henry Cabot Lodge.

At 8 P.M. this Vietnamese channel signed off and AFVN-TV Channel 11 began service with introductory remarks by General William Westmoreland and Secretary of Defense Robert McNamara. A two-hour videotape produced at KTLA, Los Angeles, was presented, featuring Los Angeles disc jockey Johnny Grant, Bob Hope, Ann-Margaret, Kathleen Nolan, and Gene Autry, owner of KTLA. The second program was the "Grand Ole Opry," videotaped in Nashville. Both the American and Vietnamese stations used American TV technical standards. (*Wall Street Journal* 1964; *Broadcasting* 1966a, 1966b, 1966d; Salazar, 1966a).

That first day, the 800 television sets at the PX were sold almost immediately. The new medium was extremely expensive to operate, airborne transmission costing about $2,000 an hour, or $750,000 yearly.

On 27 June 1966, an agreement was signed between the governments of South Vietnam and the United States providing for the construction of a four-station network. The United States was to provide all the equipment, training, and additional receivers for community viewing, while the Vietnamese were responsible for the land, buildings, staff, and an operating budget. Progress was slow. Temporary ground stations in Saigon and Hue were in operation by October 1966 and September 1967, respectively.

In 1970, THVŃ—literally "Vietnam broadcasting with pictures"—employed 190 persons at stations in Saigon, Can Tho, and Hue, operating on a budget of $1.3 million. The lack of trained personnel was always a critical problem. NBC International supervised the technical training and between 1968 and 1970, it was estimated that more than $100 million was spent providing American personnel to operate THVN and to train the Vietnamese (*Wall Street Journal* 1966; Salazar 1966b; *Los Angeles Times* 1966a; R. Hull 1970).

Program tapes and film from Saigon were mailed to regional stations by air. No interconnecting network existed, but by July 1971, Can Tho and Hue stations had their own news film and local origination capability.

According to a 1970 analysis by the Joint U.S. Public Affairs Office (JUSPAO), THVN content consisted of 51% entertainment, 30% government, and 18% news and commentary. In the same year, THVN was 75% videotape, 15% live; externally produced content amounted to less than 10%.

From the beginning of United States assistance in January 1966 to its termination on 30 June 1972, the total United States investment in Vietnamese television amounted to $8.2 million. South Vietnam contributed another $2 million in the form of land and building costs. By 1970, the five THVN facilities were costing about $1.3 million a year to operate, including salaries. THVN in Saigon alone had a yearly budget of about $400,000. Funds for operating THVN were derived through the Commercial Import Program, which, in effect, meant the United States paid the money.

A variety of government and private elements provided program material for THVN on a regular basis. For example, THVN news programs were supplemented with film purchased from American Broadcasting Company, as well as with free material from the British, French, Australian, Dutch, and American embassies, and from the regional stations in Can Tho and Hue. The Vietnamese motion-picture center supplied a 10-minute weekly film wrap-up. Government programs were produced by the Ministry of Rural Development, National Police Directorate, Ministry of Chieu Hoi, Ministry of Agriculture, Health Bureau of Saigon, Ministry of Defense, Vietnam Press, Ministry of Education and other agencies.

Buddhists, Catholics, and Protestants also provided a few programs monthly for THVN television, as did the Tuoi-Xanh Group — comprised of teachers, professional artists, military men and government officials — which produced children's shows.

Popular Cai Luong dramas telecast on Friday evenings, usually three or four hours in length, were performed by a professional drama group under contract to THVN. Reform theater programs and classic drama attracted the largest viewing audiences, and as on radio, political content was sandwiched within the long TV dramas. Private professional groups also contracted with THVN to produce talent, variety, and musical programs, and a limited amount of school programming was broadcast. The largest amount of THVN content — almost 25% of all programming — consisted of psychological warfare, embracing objectives contained in a 1969 pacification plan, e.g., programs for refugee resettlement and the Chieu Hoi program.

Except for an attempt to dismantle the Hue TV station by unsuccessful fleeing ARVN forces, the southern Vietnamese television system built by the United States seems to have survived the 1975 change of government. During the takeover of Saigon, the new government broadcast appeals for station workers to continue in their jobs. Naturally, TV content changed to include, in Hue for example, newsreels and "artistic performances by students" (FBIS 1975, IV, p. 85). In the summer of 1975, Saigon TV signed on about 5:30 P.M. and signed off about 8:45 P.M. Much of the content consisted of cultural offerings, short plays, and several films, especially a Ho Chi Minh biography repeated many times. When the Saigon TV stations were seized, the new regime telecast films of the 1954 fall of Dien Bien Phu, intercut with clips of U.S. planes dropping their bombs over the battle — accompanied with the narration: "this shows American support of the French colonials to hold the last foothold in North Vietnam." According to a UPI reporter, the inaccuracies didn't seem to bother the new Saigon propagandists, but the film with the false intercutting made their point.

As it had been used to emphasize every major propaganda program of the Thieu regime, Saigon television showcased the "victory" and May Day parades together with numerous repeats over a four-day period. The victory parade was telecast live and repeated via videotape a number of times. While there is not detailed information, it appears that by the summer of 1975, Saigon television, and probably the other TV stations built by the United States, were being operated by former THVN employees. Programming was very limited compared with the schedule before the fall/liberation of Saigon; the schedule was more like that of television in Hanoi.

3.1.5 External Broadcasting

South Vietnam's external service, Voice of Freedom (VOF), was aimed at North Vietnamese audiences. From Saigon headquarters, VOF broadcast 24 hours daily by the end of 1969. Operated by the ARVN Political Warfare Department with training assistance provided through 1972 by the Military Assistance Command Vietnam (MACV) personnel attached to JUSPAO, VOF received most of its financing from the United States.

By June 1967, VOF broadcast from a short-wave transmitter near Saigon and from both a short-wave and two medium-wave transmitters near Hue. Heavily guarded studios located near Saigon utilized about 122 employees.

A new external-service transmitter complex was constructed at the mouth of the Perfume River near Hue in late 1969. The power of VOF by 1969 had been increased to 200 kw. during the day and 100 kw. at night, in addition to short-wave service.

Psychological warfare policy guidance for VOF was provided from JUSPAO through United States command channels, although there was considerable variation in adhering to psywar policies, since the Vietnamese had never formally approved the basic policy guidelines in psychological warfare promulgated by the United States in 1966.

During its first year of operation, VOF operated both as an openly acknowledged and a clandestine station. Content included news, commentary, youth panels, talks, drama, and music of particular interest to North Vietnam. The North Vietnamese and NLF in 1967 jammed VOF services — particularly news and some features — but music shows were usually not tampered with, according to a report from a JUSPAO advisor.

Apparently South Vietnam also operated some stations that were either clandestine or South Vietnamese stations pretending to be Liberation Radio, the NLF service.

Following the 1964 Gulf of Tonkin incident, VOF and similar clandestine broadcasts were increased. For example, it was estimated that VOF broadcasts pretending to be those of North Vietnam averaged 8–10 hours weekly; regular VOF broadcasts amounted to about 60 hours weekly. Using techniques developed in World War II, the Americans and South Vietnamese broadcast very near Liberation Radio frequencies, conveying reports of resistance activities, opposition to the North Vietnamese regime, and battle losses.

As of summer 1975, the external and internal radio services of southern Vietnam appear to broadcast the same content as indicated below in the Radio Giai Phong (Liberation Radio) schedule for July 1975:

Fig. 3

0500	News		
0530	Music		
0600	News in the Cities	1600	Children's Program
0630	Children's Program	1630	Liberation Army Program
0700	Liberation Army Program	1700	News
0730	News	1730	Music or Drama
0800	Silent	1800	Agricultural Program
		1830	Music
1000	News	1900	News
1030	Music or Drama	1930	Women's Program
1130	Agricultural Program	2000	News in the Cities
1200	News	2030	Liberation Army Program
1230	Silent	2100	News
		2130	Drama
1400	Songs and Music for Children	2200	News
1500	Music or Drama	2230	Storytelling

Schedules and translations were obtained by Lichty from Agence France-Presse, Hong Kong, BCC, AP, Bangkok, and an unattributable U.S. government agency.

3.1.6   Giai Phong (Liberation Radio)

Broadcasting by the National Liberation Front (NLF), Radio Hanoi, and the then clandestine Liberation Radio included party doctrine, news commentaries, and entertainment. Broadcast channels were also used to disseminate news at dictation speed and operational instructions from Hanoi or the Central Office in

South Vietnam (COSVN) – also reported to be in Cambodia. These messages were redistributed by a network of couriers. Occasionally broadcasts ostensibly aimed at South Vietnamese publics were actually covers for transmission of party orders. Village and hamlet propagandists were instructed to listen to broadcasts and then disseminate the themes through interpersonal channels. An unidentified captured document stressed that propaganda and indoctrination tasks in towns should

[guide] the people to listen to our broadcasts to be aware of current events and the general policy lines of the Party. After that, the people will legally spread the news among the masses. Propaganda agents posted in public places such as: barber, tailor, bicycle repair, and coffee shops, etc. ... should [encourage] broadcast listeners to [act upon the] propaganda. [Conley 1966, pp. 308–9]

Broadcasting of operational messages and propaganda appeals of so-called spontaneous front organizations increased during the February 1968 Tet attacks. The effort to link mass-media channels to interpersonal ones probably had some success because of the Party's varying control over the social and political environment at the receiving end; at least the articulated attempts were very similar to techniques used in mainland China.

Liberation Radio began broadcasting in February 1962, identifying itself as "Liberation Radio, the Voice of the National Front for Liberation of South Vietnam." On 26 June 1969, the identification was changed to the Liberation Radio broadcasting station, "the Voice of the Provincial Revolutionary Government of the Republic of Vietnam."

Initially, Liberation Radio broadcast 90 minutes daily, about a third in Vietnamese, the remainder in English, French, Cambodian, and Chinese. By late 1964, programming was increased to about five hours daily with some material repeated. Although the station was frequently jammed by the Republic of Vietnam, a 1966 survey revealed that up to 60% of Liberation broadcasts were audible in Saigon.

By 1970, Liberation Radio broadcasts had increased to 107 hours weekly in Vietnamese, and at least three hours weekly in English, French, and Cambodian (see Table 11).

Table 11. Average Weekly Hours, Giai Phong (Liberation Radio)

Language	1965	1966	1967	1968	1969	1970
Vietnamese	56:00	52:30	40:00	75:30	106:45	107:00[a]
Cambodian	3:30	3:30	3:30	3:30	3:30	20:15
Cantonese	3:30	3:30				
Mandarin	3:30		3:30	3:30	3:30	3:30
English		1:00	:15	:45	::45	7:00
French					7:00	10:30[b]

Source: Unattributable U.S. government agency.
[a]Vietnamese to Europe = 10:30 of this total.
[b]French to Europe = 3:30 of this total.

Some broadcasts were aimed at minorities in the South Vietnam highlands. There was a considerable increase in weekly hours of Cambodian programming in 1970 linked to the United States — South Vietnamese invasion and North Vietnamese presence in the country. Also, during the late 1960s, Liberation Radio increased English and French programming, essentially aimed at United States forces in South Vietnam and European audiences overseas. Short-wave services — apparently broadcast from North Vietnam — were aimed at expatriates living in France to demonstrate the legitimacy of the revolutionary movement.

In June 1969, Liberation Radio, unlike VTVN, aimed more programs at specific audiences, including the ARVN, Viet Cong, Montagnards, students, women, urban listeners, and those in the countryside and in traditional Hue. Although it was unlawful to listen to Liberation Radio in areas controlled by the Republic of Vietnam, many South Vietnamese with missing relatives often listened to the station hoping for news of their families.

Giai Phong Radio (Liberation Radio) was often reported to originate in the jungle areas and rural countryside of South Vietnam, but the services probably always originated in North Vietnam and Hanoi in particular. Much of the content on Giai Phong was the same as that heard over Radio Hanoi, except Liberation Radio would not always attribute the source to the North Vietnamese. Content originated by Giai Phong was picked up and used by the North Vietnamese News Agency (VNA).

3.1.7 U.S. Forces Broadcasting

The United States Armed Forces in Vietnam Network began radio broadcasting in Saigon on 15 August 1962. At first, the Armed Forces Vietnam Network (AFVN) was on 18 hours daily; it went to around-the-clock programming in February 1965. By August 1970, radio services had been expanded to six combination AM and FM stations, two of the latter broadcasting in stereo. By that time, there were also eight VHF television stations and two low-power UHF translators. By 1973, they were all gone, although American diplomats were lobbying to have the radio section turned over to American and Vietnamese civilians (*Penang Star,* 23 March 1973).

Additional repeater transmitters were installed in Qui Nhon, Danang, Pleiku, and Cam Ranh Bay. Throughout much of the heaviest fighting in the northern-most region of Military Zone I, troops could barely receive radio signals until a repeater transmitter was installed there in the fall of 1968. A number of ships off North and South Vietnam also had their own radio and television stations, sometimes originating live programming.

Armed Forces television, after the initial airborne transmissions (described in §3.1.4), expanded by late 1966. Stations operating out of temporary vans covered the Qui Nhon and Danang areas, supplementing a permanent station in Saigon. The next year AFVN television stations were begun at Pleiku, Cam Ranh, Tuy Hoa, and Hue, the latter destroyed in the 1968 Tet offensive.

Additional stations were then built at Quang Tri and Danang. Television translator stations operated with low power in Can Tho in the Delta and Phan Rang.

AFVN radio programming was primarily news and music; about 40% of the music was standard and pop, about one-third was contemporary top-40, and another 10% was country and western. Many programs were prerecorded in the United States by well-known American disc jockeys. Twenty-four hourly newscasts were aired with material from United States news wires, the Armed Forces News Bureau, as well as newscasts from the four American radio networks, recorded in Washington, D.C., and relayed via short-wave to Saigon by AFVN. Most locally originated music was from discs specially prepared by AFRTS, often with controversial or antiwar music deleted.

About three hours daily, the stations in the outlying regions did their own programming to units in their areas. A 1968 survey indicated that 99% of all American soldiers in Vietnam owned or had access to a radio and more than 67% to FM sets. Top-40 music and pop standards were the most preferred shows. Some AFVN radio programs were reminiscent of the earlier days of the medium, e.g., "Gunsmoke," "Hawaii Calls," and "Escape."

By 1968 in Saigon and by 1969 at other locations where large numbers of U.S. troops were stationed, separate FM programming was available. FM programming emphasized background music. In season, a large number of sports events were carried by AFVN and were among the most popular programs (Bayliss 1969; Wentz 1969).

As mentioned above, some censorship took place. One source reported, "Every few days the station receives a disc similar to an oversized long-play record on which one or two songs have been carefully removed with what appears to be nail polish" (Weinrab 1967). Protest, drug, and sex songs, however, were "sliding through," according to one draftee announcer. By early 1970, public attention was drawn to the question of news censorship after several AFVN newscasters quit, were relieved, or were given other duties after complaining of censorship in September 1969. For example, Specialist 5 Robert Lawrence, in early 1970, ended his newscast with, "We have been suppressed and I'm probably in trouble for telling you tonight the truth. I hope you'll help stop censorship at AFVN."

Separate analyses indicated that the main conflict was between AFVN's attempt to report the news and the Military Assistance Command Vietnam (MACV) Office of Information's concern with public relations (see Moore 1971, p. 393; Moody 1970, p. 29).

AFVN radio also broadcast programming for the forces of other countries in the area, such as a daily program of Australian news. Several low-power radio stations also were operated by the Republic of Korea Army for its own troops.

Most AFVN television consisted of films and videotapes of regular United States programs, although some live fare was included, such as news, shows featuring entertainers visiting Vietnam, talk programs, and those produced by and for special units. The most popular program on AFVN television in 1966 was "Combat" (see *Los Angeles Times* 1966b; *TV Guide* 1967). In 1968, however, a survey indicated that the most popular types of programs were comedy, sports, drama, and westerns, in that order. That survey also indicated that about 20% of all American soldiers had their own television sets.

Frequent spot announcements provided information on the G.I. Bill and urged the forces to take malaria pills, practice fire safety, be aware of the dangers of veneral disease and marijuana, and promote good United States-Vietnamese relations.

Vietnamese and American television obviously were aimed at different audiences. As indicated in Table 12, the Vietnamese service offered more news and fine arts content; AFVN emphasized drama, variety, and sports. Nearly a quarter of the Vietnamese schedule was devoted to psychological warfare programs. The Vietnamese schedule aimed to help audiences remember war and the need for sacrifice. AFVN schedules tried to help the American soldier forget the war by providing entertainment.

Table 12. THVN and AFVN-TV Saigon Television Programming (in percentages)

Program Category	$THVN^a$	$AFVN\text{-}TV^b$
Variety	2	17
Music	11	5
Fine Arts	3	1
Drama	21	42
Quiz/Contest	1	1
Sports	–	11
Personalities	–	6
Children's	–	–
News	14	7
Public Events	8	5
Information/Education	5	4
Religion	–	1
Psychological Warfare	24	–
Other	2	–
Unaccounted	9	–
Totals	100	100

Source: Based on content analysis of August 1969 program schedules.
[a]THVN telecast from 7-11:30 P.M. five days per week; 6:30-11:30 P.M. on Saturday and Sunday.
[b]AFVN-TV (Saigon) telecast from 1:45 P.M.-12 A.M. seven days per week.

3.1.8 Other U.S. Broadcast Activities

In addition to providing technical and program help to Vietnamese broadcasting, JUSPAO also prepared material for the world-wide broadcasting facilities of Voice of America, which had stations serving Southeast Asia in the Philippines, South Vietnam, and Thailand. In the Philippines, 20 short-wave transmitters ranging in power from 35–250 kw. and a 1,000-kw. medium-wave transmitter provided coverage from Korea to Indonesia.

These services fed relay stations in Hue, which beamed Vietnamese programming to North Vietnam. A third relay station in Bangkok used 1,000 kw. on medium-wave to provide VOA coverage from Bangladesh to Western Indonesia. For the East Asia and Pacific areas, VOA programmed various schedules attuned to regional interests, including broadcasts in English, Burmese, Cambodian, Indonesian, Lao, Chinese, Korean, Russian, Thai, and Vietnamese.

Before 1970, VOA broadcast about seven and a half hours daily, or more than 50 hours weekly, in Vietnamese. With the advent of the 1970 Cambodian incursion, however, VOA broadcast up to 10 hours daily to both North and South Vietnam.

Daily news reports originated in Vietnam and were relayed to VOA headquarters in Washington, D.C.; other material for the Vietnam broadcast was drawn from Agence France-Presse, Reuters, Associated Press, and United Press International. VOA usually had one reporter stationed in South Vietnam for English broadcasts and several others who came in from Bangkok when necessary. VOA also worked very closely with JUSPAO in preparing Vietnamese programs for domestic stations. During the late 1960s, JUSPAO prepared about 15½ hours of programming daily, mostly in Vietnamese, and produced one 10-minute newsreel weekly, as well as special documentaries.

In addition, a huge psychological warfare program was carried out under JUSPAO that included MACV, U.S. Agency for International Development, USIA, and a number of South Vietnamese offices. Psychological warfare priorities initially emphasized the inevitability of South Vietnam's victory, Viet Cong "banditry" and weaknesses, and U.S. strength. At the time of Tet 1968, greater emphasis was given to promoting newly evolved political structures from village to national levels and to improving relationships among personnel in various government agencies. Two years later, the emphasis had shifted to themes of political and, to a lesser extent, economic development. Radio and television were used in propaganda, of course, but a very heavy emphasis was placed on leaflets, loudspeakers, touring theater and puppet companies, and other more traditional techniques (Hoffer 1972, ch. 4).

JUSPAO was phased out in June 1972, the major information program being taken over by USIS, whose Vietnam staff had been slashed from 700 to 33. All Armed Forces radio and television facilities were dismantled and removed from Vietnam as were the Korean stations.

What was the ARVN-FM station in Saigon after 1973, however, was operated by the Defense Attache Office (DAO) and was known as "American Radio Service Saigon" (ARSS). The station was automated and broadcast "background" music, mostly middle of the road, and news. Many news items were recorded from radio network newscasts in Washington and relayed to Saigon and rebroadcast. But, during the two weeks immediately before the U.S. evacuation in April 1975, these news reports were no longer carried because it was felt that many were too critical of the United States or too pessimistic. ARSS was to broadcast the signal for the evacuation of Saigon by playing "White Christmas" after another signal. Because it was automated, ARSS was apparently on the air, repeating the Bing Crosby song, for some hours even after the Americans left.

In late July 1975, the new Saigon government reopened this station, calling it the "Time Announcing and Music Station," broadcasting from Ho Chi Minh City. The FM service, apparently the only one in Vietnam, operated 18 hours daily, beginning at 6 A.M. with time checks every hour on the hour, news highlights, and Vietnamese and classical music (UPI, 31 July 1975).

From the mid-1960s through 1972, upgrading of the VTVN network and construction of the THVN television system resulted directly from United States advisory assistance and money administered through JUSPAO. Also USIA, one of three major agencies within JUSPAO' was responsible for considerable programming and technical assistance to the Vietnamese broadcasting system, carried out under an executive order of the United States president and the National Security Council. The statutory authority describing the parameters of USIA information activity did not extend to this kind of overt propaganda, executed in Vietnam over a five-year period. In effect, USIA had acted as a surrogate information ministry for the Republic of Vietnam, 1965–72.

3.1.9   Audiences

By 1970, at least one radio signal was potentially available to about 95% of the South Vietnamese population; a television signal to 75%, especially those living in major urban areas. Throughout South Vietnam, radio is the most widely used medium, except in Saigon where a slightly higher percentage supposedly view television. A 1970 study indicated that newspapers were the main source of news in Saigon, but radio and television were more important in other cities. Urban Vietnamese listened to radio an average of 4–15 hours weekly; a substantial number listened more frequently. Most radio listening is within the home, and peak listening times are the noon rest period, early morning, and evening. VTVN Channel A has been the most popular station; only in Hue has local programming been ranked as more popular than VTVN Channel A. BBC listenership has been considerable, but that of VOA comparatively low. Based on a 1967 study, about 65% of rural listeners owned radios, more than those who owned bicycles or any household appliances (see Simulmatics Corporation 1967; JUSPAO 1970). Nearly 64% of the respondents said they listened to radio daily, considering it not so much a recreational activity as a serious information or educational function. In rural areas, respondents preferred news programs to drama and music (see Table 13).

Although a television signal was available to 75% of the South Vietnamese population in 1970, only about 40% of survey respondents apparently had a television set in their homes. In Saigon and major urban centers with television stations, nearly half of the respondents said they viewed television "almost everyday," while in smaller provincial cities, a third said they viewed it that

Table 13. Media Use in South Vietnam Urban Areas, 1970 (Figures show percentage of respondents replying yes to question: "During the last year have you done any of the following in your leisure time?")

Media	Saigon (N = 519)	Other TV Cities[a] (N = 714)	Provincial Cities[b] (N = 956)
Radio	75	81	86
Television	77	75	59
Newspapers	66	53	54
Movies	32	40	30
Magazines	24	32	27
Books	23	27	19
None	8	9	7

Source: JUSPAO 1970.
[a] Hue, Danang, Qui Nhon, and Can Tho.
[b] Quang Tri, Dalat, Phan Thiet, Phu Cuong, Vung Tau, Chau Doc, Truc Giang, and My Tho.

often. Much TV viewing was done in groups, particularly in provincial cities which did not have local transmitters. Most Saigon TV viewers watched at home, but about half of those in smaller cities watched in a friend's home or public place. Rural area television was seen by very few South Vietnamese, although shortly after its introduction the medium attracted large community audiences in some of these regions.

Advisors and reporters were often given to puffery in describing Vietnamese audiences attracted to the new medium. Some villages, however, did own receivers kept outdoors on raised platforms for optimum viewing. The Ministry of Information estimated in 1970 more than 2,300 community-owned sets in South Vietnam, but some were unused and others had been taken by village officials to their own homes. Less than 2% of the villagers had home TV sets. Accurate figures are unavailable, but 1971 estimates put the number of television sets in South Vietnam between 300,000–500,000.

By far the most popular THVN program had been the renovated opera, Cai Luong. On Friday nights, South Vietnamese usually clustered around the nearest TV set to watch these shows of "over-blown characters," attired in sequined robes and chandelier-like headdresses, appealing to the Vietnamese love of pageantry. One such program was described as follows:

"Lasting Sorrow," about a Chinese king who courts a fairy princess, takes place on the "Mountains of the Moon." [To create a lunar landscape in the tiny TV studio, two stage hands pumped dry ice machines to send smoke swirling on stage, while another trickled paper snow from overhead beams.] In the final act, the King kills the woman he loves because she has betrayed him. The Vietnamese, traditionally sentimental, delight in such melodrama. [Steinle 1970; Emerson 1970; USIA 1970b; Variety 1966]

Another was portrayed in this fashion:

... a beautiful blind girl, raised by a devoted foster father whose enemy, the wicked district chief, wants to kill her. She flees and meets a teacher of swordsmanship who trains her to defend herself. She is wounded by the district chief, but rescued by her teacher — who, it turns out, is the district chief's long-lost son; she marries the son, and the district chief promises to mend his wicked ways. [White 1971, p. 329]

Apparently only a very small "eavesdropping" Vietnamese audience existed for AFVN radio, about 5% in Saigon, even less in other cities. In 1970, however, nearly half of Saigon television viewers watched AFVN television. According to one source, the United States channel "is by far the most popular among the Vietnamese, who, even if they don't understand the dialogue, enjoy action of such shows as *Mission: Impossible; Wild, Wild West;* and *Batman* (Shaplen 1971). United States programs attracted younger Vietnamese, especially those who had been trained by or worked for Americans. The American TV programs were popular enough to lead to the publication of a number of comic books in Vietnamese, such as *Wild, Wild West; Mission: Impossible;* and *Star Trek.* Evidence was not available to determine the amount of radio listening and television viewing by Viet Cong or the North Vietnamese Army. Apparently these audiences gave some attention to BBC shows and South Vietnamese stations. Captured documents, interrogation of POWs, and evidence from defectors indicated there were repeated warnings from Hanoi and Viet Cong leaders not to listen to South Vietnamese stations (Hoffer 1974, pp. 63–80). Such warnings led some to believe there was considerable listening, which increased after Tet and the beginnings of the Paris peace talks. A limited amount of evidence showed that although most NLF listeners did not place much credence in the South Vietnamese broadcasts, nevertheless they were motivated to listen for news of their families (JUSPAO 1970).

3.1.10 Freedom of Expression

Since 1954, various South Vietnamese constitutions have guaranteed freedom of expression but to no avail. Press freedom promised by the 1956 constitution was certainly not achieved. The Vietnamese constitution of 1967 contained similar lofty promises, but a 1969 press law limited the kinds of stories that might appear and imposed fees on publishers. In the last months of the Nguyen Van Thieu regime, the few newspapers that continued to publish despite heavy censorship abided by the government line (Sutherland 1975, p. 1). The same phenomenon appears to be repeating itself with the new government in 1975. Movie houses that once ran U.S. and French films, in 1975 projected the "Life of Ho Chi Minh" and other propaganda films. Bars and nightclubs, an American legacy, were closed. Campaigns against what was called a depraved culture were led by students, exhorting the public to eradicate American music, books, and comics (Fenton 1975a; Esper 1975). The new government sought persons formerly employed by the Thieu regime, "reeducated" many, and campaigned against lawlessness, punctuating its stern policy with summary executions of suspected thieves "tried" by so-called "People's Courts." Initially, news channels to the outside were cut. The number of Western correspondents reporting on the new government became severely limited. Reporter James Fenton, upon departing Saigon in August 1975, concluded: "There is something underhand about the methods of the authorities. Something sordid. And it all begins with their inability to tell the truth" (Fenton 1975b).

While it is clear that radio listening and especially television viewing have increased greatly in Vietnam, it is extremely difficult to assess the impact of these media. Broadcasting was harnessed to trumpet government programs and policies. But, according to 1966 and 1967 surveys, few respondents could recall very much about the substance of the programs, such as the 1967 constitution — an event which was the subject of considerable propaganda. There was some evidence that villagers who owned radios and listened regularly were more likely to desire other modern appliances and tools contrasted to villagers who did not own radios. Potentially, the Vietnamese radio and television media served to help them remember the war and the sacrifices required; for the American G.I., his media potentially served to help him forget the war.

Despite the availability of American radio and television services for a substantial period and American aid and influence in producing South Vietnamese programming, broadcasting per se did not have much direct influence on Vietnamese cultures. While the notion persisted that world-wide United States "electronic imperialism" has had some devastating effects on local cultures, the evidence is far from clear cut. In the case of South Vietnam, cultural variations and change had begun long before American radio and television operations were introduced there.

3.2   North Vietnam, Khmer, and Laos, *by Lawrence W. Lichty and Thomas W. Hoffer*

The Democratic Republic of North Vietnam (DRVN) was proclaimed 2 September 1945, by the charismatic leader Ho Chi Minh. After nearly eight years of fighting against the French, the DRVN was allowed, under the Geneva cease-fire of 1954, to receive the land north of the 17th parallel. By the spring of 1975, DRVN had conquered all of Vietnam.

The population of North Vietnam in 1974 was slightly larger than that of the South — 23.8 million; major cities included Hanoi, Haiphong, Nam Dinh, Nam Hoa, Thai Nguyen, and Vinh Phu. DRVN was divided into 23 provinces plus the two municipalities of Hanoi and Haiphong, two autonomous zones (Tay Bac and Viet Bac) and one special zone (Vinh Linh). About 85% of the population is ethnic Vietnamese concentrated in the delta of the Red (Hong) River. This rich rice-growing territory is also the industrial heart of the nation.

Hanoi in recent years has renewed its efforts to integrate different ethnic minorities living in inaccessible mountainous zones into the political and economic mainstream. In 1974, the government promoted a "new way of life" campaign for these people, hoping to teach them new ways of agriculture, to persuade them to give up their nomadic lifestyles, but at the same time trying to preserve "their fine traditions."

Since 1970 officially known as the Khmer Republic, this country of 7.3 million people is still most frequently called Cambodia. At its height between the eighth and fifteenth centuries, the Khmer Empire conquered much of Southeast Asia, including Thailand and Vietnam, and had a population of nearly ten million, nearly twice the size of England at the time. In 1864, it too became a part of the French Indochina empire. Independence was declared in March 1945, but after World War II the French returned. After a campaign for total independence, waged by King Norodom Sihanouk, Cambodia became self-governing in 1953. For nearly a decade and a half, Cambodia seemed to avoid the war that flared in Vietnam and Laos. Prince Norodom Sihanouk, who stepped down as king in 1955 when he was 33 years old to become chief of state, seemed able to hold his nation together as a neutral and tranquil relic of the past. An election was held in 1966 in which for the first time Sihanouk did not personally select all the National Assembly candidates. At the same time, General Lon Nol became prime minister. Beginning in 1967, attacks by "bandit elements," known as Khmer Serei, and others, apparently related to the Viet Minh and North Vietnamese, increasingly plagued government forces and took over more territory.

On 18 March 1970, Lon Nol and other pro-Western generals and politicians overthrew Sihanouk, and he fled to China. On 30 April 1970, South Vietnam and United States troops invaded Cambodia, apparently searching for secret headquarters of the North Vietnamese and Viet Cong. After five years of bitter fighting, the Khmer Rouge successfully conquered the Khmer Republic in the spring of 1975.

About 80% of the Khmer population is made up of Khmers; Chinese and Vietnamese each represent 7% of the population. The Khmers are usually farmers living in small lowland villages, while the Chinese are often merchants and businessmen concentrated in the main urban areas of Phnom Penh (the capital), Battambang, Kompong Cham, or Kampot. Reports in mid-1975 indicated that cities were being emptied of people who were encouraged to work in rural and jungle areas for the development of the country. The income per capita in 1971–72 in Khmer Republic was a dismally low $90.

Laos was first unified in 1353 under the powerful kingdom of Lan Xang (Kingdom of the Million Elephants). After a brief period of glory, however, the kingdom fell prey to the Thai and Vietnamese and was not much more than a Thai vassal state when the French established a protectorate in the 1890s. Full independence was received in 1953. By 1957, the Pathet Lao (pro-Communist) forces were bidding for power, and by the early 1960s, these troops were receiving aid from the U.S.S.R. and North Vietnam. The United States Central Intelligence Agency (CIA) in the meantime was helping the opposing Royal Laotian Army.

Another Geneva conference was held in late 1961 in an attempt to end the Laotian crisis. The following June, an agreement was announced and a coalition government created. Since 1962, Laos was roughly divided in half on a north-south line along the mountains: the eastern half controlled by Pathet Lao, the western by Prince Souvanna Phouma's forces. What government existed can be described as a constitutional monarchy with a coalition. In early 1971, South Vietnamese troops invaded Laos to add to the turmoil. On 21 February 1973, a cease-fire was signed, ending the war in Laos for the third time in two decades, and the way was paved for the third coalition government, set up 5 April 1974.

Half again larger than the Khmer Republic or either North or South Vietnam, the rugged mountainous terrain of Laos is inhabited by only 3.26 million people. About half the population is made up of the politically and socially dominant Lao (Laotian Thai), who live chiefly in the southern and western portions in the Mekong River Valley. The mountain Mon-Khmer, Meo, Muong, Khmu, Red Thai, and other tribes dominate the northern part of Laos. Major cities are Vientiane (capital), with 176,000 population, Luang Prabang (44,200), and Savannakhet (50,690).

3.2.1 North Vietnam

Face-to-face indoctrination and radio are apparently the most important channels of communications in the Democratic Republic of Vietnam, commonly known as North Vietnam. The role of the press, and particularly motion pictures, however, is said to be increasing. All media are controlled by the Lao Dong (Worker's Party).

News for the Vietnam radio network, as well as all printed media, is supplied by the Vietnam News Agency (Vietnam Thong Tin Xa or VNA). VNA transmits material in French, English, and Vietnamese via radio teletype to Southeast Asia and Europe. It also has a Morse code service in English to the same areas; Morse code is supposedly used to transmit domestic news within the country as well.

Origins of Broadcasting. On 7 September 1945, just five days after Ho Chi Minh, leader of the Viet Minh, established the Democratic Republic of Vietnam, Voice of Vietnam went on the air in Hanoi with the use of old French equipment. With the outbreak of conflicts after 1946, the station was moved from Hanoi, apparently broadcasting from various places in Viet Bac — the northwest provinces. During that period, four other stations were operated by the Viet Minh in Central and South Vietnam.

After the Geneva Accord in 1954, all stations were merged into one, operating out of Hanoi as Voice of Vietnam. By the early 1960s, Voice of Vietnam broadcast from about nine transmitters on both medium- and short-wave.

Today Radio Hanoi, operated as a government agency under the Broadcasting

Department, maintains two networks of both short- and medium-wave stations. Domestic service, broadcast in Vietnamese only, operates about 12 hours daily.

Programming has been designed primarily for peasants, children, and farmers; in particular, extensive efforts have been made to introduce more modern agricultural techniques and collective farming developments. Directed mainly at the people of North Vietnam, some Radio Hanoi domestic programming up to 1975 was also intended for the South Vietnamese, this in addition to regular international short-wave programs beamed to the South. News, including bulletins read at dictation speed, music, and propaganda are the main fare of Radio Hanoi. Home service has been using three short-wave and one medium-wave outlet and a secondary program (for repeating purposes) from the other transmitters.

The second network providing international broadcasting by 1972 used a maximum of one medium-wave and 11 short-wave transmitters. The network directs about 300 hours weekly of broadcasts to Asia and Europe, primarily in Vietnamese, Cambodian, English, and French, and another 150 hours per week specifically to listeners in South Vietnam. The latter programming often includes relays of programs from Radio Hanoi's domestic service.

In 1963 it was estimated that there were about 130,000 radio receivers; although accurate figures do not exist, the estimate was 550,000 by 1975. Agence France Presse reported that Hanoi "exploded with joy" at the announcement of the collapse of the Saigon government on 30 April 1975 and that people listened on "transistors all over the city."

Wired distribution systems exist in major cities and towns of the most populated provinces. One estimate in *Nanh Dan,* official newspaper of the Lao Dong Party, reported 125 such systems with 100,000 loudspeakers, serving an audience of over three million in 1964, or about 20% of the population. Additionally, there were said to be nearly 100 wired systems in the eight highland provinces, another 65 in the Red River Delta, plus more than 600 private relay broadcasting systems in collective farms, factories, schools, and hospitals. Another 13 villages in the provinces immediately north and south of Hanoi — Vinh Phuc and Hadong — were reported to have their own relay systems. This "megaphone system in all major towns" was established with the help of other Socialist countries. The wired system has been considered the most important method of domestic communications, because it can be operated in areas without electricity, is inexpensive to install, and the receiving loudspeaker is much less expensive than radio sets.

Two additional stations have been set up for the "nationalities," one in Viet Bac broadcasting about four hours daily, the other in Tay Bac, which in the late 1960s was on the air about three hours daily (Smith et al, 1967, pp. 229–30). The Viet Bac station, "The Voice of the Nationalities," broadcast in the mid-1960s on a 24-hour basis, primarily in the dialects of North Vietnamese minorities, including Thai and Nung.

In December 1972 Voice of Vietnam was off the air for a short time after being hit by "eight large American bombs" (*Wisconsin State Journal* 1973).

Table 14. Average Weekly Hours of Voice of Vietnam: North Vietnam International Service, 1965-72.

Language of Service	Nov.[a] 1965	Nov.[a] 1966	Sept.[a] 1967	Dec.[b] 1968	Dec.[b] 1969	Oct.[b] 1970	Sept.[c] 1972
Vietnamese	48:15	48:15	48:15	71:30	95:30	71:45	60:00
Cambodia	8:30	7:00	7:00	14:00	14:00	28:00	21:00
Cantonese	7:00	7:00	7:00	7:00	14:00	14:00	14:00
Mandarin	7:00	7:00	7:00	7:00	10:30	10:30	10:30
English	14:00	14:00	14:00	27:00	31:00	35:00[e]	31:30
French	–	8:45	8:45	8:45	17:30	17:30[f]	17:30
Lao	10:30	14:00	14:00	17:30	21:00	21:00	21:00
Thai	7:00	7:00	7:00	14:00	17:30	17:30	17:30
Indonesian	–	7:00	7:00	7:00	10:30	14:00	14:00
Japanese	10:30	10:30	10:30	14:00	14:00	10:30	14:00
Korean	10:00	14:00	14:00	14:00	28:00	28:00	7:00
to Montagnards				33:15	33:15	33:15	31:30
Other[d]				21:00			
Vietnamese & English to South and/or North Vietnam						16:30	
Music	1:45					5:30	

Source: Unattributable U.S. government agency.
[a] Did not include Hanoi broadcasts to South Vietnam.
[b] Included broadcast to South Vietnam.
[c] We do not have specific figures for 1975, but monitors' schedules show little change from 1972.
[d] Other includes Hanoi broadcasts in several languages direct to Europe after peace talks began.
[e] Included 3:30 hours to Europe, Africa, and Middle East.
[f] Included 14:00 hours to Europe, Africa, and Middle East.

Strict censorship of broadcast materials is enforced in North Vietnam. For example, in 1969, Phan Than Hoan and seven of his associates were arrested and sentenced to 15 years for playing "depraved reactionary" music, described as a mixture of French influence, Vietnamese love ballads of the colonial days, and the music of Saigon and American radio stations (Harvey 1971).

"Hanoi Hannah." Although the name "Hanoi Hannah," given to several women announcers on Radio Hanoi, may call up memories of "Tokyo Rose" and "Axis Sally," the similarity ends there. At the beginning of intensive American involvement in the war in the mid-1960s, about a half-hour of daily programming was designed for "American servicemen involved in the Indochina war." In 1970, there were three half-hour segments, one each in the morning, afternoon, and

near midnight. Several women read these broadcasts, including Thu Hueng ("Autumn Scent" or "Autumn Fragrance"), Chi Mai ("Sister Love"), and "Perfumed Orchid," who, according to correspondent Wilfred Burchett, was Cambridge-educated.

The broadcasts began:

This is the Voice of Vietnam, this is the Voice of Vietnam, broadcasting from Hanoi. . . . the following broadcast is for American servicemen involved in the Vietnam war. . . . Americans why, and for whom, are you dying 10,000 miles from your youth?

The format of the program usually included this or a similar welcome, some international news particularly relating to the war, American popular music, and sometimes a commentator — usually a male — discussing politics. Occasionally tapes from anti-war groups in the United States were played, as were United States folk songs, especially protest and union songs of the 1930s. "Hanoi Hannah" often asked "How many of your buddies were killed today?"; said "Greetings, dirty imperialists"; and listed the most recent American soldiers killed in Vietnam or those that were said to have deserted or had refused to fight (Lieber 1966; *Los Angeles Times* 1967).

At least one American, Ronald B. Ramsey, broadcast regularly for Radio Hanoi. His programs, however, prepared in the United States, shipped through a Quebec post office, and broadcast from Hanoi beginning in January 1966, lasted for only a couple of months. Ramsey claimed he represented "a group of working guys and students who were seriously concerned about Vietnam" (*Broadcasting* 1966b, 1966c, 1966e; *Newsweek* 1966; *Wisconsin State Journal* 1966).

Frequently, speakers identifying themselves as Americans but seldom giving their names, said over Radio Hanoi that they opposed the war. The voices sometimes appeared to be those of individuals with a British accent affecting a southern United States drawl.

During the summer of 1975, it was announced that the home network had begun broadcasts of language lessons in English, Russian, and French ("Sweden Calling Dxers," 12 August 1975, monitored in Stockholm by Lichty; and *Washington Post,* 3 July 1975). A Radio Hanoi schedule in the summer of 1975 (Associated Press monitor, Bangkok; AFP, Hong Kong) follows:

List 2

0355	National Anthem
0400	Socialism in North Vietnam
0430	Music Followed by News
0515	Music for Exercises
0525	Weather
0530	Agricultural Program
0545	Music Followed by News
0630	People's Army Program
0700	Culture and "Way of Living"

0700	Culture and "Way of Living"
0715	"Introducing Socialist Countries." History, geography, and stories about foreign countries that are "socialist."
0730	Music (on Sunday from request letters)
0800	News
0815	Music for Children
0830	Music Around The World (classical) Followed by News
0915	Program for children in kindergarten school
0930	Music Followed by News
1030	Drama
1100	News
1130	Folk Songs
1200	Agriculture Program
1215	Science Program
1230	News
1245	Music
1300	"How To Sing" (music education)
1330	Silent
1500	News
1515	Children in Kindergarten Program
1530	Music Followed by News
1615	Culture
1630	Folk Songs of North Central and South Vietnam
1700	Press Review (from local regional newspapers)
1715	"For the Sake and Security of the Country." (Stories of sacrifice of the people "for peace and order.")
1730	Music for the Soldiers
1800	News
1830	Children's Program
1845	Agriculture
1900	Socialism in North Vietnam (repeat) 1930=2230 Saturday Live Drama
1930	Music Followed by News from Theater in
2015	Women Hanoi
2030	Music
2045	Youth Program
2100	Program for the People's Army
2130	News
2200	Drama
2230	Modern Songs
2300	News
2315	Story Telling

Television. East Germany and other socialist countries apparently helped build a television system in Hanoi but little is known of the details. American Folk Singer Pete Seeger said he did a 15-minute TV show in Hanoi in March 1972. In her film "Introduction to the Enemy" Jane Fonda is seen observing a TV production — a classical play and dance — in Hanoi. In the 1974 film "The Year of the Tiger" the studio is shown. According to the film, the station broadcasts two nights a week to about 1,000 sets in public places. There were live and film programs and one evening schedule included a 30-minute program called "Science Serves the People," a demonstration on health and baby care, an algebra lecture, and a children's puppet show.

Beginning in May 1975, some films – and probably TV programs – originating in Hanoi were broadcast from Saigon. There was interconnection of radio lines – some programming from Giai Phong produced in Hanoi was broadcast from Saigon – and on May 8, North Vietnam newspapers were distributed in Saigon and the surrounding area formerly held by the Republic of Vietnam.

3.2.2 Khmer Republic

In 1975 Khmer Republic seemed to cut itself off from the rest of the world, even the rest of Asia. With the takeover of the government by the FUNC (Front Union National du Cambodia, or variously, Cambodia People's National Liberation Armed Forces, or Royal Government of National Union of Cambodia), some Cambodians fled to Thailand. Prince Sihanouk who returned to Phnom Penh for the first time since 1970 announced that more than 100,000 Vietnamese who settled in Cambodia had returned to the North, and only 10 North Vietnamese remained at the DRVN embassy "including the cook." Apparently many city residents were forced into the countryside to work in the fields. But, according to Sihanouk, by fall many had returned, and industrial work and public services were restored. At this writing, credible firsthand accounts cannot confirm any of this.

It is likely that radio is, as it was, the most widely used communication medium. In 1974, there were only about nine newspapers in the entire country; none exceeded 8,000 circulation. Total movie seating capacity was estimated at about 25,000. But the number of radio receivers was put at about 100,000, a substantial increase from 1957 estimates of 20,000. (We have seen estimates of 400,000 and of one million radios, but do not believe them.) Most tribal villages are said to have at least one receiver.

During Prince Norodom Sihanouk's term of office, radio was used extensively to cover the chief of state's frequent trips and speeches. His speeches sometimes took up as much as one-third of the daily broadcast time.

Radio and television were controlled by the Ministry of Information, as were nearly all of the newspapers. Radio Diffusion Nationale, Khmere (RNK), the national system, operated from the capital, Phnom Penh, about 13 or 14 hours daily. Most domestic programming was news, "commercial announcements and music," entertainment, political commentary, and obituaries. Government limited advertising to about 3% of broadcast time and supplied news through Agence Khmere de Presse (AKP), operated under the information ministry. Newscasts were aired in the early morning, at noon, and twice at night. There were also 10-minute programs of "civic education" and instruction in the English and Russian languages.

Relay stations operated in major population centers outside Phnom Penh, especially in provincial capitals. The two medium-wave and two short-wave transmitters in Phnom Penh apparently used 50,000 w., but in 1972, with the nation at war, the location and power of all relay stations was not revealed. All transmitters and other radio equipment were given to the Khmer Republic by the People's Republic of China.

International broadcasting was carried out for about six hours daily on one medium-wave and one short-wave length. Languages of broadcasts were French, English, Lao, Vietnamese, Thai, and three Chinese dialects. Music and news in French and English were the dominant fare; broadcasts in other languages were limited to just a few minutes daily.

Construction of a television station (TVRK) was begun in 1961 and apparently completed in 1965. The standards were American, 525 lines, on Channel 8. The station began programming 2 February 1966, using 40 kw. and was said to reach about 60 miles from Phnom Penh. Programming in 1974 was three days weekly — Monday, Tuesday, and Saturday, for a total of eight hours. Programs have included a "television journal," musical variety, drama, an international magazine, and local "actualités." At the beginning of transmission, there were an estimated 300 receivers, but by 1971 it was said there were nearly 7,000 (So Woon 1971a; Kamm 1970, p. 28; *Television Factbook* 1971–72, p. 1050b; Munson 1968). Estimates for 1974 were of 25,000–30,000 sets.

While 1951 and 1957 laws presumably assure press freedom, considerable suppression existed. In 1971, publication or broadcasting of an item from an unapproved source could mean government reaction ranging from a "polite warning" to imprisonment and fines.

"Clandestine" Stations. The Khmer Rouge station VNUFC ("Voice of NUFC of Phnom Penh" or Vithayu Phsay Samleng Ronnacse Ruab Cheat Kampuchea) probably always broadcast from Hanoi (at least until late April 1975). Several other stations claiming to be located in the Khmer Republic were also broadcasting from Hanoi according to United States monitors. One Khmer-language, pro-Communist station, however, was possibly located in northeastern Khmer.

The CIA distributed hundreds of transistor radios in the Khmer countryside in 1970. Apparently these were to listen to a black clandestine station operated briefly by the CIA (possibly with USIA help). The station was at a location reported to be "PS-18," the CIA camp at Knorn Sin, northwest of the southern Laotian city of Pakse. This station carried broadcasts impersonating Prince Sihanouk. At first the imitations were done by a woman, then his high pitched voice was simulated by using various electronic devices. Reports also indicated other stations operating from this base claimed to speak for the NLF in South Vietnam, Laos, and Thailand but were pro-U.S. (*Washington Post,* 5 August 1971; *Milwaukee Journal* 1971).

Radio and TV after April 1975. Before the fall of Lon Nol, the government had no regular news service, but only produced handouts. There was a "clandestine" service — Agency for Khmer Information — but it was believed that this actually originated in Hanoi. AKI was suspended on 6 May 1975.

On 13 April 1975, the Phnom Penh Domestic Service (referred to as Home Service in the BBC monitoring reports) stated that "even though the U.S. has temporarily withdrawn it continues to give aid to our Khmer Republic as usual." Two days later, it reported that three rockets had hit the west side of the TV station. On 17 April, the Phnom Penh Radio came on as usual at 5 A.M.; following the opening announcement, it went off the air, and returned at 7:20 A.M. for about 20 minutes. Then at 1:30 P.M., another announcer identified himself as the voice of the nationalist movement. That evening, the station was identified as representing the "National Liberation Front, including the comrades from the North and East region."

Beginning in May 1975, the Phnom Penh station seemed to establish a regular schedule of about six hours a day — one hour each in the early morning and at noon, and from 6–10 P.M. Sometimes there is only one hour of original programming — news, announcements, and folk music — with the other hours just repeats (apparently on audio tape). But there were some special programs, such as an eight-part "documentary" recalling the "final drives" to Phnom Penh, broadcast in May. Through the summer and fall of 1975, these brief broadcasts — such as those that announced Sihanouk's return in September — provided almost the only news the world heard from Cambodia.

3.2.3 Laos

For years, the primary communications system of Laos depended on bonzes moving from pagoda to pagoda and traders, boatsmen, and ballad singers following a circuit of popular festivals. In the 1960s and half of the 1970s, even this was limited because of hostilities between the government and the Pathet Lao. In the summer of 1975, the Pathet Lao completely took over the government and the operation of broadcasting.

Only 6–10 newspapers existed in Laos, usually mimeographed sheets containing 4–8 pages (see Lent 1974c). Motion pictures have become popular, but in the mid-1960s there were only about a dozen theaters in the nation.

Under the French, especially while they were fighting the Viet Minh, more formal media were placed under strict censorship by the Ministry of Information. While official censorship was not exercised, "self-restraint" which came with many years of war was apparently fairly tight. Further, major private newspapers were owned by Laotian military officers and strongly anti-Communist aristocrats. Neither newspapers nor films can be regarded as principal means of communications in Laos, where the media remain among the most underdeveloped of all Asia. In Vientiane, however, Hong Kong Chinese movies do play regularly and during the summer of 1975 "Judge Roy Bean" was among the few American films shown in the country. Recently, U.S.S.R. newspapers and news from TASS are more widely used than American publications or wire services.

Broadcasting. The first radio station in Laos was established in 1950, broadcasting on short-wave with 1 kw. of power from a transmitter donated by the French. Not until April 1952, when the station was opened officially by Prince Souvanna Phouma, was broadcasting done on a regular basis.

External broadcasting is nonexistent, but at least one regular domestic program was entitled "For Lao People in Enemy Hands." Also, a major activity of the Ministry of Information, Propaganda, and Tourism appeared to be rebutting Radio Hanoi and Radio Peking.

While Lao National Radio (LNR) is the only official broadcasting system in the country, several unofficial stations are operated by the army, some with the backing of Thai businessmen (So Woon 1971b; UNESCO 1967b).

In addition, at least three propaganda or "psywar" stations — each using 20-kw. medium-wave transmitters — were operated by the Force Armée Royale (Lao Army) at Vientiane, Savannakhet, and Pakse. Another station was run by the CIA-supported army of General Vangpao at Long Cheng. It used two 5-kw. transmitters on both medium- and short-wave and broadcast in Lao, Vietnamese, Meo, Thai-Dam, and Yao. By 1972, a 20-kw. medium-wave station, sponsored by the Association of Lao Police, was planned at Thadeua, just across the border from Nong Khai, Thailand.

As in other parts of Indochina, the United States became heavily involved in Laotian broadcasting, donating a second transmitter in 1954. The two transmitters then in operation were under Lao National Radio. The United States loaned Laos a 5-kw. medium-wave transmitter in 1957 and donated two additional 10-kw. short-wave transmitters in 1960. The British government gave additional transmitters in 1964 which were subsequently destroyed in the *coup d'état* of February 1965. A 50-kw. transmitter was donated by USAID after the coup and additional transmitters were given by Australia in 1965.

In 1966 the Lao National Radio station was on from about 6:30 A.M. until 2 P.M. and from 5 P.M. until about 11 P.M. Programs included music, fare for the army, classical and modern songs, farm programs, and shows in Vietnamese and French; about 10% of the program hours were educational.

By 1968, Radio Laos was operating with a new 25-kw. German short-wave transmitter from Vientiane and three medium-wave transmitters — in Vientiane (10-kw.), Luang Prabang (2.5-kw.) and Pakse (10-kw.). All programs originated in Vientiane, and the same programs were carried on both short- and medium-wave stations simultaneously. In 1972, the four stations mentioned above plus an additional station in Luang Prabang were reportedly broadcasting, while still another station was under construction at Savannakhet.

LNR stations broadcast about 12 hours daily, generally from 6–9:30 A.M., and noon until 9:30 P.M., with added program hours on Saturday and Sunday. Programs are primarily in Lao, but some, mostly prepared by the French Embassy, are in French. The schedule includes traditional and modern Lao music, political talks, broadcasts from the National Assembly, news in French (obtained from Lao Press, the national news agency which in turn receives its international news from Agence France Presse), children's stories, special programs for housewives, and several hours of in-school programming and adult education. A large amount of the fare was prepared by other government agencies, such as the Ministry of Health or Red Cross.

List 3: Schedules of Four Laos Stations

Hour	Radio Pathet Lao	Laos Second System	Lao Kingdom/ Luang Prabang	Sieng Santisouk Slash Voice of Peaceful Laos
0530	Music			
0600	News	Khamu dialect	Local News	Pathet Lao
0630	Liberation Army	Lao Soung dialect	Lao songs	Local News
0700	Neutralist Forces	La-Ve dialect	Announcements for Chieng Kwang dist.	Relay Vientiane
0730	National Construction	Popular Music, French language	Relay Vientiane	Magazine article
0800	Call of the Country	Silent	Conciliation of Compatriots	Relay Pathet Lao
0830	Dictation-speed news		Lao Soung	Music
0900			Silent	Silent
0930	Silent			
1100	(Repeat of 630)			
1130	News			
1200	Drama/Music		Relay Pathet Lao	
1230	National Construction		News	
			Relay Vientiane	Local news
1300	Silent			Relay Vientiane
1330			Announcements for Chieng Kwang dist.	Magazine
1400				article
1600	Dictation-speed news		Silent	Music
1630				Silent
1700	National Construction			
1730	Entertainment			
1800	News		Lao Soung	
1830	Neutralist Forces		Ann. Chieng	
1900	National Construction	Vietnamese	Kwang	
			Relay Pathet Lao	Relay Pathet Lao
1930	Call of the Country	Cambodian Khamu	News	Local news
		Popular Music	Relay Vientiane	Relay Vientiane
2000	Literature	French		
2030		La-Ve dialect	National Revival Buddhist program	News analysis
2100	(Repeat 630)	Lao Soung	Stories	Local News
2130	News	French	Lao Soung	Music
2200	Silent	Cambodian Vietnamese Silent	Silent	Silent

In 1975 stations were often carrying programs both from the Pathet Lao and from the government — at least until August 1975. By autumn 1975, the similarity of broadcasting schedules for stations in Laos, Hanoi, and Saigon was obvious.

In 1966, more than 70,000 radio sets were reported in Laos with the number "rapidly increasing." An estimate in 1971, however, was only 50,000. One 1974 estimate was 100,000. Most sets are capable of receiving short-wave, an important factor since both North Vietnam and China broadcast to Laos several times each day. Radio Hanoi and Radio Peking reception is as clear throughout Laos as Lao National and Pathet Lao reception. Broadcasts from Saigon were widely listened to by the 30,000 or so Vietnamese in Vientiane (at least until June 1975). Some Thailand broadcasts can also be heard.

There are no television stations in Laos. But in 1966 there were said to be about 40 TV receivers capable of receiving the Thai station at nearby Nong Khai. One source reported in 1972 that "many people" did watch, and a 1975 estimate put the number of television receivers at 3,000.

One correspondent told Lichty in October 1975 that whatever was written then about Laos, Cambodia, and Vietnam may not be true in a year. (Lichty interviews in Hong Kong, Bangkok, July–August 1975.)

3.3 Thailand, *by Guy B. Scandlen*

Thailand is unique in Southeast Asia, never having been under colonial rule. Since 1932, when Pibul Songkhram ended the Thai monarchy's absolute power in a coup, a number of military dictators have led the nation. In October 1973 the corrupt military rule of Thanom Kittikachorn and Prapas Charusathiara collapsed following mass student demonstrations. The leaders fled into exile and King Bhumibol appointed an academician, Sanya Dharmasakti, as prime minister. Sanya formed an interim government and drafted a new constitution. In early 1975, after an additional interim government, Kukrit Pramoj, publisher, politician, and actor (who, by the way, played the role of the prime minister in the movie *Ugly American*), became prime minister of Thailand.

Thailand is made up of 71 provinces and in 1972 had a population estimated at 38 million. The chief city is the capital of Bangkok with four million population. Other important cities are Chiangmai (90,000), Korat (86,000), Udorn (58,000), and Haadyai (57,000). Thais form 82% of the population and speak different dialects; the official language as used in Bangkok is widespread. About three million Chinese have been assimilated into Thai society and have been granted citizenship. Nearly a million Malay-speaking people live in the extreme south. Other non-Thai groups are Indians, Pakistanis, Cambodians, and Vietnamese. The income per capita of the people in 1972 was estimated at $200.00.

The nation has a large mass-media setup, with at least 77 daily newspapers in addition to the broadcasting stations. Thailand is probably the only nation in all

Guy B. Scandlen is Lecturer in Communication, Chulalongkorn University, Bangkok; he was formerly language supervisor-consultant in Thailand in the early 1960s.

of Asia, except for Japan, that was still practicing freedom of expression. A bloody coup in October, 1976, ended this.

3.3.1 Introduction

It would be easy, and not unusual, to be cynical about Thai broadcasting. The temptation is to take Rama VI's optimistic 1919 statement broadcast by radio for ship-to-shore telegraph ("Greetings to you on this, which will be one of the most important days in our history") and patronizingly show how broadcasting has missed its chance; how it has become a commercial enterprise, sloppily executed, poorly maintained, but profitable. It would be easy; it would also be wrong.

In the context of Thai history, informational mass media are new phenomena, borrowed and adapted from essentially Western societies and traditions where mass media have evolved from forces within the cultural and historical processes.

But what about such media in an Asian culture still largely agrarian and authoritarian, where information still flows according to traditional means and where the majority of the people follow codes of social behavior rooted in the past? How can a media system derived from Judaic-Christian cultures, blended with traditions of concerned citizen participation in the governmental process, be incorporated into a society with traditions from which commands and information flowed downward to the people only at the will and grace of the king?

It would not be fair to judge broadcasting in Thailand under these conditions. Nor would it be completely fair to judge its performance by the government's codified and stated intentions. Far better to judge the broadcast media by the societal requirements of both traditional and contemporary Thailand and see if the needs of the society are, in fact, being fulfilled.

3.3.2 Governance and Facilities

Broadcasting started in 1931 as a state monopoly operated by the Thai government. Originally, there were four broadcasting stations: Thai National Broadcasting Station and the experimental stations of the Post and Telegraph Department, the Military Signal Corps, and the Territorial Army. The National Broadcasting Station, under the Government Publicity Department — now the Public Relations Department (PRD) — operated a medium-wave Thai service, a medium-wave experimental station, and a short-wave overseas service (see Rowland 1973, pp. 4—5).

Since 1938, the PRD has been entrusted with the coordination of broadcasting policy. The National Broadcasting Station is financed by government grants and advertising revenues. Originally, income from receiver licenses — ten cents per receiver — went to the government. In 1952, the radio license fee was lifted on the assumption that broadcasting is a free service to the public.

Broadcasting in Thailand is governed by the 1955 Radio Communications Act enforced by the Post and Telegraph Department, and the Radio Broadcasting Act of 1965, under the charge of the PRD. The Radio Communications Act deals with technical aspects of broadcasting, such as licensing regulations, definitions as to who shall broadcast, broadcasting restrictions, punishments for violations, and procedures for both appealing revoked licenses and license substitution.

The Radio Broadcasting Act, which also covers television, includes legal definitions and objectives of Thai broadcasting, regulations for establishing broadcast facilities, definitions and descriptions of broadcasting personnel and their duties, and operational guidelines for stations.

According to a PRD release of November 1970, the Radio Broadcasting Act

does not give the Public Relations Department the authority to direct a station to put a particular program off the air; neither does it invest the Public Relations Department with censorship authority. Nevertheless, the Public Relations Department takes as its responsibility . . . to see that the programs broadcast are in good taste and do not threaten public safety and security. [See also Glunt and Stelzenmuller 1966, p. 19]

Because, as stated in the premable to the Radio Broadcasting Act, broadcasting is "looked upon as a powerful instrument for information and enlightenment in a democratic society," the government in 1962 established the Committee of Radio Broadcasting and Communication of Thailand — the National Board of Broadcasting, composed of the directors or their representatives from every branch of government. The committee can make policy, fix rules, consider and approve new radio stations, and supervise, advise, and warn radio stations about regulations and procedures, but in cases where a violation has occurred, the committee can only refer the matter to the prime minister for consideration and orders.

One of the committee's first acts was to recommend in 1966 the banning of all commercial advertising from stations operated by the PRD. Soon after, according to Khun Chamnon Rangsikul, PRD news director, commercial radio advertising was banned from all stations, following a crisis in which the government accused certain radio stations of being run by unscrupulous people using advertisements to transmit messages to aid foreign powers. The ban forced most stations to cut programming drastically, but few closed. Since at least 1969, however, there has been radio advertising.

In 1970 an attempt was made to define broadcasting rules more clearly and to give greater authority to the supervision of broadcasting in Thailand, especially that concerning foreign news. Through subcommittee, rules were drafted to standardize the reporting of foreign news.

A Regulation of Radio Broadcasting Law was instituted 4 September 1974. It specified broadcasting's purposes as: promoting national policy and public advantages in politics, the military, economics, and society; persuading people to have faith in the nation, religion, and king; promoting unity among Thais;

encouraging resistance to enemies foreign and domestic; supporting national education activities; providing news and government information to create understanding; persuading the public to practice Thai customs, traditions, and language; and providing people with decent knowledge and entertainment. The law specifies required qualifications for stations and personnel. A Radio Broadcasting Executive Commission was set up, including the prime minister, directors-general of the PRD, Police Department, Intelligence Department, Post Office Department, general secretary of the National Security Council, chief of the General Staff, representatives of the ministries of education and foreign affairs, Royal Army, Royal Navy Forces and Royal Air Forces, Legislative Commission Office, and the heads of the Internal Radio Broadcasting of PRD and Radio Frequency Administration Offices. The commission has the authority to set conditions and grant licenses for the establishment of stations, establish advertising and business policies, give advice, and supervise broadcasting stations in carrying out these regulations. If any station violates these regulations, the commission has the power to issue warnings, cancel offending programs, withdraw broadcasting licenses, or close the station.

Furthermore, broadcasting stations must classify their programs into news, information, entertainment, and commercials. All stations are required to broadcast news from the PRD and programs supportive of government policy. News that discourages the public, tends to cause riots or break down unity, or affect national security and relationships with foreign nations is outlawed.

Except for the Royal Household, Post and Telegraph Department, and Ministry of Foreign Affairs, each government agency has broadcasting affiliates which may or may not be directly controlled and administered by the governing agency. For example, university radio stations are administered by the University Bureau and supervised by the host university, but the radio station at Khon Kaen University is governed by Kasetsat (Agricultural) University in Bangkok, as is the station at Kasetsat University in Chiangmai.

Technical-school stations are the responsibility of the vocational education department under the Ministry of Education, although operated on the local level. Some municipalities have stations, but employ military personnel as program directors.

Some agencies administer stations under their names, but borrow the frequency from the army or navy; others, the army for example, distribute radio stations to its branches throughout the kingdom and therefore are not completely in control of programming (see Thompson 1975, p. 6).

The Thai Television Company Limited, operating both radio and television, was initiated by legislation in 1953 and began broadcasting in 1954. Nine government agencies are shareholders; PRD is the largest with 55%. 45% is divided among the army, navy, air force, police department, Thailand tobacco monopoly, Thai sugar organization, liquor factory, and state lottery bureau.

In January 1958 the Army television station, Channel 7, was created (see Green 1972, p. 246). For four years, the station functioned without government support, but since 1963 an annual $25,000 subsidy — since increased to $50,000 — has been appropriated for the expansion of operations. Programming is completely of a non-military nature, and as one source states,

The name Army Television gives the newcomer the impression that it is a television station run exclusively by the Royal Thai Army for the Army. An Army spokesman insists that 99 per cent of its programmes consist of entertainment, news and educational programmes, while only one per cent deals with military affairs. [Fernando et al. 1968, p. N – 14]

Bids were accepted for a color transmitter in September 1967 — also to be controlled by the army in return for the privilege of buying airtime; within a month, equipment was airmailed to Thailand and the system was operating in time to record the crowning of Miss Thailand, 59 days after approval had been given to broadcast in color.

A second color transmitter, that of Thai Television Channel 3, was established in 1970 under an unusual operational procedure; the station is partially owned by PRD but operated entirely by the Bangkok Entertainment Company Limited, a private commercial enterprise.

Technical and programming functions in Thai broadcasting are separated by law; personnel are not supposed to double up the jobs. But in tens of stations throughout the kingdom, broadcasting is left to the whim of whichever engineer or technician happens to be on duty. The shortage of manpower does not allow otherwise. As one source indicated,

Most of the radio and television studios need manpower . . . (perhaps) five to six more persons working as announcers, news staff, technicians, in the financial section, etc. But the budgets are not large enough to develop the stations. Some depend administratively upon the central Bangkok authorities, but there is no cooperation between stations. In the stations themselves, there is no effective division of labour. Mechanics may work as radio technicians and radio technicians may work as announcers. They do not work conscientiously in order to serve the public. [Kaviya 1971, p. 467]

With the exception of morning and evening news broadcasts produced by PRD and relayed to every station in Thailand, personnel may play any records which suit them and occasionally play tapes supplied by the governing agency in Bangkok or by one of the two major advertising companies.

No formal radio censorship exists although the Radio Communications Act specifies:

Every broadcast, regardless of whether it is a tape recording or a gramaphone record, except in the case of a program relayed from outside, and including programs of interviews conducted by permanent announcers, news programs, official programs, amusement programs and programs of talks given on technical subjects, must be recorded on tape or on gramaphone records to be kept as proof . . . for a maximum of 15 days from the day of broadcast.

It is safe to say that, with very few exceptions, this regulation is totally ignored.

A television censorship committee, however, composed of representatives from the Government House Secretariat, the Ministry of Education, the Ministry of Public Health, and the Police Department screens all television films prior to airing. Play scripts are censored by the staffs of television studios before performances.

Thailand uses medium-wave AM and VHF FM transmissions for its domestic broadcasting service. It is difficult to gauge at any moment the exact number of radio stations in Thailand, the figures varying with each reporting agency. For example, one source in 1974 reported 132 medium-wave stations alone (*WRTH* 1974, p. 170), while another claimed the number of transmitters to be 108 long- and medium-wave, 26 short-wave, and 10 FM (UNESCO 1975, p. 345). Still another source claimed there were 113 radio stations in 1974, all government-owned and leased to businessmen (*Media* 1974b, p. 4). One possible reason for this confusion relates to the sporadic births and deaths of stations under military auspices. Also, definitive information is hindered because some stations switch call letters and frequencies during a broadcast day. This has led to constant overlapping of stations in spite of Radio Broadcasting Act regulations requiring

Table 15.   Radio Stations in Thailand, 1970-71

Administrative Agency	Bangkok-Thonburi Region				Provincial Regions			
	By Agency			By Frequency	By Agency			By Frequency
	AM	FM	Total		AM	FM	Total	
Public Relations Dept.	3	8	11	24	18	11	29	34
Ministry of Defense								
Army	18	6	24	27	31	1	32	35
Navy	0	3	3	4	4	0	4	4
Air Force	4	1	5	5	12	2	14	15
Supreme Command	1	1	2	2	2	1	3	3
Ministry of Interior								
(Police Department)	4	0	4	5	3	0	3	3
Ministry of Education	1	2	3	5	6	2	8	9
Ministry of Foreign Affairs								
(Public Relations Dept.)	1	0	1	2	0	0	0	0
Ministry of Agriculture								
(Public Relations Dept.)	1	0	1	2	0	0	0	0
University Bureau	2	1	3	3	3	1	4	4
Post and Telegraph Dept.	1	0	1	1	0	0	0	0
King's Service	1	0	1	1	0	0	0	0
Unknown, unidentifiable	?	?	1	1	?	?	1	1
Total			60	82			98	108

Source: USIS (Bangkok) listing in a private memo, 1971; Public Relations Department listing (untitled), 1971; National Statistics Office, *1969-70 Census, Final Report,* Bangkok: Office of Prime Minister, 1970; Kaviya 1971. The author also mailed letters and made phone calls to administrative agencies to obtain information. 52 of 98 letters were unanswered and seven phone calls were refused information.

at least "sidebands of the minimum of five kilocycles under the AM system, and frequency deviation to the maximum of 100 kilocycles under the FM system."

For example, a PRD station in Tak broadcasts from 6 A.M. to 9 A.M. as Radio Thailand Tak "Regular" (AM), becomes Po Cho So Tak AM "Special" from 9 A.M. to 2 P.M. and again from 4–7 P.M., after which it reverts to Radio Thailand Tak "Regular," broadcasting until 10 P.M. The primary difference between special and regular stations is that, under the law, special stations may accept advertising. All FM stations are permitted to accept advertising.

Despite these data-gathering drawbacks, Table 15 is presented as a tentative listing of radio stations in Thailand, although the results are by no means definitive.

Obviously, the concentration of media is greatest in the Bangkok-Thonburi capital region; there, nearly half of the nation's radio stations serve about 3.05 million people or slightly more than 8% of Thailand's total population of over 38 million.

Television, too, is concentrated in the Bangkok-Thonburi region, viewers sometimes having a choice of five channels. On the other hand, provincial residents have very little choice of programming except for rare faint signals received from neighboring regions.

Among the five Thai television operations are those administered by Thai Television Company, under PRD, which include Channel 4 in black and white and Channel 9 in color. These channels program both independently and jointly depending on the programs. The newest station, Channel 3, Bangkok Entertainment Company, broadcasts in color exclusively with Japanese equipment. PRD is a large shareholder in Channel 3. The Royal Thai Army Television Company operates Channel 7 in black and white and Channel 7 in color. The four provincial television stations, all operated by PRD, do not have color facilities. The stations broadcast from Khon Kaen, Lampang, Surathani, and Haadyai, the latter serving Songkla. Provincial stations and certain ones in Bangkok have repeater facilities to transmit signals to more remote municipal areas.

Besides these domestic broadcasting facilities, Thailand also has an external service, directed by PRD, which broadcasts from Bangkok on 11905 kHz (50 kw.) and 9655 kHz (100 kw.). Short-wave programming to Europe and North America is in French, English, and Thai, while the Asian service broadcasts in Lao, Vietnamese, Cambodian, Malay, Mandarin, and Thai.

Thailand joined Intelsat in 1966 and established a transportable earth station in April 1967. At Sri Racha district in Chonburi Province, stations one and two worked with satellites over the Indian Ocean in 1968 and 1970. Thailand participates in Intelsat IV, renting satellite time primarily to major United States and European communications networks. This service is provided weekly, and television companies are given the use of army television Channel 7 (color) and Thai Television Channel 4 (black and white) which relay the signal to Sri Racha via a two-hop wide-band microwave link (Sharuprapai 1972).

From the beginning, Thai broadcasting has been dependent upon materials purchased abroad; today, most of it is purchased from Japan, Germany, and Great Britain. Manufacturing and assembling of locally produced equipment is commencing at various army stations which otherwise have neither funds nor credit to replace American World War II equipment.

Very few stations — even the five or six largest ones in Bangkok — have any emergency stand-by equipment, nor do they have the basic tools for testing operating equipment. In cases of difficulty, foreign military personnel and their equipment are hired for short periods. Other problems with broadcasting facilities include the inadequate maintenance of studios, lack of soundproofing, antiquated equipment, and extremely dirty working conditions. Provincial stations face problems in repairing equipment; they are never sure parts they send to Bangkok for repair will be returned.

National electrification under these conditions also presents problems such as the following:

the difficulty is the irregular current and the inefficient electric system. .... Radio Thailand in Chiangmai, for example, often has to stop service because of the inefficient electrical system. Each time it has had to stop service for long periods of time: in October, 1970, it stopped for 29 days, in April of 1971 for 21 days. [Kaviya 1971]

In Prae, electric current dims throughout the municipality every evening, and in Trang, relay signals cannot be received during cold weather.

As for the availability of radio and TV receivers in Thailand, one can only rely on estimates drawn from statistical inferences which claimed the number of radio sets to be over four and a half million in 1971. UNESCO used a more conservative estimate of three million in 1975 (UNESCO 1975, p. 345). The number of TV receivers, inferred from a 1972 sample of urban areas conducted by Deemar Marketing Research, varies from 532,000 to 600,000. UNESCO estimated the number to be 350,000 (UNESCO 1975, p. 345); another source put the figure at 650,000 (*WRTH* 1974, p. 297).

Television reception does not extend much beyond the major urban areas. For example, in southern Thailand, there is little or no television in rural areas; in the North and Northeast, approximately 2% of rural households have television; and in the Central Plain, about 7% of the rural households.

The same does not hold for radio. Transistors are found in the most remote hill-tribe villages. That the government recognizes the potential for penetrating these areas may be seen in the installation of a 100-kw. omni-directional station in Chiangmai, devoted exclusively to broadcasting to the hill tribes living in politically sensitive regions. Built by Thailand and equipped by the United States government, this station is operated by PRD and staffed by hill-tribe personnel who broadcast only in seven of their own dialects.

3.3.3 Advertising

Thai broadcast advertising, according to the director of Diethelm Advertising, "lacks a clearly defined relationship between the media and advertising agencies." No standard rates and charges exist and advertising "depends on advertiser's credit position and on his personal relationships with colleagues in the media," he said.

It is probably true that in some cases there are no standard or fixed advertising rates. The media publish monthly rates, applicable primarily to television advertising, although there are "secret" radio advertising rates available as well. The average advertising cost of 34 Bangkok-Thonburi radio stations for a half-hour time slot is $187.50; of 66 provincial stations, $132.77. The mean cost per one-minute spot of the five Bangkok-Thonburi TV stations is $125.

It is not surprising that prices are negotiable as in any buyer-seller relationship in Thailand. Rates are kept secret so that a client may have exclusive control of certain time slots. Heavy time buyers who reserve yearly amounts of time sometimes are not charged for unused time. Advantageous payment schedules are also extended to quantity buyers of media time.

Large radio and all television stations in Bangkok have sales divisions; smaller radio stations often assign a person with other duties to keep advertising records. Although advertisers may approach stations directly, there are a few media brokers who negotiate sale of airtime.

One source lists the problems dealing with broadcast advertising as the lack of control by local stations over programs sent by advertising agencies in Bangkok, the collection of advertising fees, and the fact there are too many sponsors for a single program (Kaviya 1971). More often than not, however, the advertising rates are too high, so unsponsored programs are not broadcast.

Few, if any, rules exist concerning program sponsorship. Characteristics of sponsorship include: news programs are unsponsored; some companies give their names to programs — "The Singha Beer Show" or "The Toyota Show" — and few foreign advertisers sponsor Thai-produced television programs, despite the fact that Thai programming dominates television, drawing the larger audiences. Thai programs are costlier to produce than foreign show importation, and consequently their advertising spots cost more.

Theoretically, advertising rates are predicated on the size of viewership, determined through surveys by two marketing-research organizations. Media executives, however, question the results of these surveys and the efficacy of using recall to elicit viewing behavior. For reasons of safety, interviewing is done in the early evening or on weekend mornings. As a result, people are asked to predict what they *will* be viewing or asked to recall what they *have* seen. More often, however, the results do not conform to what an executive might believe concerning viewing behavior. Similarly, stories are told by advertising and marketing people attesting to arbitrary practices in deciding time slots to be given an advertising account. For example, a time slot was taken from one account and given to a lesser-paying one because the former had had it too long.

Advertisements must conform to broadcasting rules, observing institutional and patriotic restrictions, such as not defaming the Royal Family nor criticizing government leaders, as well as observing social niceties such as avoiding "impolite" language.

Certain taboos are specifically Thai: a statue of the Lord Buddha should not be used as a set decoration for a cold cream commercial (it happened once); tatooed male bodies are "impolite"; stroking of heads (to the Thai, the head is sacred) and pointing at people with one's feet (the "lowliest" part of the body) should not be shown. Rival products cannot be disparaged.

The major complaint against broadcast advertising, however, relates to the large number of commercials. Regulations governing broadcasting permitted nine minutes of advertising per program hour, or 15% of program time, on both radio and television. The 1974 radio broadcasting law, however, stipulated that commercial stations cannot use more than six minutes of advertisements per hour. The Radio Communications Act specifies further that "there must be a suitably long period of time between these categories of programs, under measures fixed by the National Board, except in the case of advertising that is part of a program relayed from outside."

Despite audience complaints, a 1970–71 content analysis by Thammasat University showed radio advertising comprised only 11.49% of broadcasting time in the Bangkok-Thonburi region and 10.76% in the provinces, both considerably less than legally permitted. Television is a different story. In Bangkok, 16.05% of airtime is devoted to advertisements; in the provinces, 18.13%.

Further, there does not seem to be any limitation on the amount of advertising permitted between programs or at station breaks. Television stations particularly tend to concentrate a large number of commercial messages during these periods, giving a liberal interpretation to the statement, "a suitably long period of time between these categories of programs." This is probably why the published listings of Thai television broadcasts seem whimsically strung together. A typical evening has programs on various channels beginning at 8:22, 8:25, 8:28, 8:33 or 8:47. The control of broadcast advertising may be one of the biggest problems facing Thai broadcasting.

3.3.4   Programming and Program Production

In spite of the Thai government's acknowledgment that broadcasting is effective for reaching "vast numbers of people immediately (and that) every official radio station is of the greatest practical use to the State and the people," broadcasting in Thailand is devoted largely to entertainment. Content analyses conducted by Thammasat University between October 1970 and June 1971 showed that in the Bangkok-Thonburi region, 58.9% of radio programs were entertainment oriented; 13.6%, news; 11.5%, advertising; 11.2%, general information; and 5.6%, commentaries. In the provinces, the figures were: entertainment, 61.4%; news, 15%; advertising, 10.8%; general information, 8.3%, and commentary, 4.6%.

Corresponding figures for television in Bangkok-Thonburi showed 62.2% of airtime was entertainment; 16.3%, news; 16%, advertising; 3.8%, general information; and 1.8%, commentary. In the provinces, 58.9% was entertainment; 18.1%, advertising; 16.2%, news; 6%, general information; and 1.6%, commentary (Kaviya 1971).

Radio broadcasts use standard Bangkok Thai as well as regional dialects. In Bangkok, four stations broadcast in English. FM stations administered by television companies broadcast original language soundtracks, a service provided only in the Bangkok-Thonburi region (see Table 16).

Table 16. Languages of Broadcasting, Bangkok-Thonburi Radio Stations (by frequencies)

Language Distribution	Number of Stations
Central Thai exclusively	51
Central Thai and English[a]	16
Thai, English, Chinese dialects, Indian dialects, and Japanese[b]	5
Thai, Chinese dialects, French[c], English, Indochinese languages,[d] and Malay	9

[a] Includes three radio stations in which programming, except for station identification, some news and government announcements, is in English. Also included in this figure are two Ministry of Education stations and the FM stations at Chulalongkorn and Thammasat universities.
[b] Includes five FM stations affiliated with television stations and playing the sound tracks in original languages. Two of these stations program exclusively in English. One Army station programs instruction in the Japanese language.
[c] Includes the seven frequencies for external service.
[d] Indochinese languages being Lao, Vietnamese, and Cambodian.

Language use in provincial stations is broken down according to Table 17.

Table 17. Languages of Broadcasting, Regional Provincial Radio Stations (by frequencies)[a]

Language Distribution	Number of Stations
Central Thai exclusively	52
Thai and unspecified regional dialects[b]	35
Thai, Northeastern dialect, and English	1
Thai and English	7
Thai and Indochinese languages[c]	4
Thai, regional dialects, and Indochinese languages	4
Thai, Muslim	4
Not reporting	1

[a] Listed by broadcasting frequency because administrative agencies may divide stations according to dialects and languages used.
[b] Northern dialect, Northeastern dialect, Southern dialect, hill tribe dialects.
[c] Lao, Cambodian, Vietnamese.

It is difficult to judge what constitutes scheduled radio programming because, aside from the English-language stations, Voice of America, British Broadcasting Corporation, and some university stations, program schedules are not distributed for publication.

Some stations are stricter than others about following a program schedule. Larger stations administered by PRD, Army Signal Corps, and Air Force have significant advertising budgets and thus take more time with programming. Other stations are more cavalier. For example, the chief engineer for one series of stations said his program schedules looked like a Chinese menu; "we just pick and choose whatever we're in the mood for," he said.

Thai-, Chinese-, and English-language newspapers in Bangkok publish television schedules, and Channel 3 prints a monthly booklet resembling the U.S. *TV Guide*. Unfortunately, published schedules are often unrelated to what is aired. Programs run late, or not at all, and substitutions are made without prior notice. One television executive explained, "Sometimes a series runs out or the contract is finished or we may have bought only ten shows to see how popular it is."

Time slots are reserved for particular kinds of programs — detective adventures, for example — and when one detective series runs out, another is found to replace it.

What kind of programs dominate Thai television? There is some debate on this matter. Programs produced abroad, despite fears of their negative effects on the public, seem to be most popular, according to one survey (see Table 18). A 1968–69 survey by the National Statistics Office showed Thai people preferred foreign films over all others (National Statistics Office, Thailand, 1970). Foreign TV programs are dubbed in Thai. Non-Thai speakers must use an FM radio to tune in on the English soundtrack (*Variety* 1975h, p. 116).

Table 18.   Television Program Preference, National Sample, Thailand, 1968-69[a]

Program Category	No. of Households Receiving Programs	Like Programs Very Much	Like Programs	Like Programs Little, or Not at All
Foreign Films	96	69	25	2
National News	96	53	37	6
Thai Films	94	61	29	4
Popular Thai Music	93	54	35	4
Foreign News/Analysis	93	44	40	9
Live Thai Drama	90	47	37	6
Sports	82	37	35	10
Thai Country and Western Music	73	29	34	10
Thai Classical Music	39	11	19	9
Other Music	38	15	19	4

[a] Modified to include only the top ten programs.

To determine what is available to the Thai TV viewer, this writer took a random sample of 18 weeks of Bangkok-Thonburi program listings over a period of three years (1970–72) and, averaging the hours together, computed a constructed week of programs. Over half of the shows, including those of primetime (about 6–10 P.M.), were produced by nationals in the Thai language.

Nearly 25% were Western-oriented and produced; 13.5% Japanese; 6.8% Chinese; 2.4% Indian; and 2.8% unknown origin. This survey showed that even when pitted against American shows such as "Wagon Train" or British favorites such as "The Avengers," Thai films attract larger audiences. In September 1971, September 1972, and March 1973, it was found that the most popular show was always Thai, and in all three instances at least 60% or 70% of the top ten TV shows were Thai.

Unfortunately, no such sequential data are available for judging viewership patterns in the provinces. There is, however, one Business Research Limited study of July 1971 which gives some idea of viewership patterns in that month across all regions. In the Central Plain, North, Northeast, and South regions, Thai programs were nearly always the most popular, followed closely by Japanese shows. From the foregoing data then, one might conclude that even though audiences prefer, or say they prefer, foreign films, in reality they do not. They watch what there is the most of, Thai programs.

Getting a pulse on radio listening in Thailand is more difficult than measuring TV viewing. First, there are more radio stations to choose from, and second, stations do not identify themselves more than the minimum government requirement of once an hour.

Furthermore, most people do not listen selectively, i.e., there are few favorite music and talk shows which attract large audiences. Instead, Thais tend to use the radio as a companion, turning to whatever sounds good, but paying little attention to the station. Soap operas attract selective audiences, but still, these listeners find it difficult to recall the name of the transmitting station. In cases where there is recall of stations, people tend to prefer PRD's special stations, some of those of the army and air force, according to a Deemar Media Report of 1972.

A 1969 survey of the National Statistics Office reported that Thais seemed to prefer Thai country and western music, soap operas, government or provincial news, foreign news, popular Thai music, and agricultural programs, in that order. The least popular radio shows were sports and Thai classical music.

Generally, the quality of Thai-produced television is poor by Western standards. Live drama is ragged, hastily produced, and full of technical flaws – microphones turned on and off at wrong times, missed lighting cues, mike booms in full sight, cameras out of focus. As one program director said, "The way we work is not like in other countries. It's always an emergency. Last minute." For example, when drama groups from outside the studio buy time to produce a play, studio technical crews are not informed of what is required until the final rehearsal.

Thai films are usually dubbed, either live during broadcast or synchronized with tape recorders. They tend to be very long and abound in subplots and intrigue. Musical shows fare a bit better when both the orchestra and singers are in tune. But as a television executive complained, "We rarely know what musical productions will contain until a few minutes before airtime."

Another source commented on this aspect at length:

Most stations are not capable of producing a well-done program. There is too much entertainment and not enough information and education. The production may be too complicated and most always depends on production centers in Bangkok. Some stations, such as the Agricultural College station in Chiangmai, run all their programming from material supplied by Bangkok. Some programs are completely produced by advertising agents, even though the basic policy is to make anti-communist propaganda. Too many outsiders are allowed to interfere in the program arrangements. The station manager may be too busy to control and supervise programs thoroughly.... For television, videotape recorded programs from Bangkok are complicated and troublesome due to delays and errors in sending them. In addition, government authorities frequently make demands for special broadcast time without previous notice. [Kaviya 1971, p. 471]

Subjects which may not be broadcast are listed in the Radio Broadcasting Act as "the loss of officials in the suppression of bandits, terrorists, or rebels; reports of movements of crime suppression officials"; news reports that would adversely affect public morale, cause panic to the people, cause merchants to increase their prices; or material that would support the interests or strengthen the status of the enemy.

The Radio Communications Act specifies that all radio stations must carry two daily news broadcasts, at 7 A.M. and 8 P.M., prepared and relayed by PRD in Bangkok. Both newscasts usually feature a summary of national and world events, but the morning news also includes documentary programs, human interest features, agricultural advice, etc. Non-PRD affiliates may choose not to carry the features.

During the October 1973 student demonstrations in Bangkok that toppled the government, the Public Relations Department's Radio Thailand was accused of broadcasting progovernment announcements and false news. The actions provoked students to attempt, on several occasions, to take over the PRD Building and burn it. After the riots, the government vowed to try to regain credibility for PRD broadcasts, by using them less as propaganda tools and more as vehicles for dialogue with the public. One of the first actions along these lines occurred in late 1973 on the "Meet the People" program, aired over ARMY TV Channel 9, when the prime minister appeared to discuss national issues. The program, simulcast by radio stations, has brought in numerous other officials for discussions of public issues (*Media* 1974b, p. 4). It is fair to say that since the overthrow of the government in 1973, Thai radio and TV stations have done much to raise the standards of news reporting and commentary. For example, the PRD broadcast all of the debate on the new constitution in the interim National Assembly (Thompson 1975, p. 6).

All radio stations begin their broadcast day with a sermon, followed by patriotic songs. Messages from the king, the prime minister, and other officials must be carried by all stations.

Regional stations are relatively autonomous, although they do depend on some packaged broadcasts supplied by Bangkok stations. Some regional television stations program portions of weekend mornings for educational purposes. Channel 5 in Khon Kaen, for example, helped prepare high-school seniors for the government examinations by providing well-known teachers to review coursework.

PRD is responsible for the external service. In addition to PRD's hill-tribe station in Chiangmai, the Thai Supreme Command Center radio station operates a 50 kw. transmitter (some say 10 kw.) relayed to three separate provinces regarded as sensitive areas: Sakonnakorn, Naratiwat and Chiangmai. Programming consists of propaganda used for counterinsurgency purposes; because the station used to relay to Thai troops in South Vietnam, it was often considered an external service. No external television service exists, although Laos, Burma, and Khmer can receive signals from Channels 5 and 8 in Lampang and Khon Kaen, respectively.

3.3.5 Educational Broadcasting

The Division of Educational Information, supervised by the education under-secretary, is responsible for producing and transmitting educational broadcasts for school children, teachers and adults. This division operates one 1 kw. FM transmitter from the Ministry of Education and three AM transmitters (one 10-kw. two 2-kw.) from the Bangkok Technical Institute. In addition, PRD transmits schools broadcasts from nine regional transmitters and also uses 17 stations for transmitting adult-education programs in the evening (see Rowland 1973, pp. 6–40).

During academic terms, there are schools broadcasts five days a week, four and a half hours daily – 9 A.M. to noon and 1–2:30 P.M. In addition, a lunch-hour program for teachers explains the use of the broadcasts in the curriculum. Broadcasts cover three subjects: English, of which there are eight levels, and social studies and music, four levels each. Programs are repeated four times weekly so that schools can fit them into their schedules more easily.

A daily two-hour program of music and views is broadcast between 2:30 and 4:30 P.M. from the FM transmitter in Bangkok, as are daily three-hour adult-education shows, aired weekdays from 6–9 P.M. and weekends, 5–8 P.M. Material includes news, health and hygiene, science, and cultural information.

The Division of Educational Information has two sound studios at its disposal, one at the Ministry of Education, the other at the Bangkok Technical Institute.

Teacher handbooks, wall charts, and other teaching aids are prepared for the 6,700 schools using the broadcasts; poorer schools receive the materials free while others purchase them at a nominal cost. Continuous evaluation of the programming is not done because of staff limitations. In-service training is provided during the school year and vacations, and division officials are sent overseas for further training and study tours.

The ministry recognizes three major problems with radio education, one of the most serious being that teachers do not know how to use the programs in class. Until recently, teacher-training colleges and schools did not include educational radio in their curricula. A second problem is finding airtime. Stations in different parts of the country make varying times available; thus, it is difficult to coordinate programming with school days, except in Bangkok where the ministry has its own transmitters.

The third problem pertains to the lack of sufficient studio space and program production and transcription equipment. The two existing studios are being used to full capacity; to replay more programs and send them to the provinces, transcription facilities must be increased.

Up to now, relatively little use has been made of television for direct educational purposes. The Bangkok municipality has been producing daily one hour of television programming for elementary schools within the municipal area. English, social studies, and music shows are produced for lower and upper primary schools and Thai, science, and math programs are transmitted daily to upper primary schools. Programs are transmitted from 10—11 A.M. every school day.

In addition, some educational institutions have closed circuit television. The College of Education at Prasarnmitr not only has a closed-circuit television system, but has also acquired television production equipment to be used for preparing programs for other branches of the College of Education, as well as for other teacher-training colleges. Already, closed-circuit television equipment exists at seven branches of the College of Education and ten teacher-training colleges. Not fully operational, the equipment is used on an experimental basis.

At Ramkamheng Open University, a considerable portion of teaching is conducted through closed-circuit television. Without it, the limited staff would be hard pressed to meet the 167-to-1-student-teacher ratio. Thammasat University also uses closed-circuit television for instruction.

There are plans for a national television network operated by PRD; by 1974, the necessary switching stations were expected to be completed, thus, facilitating the regulation of educational broadcasting throughout municipal areas of Thailand ("Request for Assistance," 1972). The PRD proposal called for a total of 17 TV stations in the north and south by 1975, while stations in Lampang and Surat Thani were to be improved to allow the transmission of a 625-line system. A television system control center will be set up in Bangkok to select programs for transmission to regional pilot stations in Lampang, Surat Thani and Haadyai (*Bangkok Post*, 27 December 1972).

3.3.6 Foreign Influences

Negative foreign influences upon broadcasting have been the subject of much debate in the Thai press for several years. Discussion revolves around the possible influence of foreign programming upon Thai children. As already pointed out, local program production is relatively more expensive than the importation of foreign shows. Broadcasting enterprises want profits, yet in Thailand, they are regarded as arms of the government in fostering nationhood. The problem is: Can promotion of nationhood (and anti-Communist propaganda) be economically profitable for a broadcasting system?

Just what influences do Western and Japanese-produced programs have? Not much solid evidence is available, but one Thai psychiatrist, Subha Malakul, feels television "teaches aggressive behavior and widens the generation gap." In Thailand, he feels this is especially serious "because violence is alien to traditional Thai culture. A certain amount of acting out of aggressive impulses by children is tolerated and even condoned in some cultures, but not in Thailand where any aggressive behavior is looked down on" (Breen 1972, p. 5). Whether aggressive behavior is un-Thai is debatable, but the forms of foreign aggressiveness have been noted by Dr. Malakul: "Formerly, Thai children indicated 'I am angry' by an upraised index finger. Now the sign is the mimicking of a karate chop."

Five graduate theses at Chulalongkorn University, dealing with television viewing behavior of second grade to high-school children, attempted to find out how children felt they were influenced by television and films. Some of the findings indicated that when viewing television alone (an uncommon practice), children tended to be selective in what they watched, using the medium for recreation rather than education. It was found that both boys and girls prefer spy and detective stories, historical plots, cartoons, slapstick comedy, and musical films, in that order. Boys also rated war movies especially high. When asked what sort of religious programs they preferred, the children chose shows featuring the activities of Satan (Yompraban in Thai folk tales) and his defeat. Rank ordering their favorite programs by source of production, girls answered Western, Thai, Chinese, Japanese, and Indian films, in that order (Jareunsak 1970; Meenpradit 1970; Sripraphai 1970; Tamrongshod 1966; Wingomint 1970). Of course, there still have not been any cause-effect relationships drawn between foreign-film violence and Thai children's social behavior.

Although Thai broadcasting is not under foreign control, there are two instances where foreigners have purchased blocks of Bangkok stations' daily time for which they have produced news, feature, and music programs. Apparently these stations program with great freedom.

One FM station in particular, renting from the Army Signal Corps, is owned under a Thai name, but has as its major shareholder the Thomson organization of London which also owns two of the three Bangkok English-language newspapers. This station has been granted permission to prepare its own morning news from wire service copy and is thus exempted from using the PRD News in Thai. It does broadcast the evening news in Thai.

Great concern has been expressed about foreign spillover in southern Thailand where Communists and Muslim separatists are extremely active. This was commented upon at great length in a report written for a public-relations management course at the Public Relations Department. A group of business executives, reporting on a survey they conducted of media in Malaysia and southern Thailand, said that in southern Thailand, 80% of the population in nondanger areas could receive the programs of the Central Safety Committee's 10-kw. station. They added, however, the four most sensitive provinces could not receive any Thai stations; instead, they depended upon Malaysian radio. Even the 50-kw. station at Yala, another southern province, has been ineffective because its transmitter is geographically lower than the Malaysian one.

Moreover, the report criticized the number of advertisments at prime time, causing southern Thais to listen to Malaysian stations which forbid advertising during this time period. Also, according to the report, Malaysian news is brief, to the point, and interesting, whereas Thai news is long-winded and boring. Malaysian psychological warfare programming is also "more interesting" than Thailand's, the writers of the report felt, as are reports of agriculture, economics, and other features. Malaysian programming has been so well received by Thai audiences that Radio Malaysia has expanded its Thai-language programming and increased its staff by three Thai nationals who work with the original Thai-speaking Malaysian (Srisamt et al. 1973). There has been no official response by the government.

3.3.7 Training

The very earliest training of Thai broadcast engineers was performed by the Radio Corporation of America in the United States. Several groups from the Royal Thai Navy were sent to observe and be trained in the late 1940s.

Today, there still is no structured and systematic way to train engineers and technical personnel in Thailand. Armed Forces technicians are training on the job after finishing vocational high schools. Other technicians are apprenticed to various media without any background. Some vocational schools and institutions such as the Nontaburi campus of Phra Chom Klao Institute of Technology and the Bangkok Technical Institute offer basic broadcast training. All media agencies hire engineering graduates with university degrees, and the media send technical personnel to Japan, Germany, Great Britain, the Netherlands, and the United States for training. The most systematic and practical instruction in programming is offered by PRD, which also has courses in advanced techniques and research methodology, designed for active media personnel and other professionals who have an interest in the media.

Regulations governing broadcasting are quite specific about the training of announcers, emphasizing they must possess "a permit of radio announcing issued by the Public Relations Department," obtainable by completing the PRD radio-announcing course. The Radio Broadcasting Act specifies that broadcast technicians must "possess a radio official's permit issued by the Post and Telegraph Department," but training does not seem to be a pre-requisite for the issuance of such a permit. Furthermore, no such courses are offered.

Universities which offer degrees in broadcasting are the Faculty of Communication Arts at Chulalongkorn University, the Independent Department of Journalism and Mass Communications at Thammasat University, and the

Department of Communications at Chiangmai University. The curricula are comprised of a combination of liberal arts education, historical and theoretical backgrounds in the media, in addition to practical internships during the third and fourth years of study. Graduates receive further on-the-job training when they enter the media (see Rowland 1973).

3.3.8 Conclusion

James Mosel has written that Thai acculturation mechanisms "are able to modify the traditional and reinterpret the new so that compatibility (between the old and new) becomes possible" (Mosel 1963, p. 185). Thai broadcasting faces a similar problem: how to reinterpret a Western phenomenon to make it compatible with contemporary Thai society.

Benedict, Kingshill, and Phillips have noted certain cultural traits that organize Thai social and, ultimately, national behavior. The first trait is that work — all life, in fact — should be fun or *sanuk* (Phillips 1965, p. 59). Thai broadcasting is certainly fun or entertainment-oriented.

Further, Kingshill has said that if something can be shown to be profitable and expedient, Thais will adopt it immediately, possibly the reason for the 158 stations in the nation and the proliferation of advertising, especially on television.

A more interesting phenomenon is that Thai people have entrusted the broadcast media with great credibility. Mosel, Noah, Jacobs, and USIS have reported that villagers put more reliance in radio than newspaper news (Mosel 1963, p. 199; Noah 1969; Jacobs, Rice, and Szalay 1964; USIA 1961; USIA, 1960a). For example, Noah wrote:

For the village elite and others as well, medium-wave radio is a far greater source, compared with publications, of information they remember and can discuss. Its growth is phenomenal and its potential, especially if linked to personal contact through local institutions, is much greater than publications. [Noah 1969, p. 6]

But this is not blanket credibility. For example, a Rand Corporation study of northern and northeastern villages found that when listening to communist programs "evidence suggests that villagers ignored or distrusted any thinly veiled political propaganda" (Phillips and Wilson 1964, pp. 4—5).

And, like the Thai social structure, broadcast media are not rigid. Blackburn commented that Thailand has a decentralized commercial media system, the decentralized character of which "in many respects mirrors that of Thailand's bureaucracy as a whole" (Blackburn 1971, p. 341). He referred to David A. Wilson's tracing of the "extraordinary organization of radio broadcasting" in Thailand to "the idiosyncratic administrative autonomy permitted within the Thai bureaucracy, in which each element keeps itself going through the manipulation of its own revolving fund" (Wilson 1962, pp. 181—85).

The disorganization, sloppiness, and lack of punctuality may be maddening to some, but it also indicates a freedom, implying the possibility for experimentation and development.

A young American composer, Bruce Gaston, reacting to complaints about the media, mentioned:

In the United States, television is slick, punctual and a closed shop. How much experimentation do you see? The other day in Lampang, I saw a study in shadows: blurred dancers weaving between light and darkness. In Bangkok drama troops are experimenting with new forms of drama on television. That's exciting. And here producers and administrators listen and aren't afraid to experiment.

Because Thai broadcasting needs strong, viable direction, acculturation mechanisms are not enough. The ultimate question is: Will the Thai government assume responsibility for guiding its own broadcasting?

3.4 Malaysia, *by Jack Glattbach and Ramanujan Balakrishnan*

The Malay States came under Portuguese and Dutch influences until the British acquired Penang in 1786 and established British rule by the end of the 19th century. Malaya acquired its independence in 1957, at the height of the Communist emergency in the nation. The Federation of Malaysia, comprising Malaya (now West Malaysia), Sabah and Sarawak (formerly British Borneo and now East Malaysia), and Singapore, was set up 16 September 1963. Two years later, Singapore was dumped from the federation.

Malaysia covers 130,000 square miles; West Malaysia with its 11 states has 52,000 square miles, East Malaysia's two states, 78,000 square miles. The 11.1 million population is multiethnic — 47% Malay, 34% Chinese, 8.5% Indian and Pakistani. The major cities are the capital, Kuala Lumpur (452,000), George Town (270,000), and Ipoh (248,000).

Politically, the dangers to Malaysia are lingering Communist insurgency along the Thai border and in the jungles of Sarawak and the possibility of racial disturbance, although the latter is becoming less threatening because of the continuing rise in prosperity and amendments to the Sedition Act in 1971 (forbidding discussion of sensitive issues such as the position of sultans and king, special rights granted under the constitution to the Malays, citizenship and the national language, Bahasa Malaysia).

Economically, gross national product has been growing at about 6.5% per annum, giving a real income per capita of $360 in 1970, the fourth highest in Asia. Under the Second Malaysian Development Plan, this figure was expected to reach $420 by 1975.

Mass media, including over 50 daily and Sunday newspapers, operate under a

Jack Glattbach is Consultant for the Press Foundation of Asia, Manila; he was formerly editorial director of South East Asia Press Centre, Kuala Lumpur. He is the author of three monographs on print and broadcasting media in Malaysia and Singapore and founding editor of *Leader: A Malaysian Journalism Review* and *Media for Asia's Communications Industry.* Ramanujan Balakrishnan is Head of the National Broadcasting Training Centre, Kuala Lumpur, and former head of Indian Service of Radio-TV Malaysia.

guidance concept in their relationships with government. Broadcasting, although the most pervasive media, faces problems because of geographic conditions: East and West Malaysia are separated by the South China Sea; West Malaysia is divided from north to south by a 5,000-foot hill range.

3.4.1 Background

Malaysia's performance in the general business of development is without doubt one of the best in Asia, and the development of broadcasting is no exception to this pattern.

Until 1940 and the imminence of war, radio in the then-British colony was the preserve of enthusiastic amateurs, most of whom were in Singapore. A small station was opened in Kuala Lumpur just before the Japanese occupation in 1942; the Japanese added three low-power stations at Penang, Malacca, and Seremban. In 1946, after Malaya reverted to the British, a department dealing with broadcasting (known as Radio Malaya) was created, using former military equipment and administered from Singapore.

The first great stimulus to broadcasting development was the outbreak of militant Communist terrorism in 1948, which forced rapid radio expansion continuing through Merdeka (Independence) in 1957, the formation of Malaysia in 1963, and right up to the present. An additional stimulus, although smaller than the Communist emergency, was the confrontation with Indonesia in 1965. On 1 January 1962, commercial radio broadcasting was introduced; a year later, the external service, Suara Malaysia, was developed partly to offset Indonesian propaganda in the nation. On 28 December 1963, television was established in Malaysia (see §3.5.1). A second TV network was set up in November 1969, when TV Malaysia moved to its new $14.9 million facility at Angkasapuri (literally translated as "space city"), four miles from downtown Kuala Lumpur. That same year, radio and TV were integrated into the Department of Broadcasting under the Ministry of Information and Broadcasting. In 1973, a $4 million six-story building, called Wisma Radio, was completed next to Angkasapuri. The completion of Wisma Radio, home of Radio Malaysia, gave the country the largest centralized radio and TV complex in Southeast asia (*AMC Bulletin*, June 1973).

The importance of radio and television in Malaysia is immediately apparent. The five guidelines for broadcasters laid down by the Ministry of Information and Broadcasting emphasize a preoccupation with national development: 1. To explain in depth and with the widest possible coverage government policies and programs to insure maximum public understanding. 2. To stimulate public interest and opinion to achieve its deserved changes. 3. To assist in promoting civic consciousness and fostering the development of Malaysian arts and culture. 4. To provide suitable elements of popular education, general information, and entertainment. 5. To promote national unity — by using Bahasa Malaysia in a multiracial society toward the propagation of a Malaysian culture and identity. Therefore, at policy level, broadcasting is recognized as a major tool in developing national unity in a multiracial, multilingual, and multireligious society. At the operating level, this means that broadcasting in West Malaysia is done in the four languages of Bahasa Malaysia (national language), Mandarin, Tamil, and English. Transmissions in the East Malaysian states of Sarawak and Sabah use even more languages, including some regional dialects. The policy toward developing a Malaysian identity, however, especially prevalent since 1972, is resulting in a trend away from the multilingualism of former days.

To cope with this diversity in cultures and languages, the infrastructure for broadcasting is developing rapidly. For example, transmitting capacity in 1972 totalled 844 kw. and should reach 1,204 kw. by 1976. Cheap transistor radios have put the medium within reach of nearly all Malaysians. Although television is still mainly for the richer urban groups, rural penetration is increasing quickly with the growth of group viewing habits.

3.4.2   Facilities

Radio Malaysia, transmitting in short-wave, medium-wave, and FM, provides six services; five domestic networks and one external service. The domestic breakdown is by language, i.e., separate services in Bahasa Malaysia, Mandarin, Tamil, and English, and the Kuala Lumpur "Siaran Ibukota" (Capital City Broadcasting). The latter service was launched in November 1973 to meet the special needs of a city population, providing instant information on traffic, weather, and cultural and social events of Kuala Lumpur. All transmitting and production centers are interconnected through microwave, thus helping relay of programs from one or more sources by any or all stations at times convenient or desired.

Transmitting and production centers are situated in ten cities; Kuala Lumpur, Penang, Ipoh, Malacca, Johore Bahru, Kuantan, Kuala Trengganu, Kota Bahru, Kota Kinabalu (Sabah), and Kuching (Sarawak), and at a few unrevealed locations (*Broadcasting in Malaysia* 1971). In 1971, Radio Malaysia had 22 medium-wave, 14 short-wave, and 2 FM 100-kw. transmitters. Aggregate power of the medium-wave and short-wave transmitters was 940 kw. More than 80% of the population can receive medium- and short-wave broadcasts, 60% medium-wave only, and 80% short-wave only (Glattbach and Anderson 1971, p. 23). All broadcasting equipment is imported, Britain being the major supplier, closely followed by Japan.

On the receiving end, there were 322,757 licensed radio sets in June 1972. Of course, the actual number is much higher, since a license entitles its holder to operate more than one set, and the usual problems of enforcing the licensing transistor sets prevail. Survey Research Malaysia, an independent market-research firm which carries out six weekly surveys over West Malaysia, estimated in mid-June 1971 that there were one million homes, each with an average of 3.4 adults, with radio sets. Over 60% of all homes have radio sets. UNESCO estimated two million sets in use (UNESCO 1975, p. 317). One reason for this relatively high radio-set ownership may be that broadcasting receivers (both radio and TV) are assembled in Malaysia by about half a dozen major international companies. Locally assembled sets, a little less expensive than in some neighboring states, account for about 75% of the domestic market.

Group radio listening was at a peak during the 1948–60 Emergency, a period when Communism posed a serious threat to the nation, but has declined since, although the government in the 1970s was encouraging formation of farmers' associations and community centers where group listening would figure prominently.

The external radio network, Suara Malaysia (Voice of Malaysia), uses three short-wave transmitters with an aggregate power of 210-kw. at Kajang, near Kuala Lumpur. The network transmits 56 hours a week in Indonesia, 17½ in English, 14 in Mandarin, 7 each in Thai, Arabic, and Tagalog to target areas in China, Southeast Asia, Australia, and New Zealand. The Thai and Tagalog Broadcasts, started in 1973, are aimed at strengthening ties among ASEAN (Association of Southeast Asian Nations) nations.

Reception of foreign external services is also extensive in Malaysia, the most important being those from Singapore (which effectively supplies the southern part of West Malaysia with four extra radio stations and two TV channels), BBC's World Service, VOA, Australian Broadcasting Commission. All India Radio, and RRI (Indonesia). Reception is good too from Japan, China, Taiwan, and Thailand.

Besides government broadcasting, the other radio facilities in Malaysia are two much smaller, foreign-owned stations. Rediffusion originates over two channels in Kuala Lumpur, Ipoh, Penang, and Butterworth, all within a 250-mile radius of each other in West Malaysia.

Daily Rediffusion Malaysia programs from 6 A.M. to midnight cater mainly to the Chinese, but English, Bahasa Malaysia, and Tamil are also used. In 1972, there were nearly 50,000 subscribers who paid a $1.80 monthly rental. Advertising is used by Rediffusion and the network also relays news from Radio-Television Malaysia. Additionally, there is a small Royal Australian Air Force station at Butterworth. A Far East transmitting station of the BBC, located at Johore Bahru, adjacent to Singapore, was ordered closed by the Malaysian government in early 1974. The decision was in keeping with Malaysia's nonaligned policy which does not allow for foreign-managed and edited news being broadcast from Malaysian soil (*Media* 1974f, p. 20).

As for television facilities, Malaysia uses the 625-line monochrome system. The major production center is at Kuala Lumpur, with a small production unit in Kota Kinabalu to serve East Malaysia. Programs are telecast through two channels, covering all West Malaysia and Sabah with a network of 38 transmitters in 22 locations within the country's microwave network, which is operated by the telecommunications department. Six transmitting stations are under construction in Sarawak, and another 16 booster stations are planned (Dyer 1974, p. 20).

Channel 1, the national TV network, telecasts 84 hours weekly in Bahasa

Malaysia, while Channel 2, in English, Chinese, and Tamil, is on the air 44 hours weekly. Channel 2 is also the vehicle for Malaysia's ETV service. As of 30 June 1972, there were 238,357 licensed TV sets in Malaysia. Group reception is, like radio, on the verge of rapid expansion, particularly with the introduction of ETV facilities.

The government announced in late 1972 that Malaysia would have color-TV facilities by 1975. For economic and technical reasons, however, color television will probably be delayed until 1976. Only foreign films will be shown initially, and it is hoped local color productions will be available by 1978. Only one network will have color TV at the beginning, the second in 1980. Part of the reason government has given for introducing color telecasts is that equipment for black-and-white film will no longer be produced (Kuala Lumpur *Straits Times*, 21 December 1972). Obviously, this is a lame reason; the equipment will still exist. Some observers feel color TV is being introduced because neighboring Singapore now has color, and it has become a matter of pride and prestige.

Two main external possibilities are available now for TV Malaysia's domestic productions: the first is the "spillover" to Singapore, northern Sumatra, Brunei, and southern Thailand; the second involves the earth satellite station at Kuantan, opened in 1970, which links Malaysia with the Indian Ocean satellite, and therefore is expected to provide links with India, Pakistan, the Middle East, Europe, Japan, Australia, and Indonesia. For Malaysian viewers, the biggest benefits of satellite usage to date have been the live telecasts of the Frazier-Ali heavyweight fights, the Malaysian soccer performance in the 1972 Olympics, and the 1974 Islamic summit conference in Lahore. A second earth satellite station in Kuantan has been constructed, again, as with the first, through Japanese funds. The new station, opened in 1975, beams Radio-Television Malaysia programs directly to Kota Kinabalu in Sabah (Coats 1975, pp. 18–19). Also, in 1974, there was talk of setting up another earth satellite station in Sarawak to improve TV programming and telephone facilities there (*Media* 1974j, p. 3).

3.4.3 Governance

Both radio and television are owned and operated by the government, except for the Rediffusion and Australian Air Force stations. The chief executive of Radio-Television Malaysia (RTM) is the director-general of broadcasting who is answerable to the Ministry of Information, coordinator of all government mass-media institutions.

The telecommunications department is the licensing authority for the operation of both radio and TV. While radio transmitters are effectively under the control of the broadcasting department, television transmitters, as part of the total microwave system of Malaysia, are operated and maintained by the telecommunications people. Funds for the additional transmitters required for telecast purposes, however, are provided by the broadcasting department. As yet, government has not permitted broadcasting to be developed by additional private individuals.

No insulation from direct political control is possible, the attitude being that all public service must act in concert with the declared policies and aspirations of the party elected to govern. Government policy on this matter was reiterated by the Minister of Information in mid-1973, when he said opposition members would not be allowed to make use of radio and television to channel political ideologies (*Penang Star,* 3 May 1973).

3.4.4 Financing

Radio-Television Malaysia is financed by license-fee payments and advertising. To possess a radio receiver, one must pay an annual fee of $5 or $10 yearly for a joint radio-TV license. Fees are collected through the country's post offices and credited directly to government revenue. In 1973, radio-license revenue amounted to nearly $2 million; for TV, the figure was about $3.1 million. The exact extent of nonpayment, of course, is not known, but newspaper reports suggest a substantial loss of revenue, particularly with regard to radio.

Advertising is permitted on both radio and television, revenue again being credited directly to the government treasury. Long-term advertising contracts enjoy a certain discount just as commissions granted to advertising agencies are allowed. In 1973, revenue from advertising was $7.04 million, of which $2.76 million came from radio and $4.28 million from television.

Advertising time is sold by the information ministry's chief commercial officer. Advertising agencies have to be accredited by the ministry; those conducting business in Malaysia are allowed a 15% discount, foreign agencies, 7.5% (see Larsen 1974, pp. 21–22).

Advertising spots are available to a maximum of one minute each during all radio and television broadcasting hours. In a 14-minute program, two commercial inserts totaling not more than 1½ minutes are allowed; in a 29-minute program, three inserts totaling three minutes with a maximum of one minute and 20 seconds in any one insert, are allowed.

RTM accepts sponsored programs, but there are very few such shows either on radio or TV. About half a dozen large companies regularly sponsor weekly radio shows. Otherwise, sponsors prefer to help reduce the cost to the government of buying occasional, high-appeal foreign programs. For example, the Frazier-Ali fight was broadcast on Malaysian television direct by satellite, sponsors raising most of the needed money. In the programs themselves, no advertising mentions are permitted, the sponsor's name appearing once in the lead-in and once in the lead-out, but it is not difficult to pick out specific products as parts of drama sets.

For block bookings, advertisers must take a certain proportion of time on radio's National Network and TV's Channel 1. Commercials are accepted only in the national language on both Channel 1 and National. In addition, since June 1972, Channel 1 has accepted commercials only if the packages of products shown carry wordings in Bahasa Malaysia, as well as the voice being in that language. Packages using other languages are shown on Channel 2. At the same time, government ruled that commercials not produced in Malaysia were subject to a 5% surcharge on airtime, it being the responsibility of advertisers to certify where the commercials were made. In mid-1973, the surcharge on foreign-made commercials was increased to 50%, with obvious advantages to the local film houses. By early 1974, it was estimated that Malaysian-made commercials accounted for 80% of all those screened on television (*Media*, January 1974, p. 20).

Radio-Television Malaysia utilizes a copy code for advertising, based on accepted international requirements with additional local requirements peculiar to a multiracial, multireligious society. Among local requirements are: television and the National Network of radio may not accept advertisements for liquor or food with pork content (offensive to Muslims); advertisements may not contain material offensive to religious, racial, political or sentimental susceptibilities of any section of the community; advertisements may not publicize political or religious meetings; and advertisements are not allowed for death notices or firms of funeral directors or monumental masons. In the 1970s, the minister of information reminded advertisers of their responsibilities to a developing country, which included avoiding "mindless aping of bourgeois values and styles of the West." A mimeographed drawing of what government considers acceptable hair lengths in commercials also was prescribed by the Ministry of Information in mid-1972.

3.4.5   Programming and Production

The number of weekly radio broadcasting hours in West Malaysia in 1973 was nearly 475, made up of 168 hours in Bahasa Malaysia, 101 in Chinese, 100 in English, 92½ in Tamil, and 14 in aboriginal languages such as Semai and Temiar. By mid-1973, the information ministry was studying the use of more local dialects, especially those of Chinese, for regional broadcasts. It was carefully explained that this was not a move against the national language, but an effort to get "messages over to the man in the street" (Kuala Lumpur *Straits Times*, 29 March 1973).

A 1969 analysis of program content on radio in West Malaysia showed entertainment fare predominating on all four language networks, and especially so on the English network (79.2%). In the 1970s, there was a definite trend toward increasing the amount of informational and educational content of both radio and television, as well as to implement more use of the national language. The information minister, speaking at one Asia Assembly in 1973, repeatedly emphasized that television in Malaysia should not be predominantly an entertainment medium, claiming that as a reason why TV must always be owned and controlled by the government alone.

From interviews with Radio-Television Malaysia department heads in March 1972, the authors of this chapter found that music constituted the largest chunk of broadcast time on both media, followed by education and news and current affairs (see Table 19).

Table 19. Programming and Production, West Malaysian Radio and Television, March 1972 (Percentage of Weekly Outputs)

	Radio	Television
Advertising/Promotion	5	5
Children's	2	3
Drama	7	6
Education	11	12
Feature Films	–	10
General Entertainment	5	10
Music	45	29
News/Current Affairs	10	11
Religion	3	2
Sport	5	5
Talks	6	5
Unclassified	1	2

Source: Interviews with Radio-Television Malaysia department heads.

The government does not have its own audience measurement facilities, relying on data supplied by an independent market-research organization. Its surveys show wrestling, usually from the U.S., as the most popular program, followed by imported detective and courtroom dramas and cowboy series. Surprisingly, high ratings are achieved by certain imported period plays such as "The Forsythe Saga" and "The Six Wives of Henry VIII" and for imported documentaries such as "Life and Times of Mountbatten" and "Valiant Years."

RTM has good facilities for outside and remote broadcasts but use of these facilities is less than optimal, probably due to underdeveloped attitudes of program directors and producers who tend to see Malaysian society only through the eyes of officialdom. Sports events, such as soccer and track, however, are reasonably well served by outside broadcasts, and the percentage of extra studio material used in programs is increasing.

RTM depends on two government agencies for some local programming materials, Filem Negara, the national film unit, and Bernama, the national news agency. Filem Negara produces documentaries that have at times been used on television, and Bernama provides most of the copy for the joint radio-TV newsroom.

Radio uses very little imported material with the exception of music in Chinese, Indian, and English. On the other hand, television has a high reliance on foreign material. During a typical week of television programming in mid-1972, it was found that out of nearly 85 hours telecast, 51% was imported, over 46% of it in English, emanating from Britain and the United States. This is likely to continue for a number of years, even though the proportion of locally made shows is increasing and despite ministerial speeches denouncing these foreign influences. No particular quotas are imposed on imported programs, although an effort is made to increase the local ones. Imported program on TV's Channel 1 are dubbed, while other imported material, particularly films, is subtitled in Bahasa Malaysia.

Although provision is set down for the acceptance of local programs made outside the broadcasting department, such material has not been forthcoming, most probably for reasons of cost. Outside contributors, however, are used quite extensively in presentation, acting, writing, composition, and contribution in specialist areas. Talent fees are paid, regulated by the Malaysian treasury. In 1972—73, there was some debate on whether these fees were adequate to attract the nation's best talent. The rate varies from $.40—$1.70 per minute.

Broadcasting has been effective in increasing awareness of indigenous arts and culture; for example, a current revival in ethnic music owes a great deal to radio-TV exposure, as does appreciation of local textiles, silverware, and painting. Radio and television maintain a 60-piece professional orchestra and regularly hire local dance troups. Local talent is encouraged through a series of competitions organized by RTM. The department of broadcasting also publishes books of traditional, modern, and children's songs.

Television suffers more constraints than radio, where it is reasonably safe to assume racially and religiously homogeneous audiences. Television, however, can make no such assumptions, and much of the conservatism and timidity of Malaysian television stems from efforts of producers to avoid the numerous areas of offense in such a diverse society.

Security of tenure for broadcasting staff tends to breed complacency and a lack of drive and imagination, resulting in a rather stereotyped radio-TV atmosphere. Bureaucracy and red-tape problems inhibit the creative spirit, as does the direct political control which often descends well down into the organization. For example, plane crashes are not reported on radio or TV for fear of upsetting pilgrims traveling by air charter to Jeddah. In fact, in 1972—73, broadcasting officials proudly talked about a RTM feature which they thought was unique: no bad news is presented in early morning radio programming so as not to upset workers before they started their day.

Because of these conditions, TV Malaysia especially attracts its fair share of criticism, most of it expressed in daily newspapers. *Straits Times,* Malaysia's biggest English-language newspaper, says it receives an average of 100 letters a week, most of them expressing dissatisfaction over the type of programs televised, screening times, interruptions, bad dubbing, poor sports commentary, low quality local productions, poor imported material, and the screening of too many old films. TV Malaysia counters by saying that such complaints come mainly from urban viewers, whereas the station is more concerned with people in the rural areas whose working day begins at sunrise and ends at about 9 P.M. Thus, from 6:30—9:30 P.M., programs are directed to rural audiences, and only after 9:30 P.M. is the emphasis switched to the syndicated productions in English, enjoyed by urban viewers.

The authorities are also strongly conscious of aligning their programs to the concepts of the Rukunegara, Malaysia's national ideology, meaning that programmers should see their primary role as one of promoting national consciousness and racial harmony. In almost "Big Brother" language, television is seen as "one of the most effective means for the guidance of the masses." But, while it is possible to see the influence of this ideology on the content of locally produced programs, it is much more difficult to observe in the selection of imported material which forms the majority of program time. For instance, there is censorship of kissing scenes, but only those scenes where the kissing is "excessively passionate."

Another problem for programmers is that the printed media give viewers easy access to news about entertainment trends elsewhere in the world. But when TV Malaysia tries to acquire the latest international programs, it finds the prices are too high, which precludes anything more than the occasional outright purchase of this material (*Malay Mail,* 15, 22, 29 October 1972). One way out of this economic bind would be to increase the number of commercials. But this would mean interrupting programs, which so far the authorities have refused to do.

Against this criticism, one has to weigh the very real problems of broadcasting in a multiracial country. Private-sector broadcasting has not always been known for a well-developed sense of responsibility in much less sensitive countries than Malaysia, and it would be a brave, perhaps even foolish, man who would advocate free enterprise in Malaysian broadcasting. Certainly there is no lobby for such a move, probably because one of the advantages of a monopoly is that listeners and viewers do not always know what they might be missing, although they can get some idea from the printed media. Thus, while there is criticism of programming on radio and TV, there is also considerable national pride in the development and performance of a broadcasting system which is head and shoulders above most of its neighbors.

3.4.6 Educational Broadcasting

Schools radio broadcasting began in May 1966 and is part of an educational mass-media service administered by the Ministry of Education in conjunction with the Ministry of Information. The information ministry's 1972 budget for schools broadcasting was $135,000, while that of the education ministry was $120,000.

All educational personnel are from the education ministry, while broadcasting technicians are seconded from the information ministry. Physical facilities are presently shared between the two ministries in the old studios of RTM, but educational broadcasting will have separate facilities by 1975.

Basically, educational radio broadcasting is a functional system, backing up established school syllabi with broadcasts in four languages to primary and secondary schools. Subjects covered include music, history, geography, health education, religion, literature, and languages, plus a general civics education program aimed at fostering national unity.

The output of this system amounts to 80 programs for a total of 40 hours per week. The programs are in Bahasa Malaysia, English, Chinese, and Tamil. Listening to educational broadcasting are 2,328 out of 4,365 primary and 341 out of 735 secondary schools, or about 65% of the total schools. Sabah is the only state that does not receive school broadcasts, although it will in the near future.

Teachers' notes and manuals on how to use the broadcasts are supplied by the education ministry's utilization section. All states, except Sabah, have an education officer responsible for utilization and liaison. Schools are informed at the beginning of every school year of the times and content of the broadcasting service. Teachers are also asked to complete an annual questionnaire in which they can request particular types of programs. In case of timetable difficulties, teachers can wait for repeats, record off-transmission, or request tapes from the audio-visual aids section of the educational media service.

An educational television system began 19 June 1972 (see also §6.3.4). Although administered by the Ministry of Education, ETV is a joint service involving also the Ministry of Information and Broadcasting, which provides technical personnel and facilities, and the Ministry of Communications, responsible for transmission facilities. ETV is on the air four days a week with a daily output of 18 15–20 minute programs. In 1973, 2,500 schools were supplied with TV receivers; the number was expected to rise to 4,000 by the end of 1974. Schools without electricity have been provided with gasoline-driven generators (Dyer 1974, p. 21).

In late 1975, the Malaysian government announced that the World Bank had approved nearly M$1 million in loans for the 1976 introduction of educational television in Sarawak (*Malaysian Digest* 1975).

3.4.7 Training

Since December 1971, the department of broadcasting has had its own national broadcasting training center (NBTC), a venture which puts the country in the pioneering class among developing (and, for that matter, many developed) nations. The center is an ambitious project supported by UNESCO and the British Special Aid Loan Fund. It is housed in the former studios of TV Malaysia and has all the facilities of a broadcasting station with the exception of a transmitter.

In-service courses are offered to broadcasting personnel in both technical and program aspects of radio and TV. UNESCO has supplied four experts – in TV production, engineering, TV operations, and film – and courses last from a few days to three months.

By 1975, the center's new home, next to Angkasapuri, was expected to be ready, and the previous facilities were to be rebuilt with additional studios to accommodate the educational broadcasting service (see § §7.1.3 and 7.2). NBTC will have two TV studios (one for color), two radio studios, two continuities, seven classrooms, one large exhibition room, a hostel for 80 people and numerous other ancillary and technical facilities for training. The center will provide training in courses of 2 days to 12 weeks in length, to as many as 150 full-time and 500 part-time students per year (*COMBROAD* 1974a, p. 62). Courses will deal with production, presentation, operations, engineering, and other aspects of broadcasting to meet both national and international needs.

It is also planned to develop a regional experts service working out of Kuala Lumpur and thereby open certain courses to regional participants (see Balakrishnan 1974, pp. 22–24).

Broadcasting employs a high proportion of its personnel from Malaysia's three universities, one of which — Universiti Sains Malaysia — offers a degree in communication. Malaysia has also sent members of its broadcasting staff for training overseas, mainly to Britain and Australia.

3.4.8 East Malaysia

The East Malaysian states of Sarawak and Sabah, although separated from West Malaysia by a thousand miles of sea, are both served by the government broadcasting networks.

RTM broadcasts 328 hours weekly in Sarawak, 73½ of which are in Bahasa Malaysia, 57½ in Chinese, 50 in Iban, 55½ in English, 64 in Bidayuh, 1 in Melanau, 7 in Kayani/Kenyah, and 14 hours for the armed forces (Dyer 1974, p. 19). Entertainment predominates on programs broadcast in Bahasa Malaysia, 43%; Chinese, 54%; English, 61%; Iban, 52%; and Bidayuh, 31%. News is the second largest time consumer, accounting for 94% of all Kayani/Kenyah broadcasts, and between 21% and 31% of each of the broadcast totals of the other five languages.

In Sabah, Radio Malaysia in 1973 aired 126 hours weekly, 61.75 of which were in Bahasa Malaysia; 24.5 in English; 18, Chinese; 16.5, Kadazan; the remainder in Indonesian, Murat, and Bajau, plus 2.25 hours for the armed forces. Beginning in January 1974, Sabah radio and TV were ordered by the state's chief minister to broadcast only in Bahasa Malaysia and English in an effort to unite the various races (Abas 1974, p. 18). Entertainment makes up the largest proportion of the radio schedules in Sabah, news being second.

Sabah has had television service since 1971; Sarawak was scheduled to have its first TV in 1974. TV Malaysia, Sabah is a state-wide service covering about 85% of the state's population, with the main transmitting station in Kota Kinabalu and five regional stations. Programming for Sabah television is drawn from three main sources: Kuala Lumpur productions, making up 29.3% of telecast time; Sabah productions, 20.5%; and syndicated overseas films, 50.2%. Commercial television was introduced to Sabah in early 1972.

3.4.9 Pressures

Most of the pressures on broadcasting will be apparent from the foregoing, the biggest single factor being the government itself with all the sectional interests it represents. Obviously, with government in direct control, the system has to reflect and promote government activity. Yet, despite this essentially bureaucratic infrastructure, the character of the system at any given time depends considerably on the personality of the minister in charge. Thus, between 1971 and 1973, both radio and TV acquired a more dynamic image as a direct result of Tan Sri Ghazali Shafie taking over the ministry. He was responsible for making RTM a strong agency for the promotion of national development campaigns.

One immediately apparent change was the improvement in news programs, which until then had been subject to a rigid division between national and foreign items — ten minutes national followed by five minutes of foreign. This ratio was scrapped, and the impact and general credibility of the news programs increased. Still, in 1973–74, international news was used only if it had a bearing on Malaysia; thus Watergate merited very little TV attention whereas news of the Middle East war of October 1973 led off most telecasts. The priority system of presenting people in the news also holds; thus, any item about the Yang di–Pertuan Agong (King) leads the news bulletins, followed by the doings of other rulers, followed by the prime minister, deputy prime ministers, and so on, down the hierarchical line — all at the expense of what is happening in the world. As one publication reported, "the net effect is of a country divorcing itself from reality" (*FEER,* 22 July 1974; see Lent 1974b).

None of the changes should be seen as reflecting any increasing belief in "freedom of broadcasting"; rather they demonstrate a greater awareness of the communication process, and, probably more importantly, how it can be used to communicate a particular message. For reasons mentioned earlier, this is not necessarily a bad thing in Malaysian circumstances. The orthodox official rationale runs something like this: "We do not see that Western ideas of freedom have produced an ideal broadcasting system in the West; so why should they here, where the structure and problems of our society are entirely different anyway?" The result has been that broadcasting is given a major job of nation-building and the whole developmental process in a young country, and if this means some curtailment of freedom and an expansion of broadcasting as a propaganda medium, then so be it. The most significant trend in the early 1970s was the realization that the propaganda has to be good to be credible, which, one could argue, is better than bad propaganda with low credibility.

Similarly, freedom of speech in relation to broadcasting should be seen within the wider context of freedom of speech within Malaysian society as a whole. Here again, national objective have imposed limitations in the form of amendments to the Sedition Act prohibiting discussion of four sensitive issues: the position of Malay rulers, special constitutional rights of Malays, citizenship, and the position of the national language. These limitations are generally accepted — if only in the short term — as Malaysia's answer to what is uniquely a Malaysian problem. Thus, although no one can pretend that this is anything but a severe limitation of freedom of speech, the alternative would appear to be much worse (see Lent 1974b).

With such legislation, therefore, broadcasting has to toe the line, probably having even less freedom than printed media. Any political discussion is heavily authoritarian, and there is little live debate on serious issues. The audience is usually lectured rather than involved. An independent approach is inhibited and the better organized pressure groups – particularly Islamic religious leaders and the women's section of United Malays National Organisation, both generally progovernment – are able to make their voices forcefully heard.

Non-political sources exert much less pressure. In the monopolistic situation, advertisers are not in a strong position, although they usually are consulted, even if the decision normally goes against them. One must be careful, however, not to read too much of the "Big Brother" approach into what happens in Malaysian broadcasting. The program areas where limitations are in force make up only a small proportion of total program output, and the vast majority of programs are a catholic selection.

It would also be unfair not to acknowledge the problems facing what is, on the global scale, a small system attempting to purchase foreign programs. Package deals are the usual business transaction in renting programs, especially in markets where rental prices are relatively low. Thus, Malaysian broadcasters cannot be blamed totally for much of the program material which they had to accept from international distributors in order to get the program they really wanted.

It would be easy for the broadcasters to make this into an eternal apology for poor service, but fortunately, this is not the case. Despite being under direct government control, with all the pressures that brings, there is still a professional belief in public service broadcasting, almost on the lines of Lord Reith's BBC. The BBC ideal is still at the heart of the system, but just as the BBC had to change after Reith, so this system had to be "Malaysianized."

3.5 Singapore, *by Wong Soon Chong and Lian Fook Shin*

This city-state became self-governing in 1959 and formed part of Malaysia from 1963 to 9 August 1965. Since April 1959, Singapore has been led by Lee Kuan Yew and his People's Action Party, which have effected strong controls over all aspects of the society, including the mass media.

The Republic of Singapore is made up of 54 islands and approximately 2.2 million people, the overwhelming majority of whom (eight out of ten) are Chinese. The pluralistic society has faced problems concerning language and education policies, but in 1974 it was becoming more apparent that English would be the language to bind all races together, while the mother language of

Wong Soon Chong is Assistant Professor of Public Administration at Nanyang University, Singapore; chief editor, *Bulletin of Nanyang University;* and author of surveys on Singaporean mass media. He received the Doctorate du Troisième Cycle at Strasbourg.

Lian Fook Shin is Secretary-General, Center for Production and Training in Adult Education (CEPTA-TV), Singapore. He was the organizer and head of Singapore Educational Television, 1967, and a Colombo Plan fellow.

each ethnic group (Chinese, Indian, or Malay) would remain as part of the bilingual pattern.

Culturally, Lee Kuan Yew has been concerned that Singaporeans tend to imitate Western lifestyles. As the *Far Eastern Economic Review* reported in 1975, because of the news media and television programs, "Singaporeans were more aware of developments in western countries, as well as western life-styles, than they were of the realities of their Southeast Asian neighbours." A move against this tendency was reflected in a press bill which came into force 1 January 1975, requiring all Singapore newspapers to be controlled by Singaporeans and to be free of foreign influences.

Economically, Singaporeans are generally well-off, having an income per capita of $4,527 in 1973.

3.5.1   Background

Ironic as it might seem when looking at the government control over Singapore broadcasting now, the first radio station in this former British city-state was a private commercial organization, established in 1935 by the British Malaya Broadcasting Corporation. Transmissions commenced a year later, in June 1936. But this venture into private broadcasting ownership was short-lived, the firm and its complex being purchased by the Singapore government in 1940. For nearly a year, the service was operated as "Broadcasting Station, Posts and Telegraph Department, Singapore and Federated Malay States"; by April 1941, responsibility for the station had been assumed by the Malaya Broadcasting Corporation, a quasi-government enterprise jointly controlled by governments of the Straits Settlement and United Kingdom.

Following the fall of Singapore, the station came under the Japanese military administration from February 1942 to August 1945, during which time it was known as Syonan Hoso Kyoku. Then, after a short period under British military administration immediately following liberation, the service was taken over by the civil government, which in April 1946 inaugurated a medium-wave and short-wave service for the whole Malay peninsula. It was renamed "Radio Malaya, Singapore and Federation of Malaya," with Singapore as headquarters.

On achieving independence in 1957, the Federation of Malaya decided to set up its own broadcasting service, resulting in the split of Radio Malaya, with Singapore operating as Radio Singapore. The two services were amalgamated once again in August 1963, when Malaysia was formed. When Singapore became a republic on 9 August 1965, the Singapore station was redesignated Radio-Television Singapore (RTS), within the Department of Broadcasting, Ministry of Culture.

3.5.2   Facilities

As in numerous developing societies, the importance attached to broadcasting can be seen in the relatively modern plant and facilities the Singapore government is willing to provide. The main building of Radio Singapore, completed in late 1974, contains an auditorium which can accommodate 400 persons, nine general-purpose studios, six continuity studios/control rooms, a main control room, dubbing and editing rooms, a rehearsal room, and a tape and record library. The complex houses program, services, administration, and finance personnel.

Radio Singapore broadcasts four language services (Channel 1, English; Channel 2, Malay; Channel 3, Chinese; and Channel 4) on medium-wave, FM, and short-wave bands. Programs are fed to the transmitter at Jurong, on the western part of the island, by land lines, and the outputs of each of the four 5-kw. FM transmitters feed antennas on a common tower.

The television complex houses four TV production studios, with all related facilities; two continuity presentation studios and related administrative units; seven multiplex islands, telecine, tape/playback machines, as well as numerous other facilities, including two outside broadcasting vans for special events. A fifth studio was completed in 1975 for local TV productions (*Variety* 1975h, p. 116).

Television programs are transmitted by a transmitter at Bukit Batok, a hill about 300 feet above sea level. Television Singapore provides programs in four languages on two channels (5 and 8). Each channel uses two 5-kw. transmitters working in parallel to give an output power of 10 kw. The television service operates on the CCIR 625-line 50 Kc/s system.

Full color transmission was launched in mid-1974. TV newsreels went to color in November 1974 in the second stage of operation. The entire color-TV project is expected to cost about $8 million spread over five years. Color-TV sets have been installed in community centers throughout Singapore, and the sale of home sets exceeded all expectations during the first ten weeks of color transmission (*COMBROAD* 1974c, p. 58; see Tan 1974, pp. 37–39).

Singapore's SENTOSA satellite earth station was opened in October 1971. The station, which has TV transmit-and-receive facilities, is designed with two antennas, one tracking the Pacific Ocean satellite, the other the Indian Ocean satellite.

Besides facilities of Radio-Television Singapore, the nation is also served by Rediffusion (see §3.5.6) and British Forces Broadcasting Service Singapore, operated by the Singapore Ministry of Defense on behalf of the ANZUK Forces to provide a service of 80 hours weekly of entertainment and information. The British Forces Broadcasting is also designed to provide a link with home for Australian, British, and New Zealand forces stationed in Singapore (*WRTH* 1974, p. 168). In 1975, the BBC relay station, set up in Malaya in the 1940s, was moved to Singapore. It broadcasts the BBC World Service in English and 13 other languages (*Media* 1975a; *Media*, April 1975, p. 4).

3.5.3 Organization

Radio-Television Singapore is solely owned by the Singapore government and administered by the Department of Broadcasting within the Ministry of Culture.

The department is headed by a director of broadcasting and assisted by a deputy. Five major divisions exist in the department: commercial, programs, news, engineering, and administration.

Total staff of Radio-Television Singapore is 1,200, of whom 2.8% are executive, 41.3% professional, 16.2% general and clerical, 27.7% technical, and 12% office attendants and apprentices.

Two types of in-service training are offered RTS staff: courses for newly recruited staff and refresher courses for veteran personnel. Under the Colombo Plan, experts from Britain and Japan have assisted in such training. Besides giving in-service training, the department occasionally sends its staff abroad for further instruction. Many technicians are trained through Singapore Polytechnic, which between 1962 and 1972, turned out 472 graduates in the electronic and communications course. With the government announcement in 1972 that Singapore would have a color-television system by 1974, Polytechnic sent one of its lecturers to Holland to study color techniques. Polytechnic in 1973 was planning to introduce a part-time or evening course in color TV as an "endorsement" subject. Also, partly because of the introduction of color TV, a new Telecentre, for training telecommunications and broadcasting staffs, has been set up (*AMC Bulletin*, June 1973).

3.5.4 Programming

Programming for a multiracial, multilingual society is obviously difficult. For example, on television, subtitling is frequently necessary; there are programs in Chinese subtitled in English and English shows subtitled in Bahasa Malaysia. Each language service also presents programs meant to promote a better appreciation of the culture of the other linguistic streams. Apart from having to strike a balance in the use of four official languages — Malay, English, Mandarin, and Tamil — there is need to cater to the varying degrees of audience sophistication and tastes. This is true of radio but even more so of television.

Also, some programs are broadcast not because of their appeal and popularity, but because they are considered necessary for a developing society. Program contents stress racial tolerance, national cohesion, and unity. The electronic media are used to promote campaigns on such themes as "Keep Singapore Clean" and "Save Water," as an integral part of a comprehensive plan to inform and motivate. For example, RTS has lent its full support to the family-planning program by using spot announcements, indirect messages in youth, women, and worker shows and discussion programs, and by sponsoring oratorical contests on the subject for secondary schools (Liew 1975, pp. 38–39).

Being implored to use their facilities for such developmental campaigns, at the same time watching what happens to printed media that do not conform to Prime Minister Lee Kuan Yew's directives, RTS does not program much in the way of criticism. One source said the main complaint about Television Singapore is "in the more subjective areas of content, criticism and leadership";

government's policy of licensing and "guarding the integrity of the press" is no incentive toward independent editorial decisions (*Asian Presss* 1971, p. 147).

Radio-Television Singapore broadcasts programs not only in the four main languages, but also in the dialects of Mandarin, Hokkien, Cantonese, Teochew, Hakka, Foochow, and Hainanese. The target audience, the republic's 2.1 million people, is cosmopolitan, the main groupings being made up of 74% Chinese, 14.4% Malay, 8% Indian and Pakistani, and 3.2% other races (*Singapore Facts and Figures* 1970).

Radio broadcasts 525 weekly hours, 126 of which are in English, 132 in Malay, 112 in Tamil, 154, Chinese; television programs 106.5 hours per week, made up of approximately 37 hours each in English and Chinese, 21 in Malay, and 11 in Tamil. These figures do not correspond to population proportions, nor do they include the 52 hours given weekly for ETV programs. In January 1974, TV transmission was cut by 11 hours and radio by 21 hours weekly in a streamlining drive by the government (*Straits Times* 1973e). Included in the program schedules of each of radio's language services are commercials and sponsored programs; advertisements, however, are not permitted during news, public service, serious music, documentaries, and feature shows. On the English, Malay, and Tamil radio networks, popular variety shows take up the largest percentage of time, 62%, 57%, and 49.4%, respectively. The Chinese network devotes its largest share of time to art songs, 32.6%, followed by popular variety, 16.3% (see Table 20). FM stereo broadcasts amount to 56 hours weekly, comprising mainly classical and light classical fare presented in English and Chinese.

Table 20. Radio Singapore Programming by Language Networks (in percentages)

Program Category	English	Malay	Tamil	Chinese
Information and Education				
News	6.4	6.3	12	12
Social and General	6.7	9.7	5.4	5
Children's	4.2	2	2.7	4
Youth	2.4	4.5	3.2	4.8
Women	1	2.9	2.7	1
Religion	0.5	2.5	2.2	0.3
Arts	1.6	1.5	3.8	6
Entertainment				
Sports	1.4	1.4	1	1
Drama	5.2	5.7	3.6	17
Popular Variety	62	57	49.4	16.3
Art Songs	8.6	7.5	14	32.6
Total	100.0	100.0	100.0	100.0

The combined program schedules of Television Singapore show that, despite government's emphasis on developmental subjects (information and education), entertainment accounts for 73.7% of content. Drama is given the largest individual percentage of time, 54.6%; followed by variety, 13.5%; news and social and general information, 8.7% each; Chinese information, 5.2%; sports, 5.1%; family-type education, 3.2%; and education arts and serious art, 0.5% each.

Local productions account for about 40% of the total RTS program load, which is low compared with the 70% local output of Rediffusion, the privately owned wired service operating in Singapore. Imported programs are mostly North American; for example, the most popular television series in 1975 included "Hawaii Five-O" and "Mannix." Of the local efforts, "Chinese Variety Show," a potpourri of songs and dance, and "Pesta Pop" (Pop Festival), featuring Malay talent, have wide appeal. Few locally produced serious plays are scheduled, the occasional efforts being generally of poor standard. In our opinion, this lack is attributed to the dearth of scriptwriters and professional actors, caused by low talent fees, as well as the lack of even minimum training and development resources. Attempts were being made by RTS in 1973 to stimulate local productions, especially in Chinese, Malay, and Tamil. Again, because of insufficient talent, these plays are usually of the domestic situation type. TV Singapore makes its own family magazine shows — ranging from personality profiles to flower-arrangement demonstrations. Game shows and quizzes are taboo; the broadcasting officials want to maintain a low commercial profile and big commercial sponsors are seldom attracted (Koh 1975a, p. 58).

All imported programs are previewed by officials in the Department of Broadcasting. More rigid censorship is imposed on television than on commercial cinema fare; this precaution is considered necessary because television audiences have less control and discretion in the choice of programs. More tolerance, however, is shown regarding TV programs designed for adult viewing during the late evening. Hippieism, drug abuse and addiction, excessive brutality, bloodshed and violence, nudity and sex, and scenes offending other racial and religious sensitivities of a multicultural society are stringently censored (Lent 1975a). In 1974, mass media, especially television, were blamed for the increasing trend in violence, delinquency, and the pursuit of immediate pleasure and extravagance on the part of Singaporean youth. The Ministry of Health and Home Affairs Committee on Crime and Delinquency based its findings on statistics available in government agencies such as the Prisons Department and Reformative Training Center (Singapore, Ministry of Health and Home Affairs, 1974). As a result of governmental concern about violence, Television Singapore is airing fewer U.S.-originated police and private-eye shows than most stations of the region (see Koh 1975b, p. 116). Only "Toma," "Harry O," "Mannix," and "The Streets of San Francisco" remained in mid-1975. Mondays, Tuesdays, and Fridays are violent-free on Television Singapore. Other U.S. programs have stayed in prime time, such as "Medical Center," "Rhoda," "The Six Million Dollar Man," "I Love Lucy," "Gomer Pyle," "The Waltons," etc. English-speaking viewers prefer United States over British entertainment shows. Because a growing number of Singaporeans prefer British documentary and serious drama, shows such as "The Ascent of Man," "The Scientist," "World at War," and "Discovery" are being shown. In 1975, 26% of the program output at Television Singapore was made up of documentaries (Koh 1975a, p. 58).

Acquisitions of special programs, especially those not on the regular Southeast Asian circuit, are few since the local station can only offer moderate rates. There is an attempt to diversify sources of supply; during an average week, Television Singapore programs originate from no fewer than ten countries. With a limited budget of $1.2 million yearly for program acquisition, the best buys were still American in 1975 (Koh 1975a, p. 58).

An interesting feature of RTS is a central production unit to deal with civics and international affairs programs. Current affairs relevant to the local scene are produced both for radio and television and are presented as features, talks, interviews, discussions, and documentaries. Current-affairs programs are usually allocated prime time. The central production unit has an exchange agreement with Asian Broadcasting Union (ABU) members for TV films and ASEAN nations, to whom it dispatches 15-minute radio tapes on agreed topics. Material received from ABU members is compiled into a half-hour "ABU Magazine."

3.5.5 Financing

Radio-Television Singapore operates on an allocation voted annually. The 1972–73 Singapore government estimates list an expected revenue of $5.85 million from the following sources: radio advertising, $446,429; television commercials, $2,678,571; Rediffusion license fees, $10,714, and radio-TV licenses, $2,714,286. Radio receiver license fees are $4 yearly; TV, $13. In January 1973, there were 280,809 radio sets licensed and 207,995 television receivers.

For its operating expenditure, which includes staff emoluments, production, and other recurrent and special items, RTS received a government allocation of $4,544,200 for 1972–73. As the staff emoluments alone amount to over half the allotment, $2,315,700, the balance does not really provide abundantly for the complex operations expenditure at RTS.

3.5.6 Rediffusion

Rediffusion (Singapore) Pte. Ltd., a privately owned wired system, commenced radio broadcasting in 1949 under government franchise. A branch of Rediffusion International of London, the Singapore outlet maintains ten recording studios and two wired networks. The services ("Gold" in Chinese; "Silver" in Chinese and English) utilize over 2,500 miles of cable, serving about 63,000 subscribers, over 97% of whom are Chinese. Two simultaneous programs originating in the Rediffusion studios are fed continuously from 6 A.M. to midnight daily. Rediffusion provides programs, over 80% of which are entertainment-oriented, in Malay, English, and Chinese dialects, mainly Mandarin, Hokkien, and Cantonese. Rediffusion in Singapore has close ties with similar operations in Hong Kong, Kuala Lumpur, and Penang; as a result, a great deal of interchange of Chinese program occurs.

Rediffusion's main source of revenue is the collection of a monthly rental fee of $2.50 for the installation of a loudspeaker in a subscriber's home.

3.5.7 Educational Television

Educational Television Service, an independent unit of the education ministry, initiated its transmissions 30 January 1967. ETV programs are videotaped and transmitted via Channel 8 of Television Singapore from 7:50 A.M. to 5:30 P.M. intermittantly Mondays through Fridays, and 8:10–11 A.M. on Saturdays.

During the first year, programming was directed to the 12 to 13 age group of the lower secondary schools, mainly in the areas of general science, mathematics, English as a second language, geography, civics, English literature, and national language. The service has since introduced programs for pre-university students, as well as subject areas for primary schools. In 1974, about 80,000 secondary students and 200,000 primary-school pupils followed the programs (Seow 1974, pp. 29–30). Except for English literature, mathematics, and science, which are broadcast in English, all lessons have Malay, Mandarin, or English versions. To overcome class scheduling problems, programs are repeated several times within the week. In 1973, the total hours of transmission amounted to 26 hours weekly; the figure was 52 hours weekly in 1974.

The on-syllabus, direct teaching approach, especially for science and mathematics series, is aimed at supplementing teachers' efforts as well as bringing about qualitative improvement in instructional techniques. Primary schools' programs are meant to enrich and promote incidental learning. Sets of teachers' guides, charts, and other teaching materials are often produced to support ETV programs. Each school is equipped with at least one free television receiver, but the individual schools are encouraged to purchase additional sets from their own budgets.

Broad guidelines, especially in regard to the choice of subject areas for programming, have been laid down by an advisory committee, made up of subject specialists, school inspectors, and representatives from schools and the Teachers' Training College, where the ETV facilities are located. The normal procedure in developing ETV programs is that after the advisory committee meets, a number of smaller sub-committees are formed to work out contents of individual programs and in particular their relationship to the school curriculum. Feedback is obtained through visits to schools by ETV producers, reports by school principals and inspectors, and data-processed evaluation returns. Since its inception, ETV has been recording its programs in temporary premises, limited by inadequate facilities.

Still in the process of growth, the ETV service plans in the 1970s to construct a new studio complex with modern technical and production facilities. Also, it is envisaged that the ETV service will become part of a new Singapore Educational Media Service (SEMS), an agency providing coordinated educational media facilities for schools and other institutions in Singapore (see also Green 1972, p. 244).

3.6   Indonesia, *by K. E. Eapen and John A. Lent*

Indonesia has had cultural implants dating at least to the 7th century, when Hindu and Buddhist kingdoms, inspired by Indian culture, arose in Sumatra and Java. By the 14th century, Islam had achieved a foothold in the nation, and in the 1500s the Portuguese established settlements during their searches for spices. The Dutch replaced the Portuguese a century later and stayed until evicted by the Japanese in 1942. In a left-handed way, the Japanese were benevolent occupiers, fostering nationalism; upon Japan's surrender, Indonesia declared its independence from the Dutch on 17 August 1945. Sukarno became president of the new republic which fought against Holland until a unitary state was proclaimed 15 August 1950. Sukarno's government was ended by a military takeover by President Suharto in mid-1966. In 1974, the government faced numerous tests to its political and economic stability, with the result that the military influence gradually waned, and freedom of expression, which had flourished briefly, came to an end.

Indonesia is an archipelago of 13,667 islands, of which nearly 3,000 are inhabited. Their total land area is 735,000 square miles, 25 times as big as the Netherlands which ruled them. Geographically, Indonesia can be split into two halves – the western (Java, Borneo, Sumatra, etc.) and eastern (Celebes, Timor, Ambon, Maluku, Irian Jaya or West Irian, etc.). Five land masses dominate the islands: Java, Kalimantan (Borneo), Sumatra, Sulawesi (Celebes) and West Irian. Java alone has nearly two-thirds of the national population on only about 5% of the land area. Yet, Kalimantan and West Irian, with a combined 5% of the population, share between them half of the land. The islands are spread over 3,200 miles.

Of Indonesia's 129 million people, 85% are Muslim, nearly 10% Christian, 2% Hindu and Buddhist, and the rest, other religions. The nation has scores of ethnic groups and languages; Sukarno's major contribution, in fact, was in tying together these diversities by making Bahasa Indonesia the national link language. Economically, the nation has not been well-off; in 1973–74, the estimated income per capita was $100.

3.6.1   Radio Background

Radio in Indonesia dates to the colonial period when, because of the difficulties of cable communication, the Dutch administration sought new ways of keeping in touch with the Netherlands during World War I. These plans did not materialize until after the war when the Malabar radio telecommunication system was developed in Bandung. The system, owned by the government Post, Telephone, and Telecommunication, stimulated interest in radio elsewhere in

K. E. Eapen is Head of the Department of Communication, Bangalore (India) University; former Director of the Zambia-Indonesia Research Project, Centre for Mass Communication Research, Leicester, England. He has conducted research in Indonesia, India, Zambia, UK, and the U.S. He was formerly journalism department chairman in India; a journalist in the U.S. and India; and the author of a monograph on communication in Zambia and Indonesia. He received his Ph.D. at the University of Wisconsin.

Java, leading to a number of experiments in Bandung, Batavia (now Jakarta), Jogjakarta, Semarang, Solo, and Surabaja, all for purposes of point-to-point radio communication.

The first broadcast of music and entertainment was attempted by Bataviase Radio Vereniging (BRV) on 16 June 1925, from a hotel room in Batavia. Programs in the Dutch language went on the air for three hours daily. In 1933, Sultan Pangeran Mangkunegara VII sponsored the first Indonesian-language broadcasts from Surakarta through Solose Radio Verenging (SRV). These broadcasts were intended to promote Javanese music, arts, and *wayang* (shadow play) programs. Earlier, in 1930, the colonial government had issued a license for a government-sponsored station, Netherlandsch-Indische Radio Omroep (NIROM), which soon after had branch stations in a number of Indonesian urban centers.

A 1964 UNESCO report provided this description of NIROM's development:

The purpose of NIROM was to maintain communications between the Dutch citizens living in the Netherlands East Indies and their homeland and to disseminate information by the Dutch administration and to introduce Western culture. For this purpose, many relay stations were established and listeners' fees collected. For the Dutch wishing to keep in touch with their homeland, short-wave receivers were imported.

During these years, the Indonesian national radio organizations operated under restrictions. For example, a maximum ceiling of 250 watts on transmitting power of stations existed and they were allowed frequencies only between 60 and 150 metre bands. These organizations were stationed in Djakarta, then Batavia (VORO), Bandung (VORL), Soerabaya (SRV), Jogjakarta (MAVRO) and Semarang. These stations were later merged into one body, the PPRK, with its head office in Djakarta. They continued in operation until 1942. [UNESCO 1964, part II-4, p. 5]

Another source reported that during 1933–36, Indonesian listeners in Java's main cities formed radio associations to organize Indonesian-language broadcasting "based on Oriental culture." In 1938, these groups amalgamated and received a government subsidy (Agassi 1969, p. 53).

When the Japanese occupied Indonesia in 1942, they reorganized the whole broadcasting structure, setting up Hoso Kanry Kyoku (HKK) in Jakarta. HKK had branches in all Javanese towns, as well as in towns such as Padang and Makassar on the major islands. The occupying forces tried to limit audiences to use of authorized receivers pretuned to Japanese-controlled stations. Regular news, commentaries, and general programs from HKK and its satellite stations were carefully controlled, except for items dealing with the arts and culture. The Japanese occupation years of 1942–45 yielded many opportunities for Indonesians to better acquaint themselves with the radio medium, which they began to use effectively for the propagation of nationalism. Agassi has credited the Japanese with modernizing Indonesian broadcasting, pointing out that the number of sets increased from 108,520 in 1941 to 213,038 a decade later

(Agassi 1969, p. 54).

The Japanese also introduced public radio, meaning loudspeakers that were installed in public places to blare all day the occupier's proclamations and other messages. It is not known when this system collapsed, but it made a reappearance — although on a much smaller scale — during Sukarno's "Guided Democracy" period, especially in the early 1960s. The Sukarno system was operated by district government officers or village headmen and propagated news, announcements, and frequent speeches of the "Great Leader of the Revolution" (Agassi 1969, p. 113). In 1956, 3,806 wired receivers were reported in the republic; by 1962, the number was up to 9,256, falling to 6,336 in 1963, and eventually disappearing. By the 1970s, they were replaced by armed-forces mobile loudspeakers, which on special occasions such as opening of parliament or special presidential speeches took the messages around large cities and crowded night fairs and markets.

The political leadership of the country declared independence from the Dutch on 17 August 1945; shortly after, Indonesian employees in the stations took over the transmitters. On 11 September 1945, a conference of radio representatives met in Jakarta and formed Radio Republik Indonesia (RRI). Eight months later, RRI was recognized as a government body by the information ministry. RRI broadcasting became an important weapon in the hands of the nationalists, the station claiming its purpose was to serve the "Revolution," the 'five-year struggle with the Dutch after independence was declared.

RRI added 21 stations to those the Japanese built, but with Dutch reoccupation of Java, these stations were confiscated. RRI went underground, broadcasting from mountain regions with mobile transmitters, until December 1949, when the Dutch transferred *de jure* powers to the national leadership.

By 1955, RRI had 25 domestic and 8 overseas transmitters; the resultant programming was designed to air nationalistic and anti-Western ideology. A year earlier, to guarantee that the main currents in Indonesian society were not neglected by RRI and to help the information ministry in improving program quality, a Broadcasting Advisory Council was formed. The council consisted of leading artists, cultural leaders, educationalists, and religious and social leaders (*Asian Press* 1971, p. 96).

By 1964, Indonesia had 38 broadcasting stations with a total power of 600 kw. Included among these were 1 central station in Jakarta, 3 inter-island, 28 regional, regional/local, or local only, and 6 stations in the planning stage. Only 30–40% of Indonesia could receive radio clearly at that time, primarily because the stations could not reach all islands (UNESCO 1964).

Four years later, RRI was broadcasting on three stations for the Jakarta area: "Ibu Kota" (Capital City), "Nasional," and "Chusus," the latter using specialized programs oriented toward the military and police. The stations were on the air 15, 12, and 10 hours daily, respectively, in 1968. In addition, Chusus broadcast a *wayang* from 11 P.M. Saturday to 6 A.M. Sunday. All three initiated broadcasting at 6 A.M., and Ibu Kota and Nasional took breaks between 3 and 5 P.M., Chusus from 8 A.M. to 3 P.M. Radio Ibu Kota broadcast the largest proportion of news and announcements: three hours dividied into 14 programs, ten of which were relayed from Sentral, the central RRI studio in Jakarta. On all three Jakarta stations, music fare predominated. This may have been a reaction to the Sukarno years when, until December 1966, Western music was prohibited as being degenerate and unpatriotic (Agassi 1969, p. 58). But in recent years, RRI stations broadcast at least twice as much Indonesian music as they do Western. Most of the rest of the programming, even in the 1970s, included the usual radio fare — quizzes, serials, talks, and shows designed for special audiences of children, teenagers, women, farmers, and scouts. Discussion, panel, and background news programs were rare. In the late 1960s, only Chusus carried a daily political commentary, and it was written by *Ang Jatan Bersendjata,* the main military daily.

In 1968, RRI was not airing political broadcasts, whether government speeches or political party broadcasts. Of course, during Sukarno's reign, his speeches, slogans, and campaigns dominated long broadcasting segments. According to Agassi, "at least during the weeks of January and February 1968, the Suharto regime seemed to make little use of it for explicit political or economic communication with the masses"; she went on to say, however, that at crucial times of the postcoup era, after 1965, as well as on national holidays, political, economic, and military leaders did use RRI to get across their messages (Agassi 1969, p. 59).

3.6.2 Facilities and Audience

In the early 1970s, there were in Indonesia about 50 RRI stations and nearly 100 Radio Daerah (regional government) stations, the latter set up by provincial administrations. Radio Daerah stations usually relay RRI news but otherwise originate their own programming. In addition, the Voice of Indonesia, RRI's overseas arm, broadcast ten hours daily in Arabic, Chinese, Dutch, English, French, Hindi, Urdu, and Indonesian, beaming mainly to Southeast Asia, Middle East, Europe, and the Pacific Islands. RRI, controlled by the Ministry of Information, has its transmitters and studios distributed among six major islands. The local/regional stations operate more or less independently, producing many of their own programs. National programs originating from Jakarta are also relayed by the local regional stations. While such national items are in Indonesian, the local/regional stations tend to produce many of their own programs in local languages and dialects. In effect, the only attempt at networking relates to national news. Emanating from Jakarta the national news is picked up by the Nusantara (Archipelago) stations and retransmitted. Despite the multitude of microwave links covering most of Indonesia, there is little attempt to utilize these facilities. Actually, the networking of national news from Jakarta to Nusantara II in Jogjakarta (1,300 miles away) is achieved by fairly primitive means. A mantel-model radio, tuned to RRI Jakarta on short-wave, receives the transmission in Jogjakarta. The program is then jacked into the operational mixer and retransmitted simultaneously.

RRI utilizes short-wave and tropical-wave for its domestic transmissions, one of the few nations in the world to do so. Because of geographical distances, the spread of over 3,000 islands, and tropical interference, medium-wave is not technically suitable, and large areas of the islands still cannot receive clear signals. There is a plan, however, to reequip RRI with medium-wave transmitters on a nation-wide basis. It was due to be implemented in 1972, but was postponed because of financial and technical problems. On 4 August 1975, the U.S.-based Harris Corporation, in a news release, announced it had signed a $20 million agreement with the Indonesian government to develop a nation-wide radio broadcasting system. The contract called for Harris to supply 10-kw. and 50-kw. transmitters, antenna towers, and related equipment at 36 separate sites along the island chain. Stations were due on the air in 1976.

Because the present short-wave coverage is inadequate, a number of foreign broadcasts, beaming in Indonesian, are very popular. In eastern Indonesia, where RRI signals are particularly weak, the Australian Broadcasting Commission's "Radio Australia Service" attracts wide audiences. Radio Australia provides a varied range of programs in Indonesian. Its service's popularity in Indonesia can be judged from mail feedback; of 17,000 foreign letters which Radio Australia received in January 1971, over 45% originated in Indonesia. Letters showed the most popular Radio Australia programs were "As You Like It," "Contact with Listeners," "Morning Show," and "Children's Programme."

Using the island of Flores as a small case study, one can readily see the importance of having programs to back up those of RRI in these far-removed areas. A priest residing on Flores told Eapen that RRI reception is often bad there and that the most popular station is Radio Australia. The people there like Radio Australia's light programs, especially for their humor and handling of ordinary situations. The whole island of 2.5 million people probably has no more than two cinema houses, and because of this lack of entertainment, the islanders are not searching for heavy fare as they fiddle with their radio knobs.

Indonesians also depend greatly on Radio Netherlands. The colonial links help Radio Netherlands produce attractive material in the national language. Many Indonesians appreciate the fact that, unlike RRI, which has a tendency to shift and rearrange programs without notice, Radio Netherlands sticks to its schedule. BBC picks up a number of listeners in Indonesia, especially from the elites and students. Even though Radio Republik Indonesia and Telivisi Republik Indonesia (TVRI) broadcast English-language instructional lessons, many students prefer programs from England for their authenticity in pronunciation. Of course, BBC's strong signal is also attractive.

Such large proportions of a national population listening to other countries' programs should spur the Indonesian government to action regarding transmitter facilities. In 1969, to increase its listening area, RRI boosted its total transmitting power to 2,000 kw., but adequate reception is still far from nation-wide because of weak transmitters, old and inadequate studio facilities, the lack of electricity in rural areas, and the high costs of radio sets, the latter because of high taxes levied on them. Agassi said the license fee of R. 10 ($.03) is insignificant in comparison (Agassi 1969, p. 56). Also, there is a shortage of spare parts and maintenance skills. For example, a 50 kw. transmitter opened in Jogjakarta in 1970 operated for only two weeks before the main valves gave out, and the transmitter has not functioned since.

The number of radio sets, to the extent ascertainable from official license records, increased from 960,502 in 1963, to 1,366,999 in 1966, and 3,191,209 in 1968. In 1971, the total number of licensed radio sets was estimated as 3.5 million, which, according to government reports, represented only 60% of the 5.85 million assumed to be in the country. Exact figures of even licensed sets are difficult to obtain because in 1969 regional registration was introduced and Jakarta has not always been promptly informed about the number of sets registered in outlying areas. Nearly 700,000 licensed sets existed in Jakarta in 1971, with an estimated additional 500,000 unlicensed. In 1975, UNESCO estimated the number of radio receivers at 13,796,277, and TV receivers, 208,968 (UNESCO 1975, p. 281). A thriving smuggling operation, increased local production of radio sets, and an improved rural economy were among the many reasons given for these increases in set ownership.

Of course, another phenomenon that spurred the increased number of radio sets was the transistor radio. Its impact in Indonesia, however, has not been as significant as in many other Asian nations, because the cost of a transistor radio is still a major expenditure, amounting to at least the equivalent of a mid-level government official's monthly salary, if bought legally. Thus, although transistor radios have been important in increasing the number of radio owners in urban centers, they have not penetrated deeply into rural areas (see Crawford 1967).

3.6.3 News and Commentary

A majority of news programs broadcast over individual RRI outlets, as well as non-RRI stations (see §3.6.4), emanate from the central RRI office in Jakarta. RRI depends almost solely on Antara, the national news service, doing very little of its own newsgathering and monitoring. A daily mimeographed "Bulletin Radio," disseminated by RRI's central office, includes texts for most of the news programs broadcast throughout the nation.

In a news survey carried out by Agassi in 1968, she found that only three of 112 daily items on "Bulletin Radio" dealt with political news commentary — all concerning Communist threats to other countries. According to Agassi, "Domestic political news is reported and commented on rather vaguely and sketchily, either quoting vague and sketchy editorials from the press, or in the form which is also typical of the Indonesian press — by quoting statements and speeches of political figures, regional governors and military commanders" (Agassi 1969, p. 101).

Analysis of a provincial RRI station in Jogjakarta revealed news programs were relatively long and varied and included some local newscasts. Local institutions, the government among them, had their own shows on Jogjakarta RRI, and about one and a half hours was programming from Sentral in Jakarta.

3.6.4 Amateur and Commercial Stations

About 324 amateur and commercial transmitters were spread over Indonesia in 1972, many of them in Jakarta. Their owners have licenses from the telecommunication and information departments, based on approval from governors of the areas concerned. Many of the so-called "amateur" broadcasting units are one-man, single-room operations; half are estimated to be Christian-owned and operated. Some of the non-RRI transmitters are located in the Indonesian universities; some in commercial enterprises.

Amateur stations first made their appearance in 1966, brought about chiefly by the new freedom and involvement many youth felt after Sukarno's overthrow. At first, the authorities did not interfere with these stations, staffed voluntarily by college and high-school students, as well as members of numerous other groups. When the stations were required to register with the regional military command after 1968 and pay registration fees of up to Rp. 60,000 ($144) yearly, the number declined. In 1968, the military authorities of Jakarta raided Kami (Students' Action Front), the most important political station, because it was critical of Suharto (Agassi 1969, p. 60). Actually, although the stations are labeled "amateur," they cannot universally be described as such; in fact, some are more professional in program design and presentation than RRI stations.

Amateur stations operate on short-wave and medium-wave, the government allowing them only 100 w. power on short-wave, 500 w. for medium-wave. At least one, ITB in Bandung, is FM. These stations usually reach an audience limited to the cities in which they are located. So, outside urban centers, only RRI and foreign stations can usually be received. By 1968, three very popular amateur stations in West Irian (now called Irian Jaya) competed seriously with RRI; two were operated by regional police and military commands, the third by the national oil company.

Many private outlets broadcast from morning until midnight. Because of the lack of local talent and high production costs, many rely heavily on recorded music and free tapes offered by Sanggar Prathivi, a Catholic radio production unit.

In metropolitan Jakarta, a distinct diversity in broadcasting patterns is emerging from private studios. For example, the commercial stations, called Elshinta and Nanggala, serve different audiences; the former is generally patronized by older people, the latter by youth. Nanggala pours out beat music, played by screaming disc jockeys; Elshinta tends to be traditional, broadcasting sweet songs that reflect traditional Indonesian culture. The Indonesian Air Force has operated its own commercial station on the RRI premises in Jakarta, and Saura Kebehasan (Voice of Freedom), another commercial station, was popular in Jakarta in the late 1960s.

3.6.5 Rural Broadcasts

The radio farm forum technique was formally accepted in Indonesia in July 1969 during a national seminar sponsored by the Food and Agricultural Organization, under the auspices of the Indonesian departments of agriculture and information. Farm broadcasting began on 24 September of the same year (see Eschenbach 1970 and 1971). By January 1972, over 4,800 listeners' groups functioned in the nation, about 3,000 of which were in Java, another 800 in Sumatra. Total broadcasting time was 165 hours weekly, split between RRI (87 hours) and regional (78 hours) studios. Forty-two of the 50 RRI studios and 62 of the nearly 100 regional studios participated in these efforts. During the period July 1969 to April 1971, 113 extension officers and 51 program producers were specially trained for the project. The broadcasts include market reports, price reports of some primary commodities, weather forecasts, on-the-spot interviews, and panel discussions. There have been a number of criticisms of the Indonesian rural radio forums, one of which bears on the apparent lack of understanding among the three principal participants as to their roles. For example, the rural audience is not necessarily a homogeneous group; the scientists lack coordination because they hail from many departments to cover the wide range of subjects, and the broadcasters sometimes do not see the significance of this highly specialized task.

Eapen's findings, after examining a few community listening centers, show that not enough listening groups exist to cover certain areas adequately. Where community sets have been installed, they are not always available to community members. Oftentimes, village leaders treat the sets as personal possessions. This finding has been supported recently by an evaluation made by the German Technical Cooperation Team in Farm Broadcasting, stationed in Jogjakarta and Jakarta. The team found that the 1974 statistic of over 12,000 registered listening groups was highly inflated, that, in fact, more than a third of the groups no longer existed and another 10% were inactive. They attributed the loss of momentum of Indonesian radio farm forums partly to the availability of inexpensive transistor radios, making individual listening more possible. They concluded:

The trend towards individual listening is such that many listening groups which were previously meeting weekly now seldom meet more than once or twice a month. These findings suggest that parallel to the increase of radio ownership in villages the incentives for group listening will diminish further in the future. [Hilbrink and Lohmann 1974, p. 38]

Eapen's observations of Indonesian radio farm forums led him to conclude that there was no research showing cause-effect relationships between listening to the programs and carrying out their messages; that the forums lacked dedicated, trained personnel, effective feedback machinery, adequate transmissions in signal, production and design, and proper timing suitable for farmers' work habits. Finally, she said, Indonesia has not shown much interest in learning from the experience of countries such as India, where success has been claimed for rural radio forums.

3.6.6 Educational Broadcasting Experiments

Schools broadcasting in Indonesia has occurred spontaneously in several areas since 1966. These embryonic attempts at the development of a middle-level technological innovation were probably stimulated by experience gained by Indonesian educators while studying abroad. Although uniformly unsophisticated and pedantic, these initial efforts served as indicators of an awareness of the potential value of radio in education. With the return of Indonesia to the United Nations in the late 1960s, educational reform and development became important, and educational radio was seen as one means to obtain rapid advancement in both areas. The need was shown for experimentation in mass delivery of educational innovation in Indonesia, and Koch (1968) specified the means for achieving it. With the continued influence of UNESCO consultants, and from experience gained by Indonesian educators working with the Australian Broadcasting Commission in 1970, a plan for experimentation evolved, and several experiments were actually begun.

Jogjakarta experiment. Various educators had dabbled in schools broadcasting in Jogjakarta from about 1966. In late 1972 studio construction was begun using local funds, and the Jogjakarta studio was equipped the following year with advanced recording equipment provided by UNICEF. With assistance from UNESCO in the form of training abroad, contracts with research institutes to prepare the experimental design, and expertise through visiting and resident consultants, the experiment was begun.

Many delays have occurred, mainly because of the complexity of the relationship between a centrally controlled experiment (under the Office of Educational Development in Jakarta) and the semiautonomous regional directorate of education. Other problems, relating to the nonexistence or breakdown of financing and personnel policies, have affected the preparation. Experimental programs have been recorded, however, and a full-scale start was planned for January 1974. Transmission was to be through RRI's Nusantara II station in Jogjakarta; the first programs were to cover the subject areas of English for junior high school, Bahasa Indonesia, social science, and music singing. Language programs are scheduled to be broadcast twice weekly, the others once a week.

In the initial stages, approximately 200 schools will participate, involving 2,500 students. Schools will be supplied with radio sets and teachers' and pupils' notes.

Semarang experiment. A much more complex experiment is taking shape in Semarang. Many of the technical and policy problems are similar to those in Jogjakarta, but the different emphasis at Semarang has caused new difficulties. Recognizing that the majority of Indonesian elementary-school teachers are not qualified to teach at the level at which they are employed, the experiment is aimed at upgrading them *in situ*. The mechanical problems are those common to most developing countries — poor ground communications hampering materials delivery, ineffective servicing, insufficient incentive, and competition for the teachers' interest. Many, in fact most, Indonesian teachers have at least one second job, usually teaching at another school.

The major problem at Semarang has been trying to reach agreement on methodology. There are many experiments in educational change and development in process in Indonesia, and the educational aims and methodology employed are not always compatible. As a result, there has been some confusion about what the broadcasts should try to do, though there is general agreement about how it is to be done. A final decision was made in late 1973, and the so-called "demonstration" method, as practised in the Malang Teachers College, is to be the basis for program design and presentation. From a Western educational view, the method is extremely conservative, even old-fashioned. In Indonesian terms, it is a revolutionary change. Programs, to be broadcast thrice weekly during school hours and repeated at night, will present the justification for the suggested methodology, illustrated in a variety of ways with actual and studio-produced lessons.

As is the case in Jogjakarta, the intention is to conduct the experiment along fairly tightly controlled lines. Experimental and control groups are being set up, and from the results of an evaluation, a determination will be made whether to proceed with the educational broadcasts. This in itself is a dangerously short-sighted view, since the criteria for evaluation are to be arbitrarily applied.

Irian Jaya project. Under FUNDWI (United Nations administered fund for the development of West Irian), a small-scale educational broadcasting project has been carried out. Some 1,000 radio sets have been distributed and 400 more will shortly follow, so that all elementary schools in Irian Jaya will have a receiver. The broadcasting has been directed toward improving the skills of the elementary teachers. An integrated program of methodology, pedagogy, and general educational content has been prepared and transmitted. At the end of 1973, an examination was administered to the participating teachers; those who passed it received promotion to a higher professional level.

Now that FUNDWI is terminating, the Irian Jaya educational broadcasting project will come under the control of Jakarta. This means a reduction in independence of operation and an increase of competition with other projects for funds. Schools broadcasts were planned to commence in Irian Jaya in 1974.

Generally, the pace of development of educational broadcasting in Indonesia has been agonizingly slow. There is a deep-seated caution, based on the fear of being associated with failure, which has made educational reform a tedious and tenuous experience. Constantly under pressure from international and bilateral aid programs, the Indonesians have maintained an imperturbable pace. Regrettably, this may rebound because the problems — growing numbers of out-of-school children, larger teacher-pupil ratios, inflation of building and service costs, and an increasingly uncommitted teacher force — will overtake and overwhelm them unless mass improvement of education and mass delivery (educational broadcasts) are adopted.

3.6.7 Christian Broadcasting

Since the demise of colonial rule, the Pacasila climate has encouraged the use of Radio Republik Indonesia by many religious groups. Pacasila, created by Sukarno and adopted by Suharto, is the national ideology, a set of five principles on which Indonesians should pattern their lifestyles. One of the principles concerns religion, i.e., belief in one God. Both RRI and non-RRI stations have provided different time slots for use by various religious groups, but, partly because of a lack of professional radio personnel, the religious programs have been mostly sermons, readings, songs, and talks, presented oftentimes in a boring fashion. In the more recent preparation and presentation of Christian programs on RRI, great care has been taken to offer fewer "churchy" items and more drama, dialogue, features, and Indonesian cultural formats.

With both a Christian and Catholic political party in Indonesia, divergent attitudes on the use of broadcasting for religion are to be expected. While Protestants have many transmitting and studio facilities, the Catholics have concentrated on the production unit Sanggar Prathivi in Jakarta. Started in 1966, Sanggar Prathivi has grown to be the best studio of its kind in Indonesia. Recognizing Indonesia's fairly wide transmission facilities and poor quality programming, Sanggar Prathivi's sponsors emphasized software aspects of broadcasting. For example, to produce better programs, they hired some of the best talent available, paying well in turn. In the more immediate future, Sanggar Prathivi will probably initiate more production centers in outer islands to capture the flavor of those areas, will continue to seek or train the best personnel available, and make use of its adequate transmission channels, rather than build new facilities. As for government control, Sanggar Prathivi scripts for RRI are approved by broadcast officials in Jakarta. This does not imply censorship, but does provide an assurance to government that inflammatory and emotional items are not aired over government broadcasting.

The manner in which the Indonesian government and other agencies use Sanggar Prathivi radio-TV production facilities shows how a communication subsystem may emerge to mutual advantage of the system, as well as the nation. Perhaps Sanggar Prathivi offers a model for other Asian countries in the use of independently produced quality programming.

3.6.8 Television

Television came to Indonesia in 1962 when the Asian Games, held in Jakarta that year, were the first major event to be televised. Telivisi Republik

Indonesia (TVRI) started with one station in Jakarta, telecasting about eight hours weekly, half of the programs devoted to live speeches or other political events, the remainder to documentaries. The Japanese lent support to the development of Indonesian television.

From the outset, TVRI was a government monopoly, subordinate to the director-general of radio, television, and film in the Ministry of Information. As such, the broad policies of television in Indonesia are laid down by the Ministry of Information, while day-to-day operations are handled by the director of television and station managers. As an arm of government, TVRI is entrusted with communicating government policies and programs to the public. This function was evident during the "Guided Democracy" of the early 1960s when TVRI concentrated on programming "patriotic-political-propagandist" items (Agassi 1969, p. 104). Today, television is expected to portray government policies that aim at "building a modern, just and prosperous society where the people enjoy a degree of well-being, in a physical-material sense, as well as in a mental-spiritual way" (Sumadi 1971, p. 2).

In 1974, Indonesia had 12 TV transmitters (five main, seven relay) providing coverage to the island of Java (with stations in Jakarta, Jogjakarta, Bandung, and Semarang), North Sumatra (Medan), South Sumatra (Palembang), and South Sulawesi (Ujung Padang). Other transmitters are in the cities of Gantungan, Cirebon, Surabaya, Cemarasewu, and Balikpapan.

Stations are financed by license fees on sets, advertising, and government subsidy. Factors limiting the extension of television services in Indonesia include the size and disperseness of the nation, mountainous terrain, and the absence of electricity in rural areas. Another limitation is the expense of television for such a poverty-stricken nation as Indonesia. For example, speaking in 1974, the information minister said the country could not introduce color television because the nation could not afford it (*Media,* October 1974). (In mid-1975, however, Indonesia signed a $40-million agreement with West German and British companies for color-TV studios and equipment.) In 1974, there were 236,828 television receivers in Indonesia (*WRTH* 1974, p. 293), of which 124,454 were concentrated in the capital of Jakarta. Whereas Jakarta had one receiver per 40 persons, the rest of the nation had one per 2,000 (*Media,* January 1974, p. 26). The number of unregistered television receivers is negligible according to the government, because their owners do not want to risk confiscation of such a high-priced luxury item.

TVRI is on the air five hours (beginning at 6 P.M.) each weekday and seven hours in the late afternoon and evenings of Saturdays and Sundays. There are no immediate plans to increase the telecast hours because of the limitations of the equipment, much of which dates to the first broadcasts in 1962. Most of the programs are relayed from Jakarta by the TVRI network of microwave repeaters and translators on Java or are sent as video tapes to the other stations. New studio facilities contemplated for Medan, Surabaya, and Palembang will allow for more local programming (UNESCO 1975, p. 283).

Trying to meet government regulations that programming should be a 50-50 split between news, information and education, and entertainment, TVRI in 1972 used 30% education and culture shows, 20% news and information, 40% entertainment, and 10% commercials. In 1975, the government, announcing tighter controls, reduced the programming devoted to commercials to 8%. No advertisements are allowed after 7:35 P.M. At the same time, the number of films allowed per week was reduced from 40 to 8.

News bulletins are telecast three times each evening; a five-minute newscast at 6 P.M. is meant for regional viewers, and two others featuring national and international news are aired at 8 P.M. and 10 P.M. for 15 and 10 minutes, respectively. About 45% of the news is gathered by the TVRI staff, another 43% comes from Antara, the national news agency, and 6% each from Radio Republik Indonesia and various foreign agencies. Breaking the news into its places of origin, it was found in 1972 that 59% dealt with Indonesia, 14% with other Asian nations, and 27% with the rest of the world (*ABU Newsletter* 1973c, p. 17).

About 30% of the TVRI programs are foreign in origin. There has been some reaction to even this small percentage, but to change to more indigenous shows will prove difficult. TVRI does not have the personnel to cope, even partially, with any radical program change. Even if TVRI does reach a stage of staff sufficiency, partly as a result of West German—sponsored training schemes, the low salary scales of producers are unlikely to draw out the best in them. High-ranking RRI-TVRI officials usually earn about Rp. 7,500—10,000 ($18—$24) a month, plus an equal amount in bonus. Middle ranks earn $12 and the lowest $5. Television actors make $5—$7 and radio artists $.50 monthly. It is not unusual for regular TVRI employees to double as actors or artists, thereby supplementing their meager incomes. Program quality suffers as a result. In 1972, Jakarta television had 600 employees, nearly a third of whom were involved in program planning and production.

3.6.9 Satellites

By the mid-1970s, Indonesia was building up its infrastructure through microwave and satellite usage, all of which should improve broadcasting in the nation. During the country's first five-year plan (called Repelita I, 1969—74), the Nusantara (Archipelago) Microwave System of three regional networks was completed. As part of Repelita II, the second five-year plan, 1974—5 to 1978—9, the Indonesian government will include a national communication satellite system. At a cost of $153 million, to be paid by the Indonesian government through a loan from the United States Export-Import Bank, the satellite system will have 12 microwave transmitters, each capable of handling 800 telephone lines or one color-television channel. There will be 50 ground stations with a master terminal control in Jakarta. Television, telephone, telegraph, and telex transmissions will make use of the system, scheduled to be put into operation in 1976 (Djajanto 1975, p. 25).

As one publication indicated, it seemed as though communication satellites were invented for a nation such as Indonesia, with its 3,000 inhabited islands stretched over 735,000 square miles of sea, its erratic population distribution, and mountainous terrain (*Intermedia*, August 1975, p. 15).

3.7 The Philippines, *by John A. Lent*

After more than three centuries of Spanish rule, the Philippines declared its independence on 12 June 1898. During a conflict not normally listed in American history texts (Fil-American War), the United States gained control and held the islands — against the wishes later of nationalists such as Manuel Quezon — until 4 July 1946. In the post-World War II period, attempts by the Communist-led Hukbalahaps (Huks) to overthrow the government were stopped by Ramon Magsaysay, who later became president. On 9 November 1965, Ferdinand Marcos was elected president; he became the only Filipino to be reelected when he secured a record majority of the vote in 1969. During his second term, increasing dissatisfaction with Marcos policies intensified, and on 21 September 1972, Marcos declared martial law in the Philippines. Thus, in one swoop, a "New Society" based on constitutional authoritarianism was established; dead was the freest mass-media system in Asia, if not the world. In 1975, the biggest problems the government faced involved Muslim conflicts in Mindanao, the economic slump, and Communist and other dissident insurgencies.

The Philippines, consisting of 72 states spread over 7,107 islands, has a population of 41.2 million. Among the largest cities are Manila (1.49 million), Quezon City, the capital (840,000), Cebu (390,000), and Davao (360,000). The country is mainly Roman Catholic. Although about 70 languages are used throughout the nation, the official language is Filipino; the most used, English.

3.7.1 Historical Perspective

Radio. Philippine broadcasting has a relatively long history, dating to June 1922, when three small stations owned and operated by an electrical supply company went on the air in Manila and adjoining Pasay City. Used mainly for demonstration purposes, the stations were operative for about two years before they were replaced by the 100-w. KZKZ station. By the time of World War II, the Philippines had four stations, all owned by department stores to advertise their merchandise.

In 1931, the Radio Control Law was passed, enabling the secretary of commerce and industry to watch over the medium. A regulatory body, Radio Control Board, was a result of the law and functioned until martial law in 1972 (Lent 1971, pp. 79–81). After the Japanese occupied the Philippines in

1942, all radio stations were shut down except for KZRH, which was renamed PIAM and used as the Japanese broadcast outlet. Liberation from Japan in 1945 heralded the real birth of broadcasting in the archipelago; before the war, 20 years had elapsed before four sustaining stations had been set up; within five years after the conflict, there were 30 stations. In fact, because of the large number of applications for broadcast permits, Congress enacted Commonwealth Act 729 on 2 July 1946, giving the President a four-year right to grant temporary permits for the establishment of stations. Another act was passed in 1947, stipulating that stations change their first call letter from "K" to "D" so not to be confused with U.S. radio call letters. Today, call letters "DZ" stand for Luzon stations, "DY" for those in the Visayas, and "DX" for Mindanao stations. One of the main problems of radio broadcasting in the postwar period was the lack of receivers. A local firm, Rehco, partially alleviated the problem in 1949 by making local sets.

Big business interests in control of large portions of Philippine broadcasting by 1972 were responsible for some of the first postwar commercial stations. Conglomerates such as those of the Elizalde, Lopez, and Soriano families developed broadcasting networks, in many cases for political purposes. Other significant changes in postwar radio were the increased use of Pilipino, rather than English, as the language of broadcast, and the extension of the medium to provincial cities. By 1964, a city of 250,000 population, such as Cebu City, had 13 radio stations, some owned by Manila networks. By 1968, there were 213 radio stations in the Philippines, 40 in greater Manila alone; in 1972, just before martial law, the number increased to about 350, 55 of which were in the greater Manila area. By geographical breakdown, there were at least 120 radio stations in Luzon, 90 in the Visayas, and 85 in Mindanao (Almario 1972). Many of the stations were part of multimedia combines. Before martial law, for example, the Lopez family owned newspapers, magazines, and ABS-CBN radio and television with at least 20 radio and five TV stations; the Roces family had newspapers, magazines, and Associated Broadcasting of one TV and five radio stations; Soriano interests included newspapers, magazines, the Radio Mindanao Network of eight radio stations, and the Inter-Island Broadcasting Network of three television channels; the Elizalde family had a newspaper and Metropolitan Broadcasting, a network of one television and eight radio stations, and Republic Broadcasting owned six radio and two TV outlets.

One criticism of radio in the Philippines was that it grew too fast and too big, the result being overlapping and poor distribution of frequencies. Because of the insular nature of the country (i.e., water offering very little impediment to radio waves), radial spread was increased, providing greater physical coverage for stations, and again, tending toward overlapping of frequencies.

Advertising alone could not support the large number of stations, many of which survived only with political party support, especially during the biannual elections. The staff competition also resulted in poor standards and unethical programming. Available advertising money was fed to entertainment shows, especially soap operas and silly joke programs (Interview, Aurelio Javellana, Mindanao Broadcasting System, 1964). Effective broadcasting was hindered by what became known as the "bakya mentality," a mind-set that favored stories about "illegitimate children, forsaken wives, abused women, moribund fathers, poor girls and rich boys, poor boys and rich girls, stories where the leading lady alternates between singing and weeping" (Avellana 1963, pp. 382—86). A 1964 survey showed that in a 12-hour broadcast day, most stations devoted four hours to soap operas, three to music, three to conversation, one to news, and one to commercials (Lent 1971, p. 90).

The keen competition coupled with the ineffectiveness of the Radio Control Board produced many unethical practices in radio. In 1961, for example, a candidate for president of the Philippines bought out an entire stations's programming; on another occasion, a sponsor regularly lampooned the Chinese minority group in the Philippines without any repercussions; at other times, presidential candidates were charged on the air with being pro-Communist, anti-Catholic, and antidemocratic. Self-policing efforts on the part of the broadcast industry or Radio Control Board accomplished very little.

Television. Philippine television took root in a clamorous political soil with very little planning and foresight. Judge Antonio Quirino, brother of the nation's president at the time, was responsible for the islands' first station. In 1952, Judge Quirino bought Bolinao Electronics Corporation, an organization which two years previously had been granted a franchise by Congress to operate a television station. The granting of the franchise to Bolinao was questionable, because at least three other groups had been refused franchises by the administration for nebulous reasons (Lent 1971, p. 95). Bolinao opened the first station, DZAQ (Channel 3 in Manila), just before the 1953 Philippine presidential elections, adding to the suspicion that its founding was a political tactic. By 1957, the only two TV stations in the country were operated by the Chronicle Broadcasting Network, owned by the Lopez family.

Television came in for much criticism during its first decade: for its poor election coverage, its use as a political tool, and its immoral and unethical program content. It was also accused of breeding envy and discontent since most people could not afford a set. In addition, there was a dearth of local programming and a prevalence of immorality and indecency in shows. Most of the problems still existed just before martial law, again, partly because of the lack of clout on the part of the Radio Control Board. In fact, after at least 15 years of television in the islands, the Radio Control Board still had not developed rules designed especially for the medium, nor had it established any specific plan for assigning television channels.

Before the declaration of martial law, television stations were so busy fighting each other for ratings that no one had time to consider more rational growth. There was no comprehensive national policy to extend the networks in an orderly manner throughout the islands, although some Manila networks did have outlets in the southern areas (Green 1972, p. 250).

3.7.2 Martial Law: Effects on Organization and Control

Before September 1972, broadcasting in the Philippines was probably as free of governmental control as any system in the world. Governments since independence in 1946 had leveled protests against broadcasting practices, but most were not taken very seriously by the broadcasters. Freedom of expression was virtually unrestricted, to the extent that no politician or public figure could hope to escape permanently from mass-media revelations. As indicated earlier, irresponsible acts were conducted by broadcasting programmers during such raucous times.

After Ferdinand Marcos was elected to an unprecedented second term as president in 1969, examples of a deliberately guided mass-media policy became perceptible. First of all, Marcos, who had been very critical of the oligarchic control of mass media, began building his own oligarchy, either through government agencies or family and friends. The National Media Production Center (NMPC) was strengthened and placed under the Office of the President; NMPC, the Malacañang (presidential palace) press office, and public information offices received budgets that equaled those of the four largest dailies combined. Malacañang, for example, had one press office outfitted with complete television studios and equipment.

By early 1972, Marcos directly, or through relatives and friends, was in control of some commercially operated newspapers and broadcasting stations. For example, his top military aide, Hans Menzi, owned the Manila *Bulletin* and its broadcast outlets, and Marcos relatives had Kanlaon Broadcasting System stations. To man these enterprises, Marcos raided staff members from commercial media. He was charged with paying radio commentators, for instance, through public funds under the guise that they were independent (Lent 1974a).

When martial law was declared in September 1972, the media were cited as a prime enemy and target of the Marcos forces. Troops in camouflage uniforms entered radio and TV studios, arrested some broadcasters, sealed the studios, and placed the stations under military control. At one station, Eagle Broadcasting, owned by the Iglesia Ng Kristo church, guards refused to accept the presidential decree declaring martial law, opened fire, and killed nine soldiers. The military returned with additional arms and killed nearly a dozen Eagle Broadcasting guards before serving the decree. Within a few hours, the government had wiped out the entire news media of the Philippines, except for the pro-Marcos *Daily Express*, Kanlaon Broadcasting, and a few other supporters. The reasons given for such drastic action were that there were too many broadcasting stations, that radio (and newspapers) had been infiltrated by Communist propagandists and were therefore guilty of distortions, tendentious reporting, speculation, and criticism that had damaged society and weakened resistance to Communism.

Immediately upon martial law, a Department of Public Information was established as an exclusive branch, designed to merge all public-information offices of the various governmental branches. Its first decree included the regulation that radio and TV shall "broadcast accurate, objective, straight news reports of the government to meet the dangers and threats that occasioned the proclamation of martial law, and the efforts to achieve a 'new society' as set forth by the President and Commander-in-Chief of all the armed forces of the Philippines" (Department of Public Information, Department Order No. 1, 25 Sept. 1972). Furthermore, editorials, "opinion, commentary, comments or asides" were expressly forbidden over the air.

On 16 November 1972, the president signed his 36th decree, calling for the establishment of the Mass Media Council (MMC) to set guidelines for the reopening of mass media. MMC was also given the task of supervising and controlling the performance and conduct of all mass media relevant to the promotion of closer coordination with the government's objectives. MMC ceased functioning in May 1973 when the governmental Media Advisory Council (MAC) was formed. MAC was to undertake the encouragement of responsible opinion writing dealing with social and economic conditions, the freeing of media from monopoly ownership, and the vernacularization of media content. Among other goals, MAC sought to provide for a national and orderly allocation of radio and TV frequencies through a system of zonification under accepted international rules, and to develop more radio and TV stations in the provinces. Broadcasting responsibilities were delineated as the education of the masses, the presentation of cultural and genuine artistic or literary materials, and the promotion of valued Filipino moral and social traits. Under a section dealing with broadcasting for children, the regulations stated that violence and sex must be deemphasized and "programs should reflect respect for parents, for honorable behavior, and for the constituted authorities of our New Society." Program standards called for wholesome entertainment and respect for the sanctity of marriage and the value of the home, disallowed profanity, smut, or obscenity, and racial, nationality, or religious slurs. Broadcasters were expected to portray the following in their programs: law enforcement must be upheld; cigarette smoking is not to be depicted in a manner to impress youth as desirable; criminality is to be presented as undesirable and unsympathetic; suicide is not justified as acceptable; illicit sex relations are not treated as commendable; drunkenness should never be presented as desirable or prevalent. Furthermore, narcotic addiction should not be presented except as a vicious habit; gambling should be used in plots only when shown with discretion; live sports programs at which on-the-scene betting is permitted by law should not be presented or discussed on the air; programs related to astrology and its branches are unacceptable; quiz and game shows must be fair. Finally, the use of horror for its own sake must be eliminated; dress and movement of actors and dancers must be decent; identification of brand names within programs is outlawed; and "the creation of a state of hypnosis by act or demonstration on the air is prohibited, and hypnosis as an aspect of parlor—games antics to create humorous situations within a comedy setting cannot be used" (Media Advisory Council, Philippines, 1973).

MAC also set down policies on news and public-events broadcasting and religious programming. News reporting must be factual, fair, and free of bias; materials tending to incite people against the government are strictly prohibited. News shows must not play up morbid or sensational details and must be presented to avoid panic and unnecessary alarm. Commentary and analysis must be clearly identified, and uniform and simultaneous scheduling of news and public-affairs programs by all stations and networks is encouraged to promote and increase their audiences. Time must be allocated for religious shows which must emphasize broad religious truths, excluding controversial or partisan views not directly or necessarily related to religion or morality.

These regulations have been extremely successful. Having jailed or discredited his opponents in the broadcast profession, Marcos can rely on favorable treatment on radio and television now. In 1973, the broadcast media were used effectively as campaigners for the New Society; for example, during a one month period, a videotape of Marcos reading a "bless this nation" prayer appeared on TV daily at 6 P.M., timed with the Catholic habit of reciting the Angelus at twilight. Marching songs to commemorate the New Society were played at least once or twice daily during any feature film on television. Other New Society promotionals on TV showed farmers reading about land reform or a misty-eyed lad before a judge learning there is no legal class privilege in the New Society. Commercials regularly stressed cleanliness and politeness and assured the people it was now safe to walk the streets.

In October 1974, Marcos decentralized mass-media censorship, after factions within MAC squabbled for control. Separate bureaus for print and broadcasting were created but operated under MAC guidelines. In fact, former director of MAC, Primitivo Mijares, who denounced Marcos after defecting to the United States, said the same controls exist in the mass media now as at the time of the imposition of martial law (*Philippine Times* 1975). The Bureau of Broadcasts, under the Department of Public Information, controls broadcasting in the Philippines and is headed by pro-Marcos newspaper columnist, Teodoro Valencia.

3.7.3 Systems Dimensions

Recent figures show that Marcos was successful in breaking up the old broadcasting networks owned by oligarchies, but not in eliminating monopolization. For example, of the 209 radio stations listed in 1975, 117 were owned by ten companies. The privately owned Nation Broadcasting Corporation has 18 medium-wave stations, followed by international religious broadcaster Far East Broadcasting Company with 17; the Marcos-owned

Kanlaon Broadcasting System with at least 15; privately owned Northern Broadcasting Company and the governmental Bureau of Broadcasts, 12 each; Radio Mindanao Network—Inter-Island Broadcasting Corporation, 11; University of Mindanao Broadcasting Network and Catholic Welfare Organization, 10 each; and Allied Broadcasting Centre and Filipinas Broadcasting Network, 6 each (PFA 1975, p. 207–13). Of all stations, 19 are government- or military-controlled, by agencies such as Rajah Broadcasting Network (3), Republic Broadcasting System (1), Bureau of Broadcasts (12), and Voice of Philippines-National Media Production Center (3). But these government stations operate the most powerful transmitters and relay stations. For example, National Media Production Center, directly under the office of the president, operates the powerful Voice of the Philippines network both domestically and externally and shares time with the Bureau of Broadcasts and KBS in running GTV-4.

Breaking down the stations by regions in 1975, there were 122 with headquarters in the greater Manila area, 50 in Luzon, 19 in the Visayas, and 18 in Mindanao. Of the stations with headquarters in the greater Manila area, 36 actually broadcast in Manila. The Bureau of Broadcasts, in an effort to disperse more stations to the provinces, ruled that beginning 1 October 1975, only 25 radio stations will be allowed to broadcast in Manila (Gozo 1975, pp. 9, 11). Of the 27 active short-wave stations, 22 were owned by religious broadcasters, such as Far East Broadcasting Company (15), SEARV (5) (now defunct), and Radio Veritas (2); and 5 by government agencies such as Philippine Broadcasting service (3) and National Media Production Center (2) (*WRTH* 1974, p. 163). The Voice of the Philippines, outlet of National Media Production Center, and Radio Veritas operate on 500 kw. while Far East Broadcasting Company has a total of 400-kw. in the Philippines (Gozo 1975, p. 9).

The ever-changing characteristic of Philippine broadcasting does not allow for exact figures on system dimensions or on government participation in the media. Data provided by a delegation of Philippine broadcasters in attendance at a 1974 conference in San Francisco indicate the government has definite plans for broadcasting. These delegates pointed out that broadcasting under martial law functions as an agent of change and development and a vehicle for government information and support. The Bureau of Broadcasts, through an organization called LINK, has planned for the development of numerous stations throughout the archipelago. LINK, an agency for purposive communication, was designed to act as a bridge for the task of day-to-day development, promoting government campaigns, and insuring a balance between information and entertainment. The delegation added that in mid-1974, the Bureau of Broadcasts had four medium-wave, three short-wave, and two FM stations in Manila and seven stations in provincial cities such as Baguio, Jolo, Dagupan, Cebu, Malawi, Davao, and Iloilo. A four-year broadcasting expansion plan implemented in 1974 called for the development of *barangay* (small community) stations, total communication reaching people all over the Philippines, and the use of a social dimension in broadcasting. By the end of 1977, the government plans to have established 43 *barangay* and 11 regional radio stations, as well as 3 TV centers and 8 TV relay stations.

Television is also controlled by the Bureau of Broadcasts. Again, figures for the number and allocation of channels vary. *WRTH* listed 22 channels in 1974, including 2 that were under construction. Radio Mindanao—Inter-Island Broadcasting Corporation owned eight, one each in Manila, Baguio, Tacloban City, Cagayan de Oro City, Bacolod City, Cebu City, Davao City, and Naga City. The Marcos-controlled Kanlaon Broadcasting System had channels in Bacolod, Pasay City, Cebu City, Iriga City, and Baguio, while American Forces Philippines Network, used for U.S. servicemen stationed at Clark Air Base, San Miquel, Cubi Point, and Subic Bay, had four channels. Privately owned, pre-martial law Republic Broadcasting System had two channels, one each in Manila and Baguio. Other TV broadcasters, each with one outlet, were Rainbow Radio and TV Corporation in Bacolod City, and the two government-owned stations, Philippine Broadcasting Service and Department of Public Information (*WRTH* 1974, pp. 296—97).

The most recent data show there are 22 TV stations; 5 in Manila and 17 in the provinces. Four of the five Manila stations control provincial outlets: Banahaw Broadcasting Corporation (BBC) has three; Inter-Island Broadcasting Corporation (IBC), seven; Radio Philippines Network (RPN), five; and Republic Broadcasting System (RBS), two. Only GTV Television Service has no provincial station. Apparently television broadcasting has been completely revamped, to the extent that by 1975 even the names of the organizations had changed. The dominant force in Filipino television is still Kanlaon Broadcasting System (KBS), which is now a broadcasting management company acting as general manager for 3 of the 5 networks — BBC, RPN, and GTV — and 11 of the 22 stations (*Variety* 1975h). Still another 1975 source listed the total number of TV channels as 24, broken down this way: KBS-RPN, eight; IBC, seven; BBC, four; GMA-7 Radio Television Arts, two; and DYAF-TV Magnitude 10 in Bacolod City, Clark Air Base, Bureau of Broadcasts GTV, one each (PFA 1975, pp. 213—14).

The Philippines has used satellite communications since 1967. Philippines Communications Satellite (Philcomsat) has transmitted and received messages via Intelsat, including the funeral of Robert Kennedy and the Apollo 8 journey around the moon in 1968. By 1976, a domestic satellite system (DOMSAT) was expected to be in existence, allowing all provinces to be able to view live telecasts from Manila or elsewhere in the nation. The system was seen as a boom to the TV industry which previously had been dependent upon Manila advertising revenue for its existence (*Variety* 1975m).

3.7.4 Programming and Audiences

Speaking before the first National Broadcasters Conference in the Philippines in 1975, Teodoro Valencia, head of the Bureau of Broadcasts, said broadcasting must redirect its efforts toward concrete contributions to the New Society, by using fewer commercials and more quality programming and by reducing the number of radio stations in the country. He instructed the conference delegates to redirect the efforts and goals of the broadcast industry to conform with the aims and objectives of the New Society, to foster stronger relationships and cooperation between broadcasters and advertisers, to formulate plans that will make it easier for Marcos to go on a nation-wide hookup at the shortest possible notice, to improve program content, to professionalize broadcast media personnel and upgrade technical skills and equipment to improve the service of broadcasting, to study government programs, and to assist in all aspects of reorganizing society and developing national unity and pride (Pines 1975, pp. 38, 56). In short, broadcasters were implored to cooperate with government in bringing about acceptable developmental goals set down by the authorities.

Of course, the broadcast industry had been doing all that Valencia suggested since the declaration of martial law in 1972. Philippine developmental news and public-affairs programming meant to keep Filipinos informed of the strides made by the authorities in economic planning and implementation have been emphasized on both radio and television; humor, music, and other entertainment have been redesigned with Philippine languages, values, and audiences in mind. According to one publication:

Radio and television now carry a fairly heavy load of propagandistic broadcasts. For instance, every now and then regular programs are interrupted to make way for a presidential speech or some official function. Once a week in the early evening a forum on grass-roots issues is simulcast on radio and TV. In the early morning every day development topics, most frequently agriculture, are discussed on almost all stations for at least one hour. News comes on TV three times a day — in the late morning, in the early evening and late at night. On radio it comes every hour on many stations. [*Media,* August 1975, p. 13]

On radio, nearly all programming is locally produced, using mainly Pilipino and English as the broadcast languages.

More information is available concerning television programs. In 1974, KBS produced 7,000 hours of shows for its three networks, of which 2,432 were devoted to series, 1,748 to public affairs and news, and the rest to sports and specials. Still, nearly one-half of the TV schedules of these three networks was devoted to foreign-produced shows, although only one-third of the foreign programs were slotted for prime time. Imports of foreign shows in 1974 totaled 5,348 hours (3,187 hours of features, 1,478 series, 282 news and public affairs, 215 specials, and 186 sports). A partial list of the 24 U.S. series used by KBS includes "Perry Mason Show," "Shaft," "The Rookies," "Hawaii Five-O," "Hawkins," and "Medical Center"; among the American specials and features KBS purchased were Oscar, Emmy, and Grammy shows, the Julie Andrews, Bob Hope, and Burt Bacharach specials, and such features as "Airport," "South Pacific," and "Dirty Dozen." The price for an hour-long U.S. series was $450–600, for U.S. features, $800–1,200 (*Variety* 1975h, p. 116).

Among locally produced news and public-affairs TV shows on the Bureau of Broadcasts channels were "Sandiwa" (public affairs), "Balita" (news in the vernacular), "Saling Pusa" (information for children), "Shape of Tomorrow" (discussion on key development topics), "Pamantayan ng Talino" (school competition), "Enterprise" (documentary on successful entrepreneurs), and "Paligsahan 74" (sports clinics). Philippine-produced music shows include "Himing ng Lipunan," "Musika," and "Do Re Mi," and local humor include "Serbisyo Sibil" (favorable satire on the government) and "Anak ng Kutsero." Other locally made TV shows stressed national development and Philippine culture and history; "Talambuhay ng Dra de Jesus" (a vehicle for developing self-reliance), "Alamat" (Philippine heroes), "Lagusan" (life in the city as seen by a journalist), and "Hangganan" (true crime stories) were among them.

Recent ratings gave KBS television stations 72.8% of the total audience; the most successful KBS network being RPN with 38.4%; the least successful, GTV with 4.4%. The number of TV receivers is still relatively low; in the greater Manila area, however, there are over 553,000 TV sets alone (*Variety* 1975h, p. 116).

Radio still ranks as the most used mass medium, there being nearly 1.65 million radio sets in use (UNESCO 1975). In 1973, for example, 60% of the Filipinos surveyed by the government received their information from radio, 36.5% from newspapers, 2.2% from word of mouth, and only 2.1% from television. Another survey of 1,960 people conducted in the nation's largest provincial urban area, Cebu City, showed 90% of the respondents owned radio receivers while 44% had TV sets in their homes. Program preferences among radio listeners in Cebu City were music, soap opera, and news, in that order (Cebu City *Morning Times*, 24 January 1975, pp. 2–3).

3.7.5 Advertising

The abuse of commercial time on radio and television in the Philippines has been a subject of controversy for nearly two decades, the main complaints being there have been too many examples of unethical, misleading, and exploitative advertisements, and too many commercials presented for long durations of time. The Media Advisory Council, in its set of guidelines, tried to deal with the problems, forbidding, among other things, the advertising in broadcasts of firearms, ammunition, fortune telling, astrology, lotteries, and betting. MAC advertising standards also stipulated that advertisements which tend to demean official slogans and concepts of the New Society must be avoided. For example, advertisements such as "New Society Bargain Sale" are outlawed. The exploitation of children and discrediting of competing products in broadcast commercials are also not allowed; other regulations deal with the use of commercials for medical products, contests, premiums, and offers.

MAC spelled out quite specifically the amount of broadcast time allowed for commercials. On prime-time network shows in Manila, nonprogram materials (including commercials and credits) cannot exceed 12 minutes per hour; on provincial stations, the limit is 14 minutes in any one hour. During all other times, nonprogram materials cannot exceed 16 minutes per hour. As for the number of interruptions for commercials, MAC regulated that for prime time, there cannot be more than two each 30 minutes or five in an hour; at all other times, up to four interruptions per hour are permitted (Media Advisory Council, Philippines, 1973). Apparently these safeguards were not adequate, and in 1974, the government and private sector set up an advertising code of ethics, retaining some of MAC's guidelines but specifying that broadcast advertising be limited to nine minutes per prime-time hour (*Media* 1974h).

Martial law has been somewhat salutory for advertising because it reordered mass media, especially broadcasting. Before martial law, one major media group, that of the Lopez family, controlled more than one-half of the advertising action, with a second layer of four media-owning groups sharing one-fourth of the field, and a third layer of 100 marginally profitable independents holding the remainder of the business. At least one publication feels this has changed since 1972 but did not provide statistics to back up the claim (*Media*, November 1974, p. 12).

A survey by Advertising and Marketing Associates of the Philippines showed that gross billings in advertising have gone up considerably every year since martial law; the total projected advertising billings in 1975 were estimated at over $45 million (*Media*, November 1974, p. 12). The total advertising revenue in 1974 for all five television networks was $14.3 million, of which Inter-Island Broadcasting got $1.7 million and Republic Broadcasting $1 million, the remainder divided among Kanlaon Broadcasting networks: RPN, nearly $6.5 million; BBC, almost $5 million; and GTV, $140,000 (*Variety* 1975h, p. 116). This enormous amount of television advertising billing is also credited to good metropolitan coverage and low rates (*Media* 1975a).

3.7.6 Educational Broadcasting

Educational broadcasting was initiated in the 1950s as a joint project of the governmental Philippine Broadcasting Service (PBS) and the Bureau of Public Schools. Initially, two lessons were transmitted over PBS and commercial radio stations. The real thrust for the program came in 1959 when the Australian government donated 500 radio receivers for use in the schools. By 1967–68, 19 elementary and high school programs were broadcast over 18 private and commercial stations into 39,000 classrooms. There were 19,168 radio receivers available for the project by then, 90% of which had been purchased by the schools themselves (Carroll 1970, p. 119). Additionally, the Bureau of Public Schools, Defense Department, Land Reform Information Service, Radio-TV Section of Malacañang Press Office, and other agencies were involved in educational broadcasting projects. Adult education, for example, was provided through the Adult and Community Education Division of the Bureau of Public Schools in a series called "The Citizen"; farm broadcasts, developed in the 1950s, were handled by a number of stations, including Republic Broadcasting which sponsored "Paaralan sa Himpapawid" (Radio Farm School). The Radio Farm School had graduated over 2,000 farmers by 1968 through its radio correspondence courses in poultry raising, vegetable gardening, and miracle rice cultivation (Carroll 1970, p. 119).

Educational television was created in the early 1960s with a show entitled "Education on TV" over Channel 9; in 1961, a physics course was televised. Early sponsors of educational television in the Greater Manila area were the Bureau of Public Schools, Center for Educational Television, Metropolitan Educational Television Association (META), and in Bacolod, Visayan Educational Radio and Television Association (VERTA). The Bureau's ETV operations have been relatively limited since they began in 1965 over Philippine Broadcasting Service. The Center for Educational Television at Ateneo de Manila University initiated a closed-circuit TV pilot project in 1964 with six receiving schools. Within three months, the service was extended to 30 public and private schools of META by microwave link to a commercial channel. The center's peak efficiency was during 1968–72, but since martial law the center has suffered from the lack of governmental emphasis on educational television. Between 1972–74, ETV services in the nation shifted to out-of-school or informal education by television, and there was a definite decline in instructional television services. Also, it has been decided in recent years that ETV on a national level must be the responsibility of the government, because the majority of the schools are government operated. Like so many responses provided by the government in martial-law Philippines, this is a poor rationale; probably the real reason is that the government in its .efforts to control all mass media, does not want the instructing of young minds left to individuals in the private sector.

The Metropolitan Educational Television Association (META) was organized in 1964 to represent elementary and secondary schools of the greater Manila area interested in educational television. META has been dissolved because of insufficient funds and its functions taken over by the Center for Educational Television. The Visayan Educational Radio and Television Association existed between 1969–73 to provide basic out-of-school education via television for sugar-plantation workers. It too ceased operations because of a lack of funds (*Educational Broadcasting International* 1974, pp. 121–26).

According to one publication, the Marcos government since martial law has shown very little interest in the development of instructional television, despite the fact that New Society campaigns require the education of masses of people for their success (*Educational Broadcasting International* 1974, pp. 121–26).

Judging from what has happened with other aspects of mass media since martial law, it is safe to say that educational television will be emphasized again once the infrastructure is developed enabling the government to be completely in control.

3.8 Burma, *by Paul P. Blackburn*

Burma's political history started in the 5th century when a kingdom was founded by the Pyus. Later, the Mons ruled the lower part of Burma until the Burmese arrived from the north in the 11th century. After numerous wars, mainly between the Mons and Thais, Burma was annexed in stages up to 1885 and became a province of British India. In 1937, Burma was separated from India and allowed to practice self-government. The Union of Burma finally won full independence on 4 January 1948, but immediately faced rebellions by Communist groups and various non-Burmese tribes. On 2 March 1962 the army overthrew the U Nu government and installed a military revolutionary government led by General Ne Win, whose political philosophy was the Burmese Way to Socialism. The nation went into self-imposed isolation until 1973. On 3 January 1974, it became the Socialist Republic of the Union of Burma, after a new socialist constitution was passed in a referendum. Two months later, the revolutionary government was dissolved and replaced by the constitutional government, still headed by Ne Win, who now held the title of president.

Burma, comprising seven states, has a population of 28.8 million, divided among many ethnic and tribal groups. The largest city is Rangoon, the capital, with 2.1 million, followed by Mandalay (520,000), Moulmein (200,000), and Pegu (250,000). The nation suffers from inadequate amounts of food, education, and health facilities, and an economy that is in rags.

3.8.1 History

In the years since Burma gained its independence from Britain in 1948, Burmese broadcasting has shown a most un-Topsy-like reluctance to grow. Just as in the early postwar period, when the Burma Broadcasting Service (BBS) was inaugurated in 1946, Burmese radio today consists of a single Rangoon facility. Moreover, there is no television broadcasting, and no plan to institute it (*Guardian* 1971).

Before describing the present form and content of Burmese broadcasting

Paul P. Blackburn is Director, Tokyo American Center, and U.S. Embassy Cultural Attaché in Japan. He served with USIA in Thailand for five years and was an analyst for Far Eastern affairs in the Library of Congress. He studied communications and national development in Burma, Malaysia, and Thailand for his Ph.D. dissertation at American University.

and trying to deal with the intriguing question of why there has been virtually no growth in broadcasting facilities since World War II, a brief survey of some of the origins of BBS is pertinent.

The first broadcasts in Burma were by the British, who in 1937 started transmitting programs on a Marconi transmitter which had been used for wireless communication between India and Burma (*Taw Daw Shin* 1971). The broadcasts could be heard only as far as the Rangoon suburbs. In 1939, the British set up a 10-kw. transmitter near Rangoon, at Mingaladon, for propaganda broadcasting in English, Burmese, and Hindustani. During the Japanese occupation (1942–45), the Japanese carried out both medium-wave (10-kw.) and short-wave (5-kw.) broadcasting in Burmese, Japanese, English, Hindustani, Bengali, and Chinese. In the later stages of the war, especially in early 1945, the Burmese resistance movement set up a secret "Burmese Revolutionary Army Broadcasting Station" and carried programs in Burmese, English, and Hindustani, especially news and music for the resistance forces. Later in 1945, with the arrival of the Psychological Warfare Team of the returning British Civil Administration for Burma, the British took over the broadcasting operations once more. These were on two 7.5-kw. and one 5-kw. Marconi transmitters for short-wave and medium-wave broadcasts, respectively, and as before, there were daily transmissions in Burmese, English, and Hindustani. BBS, known then as the "Voice of Burma" (or Myarma A-Than), was born 15 February 1946, when the facilities were turned over to the pre-Independence Burmese Civil Government (Provisional).

Although Burmese broadcasting in the late 1940s was not unlike that of other countries in the region, most others greatly expanded their radio facilities and programming efforts and started television stations during the 1950s and 1960s. Meanwhile, Burma remained content with its single Rangoon radio station, its modest level of programming, and its complete isolation from the growing influence of television. This relative non-development has been due not so much to a lack of technical resources or trained personnel, as to a conscious policy by the Burmese government (GUB) – particularly since the takeover of power by Ne Win's Revolutionary Council in March 1962 – to apply the bulk of its resources for information activities to other forms of programming, especially the print media.

3.8.2 Ideology

The Burmese mass-media system, in general, is highly ideological in content and aimed primarily at elite audiences. The government owns and operates all but one of the eight daily newspapers (there are no weeklies) and keeps circulation levels down by newspaper rationing and other measures. The newspapers and supporting government periodicals are primary vehicles for articulating official policy; radio is intended to play a contributing role by reinforcing messages carried in the print media.

Whether the medium is newspapers, periodicals, radio, or film, and whatever the ratio of private to government ownership and operating responsibility, all messages carried by the media are expected to support and advance "The Burmese Way to Socialism." These messages emphasize Burma's independence, neutrality and self-reliance, and its successes in developing its own variety of socialism. A very clear and persistent element in these messages is that whatever economic hardships may accrue to Burma because of its anticapitalist domestic policies (which most strongly affect the once-powerful Indian, Chinese, and European financial interests) are well worth the price in terms of national self-reliance and independence.

Under current ideological guidelines, workers and peasants receive doctrinal priority, but this emphasis has extended mainly to the leaders rather than to the masses of these groups. Other elite audiences include military and civilian officials, cadres of the Burma Socialist Programme Party (BSPP), and advanced students. Indigenous minorities, from whose ranks come most of the insurgent forces which pose a continuing threat to domestic tranquility and national unity, receive little attention from the Ministry of Information, except for a few radio broadcasts. The Indian and Chinese minorities, numbering perhaps half a million persons and containing many of the most prosperous, best-educated, and talented members of the society, are completely ignored in today's media output in Burma.

3.8.3 Finance and Facilities

Within the overall GUB budget for information, the proportion allocated for radio broadcasting is very modest indeed. Out of an information ministry budget estimate of $7.3 million in 1967 (the total GUB budget was $273.2 million at the then-existing rate of 4.76 kyats to a United States dollar), of which $6.1 million was earmarked for operating expenditures, only $.5 million (about 8.2%) went to broadcasting operations. At the same time, the budget for press activities was nearly five times as large (Union of Burma 1966, pp. 116, 121–22). Unpublished GUB budget figures for 1970 indicated that radio accounted for approximately 14% of the total funds allocated to the information ministry for operating expenses and capital improvements that year.

The BBS staff consists of about 120 administrative personnel and some 300 program and technical specialists. All programming is done at the Prome Road facilities (completed in 1960) in Rangoon, while all medium-wave and short-wave broadcasting is handled by five 50-kw. and one 250-w. transmitters located at Yegu, about eight miles outside the capital (*WRTH* 1974, p. 140). Medium-wave broadcasts, simultaneously carried on short-wave, are aired 12½ hours daily, with an extra hour on Sundays, for a total of 88½ hours per week. "Burmese Programme I" in Burmese and English is on the air daily from 7–9 A.M., 10 A.M. to 2 P.M., and 4–10:30 P.M., while "Burmese Programme II" broadcasts on short-wave only, aimed at minority audiences from 5:30–8:45 P.M. daily. As implied from the above figures, BBS is shut down from 9–10 A.M. (except on Sundays), 2–4 P.M., and 10:30 P.M.–7 A.M.

An FM transmission links the Prome Road offices and the Yegu transmitters, but it is not used for independent programming. Likewise, there are no repeater transmissions, provincial stations, or wired speaker/rediffusion facilities.

Although in the early 1960s, an army-run broadcasting operation transmitted to troops in the field and regional minority groups, the facility was closed in 1965, its programming turned over to BBS. Security considerations, as well as cost, appear to be the major reasons for GUB's reluctance to open regional stations. Mandalay would be the most likely site for such a station, should BBS decide to establish one on a permanent basis. As there are currently no originating or repeater stations outside of Rangoon, only a limited part of the country − about 100 miles in radius − can be reached by medium-wave, while the rest of Burma has to rely on short-wave transmissions. Short-wave broadcasting is said to have a clear signal throughout Burma and can be received by about 90% of the sets in use (USIA 1966, p. 27).

3.8.4 Radio Receivers

The number of radio receivers in use in Burma totals perhaps between 800,000 and one million, or, estimating Burma's population at 27 million, from 2.7–3 sets per 100 persons. The number of licensed sets has risen from 117,000 in 1960 (UNESCO 1964, p. 202) to 400,000 in 1974 (UNESCO 1975).

A radio license costs nine kyats (about $1.68 at the official exchange rate of 5.3487 kyats to a dollar), is good for three years, and allows the holder to have as many as three sets in his household.

In calculating the total number of sets, it would seem possible to look at imports and local production, but reliable data on these aspects are not available. It is known, however, that imports have dropped from many thousands annually to perhaps only a few hundred, a figure which may represent the number brought in by GUB officials returning from abroad and those imported for specialized purposes by different government departments. Normal duties applied to such imports are about 150–200% of cost. In essence, there is virtually a complete ban on receiver imports. Local production, on the other hand, consists mainly of some 2,000–3,500 Japanese (National) sets, assembled monthly by the GUB's Defense Services Institute. The sets are sold commercially through Trade Corporation 14 and also are distributed free to village headmen, schools, military units, and the like. The four different models produced domestically and sold through Peoples' Stores cost between 250 kyats ($46.74) and 464.55 kyats ($86.85). Despite such high prices − and black market prices are even higher − the shops are unable to keep up with the demand. In fact, there are reported many instances of raffles in which the winners receive coupons giving them the right to buy radios in the state stores.

Because of the high prices and limited quantities of locally made sets, there is a strong incentive to smuggle in cheap transistor sets from nearby countries such as Thailand and Malaysia, where the supply is plentiful. In Burma, such sets sell for several times their original market value.

The writer's estimate of 800,000 to one million receivers is derived by adding 25% to the 400,000 licensed sets (to allow for multiple-set households), and then calculating that 300,000–500,000 is sufficient to account for not only illegally imported sets, but also those previously imported legally but not currently licensed, as well as unlicensed sets produced locally from cannibalized old sets and spare parts.

Despite sharp increases in the number of licenses since 1960 and signs that the transistor revolution may be coming to Burma via the back door, the country does not have as extensive a mass radio audience as other nations in the region. Expansion of radio receivership in Burma is held back not only by the GUB's curtailment of imports and modest production levels, but also because prices of both legal and black-market sets are too high to be within the reach of the masses.

3.8.5 Programming

In 1970, international broadcasting in Burmese totaled over 93 hours per week. Radio Peking transmitted 24½ hours to Burma; VOA, 21; All India Radio, 11; Radio Moscow, 10½; BBC and the Voice of Patriotic Youth (clandestine), each 7; Radio Pakistan, 5¼; and Far East Broadcasting (based in the Philippines) and NHK (Japan), both 3½ (USIA, March 1970, pp. 1–2). It is worth noting, for the sake of comparison, that BBS itself was at that time broadcasting only 65 hours weekly in Burmese, and thus some 60% of the total Burmese-language airtime was accounted for by transmissions from other countries. The only foreign broadcasts which appear to concern the GUB are those coming from the Voice of Patriotic Youth, which started broadcasting in April 1970 and is said by GUB to be associated with deposed Prime Minister U Nu and his supporters living in Thailand (*Working People's Daily* 1970a and 1970b).

Although precise figures are lacking, the Burmese have a high propensity to listen to foreign broadcasts. In 1960, a USIA survey found that about half of those who could be called radio listeners "regularly listen to foreign radio programs," especially the BBC, VOA, All India Radio, Ceylon Broadcasting, Radio Pakistan, and Radio Peking (USIA 1960b, p. 7). And a 1966 USIA study concluded that:

15% of the Burmese radio audience listens to foreign radio broadcasts, from both communist and Free World nations. In fact, there are indications that more Burmese have been listening to foreign stations in recent years because of the relative paucity of international news on BBS broadcasts. [USIA 1966, p. 27]

Voice of America, which receives a high volume of audience mail from Burma, estimates its total audience in the country to be as high as 4 21 million (USIA 1970a, p. 1). Despite the fact that currently a substantial segment of the population is exposed to transmissions from abroad, GUB has not attempted to place restrictions on such listening, nor has it showed an inclination to respond to the competition by increasing its own level of output.

BBS broadcasting time is divided by language according to a daily schedule of ten hours in Burmese, 2½ hours in English on medium-wave/short-wave, and one-half hour each on short-wave in the majority languages of Kachin, Kayah, Sgaw Karen, Pwo Karen, Chin, and Shan (plus another 15-minute Burmese news program sandwiched in the middle of the minority-languages transmission).

Hindustani programs, transmitted from the earliest days of Burmese broadcasting, had been dropped by 1966, which coincided roughly with the withdrawal of licenses for Indian and Chinese newspapers on 1 January 1966. Indigenous minority-language broadcasting is now the only locally originated mass-media activity aimed at a non-Burman audience.

Burma has no commercial broadcasting. Though the practice was gradually being introduced during the latter part of the U Nu period, the Ne Win government stopped it upon taking power, and there appear to be no prospects for its reinstitution. The absence of radio commercials on BBS may be an important factor contributing to the relative weakness of radio in the Burmese mass-media system. Without any means of earning revenue (aside from license fees), radio is the weakest of the GUB-employed media when it comes to demonstrating a tangible financial return on government investment.

The distribution of program time in the early 1970s differs considerably from that reported by Fagen and UNESCO for the early 1960s. Fagen said that BBS content consisted of 25% news, 50% entertainment and 25% educational programs (Fagen 1962, p. 53). The proportions reported by UNESCO were 30% news, 60% entertainment, and 10% "talk shows" (UNESCO 1964, p. 203). UNESCO in 1975 reported that of 111 hours broadcast per week, 24 were devoted to news and information, 59 to folklore and popular music, and 5 to educational and cultural programs (UNESCO 1975, p. 263). The proportion of news content relative to entertainment declined considerably between 1962 and 1972, with entertainment accounting for some three-fourths of the total and news down to one-sixth of airtime in 1972 (see Table 21).

The BBS news broadcasts emphasize official statements related to the progress of government programs and rely almost exclusively on the output of the News Agency Burma (NAB). NAB (Domestic) collects and distributes national news and issues official pronouncements and announcements, while

Table 21. Burmese Radio Programming, 1972 (minutes per week, medium-wave)

Program Category	Burmese	English	Total	Percentage
News (including sports)	610	270	880	16.6
Music/Entertainment	3146	780	3926	73.9
Education	155	–	155	2.9
Information (general, women's shows, youth, armed forces, worker's and peasant's programs)	300	–	300	5.7
Other (program announcements)	49	–	49	0.9
Total	4260	1050	5310	100.0

Source: Program schedules in *Working People's Daily,* 5–11 July, 1972.

NAB (External) screens, reproduces, and provides the sole legal distribution channel for the daily intake from international wire services. Because of this heavy reliance on NAB, radio news essentially duplicates the content of Burmese newspapers. International news tends to be sparse, and treatment of these items is notably cautious, in keeping with the GUB policy of passive neutrality and noninvolvement in the disputes of other countries. Consistent with this same policy, BBS rarely accepts tapes or other programming from foreign embassies in Rangoon.

Music/entertainment programs consist of about 90% music and 10% light drama. Many of these programs are aimed at specific minority or occupational audiences and thus cannot be considered "pure entertainment." That GUB evaluates all programs in the light of their contributions to "The Burmese Way to Socialism" is indicated by an official analysis – carried out by a Modern Songs Scrutiny Board under BBS – of the words of Burmese songs played over radio during 1965. The study found that of 1,344 songs used by BBS during that year, 987 dealt with love, 177 with beauties of nature, 90 with social problems, and 99 with nation-building. It concluded that "only 7% of modern songs serve the people," while "73% have been sentimental songs which would have a detrimental effect on the revolution" (*Working People's Daily* 1966). As a result of such studies, GUB between 1965 and 1970 banned 588 Burmese records from BBS because of their unsuitable content (*Working People's Daily* 1970c).

Schools broadcasting is the major component of the education programming. The broadcasts consist of 20-minute mid-day transmissions (repeated in the evenings) three times weekly, aimed mainly at students in some 900 middle schools and 500 high schools. Program content has been devoted to subject areas such as English lessons, Burmese natural resources, school health, and the dignity of labor (*Working People's Daily* 1969).

The information programs, aimed at women, youth, armed forces personnel, workers, and peasants, are both informative and exhortative. Current programming content probably does not differ appreciably from that noted by one source, which in the mid-1960s offered an information/education content breakdown of 32% rural development, 37% civics, 23% science and art, and 8% health and hygiene (*Area Handbook for Burma* 1968, p. 205).

The preceding program breakdown applies only to medium-wave programs; the short-wave service for the indigenous minorities has a somewhat different mix. The six 30-minute shows in minority languages (and 15-minute Burmese news show), which run from 5:30—8:45 P.M. daily, consist of about one-half news, the other half divided among music, light features, and information.

3.8.6 Retarded Expansion

This study ends where it began: with the question of why Burmese radio has shown so little expansion and is today probably the least developed national radio operation in the region. One answer is financial: it costs a great deal of money to operate a radio network, and Burma has neither the foreign exchange nor wealthy allies necessary for sustaining such an operation. Second, there is a strong desire to maintain control. Provincial stations are undesirable because of their vulnerability to attack and takeover by insurgent and/or dissident political groups outside the capital. In a similar vein, advertising is not accepted, at least in part, because of a fear that commercialization would lead to undue influence and perhaps control by the dreaded Chinese and Indian minorities.

Third, and perhaps most important, GUB pays little attention to radio for ideological reasons. Since its efforts have been focused on reaching an elite audience of officials, party cadres, advanced students, and worker and peasant leaders, radio has been seen primarily as a means of reinforcing print-media messages. That this policy might be undergoing some change was suggested by Information Secretary Lt. Col. Tin Tun's comment in 1971 that a greater effort would be undertaken to reach a larger mass audience through broadcasting, in line with the widening of the mass base of the BSPP. Nonetheless, the actual operating policy of BBS shows clearly that rather than allowing radio to develop into a mass medium, programmed largely on the basis of the wishes of general audiences, GUB prefers to keep the medium limited, carefully controlled, programmed with heavy infusions of ideological content, and focused on the informational requirements of the elite, rather than mass audiences.

Television has not been introduced primarily for the same reasons, but also because the nation does not have technological and economic subsystems needed to use and maintain this medium (Nakajima 1974, pp. 110—13).

4. South Asia

The countries of South Asia have at least one common characteristic; they were all closely controlled by or linked to Britain at various times. In fact, to study the history of what has been called the subcontinent is to take note of splits of territories and governments — e.g., India from Britain, Pakistan from India, and Bangladesh from Pakistan.

South Asia represents one of the most populated areas in the world, with 744 million people, 581.2 million of whom reside in India, the world's second largest nation. The region has been hindered for years by economic starvation, cultural and linguistic strife, territorial disputes, and political and governmental instability. In the 1970s, strong one-person rule predominated in at least India, Pakistan, Bangladesh, and Sri Lanka.

Although not covered in separate contributions in the following pages, the meager mass-media operations in Bhutan and Sikkim are mentioned here.

Bhutan, a Himalayan state connected with the British East India Company in 1774 and after 1947 with India, has been greatly assisted by outside forces. In 1974, for example, India provided 75% of Bhutan's annual budget. As for mass media, Bhutan is served by one weekly, *Kuensel,* a government paper in English, Bhutanese, and Nepalese, and about an hour daily of broadcasting directed to Bhutan and Sikkim by All India Radio External Services. Among United Nations Development Program funds directed to Bhutan in 1974–75 are those for communication and transportation. The largest portion of these funds will go toward a radio network and telcommunications system, $380,000.

Sikkim, a British protectorate from 1890 until India took over in 1947, was made an associate state of India in 1974–75. In an August 1974 bill, it was specified that India will have exclusive right of constructing, maintaining, and regulating all infrastructure facilities, including telephones, telegraph, and wireless installations. The capital, Gangtok, sizzled with anger after the annexation, many critics feeling because of India's extensive control of communications with Sikkim, New Delhi had been able to monopolize the flow of news and views. All projects in Sikkim have been financed outright by India, although there have been no indications that communications was among the development priorities.

In 1974, the country of 300,000 (65% of whom are Nepalese) was served by one newspaper and shared one hour of external broadcasting of All India Radio with Bhutan.

4.1 India, *by G. C. Awasthy*

The British East India Company gained control of Bengal and the Coromandel coast of India in the 1760s, and after wars with the Marathas, Mysoreans, and Sikhs, became supreme throughout the subcontinent. The British crown was given control over India in 1858. Independence was granted on 15 August 1947, when the subcontinent was divided into India and Pakistan. India has been involved in hostilities with China (1962) and Pakistan (1965 and 1971) over the past decade and a half. The government of Indira Gandhi and her Congress Party has met numerous crises, the latest of which occurred in mid-1975 when opposition parties threatened her control. The reaction was the declaration of a state of emergency, during which media were severely censored and thousands of political opponents jailed.

India is made up of 21 states and 9 union territories, comprising the world's seventh largest country in land area. It has nine cities with over one million people, the largest being Calcutta (7 million), greater Bombay (6 million), Delhi (3.6 million), and Madras (2.5 million). With ethnic origins traceable to races such as Aryan, Dravidian, and Mongol, Indians speak a wide diversity of languages. India's constitution recognizes 16 different languages, including English. The multilingual characteristic, however, is much more frightening than is officially recognized, especially in regard to broadcasting. To reach the masses, nearly 75% of whom are illiterate, languages and dialects otherwise without any official status must be pressed into service.

The 1961 Indian census, for example, recorded 1,952 mother tongues; constitutionally recognized languages alone can be divided into 380 mother tongues. To emphasize the complexity of the language situation, there are 17 languages, each spoken by more than 500,000 people, further sub-divided into 241 mother languages; 19 other languages, each with 100,000 to 500,000 speakers, and subdivided into 69 mother-language groupings, and hundreds of others, with or without subgroupings, plus 103 non-Indian languages spoken by over 500,000 people.

India is also a land of many faiths — Hindus, Muslims, Christians, Sikhs, Buddhists, and Jains, among numerous others. The constitution guarantees

G.C. Awasthy is a partner in a sales corporation in New Delhi. He was formerly with All India Radio for 15 years, serving at nine radio stations, and the author of *Broadcasting in India*. He has also studied broadcasting systems in about a dozen other nations through on-the-spot observation. He is founding editor of the *Indian Journal of Communication Arts*.

equality, freedom of speech, freedom of assembly, association, or union, freedom of conscience, profession, practice, propagation, and worship, and above all, the right of minorities to conserve their culture, language, and institutions.

4.1.1 Overview

India is a union of states and territories, the states having been formed largely on linguistic lines. Each Indian language recognized by the constitution has a state of its own, the only exception being Urdu, second language in two or three states. Unlike the states, union territories, being smaller in size and poorer in resources, are administered directly by the union government. All states have their own legislatures, to which representatives are elected for five-year terms on the basis of adult franchise.

According to India's constitution, the state governments enjoy within their respective territorial jurisdiction complete freedom in 66 subjects. These subjects include education, local self-government, land revenue, police, jails, public works, forests, fisheries, and public health, among others (see §4.1.10).

Important to note is the fact that defense, foreign affairs, communications, and currency, as well as broadcasting, have been assigned to the union government. Indian broadcasting is operated and managed by the nation's Ministry of Information and Broadcasting, and the only broadcasting organization in the nation, All India Radio, is a government department.

For years, persistent demands have come from political parties, the intelligentsia, and broadcasting experts to convert AIR into an autonomous corporation. The government has been resilient to these demands for change; recently, however, it has toyed with the idea of making AIR seem more autonomous in operational matters, at the same time retaining its administrative control over the station.

4.1.2 British Influence

Curiously enough, during the British colonial period, broadcasting existed somewhat privately. For example, amateur radio clubs were first permitted to operate in 1924, but only in towns not covered by official broadcasting stations. In 1927, the Indian Broadcasting Company (IBC), a private enterprise, established radio stations in Bombay and Calcutta, but soon ran into financial difficulties. After attempts to resuscitate IBC, the Indian government in 1934 decided to run broadcasting as an official activity under the name Indian State Broadcasting Service. A year later, Lionel Fielden of BBC became the first broadcasting controller in India, and soon after, at his insistence, the service was redesignated All India Radio (AIR) (see Awasthy 1965).

Thereafter, broadcasting in India never had more freedom than what the British government chose for the medium. Fielden tried to keep AIR functionally free of government, succeeding to a large extent because he was able to cut across bureaucratic control and go straight to the viceroy, if necessary. Fielden's exit, World War II, the British ban on political and controversial broadcasts, and the denial of broadcast access to Indian National Congress leaders, however, made All India Radio suspect in the public's eyes. The British used AIR to serve their own interests to the extent that during World War II, listeners in India had more faith in Radio Berlin than in AIR (see B. Rao 1974).

Independence in 1947 did not help the situation much as AIR still has not been able to shed some of its British influences. Although AIR is now very popular with the masses and public interest matters are generally discussed frankly and freely, governmental control continues to be rigid, giving rise to the charge that the ruling party uses broadcasting for self-publicity and propaganda.

One aspect of the British inheritance has since proved to be particularly useful. When the India Bill was being drafted in 1935, considerable pressure was mounted to make broadcasting a state subject. Lord J. C. W. Reith, BBC's first director-general, strongly opposed this move, thus saving India from possible future political chaos. For, had the move succeeded, India, a multilingual country, poorly developed in communications and abounding in fissiparous tendencies, would suddenly have had as many broadcasting authorities as it had languages and dialects, each interfering with the others. But, under the union government, All India Radio has played a laudable role in keeping the country emotionally united.

4.1.3 Programming

Because of the multiplicity of languages, broadcasting in India is necessarily multilingual. Each language area has a broadcasting station in the capital city and/or important cities of the state. Besides 16 languages recognized in the constitution, All India Radio presses into service 91 dialects from 17 stations to foster communication links with tribal communities.

AIR Home Service program units include News, Vividh Bharati (Light Entertainment), and General Cultural, while stations are broken down into the zones of north, south, east, and west. Delhi (north), Madras (south), Calcutta (east), and Bombay (west), being the principal stations in their zones, are known as zonal stations.

The News Service feeds news from the central unit in New Delhi and from regional units. About 232 news bulletins are issued daily: 50 in 21 languages in the External Service and the other 182 for the Home Service. In the Home Service, the central unit in Delhi originates 83 bulletins in 18 major languages; the regional stations produce the remaining 99 bulletins in 18 languages and 33 tribal dialects (Baji 1974, p. 15). All language-area stations receive from Delhi at least two to three daily news bulletins of five to ten minutes. The Delhi AIR News Service has domestic newsgathering personnel as well as a small monitoring unit which feeds the general newsroom with items from foreign stations. The monitoring unit also supplies transcripts of these broadcasts to all government ministries in addition to AIR. News bulletins in all major Indian languages are prepared and broadcast by the News Service 24 hours daily. Also, four major bulletins in English and four others in Hindi are broadcast daily, in addition to the two-minute Hindi and English bulletins broadcast hourly. Regional stations with more than one channel relay all these bulletins, while others relay according to local requirements. Besides these bulletins in Hindi and English, the News Service prepares and broadcasts at least two to three others daily in each major language of India. Regional news bulletins are prepared and broadcast by the principal station in each language area. The News Service also prepares other programs for broadcast and relay by AIR stations, including newsreels in both English and Hindi twice weekly; "Spotlight," a daily discussion show pertaining to major news items of significant political and economic developments; and "Current Affairs," once weekly. The quality of AIR national news programs has been criticized often, the most frequent complaint being that the news is presented in a partisan manner, playing high the party and personalities in power (B. Rao 1974, p. 20; see Baji 1974).

The Vividh Bharati Service is centrally produced in Bombay. Spread over four transmissions, it is aired for more than 12 hours daily, containing mainly film and light music. Thirty-six AIR centers broadcast Vividh Bharati programs, 18 of which carry a commercial service (B. Rao 1974). Because of Vividh Bharati's commercial success, the number of centers carrying the commercial service is expected to increase to 28 (Singh 1974, p. 7).

Basically a library service, Vividh Bharati sends dubbed programs to originating stations ten days in advance; the shows are broadcast according to a uniform schedule. The service has been criticized for its centralized nature (not providing enough regional appeal) and for its poor reception because of an insufficient number of channels (B. Rao 1974, p. 21).

Programs in the General Cultural Service also are fed from the national and regional levels. The four types of national programs broadcast regularly are: talks/discussions, music, plays, and features. One may wonder how AIR manages to have national programs in the face of so many languages (see Chatterji 1974). The answer is that these programs − except for the national music program − are multi-lingual. For example, an English or Hindi version of a drama selected for the national broadcast hook-up is circulated in advance to all language stations for translation. The translated script is then produced locally, and on the scheduled date of broadcast, the stations originate their own language versions of the drama simultaneously.

Music really does not present a language problem, even though two distinct styles of music exist − Hindustani and Carnatic. The national music program, broadcast on Saturday nights, features in turn vocal and instrumental recitals by top-ranking artists in both styles; the program is relayed simultaneously from Delhi by all of the regional stations.

Roughly speaking, 60−65% of AIR transmission time is utilized for music broadcasts, 35−40% for spoken-word items, including news and composite shows meant for specific audiences. This ratio holds true for nearly all General Cultural program channels in the Home Service network. The percentage of music on the Vividh Bharati program channel, however, is almost 90—95%.

In both the Carnatic and Hindustani styles of music, many subdivisions exist. For example, Hindustani style is divided into classical, light classical, light, folk, and film music. Each language area has its own fund of light songs, and in practically every language, new songs are being written and set to music. Similarly, each language area has a rich heritage of folk songs and devotional music; the latter is utilized by virtually all stations in their first morning transmissions.

As for spoken-word shows, AIR stations broadcast talks, discussions, plays, features, newsreels, sports reviews, and commentaries, mostly in the regional language, but also in English and Hindi when the number of listeners knowing these languages warrants such usage. Additionally, nearly all important stations in each language area broadcast composite programs for specific audiences, such as children, women, rural dwellers, armed forces, schools, and universities. Radio farm and home shows, planned in consultation with the agriculture and health ministries, are permanent features with a number of AIR stations. During the past decade, there has been an emphasis on field-based programs, where the microphone is taken into fields, factories, and homes to get audience participation. The impetus was the development of Farm and Home Units in 1966, Family Planning Units in 1967, and the Youth Service (Yuv Vani) in 1969. AIR has 38 Farm and Home Units, 37 Family Planning Units, and 48 centers which broadcast programs for youth, 4 of which have separate channels used exclusively for this service (Das 1974, pp. 15—16). Intended for the 15- to 25-year age group, the Youth Service is very popular, probably because it takes a liberal and emancipated approach to youth problems. The service allows youth to air their views on all important topics concerning them and their nation.

Other specialized audiences are also served by AIR. Almost all stations broadcast weekly a few items in English and Hindi, besides the news relays mentioned above. English programs are still broadcast substantially from the four zonal stations at Delhi, Bombay, Calcutta, and Madras.

Educational programs, initiated by broadcasting pioneers in 1929—30, are now broadcast from 27 stations, two to five days weekly. The daily program, varying from 20—40 minutes, is addressed predominantly to students of higher secondary classes. Stations originating educational programs maintain consultative panels, made up of well-known educationalists, teachers, and officers of the state education department, which offer planning advice. Schedules, drawn up with due care, are sent in advance to schools with listening facilities, but unfortunately, except in two or three states, the programs have failed to make much impact. Not much interest in educational programs exists among teachers or students. Broadcast materials do not reach schools in time to be relevant; teachers do not prepare themselves for guiding students; programs are not dovetailed into school curricula, and listening conditions are far from satisfactory. Apart from programs for school children, AIR was broadcasting material for university students, but the audience was extremely small.

AIR produces its own programs, there being no other agencies in India engaged in broadcasting production. Because the question of competition does not arise, program quality varies with each station, depending upon the talent available. AIR is quite adequately equipped with program planning and production staff; for example, the number of instrumentalists and other artists (script writers, drama voices, producers, and composers) on the total staffs of all stations is about 2,000. Musicians are booked by AIR on a casual basis, their fee varying from Rs. 30 (about $4) to Rs. 200 (about $29) per broadcast, depending on the artist's grading, determined by regular audition committees functioning at each language center.

Normally, All India Radio does not use foreign broadcasts or syndicated materials. India, however, does have cultural program-exchange relations with other nations, carried out in a program-exchange unit. When received, such programs are properly screened and circulated to stations for possible use. The program-exchange unit also facilitates the internal exchange of programs among AIR stations. Each AIR station must send periodically to the unit, recordings of its select items, details of which are circulated to all stations, and copies of the recordings supplied to stations desiring them (see *Variety* 1975h, p. 112).

4.1.4 Transmitters

Only AM transmission and reception facilities are used by AIR; the two FM transmitters (at Delhi and Calcutta) are used only in cases of a breakdown in power supply. All India Radio presses into service 138 transmitters, 106 of which are medium-wave and 32 short-wave, for home and external broadcasts (B. Rao 1974, p. 18).

Most broadcasting equipment must be imported into India, either in its manufactured state or in parts to be assembled. Bharat Electronics, a government undertaking, has the monopoly for supplying all electronic equipment to AIR; it fulfills its functions by assembling radio equipment brought to India from Japan and Holland in unfinished forms.

Seventy medium-wave and short-wave transmitters are used to broadcast in different languages and dialects. All transmitters do not carry original programs. Forty-five principal broadcasting stations function and at least 27 auxiliary centers relay programs from their respective principal stations. Three towns, however, Baroda, Darbhanga, and Shantiniketan, have only studio and recording facilities; programs produced and recorded at these centers are sent to Ahmedabad, Patna, and Calcutta, respectively, for broadcast. New stations were being set up in 40 different centers in 1975, and it was estimated India would have more than 100 stations by 1977 (*Variety* 1975h, p. 112).

As indicated earlier, AIR domestic stations are broken down into the zones of north, south, east, and west, with Delhi, Madras, Calcutta, and Bombay being the principal zonal stations. Such grouping is only for relay purposes and does not interfere with programming patterns of regional stations, which may or may not have the same language as the zonal station.

Stations at Delhi, Lucknow, Simla, Bhopal, Jammu, and Srinagar in the north zone; Calcutta, Gauhati, Kohima, Kurseong in the east zone; Madras and Hyderabad in the south zone; and Bombay in the west, also have short-wave transmitters, varying in strength from 2–100 kw. (*WRTH* 1974, pp. 145–46).

Generally, AIR stations located in the state capitals put out three transmissions daily, usually between 6–10 A.M., noon to 3 P.M., and 5–11 P.M. Auxiliary centers located in less important cities have two transmissions daily, and in some cases, only one.

Each AIR station has attached to it a receiving center which helps in relaying news, national programs, and other important broadcasts originating from Delhi.

4.1.5 Organization and Control

As a government department, all AIR sanctions flow from the minister, who is assisted and advised by a secretary and joint secretary. All policy decisions are made at the level of the ministry and communicated to the directorate general of All India Radio for implementation. AIR is headed by a director general who depends on the chief engineer and four deputies for assistance. Immediately below the deputies are a number of directors, assistant program directors, and program and administration branches, where all matters are processed in the usual bureaucratic fashion. Similarly, the chief engineer is aided by an "additional chief engineer," and a number of deputy and senior engineers. AIR technical and program matters are not separately controlled; formally, both are administered by the director general, as are all radio and TV stations and subordinate offices, such as project circles, research department, maintenance department, and the office of editor of program journals.

Each Indian station is headed by a station director who controls the work of the program staff and, with the help of a station engineer, that of the technical staff. At stations having high-power transmitters, the engineering staff is under an engineer-in-charge or deputy chief engineer, while an auxiliary station is headed either by a station engineer or an assistant station director. One of the station director's most important duties is to maintain close liaison with the state government and to help publicize state policies and plans.

Because of AIR's government department status, it need not be supervised by any licensing body. All AIR accounts, however, are subject to audit. For example, within the directorate general itself, an inspection unit, under a deputy director general, conducts periodic inspections of the accounts, administration, and program activities of all broadcasting centers. Such inspections have a salutary effect.

Very little scope exists for AIR to be subjected to direct political party pressure, except through questions in parliament, which do sometimes lead to some soul-searching. Of course, the ruling party is always in an advantageous position as far as AIR is concerned. At the same time, AIR has developed a code by which it is guided in matters of political broadcasts. If the ruling party at the center is the same as that in the different states, AIR does not have any difficulty. When a party in power in a particular state, however, is not the same as the one at the center, AIR's role in that state is hard to cope with. The AIR code stipulates that stations may not broadcast criticism of friendly nations, attacks on religions or communities, obscenity or defamation, attacks on political parties by name, or hostile criticism of any state or the center. Also forbidden by the code are broadcasts tending to be against maintenance of law and order or inciting to violence, those amounting to contempt of court, aspersions against the integrity of the president, governors, or judiciary, or anything showing disrespect to the constitution or advocating change in the constitution by violence (see Baji 1974).

When the code is violated, the station director brings to the notice of the violator the relevant script passages. If the violator does not accede to the director's suggestions, the latter may justifiably cancel the broadcast.

Cases of opinion differences between a state minister and an AIR station director have occurred. The code provides that at such times, the ministerial talk to be broadcast is referred to the Minister of Information and Broadcasting of India who decides whether any change in the text is necessary to avoid code violation.

4.1.6 Financing and Advertising

Each station's budget varies according to its importance and the multifariousness of the station's activities. Budget grants are from Rs. 100,000 ($14,300) to Rs. 1.5 million ($214,285) annually. The grants make provision for program and salary expenditures. Stations in Bombay, Madras, Calcutta, and Delhi are the most expensive to the government.

Overall, AIR is no longer a financial burden on the government, supporting itself mainly through license-fee revenue. A secondary revenue source comes from sales of publications and program journals. Customs duty levied on the importation of broadcast receivers and spare parts is also treated as indirect revenue for purposes of assessing AIR's working as a commercial department. Receipts from customs duty, however, are credited to the customs department in government books and do not find a place even in the *pro-forma* accounts of AIR.

There are 12 types of radio-receiver licenses in India. Under the category of domestic broadcast receiver licenses, BRLs, four subdivisions — domestic, village, inexpensive radios, and tourists — are in force. Licenses are issued by posts and telegraphs for private and domestic operation of radio sets; they are not transferable. The annual radio license fee is Rs. 15 (about $2) per set in urban areas and Rs. 10 (about $1.40) per set in rural areas. An additional fee of Rs. 3 (about $.40) is charged for every additional set owned by a licensee. For inexpensive domestic sets, the annual fee is Rs. 7.50 (about $1), and Rs. 2.50 (about $.33) for every additional set of that type. The tourist fee is Rs. 7.50 per set. The Posts and Telegraphs Department retains Rs. 2 per set from the amount collected to defray collection costs and to finance antipiracy work that it carries out. In mid-1975, the Department of Electronics recommended to the Indian government that license fees on inexpensive radio sets be dropped to encourage rural people to use more of them (*Variety* 1975i).

During the year April 1971 to March 1972, for example, the number of receiving sets licensed was 12,772,225, yielding a total revenue of Rs. 172,700,000 (nearly $25 million). Similarly, the number of television sets licensed during this period was 44,055, accounting for a revenue intake of Rs. 1,103,000 (about $150,000). By 31 December 1973, the number of licensed radio sets had increased to 14,033,919 (B. Rao 1974); the number of TV receivers was estimated at 65,000 (Chander 1973, p. 16).

An additional income source results from the Commercial Broadcasting Service, introduced in Bombay in 1967. The government, reluctant at first to introduce commercials, shed its inhibitions as it watched the Commercial Service of Radio Ceylon being heavily patronized by Indian goods and products, thereby causing a loss of foreign exchange. Of course, revenue that accrues from commercials was also in great demand.

The Commercial Service is broadcast from 18 centers, which are the eight entertainment channels converted into commercial centers. The conversion has been effected without any change in the basic pattern of fare broadcast in the light entertainment service; spots, jingles, and time checks the majority of which are 15-second duration, are inserted between two or more phonograph records. Total AIR income resulting from commercial broadcasts is nearly Rs. 40 million (between $5.5 and $6 million). In 1974, AIR officials, feeling there should be more demand for sponsored programs, set up a committee to investigate radio advertising in India (*Vidura* 1974c, p. 742).

Broadcast time is sold centrally by the central Sales Unit in Bombay; 10% of each commercial center's broadcast schedule is available for sale. On an average, it comes to 75 minutes per day per center. The Central Sales Unit accepts bookings of time on behalf of each center; CSU informs each center of its bookings for the month at least 15 days in advance. The 18 commercial centers, located in eight language areas, create advertisements which are largely in the language of the region, in addition to English and Hindi ads common to all centers.

Programming time is divided into "A" and "C" segments, the "A" block regarded as peak listening time. Costs for each block of time vary, of course, and Sunday time is more expensive.

10- to 30-minute sponsored programs are accepted for broadcast. Sponsored shows must be strictly entertainment-oriented. The sponsor's name or product is mentioned at the beginning and end of 101—15-minute programs. In longer shows, there is no objection to the mention of the sponsor's name in the middle of the program as well, provided there is a natural break.

Standards established for the benefit of sponsors follow the spirit of the programming code. They stipulate that programs should not: abridge Indian laws; offend against morality, decency, and religious laws; bring "into disrespect the rights and susceptibilities, dignity and brotherhood of all people residing in this country"; or bring any dishonor to the sancity of marriage and family life. Programs should not incite people to commit violence or crime or promote disorder or breach of the law; make any reference which may adversely affect friendly relations with foreign states and their people; or exploit the national emblems, any part of the constitution, persons or personalities of India, national leaders or state dignitaries. Additionally, the matter, content, and type of sponsored programs shall be subject to the approval of the AIR director general, or any officer deputed by him, and "he shall have absolute discretion to reject or refuse to broadcast any programme without assigning any reason and without incurring any *liability* by reason of such refusal."

Standards for the length and advertisement content of sponsored programs regulate that a proportion of one to ten be used in determining maximum duration of commercials to program time. Programs permitted to accept commercial sponsorship include Indian and Western music shows, dramas and skits, brains trust, quiz and similar varieties, musical variety, personality programs with audience participation, and those specially designed for women, children and youth. Also, talks on noncontroversial topics of general interest, sports, events, and education and culture fare can be sponsored.

Programs of a religious and political nature, however, as well as news and commentaries, are not acceptable for sponsorship. If the sponsor uses phonograph records in any of his programs, he must indemnify All India Radio against all claims, loss, and damage arising out of, or in consequence to, copyright on the records. Where programs contain music, sponsors must state whether the music content is original or dubbed from commercial discs.

All India Radio has the right to censor, edit, or amend the text of any sponsored show. The sponsor must submit all program scripts, along with continuity sheets, to the sales director of Central Sales Unit and obtain his approval six weeks in advance of the broadcast date. He must also supply a tape recording of his program two weeks before airing (see also Singh 1974).

4.1.7   External Broadcasting

The AIR External Services Division in Delhi started in 1939, is headed by two directors, each having a well-defined sphere of responsibility. Directors are assisted by deputies and language supervisors who are helped by translators, announcers, and language assistants. Each Indian-language unit is headed by a program officer.

AIR external broadcasting is accomplished in 24 languages, 16 of which are foreign, including the general overseas services in English, and 8 which are Indian. Foreign languages used are Burmese, Cantonese, Kuoyu, Indonesian, French, Thai, Sinhala, Nepali, Tibetan, Pushtu, Dari, Persian, Arabic, Russian, Swahili, and English.

Roughly, external broadcasts may be categorized according to the 15 foreign-language services and the General Overseas Services in English; services in

Hindi, Tamil, Gujarati, and Konkani, directed to more than five million Indians living in Africa and Southeast Asia, and those broadcast in Urdu, Bengali, Panjabi, and Sindhi for listeners in Pakistan and Bangladesh. Foreign-language broadcasts are on the air 17 hours and 20 minutes daily, and General Overseas Services for 9 hours and 45 minutes per day. Services for Indian listeners in Africa and Southeast Asia are broadcast 5 hours and 25 minutes daily, and those for listeners in Pakistan and Bangladesh, 18 hours.

4.1.8 Training

Training at AIR is carried out through its schools: two meant for radio − one for engineers, another for program personnel − and one for television. Except for the television-training school, which is aided by UNDP funds, the other two merely conduct refresher courses periodically. For example, the program-training school, headed by a director and two program instructors, plans refresher classes of one to six-weeks duration for various staff categories.

4.1.9 Television

When Indians discuss television for India, they do not talk about past or present development, but about future growth and possibilities. As a mass medium, television has not had impact on the Indians, mainly because this giant and populous nation only had two television stations by 1972. At that rate of development − 13 years between the first station at Delhi in 1959 and the second in Bombay in 1972 − it would take almost a century for TV to extend to the entire length and breadth of India.

Television had been given a low priority because of the poor state of the Indian electronics industry, the absence of broadband telecommunication links in the country, the immense expense of television to viewers, and the desire on the part of AIR to develop its own corps of trained manpower to produce indigenous programming (Chander 1973, p. 16). By 1973, however, part of the situation had changed: India was manufacturing TV transmission and reception equipment, a TV training institute was set up, and nation-wide broadband microwave linkages were planned. By the end of 1973, additional television centers in Poona, Srinagar, and Amritsar (see Mohan 1974, p. 579) were already in existence; a year later, Madras, Lucknow, Calcutta, and Jullundur stations with relay transmitters were to be on the air. By early 1975, AIR proposed another 11 stations with 48 relay transmitters (Chander 1973, p. 16). There have been delays, however, in the establishment of many of these stations; for example, the Calcutta station was still not telecasting by early 1975 (Sengupta 1975, p. 53), and the Patna television center in 1975 was still selecting a site.

When the question of introducing television to India was publicly discussed in the mid-1950s, a number of misgivings were expressed: Was television to be merely a status symbol, a matter of national prestige? Or was it to impress the outside world that India was becoming progressive? Others felt that if television was to be developed into a national network for the education, information, and entertainment of the people, two basics were necessary: adequate financial resources and a regular, rapid recruitment and training of program and technical personnel. Many others strongly suspected that television's introduction would divert financial resources from sound broadcasting. In a country which has reached an optimum level of sound broadcasting development, that would not have been a problem; but after nearly 50 years, broadcasting in India still does not cover the entire nation. Backwardness, ignorance, illiteracy, and poverty make it imperative that government communicate its development programs to the masses in outlying border areas, as well as in the inaccessible villages of the interior; for many decades, this will have to be accomplished through sound broadcasting. Hence, many fear that TV development at the cost of radio would damage the country's interests.

Experimental Television Service in Delhi was inaugurated on 15 September 1959, as part of a UNESCO "experimentation, training, and evaluation" project. Designed to evaluate the effectiveness of social education TV programs on organized groups of viewers, the project at the outset, had encouraging results.

As a result of an agreement with the Ford Foundation, television programs for Delhi schools were started in October 1961. Today, telecasts generally cover subjects such as physics, chemistry, general science, social studies, and English. Programs of 20–30 minutes are telecast Monday through Thursday at 9 A.M., 9:40 A.M., and 11 A.M., and repeated for afternoon schools at 2:35 P.M., 3:15 P.M., and 4:45 P.M. On Fridays and Saturdays, the programs are shown at 9 A.M. and 9:40 A.M. and repeated at 2:35 P.M. and 3:15 P.M. Occasionally, teachers' training programs are carried on television. Teleclubs were formed to discuss televised topics such as community health, traffic, adulteration of foodstuffs, and citizenship. By the early 1970s, as the number of privately owned TV sets increased, the number of teleclubs dropped sharply (Chandiram 1974, p. 730).

In addition to the above-mentioned education fare, Indian television in 1967 created "Krishi Darshan," instructional programs designed for agriculturists in the Union Territory of Delhi and those in border areas of the neighboring states Haryana and Uttar Pradesh (*Media* 1974m, p. 11; also see Green 1972, p. 241). Television in India also provides magazine programs, news and news reviews, folk music and dance, discussions and talks on topical subjects, literary programs, and children's shows. Of course, the most popular fare is the screening of feature films on Saturday and Sunday. Programs from Delhi, all in Hindi and English, are telecast from 6:30–10 P.M., except on Friday (6:30–10 P.M.) and Sunday (6–10 P.M.). The Bombay station, functioning since 2 October 1972, has the same overall program pattern as that of Delhi. To cater to Bombay residents' needs, however, programs are telecast in five languages for 3½ hours each evening. Based on a 1974–75 survey, Hindi and English programming were the most popular, preferred by 70% of those sampled. As for the Bombay viewers' program preferences, they chose sports, films and film songs, science reports, Indian and world affairs, music, drama, and children's shows, in that order

(Noorani 1975).

Despite television's slow growth from 1959, there had been those who recommended expansion of the medium. For example, on 4 December 1964, the Ministry of Information and Broadcasting appointed a committee to evaluate the work of the ministry's various media units. In a report submitted over two years later, the committee recommended that "a country-wide coverage by the end of the Fifth Plan should be attained by entrusting the planning and execution to an independent TV authority." The committee urged that TV services be extended to 113 other towns, as well as provide a daily school service, in-service training for teachers and village-level workers, farmers' shows, social education programs for adults, children's fare, and entertainment. While this committee conducted investigations, a technical committee, under the chairmanship of Dr. S. Bhagavantam, was constituted in 1965 to study technical aspects of television development, and new methods and techniques to provide TV services equivalent to the highest international standards.

The Bhagavantam Committee recommended that .5-kw. pilot transmitters and corresponding transmission towers be "put up at existing installations of AIR to facilitate the very early inception of television in the selected centers." These transmitters were to be replaced later by more powerful ones, and pilot transmitters were to be shifted to the other centers.

Also in the 1960s, AIR's planning and development unit emerged with a master plan which envisaged an earthbound network of TV stations, transmitters, and relay centers to be set up in India, city by city, over a period of 20 years. According to AIR's plan, interstate, intra-state, and national TV interconnections were to be provided the TV system by the Posts and Telegraphs Department. The plan, conventional in concept, is heavily conditioned by India's resources. The time period required to achieve AIR's target is suggestive of a relaxed and leisurely approach to the problem.

The rival plan is that prepared by the Indian Space Research Organization scientists under the leadership of the late Dr. Vikram Sarabhai. ISRO's plan foresaw a single synchronous satellite capable of transmitting directly to sophisticated receiving sets and indirectly to conventional sets through rediffusion by earthbound relaying stations. The five-channel, geo-stationary satellite will operate on five different frequencies to reach five artificially divided zones covering the entire country. Through its receivers, the satellite will be fed programs from Delhi, Madras, Bombay, Calcutta and Srinagar. The synchronous satellite, together with the existing and proposed terrestrial network, will provide television coverage to virtually every one of India's 3,000 towns and 560,000 villages. If all goes well, the satellite, built and launched wholly by Indians, will be placed in orbit by the end of 1981. By 1985, the ISRO plan will have achieved its target, being a ten-year plan beginning in 1975.

The plan's main drawback is that five channels are insufficient to meet the varied needs of a country with such baffling cultural and linguistic diversities (see Masani 1975). Also, the sophisticated sets designed to receive programs directly from the satellite will likely be too expensive for the common viewer. As it is, even conventional receiving sets, costing about Rs. 2,500 (about $350), can be afforded by only the upper middle class.

Both the AIR and ISRO plans were studied at length by the planning commission. While the government decided in early 1972 to emphasize TV in a really big way and in the time frame of the 1970s, the choice of plan was left to experts convening during 1972–73 in a series of seminars, meetings, and group discussions. On the basis of the experts' recommendations, the government agreed upon the coexistence of the proposed satellite with a substantive earthbound network. This hybrid plan was favored because of India's size and cultural and linguistic diversity which earth-based TV originating centers in each language region could satisfy.

The hybrid plan is estimated to cost the government over Rs. 4 billion ($570 million), including costs of sophisticated receiving sets which the government plans to install in centers in about 150,000 villages, and conventional sets to be provided the remaining 411,000 villages and 3,000 towns.

The project will employ about 5,000 engineers and scientists, 20,000 technicians, 20,000 persons required to produce TV sets — at the rate of 100,000 a year — and 12,000 technicians to maintain the receiving sets.

In August 1975, as the first phase of this satellite plan, Satellite Instructional Television Experiment (SITE) began beaming instructional TV programs via an Applications Technology Satellite (ATS-F) to 5,000 selected villages in Orissa, Madhya Pradesh, Mysore, Andhra Pradesh, Bihar, and Rajasthan. Half of the villages received the broadcasts directly from the satellite, the other half by a rediffusion cable network of wireless transmission from a relay station (*Intermedia*, August 1975, pp. 11–12). The ATS-F has two audio channels on one video channel for this experiment. The satellite is on loan to India from the United States to test the efficacy of television in modernizing agriculture, population control and national integration, upgrading and expanding education, and bettering the lives of rural people (Chander 1975). The one-year experiment involved four hours of broadcasts daily; of the total 1,500 broadcast hours during the year, 360 were for children's viewing in schools (Chander 1974a, p. 546; see Karamchandani 1974). The experiment has aroused a great deal of enthusiasm, as well as criticism (see Krishnamoorthy 1975; Nelson 1974; Nickelson 1974; *Vidura* 1974a, b, c; Kale 1974; Rana 1974; Kamath 1974; Mulay 1974; Dhawan 1974; Gupta 1974).

Little doubt exists that India desperately needs television, inasmuch as it requires powerful and effective means to achieve economic development and social transformation. The nation's ambitious TV plan must obviously be piloted with utmost care and competence; any shortfall at any point is likely to have disastrous consequences. Take, for example, TV community-viewing sets which the government has undertaken to provide. Repair and maintenance of these sets, particularly in remote areas, will require extraordinary loyalty to purpose. (AIR's experience in the maintenance of radio community-listening sets has not been a happy one.)

In the particular context of the initiation of television on a grand scale in India, the paradox remains: in 50 years of radio broadcasting, there have been only 150 million radio sets for 540 million people; therefore, how many television sets can be expected to be in India after a decade or two? Social transformation may be the objective of television in India, but will it be achieved without economic prosperity?

4.1.10 The 1975 Emergency

In mid-1975, Prime Minister Indira Gandhi, in a crackdown on her political opponents, imposed a state of emergency in India. Thousands of political opponents were jailed, and a strict censorship policy was put into force. AIR was duly affected. A few days after Mrs. Gandhi went on AIR to announce her move, a fire, suspected of being an act of sabotage, destroyed the TV-film library in the New Delhi AIR Building. Opposition forces had accused AIR of being biased in favor of the prime minister. While firemen battled the flames, neither AIR's radio nor TV services made any reference to the fire. For two days after the emergency was declared, AIR was the only source of news for many Indians, all newspapers having been suspended temporarily (*Philadelphia Inquirer* 1975, p. 3-A).

One source said All India Radio since the emergency sounds like All-Indira Radio (*Variety* 1975j). AIR listeners in Pakistan, who claimed that in the past they distrusted their own official broadcasting station and depended on AIR, said AIR now was worse than Pakistani radio (London *Times*, 29 July 1975, p. 5). The BBC, declaring Indian censorship regulations were unacceptable, suspended its news operations in India and withdrew its correspondent (London *Times*, 24 July 1975, p. 1).

4.2 Pakistan, *by Sharif al-Mujahid*

Since at least 1930, the idea of a separate state for the Muslims of the Indian subcontinent had been proposed. It was formally adopted by the All-India Muslim League in 1940. A Muslim state called Pakistan consisting of east and west wings, emerged from the partition of India 15 August 1947. The nation had a parliamentary form of government until Field Marshal Mohammed Ayub Khan seized power from 1958 to March 1969. In the first free elections in December 1970, Zulfikar Ali Bhutto's People's Party dominated the west while Sheikh Mujibur Rahman's Awami League gained control in East Pakistan. Mujib stepped up demands for autonomy in East Pakistan, civil war broke out, and on

Sharif al-Mujahid is chairman of the Journalism Department, University of Karachi and editor of *University of Karachi Gazette* and *Pakistan Journal of Social Sciences*. He has professional experience with seven media in Pakistan, the U.S., and India. He has been a visiting lecturer in the U.S., is the author and editor of many books, and received his Ph.D. from Syracuse University.

26 March 1971, the east became the People's Republic of Bangladesh. Pakistan quit the British Commonwealth in January 1972, upon learning that Britain would recognize Bangladesh.

Geographically, Pakistan in the form it was conceived in 1947, was unique in the history of state structures, as it consisted of two large blocks. Not only were about 54% of the people concentrated in East Pakistan, comprising only one-seventh of the area, but, more importantly, the two regions were separated by almost 1,000 miles of alien Indian territory. Poor transport facilities in both states, high mountains of 12,000–25,000 feet in West Pakistan, and numerous streams and waterways in what is now Bangladesh rendered a number of places within the two states normally inaccessible during certain periods of the year.

Linguistically, Pakistan had two national languages (Urdu in West Pakistan and Bengali in East Pakistan); English, which continues to be the chief language for inter-wing communication and administrative and court functions; five regional languages; and a host of dialects.

The Pakistani society is in a stage of transition, and its communications systems reflect this trait, being bifurcated and fragmented and tending toward urban-centeredness and unequal development. Pakistan is about seven-eighths rural and has about 101,500 villages. In 1961, the entire nation was only 13.1% urban and 15.9% literate.

Economically, the country is underdeveloped, with income per capita in 1971 being less than $100. Since newspaper prices are still high for Pakistani incomes, people naturally turn to radio if they can make the initial investment in a radio set.

Pakistan today is made up of the provinces of Baluchistan, Sind, Punjab, and the North-West Frontier. It has a population of 64.9 million, with three cities over a million — Karachi (3.5 million), Lahore (2.2 million), and Layalpur (1.1 million). The capital is Islamabad.

Since the data for these chapters were collected for the most part in 1971–72, in some cases it has been difficult to separate Pakistan and Bangladesh. Technically, Bangladesh could not be treated separately for the 1947–71 period. Mentions of East Pakistan, therefore, denote present-day Bangladesh.

Of all Pakistani mass media, radio alone is capable of overcoming the limitations imposed on that country by geographical discontinuity and bifurcation, distance barriers, multilingualism, high illiteracy, low urbanity rate, and socioeconomic underdevelopment (see Kalimullah 1975, pp. 7–11). Therefore, more and more, government and societal agencies have been turning their attention to this electronic medium as a panacea for all national problems.

4.2.1 System Dimensions

Expected to carry out these mammoth developmental roles in 1975 were eight regional broadcasting stations, located at Karachi, Hyderabad, Multan, Khairpur, Lahore, Rawalpindi-Islamabad, Peshawar, and Quetta, and smaller stations at

Azad Kashmir and Muzaffarabad. Their combined power was 3,130 kw., relayed over 33 transmitters (17 medium-wave and 16 short-wave) (see UNESCO 1975, p. 327). A new radio station at Bhawalpur, probably with a 10-kw., medium-wave transmitter, was expected to be commissioned in April 1975. Major stations at Karachi and Lahore also broadcast on a second channel to provide a wider program choice. In addition, short-wave transmitters are used extensively for domestic broadcasts in Pakistan, because expected coverage areas often are too vast to be fully covered by the medium-wave transmitting network.

Radio Pakistan (renamed Broadcasting Corporation of Pakistan on 20 December 1972), centralized at Karachi since 1949, was recently shifted to the newly built station at Rawalpindi. Until then, the central news desk was still located at Karachi; national news bulletins, commentaries, and other broadcasts of an all-Pakistan nature, such as presidential and ministerial speeches originating from Karachi, were relayed by regional stations.

During 1969, Radio Pakistan broadcast in both wings of the nation 52,200 hours on short-wave, 53,910 on medium-wave. The primary service in 1965 covered 25% of the area and 62% of the population in West Pakistan, 95% of the area and population in East Pakistan. Projected development and expansion under the Third Plan (1965–70) called for an increase of coverage by 1971 to 98% of the area and population in the east, and 65% area and 85% population in the west (*Twenty Years of Pakistan* 1967, pp. 554–55). Of course, the conflicts between the two wings of Pakistan probably hindered such expansion, but by 1974, medium-wave covered 70% of the population and 33% of the area, and short-wave covered almost the entire country. Some regions are in a vantage position, whereby they receive broadcasts from more than one station. Areas close to Karachi, Rawalpindi, and Hyderabad fall into this category.

In 1974, a 150-kw. medium-wave transmitter was opened near Quetta as part of a new expansion campaign on the part of the government to use radio as an "instrument of the people" (*Data for Decision* 1974c, p. 1802). Previously, huge areas such as Baluchistan had inadequate radio coverage; the Quetta transmitter, the first of a series of Russian-made transmitters under installation in Pakistan, is designed to fill that gap. At night, the Quetta-transmitted broadcasts can be heard within a radius of 500 miles; in the daytime, the reliable coverage can extend to about 40,000 square miles.

The Broadcasting Corporation of Pakistan in 1973–75 was in the midst of a vast expansion plan for both home and external targets. In 1973, two of Radio Pakistan's most powerful short-wave transmitters, 250-kw. each, were commissioned at Rewat and Islamabad to lend support to the external services. The Rewat station is to have two additional Russian-made short-wave transmitters. The Islamabad complex also houses three 100-kw. short-wave transmitters. The Karachi setup now has two 50-kw. and two 10-kw. short-wave transmitters, plus a 1-kw. transmitter used as a second local channel. In addition, by 1974, Radio Pakistan had a network of high-powered medium-wave transmitters throughout the nation: Hyderabad and Multan each with 120-kw.,

Lahore 100-kw., Karachi, Peshawar, and Rawalpindi each have a 10-kw. transmitter. One 100-kw. transmitter was expected to be installed in Karachi in 1975; a 1,000-kw. transmitter at Islamabad and a 300-kw. transmitter for zonal coverage near Peshawar were planned during the same period (*Data for Decision* 1974c, p. 1803).

Also, a pilot project to set up ten small, low-powered transmitters at the Integrated Rural Development Program (IRDP) centers in the countryside was underway in 1975. Covering an area of seven to ten miles, these self-contained broadcasting stations would be devoted wholly to development programs oriented toward the agricultural and industrial aspects of the area, and to the projection of village life and problems.

Of all the factors working against universal radio listening in Pakistan, the most serious perhaps involve the price and scarcity of receiving sets. Initially, until the mid-1950s, sets were imported and in the price range of only a small fraction of the population. Owning a set, therefore, was a status symbol. This situation has changed, though slowly, since the first assembly plant was established in 1953. By the mid-1960s, Pakistan had 21 assembly plants (11 in the West, 10 in the East). Whereas in West Pakistan, the radio industry was nearly self-sufficient in all components, local manufacture in East Pakistan was rather meager. Thus, in 1964, 208,600 sets were manufactured in West Pakistan as against 81,000 in East Pakistan, for a total 289,600 ("Survey of Radio Industry" 1965). The local radio-set industry has made further progress since 1964, although statistics are not readily available.

Despite such growth, radio sets continue to be imported on a small scale, partly because the local industry restricts itself to producing inexpensive transistor receivers, ignoring costlier, high-quality, bandspread sets.

Prices for locally made or assembled sets vary from $24—$80, depending on whether they are one-, two- or three-band receivers. Though locally manufactured, the receivers are still rather expensive in terms of Pakistani wages, the cheapest costing the equivalent of a factory worker's average monthly earnings (*25 Years of Pakistan* 1972, pp. 36—37).

Primarily because of the limited number of sets, the actual radio audience is far less than it could potentially be. In the absence of reliable data, radio-license issuance or renewal figures must be used as guides to the number of sets.

In Pakistan, a radio-set owner is required to pay a yearly Rs. 10 ($2.10) to the postal department for a license. But because a license may include more than one set in a single household and because of a high incidence of unlicensed sets, official figures tend to be inaccurate. It is estimated there are as many unlicensed receivers as licensed in Pakistan. Thus, on the basis of 1,870,503 licenses (West, 1,339,140; East, 531,363) issued during 1968—69 (*25 Years of Pakistan* 1972, p. 142), the total number of sets then could be estimated at 3,740,000. This disparity in the number of sets in the two wings reflects the fact that West Pakistan was about 4.5 times as urban as East Pakistan (22.5%—5.2%), and its income per capita was about 30% higher.

Of course, such figures in transitional nations fail to provide an index to audience size since:

Radio listening is a community habit in Pakistan. People sit in restaurants to listen to music and news; they collect in front of shops which use radio to attract people; they expect their neighbours, who have radio sets, to let them listen if some big event is taking place. In key villages throughout the country, and the strategic tribal areas of the north and northwest, government-installed community sets broadcast music and news. Many schools have their own sets. [Olson and Eirabi 1954]

Under a 1965 scheme, community-listening centers were established at offices of the union councils (lowest tier in the local government hierarchy), mostly in rural areas. At that time, 4,500 transistorized sets were sanctioned for East Pakistan centers, 3,500 for West Pakistan. Audiences at such centers vary between 20–50, depending upon the day of the week and weather conditions.

Schools have remained largely neglected. Only 5,000 out of 70,000 primary and secondary schools owned sets in 1967; of these, 3,000 were in East Pakistan. Plans in the 1970s call for distribution of 150,000 receivers to schools and adult education centers.

Although an earlier study (Mujahid 1952, pp. 82–83) calculated the average audience per set at 17.33, in the 1970s, the figure is more like ten. Therefore, the 1972 radio audience in Pakistan was in the neighborhood of 25.8 million; in 1974, with an estimated five million radio sets, the audience was about 50 million (*Data for Decision* 1974c, p. 1803).

4.2.2 Origins, Growth, Expansion

Although broadcasting in the subcontinent dates to about the mid-1920s, its development in what is now known as Pakistan began on 14 August 1947, when the nation was created. Pakistan actually inherited only three weak medium-wave stations at Lahore, Dacca, and Peshawar, with a total power of 20 kw., broadcasting 27 hours daily. The Lahore station was established in 1937 as part of All India Radio (AIR), Dacca in 1939 to complement the Calcutta AIR station, and Peshawar in 1935 as an experimental station under the North-West Frontier Province government. Designed primarily to help educate the vast illiterate rural population in the region, Peshawar programs were still predominately rural after its takeover by the Indian government in July 1942. Originally meant to cater to local needs, each of these stations had a 40-mile range; together, they covered only about 8% of the area in East Pakistan, 6% in West Pakistan (*Three Years of Radio Pakistan* 1950, pp. 10, 108, 110).

During its initial year, Radio Pakistan worked under extremely adverse conditions. First, denial by India of Pakistan's share of short-wave transmitters from AIR assets not only prevented an organic link-up of the three Pakistan stations, but also put off the setting up of a central news organization. In consequence, India's denial also forced the stations to operate independently, although Lahore was made the headquarters. Second, the stations were seriously hindered by understaffing and acute shortages of technical staff, equipment, and buildings. At Lahore and Dacca, for example, studios were converted from residential rooms in small rented buildings.

Whereas communal warfare in the Punjab adversely affected the Lahore station, those at Dacca and Peshawar were hamstrung by an absence of teleprinters. For many months, the Dacca station's news supply depended on monitoring bulletins from Lahore and BBC, receipt of Reuter messages by phone and air mail from Calcutta, and collection of provincial news through its own editors. The Peshawar station for quite some time depended on monitoring Lahore bulletins. These bulletins had to be taken by the Peshawar transmitters on telephone lines, resulting in staggering telephone bills amounting to Rs. 150,000 ($45,000) per month.

In 1948, Pakistan had its first broadcast unit which did not have roots in the colonial period, a low-power medium-wave station in Karachi, then the federal capital. The Karachi station started operations in a single barrack with offices in five tents. A 10-kw. medium-wave transmitter was added later, expanding the Karachi station's coverage to 60–80 miles. The first big breakthrough for Pakistani radio came in August 1949, when, with the installation of one of two 50-kw. short-wave transmitters, a central news organization was developed at Karachi. Simultaneously, headquarters were shifted there from Lahore, along with the editorial staffs from the other three stations, thus accomplishing the centralization of news. Also during this period, external services, four initially, were established in Karachi, plus a reliable link between the two wings of Pakistan. Another 50-kw. short-wave transmitter was installed at Karachi in December 1949.

When Rawalpindi came on the air in 1950, Pakistan had five stations with a total power of 137.6-kw., broadcasting 105 hours daily in 17 languages. A decade later, the number of stations had doubled, with new outlets at Hyderabad and Quetta in the west and Chittagong, Sylhet, and Rajshahi in the east. Correspondingly, the number of transmitters had increased to 19 with a total power of 204-kw., but total broadcast hours daily had risen only to 143 (*Second Five Year Plan* 1959, p. 315).

Possibly because of the rise of a modernizing autocracy under Field Marshal Ayub (late 1958), radio went through a period of considerable growth and expansion in the 1960s. For instance, total broadcasting time, which was 24,547 hours on short-wave and 24,868 on medium-wave transmissions in 1958, increased to 50,082 and 52,910 hours, respectively, in 1969 (*Pakistan Year Book* 1969, p. 464). Likewise, the number of transmitters had increased from 19 in 1960, to 29 in 1965, with a total output of 664.5 kw. of power. An upward trend was also noticeable in financial allocations granted by the government for the development and expansion of broadcasting. From a yearly budget of $330,000 in 1947, Radio Pakistan's allotment was increased to $18.95 million during the Third Plan, 1965–70, and $26.3 million for the Fourth Plan,

1970—75 (*Pakistan Year Book* 1971, p. 656).

Radio Pakistan's first external service was operated from Peshawar on a 10-kw. medium-wave transmitter during 1947—49. Directed to Afghanistan, it comprised one news bulletin in Afghan-Persian, along with musical items. Later, in August 1949, the external service was formally inaugurated at Karachi, with five services in four languages (*Sixth Year Pakistan* 1953, p. 211). Finally, by 1971, external broadcasts accounted for 185 program hours a week in 15 languages, including Swahili. Until the 1973—75 expansion, the service was seriously handicapped by a weak transmitting network and the absence of skilled technicians.

On 25 March 1974, the first earth satellite station was launched in Pakistan at Deh Mandroo, 35 miles north of Karachi. It provides direct international telegraph, telephone, telephoto, telex, radio broadcast, and television services to and from a number of countries via the Indian Ocean satellite. Completed at a cost of $9 million, the project benefitted from $6 million in loans from Canada (*Data for Decision,* 1—7 April 1974, p. 1735).

4.2.3 Governance

Broadcasting in Pakistan is a state monopoly operating through only one organization, the Broadcasting Corporation of Pakistan (BCP), a statutory corporation that replaced Radio Pakistan in December 1972. BCP was headed by a director general and attached to the Ministry of Information and Broadcasting; each of its regional stations was headed by a regional director. In 1974, the radio and television networks were turned into autonomous government-owned corporations, the corporation chiefs taking orders directly from the prime minister's secretariat. That same year, following criticisms of the information minister, Prime Minister Bhutto turned the Ministry of Information and Broadcasting into a division of his secretariat (*Asia Yearbook* 1975, p. 249).

Separate operational units function for the external, home, commercial, transcription, and monitoring services and for staff training and technical training. BCP employees rank as civil servants. News staffs are drawn from the newly constituted Information Service of Pakistan.

BCP publishes fortnightly or monthly journals in six languages (Urdu, Bengali, English, Arabic, Persian, and Burmese), presenting program guides, radio talks, and articles. The monitoring unit prepares news and commentaries from 18 foreign stations, used by the central news organization at Karachi and other government agencies. BCP's transcription service collects broadcasting material on various aspects of Pakistani culture, and, in turn, supplies such materials to domestic and foreign broadcast organizations. Some 80 nations are on the mailing list. The service also coordinates inter-station exchange of programs.

Each regional station is assisted by an advisory committee of six to ten members, some of them drawn from the public. Each committee meets at least yearly under the chairmanship of the director general for purposes of evaluating radio performance and suggesting improvements to meet regional requirements and listener preference. This, in turn, is assessed through audience research conducted by listeners' research units at all major stations. A director of listeners' research at central headquarters guides and coordinates all BCP research activities. On the basis of suggestions from interviews with the public, a 1967 broadcasting committee compiled a report detailing its findings and recommendations, some of which have since been acted upon.

Because it is state-controlled, and its officials are appointed by the central government, radio definitely reflects official viewpoints. As in most developing countries, radio in Pakistan is used as an agent of political socialization and mobilization, designed to sell the regime in power and project presidential and ministerial personalities, as well as the president's policies, achievements, and political party.

Broadcasters are not permitted to discuss opposition parties and leaders, or viewpoints of provincial governments, if they are in disagreement with the federal government. At times, politicians and leaders out of favor with the regime are blacklisted from broadcast privileges. During the 1964–65 presidential elections, not only was opposition candidate Fatima Jinnah refused radio access while her opponent, President Ayub, used the medium freely and frequently, but radio coverage of the election campaign itself was highly tilted in Ayub's favor. An analysis of news broadcasts at the time showed Ayub received almost five times the coverage of Jinnah. Radio's blatantly pro-government role (especially since 1958 when Pakistan abdicated parliamentary democracy in favor of constitutional autocracy) has come in for serious criticism over the years. Chief among such criticisms is a demand that various political viewpoints be accommodated, and that, furthermore, Radio Pakistan be converted into a truly autonomous corporation on the lines of the BBC. The latter demand was carried out in December 1972, when the Broadcasting Corporation of Pakistan was formed.

4.2.4 Financing and Advertisements

Pakistani radio is partially financed by the annual license fee on receiver sets. In recent years, there have been increased incidences of nonpayment of the fee, mainly because proliferation of sets lately has been mostly among lower income classes who ignore the law more readily, and are more difficult to apprehend by law-enforcing agencies. Also, the collection agencies are understaffed.

Another financing source is advertisements. During 1971–72, the total advertising revenue earned by six commercial stations in West Pakistan amounted to Rs. 4,965,366 ($1,043,700), about 70% of which was earned by the Karachi station. Radio advertising is handled by a commercial service of BCP. Until June 1972 an excise duty of 10% on all advertising was charged clients, but this has since been discontinued.

The net amounts earned through receiver license fees and advertising constitute only a mere fraction of BCP's annual budget. Each year, the federal government allocates considerable sums to meet capital and recurrent expenditures. For 1971—72, the allocations totaled $3,941,400, all but $65,000 of which was for recurring expenditure (*Budget 1971—72*, p. 356).

Radio airtime is generally sold through advertising agencies which receive a commission of 15%. Although advertising can be booked directly with a station, the agencies account fo 90% of total advertising time. A client can buy spot announcements or sponsor a full program.

The sponsored program is entirely the advertiser's show and is presented under his name. For this reason, the advertiser not only pays for airtime consumed by the program, but also for its production cost. Sponsored programs are of 15 or 30 minutes. In a 15-minute program, two commercial announcements of not more than one minute each, placed at the beginning and end of the show, are permitted; in a 30-minute program, a third one-minute announcement is inserted in the middle. Efforts to obtain sponsorship for nation building programs have been unsuccessful.

Although no written code exists for radio advertising, certain materials are barred, such as cigarettes, liquors, restaurants, ladies' foundation garments, professional or personal testimonials regarding medicines, and political or religious propaganda. Likewise, advertisements not in good taste are rejected. Advertising is not allowed on *Youm-i-Ashura,* a day of mourning in the Muslim calendar, or on the Prophet's birthday.

Advertising on BCP was initiated in 1961 on an experimental basis from the Karachi station. Because of its popularity, the service was introduced to five other stations in the west (Lahore, Hyderabad, Rawalpindi, Peshawar, and Multan) and two in the east (Dacca and Chittagong). Each station designates times during which advertising is allowed. For instance, Karachi generally allows advertising between noon and 1 P.M. and 1:20—4:30 P.M. Total time available for advertising also differs at each station; in 1971 it ranged from 7 hours weekly at Rawalpindi to 31 hours at Karachi and Lahore.

BCP advertising is governed by standardized rates which vary according to the time of the day and whether broadcast on a weekday or Sunday. Between noon and 1 P.M. on weekdays and 11:10 A.M. and 1 P.M. on Sundays are "preferred channel" time — comparable to prime time — because programs during those periods are broadcast on more transmitters to a wider domestic and foreign audience. Originally very low, the rates have been increased gradually to keep pace with airtime demand and rising costs.

4.2.5 Programming

Even though programming hours differ from station to station, materials broadcast remain essentially the same, including most of the general fare of stations elsewhere.

As in most developing countries, BCP's function revolves around providing news, information, and entertainment and molding public opinion. And, as in premobilized states, the guiding function takes precedence over that of informing. Talks and discussions are designed to guide public opinion to fit the official viewpoint; news selection is regulated by the same philosophy.

In its home service, BCP broadcasts news in 24 languages, two-thirds of the total daily newscasts emanating from the Karachi station. Karachi's national newscasts are relayed by all stations, whereas its regional news programs are relayed by only some West Pakistan stations. Other regional broadcasts are beamed from Rawalpindi and Peshawar in various languages.

Most programs broadcast from Karachi are in Urdu, but the proportion of shows in regional languages at other West Pakistani stations has increased considerably of late. Thus, Hyderabad broadcasts over 50% of its programs in Sindhi; Peshawar about 40% in Pushtu; Multan and Lahore 40% and 30%, respectively, in Panjabi. Except for Western music and occasional talks, discussions, debates, and students' programs in English, all other programs are either in Urdu or a regional language.

Religious shows are broadcast on the national hook-up every morning and afternoon. They comprise recitations from the Koran with Urdu/Bengali translations, followed by talks and discussions relating Koranic teachings to everyday problems of individual and community life. In addition, on the regional stations, there are local religious talks and features. During 1973–74, the Broadcasting Corporation of Pakistan and Pakistan Television Corporation together spent $217,032 for programs related to Islamic teachings. They also spent $267,576 for coverage of the Islamic Summit held in February 1974 in Lahore (*Data for Decision* 1974c, p. 1803).

Separate educational programs are broadcast for primary/secondary and college/university students. During school terms, all major stations broadcast these programs six times a week. While Karachi and Lahore broadcast a daily 30-minute program for university students on their second channels, all stations broadcast a 30-minute "university magazine" once a week. All educational broadcasts seek to impart direct instruction based on school curricula. Subjects covered include history, geography, general science, civics, home economics, and health/hygiene. Because so few schools have radios, the lessons are aired at such times to allow students to use their home sets. The failure to exploit fully this powerful medium for educational purposes, especially in an overwhelmingly illiterate nation, is tragic.

In addition to a bed-time story broadcast every evening, all stations feature 30–60 minute weekly shows for children. A 30-minute weekly program for women is devoted largely to discussing family budget, cooking, knitting, child rearing, and women's careers. Rural programs are broadcast daily from all stations, ranging from 15 minutes in Karachi to one hour on rural-oriented stations at Peshawar, Hyderabad and Quetta. They deal with livestock care, use of artificial fertilizers, cottage industry, and cultivation methods. Rural programs are broadcast in the language of the region, and active participation by those engaged in rural-development work is sought. Also, a 30-minute daily program for the armed forces is aired.

A 1971 analysis of programming at the Karachi station, which provided a basic pattern for most BCP stations, showed that out of a total 156 hours broadcast weekly in its home service, about two-thirds was taken up by music, entertainment, and news, or about 41%, 13%, and 11%, respectively. The station airs three five-minute news commentaries daily in Urdu, Bengali, and English, as well as religious shows, 4% of total weekly hours; informative, about 7%; business, 1.5%; students', 9%; children's, 1%; and armed forces, 2%.

UNESCO reported in 1975 that of the total 800 weekly hours over Pakistan's home-service stations, 254 were set aside for ethnic minorities, 158 for news and information, 150 for light entertainment, 88 for advertisements, 37 for arts, letters, and science, and 30 for education (UNESCO 1975, p. 327).

External-service programs, consisting largely of recorded music with occasional news commentaries, are primarily designed to create an understanding of Pakistan's problems and policies, present the nation's social and cultural heritage, and build good will by stressing common ties and affinities. Target areas for these services are Great Britain, Western Europe, the Arab Middle East, Turkey, Iran, South and Southeast Africa, Burma, Indonesia, and South and East Asia. Apparently India was a target as well, for in 1975, Prime Minister Bhutto wrote to India's Indira Gandhi, agreeing that the two nations should stop the radio propaganda war against each other. A suggestion that Pakistan and Afghanistan should stop their radio propaganda war was accepted by Pakistan but rejected by Afghanistan. Pakistan then accused the Afghan government of using the official radio to promote feelings of hatred against Bhutto and his government, especially in the Pakistani regions of Baluchistan and North-West Frontier Province (London *Times*, 29 April 1975, p. 6).

Feedback on both domestic and external programs is provided by listener mail. For example, 369,243 letters were received from within Pakistan during 1971–72, another 1,800 from abroad during the same year for the external service.

Programs are produced by BCP, which has its own studios, orchestra, program producers, composers, and other artists. Some are employed as "casual artists" for specific purposes or programs for which they are paid honoraria. Talent is secured through a talent utilization board which tours the country periodically, selecting candidates on the basis of audition and other tests. Except for news readers employed on a contract basis, all other news unit personnel hold tenured posts. Finally, talks, news commentaries, skits, and plays are written by paid "outsiders."

To train staff in programming and production techniques, a training school was developed in 1960. Courses given also touch upon listener research, development of drama, and music history. Others receive training in the journalism courses at the universities in Karachi and Lahore, as well as with BBC in London.

Rebroadcasting of programs produced abroad has declined considerably on BCP. Foreign syndicated materials, however, especially about international events such as moon landings, continue to be broadcast.

The geographical location of the nation, coupled with the fact that about 90% of all sets in Pakistan can receive short-wave, provides the radio audience a wide choice of external programs. Over 80% of the urban radio audience of Pakistan listens to foreign broadcasts. Stations listened to frequently include BBC, VOA, and the external services of India, Sri Lanka, China, USSR, Afghanistan, Iran, United Arab Republic, and Australia. Domestic signals from Iran, Afghanistan, and India also can be heard clearly in Pakistan.

4.2.6 Pressures

Being state owned, BCP is open to an assortment of governmental pressures. Its priorities, policies, and programming patterns are all determined by information mininstry officials with a view to meeting the exigencies of a given situation. Since Ayub Khan seized power in 1958, radio has been looked upon primarily as an invaluable propaganda machine which modern technology has unwittingly put into the hands of rulers to build up their image and personality cults. Increasingly, BCP is being used as an agent of political socialization, satisfying the regime's desire to guide, mold, and pressurize public opinion.

Freedom of speech is rather low on BCP's scale of values. Nongovernmental personnel, opposition spokesmen, and dissidents are scrupulously barred from its portals — except in times of crisis, such as the 1965 Indo-Pakistan War, when the regime is forced to seek their active support in galvanizing the whole nation to meet dire threats to its very existence. Speakers and discussants on nonpolitical programs are allowed considerable freedom, but in respect to political controversies, their talks and arguments must fall within the framework of governmental policies. Scripts are checked and approved before recording, and in the case of discussions, recorded tapes are edited to wipe out any unpalatable remarks. For some years now, BCP has discarded, with rare exceptions, its previous practice of broadcasting live discussions. Prerecording is, after all, much more convenient for overworked radio staffs and otherwise busy speakers, but, perhaps, more importantly, for editing purposes.

4.2.7 Television

In 1975, Pakistan had five main television stations, located at Karachi (36-kw.), Lahore (50-kw.), Rawalpindi-Islamabad (25-kw.), Quetta, and Peshawar, the latter two opened·in 1974. Repeater stations existed at Sakesar, Murree, and Thana Bola Khan (*WRTH* 1974, p. 296). Five additional repeater stations were being developed in 1974—75. When completed, the total coverage will rise to 60% of the population and 50% of the area. A microwave link-up of all TV stations in the nation was scheduled by December 1974 (*Asia 1974 Yearbook*, p. 251). Although the Karachi station is more developed, all other stations are self-contained units with their own production facilities, including videotape recorders and mobile units.

In 1972, the reception range of the Rawalpindi-Islamabad station was over 100 miles, including such important towns as Peshawar, Sialkot, Gujrat, and

Sargodha, while that of the two other stations developed then was about 40–50 miles. With a view of extending television coverage to outlying areas, boosters are being installed at convenient locations. Thus, towns in Sind, such as Hyderabad, Nawabshah, and Sukkur, are able to receive Karachi signals. By mid-1970, 26 cities and towns in West Pakistan (16 in East Pakistan) were covered by television; more have since come within TV range. By the end of 1970, about 25 million people (or 50% of the population of West Pakistan) were estimated to be covered by TV.

The main difficulty is that people cannot afford to own TV sets to take advantage of this coverage. Although nine assembly plants (West, six and East three) were set up in 1966, most components are still imported (*Twenty Years of Pakistan* 1967, p. 561); locally assembled sets have not made any significant impact. There were eight TV assembly plants in Pakistan in 1974: five in Karachi, two in Lahore, and one in Hyderabad Their total production per year is 70,000 sets (*Data for Decision*, 1–7 April 1974, p. 1735). Imported TV sets, despite being duty free, are out of the price range of most Pakistanis. In 1970, about 80,000 sets existed in both wings of the country (*Basic Facts* 1970, p. 5), most of them owned by governmental and professional people with incomes of over $148 per month. Estimated audience per set in 1970 was ten, making a total of 800,000 viewers in what was then West and East Pakistan. In October 1974, the number of licensed TV sets in Pakistan was 225,240 (*Dawn* 1974, p. 1).

Pakistan entered the television world not only late, but also in a modern way. Pilot stations were established at Lahore and Dacca in late 1964 on a three-month experimental basis. Later, in 1965, a Television Promoters Company (TPC) was developed, with an authorized capital of Rs. 50 million ($10.5 million); two years later, TPC was converted into a public limited company and renamed Pakistan Television Corporation Limited (PTC).

The Rawalpindi-Islamabad station came on the air in January 1967, with a three-hour program six days a week; the first well-equipped, modern station opened in Karachi later that year. A central film unit was established at Rawalpindi in mid-1970. Main stations were connected through microwave links with the five retelecast stations – three in what was then East Pakistan, at Chittagong, Khulna, and Rajshahi; two in West Pakistan at Hyderabad and Layallpur. A sum of Rs. 55 million ($11.55 million) was allocated for expansion during the Third Plan (1965–70) period, and a further sum of Rs. 157.8 million ($33.4 million) was earmarked by the National Economic Council in 1968 (*Pakistan Year Book* 1971, p. 657).

Television networks in Pakistan are operated by PTC, and controlling interest is held by the Pakistan government. Nippon Electric Company (NEC) of Japan and Thomson Television (International) Limited of England are the other major shareholders. As PTC makes a profit, the foreign investors will be repaid gradually until the company is owned entirely by Pakistani nationals (Nakajima 1974, p. 105). The Karachi station was built by Japanese money, while those in

Lahore and Rawalpindi-Islamabad were aided by the Netherlands and West Germany, respectively. Because of this foreign assistance, there has been some difficulty in unifying technical standards between stations.

Management is vested in a board of directors, five of them, including the chairman and managing director, being nominated by the government, three by NEC. Each station has its own advisory committee.

Although a public-limited company, PTC works under the aegis of the Ministry of Information and Broadcasting, the ministry secretary serving as chairman of the board of directors. Because PTC is under direct government control, not only does it seek to reflect the official viewpoint, but also allows itself to be used extensively and deftly as an agent of political socialization and mobilization. PTC's partisan role has been seriously criticized in recent years by the opposition, demanding that its own viewpoints be projected. As with radio, TV programs were used to debunk oppositionist parties, especially Jamaat-i-Islami Party, during the 1973 controversy on the future constitution of Pakistan. Opposition leaders, for the only time during the previous three years, were interviewed on television during the crisis period, but only so that they could be embarrassed by progovernment interviewers (see also Green 1972, p. 245).

PTC has an authorized capital of Rs. 50 million ($10.5 million) and a paid-up capital of Rs. 26.4 million ($5.56 million), of which the government contributed over 80%, the private sector, the remainder. The government has also advanced a loan of Rs. 14.7 million ($3.05 million), a portion of which will be converted into equity. Overall, governmental participation in PTC has been fixed at 51% of total authorized capital.

Advertising provided the only outside source of revenue until October 1970, when an annual license fee of Rs. 50 ($10.50) per set was introduced. In 1975, the Pakistan Television Corporation decided to double the fee in an effort to offset some of the corporation's expenditures (*Variety* 1975f). Extent of nonpayment was estimated to be considerable, but by 1972, it was estimated that 85% of set owners were paying the fee. Advertising continues to be PTC's major source of revenue. It is generally sold through accredited advertising agencies which receive a commission of 15%. TV commercials may be broadly classified as spot announcements, live commercials, sponsored-live, and sponsored-film programs. In sponsored-live programs, the commercial appears at the program's beginning and end – in the case of longer programs, in the middle as well. Feature films, telecast once weekly, are sponsored, as are sports events.

Commercial breaks are provided at suitable points between the programs during which spots are telecast. Usually, there are ten such breaks in a four-hour transmission, and the ratio between advertising and program time is one to six. Peak times are determined by program popularity; no special peak-time rates are assessed. But, peak timings are heavier on Sundays, hence, a surcharge on Sunday advertising. TV advertising has increased at all stations, the number of advertisers registering a 244% increase between 1968 and 1969 (*Guide to Television Advertising* 1970, p. 15). The Karachi station leads in advertising volume. By 1975, the advertising volume was not so high. Part of the reason given for the increase in TV-set license fees that year was that the TV stations were not meeting their advertising targets. In fact, the Karachi, Lahore, and Rawalpindi-Islamabad stations met 60%, 50%, and 40%, respectively, of their proposed advertising budgets in 1974. The government had to subsidize each of the stations (*Variety* 1975f).

A written code governs television advertising, its general principle being that all advertisements should not only "conform to the law of the country and best traditions of our people," but also should be based on truth. Products and subjects barred include liquors; ladies' foundation garments and sanitary towels; offers of products, medicines, and treatment of disorders or irregularities peculiar to women; clinics for treatment of hair and scalp; slimming, weight reduction or limitation, and figure control; and religious and political propaganda (*Guide to Television Advertising* 1970).

In order to promote healthy competition and provide an incentive for improvement of advertising standards, yearly commercial merit awards were instituted in 1969.

Programming is generally designed to realize objectives which inspired the development of the medium in Pakistan, namely: to provide information and education through wholesome entertainment, to make the various regions and peoples of Pakistan better known and understood to one another, and to purposefully develop the Pakistan way of life (*Guide to Television Advertising* 1970, p. 5). It is not surprising then that materials programmed are more-or-less standardized throughout Pakistan.

Initially, because of the dearth of trained personnel, technical facilities, and equipment, TV stations depended heavily upon foreign programs, to the extent that in 1965, the ratio between foreign and domestic shows was 60 to 40. Imported foreign films accounted for 35% of the total fare in 1972, most of them originating in the United States. More popular foreign shows included "The Avengers," "Disneyland," "Perry Mason," "Bewitched," "Pride and Prejudice," "Adventures of Huck Finn," "Call Mr. D," "Get Smart," "Mission Impossible," and "The Invaders."

Generally speaking, in 1971, the total weekly telecasts for all four stations, including that of Dacca, came to about 35 hours a week, 13% of which were dramas and features, 7% dance and music, and 14% news. Among other programs, full-length feature films are telecast late Saturday night, alternating between English and Urdu/Bengali films. Plans are in the offing for afternoon rural shows. During the December 1970 general elections, PTC produced a special nonstop election telecast from all stations. A similar program was telecast for the subsequent provincial elections later that month. In late 1974, the percentage breakdown of locally produced programming on the three main Pakistani stations included: drama, 11.7%; music, 6%; children's shows, 5%; light entertainment, 6%; documentaries, 2%; religion, 6%; youth, 0.5%; sports, 3%; news, 14%; current affairs, 10%; and commercials, 9%. Of foreign-produced shows, the percentage figures were: drama, 12%; documentaries, 2%; light entertainment, 5%; and feature films, 7%. About 127½ hours per week of programming were telecast over the three stations; 94 hours (or 74%) were locally produced (*Dawn* 1974, p. 1). UNESCO reported in 1975 that nationally produced programs came to 82% of the total; most imported programs emanated from the United States and West Germany (UNESCO 1975, p. 328).

All local programs are either produced by the stations, the Central Film Production Unit (CFPU), or Asian Television Service (ATS). Karachi and Lahore have facilities to produce 30—40 hours of programming weekly, while production facilities at other stations are somewhat limited. For the most part, the latter relay programs produced at Karachi and Lahore, only producing smaller segments which lend local color to their telecasts. Lahore feeds programs to Islamabad and Peshawar through translators.

CFPU, established at Rawalpindi to provide balanced programs and ensure quality control, produces specialized and complex fare, including drama, documentary, educational and rural-oriented programs. CFPU will, in the 1970s, produce 500 hours of programs per year, resulting in centralized and economized production of PTC material. A videotape exchange among Pakistan, Iran and Turkey provides program variety.

Developed in 1967 as a subsidiary of PTC and in collaboration with Ifage of West Germany, ATS is designed to provide national and international film coverage to main domestic stations, as well as to supply newsfilms abroad. ATS has five film units, one at Lahore and two each at Karachi and Rawalpindi. ATS not only releases newsfilms to some 60 countries through the European television network, but also exchanges them on a reciprocal basis with Iran, Turkey, China, and the USSR.

ETV in Pakistan is being planned on a phased basis to supplement formal classroom education; a start has been made with science subjects. Provision has also been made for distributing community TV sets. In October 1975, an educational television project was begun, designed to make thousands functionally literate. Developed by the Adult Basic Education Society, with help from UNICEF, the project included the airing of 156 ETV lessons, each of 35-minute duration, over a six-month period. A total of 1,300 trainee teachers supplemented the broadcasts, teaching in 210 villages (*Action*, September 1975, p. 5).

Possibly a reason why TV has not progressed rapidly in Pakistan, aside from the cost factor, relates to the serious lack of trained personnel. An effort to remedy the problem was initiated in 1967 when the Central TV Training Institute was established at Islamabad with the assistance of West Germany. The institute has facilities to train 40 programming and engineering personnel yearly, as well as to run specialized short courses on floor management, stage supervision, film editing, and routine operation of technical facilities. Besides the institute courses, maximum on-the-spot training is also given to the staff at various stations.

West German equipment, provided as a gift to the institute, became the nucleus of the Rawalpindi-Islamabad station. West Germany also donated the equipment for ATS, while NEC gave 2,000 TV sets for free distribution to community centers. Along with Thomson Television (International) Limited, NEC also provided assistance in the field of engineering programming and sales promotion.

4.2.8 Conclusion

Two specific roles that BCP has fulfilled considerably well relate to Pakistan's quest for modernity and a feeling of nationhood. In a largely illiterate and rural society such as Pakistan, radio is a most important medium in transcending barriers of illiteracy, distance, and poor communications, and, in turn, leading the country to a modern stage.

BCP, and earlier Radio Pakistan, has also played a crucial role in nation-building. For example, during the catacylsmic partition days, radio produced programs to rehabilitate, mentally and morally, millions of displaced persons in West Pakistan. It broadcast some 37,000 messages to and about lost persons, helping to bring thousands of displaced and stranded persons in touch with each other. Radio also helped to foster among the racially and linguistically diverse population a sense of shared culture, overcoming potentially dangerous population splits and thereby building a sense of national identity and promoting national integration.

During the 1960s and today, however, broadcasting's blatant projection of the regime in power has resulted in an increasing credibility gap for electronic media. The 1970–71 crises in East Pakistan, and that wing's sundering away to become Bangladesh, may be partly traced not only to this credibility gap, but also to the fact that for a long time, people in East Pakistan were subjected to telling propaganda from the more-powerful Indian stations around the region. To the extent that the East Pakistani stations had failed to win over the AIR audience within their midst and create trust in their own spoken words, Radio Pakistan might be considered to have failed spectacularly in one of its fundamental tasks.

4.3 Bangladesh, *by Sharif al-Mujahid*

Eastern Bengal prospered in the 17th century because of its fine muslin and silk weavers and rich rice harvests. Machinery introduced to India by the British wrecked the weaving industry and started the decline that made East Bengal into a backwater by the early 19th century. In 1947, it became East Pakistan, and on 26 March 1971, Bangladesh. Sheikh Mujibur Rahman was elected to lead the new government. He was swept back into power in March 1973; after that, his problems multiplied. After numerous economic and political crises, he declared a state of emergency in December 1974 and, within two months, had banned all political parties except his own and changed the government from parliamentary

to one-man rule, declaring himself president. In mid-1975, he banned all
newspapers except four progovernment dailies (see Lent 1975b). On 15 August
1975, Sheikh Mujibur Rahman was assassinated in a *coup d'état*. The new
president was Khondakar Mustaque Ahmed, former minister of commerce.
Martial law was declared immediately, and the name of the country was changed
from "People's Republic of Bangladesh" to "Islamic Republic of Bangladesh."
Radio Bangladesh was the most frequently named source on the events of the
governmental change (*Philadelphia Inquirer,* 17 August 1975, p. 13-A). By
November 1975, another coup saw the top administration changed again.

Bangladesh is comprised of 19 districts and literally hundreds of islands, most
of which are in the Bay of Bengal. The population is estimated at 71.3 million;
the largest cities are Dacca (the capital), Chittagong, Khulna, Narayanganj, and
Chalna.

In terms of geography, population-land ratio, communications, and
socioeconomic conditions, Bangladesh is adversely situated, but language-wise, it
has an edge over most other Asian nations. On a land area of 55,126 square
miles, the density of population is over 1,000 per square mile. With only 5.2% of
the people urbanized, four cities of 100,000-plus population, and some 64,500
villages, Bangladesh is predominantly rural and agricultural; industrialization is
still low. Its rivers, numerous streams, and rather confused network of
waterways render many areas inaccessible.

Economically underdeveloped, the income per capita was about $78 in
1968—69, one of the lowest in the world. Power supplies are limited. Literacy in
1961 was 17.6%, and only about 20% of the literates had gone beyond five years
of school. Linguistically, Bangladesh is fortunate to be almost unilingual. Bengali
is the language of masses and elite, although there are speakers of Urdu and some
dialects. (For background information on East Pakistani broadcasting see §4.2.)

Geocultural and socioeconomic conditions in Bangladesh certainly favor the
growth of radio over other mass media. The extremely limited number of sets in
the new nation, however, plus their high price, mitigate against radio listening
becoming universal. Until the first radio-assembly plant was opened in 1953, all
sets in the region were imported and expensive, out of the reach of all but a small
fraction of the population. Although by the mid-1960s, East Pakistan had ten
radio-assembly plants, the number of sets assembled was much less than demand.
For instance, in 1964, 81,000 sets were locally produced, another 10,000 were
imported.

4.3.1 System Dimensions

Bangladesh in 1975 had six radio stations broadcasting over seven medium-wave
transmitters in Dacca (5 and 100-kw.), Chittagong (10-kw.), Rangpur (10-kw.),
Rajshahi (10-kw.), Khulna (10-kw), and Sylhet (2-kw.), four short-wave
transmitters (including two of 100-kw.) and five FM transmitters in Dacca
(2-kw.), Rajshahi, Chittagong, and Sylhet (*WRTH* 1974, p. 140; UNESCO 1975,
p. 259). Central offices and studios of Radio Bangladesh are located at Dacca.

Altogether, Radio Bangladesh broadcasts approximately 83 hours daily from all six regional stations; the Dacca station, broadcasting on two domestic channels, operates about 100 hours weekly, while units at Sylhet and Rangpur broadcast less than ten hours daily. The figures include broadcasts of Radio Bangladesh's external services (see §4.3.5). In 1965, the primary service covered 95% of the area and population of the region; it had been predicted to rise to 98% by the early 1970s. Areas adjacent to Chittagong, Sylhet, Rajshahi and Rangpur can receive broadcasts from more than one station. By 1974, Bangladesh broadcasting was expanding under the nation's five-year development plan. Khulna's transmitter was expected to receive a boost in power, while Dacca was to receive a 1,000-kw. medium-wave transmitter. Also included in the development plan are the addition of four high-power short-wave transmitters with a new aerial system, two high-power medium-wave transmitters earmarked for the coastal areas and the cyclone belt, with a similar transmitter for the western zone, and three medium-power medium-wave transmitters for coverage in the central and eastern regions. Also, a National Broadcasting House was being constructed at a new Dacca site (*COMBROAD* 1975c, p. 65).

In June 1975, Bangladesh opened its first earth satellite station at Betbunia, 140 miles southeast of Dacca. The $8-million station was built with help from the Canadian International Development Agency (*Media*, August 1975, p. 22).

As with Pakistan, the actual radio audience is far less than its potential. Postal department figures for radio licenses issued or renewed provide the basis for estimating the number of radio receivers in use. Thus, on the basis of 531,363 licensed receivers, and assuming an equal number unlicensed, East Pakistan during 1968–69 had an estimated 1,062,726 sets, or about 1.5 per 100 persons.

The actual audience, however, is considerably more because of large families and the prevailing joint family system still in vogue. Therefore, one might estimate about ten listeners per household. In addition, audiences at community listening centers are about 50 persons on some days and, at the schools, about 100 per set. About 4,500 transistorized receivers were distributed to community centers in 1965; another 3,000 sets have been obtained by schools. In view of all this, the average audience per set may be estimated as at least ten, giving a total audience of 10.6 million.

4.3.2 Origins, Growth, Expansion

The first station in the present Bangladesh area was established at Dacca in 1939 as a complement to the Calcutta AIR station. Meant to cater to local needs, the listening range of the 5-kw. station was about 40 miles. Until 1948, the Dacca station was housed in a small rented building with extremely meager accommodations, studio, and equipment resources. It could not even claim a teleprinter of its own until 1947.

Probably the most important consideration in the development of East Pakistani broadcasting was to provide the radio link between East and West Pakistan so essential for administrative purposes. As a result, a great deal of attention was paid to the expansion of the Dacca station and establishment of new ones, thus, explaining why the first short-wave, 100-kw. medium-wave, and 1,000-kw-medium-wave transmitters to be installed anywhere in Pakistan were at Dacca. Additionally, another short-wave transmitter, the first Pakistani broadcasting house incorporating latest technical and studio facilities, and the most effective receiving center were all built at Dacca between 1959 and 1963. The result was that almost all of East Pakistan was brought within the Dacca range.

Development of broadcasting in other areas of East Pakistan began with the first relaying station in Chittagong in 1954; a 10-kw. medium-wave transmitter was installed eight years later. The broadcasting building was completed at Rajshahi in 1960, followed by the installation of a 1-kw. medium-wave transmitter. With an initial 2-kw. medium-wave transmitter, Sylhet began relaying programs from Dacca in 1961; a 10-kw. medium-wave transmitter was added the following year. Rangpur came on the air in 1961 with a 2-kw. medium-wave transmitter; it was strengthened during 1964 with a 10-kw. medium-wave transmitter and facilities to originate two hours of programs daily. Finally, a 10-kw. relay transmitter was built at Khulna which began functioning in 1971.

Except for national broadcasts of news and commentaries from Karachi, the East Pakistani network, before 1971, carried on independently of its western counterpart, and, because of geographical and linguistic differences, was developed as a self-contained unit over the years. Therefore, Dacca had facilities for an external service, the monitoring of foreign broadcasts, a commercial service, and a transcription facility. All of this helped transform the East Pakistani network into a completely independent and self-contained network for the new nation of Bangladesh.

The war of liberation with Pakistan in 1971 was responsible for the destruction of numerous broadcasting installations, including the transmitter and studios in Khulna. After the hostilities ended, broadcasting was hampered because many of the senior, experienced Bengali program and engineering officers had been detained in Pakistan. From an engineering point of view, the situation was serious because the central stores previously had been in Karachi, and orders for spare parts were processed there. Therefore, existing orders were canceled or diverted when independence was proclaimed, and new orders by the Bangladesh government were delayed because of administrative processing, allocation of foreign exchange, and lack of local agents. Spare parts for broadcasting equipment dwindled quickly (*COMBROAD* 1975c, p. 65). The situation was still serious in 1973; it was estimated in that year that one-third of Bangladesh's 15,000 TV sets were out of order because of spare-parts shortages. A limited quantity of parts were allowed into the country in 1973, but with a 100% duty attached (*Media* 1974a).

4.3.3 Governance

As in all nations of South Asia, broadcasting in Bangladesh is a state monopoly. There is one broadcasting organization, known as Bangla Betar, or Radio Bangladesh, and headed by a director general, which has its headquarters at Dacca. Since the split with Islamabad, certain operational units for services such as external, monitoring, commercial, music and transcription, educational broadcasting, and publications — whose Radio Pakistan headquarters had been in West Pakistan — have been either strengthened or created at Dacca. The Educational Broadcasting Unit broadcasts a half-hour show daily from the six regional stations for students at different grades. The Publications Unit was developed into a Directorate of Radio Publications in February 1972, responsible for publishing three program journals, two in Bengali for domestic audiences and one in English for overseas listeners. A Staff Training Institute has been opened, providing instruction for program and technical staffs (see *COMBROAD* 1974e, p. 65).

Each regional station of Radio Bangladesh is headed by an assistant director, aided by an advisory committee of six to ten members, some of whom are drawn from the public. The radio staff itself is appointed by the Ministry of Information and Broadcasting. As in most Asian countries, radio in Bangladesh reflects the official viewpoint and is used extensively as an instrument of government policy.

The Dacca radio staff, however, has rejected government policy on two notable occasions. On 7 March 1971, the entire staff went on strike, rebelling against a decision of the Dacca authorities to ban broadcasting of Sheikh Mujibur Rahman's historic speech at the race grounds that afternoon. As a result, the Dacca station went off the air unscheduled. Because the staff would not return unless Mujib's taped speech was broadcast from Dacca and relayed by other East Pakistani stations, and since, moreover, no stopgap arrangement was immediately possible, the authorities were forced to accept their demand. The staff returned to work the next morning.

Again, during the height of the Awami League movement in March 1971, the Dacca station for three weeks registered its protest against government by signing itself off as "Dacca Radio Center," instead of its usual "Radio Pakistan, Dacca," and by highlighting the movement in newscasts, as well as interpreting other news and events from the Awami League angle. To say the least, this sort of revolt on the part of a radio staff is probably unprecedented in the Asian context.

4.3.4 Finance

Financing of Radio Bangladesh, like that of the Broadcasting Corporation of Pakistan, depends on receiver license fees, advertising, and a government allotment. In Bangladesh, a licensing fee of Taka 10 ($1.50) per annum is charged for the use of one set in a single household or establishment, the fee being deposited with the post office before the beginning of a calendar year. Nonpayment of the fee has increased, especially since 1970 when lawlessness became widespread in the nation.

Because commercials are accepted only at Dacca and Chittagong, where the combined total time available for them is only 17½ hours per week, advertising revenue is rather meager. In fact, it is estimated to be under Taka 50,000 ($6,667) per annum.

The commercial services at Dacca and Chittagong follow the same pattern prevalent in Pakistan. Commercials were first introduced at the Dacca station in 1967 — initially for one hour daily — and became so popular that advertising time was progressively increased to 11½ hours weekly. A six-hour weekly service was introduced at Chittagong as well. Though advertising rates have increased over the years, they are still relatively low. Spot announcements of seven seconds duration cost about $4.67 and $9.33 on weekdays and Sundays, respectively.

Until 1971, allocations to meet capital and recurrent expenditures at the East Pakistani stations were made in Pakistan's central budget; now, they come directly from the Bangladesh treasury.

4.3.5 Programming

With some variations, Radio Bangladesh programs closely resemble those broadcast when the region was East Pakistan. Programs today provide the usual fare of news, information, and entertainment, plus a rather heavy dose of "guidance" shows, designed primarily to mold public opinion as the government deems fit. Bengali broadcasts predominate, but some programs are aired in English, Hindi, and Urdu. Schools broadcasts, timed to reach students in their homes, are given several times a week during the school terms from Chittagong, Dacca, and Rajshahi. Rural programs are broadcast one hour daily from Dacca, the amount differing from station to station. All programs are produced by the stations themselves. Procedures evolved and followed until the 1971 governmental split still hold true to a very large extent.

Since about 90% of all sets can receive short-wave broadcasts, people often listen to some of the world's major stations. Listened to regularly or frequently are AIR, BBC, VOA, Radio Moscow, Radio Australia, Broadcasting Corporation of Pakistan, and Radio Peking. Domestic signals from AIR stations near Bangladesh can be heard clearly, and for various reasons, the people have developed a habit of listening to these broadcasts, especially from Calcutta and Gauhati. Until Radio Pakistan strengthened and extended its services to new East Pakistani areas during the 1960s, the region, except for around Dacca and Chittagong, depended almost entirely upon the more powerful stations in neighboring India. As mentioned earlier (see §4.2.8), the powerful propaganda from AIR stations was, among other things, partly responsible for eroding the passion for unity with West Pakistan, and promoting the sentiment for regional separatism.

Bangladesh also transmits external broadcasts. Until December 1971, Nepali and Burmese external services broadcast from Karachi were relayed from Dacca. Since the launching of the Overseas Broadcasting Section on 1 January 1972, Dacca has provided external services to Southeast Asia, Europe, South Asia, and the Middle East. Languages used are English, Arabic, Hindi, Nepali, Urdu, Panjabi, Pushto, and Bengali. German, Burmese, and Chinese were expected to be added by the mid-1970s. The principal aims of the overseas services are to project the image of Bangladesh to the outside world, to report on the nation's progress and problems, and to indicate the Bangladesh government attitude on important national and international issues. Programs include news, commentary, editorial comments from various national daily newspapers, talks on the economy, culture, music, tradition, heritage, and history. One of the programs, "Onak Subho Kamana" (Calling Bengalese Stranded in Pakistan), transmits messages sent by relatives in Bangladesh to their family members stranded in Pakistan since the war (*COMBROAD* 1975c, p. 66). Since late 1973, the Publication Unit of Radio Bangladesh has published a monthly magazine, *Bangladesh Betar,* in English for overseas listeners. It lists program schedules of the overseas service and includes short articles on the country. *Bangladesh Betar* is distributed to broadcasting organizations in friendly countries and to Bangladesh embassies abroad.

4.3.6 Pressures

Being state owned and managed, Radio Bangladesh is open to all sorts of governmental pressure. Actually, because of the revolution and war during most of 1971 and the treacherous circumstances attending Bangladesh's birth, the authorities use radio all the more readily as an agent of political socialization and mobilization. For one thing, they have had to galvanize the newly created nation for the task of national reconstruction ahead, instill in the people a respect for law, breathe realism into people's thinking, and goad them to accept the harsh realities of the situation, which are, of course, completely at variance with what they had envisioned in 1971. For another, the regime has had to keep a firm hold over the people during the initial period of higher prices and scarcity of food and housing, when rising expectations turned into rising frustrations, in order to bring economic and political viability to the disturbed state of Bangladesh.

Since a state of emergency was declared in Bangladesh in December 1974, all mass media have been strictly controlled. The government reserved for itself the right to make orders against the "spread of false reports or the prosecution of any purpose likely to cause disaffection or alarm, or to prejudice relations with any foreign power" (*Index on Censorship,* Summer 1975, p. 85). When Prime Minister Sheikh Mujibur Rahman reshuffled his cabinet in July 1974, he assumed the portfolio of information and broadcasting, thus indicating the importance he placed in mass media. As 1975 dawned, the prime minister moved swiftly toward totalitarianism. On 26 January 1975, parliamentary rule was abandoned, and the following month all political parties, except Sheikh's Krishak Sramik Awami League, were banned (Lent 1975b). Sheikh Mujibur Rahman was assassinated in August 1975.

4.3.7 Television

For a poor nation such as Bangladesh, television is a luxury. The infrastructure for an extensive TV network is sadly lacking, levels of urbanization (about 6%), industrialization and income per capita ($63) being, by any standards, extremely low. Even highly urbanized and industrialized West Bengal, which borders Bangladesh and includes huge Calcutta, could not, as of the early 1970s, afford a TV network. Little surprise is it, then, that television in Bangladesh is still largely confined to the capital, Dacca.

Dacca television started as a pilot project in late 1964, on an experimental basis for a period of three months; it was the second station to be started in Pakistan. With a 3-kw. transmitter, it operated initially for three hours daily, six days a week. By the late 1960s, Dacca TV was feeding a newly established satellite station at the port town of Chittagong, some 200 miles away; this has since been discontinued. Two additional retelecast stations have since been inaugurated at Khulna and Rajshahi, their viewing range about 40–50 miles each. By 1970, these stations covered some 16 cities and towns and over half of the population, that is, assuming those people could afford sets. Weekly telecasts in the early 1970s totaled about 35 hours, the bulk of which was in Bengali.

In November 1974, the Ministry of Information and Broadcasting announced that the Dacca TV station would be transferred to Rangpur where it would become one of the largest stations of South Asia. He also announced that a 10-kw. transmitter for the Sylhet station will be developed during the current five-year plan (*COMBROAD*, January–March 1975, p. 57).

Although three assembly plants for TV sets were opened in what was then East Pakistan (in 1966), most sets were still imported, the majority from Japan. By 1973, importation of new TV sets was banned, even though only 1,000 sets were produced within the country that year (*Media* 1974a). The extreme expense of sets allows only those in the middle and higher income brackets to afford them. Thus, in 1973, the total number of sets in Bangladesh was estimated at 15,000, accounting for an audience of 150,000 at the rate of ten persons a set (*Media* 1974a). Community viewing has not become widespread because initially only 200 receivers were distributed free for this purpose.

The television network is operated by the Bangladesh Television Corporation, with controlling interest held by the Bangladesh government. The other major shareholder is NEC of Japan. Management is vested in a board of directors, most of whose members, including the chairman and managing director, are nominated by the government. The corporation works under the aegis of the Ministry of Information and Broadcasting, and, like Radio Bangladesh, it is under the direct control of the government. It too is used extensively, rather unabashedly in fact, to promote and mobilize for the government.

Initially finances to meet development, as well as recurring expenditures, came out of Pakistan Television Corporation funds. The Bangladesh government has since taken over the rights and interests of the Pakistan government in the corporation which amounted to 51%. A yearly license fee of $10.50 ($6.66 at the 1972 rate of exchange) per set was introduced in 1970, but the extent of nonpayment, especially in the rather chaotic conditions during 1971–72, must be considerable.

Advertising at the Dacca TV station, though meager compared to that of Pakistani stations, continue to be a major source of revenue. Advertising practices, developed during the erstwhile Pakistan era of 1964–71, are still prevalent. Likewise, TV commercials follow the same pattern as in Pakistan. During 1969–70, some 126 clients advertised their products. The rates are relatively low, only $14.30 for a spot seven-second announcement, $122.30 for a ten-minute sponsored program which includes a one-minute commercial. Surcharges of 20% and 10% are levied for Sundays and specific weekdays, respectively. TV advertising is governed by standardized rates and by a written code barring commercials not in good taste.

4.4 Afghanistan, *by Gordon C. Whiting and Mehria Rafiq Mustamandy*

Afghanistan is a land about the size of Texas with a climate and topography roughly resembling that of Wyoming. It is landlocked and shares borders with the Soviet Union, Iran, China, and Pakistan, although Afghans hold that their border is with Pushtunistan and not Pakistan. Its population in 1972 was officially estimated at about 17 million, 2 million of whom are nomads. About 90% of the people are engaged in basic food production, and at least that proportion are functionally illiterate in any modern language.

Four major language families are represented in the country, with Dari, a form of Persian, and Pashto, the language of the Pushtuns, as two major and official languages. Regional dialects abound.

Kinship units and obligations dominate Afghanistan society. Kin provides the individual with identity, social services, and support and constitutes his first and highest loyalty after Islam. In addition to the extended family, kinship-related ties of clans, tribes, and ethnic groups remain strong. Personal independence and group honor are also accentuated. Religious sentiment is extremely strong and tends toward conservative interpretations of social change. Islam and the monarchy represent the major unifying forces of the nation. Islam is above partisan squabbles and the monarchy almost so. The nation has succeeded in

Gordon C. Whiting is Associate Professor of Communication, Brigham Young University; he was formerly at the University of Wisconsin. He conducted research in Brazil and Afghanistan on the role of communication in development, and received his Ph.D. at Michigan State University. Mehria Rafiq Mustamandy is Information Advisor for the USIS, Kabul. She worked in a variety of journalism assignments in Afghanistan and studied at Kabul University and in Australia, England, Iran, and India.

maintaining an unaligned foreign policy and has successfully extracted foreign aid from a wide variety of donors. Afghanistan carefully guards its neutrality (Fraser-Tytler 1967; Caroe 1958).

4.4.1 Introduction

On 14 November 1969, the newly elected Afghan lower house of parliament, the Wolesi Jirgah, met to consider guidelines for its coming vote of confidence on the new cabinet. Agreement was reached on only one matter. The entire proceedings would be broadcast live over Radio Afghanistan. As it happened, the debate fell during Ramadan, the annual month-long, sunup-to-sundown fast observed throughout the Muslim world (Dupree 1971, p. 3).

The broadcasts provided more than distraction to the fasting nation, however; they fed its hopes for a better future and contributed to shaping a more unified state with common concerns, allegiances, symbols, and identity. Further, they began to establish as a tradition the broadcasting of parliamentary crises, first tried two years earlier. The innovation had been so favorably received by the masses then, that the opportunity of the 1969 broadcast stirred the members of the Wolesi Jirgah to daring criticism of the outgoing government and more explicit demands on the incoming one. By 1971, when a government was again being formed, the broadcast of the parliamentary debate had become a firmly established tradition, bordering on a parliamentary prerogative. Another effect was noted. The speeches of delegates had averaged perhaps ten minutes in 1967; their length increased to as much as three hours in 1971.

This example suggests the potential, for better or worse, of broadcasting in Afghanistan. It can scarcely be denied that the airing of the debates held national attention, provided citizens with vicarious involvement in their government, and increased their political awareness. What might be doubted is the functionality of that effusion of rhetoric the presence of radio seemed to stimulate. The members of the Wolesi Jirgah seemed very conscious of their national audience. Rules of rhetorical restraint and parliamentary responsibility were more difficult to establish than the decision to broadcast every member's comments. And practically every member wished to comment, frequently at length. While it is difficult to say whether a tradition of broadcasting national debates will be functional in the long run, it cannot be doubted that when program content seems relevant to the average Afghan, he will seek exposure.

Radio in Afghanistan has not always had such an attentive audience. In its infancy, this was primarily because of technical difficulties and disruptions, the shortage of receivers, and the unfamiliarity of the audience with the phenomenon. To an extent, some of these same problems persist. But more and more, the difficulties of attracting and influencing a large audience seem to turn on the problem of obtaining high quality program content 100 hours per week out of what is essentially an underpaid and somewhat demoralized government bureaucracy, subject to the usual pathologies of bureaucratic life.

4.4.2 Historical Perspective

The origins of radio broadcasting in Afghanistan go back to 1925. This is a remarkably early date, considering the relative isolation of the country and the emergence of regular broadcasting in the Western world only a few years earlier. Technical difficulties, the scarcity of receivers, and the absence of Afghans trained either in electronics or programming made broadcasting during those early years a sometime thing. From the beginning, radio was a government-sponsored enterprise with the initiative coming from the top for equipment purchase, training, and even the distribution of receivers. Three years passed before one of the two 200-w. transmitters, purchased from Telefunken in Germany in 1925, was successfully operating on a sustained basis from Kabul, the capital (see "Radio Afghanistan" 1967). The other transmitter, slated for installation in Kandahar, Afghanistan's second city, never became operative due to technical difficulties. The government distributed 30 receivers to the people of Kabul initially and, by 1930, supplemented these with about 1,000 simple and inexpensive sets.

The introduction of broadcasting fit into the general modernizing plans of King Amanullah Khan, sovereign of Afghanistan from its recognition as a sovereign and independent state in 1919. The king was bent upon bringing his country into full membership in the family of nations, and he believed rapid cultural changes were necessary if the requisite technological advances were to be achieved. But his program of defensive modernization was too rapid for the sensibilities of many. As a result of some of his cultural proposals, civil disturbances broke out in 1929, during which Amanullah was deposed and escaped into exile.

Radio Kabul, as it had been called, ceased to exist during these upheavals. Its transmitter was damaged and the facilities were destroyed. In 1931, after consolidating his position, the new monarch, Mohammed Nader Shah, purchased another transmitter from Germany, this time one of 100-kw. The purchase was consummated in 1932, and the transmitter is still operating, flanked by three other 100-kw. transmitters, two of which were obtained in 1966 — one short-wave, one medium-wave. There are also two smaller short-wave transmitters of 20 and 50 kw., obtained in the late 1950s, and three other 50-kw. and two 10-kw. transmitters, all new in the 1970s (WRTH 1974, p. 139).

In 1940, broadcasting passed from the Ministry of the Interior to the newly created Department of Culture and Information, which eventually evolved into a ministry in its own right with broadcasting as only one of its functions. Major expansion of broadcast hours and program diversification came in the decades of the five-year plans, begun in 1956. Simultaneously, technical facilities were expanded and improved, new quarters constructed, and an augmented program of national and foreign training instituted for both technical and content aspects of broadcasting. During the second five-year plan, for instance, the Royal Afghan government spent about $300,000 and obtained credit from West

Germany for an additional $1.5 million to purchase and install equipment and to build modern facilities. Germany has from the beginning been a major source of equipment and technical advice and has sent advisory personnel to assist in both technical and programming matters since 1963. In addition, scholarship programs and technical assistance have been obtained from the British, Americans, Australians, Soviets, and Asian Broadcasting Union, as well as from West Germany.

4.4.3 Programming

The planners and intelligentsia seem to see broadcasting essentially as an instrument of enlightenment, integration, information, and entertainment. Enlightenment provides the rationale for programs dealing with culture, history, the family, and proper behavior toward the police. Integration is achieved by these programs and by those dealing with national political affairs; religious broadcasts also serve to unify and placate the criticism of the conservative religious leaders. Informational programs include those dealing with health, agriculture and, of course, current national and international events. Entertainment is found in the extensive musical offerings and in some dialogue and drama (see Table 22).

Table 22. Radio Afghanistan Programming, Mid-1972 (by aggregate weekly totals)

Program Category	No. of Different Programs	No. of Broadcasts Per Week	Percentage of Broadcast Week (No. of Hours)
Music and Miscellaneous	10	70	53.5
Religion	6	18	8.4
Agricultural/Farm	1	7	5.8
Domestic/International News & Weather	19	133	5.7
Advertising	3	20	4.6
Music/Poetry	6	6	4.5
Health/Family Life	4	15	4.2
Drama & Serialized Reading	5	7	3.4
Editorials	2	14	3.0
Children's & Youth	3	4	1.9
Language Lessons	5	7	1.8
Broadcasting for Teachers/Schools	1	2	1.5
Historical, Cultural & General Enlightenment	3	3	1.0
Listener Response	1	1	.5
Totals	69	307	100.0

Radio Afghanistan is on the air 14 hours a day Saturday through Thursday and 16 hours on Friday, the Muslim day of rest. More than half the total broadcast hours, in the form of ten daily programs, feature folk or classical

Afghan music, native music performed by amateurs, as well as a few programs offering European and North American music. Much of the music broadcast is performed by artists in the employ of the Ministry of Culture and Information and on more or less permanent assignment to Radio Afghanistan.

Independent observers claim that music is the most successful aspect of Radio Afghanistan, particularly as it features classical and folk Afghan selections. The abstract character of instrumental music successfully sidesteps the difficulties of government approval. Thus, the lives of those engaged in providing music for the broadcast day is less fraught with complications than the lives of the balance of the program personnel. Correspondingly, the producers and talent occupied with music are probably more content and experience more satisfaction in their assignments.

Religious programs rank second in total hours. The broadcast day opens and closes with religious offerings, including Koranic readings, thoughts for meditation, and sermons. On Friday, religious programs are featured. Religious sensibilities and symbols permeate the entire broadcast offering.

News and weather are the most frequent types of program. News is broadcast hourly in five-minute segments, both in Dari and Pashto. There is an 80-minute evening broadcast and a selection of news from the Afghan press is read to listeners each morning. News is supplied to the station through Bakhtar News Agency, the official Afghan news source. Bakhtar has links to Agence France Presse, Reuters, Associated Press, Deutsche Presse Agentur, Tass, and New China News Agency. Reporters and stringers in the provinces also feed Afghan news into the agency. A study of four randomly selected weeks in 1967 indicated that Bakhtar transmits about 43,000 words of international news per week in about 50 stories. Foreign relations is the most common type of news story transmitted to Bakhtar, followed by internal politics of particular countries, e.g., Great Britain, United States, or Vietnam. Sports stories are the third most common type reaching Bakhtar (Snider 1968).

Much of the material emanating from Bakhtar is taken off monitored radio copy. Transmissions show an interest in international relations with emphasis on Muslim concerns. Sports stories tend not to be transmitted and most of the agency's output is brief, of 200 words or less. Bakhtar attempts to present a relatively neutral stance on international affairs, at least neutral *vis-a-vis* the great powers, and to cater to audience interests.

The programs for farmers, home and family life, youth and children, teachers, and listener response are prepared by the Department of Education within Radio Afghanistan. Time devoted to home and family life has increased recently in response to a budding concern on the government's part with the pressures of population on Afghanistan's resource base. Family and farm programs are the oldest daily programs on the station. Farmers are served by an hour-long show which is the major daily offering of Radio Afghanistan, other than news. The farmer's program provides information about government policies relevant to the agricultural sector and discusses various aspects of modern farming. A variety of techniques are utilized in an effort to hold farmer interest, including the use of colloquial forms of Dari and Pashto. In addition, a quiz program is featured periodically with gifts offered participating farmers. Remote recordings of farmers in outlying areas are worked into shows whenever possible, and use is made of dramatization of "old" and "new" farmers discussing farm problems. Folk music provides fill and entertainment.

Farmer response is one of the few areas to have received some research attention. Radio Kabul itself sampled the opinions of farmers who came to Kabul for the Jeshen (national independence day) celebrations in 1968–69; 45% of those interviewed like the program. In 1970, an independent survey of 520 farmers in seven provinces found that 40% had access to radio, 20% through set ownership (Whiting 1971). Of those with access, 17% listened more than once a week, 45% weekly, 20% monthly, and 18% not at all. Since this sample of farmers was selected from the more accessible and prosperous rural regions, the penetration of radio on the rural level is probably considerably less. Radio is much more available in cities and towns, which often utilize loudspeakers in the bazaar to draw and hold crowds.

The frequency of listening found in the 1970 survey is our best current estimate of farmer interest. If more than weekly listening indicates interest, then about 3% of Afghanistan's farmers show interest in the farm broadcast. The 1970 survey turned up criticism having to do with the irrelevance of most of what was broadcast, but in the main, farmers were reluctant to express their complaints to strangers.

The only other source of feedback is through mail received. When the mail was being analyzed, it appeared that the music programs and some of the external services were the most appreciated. Since 1968, the public relations department has not been functioning, however, and analysis of mail is now *ad hoc*. Given the illiteracy of most of the populace, the expense of obtaining writing materials and posting letters, and the uncertainties of the postal system for outlying areas, the volume and content of letters received cannot give much of an idea of the relative value of programs.

Commercials are aired separately in three concentrated doses for a total of 40 minutes daily. They are divided into three types sold at different rates according to their sources. Foreign firms pay the most, followed by domestic industries and products, and finally by personal or individual announcements.

Revenues from commercials have slowly increased over the years, from about $80,000 in 1967 to about $127,000 in 1971. Some commercials are supplied by the Afghan Advertising Agency, while others are produced independently. The station does a limited amount of advertisement soliciting on its own initiative. In fact, it seems to make some efforts to discourage advertising, probably attributable to the fact that the money goes into general government coffers, instead of directly to the station's budget. It may also represent an ideological or aesthetic aversion to advertising. Since advertisers cannot sponsor programs, the service is more like a radio version of the classified ads than commercial broadcasting.

Radio Afghanistan's department of arts and letters prepares six weekly programs on poetry and culture and is responsible for special programs on national holidays and recognized religious festivals. In common with most Radio Afghanistan programming, the shows are presented about half in Dari, half in Pashto. The production staff, hampered by limitations in technical facilities, scripting, and available talent, feels financial resources, rather than good ideas, are the major block to improvement of program quality. Production personnel also find it difficult to pursue the official government line and to avoid embarrassing censorship or expensive reworking of their programs, in order to conform to decisions arrived at after the fact. In the producer's view, governmental guidelines are too imprecise, and the cautious instincts of the censors too hard to anticipate or to reconcile with artistic decisions.

After a program has been finally assembled, censors at three strategic decision points may decide to alter the contents, sometimes destroying the show's integrity. The three points are the department which originates the program, the programming department, and the directorate-general of programs, which monitors all radio fare before broadcast. Precautions taken by censors are to assure that nothing potentially controversial or offensive to official policy is aired. The precautions easily lead to friction with the production departments, producers, and talent who feel that their artistic sensibilities are violated by the uncomprehending·and senseless deletion of material. Because of time pressures, the edited tape sometimes is broadcast without repair, the gaps being filled by music, thus producing peculiar effects.

4.4.4 A Typical Production

To grasp what is unique about the programming process in Radio Afghanistan, a review of the production of a typical, if somewhat complicated, program is presented. The "Rural Program" fits this description, since it must be coordinated to some extent with the various government ministries affecting Afghan rural life. About a month before a series of programs is aired, the producer meets with his superior to decide content. The producer also seeks out publicity-office heads of various ministries, especially the Ministry of Agriculture, to obtain their output and desires. Sometimes the ministries prepare a rough script that they wish broadcast; at other times, they provide only general ideas. The producer, with the aid of at least two contracted writers, then works up rough scripts for a week's programs.

About two days before the broadcast, a draft of the script must be available for screening. First, the head of the rural programming department reads the script, looking for errors from the standpoint of political or religious sensitivities, and checks the message for consistency. The director-general of the education department scrutinizes it next with the same criteria in mind. If the program as edited and amended is still sufficiently intact to be coherent, it is returned to the producer who then requisitions announcers and talent, obtains his music, and schedules a studio for use.

Usually without rehearsal, but with some prior reading by the talent, the program is recorded. According to station guidelines, recording should take place a day before broadcast at the latest, but sometimes censorship and repair delay the process such that the recording will occur less than an hour before airtime. After editing, the tape is sent to the director-general of the program department where an employee monitors the entire program for length, content, and mistakes in editing. If the program is approved, it is put on the air; if not, and should there be sufficient time, the producer is asked to make changes. In cases of too little time, the programming department does the editing, substituting music or other fill where materials have been deleted. Then the program is broadcast through the technical department, the control section recording off-the-air all station broadcasts.

The necessity of planning and integrating the various details of the "Rural Program" are, of course, constants in broadcasting. Likewise, the time pressures are standard. But three interesting characteristics of Radio Afghanistan show up here. First, the necessity of working in two languages dooms at least half of the program's spoken part to unintelligibility for the majority of the audience. Second, the necessity of censorship before, during, and after program airing turns attention inward, toward pleasing the bureaucracy and not offending the elite. The station does not receive government support to stir things up; the view it tries to present is thus more placid and sanguine than realities might warrant. Third, although there is great concern — an outsider would say excessive concern — with assuring that nothing offensive is programmed, there seem to be almost no procedures of system for assuring that something useful or interesting is broadcast. Thus, the program turns inward, toward the perpetuation of the source's prerogatives and maintenance of its power base with the audience which really matters, the urban elite. Despite the good intentions of individuals concerned with its conception and production, the program, through organizational processes and precautions, is deflected from its avowed purpose of serving the rural audience.

4.4.5 Dual Language Policy

The dual language policy dates from 1964. Before then, Pashto was the official language of the country, but Dari, a form of Persian, was the language of the bureaucracy and of Kabul. Because of the literary and classical developments that have occurred in Persian and the relative absence of a written tradition in Pashto, Dari fluency had greater status. On the other hand, the nationalistic desire to keep distinctions between Afghanistan and other Persian-speaking countries encouraged the continuance of Pashto. Some critics claim that the equating of Dari with Pashto is still insufficient, because Pashto is neither the language of a majority nor a language in which modern ideas and concepts are easy to express. Nevertheless, it is now a language politically expedient to promote, and Radio Afghanistan supports government policy.

The dual language policy is justified by station personnel purely on the basis of their upholding a political decision. To suggestions that other bi- or multi-lingual nations broadcast in different languages on different channels, or at least in large blocks of time in a particular language station, spokesmen comment that Afghanistan does things differently. They point to a parallel in the broadcasting situation of Wales where both English and Welsh are sent over the same frequency in alternate doses. The rationale for the practice is probably similar in both situations — national pride. But what complicates matters in Afghanistan is that the two main languages utilized represent far less than the total linguistic mix. Consequently, the national pride of only certain groups is assuaged, while others tend to be offended by exclusion. For example, there are at least eight other mutually unintelligible languages native to the country that have as yet no broadcasting representation. Some changes, however, were forthcoming in early 1972, when political representatives persuaded Radio Afghanistan to begin at least token broadcasting of news, commentary, and music in their languages. As a result, Radio Afghanistan broadcasts in Pashayee and Baludir, each for 15 minutes daily, and Uzbeki and Turkomani, each for 45 minutes daily. These programs are very popular in the areas where these languages are found and represent something of a victory for the deputies from those areas.

Criticism on the ineffectiveness of broadcasting in a language people do not understand is parried with the suggestion that people should learn the national languages of the country. The critic has assumed that communication of content is the main aim of broadcasting. Indirectly, the defense engaged in by station apologists seems to throw doubt on this assumption.

The necessity of broadcasting in equal amounts in two languages on the same channel, typically during the same program, clearly mitigates against the development of a single standardized code, although it might serve to standardize the two codes. There is a tendency, particularly with Dari, to broadcast in an elevated form of the language which, at least some critics of the station claim, is not intelligible even to most Dari speakers. On the other hand, dialogues and dramatizations are presented in colloquial versions of the two languages. Informal checks with a few poorly educated followers of the station's materials did not uncover discomfort with the language level used. The station apparently aims at a middle level of eloquence and there is evidence and opinion to suggest that it achieves intelligible output for most users of the language.

The policy of two languages during the same program complicates the life of producers, for the parts of a particular program are not necessarily translations of one another. For example, in a program featuring poetry and music, the Dari poetry will not be a translation of the Pashto poetry, and vice versa. Further, what is sensitive and censorable is at least partly related to the language in which it is formulated. These kinds of complexities keep producers alert for alternative areas of employment or anxious to rise in the station's hierarchy and so avoid such agonizing decisions.

The alternative of assigning broadcast frequencies to particular languages and programming separately is regarded as potentially divisive, not fulfilling the government's desires for national unification. The difficulty is not a lack of technical facilities, for simulcasting on several frequencies occurs now, and the available studio facilities would allow the production of separate programs, perhaps with less difficulty than in the present system. There seems no question that the decision is based on political policy, reflecting the station's concern for conformity to government directives, even at the expense of communicating effectively with the people. Those who have observed audiences listening to radio broadcasts in Afghan tea houses and other gathering points, notice a fluctuation of attentiveness and talk according to the intelligibility of the message.

Although they occupy a relatively small portion of total broadcast time, language classes may be one of the most functional of Radio Afghanistan's offerings. The most extensive instructions are provided in Dari and Pashto where comments on writing and grammar are included. For the other languages, the station utilizes tapes provided by BBC and cultural affairs offices of the German, French, and Soviet embassies. The Russians are the only ones translating their lessons into both Dari and Pashto; the other tapes provide translation only to Dari. There is no estimate of the number of listeners to these programs or of the value the audience places on them. Doubtless only a minority have the interest, motivation, or time schedule to stick with a series of lessons, and the lessons remain necessarily rather elementary.

4.4.6 Bureaucratic Organization

Radio Afghanistan fits the definition of a bureaucracy. Its output is not evaluated in any immediate market, and direct feedback on quality is defective. Its employees are, in the main, civil servants, protected and rewarded according to standard civil service rules and schedules. Control over employee behavior does not extend to dismissal unless the superior can find an alternate position for the employee in some other government operation. And the number of employees is large enough to assure a certain degree of anonymity and impersonality.

Although not apparent from the organizational chart (see Figure 4), Radio Afghanistan is a highly centralized bureaucracy, wedded firmly to a broadcasting theory that emphasizes the development of a single, centralized voice for the government. This theory is embodied in the constitution which gives public broadcasting a monopoly by law over the use of the airwaves. Some ideological critics of the station argue that since it amounts to "government broadcasting" rather than "public broadcasting," the present system is really in violation of the constitution. In any event, the constitution clearly precludes private broadcasting.

There are about 625 civil service protected employees working for Radio Afghanistan, about 50 of whom are college graduates. About 215 work in

MINISTER OF INFORMATION AND CULTURE

DEPUTY MINISTER

PRESIDENT OF MEDIA

PRESIDENT OF RADIO AFGHANISTAN

PROGRAM DIVISION	ADMINISTRATIVE DIVISION	TECHNICAL DIVISION
Programming and Continuity	Accounting and Payroll	Transmitter and Studio Maintenance
Continuity	Purchasing	
Censorship		Training Center
	Personnel	
Information		Security and
News and Commentary		Janitorial
Reportage		
Pushtunistan Affairs		
External Services		

Education
   Family Life and Health
   Vocational and Agricultural
   General Education

Arts and Letters
   Radio Magazine
   Poetry and Music
   Dialogues
   Drama
   Serialized Stories

Music
   Folk
   Amateur
   Classical
   Western

Public Relations (not functioning but still in the formal organization structure)
   Monthly Magazine
   Listener Correspondence (for external services)
   Foreign Travel of Personnel

Advertising

Archives

Figure 4.   Radio Afghanistan's formal Organizational Structure

programming, 200 in technical services, and the remainder in administration and support. Most personnel work an 8–5 day, but about 60 are needed for overtime until 7:30 P.M., and another 40 until 10 P.M. Because of overtime opportunities, the Radio Afghanistan staff earn a little more than people in similar civil-service grades in other ministries. Also, because of the visibility of their work, as compared with that of the typical bureaucrat, they are more likely to receive bonuses or reductions. The successful station official may, upon comparison with his peers elsewhere, feel satisfied, but the nature of the work situation has great potential for interpersonal conflict, frustration, and tension.

Promotion in Radio Afghanistan is almost universally from within and is determined to a large extent by educational background.

The great majority of those working in technical broadcasting are high-school graduates with on-the-job training, largely under the tutelage of a West German advisory team. The career of a typical technical employee includes technical-school training after high school, selection for work on the station by competitive examination, and a combination of part-time schooling and on-the-job training in maintenance and repair.

For those in the programming division with college training, the most typical pattern is a degree from the journalism department at the University of Kabul. Personnel at key points have had this supplemented by training in foreign countries. Most of the journalism staff of the university were originally drawn from journalism or broadcasting, thus a substantial amount of a student's college experience is obtained by interning with local newspapers, the Bakhtar News Agency, or the station itself.

The Afghan government is virtually the only employer of a college graduate in journalism; about 95% of the graduating students are hired by the Ministry of Culture and Information. Salaries and incentives being what they are in the civil service, many students are disinclined to put forth their best efforts even as students. The monthly starting salary of a college graduate with the ministry is about $18, while the starting salary for a high school graduate — a more typical level of training for those in the technical department — is $16. Officials who have risen to the top positions in the station because of seniority, political connections, training, and experience make about $50 per month. While the cost of living is low, these pay scales are small enough that an employee who must take a taxi to and from work daily, at about $.50 a ride, finds himself with almost nothing to show for his labors.

For at least some of the dedicated and initially enthusiastic Afghans at the station, the considerations of low pay and tension-ridden work lead to the performance of their tasks in a somewhat desultory fashion. To their dissatisfactions with remuneration, they may add insufficient recognition, lack of any indication that conscientious efforts make a difference, frustration with inadequate and uncertain facilities and supplies, and impatience with the seniority system.

On the other hand, the employee may undertake to please his superior by producing programs that do not trouble highly placed figures, by being cooperative, accommodating, and willing to serve long hours and by undertaking unpleasant tasks. To be successful, he would have to look inward to the internal politics of the station rather than to the adequacy of his work, as evaluated by the mass audience whose welfare provides the public rationale for his activities, but whose opinion matters scarcely a whit in his personal fortunes. If he is fortunate, his rewards will include bonuses, promotions and opportunities for foreign travel and training. But if his superiors find his work unsatisfactory, he may be switched to a less difficult and less visible job in the station with a more dismal career line or, as a last resort, returned to the ministry. If his duties are sufficiently unpleasant and he can find alternate employment, he may resign, but, as mentioned, he cannot be fired for incompetence.

4.4.7 Foreign Training

The various opportunities for foreign travel and study probably function as a major inducement to Radio Afghanistan employees. Under the Colombo Plan, certain members of the British Commonwealth have extended both technical and journalistic training to Radio Afghanistan. The first trainee under this program went to Australia in 1964; since then, 16 people have received training in at least one, and sometimes more than one, Commonwealth country. The U.S.S.R. has provided training scholarships in Soviet universities; in fact, Radio Afghanistan's president received his doctorate in Asian history from Moscow University. The Soviet Union has also undertaken to support a few young artists in their study of music and theatre. USIS has supported excursions for a few top-level personnel to visit U.S. facilities, and about ten Fulbright professors have participated as journalism teachers at Kabul University.

West German assistance to the station has been the largest, longest, and most important to its development. While its major thrust was for a time on the technical side, it has more recently provided journalistic training. Since 1966, West Germany has provided scholarships for two years of journalism study. Fifteen Afghans have finished this training, but the majority, upon return, have moved out of programming and into administration, or into more lucrative positions not relating to broadcasting. Thus, their training has had little impact on the station's output.

In technical training, which has been systematically provided since 1963, a similar picture presents itself. Of the 43 individuals sent to Germany, 7 are still in training, 15 have remained in Germany in more profitable posts, and 4 of the 21 who returned to Afghanistan have left the station since their return. Excluding the 7 now in training, only about 50% of the training effort can be regarded as resulting in a contribution to the station's operations. Those who do return to the station often become disgruntled quite soon. It seems very possible that effective training in Europe contributes more to depressing than improving the enthusiasm of trainees upon return, for they are then confronted with a technical and social system less easily managed than they have become accustomed to during their training.

4.4.8 Financing

Station apologists and critics alike agree that at least some of Radio Afghanistan's difficulties are attributable to its limited budget. The station depends completely upon government appropriations, which in 1971 totaled about $212,000 for salaries, maintenance, supplies, and miscellaneous. Variations in support from year to year constitute one of the uncertainties of life for administrators and employees. Advertising and receiver sales bring in some revenue, but it is not earmarked for use by the station. The excise tax on receivers being a miniscule six cents, 1971 sales of about 43,000 legally purchased sets brought in only about $2,700. In 1975, UNESCO estimated 108,000 radio sets in use in Afghanistan (*UNESCO* 1975, p. 255).

While it is certainly true that the station's budget is woefully inadequate by the standards of most broadcasting operations, the felt need of virtually non-stop broadcasting, wide program variety, and a large staff contribute to lessening the quality of most programs. Suggestions that the program schedule be made less ambitious and that resources be poured into improving the quality of a few offerings, run into political objections. If citizens have nothing to listen to on Radio Afghanistan, they might spend more time listening to foreign broadcasts. Besides, neighboring nations and those which provide a model for Afghanistan keep their broadcast outlets going full time (see discussion of this cycle in Katz 1972).

The model of broadcasting adopted by Radio Afghanistan assumes that operations should be centralized. This serves, at least in theory, to minimize control difficulties and maximize quality of station output. The latter rationale is most likely to be mentioned when apologists explain why there are no regional stations originating programs for outlying areas. The budget does not allow sufficient quality for the single station in Kabul, let alone for regional ones (for a general counter-argument, see Brown and Kearl 1967). The first, and apparently last, consideration of the possibility of regional originating stations was in 1928, when it was thought that an outlet in Kandahar would be opened. If the possibility has come up since, it was defeated by budgetary considerations.

On the other hand, plans are going ahead for the establishment of three or four booster stations (transmitter and antenna installations) in regions where the current signal does not reach effectively. Some urgency is felt about this construction, for considerable segments of the population, unable to receive a strong Kabul signal, tune instead to foreign transmissions. The single centralized station makes political sense to the degree consolidation and establishment of national identity and loyalties is still a problem, as it very definitely is for Afghanistan. Whether the station is being used most effectively to this end is hard to judge. Likewise, it is difficult to tell how far broadcasting by itself can go to overcome the nation's ubiquitous rivalries and divisions.

Finally, it would probably be somewhat difficult to keep technically or professionally trained personnel happy in regional stations. The attraction of the capital city with its services and entertainment possibilities might overwhelm personal dedication to regional needs. The solution would be to find people with ethnic or family ties in each region, but the difficulty of including these criteria with those of technical competence and the possibility regional stations might be used to help fragment the nation, argue strongly against the establishment of regional originating outlets. The argument is academic anyway, for in the foreseeable future all broadcasting in Afghanistan will originate in Kabul.

4.4.9 External Broadcasting

As would be expected, most external broadcasts are intended to tell Afghanistan's story and views in favorable terms. Radio Afghanistan broadcasts an hour daily to India and Pakistan in Urdu, as well as an hour of Afghan news, music, analysis, and response to letters, in Dari and Pashto, for Afghan residents living abroad. It also presents three programs of a half-hour each daily in English, German, and Russian; the English program is rebroadcast once in the evening. These half-hour programs are similar in format to the program for Afghans abroad and similar to each other on any particular day. The general tenor is one of information and friendly communication.

Perhaps the most important broadcast aimed at a foreign audience is that directed to Pushtunistan. Afghanistan regards certain bordering provinces of Pakistan as, by rights, constituting a separate, autonomous country with much closer ties to Afghanistan than to Pakistan. These areas are inhabited by Pushtuns with ethnic and tribal affiliations that link them to the dominant groups of Afghanistan. Radio Afghanistan broadcasts an hour daily during prime time, both on medium- and short-wave, to Pushtunistan. The program stops short of fomenting revolution or promising armed support of liberation movements in Pushtunistan, but it does proclaim the close ties that many Afghans feel with the Pushtuns and attempts to keep them abreast of what Afghanistan is doing for them. The program functions to keep alive what sentiment there is for independence and to mollify domestic Afghan criticism of the government's cautious approach to the issue. The Pushtunistan issue is sensitive enough that a separate section for Pushtunistan affairs has been set up under the director-general for information and the program's content is closely monitored by the Foreign Ministry. A special government directive was recently issued calling on Radio Afghanistan to upgrade the quality of its propaganda regarding the Pushtunistan question. To follow through on this, a special committee has been appointed.

The section for Pushtunistan affairs is charged with providing information about Pushtunistan for domestic consumption, as well as with the daily hourly broadcast. For instance, special domestic and foreign broadcasts occur on Pushtunistan national holidays. Although a certain tension exists between Afghanistan and Pakistan, it does not appear likely that organized conflict will again break out over the issue. Indeed, for some time, a tacit agreement to tone down mutual criticism on the airwaves has been observed between the two countries, although with occasional lapses. The issue is still a sensitive one and close to the surface.

4.4.10 Technical Problems

The maintenance of broadcasting facilities is complicated by the dusty conditions surrounding transmitter sites and by established routines of work procedures. As in all Afghan government activities, a special official, known as *tahweeldar*, presides over the storeroom and must account for every piece of equipment drawn upon. By law, only the *tahweeldar* dispenses materials needed to maintain the station. His training and orientations are not technical, and he tends to jealously guard his hoard and his rights to the administration of its treasures. Where the transmitter's technical personnel remain on friendly terms, few problems arise. But if a breakdown occurs when the *tahweeldar* is away, the station must either go off the air or the personnel must bend the rules to obtain the needed parts.

4.4.11 Television

While the matter of a television service is under discussion, and preliminary steps to procure land and facilities have been taken, the dominant mood at present is to delay its establishment. Technical personnel look to it with some enthusiasm; programming sections are more cautious. The government would like to establish television, in part to compete with the invasion of signals across Afghan borders. In the north, for instance, some Afghan homes blossom with television antennas, receiving signals from Soviet Central Asia. But the government is rightly wary of the costs of quality television. The expense of maintaining transmitter sites in the rugged terrain of Afghanistan would be in itself sufficient to give an administrator pause. And if transmitting satellites were relied upon to reduce these kinds of problems, the difficulties and expenses of television production for the Afghan market would be staggering.

The claim has been made by some that the visual aspects of television are in conflict with Islamic Afghan cultural traditions. This seems far-fetched given the popularity and prosperity of cinema and pictorial representation in the country. On the other hand, the utilization of large amounts of foreign television programs, a typical means used in developing nations to fill broadcast time economically, might run into difficulties because of different standards of feminine dress and deportment. The main reluctance of programming personnel probably lies in the feeling that they have not yet managed to produce radio materials of consistently high quality. The coming of television would bring more burdens than opportunities, at least in the minds of some. But television is doubtless coming.

When it is introduced, technical rationale will suggest the adoption of a Japanese standard. In 1975, a group of Japanese broadcasting technicians visited Afghanistan to discuss the feasibility of installing a television station and to work out an agreement with the government departments involved. As a result, there has been assurance given that an agreement with the Japanese is forthcoming and that Afghanistan will have a television station by 1977. Already, Radio Afghanistan personnel have left for Japan for short-term training in television.

4.4.12 Educational Broadcasting

In 1967, the Afghanistan government requested UNESCO's help in establishing a national educational broadcasting service. A tentative plan was approved by 1971, and broadcasts commenced by 1973. The plan worked out between the government of Afghanistan and UNESCO envisaged the development of educational broadcasting in three phases — use of radio for training pre- and in-service primary teachers, for functional literacy and rural development, and for direct teaching in primary schools. In 1972, a National Educational Broadcasting Board (NEBB) was established under the Ministry of Education with representatives from all ministries, departments, or projects interested in using radio for education (Wilson 1972). A four-year plan, 1973—76, for the implementation of the development of educational broadcasting was one of the first actions of NEBB.

All three phases of educational broadcasting were operative by 1975. Radio Afghanistan was airing as many as three hours weekly of programs to train primary teachers; the programs were in both Pashto and Dari. In the area of rural development/functional literacy broadcasts, progress was made when experimental village study groups were created and radio sets were made available for their use. By 1976, 3,900 radio receivers will have been placed in villages for listening by such study groups. The third phase went into effect in 1974 when programs in health, language arts, and social sciences were broadcast over Radio Afghanistan into the primary schools. By 1975, three hours weekly of schools broadcasts were expected. Approximately 5,000 radio receivers were to be in place in schools and colleges of Afghanistan by that time (Wilson 1973).

.4.13 Coup d'Etat and Broadcasting

On 17 July 1973, Afghanistan's King Mohammed Zahir Shah was overthrown in a political coup and the kingdom was changed into a republic. At the same time, martial law was proclaimed. It is significant that the leader of the coup, General Sadar Mohammed Daud, announced the change of government first in a Radio Afghanistan speech, interspersed with martial music. One newspaper reported the event in this manner:

Kabul Radio broadcast martial music this morning instead of the usual news bulletin in Pashtu. . . . Gen. Daud then came on the air and told the nation that he was declaring Afghanistan a republic and charged that the former Government was leading the country towards bankruptcy. [Kuala Lumpur *Straits Times,* 18 July 1973, p. 1]

For three days after the coup, newspapers and magazines were suspended, and the people depended upon Radio Afghanistan for information. Radio

Afghanistan broadcasts tried to persuade the masses to live peacefully, through news comments, and military and martial music.

As the national situation stabilized, Radio Afghanistan continued its policy based on nonalignment integrity and national unity. Subject matter of most programming is uniform, designed to reflect the movements toward nationalistic unity and public respect for the new regime. The radio stations are still owned by the state, and there have been no changes regarding advertising policy or the use of two languages — Dari and Pashto. Since the coup, however, the Pushtunistan programming is much more intense, Radio Afghanistan commenting regularly and fiercely on the rights of Pushtuns. As a result, Radio Afghanistan has been criticized several times recently by the Pakistani government.

4.4.14 Summary

Radio broadcasting in Afghanistan stands in an essentially paternalistic position toward the populace. It functions as an apologist for the government and seeks more to avoid, than to expose, controversy. Its greatest successes probably lie in the dissemination of folk music and other entertainment and cultural materials. Critics claims that broadcasting news and information are not highly regarded by a domestic audience who see foreign sources as more credible. The station's apologists admit that the signal itself scarcely reaches outlying areas of the country and that inhabitants of major cities in the east, west, and north are being enticed by foreign broadcasters. Perhaps the 40-year survival of the station over a turbulent period should be regarded as its basic achievement. As in so many other countries, the visionary potential of broadcasting for uniting and educating people seems far from fulfillment. In at least the near future, it would appear that Radio Afghanistan is more likely to be changed and shaped by external influences and events than it is to play a major and autonomous role in effecting change.

4.5 Nepal, *by Margaret Sheffield and John A. Lent*

Nepal from 1846 to 1951 was ruled by a family of hereditary prime ministers, the Ranas, who kept close ties with the British in India. The Nepal Congress Party, campaigning for a more democratic government, led a revolution, the outcome of which was a restoration of the royal line, represented by King Tribhuvan. A 1959 general election resulted in an overwhelming victory for the Congress Party, but by 1960, King Mahendra, who had succeeded Tribhuvan, dismissed the ministry and established personal rule. Mahendra died in 1972 and the seat of power went to his son, Birendra.

Nepal has a population of about 12 million; its capital, Kathmandu (165,000), is the only major city. The people are genetically and culturally a

Margaret Sheffield is advisor to His Majesty's Government of Nepal on setting up school broadcasting; she worked for some years as producer of educational programs for BBC.

well-mixed stock. They range from the distinctly Mongolian type in the northern hills, whose religion is Buddhism, through the various tribal groups of the middle hills, whose features are Aryan and religion Hindu, to the people of the Tarai, who resemble Indians. There are also Muslims in Nepal. The people, therefore, are characterized by their devoutness and religious tolerance.

Nepal has been classed as one of the 25 least developed nations of the world in terms of statistics such as literacy, income per capita, schooling, hospitals, newspapers, infant mortality, etc. But the country has a well-established agricultural routine and a secure sense of its own identity. It has never been a colony per se, although British India had expanded as far as its southern borders. It has both benefitted and suffered because of this: benefitted in that it has a sense of pride for not having been colonized, suffered in that the strong ruling families have rarely been able to act for the good of the entire nation.

4.5.1 Background

Anywhere one travels in Nepal — in the flat, fertile parts near the long Indian border, the hills of the middle region, or in the Himalayas themselves — he comes across people with radios (see Parajuli 1972, p. 1). Not very many people, because most of the population is low-income, and radio receivers and batteries are expensive. But nearly every village that can be considered more than a mere hamlet has a radio owner. Often, he is a shopkeeper, who keeps his radio on all day, indirectly benefitting the passers-by in the bazaar. Often, he is a government official, either in the local *panchayat* (the smallest administrative unit), or the central government. In the latter case, he is likely to be a Kathmandu man sent up-country for a year or two to assist with the administration. Often, he is an ex-soldier, a Gurkha from the British or Indian army, who has returned to his village, possessing a transistor radio. Whoever he is, he is likely to be distinguished from the rest of the community by having, or having had, at least temporarily, some little money to spare.

That he has chosen to spend his money on a radio set is not surprising, at least not in Nepal, where, next to wristwatches, radios are the commonest symbols of affluence and modernity. Radios, like watches, are easy to incorporate into the otherwise medieval conditions of Nepali village life. They do not require electricity, plumbing, or liquid fuels, most of which are nonexistent in the kingdom outside the Kathmandu Valley and larger towns. They are small and easily portable, important factors in a country mainly traversed by footpaths, and, finally, they can be used and enjoyed by all people, whatever their standard of education. In particular, they can be enjoyed by the illiterate population, who represent approximately 70% of the people.

Despite these advantages of the medium, it is still rather exceptional for Nepalis living in rural areas — about 90% of the population — to possess a radio receiver. Radios are not manufactured or assembled in Nepal, all of them coming from Japan, Hong Kong, or Singapore, and imported sets bear both freight and import charges which approximately double their duty-free costs in the country of origin (see Singh 1975, p. 29). As the average income per capita of the Nepali people is less than $100 per year, radio sets are generally out of their financial reach. No official figures are available for the number of radio sets in Nepal, but assuming each of the 4,000 village or town *panchayats* contains, say, three radios, and that the urban populations of Kathmandu, Pokhara, and the Tarai towns between them own 50,000 radios, a figure of 62,000 is derived. A 1974 survey estimated the number of sets at 115,000, or one radio receiver per 100 people (*Media* 1975a, p. 23), while UNESCO estimated 70,000 sets in use (UNESCO 1975, p. 324).

Radio Nepal, the government-owned, -staffed, and -administered station, is the only broadcasting channel in Nepal. As a government station, operating within the constitution and law, Radio Nepal is not permitted to criticize the government or its policies. The station is divided into national and commercial services, each averaging about five hours on the air daily. Not fully autonomous, the commercial service uses Radio Nepal's studios.

Radio Nepal broadcasts on two medium-wave (0.25 and 10 kw.) and two short-wave (5 and 100 kw.) transmitters. (*UNESCO* 1975, p. 324). Additionally, a normal short-wave transmission on 60 meters carries an external service into India, Bangladesh, and China. The external service languages used are Nepali, English, Newari, and Hindi. These programs can be heard within Nepal as well, on both short-wave and medium-wave. The medium-wave transmission is preferred in an area such as the Kathmandu Valley, which benefits from a medium-wave transmitter.

Financing of Radio Nepal comes out of a direct government allocation, figures of which are not made public. Revenue from the commercial service is apparently irrelevant to the allocation given to the national service. An annual license fee of Rs. 10 ($1) is assessed each radio set owner; however, collection of the license fee presents tremendous difficulties. Fees paid by Radio Nepal to contributors and performers seem to be fair and adequate in comparison to average wages earned in other jobs. For example, a fee for a half-hour script is about Rs. 75 ($7.50), for an actor performing in such a script, about Rs. 25 ($2.50). In comparison, a teacher earns about Rs. 150 ($15) per month. As a result, Radio Nepal has been a significant patron to Nepali artists since the station began.

Television has not appeared in Nepal, although occasionally, the possibility of inaugurating the medium is discussed by commercial firms which would like to see government invest in it. The government realizes the difficulties of having TV in such a mountainous terrain as that of Nepal. Line television would be possible immediately in the Kathmandu Valley but would be a solution only to the engineering problems of a very small area. But government thinking is that it would not be wise to spend government money providing yet another service for Kathmandu when the rest of the country needs help in more basic ways. Also, there are economic and political aspects to be considered in that TV, because of the expensiveness of sets, would become the prerogative of only the Nepali elite.

Additionally, the government would be hard-pressed to create beneficial program material, because of high production costs and the absence of trained personnel. The Royal Nepal Film Corporation was set up in the early 1970s and began production of documentaries and a feature film. When television does arrive eventually, it will probably draw upon the expertise and actual products of this national film unit. Fortunately, radio is cheaper and more democratic, and as such, will remain the sole broadcasting medium in Nepal for the time being.

4.5.2 Programming

A cheap short-wave receiver just about anywhere in Nepal can receive Radio Nepal, as well as All India Radio, Radio Peking, Radio Bangladesh, Radio Sri Lanka, the external services of BBC, VOA, Radio Moscow, and others. Radio Nepal itself is heard in all corners of Nepal, as well as in India and the Tibetan region of China. An unofficial survey indicated that Radio Nepal was the most popular station of the Nepali people, closely followed by All India Radio. The survey area, however, was in the Tarai, which lies along the frontier with India. A survey conducted over the whole of Nepal would most probably reveal that Radio Nepal is very clearly the most frequently listened-to station, with others rather distant second choices.

It is, after all, necessary for a Nepali to listen to the national radio station for news about matters that concern him, Nepali news not being extensively covered by other stations. Most of the news used by Radio Nepal comes from the national news agency, which is affiliated with Agence France Presse, and from BBC newscasts which, together with those of AIR and to a lesser extent of other countries, are monitored by Radio Nepal. It is also necessary for a Nepali to tune to Radio Nepal because its programs are in Nepali, perhaps the only language he understands. Other stations have a very small output, if any at all, in Nepali, BBC once a week and Radios Bangladesh, Moscow, and Peking occasionally. Specific data on these external broadcasts in Nepali are hard to come by, because the transmissions are always changing. Radio Nepal, however, broadcasts ten hours daily in Nepali. Another reason for the eminence of Radio Nepal is that Nepal's cultural identity is very pronounced, in particular as regards music. The sense of familiarity the average Nepali experiences when tuning in Radio Nepal's rather extensive musical broadcasts is probably responsible for his preferring Radio Nepal to AIR, for example, where the cultural offering is distinctly Indian.

Thus, Nepalis listen to Radio Nepal mainly to hear news and Nepali music. Other Nepali programs they favor include drama, an extremely popular radio form because of the great acting talent of many Nepalis, and special interest shows, e.g., agricultural and teachers programs. Subjects of dramas are generally family or historically based and often include developmental themes, pointing out in dialogue forms, pros and cons of new methods of agriculture, education, and family planning. Agricultural and educational broadcasts have no set pattern, the director choosing a format appropriate to the material to be communicated. Speech and music are present in about equal parts in Radio Nepal programming. Music is used frequently in what are basically talk programs, in addition to being broadcast several hours daily in purely musical shows. In particular, the commercial service fills a large proportion of its schedule with Nepali and Western music, interspersed with advertisements and announcements. The commercial service is perhaps the most popular part of Radio Nepal, in that it is painless and undemanding entertainment. Information programs of a competitive nature, such as inter-school quiz contests, also have great audience appeal, perhaps because of their dramatic element.

Entertainment aside, however, Radio Nepal's importance as a main provider of information cannot be overemphasized. Nepal is a country with many ancient footpaths, but few roads for motor vehicles. Manifestations of the printed word (newspapers, books, or letters), on their journey to communicate to rural folk, must be carried on human backs. As a result, the mails can take three weeks to reach their destinations, even when there is no special reason for delay. Part of the reason for this might stem from the fact that the quickest way to traverse the country in an east-west direction is to enter the flatlands of India in the South, and reenter Nepal at a point below your destination. Roads now being constructed, in particular the East-West Highway, will help remedy the situation, but it is likely that, because of the jumble of hills and mountains that make up the central and northern parts of Nepal, roads will never completely solve the communication problem. The network of footpaths, and aerial space above carrying radio waves, will for a long time remain the communication network. Taking these factors into consideration, one can realize why Radio Nepal is so important as an information medium. Three daily newscasts are aired by the station, each of 10–15 minutes. Two of the news readings are followed by 10–15 minutes of news in English. Altogether, half an hour is set aside for news in the morning and evening.

Apart from Nepali-language programs and the two daily English-language newscasts, Radio Nepal also produces an external broadcast in English daily, for foreigners within Nepal and non-Nepali speakers outside the country. The station does not normally broadcast in any of the 25 regional languages and dialects of the country, except in folk-song programs. Nepali, the official language, is spoken and understood by most of the population, if it is not too heavily "Sanskritized," i.e., if there are not too many formal and ancient Sanskrit words included. Radio Nepal is not using "Sanskritized" Nepali, although for a time farmers shows were aired in that manner, until it was realized they had no appeal. Nepali frequently is not the first language people learn. Because of the sedentary, agrarian nature of Nepal, population movement has not been extensive, resulting in people developing and passing on regional languages. With the development of Radio Nepal, villagers' horizons were expanded, one result being more and more of them learned the national language.

4.5.3 Radio and National Development

Nepal is a recently arrived member of the modern world. It was only in 1950 that King Tribhuvan abrogated the power of the vast Rana family and laid the basis for Nepal's first democratic constitution. During the Rana days, only the ruling family and top officials could keep radios to listen to outside broadcasts. Apparently, it was a crime for the public to own sets (Parajuli 1972, p. 3). Radio Nepal came into being in 1950, broadcasting only a half-hour program daily on medium-wave. In fact, it is interesting to consider broadcasting in Nepal from this viewpoint. The national radio station of a country is always more than a vehicle for program material, being, in addition, an identifiable intellectual activity of the government, a mirror of the nation's culture and an index of the state of the country's technological, administrative, and political development. Thus, the recent development of the station was laid down in the government plan, "Communications for Development," which specified that daily broadcast hours should be upped to ten, greater program variety should exist, and broadcasts for special audiences should be planned.

The "Communications for Development" plan has fulfilled most of its original objectives, and as yet no further plan has been proposed. King Birendra, however, is devoted to the idea of well-planned development and will continue action in that direction, at the same time, expecting to count on Radio Nepal's assistance. Thus far, the station's roles in implementation of developmental programs have included informing the public of new policies and decisions of the king and his government, reporting on the progress of various plans for development and reflecting a developmental attitude in all sorts of programs. Developmental reporting has been increasingly carried out in recent years, the programs being produced either by Radio Nepal itself, or small production units within ministries concerned. Dramas, for instance, often exploit the conflict between the old and the new.

Another area where Radio Nepal attempts to fit its programming to the needs of the culture is in religion. The station reflects the devout nature of the people, who are Buddhist, Hindu, or Muslim, by presenting a half-hour religious program every morning. Any religion can be treated in these daily broadcasts, but naturally, due to the Hindu majority, more often than not that religion is featured. The program takes the form of a prayer, accompanied by devotional music. Religious music is also played in programs mourning the death of someone important. Apart from these direct presentations, religion, like the themes of change and development, is a constant influence on all program material. For example, characters in dramas invoke the gods as naturally and often as they do in real life.

In a country such as Nepal, where there is not the wealth of social organization found in developed countries, broadcasting for minority interests is naturally also not well developed. For example, minorities in the form of political parties are nonexistent, because constitutional amendment in 1967 made illegal not only the parties, but also the suggestion that there should be parties. Minorities classified and catered for on Radio Nepal are either obvious ones such as children or women, or groups such as farmers and teachers. The very real minorities of different regional, tribal, and caste groups — of which the whole population consists, and to which every individual knows he belongs — cannot be accommodated in broadcasts in this time of nation-building and development. Broadcasting to special interest groups is permitted, there being a daily children's program, a weekly family-planning show, school broadcasting, farmers and women's programs, and rural broadcasting. For example, educational broadcasts emanate from a separate unit with its own studio, as do farm broadcasts. One can expect broadcasting's output to become more varied — and the audience wider — exactly in proportion to the development of the different interest groups.

4.5.4 Problems

Despite the expansion of Radio Nepal during its first two and at half decades of existence, the system still faces problems of great magnitude. Improvement is necessary in a number of areas, particularly in the station's philosophy of broadcasting and more practically in its programming competence. In the first area, it can never be forgotten that Radio Nepal is a government agency and as such is a microcosm that repeats government practices as a whole. The ideal of public-service broadcasting — being an ideal, rather than a pressure — often does not play a large part in the expedient decisions Radio Nepal administrators are called upon to make. The public to be served is, in fact, 12 million people, too poor and illiterate to make their demands known. Until the government becomes aware of the meaning of public-service broadcasting and invokes it as the first principle in all programming decisions, this public will not be adequately served.

In the second area, Radio Nepal lacks ancillary services necessary to ease the burden of program making. For example, in the absence of a comprehensive library, it is difficult to check the accuracy of program material; in the absence of an indexed collection of sound effects, it is virtually impossible to include sound effects in dramatic programs. In addition, there are no formalized methods of audience research or program publicity. On the engineering side, studio efficiency is sometimes hampered by machine failures due to both the difficulty of obtaining spare parts and the lack of trained personnel.

Such handicaps are normal characteristics of broadcasting underdevelopment in many parts of the world. Some features of this underdevelopment are especially pronounced in Nepal, arising primarily from its unique geography.

For example, audience research on a Western scale is nearly impossible in Nepal, because the nature of the landscape makes any process of communication — other than by radio itself — an extremely lengthy process. A large proportion of the population cannot write, thus, listener response would have to be solicited by verbal questioning, a very long procedure indeed, because researchers would have to walk through mountainous terrain to reach their samples, there being so few roads. As a consequence, listener research is limited to evaluation of letters sent to the station. Some programs, such as those for farmers, are creating special listening groups, responses from which could be useful in future programming policy.

Program publicity faces similar problems. So far, nothing in Nepal can match radio for publicity purposes, and the medium is used to publicize its own programs. The commercial service accepts paid announcements from government and private agencies but is not used much by the national service which advertises its own programs. Newspapers are used as program guides, but again, the penetration of this medium, including national papers from the government-controlled Gorkhapatra Corporation, is miniscule compared to Radio Nepal's coverage. Although the state of audience research and program publicity is often deplored, neither is regarded as a pressing necessity in Nepal since there are so many more immediate problems to worry about.

A major problem relates to the nature of radio itself, contributing to day-to-day, rather than long term, ways of thinking. The rather undifferentiated nature of positions at Radio Nepal allows for no echelons of planners with time to consider and act upon underlying issues of underdevelopment. Therefore, the "Communications for Development" plan, prepared by the Ministry of Communications, was a welcome document.

Problems facing Radio Nepal are probably those that national radio stations in any developing country must contend with. First, a difficulty that exceeds and underlines all others relates to the lack of trained and confident personnel on both program and technical sides. Training facilities do not exist at Radio Nepal; most training results from on-the-job experience, a long, expensive proposition. Overseas training, usually at BBC, but also in the United States, West Germany, and Malaysia, is provided in some cases. But, because of the teamwork nature of broadcasting, oftentimes trained personnel find their own excellence submerged or masked by inferior work of colleagues. Related to the training problem is the fact that the modern Radio Nepal equipment is not maintained properly for lack of technical know-how. Thus, frequent machinery failures cause frustration, inefficiency, and a poor quality of recorded sound.

From an outsider's viewpoint, there is a problem of attitude, a lack of awareness of what may be called "greater Nepal." Nepal is much more than the Kathmandu Valley and its approximately half-million people. Yet broadcasting is, no doubt unconsciously, very much a reflection of valley ideas and concerns. For example, when, in 1972, 15 Sherpas were killed in a mountaineering accident — an event that warranted detailed mention on BBC's World Service — Radio Nepal carried no more news or comment than BBC. The problem of language also relates to the concept of "greater Nepal." It is perhaps an insoluble problem, for while it is obvious the national broadcasting system must program in what has been decided as the national language, citizens who speak another tongue are not served.

A final problem concerns the maintenance of receivers in rural areas. Batteries are rare and very expensive, because they must be carried to rural bazaars on men's backs. Maintenance of radio sets has been partially remedied by durable transistors, but still, if a set does not function, it is either made worse by an attempted repair or is inoperable for weeks.

It is a characteristic of a vigorous broadcasting organization that it encounters such problems and still progresses. This is happening in Nepal. Like many institutions in the kingdom, Radio Nepal is in a period of its development when beneficial works can be achieved. Already, the station is in an enviable position, being an essential service for most of the population.

4.6   Sri Lanka (Ceylon), *by Shelton A. Gunaratne*

Since the beginning of the 16th century, when Portuguese settled on its west coast, until 4 February 1948, when it became independent of British rule, Ceylon (called Republic of Sri Lanka since 22 May 1972) had been a colony. In between, the Dutch also ruled from the early 17th century until being evicted by the British in 1815. Since 1972, the country has witnessed the passage of a number of radical socialist measures by the coalition government of Mrs. Sirimavo Bandaranaike. During the same period, the prime minister also made overtures at nationalizing the newspapers of Sri Lanka.

The population of Sri Lanka is 13.2 million, the major cities being Colombo (the capital), Kandy, Galle, and Trincomalee. Sinhalese is the mother language of approximately 70% of the people; Tamil is spoken by about 20%, primarily those living in the northern and eastern provinces and in the tea-estate areas of the hill country. English is the language of the elite, cutting across ethnic groups.

Newspapers in Sri Lanka tend to be owned by groups, four such chains owning all 16 dailies. Total estimated circulation is 502,579.

4.6.1   Overview

Sri Lanka broadcasting is a state monopoly, organized under the Sri Lanka Broadcasting Corporation (Ceylon Broadcasting Corporation until mid-1972), which, in turn, is split into three language services: Sinhalese, Tamil, and English. Each language service has a National (Channel 1) and Commercial (Channel 2) outlet. In addition, a separate Education Service, broadcasting in all three languages, is in operation.

External broadcasts of Sri Lanka Broadcasting Corporation (SLBC) are carried by four services: All Asia English Commercial, All Asia Hindi Commercial, All Asia Tamil Commercial, and Overseas Service. Eight short-wave transmitters generating 335 kw. are used for external broadcasts.

Broadcasting in Sri Lanka is primarily financed by license fees and revenue

Shelton A. Gunaratne is Lecturer in Mass Communication at Universiti Sains Malaysia, Penang; he was a Ceylonese journalist for five years with their largest circulation newspapers. He was a World Press Institute fellow, has written articles on Sri Lanka and Pakistan, and received his Ph.D. at the University of Minnesota.

from the Commercial Service. In 1969–70, the then Ceylon Broadcasting Corporation (CBC) received $849,650 from license fees, a payment of $49,830 from Voice of America for use of transmitters and other facilities, and a profit of $450,000 from the Commercial Service. Sponsors of the latter service include public-sector corporations and government departments, such as National Lotteries Board, Ceylon Transport Board, National Milk Board, Ceylon Leather Corporation, Department of Small Industries, and Department of Agriculture.

It is estimated radio reaches about one-fourth of the island's population. Eleven medium-wave transmitters located in six different towns and generating 266 kw. of power, cover about three-fourths of the island's area; 11 short-wave transmitters totalling 110 kw. are also employed for domestic broadcasting (*WRTH* 1974, p. 169). The number of radio receivers in Sri Lanka has been estimated at 846,000 (UNESCO 1975, p. 341), but the number of licensed receivers, including 22,000 rediffusion units, was approximately 415,000 in 1973. Radio is listened to, at least once a month, by 52% of Sri Lanka's adult population; 39% listen daily.

Because of unaffordability on the part of the public, FM broadcasting has not been seriously undertaken by SLBC. Inasmuch as medium-wave transmitters have been linked together by a network of VHF transmitters, however, owner of FM radio receivers can pick up programs within 30 miles of Colombo. The country does not have a television service, although preliminary planning for the introduction of television was underway by 1974 (UNESCO 1975, p. 342).

The British-owned Ceylon Rediffusion Service Ltd., which operated a four-channel wired network under Sri Lanka government contract and participation, folded at the end of 1973 because of a gradual fall in the number of subscribers (*Straits Times* 1973d). Rediffusion, which rebroadcast the Sri Lanka Broadcasting Corporation programs in Sinhalese, Tamil, English, and Hindi, had 22,250 subscribers in 1969 (UNESCO 1975, p. 342).

4.6.2 Historical Background

Technical development. By 1923, the Ceylon Telegraph Department was broadcasting gramophone music from a small transmitter built by that department from the radio set of a captured German submarine. Shortly after, a committee headed by the postmaster-general reported on the introduction of the new medium, recommending that broadcasting be controlled, but not necessarily operated, by the government through a board made up of the postmaster-general and five deputies. The recommendations were accepted in May 1924. The first public demonstration of broadcasting occurred 27 July 1924, when the governor's speech was broadcast.

Actually, the formation of the Ceylon Amateur Radio Society in 1922 was the earliest indication of organized interest in broadcasting. In that year, wireless telegraph rules under the Telegraph Ordinance were framed in order to enable the issuance of licenses to work radio apparatus.

On 16 December 1925, the initial experimental stage was transformed into the Government Broadcasting Station. Although shifted from the Central Telegraph Office to new studios and control rooms in 1927, broadcasting continued to be an incidental responsibility of the Ceylon Telegraph Department. A separate broadcasting transmitter was built in June 1930, and two years later a receiving station was opened to pick up British Empire programs beamed by short-wave from Daventry. Local experiments in short-wave broadcasting began in 1934 to provide better reception to listeners in outlying provinces. Short-wave transmissions were discontinued in June 1938 on economic grounds.

With the commencement of World War II, Britain set up Radio SEAC (South East Asia Command) in Ceylon; the station was transferred to the Ceylonese government after the granting of independence in February 1948. Under this agreement, Radio SEAC's 100-kw. transmitter, as well as one of 7.5 kw., was transferred to the Ceylon government in March 1949.

In May 1951, Ceylon signed another agreement, this time with Voice of America, enabling VOA to install at its own expense three transmitters of not less than 35 kw. The agreement was based on the understanding that Ceylon would have secondary use of all equipment installed by VOA, and vice versa. VOA broadcasts over the new transmitters were begun two years later.

Installation of a medium-wave station at Diyagama in 1958 and another at Senkadagala in 1960 further extended Radio Ceylon's facilities. And in 1963, Australia donated five VHF transmitters and receivers to Radio Ceylon, allowing the transmission of programs from the studio center to transmitting stations at Ekala and Diyagama.

A rapid expansion of medium-wave broadcasting coverage, aided by West Germany, was achieved between 1967 and 1971. In 1973, medium-wave transmitters were located at Senkadagala (10 kw. and 1 kw.), Weeraketiya (50 kw.), Maho (50 kw.), Anuradhapura (10 kw.), Galle (10 kw.), and Diyagama (three 20 kw. and one each of 25 kw. and 50 kw.). To achieve complete medium-wave coverage, plans were afoot in 1973 to install medium-wave transmitters in Jaffna, Trincomalee, Amparai, Welimada, and Ratnapura. VHF transmitters at Uda-Radella and Senkadagala link the medium-wave transmitters to SLBC studios and control rooms in Colombo.

All SLBC short-wave transmitters are located in Ekala, 13 miles from Colombo. In 1974, there were two 100 kw., three 35 kw., and twelve 10 kw. transmitters, the more powerful ones being used for external services (*WRTH* 1974, p. 169).

Institutional development.   Originally broadcasting came under the authority of the postmaster-general and director of telegraphs (later director of telecommunications). In February 1932, the minister of communications and works appointed a Wireless Broadcasting Advisory Board to counsel the postmaster-general, especially on broadcasting content. The chief engineer of telegraphs was chairman of this board until 1937, when the position was transferred to the postmaster-general himself. Thus, a board developed to advise the postmaster-general was chaired by him. An officer designated superintendent of the Government Broadcasting Station was appointed the same year.

A special committee, under the chairmanship of Kanthiah Vaithianathan, was appointed in 1940 to report on all aspects of broadcasting. The committee's view was that radio should be "an instrument of advanced administration, an instrument not only and perhaps not even primarily for the entertainment but rather for the enlightenment and education of the more backward sections of the population and for their instruction in public health, agriculture, etc." The committee said programs must be designed "to conform to the requirements of the people as a whole and thereby have a wide mass appeal." It also proposed a separate news service for Government Broadcasting Service to expedite immediacy in radio newscasting.

An executive committee of the Ministry of Communications and Works considered the Vaithianathan Committee Report and made its own recommendations to the then State Council in February 1942. But nothing was done until the cessation of hostilities. Following the end of World War II and the granting of independence, a separate Department of Broadcasting was set up in 1949, under the name Radio Ceylon, amalgamating Government Broadcasting Station and Radio SEAC with a director-general of broadcating as the chief executive.

Some of the more important events and new features in the implementation of the Vaithianathan Committee recommendations were:

Extension of the hours of broadcasting; augmentation of live programmes in general and enhancing the quality of Western live programmes in particular by engaging the services of talented artists drawn from the Service personnel; appointment for the first time of a Programme Committee and reorganization of the Broadcasting Advisory Board; introduction of portable short-wave transmitters for relaying broadcasts from remote places; recording of over 200 Singhales folk songs in typically rural districts; and operating three transmitters for the first time in order to cover special occasions and to serve simultaneous broadcasting needs. [*Report of the Commission* 1955].

An experimental venture carried out in 1950 dichotomized the organization of Radio Ceylon into National and Commercial Services; the same year, the first directors of programs and commercial broadcasting were appointed. Another recommendation of the Vaithianathan Committee was implemented in 1951 with the broadcasting of rural programs.

Another broadcasting commission, appointed in 1953 under the chairmanship of N.E. Weerasooria, recommended discontinuance of the Commercial Service, abandonment of the Western bias in imported programs and the introduction of features based on Eastern life and culture, establishment of a local news service by Radio Ceylon, and introduction of political and controversial broadcasts. While the recommendation to discontinue the Commercial Service was brushed aside, Radio Ceylon did accept the suggestions for a listener research section and a Muslim program attached to the Tamil Service (*Administration Report* 1957).

Most of the other recommendations of this commission were disregarded.

With the inauguration of a new Sinhalese light service in 1963, Sandhya Sevaya (now defunct), it seemed Radio Ceylon was emulating the BBC program pattern. A new European Service, also defunct now, was also inaugurated for the benefit of Ceylonese abroad, in addition to continuing the program for Southeast Asia stated in 1961 (*Administration Report* 1962–63).

The Dudley Senanayake government appointed still another commission in 1965, under the chairmanship of H.A.J. Hulugalle. The Hulugalle Commission noted that "had the recommendations of the 1953 Commission been even partially acted upon, Radio Ceylon would today have a more positive record of achievement" (*Report of the Commission* 1966). Its main recommendation was that Radio Ceylon be placed under a corporation on the lines of New Zealand Broadcasting Corporation. With great haste, the government passed legislation setting up the Ceylon Broadcasting Corporation, which came into existence 1 January 1967. CBC differed from NZBC only in a few areas: CBC members would be appointed by the broadcasting minister and the government would have control over CBC in broadcasting service matters (*Parliamentary Debates* 1966).

The Sirimavo Bandaranaike government appointed the latest commission of inquiry on the Ceylon Broadcasting Corporation in 1970, under the chairmanship of V.C. Jayasuriya. Two dissenting reports from the commission were presented to the government in mid-1971, and were published as one a year later. One of the recommendations of this latest commission of inquiry was to establish a mass-communications institute affiliated with one of the Sri Lanka universities (*Report of the Commission* 1972).

4.6.3   Developmental or Propaganda Broadcasts?

Since evidence is available that on the average, there are six owners of radio receivers per 100 Ceylonese people, it becomes apparent radio can be successfully used, if properly handled, for purposes of national development. This realization of the potential of radio as a catalyst for development came only with the formation of the Ceylon Broadcasting Corporation.

Neville Jayaweera, the first chairman and director-general of CBC, felt that in Ceylon, the contribution mass media could make to developmental efforts was not adequately appreciated because of a lack of awareness of the magnitude and scope of Ceylonese media. Jayaweera pointed out that the cumulative effect of universal franchise and free education, which Ceylonese have enjoyed since 1930 and 1946, respectively, "has been to narrow down severely the area of manoeuvre available to any government plan." Therefore, he argued that "the effective utilization of mass media for kicking off and sustaining economic growth" depends, beyond any other single factor, on the nature of ownership of media, and partly as a corollary to this, on credibility (Jayaweera 1970; Cherry 1971, p. 197). Jayaweera elaborated further that:

In a community violently divided by party politics, government-owned media are singularly ill-equipped to advance the interests of development, and paradoxically, in such an environment, can only retard and impair the effort.

Therefore, he felt mass-media operations in developing countries such as Ceylon should immediately disengage themselves from too close ties with government. Apparently, basing his conclusions on experience as broadcasting boss for four years, Jayaweera realized governments of developing countries are

notoriously loathe to part with the ownership and control of media. This attitude, while partly an aspect of immaturity generally characteristic of developing countries, arises also from a misinterpretation of the potentials of mass media. [Jayaweera 1970]

Following the formation of the CBC, objectives were outlined to use radio in helping the country in its "terrible ascent" from stagnation to growth (Jayaweera 1967; see Wavell 1969, pp. vii-ix). This was a departure from ordinary broadcasting practice whereby radio was treated essentially as a means of entertainment. The CBC commitment to developmental goals included a mass reorientation of all programs to explain economic and social reconstruction in ways that people would see benefits from their participation. Abandoning conventional radio talks in the studio, CBC decided to go into the field and involve farmers, in their living environment, in discussions and quiz programs. CBC strategy was widened further to use drama and music to create a climate of awareness and enthusiasm.

A separate Rural Service was created to discuss "Food Drive" and "Grow More Food" campaigns, as well as to popularize new agricultural techniques. Rural Service programs included contests among young farmers' clubs; "Goviliya" (Peasant Woman); "Sandwardhana Yugaya" (Development Era), a drama, narrative, and music feature; "Henyaya," a drama program to demonstrate the importance of hard work, sacrifice, and self-help; agriculture in other lands; social and economic problems; and discussion between government and farmers. With the 1970 change of government, the Rural Service was eliminated and the time devoted to rural programming was vastly curtailed.

As a result of the new program strategy, CBC was criticized as being a tool or propaganda instrument of government (*Administration Report* 1970, pp. 5-6). But, can developmental broadcasting be separated from government propaganda in the context of government's radio monopoly? On the basis of CBC's experiment with developmental broadcasting, the need for radio to be freed from government control appears extremely desirable, enabling the people to develop trust and credibility in the medium. Hence, developmental broadcasting could be meaningfully pursued without being the victim of constant government pressure that gives it the appearance of "His Master's Voice." Every Ceylonese government has used radio to promote itself, yet at every general election the electorate has ousted the government in power. But major political parties in Ceylon greedily hang on to radio, making it a tool for propaganda.

In the 1970s, political propaganda reached absurd heights in Ceylonese broadcasting. The software structure of the Jayaweera era has been dismantled and replaced by programs with a new political flavor. For example, "Veda Karamu Rata Hadamu" (Let Us Work and Build the Country) stresses worker participation; "Wurthiya Samithi Sangrahaya" (Trade Union Program) is a mixture of news and discussion; and "Yawwana Lokaya" (World of Youth) provides news, views, discussions, and music. "Idiri Gamana" (Forward March) emphasizes achievements of public-sector corporations, government departments and agencies and subtly attacks the slow progress during the previous regime. "Pravurthi Pasubima" (News Background) provides extracts of ministerial speeches and interviews with officials, although opposition views are rarely presented.

According to Susil Moonesinghe, chairman and director-general of SLBC until his removal for "impropriety" in August 1972, broadcasting in the 1970s was definitely attempting "to project the attitudes of the government toward development" and to create "the feeling that we and the state are the same" (Interview, Moonesinghe, 1972). After Moonesinghe's firing, more important changes were expected in SLBC "to create a development consciousness" among the people (*Ceylon Daily News* 1972).

While the intentions of broadcasting authorities are laudable, their means of implementation are undoubtedly the more important factor. It seems clear that a team of communication experts, sociologists, anthropologists, economists, and others of high professional and intellectual caliber should be involved in building up the software for developmental broadcasting. But this is unlikely to happen in Sri Lanka. The SLBC board membership is changed frequently, but not to bring in these specialists. For example, the Bandaranaike government, after the youth riots of 1971, removed the full board and took two members into custody, suspecting their collusion with the rebels. Nevertheless, an SLBC board comprising mediocre political loyalists who know very little about the effective handling of broadcasting, will not be able to deliver the goods.

4.6.4 Political Broadcasting

The Weerasooria Commission, in recommending political and controversial broadcasts, suggested the appointment of a committee to work out exact rules and conditions governing such broadcasts.

It was, however, left to a lameduck prime minister, W. Dahanayake, to provide radio time during the 1960 elections for all political parties recognized by the commissioner of elections. Dahanayake allowed four 15-minute programs in each language service for each of the 23 recognized parties; the first for broadcasts of manifestos, the other three for explanation of party programs and policies. This rare concession was not repeated by any succeeding governments (*Radio Ceylon* 1960, p. 21).

The Hulugalle Commission did not favor political broadcasting, rationalizing "party politics is admitted into broadcasting, and within well-defined limits, only in countries with a mature democratic tradition and a consensus among the political parties." The commission, however, did grant that listeners were entitled to an objective report of what goes on in parliament (*Report of the Commission* 1966).

More leeway was made for political broadcasting during the Jayaweera era. Perhaps for the first time, CBC allowed criticism of government ministries and departments on the grounds that "constructive public review and scrutiny would not only prevent the country's administrative machinery from going to rust, but would also enable it to enhance its efficiency and output by making it more responsive to public need." This was done through a "Roving Mike" broadcast every other day over the Sinhalese and English Services. Moreover, opposition members of parliament also were allowed to express their criticisms of the administration and to participate in "panels, constituted entirely of themselves, discussing the teachings of Leon Trotsky, Mao Tse-tung and Lenin and the significance of the Russian Revolution of 1917" (*Administration Report* 1970, pp. 7-8).

The Jayasuriya Commission appeared to favor live broadcasts of parliament only on dates determined by the speaker, the selection of speakers being decided by political party leaders. Under the state of emergency, however, that followed the April 1971 youth rebellion, the administration completely disallowed radio time to the opposition; it is not likely to be lenient in this direction for some time (see Gunaratne 1970, pp. 530–43).

4.6.5 Culture and Religion

Broadcasting became enmeshed in national culture following independence and the formation of a broadcasting department (Radio Ceylon) in 1949. Earlier, broadcasting was conducted as an isolated exercise with a colonial or Western orientation. With the realization that the pace of social and cultural change had bypassed broadcasting values, demands were made for Radio Ceylon to reflect the new national consciousness. The transformation in broadcasting values "was particularly visible in the new music and drama that came to dominate radio and in the quality of religious and talks programs that were increasingly diluted in Radio Ceylon's transmissions" (Jayaweera 1970, pp. 1217–22). Drama, features, and talks based on Eastern life and culture, as recommended by the Weerasooria Commission, were then broadcast over the English Service of Radio Ceylon. Vernacular folk songs and poetry were also included in broadcasting programs.

In 1955, a program called "Geetha Mala" was introduced to demonstrate how Sinhalese poetry could be set to music and sung in place of light songs (*Administration Report* 1956). Five years later, a special advisory board was appointed for the improvement of Sinhalese music programs (*Administration Report* 1961). Later, the Hulugalle Commission recommended more broadcast time for Sinhalese folk songs and the addition of *Nadagam* music. It also suggested that the Tamil Serice make more of an effort to broadcast folk music of the Tamils living in the agricultural areas of eastern Ceylon (*Report of the Commission* 1966). Also, the Jayasuriya Commission heard evidence that feature programs did not depict important aspects of Tamil culture.

By the 1970s nearly every week the Sinhalese National Service was broadcasting programs by local folk artists, *Nurti* and *Nadagam* songs, experimental folk music, poetry, and violin and sitar recitals. "Nawa Muwan Pelessa," a popular drama broadcast weekly by the Sinhalese Commercial Service, depicts various cultural aspects of Sinhalese life. Weekly literary forums are also broadcast. But allegations have been made for years that music broadcasts of the Commercial Service have contributed to the debasement of national culture. SLBC has two orchestras, Sinhalese and Tamil, which on occasion, play together for special compositions.

The English Service has also adapted itself to depicting the indigenous culture, broadcasting programs such as "Facets of Lanka" and "Folk Song Scene." The Jayasuriya Commission was of the belief that CBC resources had been severely taxed, catering to a small segment of the nation's English-speaking society. With the de-Westernization of the English Service, Western-oriented elites have had to turn to sources outside SLBC for their cultural fare.

Since Sri Lanka is predominantly a Buddhist, Sinhalese country, Buddhist religious broadcasting has assumed a major role in the Sinhalese Service. The broadcasting service starts daily at 6 A.M., the first 30 minutes devoted to religion comprising *Hewisi* tom-toms, recital of the five precepts, chanting of *seth pirith*, and Buddhist and Christian sermons.

At least two broadcasting commissions, Hulugalle and Jayasuriya, noted the popularity of Buddhist programming, the latter commission taking the position that the station should commit itself to upholding Buddhist values, just as BBC promotes Christian values.

4.6.6 Recent Changes

The Bandaranaike administration made a major CBC structural change in 1971, when it separated the broadcasting services on a language basis, thereby enabling National and Commercial Services to function under the same director for each language medium. Previously, National and Commercial functioned as separate entities. Apparently, the change was meant to break the three levels of culture and to avoid duplication in the same language. As a result, the National Service broadcasts 141 hours weekly, compared to 233 previously, and Commercial is on the air 253 hours per week, compared with 198 previously. A breakdown by language services shows National devotes 60 hours weekly to the Sinhalese Service, nearly 51 to the Tamil Service, and over 30 to the English Service. Figures for Commercial are: Sinhalese, nearly 108 hours weekly; Tamil, 68, and English, 77½ hours. Weekly broadcasting hours for All Asia English, All Asia Hindi, All Asia Tamil, and Overseas Services are 48, 65, 21, and 7, respectively.

As for newscasts, both the Sinhalese and Tamil Services broadcast four major ten-minute daily news bulletins at 6:30 A.M., 12:45 P.M., 6 P.M., and 9:15 P.M., as well as world news bulletins at 7:30 A.M. (five minutes) and 10:30 P.M. (ten minutes). The English Service is more world news-oriented considering its elite clientele (see Table 23).

Table 23. Sri Lanka National Service (Channel One) Programming, 1972

Program Category	Sinhala		Tamil		English	
	Hrs./wk.	%	Hrs./wk.	%	Hrs./wk.	%
Music						
Light (including devotional & Geeta Nataka)	17:30	29.6	15:25	30.0	9:55	32.3
Islamic Gee/Quran recital	–	–	1:30	2.9	–	–
Folk	1:00	1.7	–	–	0:45	2.4
Classical	3:15	5.5	6:30	12.6	3:30	11.4
Religious						
Buddhism (including pirith)	8:40	14.7	0:20	0.6	1:40	5.4
Christianity	1:05	1.8	1:00	1.9	0:35	1.9
Hinduism	–	–	2:10	4.2	0:05	0.1
Islam	–	–	0:50	1.6	0:20	1.1
Spoken Words						
Children's (including Lama Gee)	6:15	10.6	1:35	3.1	–	–
Women's	1:00	1.7	0:55	1.8	0:30	1.6
News/announcements	9:55	16.8	5:45	11.2	3:20	10.9
Sports news	0:15	0.4	–	–	–	–
Talks	1:00	1.7	0:35	1.1	2:15	7.3
Poetry	0:30	0.9	0:45	1.5	–	–
Discussions/interviews	2:25	4.1	0:30	1.0	0:30	1.6
Quiz/competitions	0:15	0.4	0:30	1.0	–	–
Short story/drama/theater	0:45	1.3	1:00	1.9	2:30	8.2
Features/magazine	3:15	5.5	1:45	3.4	2:45	9.0
Special Muslim programs (music, drama, spoken words)	0:30	0.9	7:00	14.0	–	–
Language lessons	–	–	0:30	1.0	0:45	2.4
Rural (folk music, provincial news, magazines)	–	–	2:30	4.9		
Others	1:30	2.5	0:15	0.5	1:15	4.1
Totals	59:05	100.0	51:20	100.0	30:40	100.0

4.6.7 Listener Research and Training

The first listener-research survey in Ceylon was conducted in 1954 by Radio Ceylon with the help of the Department of Census and Statistics. The sample included Colombo and principal outstation towns. Another listeners' survey was conducted in 1959. To evaluate programs, Radio Ceylon used the diary method and listening-in panels.

The Audit Bureau of Circulations conducted two media surveys in 1964 and 1967, using an all-island sample, and CBC itself carried out an all-island audience-research survey in 1967. The audience survey revealed that urban listening is far more intensive than rural, males listen more often than females, upper and upper-middle classes have the highest rates of listening and the peak listening hours are 7–9 A.M. and 6–9 P.M. Other characteristics brought out by the survey included: 82% of the radio audience listen to commercials, 34% of households have radios, and radio has the lowest audience penetration of the mass media (52%) as against 74% for newspapers and 59% for cinema.

A radio listenership survey, conducted by a government department in the early 1970s, emphasized SLBC's failure to reach the bulk of the rural areas. In fact, 35.7% of the rural sample did not listen to radio at all. The survey found that communal listening still played a key role in Sri Lanka; 18.5% of the rural sample listened to radios at the bazaar, compared to 6.4% of the urban sample. Most respondents to the survey felt radio listening could change attitudes and opinions.

Formal broadcast training was initiated when, in 1968, CBC set up a training institute with the guidance of a BBC official. Initially, it was necessary "to get top management to slough off old attitudes and values entrusted over years of professional complacency," and "to get middle flight professional and production staff to climb out of their myopic and enclosed world of dull routine," before the institute settled down to a series of regular discussions, workshops, and practical training courses (*Administration Report* 1970, p. 43). Because of a serious shortage of technical staff, SLBC must concentrate on more training in this area.

4.6.8 Education Service

The idea of schools broadcasting was first presented in 1927, and by 1931 the School Broadcasting Service was inaugurated. Ten years later, an advisory committee was appointed for instructional broadcasting, and by 1951 schools broadcasting became a separate section of the National Service under a school program organizer.

Following the formation of CBC, it dawned on broadcasters that the Education Service — earlier called the School Service — had made only negligible impact because of programs being broadcast at inconvenient hours and because of the limited number of schools (only 300) with radio receivers. Moreover, subjects taught on radio were already being taught in schools. Therefore, the main function of the service was restricted to teaching English and science.

Currently, SLBC and the education ministry have opted for a series of pilot projects to cater to "adults as well as school children, teachers as well as parents, in-school as well as out-of-school audiences" (Barlow 1971, p. 4). SLBC has allocated six hours a day, including two in prime time, for educational broadcasting.

4.6.9 Future

Sri Lanka remains one of the few Asian nations without television services. Politics of socialism has been the primary reason for the exclusion of this medium. Its introduction, however, seems inevitable in the near future. A television service was approved in principle as early as 1959, and the Hulugalle Commission recommended "that a limited television service be started as soon as possible" (*Report of the Commission* 1966). And a UNESCO observer recommended in 1967 that:

if Ceylon is able to use television to its best advantage . . . then the time to introduce television is as soon as possible consistent with thorough planning, adequate training and suitable rationalization of the financial involvement. [Goodship 1967, p. 7]

Yet, when West Germany offered a gift of television equipment worth $1.3 million in 1966, the government decided to use the funds, with the approval of Bonn, to expand the island's medium-wave radio coverage, even though it was recognized that the introduction of television could not be delayed indefinitely. The Jayasuriya Commission reportedly recommended launching an experimental TV service hoping, through its use, to make a substantial contribution to education. The position of many Ceylonese might have been expressed by the dissenting member of the commission who said, "The very talk of television will be repulsive in the present context of things where the purpose of good government must be to reduce the gap between the haves and the have-nots."

With the launching of Application Technology Satellite F 22,000 miles above the equator, television could be introduced to Sri Lanka with relatively little cost. As of 1973, Sri Lanka had not shown any interest in joining the project. But, since technology for cheaper television is within sight, Sri Lanka broadcasting authorities may well think in terms of creating the software that could usefully meet the urgent needs of development. Considering the small size of the country and scarcity of foreign-exchange resources, Sri Lanka might well enter into a cooperative agreement with India for joint developmental telecasting.

It was announced in 1974 that Sri Lanka's first earth satellite station would be operative by 1975 at a site in Padukka. The station will connect to the Indian Ocean satellite of the Intelsat Consortium (*Media* 1974i). Once satellite broadcasting is introduced, government's monopoly of broadcasting will be threatened as the public will be able to tune in outside sources with greater ease. The government should resign itself to this inevitability and take steps to build an independent broadcasting organization, comprising qualified personnel of high integrity appointed without regard to political influence. Developmental broadcasting can be more effectively managed by an independent authority, once trust and credibility are established.

In the short run, regional broadcasting offers great possibilities in Sri Lanka. The availability of medium-wave transmitters in various parts of the island facilitates opening regional broadcasting stations better able to cater to needs of regional populations.

With the continued de-Westernization of the English Service and the ability of improved radio receivers to pick up English-language broadcasts from abroad, one can predict the further curtailment, or even abolition, of the English Service of SLBC. Such action would enable resources used by this service to be diverted to the greater improvement of vernacular services. Broadcasting in three languages, using three separate services, is a very expensive matter for a hard-pressed small country.

Medium-wave radio coverage for the entire country, accompanied by a relative increase in numbers of receivers, is foreseen in the near future. Upon realization of how best to employ mass media for development, government may allocate for the expansion of communication media, in which case more foreign exchange may be released, making radio receivers available in greater abundance.

5. Oceania

The islands of the Pacific are included in this book because of their diversity, their strong dependence on broadcasting, in some cases as the only formal mass-media system, and their close ties with Asia. The latter point is brought home by the fact that the Asian Broadcasting Union includes many Pacific nations as members and that the islanders are involved in numerous training schemes with Asians, e.g., those of ABU, UNESCO, and the National Broadcasting Training Centre.

This section will deal with broadcasting in Australia, Papua New Guinea, New Zealand, and finally 14 Central South Pacific island groups. The authors of these three chapters obtained first-hand data from interviews and observations during field trips and work experiences in Oceania, as well as from correspondence with top broadcasting personnel and secondary sources.

5.1 Australia and Papua New Guinea, *by Alexander F. Toogood*

Depending on their brand of chauvinism, Australians proudly claim that they live on the world's largest island, or on the only continent under one nation's flag. This vast land mass is almost the size of continental United States, yet its population is only 13 million. Most of the people are concentrated into a 700-mile strip in the southeast corner. The two states of this area, New South Wales and Victoria, provide 65% of the total population, the country's two largest cities (Sydney and Melbourne with total population of over 4.5 million), and the federal capital, Canberra.

Politically, Australia is a commonwealth — a federation of six states and two

Alexander F. Toogood is Associate Professor of Radio-TV at Temple University; former TV producer/director at NZBC and WKGB-TV, Boston; and also worked for TV stations in Ohio, North Carolina, and Texas. He was a Johnson Fellow and the author of a book on Canadian broadcasting and articles on Commonwealth broadcasting system. He received his Ph.D. at Ohio State University.

federal territories. Unlike many new nations, Australia has not been obsessed with forging a national identity. Initial turning to Britain was skewed by World War II, the declining colonial influence, and a changing international power structure. The resultant flirtation with the United States is not so much a security measure as an endorsement of a certain lifestyle. By always looking outward, the Australian has been made particularly paranoid by his accident of geography; the great fear is isolation.

As a result, Australia was quick to endorse twentieth-century communication systems. This has included the development of one of the world's most sophisticated broadcasting patterns. It is a dual system whereby the continent is provided public and commercial services in radio and television. Its television programming is on the air for a longer period each day than any other country's, except for those of the United States and Japan; and there is a choice, for more than half the population, of more TV stations than offered in any European system.

The former Australian territory of Papua New Guinea is the eastern half of the large 2,000-mile-long island to the north of the state of Queensland. The western portion is the Indonesian province of West Irian. Papua is the southeastern area which came under Australian influence in the nineteenth century out of a lust for expansion and a fear of spreading German influence. New Guinea refers to the northern portion and its neighboring islands to the northeast. Previously a German possession, New Guinea and the smaller islands were mandated to Australia at the end of World War I. In 1949, the two areas were joined administratively, but any concept of national unity is only theoretical. Papua New Guinea was fully independent from Australia, with a Westminster-style political system, by the end of September 1975.

The total land mass of the territory represents a relentless, rugged environment; range upon range of mountains are covered with dense tropical rain forests. The area is one of the least developed in the world. Income per capita for the 2.3 million inhabitants is $230 a year, and most of that is earned by the 30,000 whites.

Broadcasting is faced not only with physical, social, and economic problems, but also with the fact that this area supports just about the largest number of different languages in a single geographic area. There are approximately 750 local languages that are mutually unintelligible. Obviously, English is out of place in this Stone Age setting; it is the main language for only 13% of the population. Pidgin is widely spoken, however, being the day-to-day tongue for 36% of the people and understood by many others. An interesting trend is toward incorporating more and more Pidgin in broadcasting, including programs designed to teach the language.

5.1.1 Early Broadcasting

With early radio, Australia pioneered a sealed set system (see Mackay 1957), whereby a broadcasting company leased to the public a receiver that was sealed to a given wave length. It was under such an arrangement that regular broadcasting began 23 November 1923, with station 2SB in Sydney. The system was disastrous. Unpopular and subject to abuse (W. Hull 1970, p. 10), it was replaced within ten months.

In 1924, the postmaster general commenced issuing two kinds of licenses, both to private broadcasters. The "A" class stations were financed by a $4 receiver license fee and limited advertising, "B" class stations relying solely on advertising revenue. Such a system flourished in the more densely populated areas, but remote locales received no service at all. There was also criticism of the programming on "A" stations. Although privately owned, the stations were regarded by the public as in the public domain because of the license fee. At the expiration of the class "A" licenses in 1928, the government announced that they would not be renewed.

The year 1929 became an important landmark. Apart from the creation of the first national service, there was the more important political endorsement of a dual system of broadcasting; in other words, the commercial class "B" stations were to remain. It was this same year that also saw the firm foundation of the current national system based on a separation of responsibility; facilities and programming was to be supplied by a private company, Australian Broadcasting Company Limited. Despite the company's impressive development of radio programming, by 1932 it became politically expedient to replace it with a government-established body, Australian Broadcasting Commission.

5.1.2 Australian Broadcasting Commission

In law, the minister responsible for broadcasting, the postmaster general, has considerable power. This has been partially whittled away by amended legislation over the years, but even today, it provides an umbrella of uncertainty for the commission's day-to-day activities. The minister may prohibit ABC from broadcasting any matter, so long as this request is tabled in parliament within seven days; parliament may direct ABC to broadcast any matter within the public interest; the government appoints the nine commissioners, as well as approves payment of any ABC salary exceeding A $7,500 ($9,000) and any expenditure over A $100,000 ($125,000), and the minister must approve the location of ABC production studios. Most restrictive of all, however, ABC financing comes solely from an annual appropriation from parliament.

Despite such an ominous list, Australia has been fortunate to escape much of the direct political pressure that similar provisions have encouraged in other countries. This might result, however because the prevailing awareness of these avenues by top ABC officials is amply intimidating. ABC is not noted for its brazen challenging of political stands, but one distinguished exception occurred in 1970. The postmaster general expressed his government's displeasure over various ABC public-affairs programs, threatening to cut off appropriations for all such shows. After much press and public criticism, the minister was forced to back down. There were fears in 1975 that the Labour government was using broadcasting for political purposes (see §5.1.10).

Part of the independence from direct government influence reflects a responsibility manifested in parliamentary decisions. Commissioners have been appointed because of their value as commissioners, not because they are political favorites or idealistic dilettantes. Parliament also gave an organizational structure to ABC that is not enjoyed by many similarly conceived bodies. For example, the commissioners, not the government, appoint all ABC executives, including the general manager.

5.1.3 ABC Broadcasting Services

The ABC undertook as its primary task the improvement of national coverage. Inheriting program responsibilities for 12 stations in 1932, the commission was responsible for 64 by the time of television's introduction in 1956. ABC provided capital cities with two networks — one in light programming, one more serious. Other parts of the country were given one network service which was a combination of the metropolitan networks. This pattern has remained, with slight modifications. There was, in 1973, a greater emphasis on service materials and cultural programming, and the single rural service, operated through 61 AM and 5 short-wave stations, was restructured so that it operated independently of the two metropolitan networks which were served by 7 stations each in 1973. With the creation of new transmitters under the Labour government, the number of radio stations transmitting ABC programs within Australia rose to 87 medium-wave and short-wave in 1974 (*COMBROAD* 1974c, p. 61). Most ABC radio stations are on the air 19 hours daily, after transmission was extended by one hour in 1973—74.

For some years, ABC has been dissatisfied with the limitations of its radio offerings. It is particularly interested in extending the alternate service to the rural areas and in providing metropolitan areas with a third service for highbrow audiences. This has been impossible because of the limited spectrum space on the AM band. The obvious solution was to move to FM, but the private sector pressured to postpone its introduction. In 1972, the government supported the introduction of FM broadcasting and endorsed ABC's plans for expansion. There is also provision for a commercial FM system and for the introduction of a new concept: the public broadcasting station. Such a station is to be operated on a nonprofit basis, withs its transmission facilities owned and operated by the government which will then apportion broadcast time among interested educational, musical, professional, and religious groups (see §5.1.10).

Television was to provide a financial and technological challenge to a young nation scattered over a massive land area. The government decided on a gradual, systematic development of the new medium with the national service, entrusted to ABC, developing alongside the commercial services. The 1956 Melbourne Olympics provided a strong stimulus for introducing TV, so services were established that year in both Sydney and Melbourne. Within a year, there were two private commercial stations in each city, offering programming in conjunction with ABC's single national service. The second stage of development took this dual service, with its national and commercial elements, to the four remaining states (see Munster 1960). Additional stages further expanded the service so that by 1972, ABC had 52 stations, each in a different center, giving a coverage that reaches more than 98% of the population. Additional TV transmitters — 11 in Queensland, 5 in Western Australia, 2 in South Australia, and 1 in New South Wales — were established in 1973–74. This stage of development, to last until 1975, will see a total of 40 additional national stations in remote areas (*COMBROAD* 1974b, p. 51). ABC stations are linked as a network for news and special events, but the expense of such an operation has meant that regular programming is "bicycled" from station to station.

5.1.4   ABC Programming

The commission's programming is governed by provisions of the various broadcasting and television acts which require that the network provide "adequate and comprehensive programmes." Such a nebulous phrase has meant that the commission has had to develop its own guidelines (Madgwick 1972, p. 24). From its earliest days, ABC has been engaged in impressive programming developments, specifically catering to various minorities: sports enthusiasts, children, women, farmers, and those seeking information and cultural enrichment. Such features characterize ABC offerings today (Kolodin 1971, p. 48). Indeed, its radio programming, 40% of which is devoted to drama, features, light entertainment, and the spoken word, is an anachronistic harking-back to the 1930s. An additional 26% of ABC total transmission time is given over to service programs.

Unlike BBC, with its authoritarian, cultural experiment and high moral tone, ABC has always tended to be more democratic in honestly striving to provide a service (Duckmanton 1970, p. 8). A new general manager in 1965 further loosened up ABC's image by deciding to compete for audiences to justify its role as a national service. It is difficult to share the commission's enthusiasm for its radio entertainment specials in 1971 with artists such as Frank Sinatra, Ivor Novello, Ted Heath, Glen Miller, and Gladys Moncrieff. At the other end of the spectrum, however, is public television programming such as "Bellbird," a racy soap opera with high production values, shown in prime time each week night just before the news. It is the only ABC production to reach the top-ten rated programs. Generally, ABC television captures only 15% of the total available audience (Gorrick 1971, p. 48).

In the realm of news and public affairs, ABC shows its greatest strength. While a minority service in any mass society, such programming attracts a reasonable following, and proves influential in providing newspaper copy and some social change. The result is that public affairs offerings are the shows that most frequently irk politicians. For example, the 1972 parliamentary election saw government charges of ABC bias in favor of the opposition (See §5.1.10).

278 BROADCASTING IN ASIA AND THE PACIFIC

Such attacks smack of undue political pressure on a supposedly independent body and fail to consider the overriding ABC public-affairs philosophy — that the network will act as a sounding board to create a climate for opinion by exploring many sides of each issue.

5.1.5 ABC Financing

The government retains the power of the purse strings. Forbidden advertising, ABC must depend on the annual appropriation for all revenue. This imposes an annual trek to parliament with cap in hand. Government does receive income derived from broadcasting matters which is placed in the consolidated fund and not earmarked specifically for broadcasting. The income is derived from licensing of receivers and licensing of private broadcasters. Each household with a radio or television receiver must pay a receiver license fee. Most radio licenses are A $8 ($9.60) annually with more remote areas paying less. Television license fees cost A $19 ($22.80) annually, although there is a combined radio-TV fee of A $26.50 ($31.80) (*WRTH* 1974, p. 176).

The fee levied on commercial stations' operations is based on a percentage of earnings, e.g., 1% for the first million dollars, 2% for the second million, etc. In 1971, earnings from this fee were A $2 million ($2.4 million).

The government then turns around and pays, out of the consolidated fund, for the national service. To pay for this service over the years, however, government has had to find additional money as well. In 1973–74, the annual appropriation to ABC was A $89,676,000 ($97,611,200), an increase of A $19.5 million) over the previous year. Receipts from other soures, A $7,000,510 ($8,400,612), exceeded the previous year by A $2.6 million ($3.12 million) (*COMBROAD* 1974c, p. 62).

5.1.6 Additional ABC Services

As with most public broadcasting bodies, ABC is also expected to provide other services. The act, for instance, requires a large number of publications, and in 1972 the commission sold 1.5 million copies of its booklets for schools broadcasts as well as its weekly editions of *TV Times* and *Radio Guide*. The commission supports an orchestra in each state and is so involved in entrepreneur activities that its cultural endeavors are considered the largest single such enterprise in the free world (ABC, 1970–71). For the government, ABC undertook two broadcasting services in Papua New Guinea until December 1973, as well as the highly developed international service, Radio Australia. Radio Australia has established such a fine reputation for its high integrity and objective reporting that it is the most widely listened-to international service in the world (Duckmanton 1971, p. 18; also see §6.1.5 for fuller discussion).

Domestically, ABC has provided an equally impressive service with its educational broadcasting. Because each state controls its own educational system, ABC merely provides production facilities for educational programming. Educational broadcasting is widely used, 90% of the schools having classroom radio receivers, 67%, TV receivers (Faragler 1971). One state, Tasmania, has radio in every school, and television in 99% of them. A full 18% of ABC radio programming time is given over to in-class instruction. Such broadcasting has been particularly valuable in a country where many regions are isolated from traditional education (Watts 1970, p. 32). Australia has been in the forefront in the development of correspondence schools, as well as rural broadcasts (White 1972, p. 19).

Supporting numerous activities peripheral to its extensive radio and television services has made ABC one of the largest broadcasting bodies in the world with nearly 6,376 full-time employees in 1973.

5.1.7 Private Broadcasting

Commercial broadcasting has always been an element of the Australian pattern. It has been encouraged in the belief that while the national service provides distinct minorities with special quality programming, commercial broadcasters should cater to the less idealistic wants of a mass society (W. Hull 1962, p. 118). Commercial broadcasting was to lend a healthy element of competition, at the same time it provided a distinctive local emphasis to balance ABC's national service. Because of this benevolent approach, government has kept itself removed from much of the activity of private broadcasting. The authorities have indulged in only a minimum of direction, although the law gives the minister considerable power; licensing is annual and the minister may revoke a private license.

In their early history, private stations did feel threatened, particularly as they viewed antiprivate broadcasting moves in all other British Commonwealth countries. They found one solution in the collective strength of networks, based on cooperatives that provided a much looser affiliate relationship than available with United States networks. The first Australian radio network, the Major, was conceived by two leading advertising agencies which bought up blocks of time on major Australian stations and then divided the time between themselves. Stations not involved felt a program squeeze that could only be countered by their forming a second network, the Macquarie. Today, remnants of these networks exist solely as selling representatives for advertising, their programming responsibilities having lapsed with the introduction of television.

Commercial radio followed the lead of the United States in coping with the new interloper, television. Today, 118 commercial radio stations owned by 104 companies (*WRTH* 1974, pp. 178–80) devote more than half of their programming to popular music presented in a hard sell, top-40 or middle-of-the-road format (ABCB 1972, p. 56). This is supported by a holdover of a programming format introduced in the mid-1960s, the popular telephone conversation programs.

5.1.8 Australian Broadcasting Control Board

Apart from resorting to collective strength in networking, the private broadcasters sought legislative redress (Emery 1969, p. 496), forthcoming in 1948 when the Australian Broadcasting Control Board was created to make recommendations on broadcasting matters and to regulate private broadcasters. In its relationship to ABC, the board is limited to making recommendations on technical matters (Maast 1958, p. 22), including consideration of the total number and location of stations, their frequency and power, and daily transmission time.

The primary concern of ABCB is with the private sector (see Cole 1966). Besides making recommendations on technical aspects of private stations, ABCB also regulates these stations through programming and advertising guidelines. Private broadcasters feel particularly constrained by the board's programming directives, often based on standards recommended by an ABCB advisory group, e.g., those pertaining to children's or religious programming (Snare 1962–63, p. 30). Australia has one of the world's most rigid public moral codes, which, of course, is reflected in broadcasting regulation (Green 1972, p. 241). Sunday morning is God's time, with all commercial programming limited to religion, news, instruction, or children's fare. Additionally, certain other periods are rigidly controlled to ensure that only suitable "family-group viewing" programs are aired.

Australia's strict film censor views all films for television and assigns viewing categories. One of the board's rule books offers such taboos as "illicit sex relations" and any matter that is "vulgar, suggestive, or of doubtful propriety" (ABCB 1967, pp. 7, 9).

Private broadcasters argue that the ABC is not subjected to such a rigid code and that the board action, therefore, is discriminatory. A claim of a dual standard is unreasonable since ABC is responsible to its commissioners on such matters, just as private broadcasters are responsible to the board. In any event, the rules appear to be chiefly a paper tiger. For example, in 1972, a prime-time serial, "No. 96," was introduced containing explicit coverage of the seamy sex life of Sydney apartment dwellers. The program has already included on-camera nudity, two homosexual leads, and free sexual discussion. With such television emancipation, the program soared to the top of the ratings.

Private broadcasters have greater problems. In 1972, the board enacted a new Australian content ruling for television which demands that, after three years of operation, a station must program at least 50% Australian-originated content. The ruling is harsher than it might at first appear. Commercial stations already make a handsome commitment to local production, and, unlike efforts in many countries, the end product frequently matches the production values of competing imported programs (ABCB 1970, p. 15). The issue of locally produced TV shows was a subject of controversy again in 1975 when the ABCB chairman announced that as of 8 February 1976, all networks would have to show an extra 30 hours of new Australian drama each year, an increase from 74 to 104. First-run Australian drama must be shown between 6 and 10 P.M. The hours devoted to children's programs must be increased from six to ten each 28 days (*Variety*, 23 July 1975). One network, Channel 9, announced it was spending A $10 million ($12 million) yearly on local productions even before this new demand (*Variety* 1975a, p. 55), airing major new productions such as "The Unisexers," "Luke's Kingdom," "The Last of the Australians," and "Shannon's Mob."

It is an endorsement of Australian standards that two of the top three TV programs for 1971 were from the Melbourne-based company, Crawford Productions. In fact, of the top 20, half were Australian. It is to be expected, however, that a limit does exist as to the number of quality programs that can result from the talents of an underpopulated country that has but a scant creative tradition on which to draw (FACTS 1970–71, pp. 8–10). Even more painful in this regard is the fact that Australian commercial television broadcasters, with their 17 hours a day in metropolitan areas, are on the air for longer daily periods than any other stations in the British Commonwealth. Even prior to the new ruling, a single Australian commercial station had more local programming each day than did the BBC.

The long hours of telecasting also mean that Australia is a bonanza for the television syndicator. The country manages to be the best market for both the United States and Britain. Among the top 20 in 1971 were, in order, the American programs, "Disney-land," "Mod Squad," "Nancy and the Professor," "Marcus Welby," "Partridge Family," and the "Mary Tyler Moore Show," and the British "Doctor at Large," "The Persuaders," and "On the Buses." In 1975, some film production people in Australia urged the imposition of curbs on the importation of United States and British television programs. Lamenting the "one-way traffic," they asked that the sale of United States and British TV programming to Australian networks be made to correspond to the volume of Australian shows used by United States and British networks (*Variety* 1975g, p. 326).

Advertising restrictions are few. All commercials must be produced in Australia; radio spots are limited to a maximum of 18 minutes in an hour; television to 11 minutes of the prime-time hour and 13 minutes at other times. Hard liquor and cigarette advertising is permitted but will be phased out between 1973–76. Previously, in 1970, the ABCB heard proposals for cigarette advertising bans or for counter advertising, but ruled out the ban and denied free time with the argument that anti-cigarette groups could buy spots. The decision was not unexpected at that time; the board had tended to be rather conservative in its regulatory function, and, when pressed, to be sympathetic to the broadcasters' stand.

The act creating the board specifically requires that it must consult with representatives of commercial stations before exercising powers and functions in relation to those stations. Thus, no new regulations can emerge until the give-and-take of prior discussion with broadcasters has been undertaken. While appearing to be a regulatory agency serving the interests of those to be regulated, the board, through this regulation, permits a healthy input from commercial broadcasters during the framing stage. Friction between ABCB and the broadcasters has been minimized as a result.

Indeed, there is a cozy ambience, possibly forced on the board by its weak position. The ABCB is virtually powerless, not having even a list of penalties it can mete out. For example, if a station breaks a rule, the ABCB merely issues a warning that if the infringement reoccurs, the minister will be informed. But relations with the minister, based in Canberra, are equally weak. The board can only advise the minister and the advice may be freely ignored. Indeed, the board's advice and special reports on such matters as color television and FM broadcasting are secret. They are released only when and if the minister so wishes.

The one-year license may look threatening, but again the board only advises, and thus far, not one station has lost its license. There are rising fears, however, among Australian broadcasters. The United States' orgy of consumer movements might well emerge in Australia in the form of an as yet unprecedented challenge to a license.

Distance between the board and broadcasters is also physical. While major broadcasting decision makers and the broadcasters' two professional organizations are in Sydney, ABCB is centered in Melbourne.

If these factors create a nonentity of the board, it has found compensating glory in publishing much responsible broadcasting research.

5.1.9 Private Television: Ownership and Scope

Major control over private broadcasters rests in their ownership structures. Fearful of early monopolistic moves by an electronics firm, AWA (Amalgamated Wireless, Australasia, Ltd.), the government developed a complex ownership formula. Single ownership is limited to eight radio stations: four of which may be in any one state, four of which may be metropolitan stations. Ownership of only one metropolitan station in any given state is allowed. Television ownership is limited to two stations. Despite these provisions, considerable concentrations of power have centered around newspaper empires. Most of the nation's leading TV stations, and even smaller rural ones, are tied to local publications. Apart from dangers of media concentration, there is the unfortunate tendency to give unabashed newspaper attention to the inhouse television station and to either ignore or attack the opposition stations.

The strict ownership requirements have prohibited the development of television networks as they are known in the United States. While common ownership gives a bond and frequent program exchange, actual hook-ups are rare. Interconnection is limited to a very few news items and special events, although various stations have banded together under the name "network" to provide an advertising sales service. For some years both public and commercial stations, in a nation-wide attempt to prevent the internecine bidding for overseas programs, engaged in pool buying of such shows. This joint venture failed when a Sydney station broke out of the pool, thus instigating the costly rivalry that, in

1971, involved A $11 million ($13.2 million) for the purchase of foreign programs for Australia.

Because the lack of a network feed demands much larger station staffs, Australian television was not an immediate money maker. It has been only recently that some stability has come to the private sector of television and that the financial situation has improved. The commercial pattern seems to have found its optimum level with its present 48 stations (WRTH 1974, p. 298), owned by 43 companies.

In 1972, the four largest state capitals were each served by three private stations, and in all, 34 television markets existed throughout the country, 5 of which had more than one commercial station.

Metropolitan stations are on the air from 7 A.M. to midnight daily; country stations from mid-afternoon to 11 P.M. With their popular mass entertainment programming, commercial stations capture four times more audience than does ABC (FACTS 1970–71, p. 17). They are left to their own devices as to program balance; little correlation between promises in license applications and ultimate performance seems to exist. This can be seen in the fact commercial stations virtually ignore the fine arts, children's shows, and educational programming. Instead, more than half their programming is classified as drama, with an additional 22% listed as light entertainment. Yet, this is what the people want, and as long as ABC provides distinguished, minority programming, the position of the private stations seems democratically responsible.

5.1.10 Recent Events

Among changes made in Australian broadcasting between 1973–75 were the introduction of color television, designing of an extensive FM stereo radio network, experimentation with cable television projects, and the inauguration of alternative television and all-rock radio.

Thoughts of color TV for Australia go back to 1967 when the postmaster general announced that investigations would proceed concerning its feasibility. On 1 March 1975, 134 transmitters and translators of the national service carried the first color television shows (Lucas 1975, pp. 3–6). Top priority in 1974 was expected to be given to the development of scores of FM stereo radio stations throughout Australia during the next eight years (Media, May 1974, p. 23). A decision by the ruling Labour Party that year, however, disallowed FM licenses to any commercial networks. Also, by 1974 the Australian government had taken steps for a pilot cable TV project in Sydney suburbs. Initially, the networks will carry normal TV channels. The concept of a "wired city," making maximum use of telecommunications, is under serious consideration by the "Telecom 2000 Think Tank," working for the Australian Post Office (Media, May 1974, pp. 22–23).

The changing trends of the Australian public were increasingly taken into account between 1973–75 by broadcasters. The formation in 1973 of a Film and TV Board of the Australian Council of the Arts led to the setting up, less than a year later, of a chain of ten Community Access Video Centers (CAVCs). The CAVCs were designed to involve local communities to the utmost and encourage open access and democratic participation in video programming (*Intermedia,* 2: 3, 1974, pp. 20—21). A new 1975 ABC radio station in Melbourne also stressed a format that allowed groups of individuals to have access to the airwaves. In both cases, part of the emphasis was in providing Australia's ethnic minorities a chance to air their views. A new fairness code, introduced in 1974 by the Ministry of Media and subscribed to by all but two commercial radio stations, also provided more access, allowing people attacked on Australian radio talk shows a chance to reply (*Media,* June 1974, p. 23).

Finally, in January 1975, the ABC, in an attempt to offset its sober image among the under-25 age set, opened an all-rock AM station in Sydney, broadcasting 24 hours daily, seven days a week (*COMBROAD,* April—June 1975, p. 67; *Media* 1975d, p. 6).

The government's role in these and other recent broadcasting developments has raised the ire of numerous critics. No doubt the election of a Labour government in 1972, after 23 years of more conservative rule, imposed a few threatening moments for broadcasting, particularly the private sector. Apart from creating a new cabinet portfolio which includes broadcasting, the Minister for the Media, the new government launched into attacks of certain commercial practices. It initially suggested the closing down of one TV station in each of the state capitals to provide a more viable marketplace for those remaining — a proposal that found little favor, so was soon abandoned. Also, in February 1975, it was learned that ABCB was preparing guidelines for radio and television journalists (Foster 1975, pp. 10—12).

In contrast to the passivity of previous ministers, the Minister for the Media has taken a forceful role in articulating policy and regulation. He has indicated that cigarette and alcohol advertisements must be off the air by 1975 (*Variety,* 6 August 1975, pp. 34, 44; *AMC Bulletin,* September 1973, p. 14) and recently threatened to cancel the licenses of television stations that were not adhering to the ABCB commercial time standards. In addition, the new Labour-appointed chairman of the ABC had actively urged a change of government before the election. His selection smarts of being a reward for a political favor. The honeymoon period of an apolitical broadcasting system in Australia seems over. Whether this is the flexing of pubescent muscles by a government that has waited too long in the wings, or a more threatening precursor for the future, remains to be seen.

In 1975, the Labour government came in for criticism for allowing monopolization of mass-media ownership to grow, especially among the Murdoch, Fairfax, and Packer groups (Bednall 1975 p. viii).

Internationally, ABC has been a major force behind the development of the Asian Broadcasting Union, and the country was quick to welcome the international link provided by Intelsat satellites. In addition to extensive use of this satellite system, there have been initial investigations to develop a domestic satellite which might well prove a satisfactory answer to the problem of the vast land mass (Duckmanton 1971, p. 5).

5.1.11 Papua New Guinea

Radio started as a commercial venture with Amalgamated Wireless Australasia catering to expatriates in the administrative capital, Port Moresby. The commercial operation ceased during World War II. Allied forces wished to establish their own transmission facilities in 1943, but the ABC pressured for its rights in this Australian territory. A compromise was reached, with the armies of the United States and Australia taking the major role in getting the station on the air in 1944, but with the understanding that ABC would take over programming control at the end of hostilities. This happened in 1946. As in Australia itself, the facilities for the ABC station are maintained and installed by the Post Office.

The broadcasting station on Papua New Guinea represented the first time the ABC was faced with a multilingual society. Despite commission claims that it felt an obligation to the entire population (Tudor 1966, p. 178), it does not seem that ABC pursued its responsibilities seriously. Radio was not viewed as an essential force to help unify the emerging territory (Mackay 1969, p. 243). The major station in Port Moresby was limited to 500 w. for its first 16 years, and the ABC turned to the territorial administration for all programming for the indigenous population, a mere 1½ hours a day (Essai 1961, p. 196). Finally, in 1962, ABC's own Papua New Guinea Service, using native Papuans and New Guineans, went into operation with a more extended service. Until then, ABC's only commitment to the area was to provide programs for the small European audience.

Working closely with the territorial administration provided its own friction. Suggestions from this government department had to be evaluated in light of their possible political relevancy. Possibly this fear of influence led the commission into an unfortunate position in the late 1950s, when a series of uprisings broke out, centered at Rabaul, the largest town on one of the islands to the northeast. Territorial officials felt ABC could assist in easing the tension by providing an expanded service through a regional station; the commission declined. The administration saw, as its only solution, the establishment of its own broadcasting service in 1961. Thus, a dual broadcasting system was created in the territory that existed until 1973 (see Naylor 1973, pp. 19–21).

In 1962, ABC did try better to meet the needs of the territory, opening a station and studio at Rabaul. The Rabaul station provided its own service in local languages and was linked to the main service at Port Moresby only for news and special events. Moreover, ABC opened a new studio and increased the power of its Port Moresby station at the same time, adding two short-wave transmitters. In 1969, a further extension of coverage was authorized, with the installation of transmitters at four new locations, and an increase in the total number of transmitters at Port Moresby to four.

The commission also broadened its programming in the early 1960s, taking the emphasis away from expatriates and giving much of it to the indigenous population. The ABC itself originated programs in Pidgin, simple English, and six vernaculars, along with regular transmissions in English. A gradual program developed to train the native Papuans and New Guineans to take responsible broadcasting positions. Out of ABC's total staff of 173 in the territory, 98 were native born. The Minister of Information of the territory seemed to have taken a reasonable approach to the localization of staff. In a speech to trainees in 1973, he said, although eager to see more positions localized, he was aware too that localization could cause damage if done for its own sake (Papua New Guinea Post-Courier, 14 February 1973).

Before 1973, about 30% of the programs were aimed solely at the indigenous peoples, 30% to sophisticated European tastes, and the remaining 40% to the community as a whole. The commission's service began at 6 A.M. daily, with a news broadcast in English, Pidgin, and Motu from Port Moresby, and in Tinatatuna from Rabaul. A breakfast session followed in which serials, Bible readings, and general information — weather, aircraft, and hospital news — were included. ABC then undertook one of its most valuable functions: broadcasts to both primary and secondary schools which took up some of the morning and afternoon programming schedules. Not until 1964 were these instructional shows designed for the territory; before then, ABC had rebroadcast programs originating in Australia. By the late 1960s, they were produced locally, in Port Moresby, and designed for the special needs of Papuans and New Guineans (Goodman 1968, p. 30ff). ABC, however, insisted in offering the instruction in English.

The commission was wedded unfortunately to the policy of promoting English as the national language of Papua New Guinea. ABC's evening program was aimed at the native population until 9:15 P.M., and included general appeal programs such as "Listeners' Choice," "Songs of the Islands," "Music of PNG," and "Talking Point," all of which were usually presented in simple English. Programs from 9:15 P.M. until midnight were for the European audience and included serious music, documentaries, and BBC transcriptions. The main function of ABC was to provide a national service; the end product, however, was more like an Australian regional service rather than the origination of distinctively Papuan and New Guinea programming (Mackay 1969, p. 243).

Partially to remedy such a situation, the territorial administration undertook its own broadcasting operation through its Department of Information and Extension Services. The first broadcasts were limited to the evening because the short-wave facilities belonged to the Department of Posts and Telegraphs, which required them during the day. The administration in 1973 had its own stations scattered in 12 districts throughout the territory and an additional second service operated by the administration in Rabaul, used to carry ABC's seven hours of daily broadcasts to schools. Three other stations were nearing completion in 1973 (Papua New Guinea Post-Courier, 7 February 1973). The

Port Moresby transmitter relayed newscasts to outlying regions; it was the only form of network service provided by the administration. The outlying stations were community setups, originating programming for local needs. Their broadcasts were in Pidgin and 19 different native languages.

The early reliance on the facilities of the post and telegraphs department instilled inferior production and technical standards which still characterize the administration's broadcasts. Localism being a strong employment policy, most station operators are natives who have been given only crude staff training, a factor that does not upgrade the degree of professionalism in broadcasting standards. Programming ranges from a Western-influenced hit parade to traditional native music.

In its earliest days, the administration's service was eyed as a possible overt organ for government propaganda. Even in 1973, programming was designed to inform as much as it was to entertain. While the administration stations did not carry formal instruction (Jeffery 1971, p. 282) (that being left to ABC), there was a strong emphasis on education in its broadest sense: agriculture, economics, health, knowledge of the political system, and a strong news emphasis.

The operations of the administration and ABC developed an efficient and comprehensive service for a relatively backward area. Although in the early 1970s, there were only 75,000 radio receivers in the territory – for which there was no license fee – it was estimated that the majority of the population had access to the alternative services provided: the ABC national service and the administration's local service. The native population also expressed an interest in broadcasting's future. A resolution in Papua New Guinea's House of Assembly in 1971 urged the establishment of a national broadcasting authority in the territory to bring together the services of ABC and the administration, and to assume responsibility for all broadcasting operations (ABC 1970–71, pp. 11–12). The authority proposal came up again in early 1973, and on 1 December 1973 the National Broadcasting Commission Papua New Guinea (NBC–PGN) replaced the dual system of broadcasting. Twenty five ABC staff members were seconded to NBC–PNG during its first two years; by the end of 1975, it was expected that nationals would replace ABC personnel (*COMBROAD* 1975a, p. 60).

During its first year of operation, NBC–PNG proceeded to dismantle the Australian-created regional program structure and began replacing it with program images that could better meet the needs of the people. Among its first changes were the employment of multilingual broadcasts, the diminution of Australia-originated newscasts, and the reorganization of technical services. NBC–PNG is deeply committed to multilingual broadcasting; each day, among the 25 stations in 17 different districts, broadcasts are made in at least 25 of the 700 languages and dialects of the nation. When NBC–PNG assumed responsibility for the nation's broadcasting in 1973, 9½ of the 17 hours of news originated in Australia. By early 1975, all news bulletins were expected to originate from the NBC—PNG newsroom equipped with its own teleprinter Also, the central newsroom was linked with those of each district station. Furthermore, NBC—PNG has worked closely with the Pacific Islands News Association to insure a steady flow of South Pacific news and current-affairs programming (*COMBROAD* October—December 1974, p. 59).

Previously, NBC—PNG was dependent upon the Department of Postmaster General, Posts and Telegraphs Department, and its own staff for maintenance of technical services. This unsatisfactory and expensive arrangement was changed with the phasing out of the role of the postmaster general, upgrading of technical services in the districts, and the gradual replacement of Posts and Telegraphs personnel at the stations with NBC—PNG manpower. The stations in the 17 districts will be grouped into four regions, each with its own control center where technical expertise will be available to stations in the regional grouping (Mackay 1975, pp. 49—50).

5.2 New Zealand, *by Alexander F. Toogood*

Because of the common heritage, there is a tendency to think of New Zealand as an Australian outpost. Yet 1,400 miles of rough seas separate the two independent countries. More important, each has its own distinctive mental outlook: Australia is a brash, emerging power; New Zealand, a tranquil, agrarian state. While Australia thrusts herself into the world, New Zealand is very content to be removed from it. This presents a dichotomy for New Zealanders, whereby they must share a nineteenth-century conformist society, yet live in one of the world's most highly developed welfare states.

The country is small, roughly the size and shape of California. Its population is proportionately even smaller, 2.8 million. A rugged terrain presents huge technical problems for broadcasting, but it blesses the country with unparalleled beauty. The people are scattered over the two major islands, with a concentration in the upper part of North Island, location of the largest city, Auckland. A welfare system's dictate of service to all has blended with the population distribution to provide a broadcasting system that, it is estimated, would serve a population twenty times as large. The system is currently in a state of great change. Private radio stations recently emerged to challenge commercial and noncommercial offerings of the public national system, and a second television service was developed.

5.2.1 Early Radio

Sharing Australia's awareness of the remote location of their country, New Zealanders were quick to see the advantages of radio. By 1922, amateurs had established seven stations which provided entertainment programs for their local communities (Marshall 1966, p. 247). Their sporadic hours, however, finally resulted in sufficient public pressure by 1925 that the government established a national public system of broadcasting. The system was entrusted to Radio

Broadcasting Company of New Zealand Ltd., a private company which was to provide a regular service to four major cities that were New Zealand's geographic and cultural centers. The company was noncommercial, drawing its income from a government-levied, annual receiver license fee of £1.10 ($3.60) and an initial government grant for capital expenditure (Mackay 1953, chapter 3). The amateur stations remained, also on a noncommercial basis, and grew in number to 40 by 1932.

Impressed by developments in Britain – as it frequently is – the New Zealand government decided that the company should be replaced by a public corporation modeled after the BBC (Polaschek 1958, p. 42). Known as the New Zealand Broadcasting Board, the corporation went into effect in 1932, taking over Radio Broadcasting Company's facilities in the process. Under pressure to expand its services, the board used eight private, amateur stations as affiliates. As a development of this move, the board later assumed responsibility for supervising all programs from private stations.

The board also faced the problem of providing an alternate service in each of the major cities. With the resultant opening of four new stations, a pattern was established in the national radio system that was still evident in early 1973: a network of major noncommercial stations supported in the four major population concentrations by noncommercial alternate programming. Although providing such impressive developments, the board was inept at the personal level. When coupled with a newly elected government during the depression, a change was inevitable.

5.2.2   State Monopoly

Labour Party governments in New Zealand started out as very socialistic, and, as a result, broadcasting fell under direct government control. Part of this came about when the 1936 Broadcasting Act abolished the board and replaced it with the New Zealand Broadcasting Service (NZBS), a government department with a minister firmly in control. The thinking of New Zealand's new government was that because broadcasting was such an important social institution, a special portfolio should be established – the Minister of Broadcasting.

All of this places a different complexion on the relationship between broadcasting and government than found in most countries. Other democracies usually parcel broadcasting into a broader area, such as posts or tele-communications, thus limiting government's concern to technical considerations. By creating the post of Minister of Broadcasting, the New Zealand government was clearly stating that the minister's responsibilities would go beyond, to matters of policy and programming. Thus, a special attitude was created that persisted into the 1970s.

As one of his first directives, the minister requested that radio, in an attempt to counter an antagonistic press, should for the first time, broadcast the parliamentary proceedings. As such directives became commonplace, it became clear broadcasting was really a government tool (Mackay 1953, p. 124). Indeed, government thought so highly of the medium's potential, that the first broadcasting minister was the prime minister himself.

NZBS continued the board's pattern of alternate metropolitan programming and a national program relying on four NZBS stations and private affiliates. The 1936 act also permitted all existing amateur stations to operate, but because of the insecurity of their financial bases — they were required to be noncommercial — eventually these stations were absorbed into the national system or folded. One did survive into the 1970s, however, to become the oldest station in the British Commonwealth.

5.2.3 Dual Services

One year after creating NZBS, the government introduced commercial broadcasting as another national system, responsible to the minister. Thus, the Minister of Broadcasting assumed responsibility for a single government monopoly in broadcasting, with a national system supported by receiver license fees and commercial stations financed by advertising. The two systems were combined into a single administrative unit during World War II and existed as such until 1973.

During Labour's years of social directives, NZBS undertook the responsibility of publishing *New Zealand Listener,* which, apart from offering program information, remains one of the country's leading cultural journals. In addition, New Zealand's only fulltime symphony orchestra was founded by NZBS. The current national broadcasting body, largest supporter of the arts in New Zealand, includes an additional smaller orchestra and a youth orchestra. Such services function at a loss, which in 1971 amounted to more than NZ$1 million ($1.2 million) (NNZBC 1970–71, p. 25). Apart from being considerably valuable in a nation otherwise deprived of cultural sustenance, these endeavors provide valuable employment for New Zealanders with creative ability (Simpson 1961, p. 113). The government also fostered the development of International Service, which was then, as now, a limited offering to Australia and western Pacific Islands.

New Zealand stood by as the rest of the world looked at television's possibilities. Although there had been some impressive experiments by private concerns interested in bringing television to the country, the first station approved by the Labour government (in Auckland, 1960) was operated by NZBS. A year later, NZBS established TV stations in Christchurch and Wellington.

5.2.4 NZBC and Government

In 1960, another new government, whose platform included a promise to end direct control of broadcasting, was elected. But in 1961 it created the New Zealand Broadcasting Corporation (NZBC) to assume NZBS functions, and the promise of government's removal from broadcasting remained an illusion (Rowe and Rowe 1968, p. 105).

Confusing lines of control were established by the 1961 legislation. As a result, ultimate authority until 1973, was vested in three different bodies: the government-appointed NZBC to give policy, the director general to provide administration, and the Minister of Broadcasting to assure a firm link between broadcasting and government.

A total, ever-present environment of political conscience for NZBC remained in force until 1973, with stipulations saying parliament must debate broadcasting estimates, questions could be asked of the minister during parliament sessions, and a cabinet committee on broadcasting should exist (Milne 1957, p. 62; Toogood 1969–70, p. 105). The Corporation was further directed to comply with government directives, and under financial provisions, expenditures in excess of NZ $50,000 ($60,000) had to be approved by the administration. While the government made only one attempt to issue a directive – an attempt that was ignored by NZBC under legal advice – the minister was particularly insistent on using his control over financial matters (*COMBROAD* 1971).

Corporation plans for a much-needed new TV-production facility had been continually frustrated by a government that considered broadcasting as just one item on a list of political priorities (see §5.2.10). Added to such direct avenues of influence was the prevailing political awareness of corporation executives (Hotchkiss 1964, p. 235). In 1961 all top personnel merely changed hats and assumed their old positions with their years of training as public servants, answerable to government. Thus a perceptible lack of boldness prevailed in managerial decisions and public-affairs programming. Because of its blandness, the corporation lost many of its senior production personnel, incuding the top producer who left in 1966, claiming direct government censorship of public-affairs programming (see Bick 1968). More recently administrative weakness caused the resignation of New Zealand's most popular TV personality, a public-affairs interviewer who had attracted the largest audiences ever received by NZBC (see Edwards 1971). Charges of political interference peaked in 1972, when the corporation fired the editor of its *New Zealand Listener*. While an official inquiry did not find any political meddling, the uproar provoked by the incident revealed public awareness of the possibility of government influence.

5.2.5 New Zealand Broadcasting Authority

An odd provision in the 1961 act required NZBC to investigate broadcasting periodically, and if its own service was found wanting, NZBC could call for applications for a private license to broadcast. It is hardly surprising that the corporation never found the need to investigate and that no private applications were sought.

Real dissatisfaction with NZBC's radio programming surfaced in 1967, however, when two pirate radio stations went on the air, operating from ships outside New Zealand's territorial waters. At first the government tried to thwart these private activities, but the public's support was so considerable that the government eventually turned not only a blind, but also a benevolent, eye. As part of its next election campaign, government promised to form a separate broadcasting authority. This was carried out in 1968 with the creation of the New Zealand Broadcasting Authority.

The Authority had three full-time members, including a chairman who must be a practicing lawyer. The legalistic overtones of this provision meant that the authority tended to concentrate on its judicial functions. The chairman insisted that he alone make announcements about authority activities, which were limited to those of a reviewing body (see §5.2.10).

Not seeing itself as an innovator or bold leader in broadcasting matters, the authority instead considered and adjudicated public (NZBC) and private license applications, granted licenses which lasted for five years, regulated public and private license holders with programming and advertising directives, and advised the minister on any matters he raised.

Although this advice shared the same fate of a similar provision in Australia — being secret until released by the minister — the other powers were considerably broader than those of the Australian Broadcasting Control Board. Not only did the authority deal with all broadcasters, including the public sector, but also acted as the ultimate authority on licensing matters, subject only to court appeal.

By early 1970, hostility had already flared between the authority and NZBC. The corporation understandably resented the interloper that had assumed many of its previous functions, and to whom it was now answerable. Contributing to this feeling was the fact that the three authority members had not had previous broadcasting experience, leading to some trouble in the courts where authority decisions were overturned.

Earliest authority regulations merely retained the standards established by NZBC. In regard to advertising, the authority was fairly liberal. Radio was permitted 18 minutes of commercials in each hour; television, 6 minutes. Television commercials were clustered so that 20-minute programs had no breaks, those of 20–40 minutes had one break, and no more than two breaks could be taken in any hour. The new private radio stations, however, felt confined by certain constraints, such as those concerning the advertising of liquor and the ban on Sunday advertising, despite the fact commercial stations broadcast on Sunday. Under pressure from the private stations, the authority investigated this provision in 1971 and found, through an extensive public survey, that the population approved of the Sunday ban. As a result, it has been retained (*Broadcasting* 1972), even after the 1975 restructure.

Programming directives are minimal. For example, there is no New Zealand content ruling; merely the request that stations should, "as far as possible," broadcast New Zealand—originated materials. No station, however, may editorialize, use political advertisements, or offer direct sponsorship of television programs. Ownership directives limit newspaper investment in private radio to no more than 30%, and private stations are prohibited from forming a network, in an attempt to ensure that they limit their service to local needs.

By 1975, all domestic radio in New Zealand was till AM. When in 1971 a hearing was conducted into the possibility of FM broadcasting, the authority recommended to the government that no need existed for its introduction at that time.

The major *raison d'être* of the authority was to foster private radio. In its first year of operation, the authority received 60 inquiries and 13 official applications. The Auckland area, with the country's largest population concentration, was the first to be considered and in 1970 received two private commercial stations. One of these had been the most successful of the pirate radio stations, Radio Hauraki. Along with the other Auckland station, Radio i, Radio Hauraki supplies the kind of popular programming characterized by American commercial radio stations: a popular music base, spiced with news and information. As in Australia, this is supported by the popular telephone call-in program. Both Auckland stations are on the air 24 hours a day.

By 1972, three additional private commercial stations were serving other areas of the country, and four other applications, each for a different area, were under authority consideration (NZBC 1971, pp. 3–4). By 1974, there were seven private commercial stations. Commercial radio, operated by private investors, is forcefully establishing itself on the New Zealand broadcasting scene.

5.2.6 NZBC Radio

NZBC was responsible until 1973, for both the radio and TV national services. Three radio networks are included under NZBC auspices: National, YC, and Commercial/ZM.

The National Network uses 17 stations to give nation-wide coverage of the same noncommercial programming. More powerful stations remain on the air late at night, making National a 24-hour-a-day service (*WRTH* 1974, pp. 182–83). The network's individual stations retain some local identity, being responsible for providing feeds to the national program. There is a news and information emphasis on National, supported by the type of radio format that characterized radio before television. NZBC still has a strong commitment to fostering locally produced drama, and to catering to various minorities, e.g., women, children, schools, churches, sports bodies, farmers, book readers, consumer groups, and the native Maori, who comprises 7% of the population.

The YC (the call sign) Network operates from four stations, offering noncommercial cultural programming for 5½ hours nightly. Clearly a minority service, YC reaches less than 1% of the population. In the summer, these stations are on the air during the day to supplement NZBC's extensive sports coverage. When parliament is in session, the major National Network station and two YC stations carry the proceedings.

NZBC's commercial activity has two outlets, the Commercial Network and the ZM stations. The 27 stations of the Commercial Network are linked only for news and a few sponsored programs; otherwise, they are considered community stations, originating most of their own programming (*WRTH* 1974, pp.

182–83). Most are on the air from 5 A.M. to midnight, offering a muted edition of commercial programming that includes panel discussions, shopping reports, and the everpersistent soap opera. Popular music is toned down by heavy dashes of music from yesteryear.

A far more popular format has recently emerged on the Corporation's ZM stations. In three strategically located centers of population, ZM stations exist to program United States – style commercial fare 18 hours daily. Private commercial broadcasters complain that this service, a recent NZBC innovation, has been undertaken solely to offer competition. The corporation counterclaims that it is merely progressing with the times, correctly noting that the prototype for these stations existed for years under the corporation's YD label.

The corporation and private stations, of which there were seven in 1974 (*WRTH* 1974, p. 183), do battle in another area, audience research. Because no independent audience research is undertaken in New Zealand, each broadcaster conducts his own, resulting in very divergent findings and claims. A three-month survey, conducted by the corporation in 1971, found that in the Auckland market the share of audience was distributed in this order: NZBC's Commercial Network station, Radio i, National program and Radio Hauraki (tied in third position), and ZM. These were total audience figures, whereas demographic studies carried out for the commercial stations show that certain target audiences are better reached on the private outlets.

5 2.7 Television

NZBC had monopolized New Zealand television until 1975 (see §5.2.10). As a public body, it developed a policy of offering television to every citizen before attempting to provide an alternate service. In 1972, this single service could reach 99% of the population, with a household saturation of 83% (*Developments in Broadcasting* 1971, p. 19). Such penetration was aided by as many as 330 private translators which carried NZBC's signal into outlying areas (Stringer 1966, p. 24). The single television service originated from a station in each of the four cities which act as New Zealand's cultural centers. One of these stations, AKTV-2 of Auckland, reaches half of the national population, whereas the smallest, in Dunedin, serves only one-tenth. In 1960, an embryo network service was established, but because of its primitiveness and inefficiency, the service was limited to the nightly news and coverage of important events.

Regular TV programming is sent from station to station with some degree of nation-wide uniformity. Television transmission is from 2–11 P.M., with one additional hour on Fridays and Saturdays. Programming reflects a public broadcasting philosophy, with a balance among entertainment, culture, and information. Two-thirds of the programming is popular mass entertainment, the remainder given over to news, documentaries, public affairs, sports, religion, children's programming, and serious music and drama. The strong emphasis on serious offerings is more popular than might be expected, and such programs are frequently among the top-rated. For example, in 1970, the most popular show was the New Zealand-produced public-affairs program, "Gallery." It was just one program from the highly developed, autonomous news service of NZBC.

5.2.8 TV Programming

Neither the authority nor the corporation had any official guidelines concerning the amount of local content on television. Approximately 25% of NZBC television programming in 1972 was produced in New Zealand, but this was chiefly news, public affairs, children's, and service programs. The corporation stressed the expensiveness of local production, particularly since the corporation and government believed the primary responsibility of TV was to offer a total service to all the country. Because of this belief, an immense financial outlay was committed to technical facilities, thus limiting the money available for production of New Zealand programs. Additionally, each of the four television production facilities was in a hastily converted building, normally not conducive to any degree of sophistication in local production (Austin 1972, p. 15).

In 1975, the bulk of the programs was still imported, the United States providing the largest proportion. In early TV days, American programs were the most popular in New Zealand. In the 1970s, however, British imports have received larger audiences, and although U.S. imports are still quantitatively the largest, they have often been relegated to the fringe hours of the early afternoon.

While television advertising was permitted, all programs were purchased and scheduled by the corporation, which also judiciously censored them for violence, horror, and sex. Despite the provision for such censorship, the puritanical standards traditionally characteristic of New Zealand television have been greatly relaxed in recent years (see Pitman 1972).

5.2.9 NZBC Financing

The highly developed broadcasting service provided by NZBC, both radio and television, was an expensive commodity for a country that has a small population, a topography imposing huge technical barriers, and an economy based on primary products and a delicate balance of payments. Despite such impositions, the corporation was forced to finance its operations without any government largess (Stringer 1964, p. 18). Broadcasting revenue was obtained from receiver license fees which, after collection costs were retained by the post office, went directly to a broadcasting account. This provision removed NZBC from the unfavorable position of the Australian Broadcasting Commission, which must request all its income from parliament each year.

In 1971, the NZ $3 ($3.60) license fee for radio sets was abolished, but TV license fees were increased to NZ $20 ($24) per household. License fees accounted for nearly NZ $10 million ($12 million) of the corporation's income in 1971. This revenue financed all NZBC noncommercial radio and television services. Commercial activities of both media are still expected to pay for themselves, as well as provide enough profit to cover losses in other areas. Commercial revenue in 1971 totaled more than NZ $14 million ($16.8 million), on which the corporation paid regular taxation (NZBC 1970–71, p. 25).

Commercial radio offers both spot buying and sponsorship, but television is limited to spot buying. TV spots must be placed in broad time bands – that for prime time being 7–10 P.M. – and the advertiser has no option as to when, within these time bands, his commercial will appear. Despite this limitation, television is very popular with advertisers. TV advertising provides the total broadcasting budget with one-third of its revenue.

On the other hand, the public is not unduly exploited by TV advertising. The corporation developed its commercial/noncommercial pattern for the single television operation in a unique way (Schroder 1961, p. 22): only 50% of total transmission time included spots and no commercials appeared at all on Monday, Friday, and Sunday, or during children's shows on other days.

This convenient blend of commercial revenue and license fees meant that the corporation showed a handsome profit each year until 1971. The 1971 reversal was blamed primarily on increased personnel costs which, in reality, were long overdue in a broadcasting body noted for low salaries.

It should be noted that the corporation's financial obligations went beyond normal business practice. NZBC's corporate status as a public body imposed strict limitations on borrowing; for example, all financing of the huge cost of introducing television came out of past radio profits. Television income not only supported broadcasting's unwieldy bureaucracy, but also covered losses of concert and publication activities, and the difference between radio income and expenditure.

Unlike many countries embracing television, New Zealand maintained, and even expanded, its radio offerings. In less than ten years, the corporation opened 14 radio stations, increased transmission power, updated equipment, and improved studio facilities of many others (Toogood 1969–70, p. 17).

5.2.10 Recent Changes

While New Zealand joined the international communications scene in 1971, by opening its own receiver station for satellite transmissions, there were indications of even more important changes. For example, the use of television for instructional purposes was under consideration upon the urging of a 1972 special committee of inquiry (*Dominion* 1972). In addition, color television was adopted in 1973, posing both pleasure and problems, in that NZBC, receiver manufacturers, and the general public are involved in additional economic outlays (*Australian Financial Review* 1971).

But the most important development concerned the second channel and subsequent reorganizational plans. In 1972, the Broadcasting Authority held hearings on two bids to operate the second television service; one from NZBC, the other from a consortium of private interests. Before the authority revealed its recommendation, a change of government occurred, with Labour returning to power. Revealing a traditional Labour interest in broadcasting, the new prime minister devoted one of his first public announcements to the fact that the corporation would operate the alternate service. Such a policy decision was to be expected from a government that has always been interested in centralization of broadcasting. But, because it was a direct government statement, unrelated to the authority's hearings, it belittled the authority and threatened its future.

The authority reacted by announcing in March 1973 that it had decided to favor Independent Television Corporation's application to run the second channel. At the same time, the authority, set up when the conservative National Party was in control, criticized NZBC, concluding ITC's conspectus was "more in the public interest than the proposals put forward by NZBC." The government said it would set aside the authority's decision; the broadcasting minister made it clear that ITC would not get the second channel but said he and his party were not in a rush to legislate.

This initial burst of government interest, however, was surpassed by a completely unexpected development in February 1973. The government revealed plans for the disbandment of NZBC, and for its replacement by three separate public broadcasting bodies: one for radio, and one each for two television channels. The initial announcement (see *Dominion* 1973; *FEER* 1973) implied that the two television services would vie for audiences and advertisers. On 1 April 1975, NZBC was abolished as the single public corporation responsible for broadcasting, replaced by three separate and independent public corporations: one responsible for Television Service One (TV-1); a second for Television Service Two (TV-2), and a third, Radio New Zealand (RNZ), responsible for sound broadcasting. Each corporation has its own three-member board. In addition, a Broadcasting Council of New Zealand was established, made up of six members and replacing the former New Zealand Broadcasting Authority. The council's many responsibilities include allocation of license fees, gathering and making available news to TV-1 and TV-2, receiving news gathered by RNZ, publication of the *New Zealand Listener,* assuring TV-1 and TV-2 programs do not clash, and advising government on receiver license fees (*COMBROAD* 1975b, p. 4). The council and the corporations are responsible to parliament and report to it annually. The Minister of Broadcasting position has been abolished.

Each corporation has its own policy, staff, studios, and financial resources, the latter still made up of license fees and advertising. The two television stations have the same mixed commercial and noncommercial character, with four advertising days per week but with nights staggered so that both carry advertising on only two nights. The TV stations are networked to give nation-wide coverage, but are decentralized: TV-1 is headquartered in Wellington, with production also in Dunedin on South Island; TV-2 is based in Auckland, with production also in Christchurch and Hamilton. Radio New Zealand is based in Wellington. On the television services, programming is structured so that normal news and public-affairs programs do not coincide (Adam 1974, pp. 162–70; see also Committee on Broadcasting 1973).

TV-2 went on the air 30 June 1975 with little fanfare and a large percentage of imported shows, mainly from the United States and Great Britain (Dubbelt 1975b, pp. 41, 46). In early 1975, *Variety* reported that television in New Zealand was heavily loaded with American situation comedies. Top-rated were "Alias Smith and Jones," "M.A.S.H.," and "The Waltons" (*Variety,* 1 January 1975). TV-1 was launched 1 April 1975 (Dubbelt 1975a, pp. 44, 56). Expected to encourage local program production is the new equipment of Avalon Television Centre, officially opened 17 March 1975, after seven years of construction. The center is equipped to transmit in color and to handle two channels. Although TV-2 now originates its network in Auckland, it will have facilities at Avalon, making it possible to inject material into its network (*COMBROAD* 1975d, pp. 21–22).

No doubt, such a change in structure will revolutionize the country's broadcasting. While adding to the already-burdensome bureaucratic structure, it introduces a healthy degree of competition to replace the previous complacency of NZBC. Unlike the relatively stable scene in neighboring Australia, New Zealand broadcasting is likely to see constant readjustment and change for some years.

5.3 Pacific Islands, *by Ralph D. Barney*

Oceania, the islands of the central, southern, and western Pacific Ocean, must be one of the most diverse regions of the world in terms of forms of government, ethnic groups, languages, and cultures.

Of the 14 Central South Pacific island groups discussed here, five are independent or self-governing; three are possessions of the United States; three of Great Britain; two of France, and one, a condominium responsibility shared by France and Great Britain. All five independent groups — Nauru, Cook Islands, Fiji, Western Samoa, and Tonga — have formerly been in close relationship with either the United Kingdom, New Zealand, or Australia.

American possessions are those commonly referred to as Micronesia; the French still control New Caledonia and French Polynesia. Niue, Cook and Ellice Islands, and the Solomons are under British control or protectorate.

Geographically, the islands represent specks in the vast Pacific Ocean. The various groups may include as many as 320 islands (the case of Fiji) or may be as scattered as the Cook Islands, 93 square miles of land sprinkled over 750,000 miles of ocean. Populations are comparatively small, Fiji being the large group with 520,000 people, most of the rest having about 150,000 people or less. Nauru, an independent state since 1968, has 7,000 people, who must be among the world's wealthiest, sharing $25 million yearly from the island's production of phosphate (see *Philadelphia Inquirer,* 7 December 1974, pp. 1A, 4A).

Ralph D. Barney is Associate Professor of Journalism at Brigham Young University. He had a varied background in the Pacific, serving in Hawaii as college director of public relations, professor, editor and publisher, proprietor of an advertising and public-relations agency, and specialist at the East-West· Communication Institute. He received his Ph.D. from the University of Missouri.

Other islands are not so fortunate as Nauru, but neither are they the world's most depressed areas financially. Most of them are endowed with a wide range of natural resources, and they have been able to attract foreign aid. In fact, the South Pacific islands find themselves in an interesting situation in which an almost-embarrassing richness of technological programs has been proposed by varied international economic aid and development groups, wanting to help solve their pressing problems of modernization. Yet, winning acceptance of these programs among the broad population groups involved is proving difficult.

5.3.1 Broadcasting History

Broadcasting in the Pacific islands is generally viewed as a means of linking the scattered groups with a common instructive or informational tie. And, as a Western communicative device introduced usually to facilitate adoption of Western institutions, it is not surprising that island broadcasting operations, content, and control are heavily dominated by Westerners.

As the most pervasive of the media in the region, broadcasting generally has the capability for reaching the peoples in a given island group with effective innovation campaigns. Most island groups have established a public radio broadcast system, and five of them have television facilities.

The history of broadcasting in the islands is neither long nor broad, since systems in 8 of the 14 groups have been established since 1961. Only Fiji had a broadcast system as early as 1935, and Western Samoa and the British Solomon Islands in the 1940s. The remainder were established between 1950 and 1969.

Besides being a spreading phenomenon throughout the Pacific, broadcasting is also growing rapidly within most island groups. One student research group noted in 1971 that just over 50 transmitters were scattered through the Central Pacific islands in the late 1960s, evenly divided between medium- and short-wave. Pointing out the skyrocketing of radio receivers between 1950 and the late 1960s, they claimed Fiji, for example, had 12 times more sets at the end of the two decades than at the beginning. Growth was computed at 1,500% in New Caledonia and 4,000% in Tonga during the same period (Henderson et al. 1971, pp. 170, 188).

Television, too, has been accepted widely in areas where that medium is available. For example, between 1966 and 1970, the number of receivers increased from 2,500 to 5,500 in French Polynesia and from 3,000 to 6,000 in New Caledonia. Television has reached Guam, American Samoa, and Micronesia as well.

In this chapter, four specific island groups (Fiji, Western Samoa, Tonga, and American Samoa) have been examined in detail because they represent the most sophisticated broadcast systems in the central South Pacific. The specific systems of each of the other groups are also described.

5.3.2 Fiji

Fijian broadcasting commenced in 1935 when Amalgamated Wireless of

Australasia Ltd. was licensed to operate under call sign, ZJV. The present independent Fiji Broadcasting Commission was established by Broadcasting Ordinance 26 of 1952; the resultant station, Radio Fiji, went on the air 1 July 1954. It remains as Fiji's only radio system.

All Fiji Broadcasting Commission programming originates from Suva, after which 13 transmitters relay the programs on two FM and 11 medium-wave frequencies. The commission claims its signals can be received in all island areas in the country.

Broadcasting for years had been divided into two networks, National (English) and Vernacular (Hindi alternating with Fijian language), until in 1972 the emphasis shifted to Hindi and Fijian channels, with English becoming a part of each. The channels were designated Radio Fiji 1 (English and Fijian) and Radio Fiji 2 (English and Hindi), with an FM channel maintaining continuous English programming (*WRTH* 1974, pp. 180–81; *ABU Newsletter* 1973d, pp. 34–35). A typical broadcast day, by mid-1972, provided nearly seven hours – of a 17-hour day – in English on each channel, the remainder in the vernacular on the channel. Much of the English programming involves news, weather, and concerts.

Changes in news presentations also occurred after 1972 as the broadcast system responded to format changes under new leadership. Generally, the local news staff consists of six, including Australian news and deputy news editors, and four Fijian-born reporters. Their responsibility is to produce nearly half an hour of local news daily, six days a week. Newscasts take the form of five-minute English-language shows at 6 A.M., repeated at 7:10 A.M. on Radio Fiji 1 and 8:10 A.M. on Radio Fiji 2 (*Fiji Times* 1972). Translated into Fijian and Hindi, the newscasts are broadcast over their respective channels during morning programming. A newscast and local news summary is produced for midday, and other Fiji news is broadcast during early evening hours in English and the vernacular languages. Forty-five minutes of international news is broadcast in English, some of which is translated and aired in Fijian and Hindi in the evening. BBC newscasts of ten minutes each are relayed through Radio Fiji 1 at 7 and 8 A.M., a ten-minute Radio Australia international newscast at 1:30 P.M., and ABC's national bulletin from Sydney at 9 P.M.

The daily local-news time allocation has been inflexible, with no special coverage time made available for news of extra significance to Fiji. Furthermore, the news staff has not participated in the preparation of interpretive or documentary programs.

Partly for this reason, FBC news policies were strongly criticized by a 1970 Broadcasting Review Committee, which, after a series of public hearings and interviews, charged FBC with "not adequately reflecting the country it serves, that it is not, in other words, Fiji-oriented" (*Report of Broadcasting Review Committee* 1970, p. 3).

The committee, noting that Fiji was small enough for "events and problems of each part to be interesting to the whole," suggested FBC should alter its news programming:

The present balance between international and local news is out of keeping with the times, and should be altered. Three international bulletins a day, in the morning, at lunch time and in the evening, would be enough. There should continue to be re-broadcasting of bulletins from overseas stations; excellent, impartial bulletins are available and the FBC has not the resources to deal with international news itself. At the same time, local news should be greatly increased.

The great majority of people in Fiji are almost completely dependent on the radio for news about their own country. The aim should be at least three substantial (ten to fifteen minutes) bulletins of local news every day in the three languages; with short news summaries (one to two minutes) every hour in between. [Report of Broadcasting Review Committee 1970, p. 3]

Also, based on a 1969 audience survey, the committee suggested a reevaluation of English-language programming and its relationship with vernacular content. According to the survey, although less than one-third of Fijian speakers and only 15% of those using Hindi listen to English-language programs, 106 broadcast hours per week are in English, 49 in Hindustani, and 37 in Fijian. UNESCO gave the figures as 119, 54 ½, and 38 in 1975 (UNESCO 1975, p. 485).

FBC is attempting to produce fortnightly documentary programs, but again they are in English. General topics of the documentaries cover contemporary problems, with a conscious effort to refrain from political discussions. Part of this results from what was called an "uphill battle to get political material" and a reluctance by government officials to participate. Despite this reluctance to become involved in political matters, FBC, along with radio on Guam and American Samoa, is the only system in the region that has even nominal independence from government.

FBC, self-supporting since 1963, is financed primarily by advertising revenue, which increased by 54% between 1963 and 1968. Radio license fees provided nearly 27% of annual operating expenses in 1968. Because of lax enforcement of licensing provisions, revenue from the source remained fairly stable despite rapid increases in numbers of sets owned (Report of the Broadcasting Review Committee 1970, p. 13). For example, the 1969 audience survey concluded that 78% of the 73,879 households in Fiji have radio sets. Therefore, as the survey team emphasized, a minimum of over 57,000 radio sets should have existed in Fiji that year, but the $2.88 license fee was paid on only 42,240. The number of radio sets licensed in the following two years dropped somewhat. In 1971, the radio license fee was abolished.

The 1970 Broadcasting Review Committee also recommended to the government that television's introduction to Fiji should not be long delayed, although "bearing in mind the heavy cost and the other calls on the country's resources." The committee recommended strongly that government finance the television system, thus ensuring the retention of all income for programming and the widest spread of the service. In the event government could not supply all the capital, the committee suggested sufficient government involvement to make sure the main loyalty of the television operation "would be to programme and not to profit." An earlier report by a former BBC man supported the notion that Fiji TV should not be a commercial concern, nor should the prime reason for its introduction be for educational purposes (*Pacific Islands Monthly* 1969, p. 3).

Should television become a reality on Fiji, the committee suggested an immediate goal of 30% locally produced programs, with an emphasis on Fijian news and sports filmed, processed, and edited in the islands. From the following paragraph, it was obvious the committee wished to pattern Fiji TV along the lines of most nations of the Third World:

But most important of all, there should be programmes to help Fiji's development as a nation, both politically and economically. Current affairs programmes, explaining and discussing the whole range of the country's problems and ambitions, could help with the first. What could be broadly described as training programmes, with agriculture, again, as an obvious example, could help with the second. [*Report of Broadcasting Review Committee* 1970, pp. 12–13, 16].

According to FBC staff, however, there is considerable resistance to the idea that television should come to Fiji. And, when it does arrive, they feel it will be financed and operated by a private enterprise from Britain.

5.3.3 Western Samoa

Radio in Western Samoa entered its second quarter century in 1973, having been established in 1948 by the New Zealand administration. To assist the effectiveness of 2AP, the station's call letters, the government installed battery-driven radio receiving sets in virtually every village, the receivers being preset to only the local station (Keesing and Keesing, 1956, p. 169). Upon independence in 1961, the radio station came under direct control of the government, with responsibility to the Minister of Broadcasting. Employees now were appointed by the Public Service Commission (rather than station management) and Samoanization (a government goal to place Samoans in all government positions) became virtually complete. The only non-Samoan at the station in 1970, for example, was a United States Peace Corps volunteer.

The station claims to be able to reach 99% of the population with its 10-kw. medium-wave transmitter at Apia. An estimated 15,000 radio sets provided almost 71% saturation, on the basis of 21,217 households in the 1966 census. In 1975, UNESCO reported an estimated 32,000 sets in use (UNESCO 1975, p. 503).

Station 2AP operates 12½ hours daily, signing on at 6 A.M. and off at 10:30 P.M., suspending service between 1:30 and 5:30 P.M. daily. As with other Western Polynesia stations, 2AP relies heavily on overseas radio services, principally Radio Australia and Radio New Zealand, for international news. In an average day, a total of one hour and 25 minutes of international news (one hour in English, 25 minutes in Samoan) and 21 minutes of local news (4½ minutes in English, 16½ minutes Samoan) are broadcast. The news day begins at 7 A.M. with a 10-minute ABC international newscast, followed by a three-minute "Information Bulletin" in English and seven minutes of local headlines, mixed in English and Samoan. At 9 A.M., another ABC newscast is relayed, followed ten minutes later with a Samoan translation of the 7 A.M. ABC file. NZBC world newscasts follow at 9:30 A.M. and 12:30 P.M., with third and fourth ABC files at 1 and 7 P.M.

At 8:30 P.M., a 15-minute world news program is broadcast in Samoan, containing selections from the ABC 9 A.M., 1 P.M., and 7 P.M. files. Samoan-language local news is broadcast from 8–8:15 P.M.

In addition, local information in Samoan is provided in small packages five other times a week. For example, "News Around Town" highlights occurrences in the Apia area, while "News from the Country" covers the rest of the nation. "Samoa on the Move" offers 15 minutes of discussion about government projects and developmental news, and "Guide for Everyone" discusses customs and other instructional material for Samoans. A weekly Saturday evening interview feature provides public discussion of government affairs. The interviews are handled in much the same way as those in Fiji; questions are predetermined and interviews are conducted by staff members.

The general evening format calls for all-English programming between 5:30 and 7:30 P.M., mixed or bilingual programs until 10:30, with sponsored time available for the last half-hour of the day. In addition, commercials are inserted through the day's schedule, providing the equivalent of 90 minutes of sponsored programming daily, enough to finance the bulk of the station's operation. Not much revenue is received through the annual 70-cent license fee on radio receivers, mainly because the ruling is not stringently enforced. According to a government statistician, in 1968, 531 of the estimated 15,000 sets were licensed.

The demonstrated ability of 2AP to support itself through advertising sales and, if raised and enforced, the annual license fee, has stirred some suggestions for granting the station a measure of independence from direct cabinet control. But the matter has not been brought before the Legislative Assembly, though it is understood to have been discussed in the cabinet.

The problems of government control surface periodically, as they did in December 1967, when a front-page story in the *Apia Advertiser* reported that the daily local news bulletin, both in English and Samoan, was suspended "reportedly . . . as a result of a Cabinet directive." The suspension was said to have resulted from a series of ministerial complaints, culminating in, among other things, the reporting of a resignation threat by the prime minister, a report which "reflected unfavourably upon the Government" (*Apia Advertiser* 1967). In the next issue of the newspaper, a letter from the broadcasting director denied the political implications of the suspension, citing a lack of funds as the reason for the shutdown.

A feature almost traditional with Western Samoan radio is the broadcast of Legislative Assembly debates, begun by the New Zealand administration and continued after independence. Four hours daily are given to broadcasting proceedings, both in English and Samoan, during the two to four weeks when the Legislative Assembly meets each year.

Although there is not a local TV service, 60% of the population is within receiving range of American Samoa television. Only 75 sets are estimated in use (UNESCO 1975, pp. 503–4).

5.3.4 Tonga

ZCO, launched 13 March 1961, is expected mainly to provide a strong international news diet for the Kingdom of Tonga to complement the local coverage of the two government newspapers. The radio operation, utilizing a 10-kw. transmitter, is in a desirable situation to provide excellent coverage through all the islands of Tonga, in that Tonga's tapu is a flat, virtually mountainless island. Coverage is such that ZCO has a relatively high listenership in Fiji and can be better received in Auckland, New Zealand, than many New Zealand stations of comparable power (*Pacific Islands Monthly* 1961, p. 65).

A 1974 station estimate for UNESCO claimed 9,000 radio receivers were in use in Tonga (UNESCO 1975, p. 502), up from a 4,900 estimate for 1967. Based on the 1966 census figure (Fiefia 1968, p. 34), the saturation of ZCO is 58% of Tongan households, though observations would lead to the conclusion that this is a conservative figure.

ZCO is controlled by Tongan Broadcasting Commission, appointed by the government and made up of as many as five members. In June 1970, the commission's composition included the premier, finance minister, secretary to government, superintendent of the Telephone and Telegraph Department, and the station manager, who is the commission's secretary.

The station's operating budget is derived generally from advertising revenue, with the manager normally serving as advertising salesman. Most of the station's advertising comes from overseas, the bulk from Fiji and Australia. Some 90% of the $33,600 annual operating costs are met by advertising, the remainder coming through government appropriation and from broadcasting paid personal messages.

The operating schedule is 7–10 A.M., noon–2 P.M., and 6:30–11 P.M., Monday through Saturday; and from 7–10 P.M., Sundays. The station averages five hours of transmissions daily in English, four in Tongan, and an hour each week in Samoan and Fijian. Commercials are broadcast in all four languages, as well as in Hindustani. Another multilanguage feature is a weekly 2½-hour record-request session in four languages, excluding Hindi.

Most newscasts are in English, particularly those picked up from overseas networks. Only the early-morning BBC news report is translated into Tongan for rebroadcast. Other international newscasts include two from Australia and one from New Zealand. Fifteen minutes of local news is broadcast daily, the first segment at 1:15 P.M., the bulk of which is translated into Tongan for evening broadcast. A new, five-minute local newscast in English is scheduled for evening transmission. The program organizer indicated the station is flexible to some degree in that it also picks up VOA or American Samoa station WVUV, if better news coverage results.

In addition, the station broadcasts live commentaries on events such as the royal visit of Queen Elizabeth in March 1970, athletic events featuring visiting overseas teams, music concert contests, and other happenings of national interest. Wiring for live broadcasts has been installed at the Royal Tombs, the Malee (a grassy, park-like area adjoining the palace), Palace Grounds, and the rugby grounds, perhaps giving an indication where nationally important events are most likely to occur.

Live broadcasting of Legislative Assembly sessions is not done, though progress reports are included in regular local newscasts. Regular quarter-hour shows during the week are scheduled for talk on family planning, health, police matters, and other instructional subjects. Speeches by the head of government and other officials are broadcast, as are campaign talks. The day prior to a recent election, each of 12 candidates for seats in the Legislative Assembly was given five minutes to present his campaign platform, illustrating the extent and type of political programming on ZCO.

Both newspapers and the radio station have found themselves in conflict with controls and pressures by nobles and, it would appear, have made some adjustments to accommodate critics. The effect of parliamentary criticism on ZCO is difficult to assess. A study of the ZCO program schedule, however, makes it evident that public-opinion outlets are not built in. The station program organizer, a member of the New Zealand equivalent of the Peace Corps, noted that a public-opinion program would probably be "selected out" by the staff, because of implicit policies and a 1969 parliamentary debate discouraging expression of public opinion.

In 1974, the King of Tonga announced that Nippon Hoso Kyokai of Japan would undertake a feasibility study for the introduction of TV to the Kingdom (*ABU Newsletter* 1974, p. 12).

5.3.5 American Samoa

In American Samoa, a government radio station broadcast as a function of the Office of Information until 1973. Additionally, a television station, as an entity of the Department of Education, operates as an educational TV medium, although it does program entertainment and news during evening hours.

A problem for both stations, however, is one of continuity, since each successive station manager adapts operations to his own view of what should be accomplished. For example, one station manager felt, after two years on the job, he was still solidifying the station's position, earning the confidence of the people, and making it a Samoan station. A media director for the Department of Education, hence director of the department's KVZK-TV, conceded he worried about the unilateral nature of his programming judgment. Advisory committees, he said, have not worked.

Contributing to the problem both managers have in this regard is the great volume of programming available from the United States, coupled with the lack of direct local influence on programming policies. American Samoa, unlike Tonga and Western Samoa, does not have locally born managerial personnel or cabinet or broadcasting commission control. Likewise, in Fiji, the program organizer for Radio Fiji has been at his post for more than a decade and is subject to the locally appointed and oriented Fiji Broadcasting Commission.

Radio station WVUV, with a 10-kw. transmitter, is able to transmit to all areas of American Samoa, as well as send a strong signal to other Pacific areas. It was estimated in 1968 that about 2,000 receiving sets were scattered through the island group; in 1975, UNESCO listed the figure as only 1,000 (UNESCO 1975, p. 475). WVUV devotes roughly one-third of its 16½ hours of daily programming to Samoan language, the remainder to English-language shows, including two and three-quarter hours of news.

The weekday broadcast schedule of WVUV begins at 5 A.M. and ends at midnight; on Friday and Saturday, service is extended to 1 A.M. The Sunday schedule is 6:30 A.M. until midnight. During the day, there are four quarter-hour world news round-ups from United Press International, all in English. There are also 15 five-minute mixed report (local, international news, and weather), six in Samoan, the remainder in English. All newscasts feature a mixture of information from individual citizens, UPI, and the Office of Information. A teletype circuit connects the information office with the studios, 12 miles away.

WVUV has five on-the-air staff members, of whom only the station manager is not Samoan. A conscious effort has been made to exclude "public issue" material from programming, because of what was termed the time-manpower problem, preventing adequate time for airing both sides of the issues. The station manager, Vern Williams, in an interview said that because of "problems of language and time we are reluctant to get into that area," and added that WVUV would not be used as a unilateral sounding board.

One project Williams threw himself into with vigor was the recording of contemporary Samoan songs, which do have political content. Two or three evenings a week, he takes his recording equipment to villages throughout the islands, recording any interested group. The resultant tapes, hundreds of them, are played regularly on the air and, as staff time permits, are translated to enable announcers to provide English commentary. Recording of Samoan music and daily broadcasting of legislative debates, when both houses are in session, are part of an effort to Samoanize WVUV.

In June 1973, WVUV's management was taken over by Radio Samoa Inc., making the station the only privately operated broadcasting station in the South Pacific. The government is leasing the station to Radio Samoa which has a 20-year option to purchase it. The move takes WVUV from government control, offers merchants a badly needed advertising medium, and saves a great deal of government money previously spent on the station.

The television system operates on six channels, from 7:40 A.M.–2 P.M. on school days, to weekly televise 200 educational lessons prepared by the staff. For three hours in the evening, an education-entertainment mix is programmed, but "pure entertainment" accounts for no more than one hour each evening.

"Sesame Street," the Children's Television Workshop educational show aimed at preschool children, was brought to American Samoa in late 1969. It was at first thought a 6 P.M. time would be most desirable, adding an hour at the beginning of the broadcast evening. The point was raised, however, that this is a prayer hour in most villages, thus such a program would interfere with local customs. The station management avoided debate on the matter and scheduled "Sesame Street" for 5 P.M., with an off-the-air hour following, before the two channels, Samoan and English, begin their evening schedule.

Local news is broadcast at 7:40 P.M., in the appropriate language on both channels, followed by the half-hour American Broadcasting Company evening news. The videotape of this program is flown to American Samoa, usually arriving for broadcast three to five days after it originates.

In addition, a half-hour "News in Perspective," produced by the National Educational Television network, is broadcast every three weeks; a locally produced, agricultural home economics instructional program is telecast for 15 minutes weekly and a half-hour "Report to the People," originating in the government's Office of Samoan Information, twice weekly. In one recent year, the system presented seven one-hour debates among Samoan leaders, who discussed problems such as independence, tourism, and agriculture. The series was well received and stimulated considerable discussion.

In the early 1970s, the television staff increased its emphasis on news. Meanwhile, government sources pointed to what they considered successes in the number and quality of remote, delayed, and studio telecasts of local events. Among these was the remote coverage of the arrival of Apollo 17 astronauts in American Samoa, after their splashdown nearby.

The station director, however, has emphasized that the "television station" aspect of the operation has always been secondary to its educational purposes. This has been reflected in the evening programming, simultaneously on both channels, of programs such as "Misterroger's Neighborhood," a children's instructional show, and the preschooler's Samoan-language "Talofa Tamaiti." In some cases, programs which obviously are not watched by a high percentage of the local population are shown opposite high-interest programs for Samoans. For example, American Broadcasting Company's "Wide World of Sports" appears on the Samoan channel at the same time the NET social commentary program, "Mason Williams," is shown on the English station.

American Samoan television does not accept advertising, although it does contain short announcements regarding agricultural innovations, a "Keep Samoa Green" campaign, and traffic safety. In addition, there are no annual license fees for radio sets.

An estimated 2,000 (UNESCO 1975, p. 475) to 3,000 (*WRTH* 1974, p. 299) TV sets exist in American Samoa. TV officials feel enough sets are in use to give access to virtually everyone. It probably would be more realistic to say, however, that viewing is high on the western side of Tutuila Island, but low on the eastern coast. TV on the eastern side is limited because of a range of rugged mountains, which separates the region from Pago Pago, as well as the unavailability of electric power.

Television was launched in American Samoa as the core of a teaching system designed to accelerate the learning process for Samoans in an effort to narrow the educational gap between American Samoa and United States school systems. Started in 1964, American Samoan TV instituted what Wilbur Schramm called "a complete reconstruction of a school system" (UNESCO 1967a, p. 17).

Although a suggestion was made that evaluation of the project should wait a dozen years or more, American Samoan ETV had become the center of political storms. Considered the major achievement of Governor Rex Lee, the concept of total education through television came under fire from Lee's successor, Owen Aspinall, who successfully sought the resignation of the National Association of Educational Broadcasters (NAEB) as managing consultants. Aspinall's complaints hinged on the difficulties he found in persuading TV educators to institute his programs.

A newspaper story at the time reported that Aspinall wanted more preschool training, adult and vocational education, and training for the handicapped, and when NAEB would not cooperate with him, he began negotiating with the University of Southern California to take over the system. The governor also charged NAEB with failing to offer English training to high-school children, thus they were not properly equipped to benefit from a high-school education (*Sunday Star-Bulletin and Advertiser* 1969).

When John Haydon became governor in 1969, he appointed Dr. Richard Balch of the University of Hawaii as the director of education and contracted with the University of Hawaii for a number of educational services, including assistance in television. In March 1970, Haydon told a congressional committee that teaching of American Samoan children by television had been an "absolute failure" (*Sunday Star-Bulletin*, 4 March 1970). Haydon reiterated some of his predecessor's complaints about the English standards of high-school graduates and the need for greater emphasis on technical classes.

In June 1970, after five months as director of education, Balch was relieved of his duties because of what he called a "personality conflict," involving the "entire fabric" of the Samoan educational system. He expressed hope for the continued use of ETV in American Samoa, contending that TV can increase the rate of development of Samoan education and enable the people to judge whether "other so-called benefits of the Western world are worth the loss of identity" (*Sunday Star-Bulletin and Advertiser* 1970).

Tension between government officials and the Department of Education was not difficult to detect earlier in June 1970, when the field trip for this study was made. The primary complaint from government officials was that the education department wrote off those students in school before the new instructional systems were installed and instead concentrated on bringing the new generation of students through the accelerated program. Educators, on the other hand, echoed Schramm that tangible results could not be appreciably measured until the first products of the program made their way through the entire program in 1975, or later.

The tension has remained. In 1974, ETV, although still an important medium in American Samoa, was deemphasized. A typical first grader who spent 44% of his school time watching TV in 1970 now spends 17%. ETV is no longer used in the high schools. Still, 45 locally produced programs, some live, are broadcast to about 3,000 school children. Subjects range from oral English to Samoan culture (Lamb 1974, p. 4-A). Governor Haydon was still a subject of controversy in 1974. His governor's term ended in October 1974, after a TV censorship incident. Haydon personally stopped the showing of the NBC film "Born Innocent" because, as he argued, it included scenes of sexual perversion "absolutely unfit for viewing in American Samoa" (*PICN* 1975b, p. 10).

5.3.6 Other Island Groups

Solomon Islands. General interest broadcasting began in the Solomon Islands in 1947, when the government of that British protectorate launched a weekly local news and information broadcast over interisland and shipping frequencies to keep island "outstations" informed (Tudor 1968, p. 443; also see *WRTH* 1974, p. 185). Such services were provided by enthusiastic government officers on a part-time, voluntary basis, until 1959 when the government established the Solomon Islands Broadcasting Service. Daytime educational broadcasts began in 1966.

In 1974 the service was utilizing two short-wave and one medium-wave band and was listened to by about 60% of the population (*WRTH* 1974, p. 185). Broadcasts are in two languages, English and Pidgin, the latter to help in a situation where as many as ten local languages may be spoken on a single island.

General broadcasting, until recently, was limited to the 6:30–10:30 P.M. hours, except for occasional programming of afternoon sports events or morning religious shows. The output in 1974 was 80 hours weekly. Governmental information services provide daily local news in English and Pidgin.

The service is financed by receiver license fees and advertising revenue in an island group with 154,000 people, fewer than 1,300 of whom are European or Chinese.

Gilbert and Ellice Islands. On one medium-wave, 10-kw. transmitter, Radio Tarawa continues a service started in 1954, reaching an estimated 8,000 receiver sets in a population of 54,000 (UNESCO 1975, p. 487). Averaging five hours daily, six days weekly, Radio Tarawa broadcasts local programs in English, Gilbertese, and Ellice. A government department, Radio Tarawa is financed by government subsidy and advertising revenue.

Guam. Patterned after U.S. practices, Guam broadcasting is privately owned and operated by Pacific Broadcasting Corporation and includes radio station KUAM (10-kw. medium-wave) and KUAM-TV. Broadcasting in Guam was started in 1950 with the establishment of a 1-kw. station by the United States Armed Forces, designed for military personnel and their families. In 1954, the station became commercial and took the KUAM call letters. Operating with 10 kw., KUAM broadcasts 125 hours weekly in English, Chamorro, and various Filipino dialects (UNESCO 1975, p. 488; *WRTH* 1974, p. 181). Eighteen hours a week are locally produced programs.

KUAM-TV was launched in 1956, and a public educational channel began broadcasting in 1970 as KGTF. Currently, KUAM-TV broadcasts in color while KGTF remains with monochrome transmission. There are an estimated 85,000 radio receivers and 42,000 TV sets on Guam, serving a population of 80,000. All television programming on KUAM-TV is in English.

Cook Islands. In 1955, two staff members of the Cook Islands Department of Education set up a tape recorder for recording and transmission purposes in one of the department's storerooms. With this start, broadcasting a half hour each Wednesday afternoon to Rarotonga school teachers, Radio Cook Islands was born (Muir 1963, pp. 34–36).

The inauspicious start led to the construction of a new studio in 1963, and 68 hours of broadcast weekly over one 1-kw. medium-wave and one 10-kw. short-wave transmitter. Extensive facilities are necessary to reach the 24,000 people on 15 islands, scattered over 750,000 square miles of the south-central Pacific Ocean. Broadcasting is primarily in English, with some Maori. The service is financed by government subvention, advertising, and radio set fees (UNESCO 1975, p. 483).

Micronesia. With a budget of nearly $4 per capita, the broadcast division of the Public Affairs Department of the Trust Territory of the Pacific Islands operates six separate broadcast stations (five of 1 kw., one of 5 kw.) to reach 100,000 people on 90 scattered inhabited islands (*WRTH* 1974, p. 185).

Each station broadcasts 18 hours daily, with a mixture of local, territorial, and imported programming. The chief of the territory's broadcast division outlined in the early 1970s a seven-category program structure: local music of the districts, locally produced record shows, American Forces Radio and Television Service material, news, religious programs, interviews, and public-information shows, as well as programs received from the South Pacific Commission, VOA, and NZBC.

Local programming and translations are handled for nine Micronesian languages, as well as English (the only one common to all districts). All but three of the division's 72 employees are Micronesian, an indication that localization is proceeding. The division chief said the entire staff will be Micronesian by 1977 and that all stations will be operating at a minimum of 5 kw. power each by 1978. The station in Truk operates on 5 kw.; those on Majuro, Koror, Ponape,

Yap, and Saipan expect to increase power from their present 1 kw. to 5 kw. before 1978.

Political resolution of control problems is expected to be implemented by 1978, and a proposal has been made to the congress of Micronesia for means of determining broadcasting's future in these islands. The bill, introduced in early 1972, calls for appointment of a commission to recommend an independent Micronesian broadcasting system to a subsequent congress (Donchin 1972). An inclusive bill, it suggests seven principles under which the commission would operate in recommending a broadcast structure. The principles are based primarily on the definition of "independent," suggested by the bill's drafters to be "clear of United States government control and a system which is not restricted by government (Micronesian) interference, but guided by government policy, not used for personal or partisan political gain and not used solely for commercial profit" (Donchin 1971).

The first radio station was established in 1964 on Majuro in the Marshall Islands, and the first commercial TV channel on Saipan in 1970. Micronesian Broadcasting Corporation is headed by the same individual who is president of Pacific Broadcasting Corporation, operator of Guam's commercial broadcast facilities.

There are an estimated 3,000 television sets on Saipan (UNESCO 1975, p. 499), but the television operation is seen as very marginal.

A media consultant to the territorial government, who was involved in the first year of Saipan television, has called attention to "the total lack of preparation or thought of the impact this powerful medium would have on these people" in changing "family life styles and social expectations," as well as "undermining the confidence of the local people in essential services such as hospitals, and medical officers' styles of patient care" (Donchin 1972). For example, Micronesians have been known to confront doctors with, "Why can't you be like Marcus Welby?" In 1975, it was announced that a California university was initiating studies on the effects of TV on Micronesian children (*PICN*, February 1975, p. 6).

New Caledonia. Operated by Office de Radiodiffusion-Télévision Française, both radio and television services are available to residents of the French colony of New Caledonia. Radio Noumea originated early in the decade of the 1960s, and television was introduced in October 1965. New Caledonia appeared to be a starting point for broadcasting in the French Pacific colonies, with radio-TV services following to French Polynesia.

Radio Noumea broadcasts daily, over three 20-kw. and two 4-kw. transmitters, to the estimated 17,000 receivers among 95,000 New Caledonians (*WRTH* 1974, p. 182). Some 30 weekly hours of televised programming are available on three channels for the 6,000 set owners. Acceptable reception is no longer limited to only the area of Noumea, the capital city; two main transmitters and four repeaters make television available to about 58% of the population (UNESCO 1975, p. 491). Programming is largely in French, particularly in television. Vernacular programming is locally produced; most services in this French colony, however, remain almost exclusively the province of expatriates.

French Polynesia (Tahiti). Tahiti radio also started early in the 1960s; television followed in 1966 for the 130 islands of French Polynesia. Six transmitters (three each of 4 kw. and 20 kw.) are used (*WRTH* 1974, p. 185). Sixty-eight weekly hours of radio programming, mixed in French and Tahitian, and 24½ weekly hours of TV, almost exclusively in French, are broadcast. The French national broadcasting organization, Office de Radiodiffusion-Télévision Française, operates the systems in Tahiti, as in the case of New Caledonia. Daily television viewing is limited to the 6–9:30 P.M. time slot. Fare includes French programs (about 60% of total) and American shows syndicated through French sources, an example of the latter being the popular entertainment program, "Flipper."

New Hebrides. The year 1972 was a banner one for broadcasting in the New Hebrides islands, a group containing nearly 78,000 people under a joint condominium English-French government. A new 2-kw. transmitter, provided by the Australian government, went into operation by mid-year, providing the station with a transmitter of its own for the first time since it was launched in 1966. A second, reconditioned 1-kw. transmitter was also placed in operation in 1972. For six years, Radio Vila "borrowed" time from a marine transmitter, thus being limited to two hours and 15 minutes of daily programming – an hour at lunch time and 1¼ hours in the early evening. Early in its existence, Radio Vila received a surplus studio from Radio Noumea, but in 1975, the service moved into new studios.

Personnel training is also moving forward, with the importation of French and English technical and programming workers, as well as the training of a local junior producer by BBC in London.

There are an estimated 10,000 radio sets to receive the English, French, and Pidgin programs. Both French and British information offices provide news programming. The service launched a series of political familiarization programs in 1975 (*PICN,* February 1975, p. 15).

Niue. With six hours of weekly shows, following the general pattern of music and news, the Voice of Niue took to the air in August 1967 on a limited schedule – 6:30–8:30 or 9 P.M. on Monday, Wednesday, and Friday – followed for four months. In January 1968, however, a 6 P.M. starting time and broadcasts on Tuesday and Thursday evenings were added to bolster the schedule. Additional hours were added so that by 1969, Radio Niue (ZZN) broadcast 16 hours a week and by 1974, 23 hours (*WRTH* 1974, p. 183). Programming is in Niuen and English.

Radio receiver sales by the broadcast services office help finance the station, but the general cost of operation is borne by the government, since the station accepts no advertising (see *ABU Newsletter* 1974b; UNESCO 1975, p. 497).

Nauru. One of the newer independent republics is phosphate-rich Nauru, an eight-square-mile island that also has a new radio station. In 1965, the Australian government appropriated more than $57,500 to construct a station; the project was completed by the time of Nauru independence in 1968. The station was started in August 1968, under the auspices of the governmental Nauru Broadcasting Services. The .13-kw. transmitter is used to broadcast approximately 50 hours weekly in English and Nauruan, as well as to include relays of Radio Australia (*WRTH* 1974, p. 182; UNESCO 1975, p. 489).

There are also small radio stations on Lord Rowe Island (50-kw.), Norfolk Island (50-kw.), Phoenix Islands (250-w.), Wake Island (150-w.), Johnston Island (100-w.), and Midway Island (250-w.) (*WRTH* 1974, pp. 182—85).

Finally, in 1975, Easter Island, famed for its archeological finds, received its own television service. Among the world's most isolated people, the 1,600 Polynesian residents can see TV shows between 7 and 9:30 P.M. daily. The program was installed by the Chilean government, owners of the island, as part of a national integration program of all Chilean territories. Programs are being carefully selected; sex and violence ruled out. The islanders, who speak their own unique language, are now learning Spanish because many of the U.S. originated programs are in that language (Padilla 1975; *TV Guide*, 31 May 1975, p. A-2).

Part 3   Cross-System Functions

6. Specialized Program Services

6 Specialized Program Services

Societal institutions which have developed and utilized broadcasting operations both within and to Asia include, among others, governmental, religious, and educational agencies. This section will deal with the specialized program services of international, religious, and instructional broadcasters in Asia.

International broadcasting to Asia had its most rapid growth during the many conflict periods that have plagued the continent — World War II, nationalist struggles, Communist ideological and physical combat, the Soviet-Sino split, and the Indochina wars. The nature of split nations in Asia — the Koreas and the Chinas, and until recently, the Vietnams and the Pakistans — has also intensified the felt need to use international broadcasting.

From such a history have developed many international broadcasters to Asia, of which nine predominate. Chapter 6.1 analyzes these nine specific organizations, largely on an examination of the English-language program services of each station, since English is the chief language employed in transmissions to Asia. The author acknowledges that while the analyses may, therefore, not always lend themselves to generalization throughout all the language services offered by each station, certain of the points raised are likely to be matters of overall station policy or approach. A great deal of Donald Browne's data for this analysis resulted from interviews he conducted with international broadcasters during 1969–70 in Europe, Asia, and the United States, as well as from short-wave monitoring.

Also extremely active in specialized broadcasting are the numerous Western religious groups, mainly Christian, that have spread across Asia and the Pacific. Their activeness resulted to a great extent from the financial support received from their world-wide membership. Although Asia is a mixture of many key religions, of which Christianity is in the minority, Chapter 6.2 deals predominantly with Christian broadcasting projects. This is so because organized activities in broadcasting by other religions are almost nonexistent, even where they are the dominant or even the state religion. The authors identify "organized activities" as programs supported by budget, staff, and perhaps facilities to carry out a planned and scheduled activity according to a stated policy with specific goals and objectives. Constantino Bernardez received his data for this chapter principally from interviews, questionnaires, and observations.

Finally, specialized use of television programming for instructional purposes is covered in the chapter written by Leo Larkin. The focus of attention here is on the use of television for formal or in-school education in basic or core subjects, rather than supplementary programs. The geographical scope is made up of 18 Asian nations, including Bangladesh, Burma, Khmer Republic, Sri Lanka, Hong Kong, India, Indonesia, Japan, South Korea, Laos, Malaysia, Nepal, Pakistan, the Philippines, Singapore, South Vietnam, Taiwan, and Thailand. An ITV regional frame of reference has been established for the discussion, some characteristics of national programs described, and observations made on the status of ITV in one of the fast-developing areas of the world today.

The chapter is based partly on the author's experiences and in-country observations and discussions, but basic facts were obtained from a questionnaire study completed by most education ministers in the region.

In each case, the reader can find additional information on these specialized program services in some of the preceding chapters. An attempt has been made to avoid duplication of information. For more up-to-date treatments of educational television, and radio, see sections in national systems chapters.

6.1 International Broadcasting to Asia, *by Donald R. Browne*

6.1.1 Brief History

International broadcasting to and within Asia dates to the late 1920s, when Radio Holland initiated short-wave broadcasts in Dutch. These were intended to keep Dutch colonial servants and other Dutch citizens in the Netherlands East Indies in touch with life in the homeland. A similar service was established by France in 1931 and by England a year later. Japan established a permanent international broadcasting service in 1935, primarily to reach Japanese residing abroad; other Asian audiences – the Chinese excepted – were secondary targets until the outbreak of World War II in the Pacific, when Radio Tokyo greatly expanded its Asian, European, and Australian services. Nazi Germany began broadcasting to Asia in 1934, but the effort was a modest one until World War II.

The creation of Voice of America in February 1942 resulted in extensive English- and Asian-language services for the Asian hemisphere, the vast majority of the broadcasts intended primarily for foreign audiences. Radio Australia's

Donald R. Browne is Professor of Speech-Communication at the University of Minnesota. He served with USIA for three years, principally in Africa and conducted field research in Africa, Western and Eastern Europe, Asia, and the Pacific. He is the author of a series of articles on international broadcasting.

predecessor, Australia Calling, had come on the air in December 1939, but its purpose at first was to broadcast primarily to Australian servicemen overseas, as well as to the major Allied powers and to Germany. By May 1942, however, it had developed a Japanese-language service, and added Thai, Indonesian, and Mandarin three months later.

The next major change in international broadcasting in Asia came shortly after the end of World War II. A number of independence movements had already started in various Asian countries, and the Kuomintang and Communist forces in China were engaged in a civil war. The Soviet Union became involved in these situations through a number of means, among them international broadcasting.

Once the Chinese Communists had conquered the mainland, Radio Peking began to assume a dominant role in Asian international broadcasting; by 1951, it was broadcasting to Asia in English, five Chinese languages, and eight other Asian languages. The Chinese government on Taiwan had set up its own overseas service in 1950 and was responding with two international operations: one for the Chinese mainland, the other for the world in general.

As Communism became a major element in Asian political life in the early 1950s, two new types of American-supported operations came into being, presumably to help combat its influence: international religious and "publicly financed" anti-Communist broadcasting systems. The Far East Broadcasting Company began its overseas service from Manila in 1951, with a stated mission to carry out "a campaign for freedom based on the teachings and principles of the Lord Jesus Christ." The same year, Radio Free Asia, an allegedly public-supported (but in reality, CIA-financed) international broadcasting station operating out of San Francisco but transmitting from Manila, was founded. Its dual mission was to strengthen resistance within China to the new Communist government plus prevent overseas Chinese in Asia from "falling victim to Communist Chinese propaganda."

Over the following decade, most operations which had been active in 1951 increased their broadcasts to Asia, both in number of hours and languages. Radio Free Asia went off the air in 1953, not to be replaced by Radio of Free Asia until 1966, but BBC, VOA, Radio Peking, Radio Moscow, Voice of Free China, Radio Australia, and FEBC all expanded their scope. They were joined in 1952 by Radio Japan which, after a seven-year hiatus because of Allied occupation, resumed overseas broadcasting, albeit modestly at first. Several of the newly independent nations (India, Pakistan, and Indonesia), as well as Thailand, also began international broadcasting in the early 1950s but were slow to develop. Both South and North Korea introduced international broadcasting services (primarily for other Asian audiences, the Japanese, overseas Chinese, and overseas Koreans chief among them) in the late 1950s, as did North Vietnam, mainly for other parts of Indochina. Additionally, other international Christian broadcasting stations were established in South Korea and the Philippines.

In the early 1960s, when the Soviet Union and Communist China engaged in an ideological struggle, Radio Peking inaugurated a Russian-language service. By the end of 1965, broadcasts in Russian accounted for 10% of Radio Peking's total schedule. Radio Moscow expanded its Chinese service from just under two hours daily in February 1962 to nearly ten hours daily by April 1964. It was joined in this effort by Radio Peace and Progress, a "voice of Soviet public opinion" operated in close conjunction with Radio Moscow, in March 1967.

Also in the 1960s, conflict over Indochina left its impact on international broadcasting in Asia; several of the operations already mentioned added Thai, Laotian, Cambodian, and Vietnamese programs to their schedules. Numerous clandestine stations, some directed to the peasantry, others to members of the armed forces, have sprung up throughout Indochina, their primary support coming from the United States, North Vietnam, and the People's Republic of China. These stations continued to be active as of the early 1970s.

The majority of Asian nations now have their own international broadcasting operations, several of them playing host, willingly or unwillingly, to international broadcasting systems of other nations or organizations. Every Asian nation also has its own domestic broadcasting service, each with radio, many with television. The radio spectrum, both medium-wave and short-wave, has become increasingly crowded over the past decade, and certain of the more powerful nations who wish to reach the area via radio — notably the United States and the People's Republic of China — have increased their transmitter power. But the increasing competition has not yet caused any of the larger international broadcasters to materially decrease their own individual broadcasts to the area; all apparently continue to feel that Asia is strategically important and that international radio broadcasting remains a viable means of reaching that area.

6.1.2 Radio Japan

Radio Japan's 22 language services and multidirectional transmissions are designed to bring it a world-wide audience, but the major share of its listener mail comes from Asia and Oceania, and its largest single bloc of correspondents, in terms of "occupation," is made up of students. Radio Japan emphasizes an informational format in its General Service which broadcasts 24 hours daily, with roughly equal amounts of Japanese and English each hour. The vast majority of broadcast time in this service is given over to news and commentary, plus occasional lessons in spoken Japanese and programs on Japanese culture. The various regional services, also in 22 languages, are more evenly balanced in this respect, and about 10% of total airtime is devoted to music, which does not appear as a separate category in the General Service.

Radio Japan has several program priorities, some varying from year to year, others relatively constant. In 1970, they were stated as: (1) active promotion of programming centered on news and information; (2) the world-wide publicity of the Japan World Exposition 1970, along with programs designed to clarify Japan's culture, arts, and sciences; (3) designing of programs to foster a deeper understanding among and about Asians and Asia; (4) consolidation and improvement of Japanese-language lessons to meet rising interest in the language by overseas people; (5) creation of programs to clarify the actual state of the Japanese economy and industries so as to contribute toward promotion of trade; and (6) expansion of sports and other programs desired by overseas Japanese (*NHK Handbook* 1970, pp. 91–92).

The second of these priorities is of limited duration, but the other five have been part of the operation for several years. It is difficult to assess these priorities in order of their importance, but the final one seems to have been of consistently high importance throughout Radio Japan's (and, for that matter, Radio Tokyo's) existence. The third priority, the promotion of greater understanding among and about Asians and Asia, is of more recent origin, appearing to have resulted from Japan's recent moves away from a "low profile society" policy, at least with respect to the rest of Asia.

In striving to fulfill these aims, Radio Japan has placed its heaviest emphasis on news and commentary, as stated above; in recent years, this category has accounted for approximately 65% of the total broadcast schedule. Chief emphasis is placed on coverage of domestic developments in Japan, particularly those of government, political and economic relationships between Japan and other Asian nations, and Asian affairs with which Japan may or may not be connected. Radio Japan officials feel the emphasis on Asia will display Japan's overall interest in its neighbors, as well as provide non-Asian nations with a means by which Asia might be better understood.

Newscasts themselves are quite detailed, although they very rarely feature on-the-spot reporting. Those in English are clearly and idiomatically written, and sentence structure is reasonably easy to follow. Staff members are keenly aware of a need to maintain simplicity of style, both as a reaction against the more complex Japanese literary style and as a recognition of the difficulties posed by short-wave transmission. They also expect that their programs will be received by an audience understanding English as a second language.

Radio Japan's greatest overall attraction in categories other than news lies in the rising curiosity and admiration of foreign listeners regarding the Japanese "economic miracle" in the 1960s, coupled with a like curiosity and admiration concerning traditional Japanese culture. Both interests are served to a modest degree by present Radio Japan programming, but neither is served very well in terms of specifically labeled, regularly scheduled programs. Music is an exception to this, and there have been several excellent series on Japanese political and cultural history, e.g , a series entitled "Japan 100 Years," which dealt with the Meiji Restoration and its aftermath. Also, Radio Japan has for several years carried a weekly "broadcast portrait" of an average Japanese citizen, "One in a Hundred Million," as well as items about economic development, cultural affairs, and social change carried in newscasts, commentaries, and as parts of such series as "Tokyo Report" and "Radio Japan Journal." Nevertheless, the overall schedule definitely favors straightforward informational programming, with a relatively minor portion devoted to extended and continuous presentation of material on culture and economic development.

Somewhat surprisingly, Radio Japan appears to be a bit reluctant to acknowledge the predominance of young people in its audience. Given the particular interest Asians display in Japan, it would appear to be sound strategy for Radio Japan to shift its emphasis more in their direction, through increased language instruction and musical request programs.

A second audience category of key importance to Japan's national interests, but rather poorly served by Radio Japan broadcasts, includes people in business, trade, and industry. Despite Japan's role as a major trading power, Radio Japan devotes but one 15-minute program weekly (translated into several languages and rebroadcast frequently) to this subject. Radio Japan officials acknowledge the potential importance of such broadcasts but feel they cannot really remedy the situation, because their tight budget leaves little money available for such highly specialized, costly programming. They also fear that Japanese businesses and industries might think the station was being unfair by singling out specific products, brands, and services. Given the alleged influencing power of Japanese business and industry on government, and the responsiveness of Japanese mass media to "establishment" pressures, this may be a justifiable reaction. A less risky approach for this particular audience would be to place increased emphasis on Japanese-language lessons, for, as with students, Asian businessmen are particularly interested in acquiring some degree of skill in the Japanese language.

6.1.3   The Voice of Free China

Taiwan's Voice of Free China (VOFC) is one of the more modest international broadcasting stations in terms of actual time on the air (87 hours daily in the 1970s), physical coverage (its signals omit most of North and South America, as well as much of Europe), number of languages and dialects employed (13), and range of program categories covered. Fifteen short- and medium-wave frequencies were used for this service in 1971. A 1,000-kw. short-wave transmitter was scheduled for 1976.

According to various analyses of listener mail conducted by VOFC, almost 90% of the station's correspondents live in Asia and Oceania; over 80% are overseas Chinese and perhaps 65–70% students and young people. The VOFC program schedule takes all of this into account, at least to some degree; it features traditional and popular Chinese music, information about economic and cultural developments on Taiwan, press summaries from newspapers published on the island, a weekly program of news and information on mainland China developments, and hourly newscasts and commentaries. The predominant attention given to official pronouncements and visits of various Republic of China government officials in newscasts and commentaries probably discourage continued listening by non-Chinese. The almost-daily criticism of the Peking regime in these same broadcasts might well have a like effect at the same time possibly alienating those overseas Chinese who would rather see the two Chinas resolve their differences.

Other VOFC programs place heavy emphasis on the Republic of China role as guardian of traditional Chinese culture, featuring Chinese classical music, Peking opera, and reports on cultural events. VOFC officials feel such shows are perhaps their strongest propaganda selling point. Occasionally, the cultural shows are coupled with reminders that the mainland government has largely replaced traditional Chinese culture with a hybrid one, but more often these programs are allowed to speak for themselves.

Along with VOA and Radio Peking, VOFC has the rather unusual distinction of offering no instruction in its national language, a natural concomitant of the station's desire to reach overseas Chinese first and foremost and other listeners only secondarily. Even English-language broadcasts are seen by VOFC staff members as intended primarily for English-speaking, second- and third-generation overseas Chinese. This is not to say that VOFC has no interest in reaching non-Chinese listeners; that interest, however, appears to be minor.

The relative success of VOFC (and, for that matter, of Radio Peking) in reaching the overseas Chinese can be assessed by a careful analysis of listener mail; their success in putting across their respective ideological messages is another matter altogether. A questionnaire survey conducted in 1965 among 166 overseas Chinese living in Japan, revealed that 25% of the sample cited "mainland newspapers, magazines and broadcasts" as a principal source of information about the People's Republic of China, while 45% made a like observation regarding "Taiwan newspapers, magazines and broadcasts." While slightly over half the sample favored the government on Taiwan, and about a fourth the mainland government, 40% of the sample felt that the two sides should negotiate their differences — an option not presented in either Radio Peking or VOFC broadcasts (Chu 1967, pp. 10, 15, 19, 31).

In addition to VOFC, the Voice of Justice (VOJ), under contract with the Commission for Overseas Affairs, maintains a limited service in Cantonese for overseas Chinese of Southeast Asia. Chiefly an intelligence and psychological warfare station, VOJ beams to the People's Republic of China as well.

Another specialized service intended for listeners in the People's Republic is operative through the Central Radio Station of the Broadcasting Corporation of China. In 1972, 13 medium-wave and 21 short-wave transmitters of a combined power of 2,281.5 kw. were used for this purpose. The government subsidizes the operation by transferring nearly all set-license revenue to the station. Broadcasting in eight Chinese dialects and Russian, among other languages, for some 44½ hours per day, it emphasizes information about life in Taiwan and the People's Republic of China.

News and commentaries occupy about 40% of its broadcast day, cultural broadcasts about 30%. Many of its programs are aimed at specific groups: university students, Communist Party cadres, military officers. A well-staffed radio monitoring service helps the station follow developments on the mainland, as these are reported by the New China News Agency, Radio Peking, and various provincialsand local radio stations. Certain broadcasts are designed to encourage defections and to aid resistance efforts. Feedback from the target audiences is extremely limited — perhaps 100–200 letters yearly — and indicates that, of those whose identity can be discerned, roughly 55% are youth and intellectuals, over 25% are government and party officials, and about 8% are workers and peasants. The feedback comes from most parts of continental China. BCC reports that 53.7% of the letters emanate from coastal provinces in the southeast, 3.75% from the northeast, 12.5% from north China, 3.15% from northwest China, 8.15% from southwest China, 11.5% from central China, and the remaining 7.5% are untraceable (*Broadcasting Corporation of China* 1972).

To counter the messages of Radio Peking, BCC has set up a special network to overshadow every audible station. This is accomplished by developing a counter station for each Communist outlet and by using the same wave length. Twelve stations with 44 medium-wave transmitters have been established to carry out this counterpropaganda scheme.

Certain military radio stations and one commercial broadcaster, the Voice of Righteousness, also provide specialized services for the mainland, intended primarily to reach the military on the one hand, intellectuals and party cadre on the other. Although nominally independent of the Central Broadcasting Station, each uses the basic news service employed by CBS.

A unique service is Voice of Kuang Hwa (VOKH), which carries on intensive psychological warfare from the offshore islands, Quemoy and Matsu. The station beams intimate messages to Mao's coast guard, only a few miles from the studios (Peng 1971, p. 129).

Whether VOFC would do well to consider expanding its mission to the level of making a wholehearted attempt to reach non-Chinese listeners is a moot point. The Republic of China is not a major trading power on a world-wide scale nor is it active in terms of purely Asian trade as are Japan and Australia. The major advantage of reaching a larger non-Chinese audience would be to win it over to Taiwan's point of view in her struggle with the People's Republic of China. This, in fact, appears to be a major goal in the present broadcasts, but it is blunted somewhat by overuse of detail, overformal sentence structure and vocabulary, and choice of specific subjects and items which are probably of little or no interest to non-Chinese listeners. This, coupled with the weakness of the VOFC broadcast signal, particularly outside Asia and Oceania (but to some extent within, particularly in South Asia), would seem to bar the station from making any substantial increases in its non-Chinese audience.

6.1.4 Radio Peking

Radio Peking started its broadcasting in six languages, seven hours a day, on 10 April 1950. At the end of 1968, its programs were broadcast in 33 foreign languages (the majority Asian) and five Chinese dialects for a total of 1,720 hours per week. The country receiving the most attention from Radio Peking is the Soviet Union. At peak hours, Radio Peking puts into operation more than 40 different transmitters with power outputs up to 240,000-w.

In terms of program variety, however, Radio Peking offers less to choose from than any other international broadcasting organization covered in this study. There is a predominant emphasis on news and talks, perhaps as much as 90% in the English-language services, and the quotations of Chairman Mao are read and repeated frequently. Music is available, often as three- to five-minute fillers, but most is in the form of revolutionary songs, and not traditional Chinese folk music or Peking opera, both of which were popular before the Cultural Revolution (Wood 1969, p. 34).

There appears to be an almost total lack of attempt to "humanize" the People's Republic of China either through programs dealing with average citizens or reports on cultural or intellectual life in major cities. Heroic deeds, however, performed by individuals "armed with the thought of Mao Tse-tung" are often mentioned. These humanistic categories are not altogether absent in Communist Chinese propaganda; *China Reconstructs* features them quite prominently. But Radio Peking appears to have a different mission, i.e., the reinforcement of the committed listener, not the conversion of uncommitted or skeptical ones. Virtually all international broadcasting stations have this as a goal, but it is seldom the only or even the primary goal.

Newscast items are generally long, highly detailed, and filled with such extended constructions as "unity and solidarity with China, North Korea, Indochina and other parts of the world will be strengthened in order to wage an unflagging struggle against the U.S.-Japanese reactionaries." This style, in fact, is typical of nearly all Radio Peking broadcasts (see Mackerras and Hunter 1967, p. 51).

Also, because of ideological disputes between Moscow and Peking in recent years, Radio Peking has devoted considerable time to presenting lengthy broadcast talks on such topics as "The True Meaning of Leninism," in which detailed comparisons have been made between statements from Lenin's *Collected Works* and statements of Soviet officials. These programs, turning as they often do on certain interpretations of these statements and frequently lasting for 40–45 minutes, would appear to be destined for audiences familiar with the works in question and in a good position to discuss or debate them with others.

Finally, the slogan-like statements with which Radio Peking's broadcasts abound, as well as its easily identified rhetorical style, have made it possible to trace some uses to which the broadcasts are put by its listeners. According to several Asian and American observers interviewed by the author, chiefly in Tokyo, Taipei, and Hong Kong, many recent demonstrations held by students and worker groups in Asia, particularly in Manila and Tokyo, have featured banners bearing slogans very similar or identical to those being broadcast by Radio Peking at that time. Yet another piece of evidence suggests that Radio Peking conceives of a very specific audience with specific uses for these broadcasts: in March 1967, the station began broadcasting a certain portion of its Russian-language service by reversed (i.e., played backwards) tapes. This was seen by United States and British authorities as a means of combatting jamming by the Russians, since the resultant broadcasts would be relative gibberish and would probably pass through unjammed (as has, in fact, been the case) (*China Topics* 1968, p. 8). In order for such broadcasting to be effective, however, an audience would have to know what to expect, and be prepared to tape the programs and play them back for the edification and guidance of themselves and their friends.

It seems clear, then, that Radio Peking thinks of its audience largely as "propagators of the faith," who must be supplied with information for their own sustenance and for use as "ammunition" in their efforts to convert others. The station also appears to be attempting to reach and influence those individuals who, while generally "Marxist-Leninist," have not chosen sides in the Moscow-Peking dispute.

Radio Peking also operates a number of highly specialized services for listeners in Thailand, Malaysia, and Taiwan, which, in contrast with most of the broadcast output of the station, attempt to report on local conditions in these areas and foment rebellion. For example, an anthropologist who lived among Meo folk in northeast Thailand told this author some Radio Peking broadcasts clumsily tried to create dissatisfaction among Meo women regarding their lot in life. The broadcasts were ineffective because the Meo men controlled the radio sets and since Meo women were already quite emancipated (see also Story 1971). Radio Peking services to Taiwan and the offshore islands of Quemoy and Matsu represent a major enterprise: over 300 hours per week as of March 1969, the last date for which figures were available. Finally, the overseas Chinese constitute a somewhat-specialized target audience, although here, in contrast with the approach followed by VOFC, the accent is placed on scientific, technological, and governmental achievements, and on statements and illustrations of the support of the people for their government. Little is said about culture or everyday life on the mainland. It is quite possible that the overseas Chinese audience is not as important to Radio Peking as it is to VOFC (see Wilson 1967, pp. 103–5; Fitzgerald 1969, pp 103–26).

6.1.5 Radio Australia

Its modest number of languages, only eight, would appear to disqualify Radio Australia from the lists of major international broadcasters active in Asia, but among these languages is a 24-hour daily service in English. Additionally, the station's impressive transmission system gives it generally good to excellent world-wide coverage.

The Radio Australia audience, as revealed through listener mail, is predominantly Asian (in fact 80% so) and young. Well over half of this percentage consists of Indonesians, probably as a direct result of the fact that the station broadcasts nine hours a day in Indonesian. There appears to have been a conscious attempt to shape the program schedule to attract this audience;

music, especially Chinese and Western popular songs, occupies from 20—80% of any given broadcast hour, much of it hosted by an identifiable personality presumably appealing to younger listeners. There are also "English by Radio" broadcasts in Indonesian, Thai, and Vietnamese, and again, the major share of the audience for these programs is presumed by Radio Australia to consist of young people, although teachers, businessmen, tradesmen, and minor government officials are also prevalent, according to analyses of listener mail.

There is a more general audience as well, probably well-educated, somewhat older, perhaps more Western than Asian, which the station attempts to attract through programs about Australian culture and economic strength. While such programs may possibly serve to attract much-sought-after immigrants, they may do at least as much to help dispel the image of the "Aussie" as a rough, uncultured individual (see Horne 1968).

Finally, some programs are geared to a small, highly specialized audience of overseas Australians, made up of Australian soldiers and sailors, businessmen, and government officials scattered around the globe, as well as Australian scientific teams in Antarctica.

Radio Australia schedules include a wide variety of program types, with music and news as leading categories, but with religion, sports, business, culture, and history available, as well. Although the accent is mainly on Australian developments, several programs do feature music of other lands, e.g., Indian folk and Chinese popular music. In addition, there is a weekly "Report to Asia" made up of items concerning Asians and Asian affairs. Most news broadcasts carry at least one or two items regarding other Asian nations, and the Indonesian service newscasts give extensive coverage to Indonesian domestic developments. For the most part, however, newscasts and commentaries deal largely with major international and Australian events, and certain newscasts consist of nothing but the latter.

In sum, Radio Australia seems to be reaching for a number of different audiences. The rationale for this can probably be found in Australian domestic and foreign policy, that is, attracting immigrants and investors while keeping Australians abroad in touch with the homeland, and also in a feeling on the part of Radio Australia that young listeners should be well served. If any audience groups are underserved by the station, they are probably the businessmen dealing in Australian-Asian trade, and a more vaguely defined group of internationally minded Asian adults, particularly teachers and government officials. Both groups are important to Australian national interests as the nation seeks closer economic and political ties with Asia. Radio Australia, like Radio Japan, gives minimal emphasis to specific programs on business, its rationale being much the same as that of Radio Japan: too much risk of objections from individual manufacturers, should a competitor receive featured treatment. Radio Australia staff, citing the lengths to which they are compelled to go in order to avoid mentioning brand names, said that on one occasion, a news item was reworded to read, "a popular, six-cylinder, four-door Australian car," instead of the brand name, "Holden."

Whether the internationally minded Asian adult looks to Radio Australia to provide fare dealing expressly with Asia is a moot point, but it seems in Australia's national interest to do so, given its increased involvement in Asian affairs. The principal obstacle to such a schedule expansion or alteration perhaps resides in the "White Australia" concept; Asians are well aware of the severe limits placed on Asian immigration to Australia. Given this state of affairs, Radio Australia can hardly place much greater emphasis on series or special features highlighting Australian interest in Asian affairs; the discrepancy will be quite evident. But a modest increase in such broadcasts seems both reasonable and wise, and the growing, visible Asian presence in Australia — in business, industry, trade schools, universities, and tourism — guarantees plenty of interesting raw material for broadcast purposes, some of which is currently used, but in a random fashion.

6.1.6 Radio Moscow

A large number of language services (73 as of 1974) and an extremely powerful and well-located transmitter system bring Radio Moscow a world-wide audience. There are few areas where its signal cannot be heard quite clearly on at least one or two days of the average week. The station broadcasts more hours daily to Asia than to any other geographical area, but a closer examination of Radio Moscow's broadcast schedule and interviews with staff members reveal that it has two chief target areas in mind, India and the People's Republic of China. It broadcasts daily to India in English and 12–14 Indian languages, and to China for more than 20 hours daily in Mandarin. In addition, Radio Peace and Progress broadcasts to the same area in Mandarin, Cantonese, and the Shanghai dialect; the Radio Moscow/Radio Peace and Progress broadcasts in Mandarin combined in sequential fashion (often employing the same frequencies) to provide a 24-hour daily service to China. Other Asian nations, particularly Japan, Indonesia, and Vietnam, also receive three to four hours daily of broadcasts in their native languages, and there are four and a half hours of daily English broadcasts to these regions.

The English-language Asian Service of Radio Moscow provides its listeners with a considerable variety of popular and folk music (usually Russian, sometimes by listener request), features on youth, science, literature, a "listener's mailbag," "Russian by Radio," and news and commentary, the latter occupying 30–40% of the average broadcast hour. The overall structure of the schedule, however, and style of language employed seem to limit the effectiveness of these broadcasts.

Unlike most other major international broadcasters, Radio Moscow does not transmit in continuous blocs of English; rather, broadcasts are broken into half-hour parcels, spaced anywhere from 30 minutes to 3½ hours apart. Furthermore, the style of English employed, as well as manner of delivery, tends to be quite formal, although not as formal as that of Radio Peking. The formality is apparently deliberate, going along with basic Soviet foreign policy objectives in Asia: to support and encourage formation of legitimate organizations which will seek and maintain close ties with the Soviet Union; and to combat "false" Communist ideology promulgated by the People's Republic of China and her followers. Because of the backgrounds of those listeners in Asia best equipped to carry out these objectives (often intelligent, currently or formerly with access to power), the decision has apparently been made to use radio to sustain them in the "faith" and provide arguments to be employed in convincing others. This bears a strong similarity to the Radio Peking approach and would likewise help to account for the fractionalization of the broadcast schedule and the language formality.

Radio Moscow's English-language service to Asia, however, is not entirely confined to this approach, furnishing material of interest to those who are simply curious about Russia, or wish to learn the Russian language. While this group may be secondary in importance, it is nonetheless important, since it very likely contains many young people. The weekly half-hour feature, "Youth Program," which presents interviews with Soviet and foreign students, Komsomol members and others, is specifically designed for this young audience, often emphasizing the more human side of student life. But it also covers official reaction to major national and international affairs, often through quotations from the major youth-organization newspaper, *Komsomolskaya Pravda.*

Listeners with specific interests in business and economic concerns are less. well served by Radio Moscow, although the weekly half-hour program, "Science and Engineering," often contains industrial development reports.

Few of the feature programs prepared by the station, it should be noted, are intended for specific audiences in specific geographical areas; "Youth Program" and "Science and Engineering" are broadcast over most of Radio Moscow's regional services. Thus, there is little attempt, aside from a weekly "Listeners' Mailbag" and some items for the news and commentary broadcasts, to cater to Asian interests and sensibilities.

6.1.7 BBC External Services

As is the case with several other international stations covered in this study, BBC provides a 24-hour-a-day broadcast service in English (World Service), as well as regional services in English to Europe, Africa, and the Caribbean. Its transmitters, located in Great Britain, West Berlin, the mid-Atlantic, the Mediterranean, the Persian Gulf, and Singapore, give it good to excellent world-wide coverage. Its staff members have a very clear notion of the types of audiences to be reached: opinion leaders (especially government officials, teachers, and journalists), college and university students, and businessmen. Audience research, these same staff members claim, indicates that the station is indeed successful in reaching these groups.

Although listeners in Asia are not the target of the English-language regional services, BBC does provide the aforementioned World Service, which, thanks to transmitters in the Persian Gulf and Singapore, is clearly audible throughout most of Asia. It also provides, through the World Service, daily 15-minute programs in the "English by Radio" series; this particular set of programs is designed specifically for Asian listeners. Most major Asian languages are also employed in BBC transmissions to the area, broadcast time for several of them having increased sharply over the past decade.

In certain parts of Asia, BBC has an advantage shared by no other major international broadcaster active in the region: India, Pakistan, Bangladesh, Burma, Sri Lanka, Malaysia, and Singapore all, at one time or another, have been under British rule and as a consequence have been exposed to British culture. Numerous citizens of these nations, as well as more modest numbers of Indonesians, Japanese, and Chinese, have studied in British universities. These nations and individuals are assumed to have a greater than normal interest in maintaining some of their ties with Great Britain, and the BBC forms a principal means of doing so.

In fact, the greater portion of the BBC World Service broadcast schedule is essentially domestic in nature; most of it concerns life and events in Great Britain, and a fair share is taken directly from BBC's domestic radio services. Approximately one-half to three-quarters of any given hour is devoted to entertainment and culture. Much of this fare is intended for a general overseas audience, albeit one with a fair speaking knowledge of English and at least a rudimentary acquaintance with contemporary life in Britain. Certain radio dramas, quiz shows, and talks demand a superior command of English and even occasional knowledge of slang and dialects. Relatively few Asians seem equipped to follow such programs, several of which are broadcast daily. Unlike Radio Japan and Radio Australia, BBC makes very little attempt to gain the favor of its Asian audiences by featuring programs likely to be of exclusive interest to them.

This does not mean that Asian music is never played on BBC, or that newscasts at hours most favorable for reception in Asia do not contain a somewhat larger proportion of items of particular interest to Asian listeners. There is nothing, however, in the BBC schedule comparable to Radio Japan's "Asian News" or Radio Australia's "Indian Film Music." The "English by Radio" service offers a weekly "Stories from Asia" segment, but this is designed to serve as a teaching aid. In fact, certain BBC staff members feel that World Service broadcasts will be more credible to Asian and other audiences because of this avoidance of any display of special interest in a given area. These same individuals point to reports concerning the high credibility in Asia of BBC news on the Indochina situation. This, they feel, is the result of Great Britain's apparent lack of direct involvement in Indochina.

There is no doubt that, compared to other international broadcasting stations, the BBC World Service offers the greatest diversity of programming. Much of this diversity, however, comes in forms and styles understandable and useful only to listeners whose command of English and understanding of British life are quite advanced; such listeners are far fewer in Southeast and East Asia than they are in South Asia.

Young people probably find less programming of specific interest to them in the BBC World Service schedule than in those of Radio Australia or Voice of America. There are popular music shows several times daily, but relatively little of the music is provided by request. Also, there are no specifically labeled programs for young people, as is the case with most other international services. High school and university students may be attracted by the "English by Radio" series, but the vocabulary and dramatic sketches employed also suit older listeners perfectly well. Certain popular music programs are hosted by personalities, some of whom are youth-oriented. A modest growth in this form of programming has developed over the past several years; apparently this has come about in response to a self-perceived need to become more human *vis-a-vis* several categories of listeners, not just young people.

Far better served by the BBC World Service than by other international broadcasters are individuals interested in science and business. BBC provides several different features weekly in each of these subjects, prepared explicitly for overseas audiences. Furthermore, these features are primarily intended for interested laymen; the weekly feature "New Ideas," for example, encourages listeners to purchase new British products discussed on the program. Other business and science features have a similar goal, although the line of approach is usually more indirect (*BBC Record* 1971, p. 7). Great Britain has strong trade ties with many Asian nations, and BBC staff members report there is much specific evidence indicating that business features are particularly successful in reaching and influencing Asian target audiences.

Thanks to the comprehensive coverage of world events available through BBC newscasts and the daily "Correspondents Reports," as well as to Great Britain's reduced role as an Asian and world power, BBC today has an excellent reputation for credibility, particularly among government officials, journalists, and university students. This, in turn, frequently makes BBC the benchmark by which other international stations are judged. Whether the credibility factor for informational broadcasts has any carryover effect on other types of programming may be debatable, but it is certainly a positive influence, if it is any influence at all.

6.1.8   Radio Cairo

In theory, Radio Cairo should be a major force in international broadcasting to Asia. Several Asian nations have large Muslim populations, therefore sharing cultural-linguistic-religious traditions with Egypt. In practice, however, Asia appears to be largely disregarded by the station. As of mid-1970, there was one daily English-language broadcast to Asia, lasting 75 minutes, available on one frequency only, and that in the 16-meter band, which few inexpensive short-wave receivers can pick up. Additionally, there were broadcasts in ten Asian languages, plus French and Arabic, most of them for one hour daily, and most of them for audiences in South Asia; only Malay, Thai, and Indonesian were used in ethnic language broadcasts to Southeast or East Asia.

Despite its relative brevity, the English-language Asian service of Radio Cairo is varied, consisting of news, commentary, a weekly press review, language lessons at several levels of difficulty, a listeners' mailbag, music (sometimes Indian or Malaysian in addition to Arabic) and, on Friday, readings from the Koran. Radio Cairo officials claim they had even more variety in the period before the 1967 Mideast War, including a weekly program entitled "My Friends," a personalized picture of an average Egyptian's life. The war, however, forced the cancellation of this program because of its expense and because of pressure from "top-level government officials" to place more emphasis on the war itself.

These same Radio Cairo staff members cite the war as the main barrier to increased audience research. The more formal types of survey research and audience mail analysis are not employed by Radio Cairo. Staff members claim they conduct periodic reviews of mail received, more to discover specific comments on technical quality and program content than to determine how much mail was received from whom and where. The staff also said that the greater share of mail received comes from Arabs residing in Asia, and that, although they are not the primary target audience (government officials and students are), they are important partly because they do write in to the station.

An Asian listener hearing Radio Cairo would probably be impressed by the variety of programs, although their brevity — few run more than 15 minutes — might be annoying. The "Arabic by Radio" lessons are very carefully prepared and can be extremely useful to Asians studying the language, as can the weekly listeners' mailbag program which solicits questions on Arabic-language structure and grammar. Also, the occasional Asian music may flatter some listeners. News broadcasts, however, become a bit monotonous, concentrating on the Mideast conflict and governmental pronouncements regarding purely Egyptian matters in which it is questionable whether many Asian listeners have a great interest.

Two other factors limit Radio Cairo's appeal: the quality of the broadcast signal and that of program production. The author's attempts to monitor Radio Cairo in East and Southeast Asia were fruitless. Program quality is also a problem, station officials said, in that they sometimes are forced to rely upon relative amateurs for many of their specialized language services. Since many of these individuals are recruited from universities and irredentist groups located in Cairo, they form an uncertain commodity in that they may leave the country with little advance notice, placing Radio Cairo in the embarrassing position of having to discontinue an entire language service until new talent is found. This has become a very real problem since the advent of the Mideast confict, in that fewer foreign students are attending Cairo universities, while many who were in attendance have returned home.

6.1.9 Voice of America

VOA, in common with Radio Australia, Radio Japan, and BBC, provides an

English-language service on a 24-hour-a-day global basis; it also resembles BBC in that it has a number of foreign transmitter locations in Europe, Africa, and Asia, enabling it to reach audiences, and in that it offers a very wide range of programs.

Unlike BBC, very few VOA programs emanate from domestic sources, partly because American radio stations offer less programming variety and also because fewer countries have been under American rule, thus there is less chance of reaching many listeners who desire to maintain a link with their "second homeland."

If VOA officials were to decide that such an audience constitutes a major target group, they nevertheless can assume this audience is already being served fairly well by the Armed Forces Radio and Television Network and many radio stations located at U.S. Armed Forces installations. AFRTS provides a 24-hour-a-day information service through short-wave to virtually all points on the globe. There are also 7 U.S. armed forces stations in Japan; 19 in South Korea; at least 7 in South Vietnam before 1975; 14 in Thailand; 6 in the Philippines; and 3 in the Republic of China (Browne 1971, pp. 31–48).

This is not to say that VOA does not use American radio productions at all. It frequently inserts excerpts from network interview shows, e.g., "Meet the Press" and "Issues and Answers," into its own news shows and the daily "Breakfast Show." Such excerpts are usually broadcast to provide listeners with a wider range of views, and, together with frequent presentations of editorial opinion from various American newspapers, allow VOA to act as more than official spokesman for the United States government.

There is reason to believe that the VOA audience in Asia may have an intense interest in learning more about the United States through the programs. This interest may even match that of Asian audiences listening to the BBC. It is not, however, based on a need to preserve cultural/intellectual ties, but much more likely, on Asian perceptions of the United States as a major influence in Asia, through American military, economic, and diplomatic activity. Along with this activity has come an increased American physical presence in Asia, including soldiers, technicians, Peace Corps volunteers, and tourists, as well as American TV programs and movies.

The Voice of America's major attraction in this setting is that it provides relatively complete, continuous, timely coverage of events taking place in the United States, as well as American reaction, official and unofficial, to events in other parts of the world. The VOA audience may in fact be well enough informed about United States life and institutions to recognize and appreciate VOA attempts to present a range of opinions on various matters, but also to attend to the rather substantial segment, roughly 20%, of the broadcast schedule given over to features and talks on American culture, science, and society.

A further examination of the VOA English-language schedule reveals that about one-third of it is devoted to music (principally American popular music, but with a sizable proportion of jazz, and a modest share of classical music), while the remaining 45% is taken up by news, commentary, and opinion roundups, usually taken from newspaper editorials. A heavy emphasis is placed on American events, while no "Asian News" or "Asian Music" programs exist. News concerning Asia is featured during those times of day when Asia is the prime target of VOA transmissions, but only within the overall context of newscasts, features, and commentaries. There is very little overt attempt to make the listener feel VOA has a special interest in his particular nation or area. A weekly 15-minute "Letters from Listeners" and the occasional reference to listeners' questions and musical requests on the "Breakfast Show" allow for a person-to-person orientation at a regional level, since these programs are prepared in distinct regional versions. But this accounts for a minor part of the total VOA schedule. By definition, then, most Asian listeners tune in VOA for information about the United States and about America's role in and views on world affairs.

The audience VOA intends to reach does not appear to be particularly young, committed to a cause, desirous of maintaining links with a "second homeland," or highly specialized in terms of interest. Certain VOA programs are designed to appeal to the young; an occasional series deals with the concept of democracy, and individual programs within the "Forum" series cover aspects of medicine and science in a very specialized manner. The bulk of the schedule, however, is intended for an audience with moderate to strong interest in the United States, but without a great deal of specific knowledge about life in America. This audience is expected to have a fair command of English, although several news and feature programs are available in "Special English," which is comprised of a 1,200 word vocabulary, delivered at a rate of 90–100 words a minute.

Undoubtedly many educated and interested Asians listen to VOA, but American involvement in Indochina, as well as its leadership in past struggles over the People's Republic of China's admission to the United Nations, have probably made many of these listeners a bit skeptical of VOA newscasts and even of features on American culture and society. VOA has covered both of these Asian issues from a variety of perspectives, some of which were critical of official United States policy. Remembrances of situations remain, however, and VOA broadcasts are quite likely, for that reason alone, to be interpreted as biased. Occasional heavy-handed censorship of negative comment concerning American involvement in Vietnam has, in the past, received considerable press coverage (*The Nation* 1967, p. 709) and has probably weakened some listeners' confidence in VOA credibility.

Based on the author's monitoring of VOA broadcasts over the past decade, however, it appears that a skeptical but interested listener would be hard put to discern any continuing pattern of censorship, and, if his skepticism should lead him to compare VOA newscasts with those from other nations, he would most often find great similarity in coverage, both in choice of events and selection of factual detail concerning these events.

6.1.10 Far East Broadcasting Company

The only international broadcasting service with a significant involvement in Asia but without any visible connection to a government, Far East Broadcasting Company receives the major share of its financial support from religion-oriented American private citizens and foundations. Its transmitter locations — in the Philippines, the Seychelles, Okinawa, and South Korea — allow for wide physical coverage within Asia. In addition, recording and production studios operate in at least Japan, Hong Kong, India, Singapore, Indonesia, and Thailand. Affiliate offices are located in Australia, Canada, New Zealand, and England. Seventy other religious organizations around the world, as well as various government embassies, regularly contribute recorded programs to FEBC.

FEBC utilizes more than 25 languages to reach its audiences, but English (11 hours daily) and Mandarin occupy the main share of broadcast time. The English-language service, although quite varied in terms of program categories, has one unifying element — Christian evangelism. Newscasts provide reasonably well-balanced accounts of world-wide events, giving considerable attention to events taking place in, or affecting, Asia; certain music programs feature popular (including American Western) and classical music, and mailbag programs contain a wide variety of letters from listeners (see also §6.2.3).

Virtually all features and most music broadcast by FEBC are religious in nature. Interviews and correspondence with FEBC officials, as well as the nature of the program schedule itself, make it clear that the station intends to reach listeners either who are members of Christian minorities — and thus need both support for themselves and "ammunition" to aid in the conversion of others — or who are in search of a faith. Although the first type of listener may be found anywhere in Asia, one major concern of FEBC is the Christian in the People's Republic of China, hence, the provision, until 1972, of a special medium-wave service in Mandarin from Okinawa for 5 hours daily, another 4½ hours daily from Manila on short-wave, and 3½ hours daily from Manila in four other Chinese languages. Some of these transmissions are also intended for overseas Chinese throughout Asia. The second type of listener can also be found anywhere in Asia but especially, according to FEBC officials, in large cities with their unsettling sociological and psychological conditions, and among young and fairly well-educated people.

The FEBC English service schedule appears to be better suited for reaching the first type of listener than the second. The preponderance of religious programming and the presentation of many of these programs in unrelieved blocs of 60—90 minutes, can be overwhelming to a listener in search of a faith. Most programs within such a bloc run no more than 15 minutes and differ to varying degrees in styles and approaches, but all contain the same basic message and a basic talk format. Furthermore, since a number of these programs are prepared for broadcast in the United States, and only incidentally find their way to FEBC, there is sometimes a problem with regional accents and specialized terms of reference. For example, a Baptist minister with a Southern accent and a habit of making reference to American TV characters is not likely to be understood very well by a Chinese office worker in Malaysia, who learned his English from BBC broadcasts or in a Kuala Lumpur school.

Several FEBC officials recognize the difficulties involved in reaching English-speaking listeners in Asia with broadcasts they can comprehend, but the station also realizes a modest income from the sale of airtime to religious groups. FEBC does attempt to space such difficult-to-comprehend programs through the schedule so they will not be clustered There are few signs, however, that the station plans to drop the programs entirely, which may or may not be due to a basic feeling that any Christian presentation is bound to make at least some positive impression on listeners, even if it is not as comprehensible as it might be.

FEBC lays considerable stress on the concept of universal Christianity and brotherhood and to this end broadcasts a number of programs containing reports on Christian activities in Australia, New Zealand, and the Philippines, as well as throughout Asia in general. In addition, a few programs each week feature the music of various Asian nations and peoples. Such programs are likely to have a more positive effect on listeners who are not committed Christians, than the more Americanized portions of the FEBC schedule. On balance, however, the station seems to offer far more interest to committed Christians than to any other audience subgroup, and it is highly doubtful that certain of the target groups so often sought by other international broadcasters − government officials, journalists, and businessmen − listen to FEBC, at least for professional reasons.

6.1.11 Other International Broadcast Services

Several other international broadcasting services are active in Asia, some of them on a major scale, at least in terms of total broadcast hours. Chief among these are the external services of Radio Pakistan, All India Radio, Korean Central Broadcasting Station (North Korea), Korean Broadcasting System (South Korea), Voice of Vietnam (North Vietnam), Radio Malaysia, Radio Republik Indonesia, Sri Lanka Broadcasting Corporation, and the foreign services of the two Germanys, Radio Berlin International (German Democratic Republic) and Deutsche Welle (German Federal Republic).

All of these services broadcast in English to South and Southeast Asia, usually for at least an hour or two daily; most also broadcast to their own citizens or former citizens residing in Asia. All of them broadcast in at least one major Asian language, such as Hindi, Japanese, Mandarin, Cantonese, Urdu, or Indonesian, and several − most notably North Vietnam, the two Koreas, Pakistan, and India − devote several hours daily to broadcasts for listeners in neighboring "hostile" countries, usually in the major languages spoken in those countries.

Certain of these broadcast operations appear to be regional in nature, beaming almost exclusively to listeners in the immediate geographical area and very seldom to those in more distant parts of the world. Malaysia and Sri Lanka confine themselves to South and Southeast Asia, while the signal strengths of Indonesia, Pakistan and India effectively impose this sort of regional limitation (see *Area Handbook for India* 1970, p. 466; *WRTH* 1974), although Pakistan and India do have a few high-power transmitters now.

The services of the two Koreas, two Germanys, and North Vietnam are somewhat broader in scope. The two Koreas, for example, each broadcast nearly 500 hours per week, in six (South Korea) to eight (North Korea) languages, including French, Russian, and Spanish in each case; Deutsche Welle airs nearly 600 hours per week, approximately 100 hours of which is directed to German and foreign listeners in Asia, in such languages as Pushtu, Hindi, Indonesian, and Japanese. Radio Berlin International's output, while considerably more modest (approximately 30 hours weekly to South Asia), includes two hours per day in Hindi. North Vietnam in 1974 broadcast largely to Southeast Asia, but employed ten languages (*WRTH* 1974, p. 173) and enjoys the advantage of a rebroadcast arrangement with Radio Havana, through which its English-language material, usually delivered by Radio Havana announcers, can be heard in North America.

North Vietnam is also the home of several clandestine radio operations directed to listeners in Laos, Khmer Republic, and South Vietnam; most of them have been in operation since 1960. The service designed for South Vietnam — Radio Liberation → was a major one by any standards, nearly 160 hours per week as of mid-1971. Radio Pathet Lao was on the air for nearly 100 hours per week in 1971 (Löser 1972, p. 36).

6.1.12 Summary

The diversity of program formats, vocabularies, and styles employed by stations discussed here make it obvious that international broadcasters seeking to reach audiences in Asia have several different types of listeners and strategic goals in mind. No single subgroup of listeners appears to be a universal target, although opinion leaders, late high-school and college students, and temporary and permanent expatriates are sought by most of the international services. Rarely do program formats, vocabulary and style, or strategic goals seem to be based largely on audience research. Many intuitive decisions, however, regarding these matters are made by individuals who have had considerable direct contact with the countries and audiences in question.

More often, program schedules appear to be determined by habit, availability of resources, or certain national campaigns, the latter because many of these stations are subordinate to government. Many of the staff members in international services profess to be unhappy with this last-named aspect, and some claim to fight and occasionally win battles over these issues. This is difficult, given the fact that most of the organizations are dependent on their respective governments for financial support and are frequently subject to supervision by various governmental ministries and/or the national parliament or congress.

Finally, most international broadcasters recognize the unique ability of radio to achieve a more personal level of communication, and the provision of programs with personality hosts, listener mailbags, and portraits of individual citizens, are fairly common features in most station schedules. It is also far more common to hear programs featuring positive accomplishments of the government and people of the broadcasting nation, than to hear programs attacking other nations or institutions. No station is entirely free of the latter, but Radio Japan and Radio Australia come very close.

6.2 Religious Broadcasting in Asia, *by Constantino E. Bernardez and William E. 'Ted' Haney*

6.2.1 Introduction

The extent and character of religious broadcasting in Asia differ from country to country, depending on the form of broadcast system in operation, the official state religion, government policies toward religious groups and their activities, and the political climate, among others.

For example, in most Asian countries where broadcasting is an exclusive government monopoly, religious groups are not allowed to use broadcasting facilities, except in very special circumstances and under very controlled conditions. In others, such as Sri Lanka and Thailand, religious groups are allowed to buy broadcast time.

None of the so-called Christian countries of Asia claim Christianity as a state religion. Indonesia, India, Pakistan, Taiwan, Japan, and South Korea are predominantly non-Christian but do not have a state religion. Sri Lanka, Burma, and Thailand are Buddhist states, while Malaysia and Singapore are Muslim. Without a doubt, most of Asia is non-Christian, even if one were to exclude the People's Republic of China.

There seems no question, however, that organized activity in religious broadcasting in Asia is almost exclusively Christian. In at least Indonesia, Australia, South Korea, Taiwan, and the Philippines, Christian groups have been granted the right to own and operate their own broadcasting stations. Christian production studios, providing programs for broadcast over public or private stations, abound all over Asia.

6.2.2 Australia

Australians belong to at least 12 religions, all Christian, except for Hebrew (0.6%

Constantino E. Bernardez is executive director of South East Asia Radio Voice in Manila, and has worked in religious-educational radio since 1952, 14 years as either program director or station manager at DYSR in the Philippines. He is a member of East Asian and World Christian conferences.
William E. Haney is director of research for the Far East Broadcasting Company. He has worked in broadcasting as a mass-media consultant since 1951 in the Philippines, Brazil, and the U.S.

of the population). The largest denominations by membership are Church of England of Australia, 34.9% of the population; Catholic and Roman Catholic, 24.9%; Methodist, 10.2%; and Presbyterian, 9.3%. The other eight denominations are smaller, ranging from 0.5–1.5% of the population.

Under the Broadcasting and Television Act, commercial radio and TV broadcasters are required to program "divine worship or other matter of a religious nature during such period as the Australian Broadcasting Control Board determines, and if the Board so directs, shall do so without charge."

This amounts to at least 1%, or one hour, of radio's weekly schedule, quite apart from sponsored religious matter. Most commercial stations meet these requirements, but at least three exceed them. One, 2CH, broadcasts over nine hours weekly of religious programs, while 5KA, in which the Methodist Church has a large controlling interest, devotes over seven hours each week to such shows. A third station, 3DB, uses over two weekly hours of religious programming.

In commercial television, the Australian Broadcasting Control Board requires that at least 1%, or a minimum of 30 minutes, of the weekly schedule be devoted to religious programs, apart from sponsored material. This time can be used in one unit or a series of units not less than five minutes each.

In each Australian state, both a Christian Television Association and Catholic Radio and Television Committee exist to provide programs to commercial stations so that they may fill the required time. The CTA units are made up of representatives of the main Christian denominations, except for the Roman Catholic Church. Attempts were made in the early 1970s to coordinate program output of the six CTA units to save money and effort, as well as raise program standards. In Sydney, a Church of England Television Society produces its own programs.

Local arrangements are made in commercial radio for live broadcasts from churches or studios; a similar procedure for TV is followed in larger towns where no CTA group functions. Both commercial television and radio allocate time, as far as possible, in accordance with denominational proportions in the area. Since Hindus, Buddhists, and Muslims do not have organized religious groups representing them, they are not allocated any airtime.

ABC national radio programs go out over three networks, the first and second made up of alternative stations in the main cities, the third network comprised of stations throughout rural areas.

The main city stations broadcast 34 religious programs weekly over the first and second networks, totaling about eight hours, or 3% of total airtime; 28 of these programs also go to third network country stations, occupying nearly 4% of their airtime. Programs usually are split evenly between the spoken word and singing.

Some main religious programs on ABC radio carry titles such as "Sacred Music," "With Heart and Voice," "Encounter," "Divine Service," "Frontier," "Community Hymn Singing," "Cross Ways," "In Quire and Places," "The

Epilogue," "Facing the Week," "Readings from the Bible," "Pause a Moment," "Religion in Life," "Evensong," and "Saturday Saints." Radio Australia, the external service, broadcasts a 15-minute Sunday program, "Churches of Australia" (including Jewish and Orthodox programs), to foreign nations.

On television, the one-hour "Divine Service" is broadcast in each state on Sundays; programs from various churches are videotaped and circulated around the states. A 15-minute youth program is televised occasionally, and on Sunday evenings there is either the series "Challenge," running from 45–55 minutes, or a series of individual units of about 25–30 minutes each. On the first Monday of each month, a 30-minute program, "Dialogue," is telecast.

To supervise and produce religious programs, ABC radio and TV in Sydney has a staff of six, in Melbourne four, and one each in Brisbane, Adelaide, Perth, Hobart, and Port Moresby. ABC sends a number of its religious radio programs to Papua New Guinea; some religious programs are locally produced in those territories.

In both radio and television, the ABC retains the right to make its own choice of persons and places for broadcasts or telecasts. It always tries to present the church on the air at its very best.

6.2.3 Philippines

In the Philippines, religious groups are allowed to own and operate their own broadcasting stations, in addition to being able to purchase broadcast time. The Radio Control Board does not specify the amount of time to be alloted to religious programs, nor the manner in which it must be shared. Instead, the primary consideration is ability to pay.

Only Christian groups are engaged in broadcasting on an organized basis. Some own and operate their own stations; a greater number produce programs or bring in packaged shows for broadcast on commercial stations.

The oldest radio station owned by a religious group is DZAS of the Far East Broadcasting Company, located in Manila. FEBC began broadcasting with a 1,000-w. medium-wave transmitter in 1948, and by 1975 was transmitting with a total power of over 600,000 w.

FEBC is a noncommercial radio network whose purpose is "to proclaim to the world the Gospel message of Jesus Christ." Broadcasts are by medium-wave and short-wave both in the Philippines and to Asia and the rest of the world.

In Manila, local FEBC service is provided by DZAS, broadcasting 24 hours daily; DZFE, a "fine music" station, and DWFM, a stereo FM station. In addition, FEBC operates five provincial stations in the islands. During the first half of 1975, FEBC completed the installation of a 250-kw. medium-wave station on the west coast of the island of Luzon, about 100 miles north of Manila. This station broadcasts to China, Khmer Republic, Laos, and Vietnam.

FEBC programs include news, special events, cultural, educational, and musical programs, as well as a very large segment devoted to the Christian message (see §6.1.10 for more on FEBC overseas service).

The Mass Communications Network of the Council of Churches in the Philippines, MASCOM, is another religious broadcasting organization. Although it is no longer involved in station operation, a brief history of the work is appropriate here. It began in 1950 with a 1-kw. transmitter, DYSR, at Silliman University in Dumaguete City. DYSR increased to 10-kw. and later added another 10-kw. station, DZCH, and a 1-kw. FM outlet, both in Manila.

MASCOM was originally noncommercial, subsidies coming entirely from the National Council of Churches in the United States. In 1969, the network's franchise was amended permitting it to continue as a nonprofit entity but to sell airtime. Foreign subsidy was gradually decreased so that by 1972 almost half of the network operating costs were met by locally earned advertising income. It was hoped that the network could eventually become self-supporting. By late 1974, however, it was recognized that this would not be possible and the stations were leased to a management corporation which now operates them on a secular, commercial, nonreligious basis. The function of MASCOM is now oriented toward the production of programs which are to be placed on commercial stations and/or its own stations, which are now operated by a secular organization.

MASCOM is the major undertaking of the Mass Media Commission of the National Council of Churches in the Philippines (NCCP). The commission, made up of representatives from member churches of the council, established policy guidelines for their work.

Another station which deserves mentioning, even though it is no longer operating, is the South East Asia Radio Voice, an international short-wave station located in Manila. SEARV was a cooperative project involving the NCCP and various church councils in Asia. It provided a 50-kw. short-wave facility for programming. Support for transmitter operations and program production came from the World Association for Christian Communication in London. SEARV was discontinued in late 1974 because of lack of funds.

Another large religious broadcaster is Radio Veritas, a radio facility under the direction of the bishop of the Philippine Roman Catholic Church. The station operates a 50-kw. medium-wave transmitter and two 100-kw. international short-wave transmitters just north of Manila. A gift of the Roman Catholic Church in West Germany, the station's equipment is German. The antenna system is designed to reach nearly every part of Asia and Europe.

The medium-wave transmitter of Radio Veritas is on the air from 5 A.M. until midnight, with news, music, educational, and religious programs. Radio Veritas is noncommercial and subsidized entirely by the Roman Catholic Church. A small resident staff from several Asian nations produces programs for the short-wave service, but since 1973 very little has been done in this area.

The Iglesia Ng Kristo, an indigenous Filipino church claiming a large membership, owns a network of commercial and noncommercial stations throughout the Philippines. Very little is known about its operations, except that the network is self-supporting.

Broadcasting systems described so far are owned and operated by churches or church-related groups; others are maintained by federations or associations. Notable among the latter is the Philippine Federation of Catholic Broadcasters (PFCB), an association of private noncommercial and commercial stations in the Philippines. These stations are either owned by Roman Catholic laymen or by local dioceses. Included in the association are Radio Veritas and 21 other private commercial radio stations. Transmitter power ranges from 1–50 kw. PFCB is the only church group which owns and operates a TV channel. Program policy is geared almost entirely toward development, and the stations average an 18-hour programming day.

There are other religious groups in the Philippines which do not operate their own stations, but do have production studios or duplicating facilities from which they produce programs for placement on either commercial or noncommercial stations.

The Lutheran Hour offices, directly connected with the Lutheran Church in the Philippines, are sponsored financially by the Lutheran Laymen's League, a lay organization with the Lutheran Church–Missouri Synod in the United States. The Lutheran Hour handles both imported and domestically produced programming. Most imported programs emanate from the United States, including the "Bringing Christ to the Nations" series, the "Lutheran Hour" itself, and "Silhouette," aimed at teenagers and featuring the top 40 tunes, interspersed with chatter concerning Christians. The locally written and produced shows are mainly two dramas in the local dialect. The Lutheran Hour office does not operate its own production studio but hires local talent and facilities for this purpose. They buy the master tape from the local artist and copy it for distribution to other stations.

In 1972, Lutheran Hour programs were aired on more than 100 stations in more than 50 cities in the Philippines, as well as in Honolulu. They claim to broadcast as many as 240 half-hour shows weekly in the four main Philippine dialects of Tagalog, Cebuano, Ilocano, and Hiligaynon, as well as in English. In a breakdown of weekly program distribution in the early 1970s, the Lutheran Hour placed 129 programs on commercial, 37 on Protestant, and 75 on Roman Catholic stations.

The Southern Baptists maintain a representative in Manila who coordinates broadcasting activity not only in the Philippines, but also all over Asia. In their Manila recording studios, the Southern Baptists produce two 30-minute programs in two major Filipino dialects for weekly broadcast on 19 stations. In addition, they produce a half-hour TV program aired in three major Filipino cities. Their local studio has facilities for producing a TV program. All their airtime is purchased.

6.2.4 Hong Kong

Hong Kong has no official state religion, the vast majority of its four-million inhabitants being Chinese and therefore Buddhists of one sort or another. Only

2% of the population is Christian.

Radio Hong Kong allows and encourages religious broadcasting. The daily English transmission includes an early morning religious spot, mid-day prayers, a relayed Sunday morning service, and special programs for religious occasions. In charge of this phase of Radio Hong Kong's broadcasting is a religious advisory committee, comprising representatives of the established denominations. Only Christian denominations broadcast with any degree of regularity.

There are at least five production studios operated by religious groups in Hong Kong. All are solely Protestant, except for the Hong Kong Christian Council (AVEC), which functions for both Roman Catholics and Protestants. Of the five studios, AVEC is the only one which prepares programs for local broadcast over Radio Hong Kong. FEBC also operates a production studio in Hong Kong, which is one of the six Asian sources for its Chinese-language programs. This studio is under the direction of its own Hong Kong board. The Hong Kong Baptist College has a department of communication where students are trained for careers in the mass media.

6.2.5 Taiwan

This country is the center of great activity in religious broadcasting. Among Protestant groups are TEAM Radio Taiwan, Taiwan Baptist Radio and Television, China Lutheran Hour, the Lutheran Voice, Joint Lutheran Television, Overseas Radio and Television (ORTV), and the Taiwan Christian Audio Visual Association (TACAVA). Foremost among the Catholic groups are Chung Sheng Station, Yi Shih Station, and Kuangchi Program Service.

Taiwan has no official state religion, and the government does not prohibit religious broadcasting.

Lutheran Voice and Joint Lutheran Television operate production studios, placing programs on local government and private stations, on a sustaining basis.

The Roman Catholic Church on Taiwan operates two commercial radio stations and one production center for radio and television. The Chung Sheng Station, initiated in 1953, has two 10-kw. transmitters in Taichung, broadcasting 22 hours daily. The Yi Shih Station, established in Nanking in 1946, and moved to Taiwan in 1950, has a 5-kw. transmitter in Keelung City, which broadcasts 21 hours a day. Both Chung Sheng and Yi Shih are commercially operated and self-supporting. Their broadcast fare is made up of news, entertainment, public service, and religious programs.

The Kuangchi Program Service, established in 1958, produces radio programs broadcast free of charge, as well as TV shows which are sold to stations on the strength of their quality. The center earns its operating costs, but must depend on church and philanthropic funds for extraordinary expenses such as equipment. The Kuangchi Service produces a few religious programs per se, but concentrates on dramas extolling Christian values in a more natural way, and educational and social fare geared at development. All in all, about 300 Kuangchi Service broadcasts per week are placed on 40 government and private stations in Taiwan; others are sent to the Philippines, Hong Kong, Singapore, and Mauritius. On television, the center produces a weekly, hour-long drama (TTV Mandarin Theater), a biweekly half-hour drama (CTS Mandarin Theater), a weekly half-hour variety program (The Singer Hour), and a biweekly, five-minute puppet show for children. Every six months, it presents a serial drama of 45 half-hour episodes.

The Baptists operate a radio-TV production studio from which they program for Broadcasting Corporation of China radio, 3½ hours a week in Mandarin, 2 hours a week in Taiwanese, and 40 minutes in Hakka. On TV, they produce one 30-minute drama every week for CTV.

TEAM Radio and ORTV both produce Chinese programs for FEBC stations in the Philippines and South Korea. Both studios also produce programs for airing on Taiwan stations. ORTV has a large facility in Taipei which includes radio and TV production as well as recording for LP records.

As for the public's reaction to religious broadcasting, a Broadcasting Corporation of China official in 1973 reported that a survey showed religious broadcasts on Taiwan were annoying because they contained too much "monotonous preaching," "too many theological terms," and were "without substance and uninteresting" (*Media Asia,* 1 : 3, 1974, p. 7).

6.2 6   Thailand

The official state religion of Thailand is Buddhism. Governmental policy towards religious broadcasting is one of tolerance, and most religious groups have no problem buying local time.

The Church of Christ in Thailand has a radio department which produces radio programs for local stations. So do the Southern Baptists, among others.

FEBC operates a production studio in Bangkok, which has sustained about 80 hours per month on approximately 20 medium-wave radio stations throughout Thailand. Most of the religious broadcast time is sponsored, and programs are mainly preevangelistic, dramatic presentations of Bible stories or lives of Christians, religious music, and the like. A small proportion of religious programming is of a teaching nature, designed for Christians and broadcast via short-wave from Manila. The FEBC studios are also engaged in TV production for closed-circuit systems.

6.2.7   Burma

Buddhism is the state religion of Burma, but other religious groups are allowed to coexist. As far as is known, however, non-Buddhist religious organizations are not permitted the use of broadcast media in Burma. Buddhism, despite its official status, does not use radio in a regular or organized way.

One religious group engaged in the broadcast ministry is the radio department of the Burma Christian Council (BCC). At one time, the BCC maintained its own recording studios in Mandalay and Rangoon, but this has been discontinued, and programs are now produced at a Bangkok studio. Not being allowed the use of the government system, the BCC uses the Manila short-wave facilities of FEBC. Tapes are sent to Manila and broadcast back to Burma over FEBC facilities. FEBC also has its own Burmese programmers in Manila.

6.2.8 South Vietnam (pre-1975)

There is no official state religion in South Vietnam; the main religions are Roman Catholic, Protestant, Buddhist, Hoa-Hao, and Cao-Dai. It is government policy to offer free broadcast time to all religions.

The Roman Catholics operate the Alexandre de Rhodes Educational Television Center, whose main function is the production of educational, nonreligious programs for television. The center is well-equipped and staffed, and its programming is of such high quality that the government has chosen it to produce much of the nation's developmental broadcast material.

The Evangelical Church of Vietnam also operates a recording studio in Saigon, which produces a half-hour evangelistic program weekly on the Saigon stations, as well as on ten provincial outlets. Broadcasts began in 1954 and are fully funded by the local church. In addition, the Evangelical Church uses government facilities free of charge to produce a 45-minute TV program monthly and employs the Manila FEBC facilities for short-wave broadcasting into South Vietnam. The Baptists operate recording and film dialogue dubbing studios in Saigon. From the Vietnamese studio, 27 programs a week are produced for airing on government stations where time is free.

FEBC has a Manila-based Vietnamese staff which produces programs for broadcast to Vietnam via short-wave. In 1975, FEBC added a 250-kw. medium-wave service to Vietnam from the Philippines.

6.2.9 Singapore/Malaysia

The official religion of both Singapore and Malaysia is Islam. Religious programs in Islam are broadcast in both countries. In Malaysia, early morning radio is dominated by prayer chants, while early evening television has frequent Koranic readings, historical treatments of the religion, and Islamic music. The time designated for such broadcasting and televising is meant for the more religiously inclined rural folk who rise and retire early.

In mid-1975, the Ministry of Information and Broadcasting in Malaysia stipulated that radio and TV programming must be interrupted five times daily for Muslim prayer calls of about three minutes each.

In Singapore, the government permits Christian broadcasts every Sunday, while in Malaysia, these are permitted only on Christmas and Easter. In Singapore, the Baptists produce programs with the assistance of Radio Singapore and also place programs on Rediffusion.

FEBC has recording studios in both countries and broadcasts to these nations via short-wave from the Philippines. The FEBC studios also produce Christmas and Easter specials for broadcast on Radio Singapore.

6.2.10 Indonesia

Indonesia has no state religion although Islam is the majority faith. Churches are permitted to operate their own stations; a typical set-up is that of the Evangelical Church of Minahassa in North Sulawesi. The church, made up of 430 congregations of almost half a million members, owns a radio station in Tomohon, which has 75 w. of power. Started in 1971, it is on the air ten hours daily, supporting itself on members' contributions.

Religious broadcasting had its biggest boost after the coup that displaced Sukarno. A system of broadcasting developed at that time, made up of amateur or student stations (usually small power tropical band short-wave transmitters put together by amateurs from junk parts). The new government permitted these stations to flourish and soon many other groups, including a number of church organizations, were setting them up. From their Indonesian studio, the Baptists produce two 15-minute programs which are broadcast weekly over 14 outlets, as well as a 25-minute program televised twice a month at government expense. (See §3.6.7 for a fuller description of Indonesian religious broadcasting.)

Many of these stations were so poorly financed, their equipment in such bad state of repair, and their program quality so poor, that by 1975 the government requested these small stations to combine their resources and personnel. This brought about a reduction in the number of stations and an increase in quality.

At the same time the Indonesian government contracted a Japanese engineering firm to prepare a five-year plan for radio and TV broadcasting. The first phase of this plan calls for these many independent broadcasters to move from the tropical and short-wave bands, where local coverage would be greatly improved. The system would then be similar to what is in use in many other countries.

FEBC has a recording studio in Jakarta where programs are prepared and placed on some 90 of these independent local stations. Programs are also sent on tape to Manila for rebroadcast to Indonesia on the FEBC short-wave transmitters.

6.2.11 Sri Lanka (Ceylon)

The Republic of Sri Lanka is a Buddhist state that maintains a very tolerant and conciliatory policy toward other religions. All religions, Buddhist, Hindu, Islam, and Christian, are allowed generous allocations of time on the state network. Little information, if any, is in hand about the work of the non-Christian religions in this field.

The National Christian Council of Sri Lanka conducts a program which is submitted to, and produced at, the studios of Sri Lanka Broadcasting Corporation. The council averages 492 hours yearly of program time in three different languages. Among programs broadcast are "Thoughts for the Day," "Christian Half-Hour," "Children's Program," and special shows during Easter and Christmas times.

The Roman Catholics in 1972 were completing the construction of a radio center. In the meantime, all Catholic programs were produced and broadcast from the studios of Sri Lanka Broadcasting Corporation. Like the Protestants, Catholics present radio time in all three major languages, English, Sinhalese, and Tamil. These include the fortnightly "Catholic Half Hour," a fortnightly 15-minute children's program, and "Thought for the Day."

"Back to the Bible" has studios in Colombo and broadcasts daily to India over the government station in Sri Lanka.

6.2.12   India

No official state religion is stipulated in India, and the government does not allow the regular use of All India Radio for religious programs. In fact, it can safely be said that AIR scrupulously shuns programs produced by religious groups, fearing that if one religious sect is permitted to use AIR facilities, others will demand the same.

At the very least, religious groups are permitted to broadcast a special program during Christmas and Holy Week. The programs, however, are planned not by the religious groups, but by AIR station directors who invite speakers and choirs to participate. The studios do provide generous assistance to these groups in program production. At the same time, AIR covers major religious events which are of general news value.

In spite of these restrictions, production studios operated by religious bodies do exist in India. Among those which might be mentioned are CARAVS (Christian Association for Radio and Audio Visual Services) in Jabalpur (M.P.), Suvartha Vani in Vijayawada (A.P.), Christian Arts and Communications Services in Madras, studios affiliated with the Lutheran World Federation. For the most part, these predominantly Protestant studios produce programs for broadcast over FEBC short-wave stations in Manila and the Seychelles, or on Radio Voice of the Gospel in Ethiopia.

FEBA (the British affiliate of FEBC) maintains two studios in India. The main one is in Bangalore, South India, and the satellite studio is in New Delhi. FEBA owns and operates short-wave transmitters in the Seychelles off the east coast of Africa.

6.2.13   South Korea

No state religion exists in South Korea. Religious broadcasting is not promoted by the government, although it is freely permitted.

Protestants are engaged in broadcasting on a very extensive basis in South Korea. Seven Protestant radio stations, five with the Christian Broadcasting Service (CBS) network, HLKX of TEAM Radio, and HLDA of FEBC, are free to air as much religious programming as they wish. Roman Catholics participate in a very limited way, and officially, Buddhists do no programming whatever. Various commercial stations sell time for acceptable religious programs, and government AM and television networks allow a small amount of free airtime for selected religious fare.

CBS, in existence since 1954, operates a network of stations in Seoul, Taegu, Pusan, Kwangju, and Iri. The central station, HLKY in Seoul, maintains a 50-kw. medium-wave transmitter, the other outlets have 10 kw. of power each. Most Christian denominations in South Korea cooperate to some degree in the use of CBS facilities.

Owned and operated by a radio committee of the National Christian Council of Korea, CBS stations function on a semicommercial basis, their licenses permitting commercial sponsors for up to 30% of airtime. Commercial income covers 75% of CBS's operating budget, the balance coming from local and overseas donations.

Each of the five CBS stations are on the air 20—22 hours a day. In general, about 83% of the programs are of a general nature — music, sports, news, education and entertainment — while 17% are Christian music, messages, or dramas.

HLKX, TEAM Mission's 50-kw. station on the air since 1956, is owned and maintained by the Evangelical Alliance Mission of the United States. Studios are in Seoul and the transmitter is south of Inchon. HLKX operates 13½ hours daily in five languages — Chinese, Russian, Mongolian, English, and Korean. Programming is largely religious, with some music and educational content. The station is supported almost entirely by gifts from abroad.

The Roman Catholic Church and its missions finance a radio/TV production studio at Sogang University in Seoul. Major radio activity of the studio has been confined to airing a daily five-minute, late evening meditation over a commercial network. No regular Roman Catholic programs are broadcast, but leaders occasionally participate in programs on government and commercial stations.

KAVCO, the Korean Audio Visual Committee of the National Christian Council of Korea, has studio facilities for preparing TV programs. Besides producing occasional television dramas, KAVCO also puts Korean-language sound tracks on religious and other films for viewing on local TV stations. Such religious films are aired on a sustaining basis on government and, occasionally, on commercial stations.

The Baptist Mission in South Korea has a mass communications department which produces weekly programs over commercial and noncommercial outlets.

In June 1973, the Far East Broadcasting Company (FEBC) began transmitting on a new 250-kw. medium-wave station, HLDA, from the island of Cheju off the southern coast of Korea. The station broadcasts programs primarily of a spiritual nature in Korean, Chinese, Japanese, Russian, and English and is on the air 11 hours a day. The station uses highly directive antennas which, coupled with its high power, provides a coverage of up to 2,000 miles. The Korean programs are produced in Seoul, while most of the other language programs are produced in other studios and sent to Korea on tape. The total letter response during the month of January 1975 was over 8,000 for 2½ hours of Korean programming on HLDA.

6.2.14   Japan

There is no official state religion in Japan. Because of codes stipulating religious freedom, each religious organization or denomination expects to be treated equally in Japanese broadcasting. The broadcasting code of the National Association of Commercial Broadcasters stipulates that freedom of religion and the viewpoint of each religious denomination should be respected. Religious groups may buy broadcast time on private stations, but the stations reserve the right to accept programs dependent upon their listener response.

Although only 1% of the total Japanese population is Christian, many Christian groups are engaged in broadcasting. Protestant groups include the Japan National Christian Council, Japan Evangelical Lutheran Church, Church of the Nazarene — Japan District, Joint Broadcasting Committee of the U.S. Presbyterian Church, Japan Union Mission of Seventh Day Adventists, Reformed Church in Japan, Swiss Pentecostal Mission, Hokkaido Radio Evangelism and Mass Communications Committee, Japan Baptist Convention, FEBC, Pacific Broadcasting Association, New Life League, Free Christian Mission, Tokyo Bible Center, and the Japan Gospel Mission. The Catholic Church of Japan also has its broadcasting program, as do Buddhist-related bodies and New Religions, such as the Nishi Honganji, Higashi Honganji, Tenrikyo, Risshyokoseikai, and the Seichono-Ie.

Perhaps the best-known Christian organization in Japanese broadcasting is AVACO, or the Audio Visual Activities Commission of the Japan National Christian Council. AVACO activities are not limited to one church or denomination, the organization being ecumenical (mainly Protestant) both in structure and personnel.

With headquarters at the new Mass Communications Center near Tokyo's Waseda University, AVACO also maintains auxiliary offices and studios at Aoyama Gakuin. AVACO has a total of seven recording and two filming studios that can be used for both radio and television. In fact, the largest portion of AVACO's operating income (about 60% of total budget) comes from renting these studios to commercial agencies. Overseas contributions amount to about 15% and are gradually being phased out.

AVACO itself produces a 10-minute daily program, "Friend of the Heart," directed to the interests of young people. The aim of this disc-jockey show is to help youth see their problems from a Christian perspective. Other regular programs are produced by AVACO, including a traditional sermonette every Sunday morning. AVACO buys commercial time in order to broadcast these programs. On occasion, however, it cooperates with Nippon Hoso Kyokai in the production of educational fare with religious content for radio and television.

In terms of service to a wider evangelical community, the Far East Broadcasting Company, along with Pacific Broadcasting Association (PBA), offer a unique ministry. PBA is a service agency which buys time and produces programs for some 30 different Protestant groups; 40% of PBA's budget is derived from donations from local Japanese.

The FEBC studios prepare programs in Tokyo which are then sent on tape to FEBC transmitting studios in Manila, San Francisco, and Korea. The first two broadcast to Japan on short-wave, and HLDA in Korea uses the medium-wave band. The FEBC Tokyo Studios produce different programs for each of these stations.

6.3 Instructional Television in Asia, *by Leo H. Larkin, S.J.*

6.3.1 Regional Profile

The progress of any ITV development program can be traced through at least seven stages, including official inactivity, study and experimentation, planning, preparation, pilot program, development and expansion, and finally, a fully developed system.

Official inactivity is a somewhat circumspect way of describing governmental unawareness, disinterest, or the inactiveness of education officials *vis-à-vis* television in formal education. Asian countries included in this category in 1972 were Bangladesh, Burma, Khmer Republic, Laos, and Nepal. Study and experimentation is a stage in which educational planners investigate the concept and implications of using television as a medium of instruction within their own educational-socio-economic circumstances. This is formally accomplished by means of literature from countries which already utilize the medium and by visiting on-going projects abroad. At this time, there may be some experimentation, usually with shared resources owned by other government or private organizations, as well as considerable fund-raising activity. At least, Afghanistan, India, Indonesia, South Korea, Pakistan, South Vietnam, Sri Lanka, Taiwan, and Thailand represented this stage of development in 1972.

The third stage, that of planning, is one in which top government officials and educational planners consider why and how ITV can be introduced into their educational system. Assets and liabilities of the medium are considered, and priorities for development are chosen. Capital costs and operating expenses are considered in relationship to other national development projects, and a feasibility study is prepared.

After a decision has been reached by government that ITV can profitably be utilized, a preparatory phase commences, including the construction and installation of plant and equipment, the preparation of a long-range budget, the designing of curricula and training programs, and the recruitment of a staff.

A pilot program is initiated in phases with the preparation of telecourses usually a year before transmission. A center providing ITV services and a relatively small number of receiving schools work out compatible and coordinated operational systems, at the same time that research is carried out for

Leo H. Larkin is director, Center for Educational Television in Manila; he has had nearly 20 years educational TV experience as administrator of an ETV center, consultant, delegate to numerous international conferences, and observer on tours through four continents. He is the author of numerous articles on instructional TV in Asia.

continual analysis and adaptation to local circumstances. This stage culminates in an evaluation of set objectives by high-ranking government officials and in a designation of more explicit future plans. Pilot programs have been established in Hong Kong, the Philippines, Malaysia, and Singapore. (Since this chapter was first written, at least Hong Kong, Malaysia, and Singapore have moved toward fully established services, meaning the coverage and range of programming excel both qualitatively and quantitatively.)

The development and expansion stage involves gradually bringing the newly harnessed educational tool to bear on appropriate educational problems of the country. Finally, a full instructional television system is evidenced by its widespread use throughout the entire nation. Even the fully implemented system is one of challenge in terms of maintaining a quality service relevant to a nation's changing educational needs. Only Japan, of all Asian nations, has a full ITV service.

Thus, it becomes evident that nearly half of the Asian nations, eight, or 44%, fit conveniently in the study and experimentation phase; five, or 28%, in the official inactivity category; four, or 22%, in pilot program; and one, or 5.5%, in the full system. Not one Asian nation belonged in the planning, preparation, or development and expansion categories in the early 1970s.

The following represent national sketches of ITV programs that either have been, or are in the process of being, launched.

6.3.2 Full System

The unique educational broadcasting leader of Asia is the nongovernmental Nippon Hoso Kyokai, possessor of excellent resources, a well-developed and efficient organization, and extensive services. In fact, it is difficult to see how NHK resources can be excelled anywhere; physical plant, equipment, personnel, and finances seem almost unlimited (see §2.5).

NHK has a separate nation-wide educational channel, providing television services for in-school, as well as correspondence telecourses. Formal education programs reach 90% of Japan's elementary and high schools, the majority being supplementary programs such as Japanese, English, science, social studies, ethics, art, music, and home economics.

No direct or official relationship with the education ministry exists; televised subjects are selected with the advice of local advisory committees composed of school teachers and education ministry officials. The National Federation of Broadcasting Education Study Societies, with eight regional federations and 54 prefectural associations, has been voluntarily organized by the school teachers. The utilization of TV lessons is well-planned in this society, where a number of other educational media are available to nearly all students. Television lessons are not intended to cover an entire curriculum, but are designed to act as supplementary aids for the discretionary use of teachers. In this respect, Japan differs from what some educators feel should be the emphasis in developing Asian nations — the use of television in basic courses. While supervisory visits are deemphasized, feedback from teachers and subsequent research analysis of this information is very well developed.

NHK provides special educational television services to nations throughout Asia. One of the more valuable contributions is its sponsorship of The Japan Prize, an international TV programming contest begun in 1965, which promotes high-standard ETV shows. NHK also offers training courses in Tokyo for production, technical, and engineering personnel, technical consultants upon special request, and filmed and videotaped materials, which are generously distributed at little or no cost to all countries (see De Vera 1967; Nishimoto 1969).

6.3.3. Pilot Programs

The four countries in Asia with ITV pilot projects in the early 1970s were the Philippines, Singapore, Malaysia, and Hong Kong. Each has a center for ETV, which provides schools utilizing ETV with services such as production of telecourses, transmission via one or more systems, publication of printed materials accompanying telecourses, training programs for school administrators and teachers, coordination with receiving schools, classroom supervision, and research.

The Philippines program was initiated in 1964 as a closed-circuit pilot project under the auspices of a private, Jesuit university and with a capital equipment grant from the Ford Foundation. In 1968, the center became independently incorporated as a foundation for public service, supported by contributions from private business and foundations.

The CETV pilot program had three objectives: to set up an ITV operation of limited scope adapted to the Philippine socio-economic-educational milieu; to evaluate this program; and to propose realistic plans for nation-wide use of in-school television. Once these objectives were accomplished, a proposal was presented to the Secretary of Education, which was favorably received and passed on to various governmental organizations which recommended an in-depth financial feasibility study. In 1973, this development and expansion program was being considered for presentation to the World Bank Group for funding (see *Educational Broadcasting International* 1974).

ETV Singapura was created in 1966, and a year later, transmitted its first programs as an essential part of the government educational system. The professional subminister of education, a civil servant rather than elected official, got it started with substantial financing from the government, while a BBC consultant guided the planning preparation and early pilot project, along with the local center director.

The "presenter" system was and still is an ingredient of the service: teachers prepare the academic content of scripts which are eventually given to a "presenter," or experienced actor, who appears on television. Regular courses of instruction on the elementary and secondary level (both compulsory in Singapore) are in four languages — English, Mandarin, Tamil, and Bahasa

Malaysia — as demanded by the diverse nationalities of Singapore. A regular supervisory and feedback system is operative.

In 1970, the service became a multimedia center when the Singapore ETV Service Instructional Material Libraries opened. This progress has been mixed with problems hindering a more rapid rate of planned growth and development of instruction by television (see Woon 1974).

For a number of years, the ministries of education and information had been studying ETV for Malaysia to provide equal school opportunities throughout the nation. In June 1972, the service was launched on a four-day-a-week schedule, with a daily output of eight 20-minute lessons. In 1973, there were 14 primary and secondary programs daily on a four-day-week cycle.

Five hundred secondary schools were provided receivers in 1972, and in 1973, another 5,000 sets were supplied to primary schools, with the help of a World Bank loan.

Administration and organization are similar to radio schools broadcasting, but the ETV system is aimed at relieving the specialist teacher shortage, particularly in the sciences and mathematics. Back-up materials are supplied to the schools (see Chong 1974).

Hong Kong opened its instructional television service in 1971, after years of careful and detailed preparation. As a result, it has great promise of steady growth and development. The Ministry of Education, budget officer, and educational planners all played significant roles in its establishment, as did the Centre for Educational Development Overseas, Thomson Foundation, BBC, and ETV Singapura. The latter four organizations provided technical, administrative, and production-staff training, as well as a full-time consultant. All financial support is from the local government.

The long-term objective of the service is a systematic series of ETV lessons in basic academic disciplines for the third to sixth years of primary schools, followed by similar series, with the addition of science subjects, from the first to third years of secondary schools. ETV, if developed and applied as planned, should improve the quality of instruction in Hong Kong schools, bring the skills of relatively few specialists to many students, supply valuable in-service training for underqualified and unqualified teachers, help relieve the lack of audio-visual aids, and facilitate curriculum reform (see §2.6.5).

6.3.4 India and the Experiments

At least eight other Asian countries are still in various stages of experimentation. They differ from nations with pilot programs in the absence of an overall plan which leads to a national program of instruction by television. Their top education officials are not committed to television as an essential element in the total educational system.

India was one of the first Asian countries to set up an ITV experiment, doing so in 1961, after the ministries of communication, education, and information had conceived a project and obtained Ford Foundation technical and financial assistance. All India Radio was the key organization not only for production and transmission but in working with educators to bring science, mathematics, English, and Hindi telelessons to Delhi secondary and middle schools. While still existing, the project never developed substantially beyond the experimental stage, seemingly for many reasons, probably the greatest of which related to a lack of involvement by educators. From the start, direction to the project was given by broadcasters. Moreover, insufficient funds and untrained personnel plagued the project. It must also be remembered that Indian television, at least until the early 1970s, was restricted to Delhi; thus, serious governmental commitment could not be justified for such a limited program, especially with the numerous other problems facing India, all of which have greater priorities. In 1972–73, India was embarking on an experiment using the NASA Indian Ocean Satellite for educating people throughout the vast stretches of the subcontinent. The satellite project seemed to indicate a government decision giving priority to nonformal, rather than formal education by television.

Neighboring Pakistan has concentrated on the use of instructional television for adult and continuing education. In 1974, Pakistan actually had several pilot ETV projects. One was the Adult Functional Literacy project, consisting of 156 35-minute lessons designed to make adults functionally literate in six months. Lessons are broadcast six days a week on sets in community viewing centers (see Zaman, 1974).

The Bangkok municipality operates an in-school TV service on a local station, but it is limited to one hour daily, five days a week. Started in 1967, the service features programs on English, science, mathematics, and Thai for post-primary grades, and music and social studies for primary students. In 1971, 102 Bangkok and 102 government and private, non-Bangkok schools used the service (Meyer 1971). The Ministry of Education, with World Bank assistance, is conducting a feasibility study on the introduction of educational mass media nationally (see Bennett 1974).

Other Asian countries have had various groups working with local broadcasting facilities which were made available on a part-time basis for educational purposes. For this, they have, or sometimes have not, obtained the cooperation of education authorities. In all cases, relatively little success has been achieved in aiding the educational systems of these nations (see also §§2.1.2, 2.1.4, 3.3.5, 3.4.6, 3.5.7, 4.4.12, 4.6.8).

6.3.5 Assistance to ITV

Asian instructional television has had to depend upon a number of major organizations for informational, financial, technical, training, and programming assistance.

Among such groups are the Asian Broadcasting Union, Asia Foundation, British Council, CEDO, Ford Foundation, INNOTECH, NHK Pennsylvania State University and Stanford University in the United States, SEATO Colombo Plan, UNESCO, USIS, CEPTA TV, and the World Bank Group.

Knowledg able individuals who have made significant contributions to developing Asian instructional TV include: Arthur Hungerford, who has acted as a consultant in Pakistan and the Philippines; Lian Fook Shin and Peter Seow, both instrumental in setting up Singapore's ETV; Alan Hancook, consultant for the Singapore, Malaysian and Hong Kong ETV services; Colvyn Haye, planner of ETV in Hong Kong; Leo Larkin, designer of the Philippine ETV project; Tadashi Yoshida of NHK;   and Jack McBride of the United States.

6.3.6   Observations

A great deal has been attempted in Asian instructional television during the later 1960s and early 1970s. For example, Japan has developed a very sophisticated ETV system, while pilot projects have been established in the Philippines, Singapore, Malaysia, and Hong Kong, and experimentation has taken place in eight other nations.

In addition, a number of important gatherings of professional educators and/or broadcasters have been convened: the Second International Conference on Educational Radio and Television in Tokyo, 1964; a seminar for education ministers in Samoa, 1967; and a seminar-workshop for Southeast Asia ministers of education in Manila, 1968. Also, NHK has sponsored annually since 1965 The Japan Prize. Still, about three-fourths of Asian countries in 1973 were not using instruction by television, and, outside of Japan, and possibly Hong Kong, Malaysia and Singapore, there has been no real success story.

Reasons for this situation of much activity with little success can be found on at least two levels. Although top government commitments to ETV are vital, obtaining such full support is virtually impossible because of a vicious circle, whereby decisions need knowledge, knowledge needs expertise, expertise needs money for travel and experimentation, and money needs decisions from the top. Furthermore, educators in Asia are in the same position (although much worse off) as their counterparts throughout the developing world; there are few educators who really understand the potential problems and techniques of an instructional television system.

On the experimental or project level, many explanations are possible for poor results, including untrained and inexperienced personnel, inadequate facilities, and hand-to-mouth budgets. Few Asian educators realize that at least three years of excellent leadership under expert consultants are necessary to develop an efficient team and quality operating project, sufficiently adapted to local circumstances, to even begin combating the priority educational problems of any developing country. Only after the pilot project period, can a basic educational development program be initiated.

Indeed, some lessons have been learned from the many and diverse experimental activities, conducted under mostly adverse circumstances, in the 12 Asian nations. (Of course, Japan is an exception.) Among such lessons are: consultations with specialists are required throughout the process of developing an ETV project; ETV is a science as well as an art, learned by training, practice, and comparison of notes with experts from different backgrounds; and basic training should be accomplished in the home country, or at least within the region, while advanced training should be abroad. Concerning the latter point, this type of training will make for less overlearning for not-easily-adaptable neophytes, less frustration when returning home to poor equipment, and less tendency to increase the "brain drain."

The ultimate explanation for much action, some progress, and no real success is that Asia is part of the Third World; it is a developing region with sufficient resources only for priority programs of which ETV is not one. Developing nations have not yet given priority to basic education, and only Japan in Asia seems to have provided sufficient funds for a successful ITV program.

The entire region, however, is rapidly approaching a stage of readiness and receptiveness for instructional television. New Asian governments are beginning to realize that quality education is needed for national development and that this quality education can be effected through TV, because it has the potential to bring the best teacher into the classrooms of a maximum number of students in a relatively short time. More senior education officials in Asia are beginning to understand that instruction by television has no mysterious mystique once it is properly studied and employed in local circumstances. There are a growing number of excellent and experienced educators in the four Asian ITV pilot projects and the many other ITV experiments. There are foundations, foreign governments, and international financing institutions, as well as the Asian Broadcasting Union, which realize the potential of this medium for uplifting education, effecting national development, and bringing about regional cooperation. The time seems right for development, and the next decade promises even more substantial and better use of television for educational purposes than the first.

Perhaps one of the most significant developments came about in February 1973, at a meeting in Al Ain, Abu Dhabi. This meeting of representatives from the seven international broadcasting unions discussed regional workshops on educational broadcasting which might lead to a Fourth International Conference on Educational Radio and Television by 1976 or 1977. The meeting was a successful and important milestone in educational broadcasting, not only in Asia, but throughout the world, because a solid basis for future cooperation was established.

Viewing instructional television in Asia is like flying into a city on the edge of a desert. Asia is the desert. Japan is the city which has all the educational conveniences of modern living — a well-developed ITV system. The four ITV pilot projects are cases where there are only the basic requirements of modern life — rudimentary ITV systems. The remaining nations of Asia are caravans of educational nomads knowing of ITV, but able to do little about it. In Asia, there is a great difference between the "haves" and the "have-nots." And this is the potential of television in education: It can be a great equalizer providing better education for more students.

7. International, Regional, and National Assistance/Cooperation

Assistance to Asian and Pacific broadcasting activities comes in bilateral, as well as multilateral packages, from outside the region, as well as from within. Areas where assistance and cooperation are offered might be categorized into training, programming, and technology. More specifically, help is provided in broadcast planning, frequency allocation, staff and program exchanges, general funding, satellite usage, news flow and dissemination, cable distribution, training seminars, and courses and meetings, among others.

The first four chapters of this section deal generally with such assistance, giving, first of all, an overall view of organizations assisting in Asian and Pacific broadcasting, followed by examples of international (UNESCO), regional (South Pacific Commission), and national (BBC) groups involved.

The last three chapters focus on assistance to Asian and Pacific educational broadcasting, a field where funding and training organizations seem increasingly willing to place their resources. Arthur Hungerford summarizes activities of such groups generally in South and Southeast Asia, after which two case studies are provided: one dealing with the philosophy relative to educational broadcasting in Asia of the Centre for Educational Development Overseas, the other detailing unique aspects of CEPTA TV's adult education project for Southeast Asia.

Primary data for most of these chapters came from interviews, observations, and in-region experiences of these seven authors, nearly all of whom spent considerable time in planning and implementing Asian broadcasting.

7.1 Broadcasting Organizations: An Overview, *by Charles E. Sherman*

7.1.1 Introduction

Most aid to Asian broadcasting emanates from international, regional, and

Charles E. Sherman is Chairman of the Department of Telecommunications at Indiana University. He is the author of articles on international broadcasting organizations in Europe, Asia, and Africa.

national organizations which, on one hand, encourages the growth of broadcasting to promote social, educational, and economic development, and on the other, provides means for improving program service quality.

Principal international bodies engaged in these activities are United Nations agencies, such as UNESCO (see §7.2), International Telecommunication Union (ITU), Economic and Social Commission for Asia and the Pacific (ESCAP), formerly called Economic Commission for Asia and the Far East (ECAFE), and the United Nations Development Program (UNDP).

Regional organizations include the 24 nations adhering to the Colombo Plan, the South Pacific Commission (see §7.3), and the Asian Broadcasting Union (ABU), a nongovernmental body formed in 1964 and composed of national broadcasting services in the Asian/Pacific area (see *ABU Newsletter,* July 1974). Examples of national groups offering extensive and frequent assistance are Nippon Hoso Kyokai (NHK), Australian Broadcasting Commission (ABC), British Broadcasting Corporation (see §7.4), and Friedrich Ebert Stiftung (FES) (see §7.7).

Working alone or occasionally in conjunction with one another, these groups have developed aid programs in the four major areas of increasing the flow of news and information, training technical and programming personnel, program exchanges, and research.

7.1.2 Increasing the Flow of News and Information

Writing in 1947, a UNESCO press counselor stated that UNESCO was dedicated to "the encouragement of the free flow of ideas by word and image" (Maheu 1948, p. 157). Since then, this dedication has been evinced in several ways.

As a result of a number of regional studies it conducted, plus a 1960 Bangkok conference on "Developing Mass Media in Asia," UNESCO initiated practical action in the area of news flow. For example, a 1961 UNESCO-sponsored seminar for Asian news agencies led, two years later, to the establishment of the Organization of Asian News Agencies. Composed of eight national groups, OANA attempts to ensure continuing cooperation among its members. In September 1974; one member of OANA, Jakarta News Center in Indonesia, started broadcasts for the benefit of OANA members through Antara News Agency's 20-kw. transmitter. The contents of these broadcasts, transmitted one hour daily, consist of news from OANA members, which the Jakarta News Center obtains by monitoring these members' overseas transmissions (*AMC Bulletin,* December 1974, p 18). Additionally, at the request of member states, UNESCO sent expert missions to Nepal, Malaysia, and Thailand to assist in the creation of national news agencies (Topuz 1970, pp. 501–4).

To train journalists to handle news flow, two seminars, held in the Philippines and India in 1961 and 1964, respectively, encouraged the development of regional training activities, to which UNESCO responded by funding the mass communication institute at the University of the Philippines. UNESCO also helped to prepare a national program for the Indian Institute of Mass

Communication in New Delhi (Topuz 1968, pp. 419–24).

Dissemination of news is also of interest to ABU. Looking to the time when costs will be low enough to use satellites for regular news exchanges, ABU met with news experts from the European Broadcasting Union in 1971 to discuss joint action. This exploratory meeting, while not producing immediate results, established contacts which could eventually produce a fast and efficient means for relaying news between these diverse regions (*ABU Newsletter* 1971a, p. 8). In 1972, ABU was invited to a meeting of EBU's Working Party for TV News, attended by regional unions representing Eastern Europe (OIRT), the Arab nations (ASBU), and South America (OTI), and held to explore the possibility of extending news exchanges into other regions (Petersen 1972, pp. 21–24).

In a more practical vein, ABU, at the suggestion of the International Broadcast Institute, organized a news workshop in 1971, attended by representatives from 23 Asian services, as well as EBU members and an American delegation. NHK hosted the conference and FES provided travel assistance, allowing many ABU members to attend. With the aim of fostering interregional flow of news, the participants discussed news judgment and selection, costs of news operations, and means for increasing exchanges. ABU organized a more ambitious workshop in 1973, bringing together representatives of regional unions, news and newsfilm agencies, and satellite and customs authorities. Particular attention at this meeting was given in reducing news flow costs and standardizing procedures both within and between regions. In January 1975, the ABU, supported by FES, held a news workshop in Teheran to examine the need to establish regular news exchanges among Asian broadcasters. A proposal was made to set up a regional feasibility study on the organization of exchanges between ABU members in the region and with other broadcasting unions throughout the world (*Intermedia* 1975a, pp. 18–19).

In a more specialized aspect of news, ABU in the early 1970s tried through two seminars to improve sportscasting in its region. Besides observing sports-reporting techniques and discussing means of improving standards, delegates to a 1971 Singapore seminar also examined the possibility of developing a pool arrangement for covering international events. Both seminars were supported by two West German broadcast services and FES. To concentrate efforts in this area, an Asian Sports Broadcasters Association was formed within the framework of ABU. Finally, again through ABU initiative, the regional unions, including EBU, OIRT, URTNA, Inter-American Association of Broadcasters (AIR), and observers from North America, met in Venice in 1972 to explore interregional collaboration in the sports field and to consider means of stabilizing the spiraling costs of TV rights for such events. It is significant to observe that the unions were generally represented at these seminars by their high officials, an indication of the apparent increasing interest in global broadcasting cooperation.

Important to effective news flow is the elimination or reduction of legal and technical barriers which impede such activity. As an example, a UNESCO seminar pointed out that news flow is hindered by governments imposing high import duties on radio sets instead of developing local industries for their manufacture or assembly (UNESCO, 23–28 June 1969). Since the late 1940s, UNESCO has striven to reduce importation tariffs on educational materials, including radios. Although somewhat successful, this effort has been hindered by many Asian governments which persist in imposing excessive duties on such items (Ragsdale 1960, pp 275–79). UNESCO has also worked closely with ITU "to draw up specifications for one or more types of (radio) receivers suitable for production in large quantities at the lowest possible cost" (UNESCO 1961, p. 12). In 1960, UNESCO requested that ECAFE study the feasibility of establishing indigenous radio manufacturers to avoid import duties and high freight charges. Limited success was achieved from such programs as evidenced by the growth of radio receivers in South Asia from approximately 16 per 1,000 inhabitants in 1958, to 33 in 1969. East Asia, excluding the People's Republic of China, had 192 radio sets per 1,000 people in 1969.

Copyright legislation can also impede news flow, and in this area, in 1971, UNESCO promulgated a revision of its Universal Copyright Convention which affords developing nations a favorable position. Although the major exemptions apply to printed matter, certain provisions impose less restrictive financial burdens on imported materials utilized in educational broadcasting. This agreement was reached concurrently with the Berne Copyright Convention and thus has greater force than if it applied only to nations adhering to the Universal Convention (Dock 1972, pp. 175–85).

Except for Japan, Australia, and New Zealand, Asian and Pacific nations are confronted by the lack of extensive telecommunication networks, thereby inhibiting information flow both on a national and international level. This situation also limits the development of national and international broadcasting networks and news agencies. Ways of solving the problem have been under investigation by both ECAFE and ITU. In 1958, seeking to connect Southeast Asia with Europe's telecommunication network, ITU surveyed telecommunication services in Asia. An international meeting, convened by ECAFE in 1969, examined the resultant report and recommended action at the national, regional, and international levels for telecommunication development. Apparently little was accomplished as ECAFE, at its 1970 session, approved a plan of operation providing for a feasibility and preinvestment survey for a South and Southeast Asia regional telcommunication network. This survey of 12 nations was also executed by ITU under a $538,200 grant from UNDP (*ABU Newsletter* 1970). Completed in 1972, it indicated that such a network was technically feasible and economically viable, that it would cost about $22 million, of which 90% would be for new radio system links, and that "soft" loan criteria be used by the funding agencies. It also urged that similar feasibility surveys be undertaken in other ECAFE areas (*ABU Newsletter* 1972). By mid-1975, ESCAP (formerly ECAFE) hoped for the development of an Asian Tele-community, to construct a vast telecommunications network across Asia, were underway. Functions of the 14-nation Asian Telecommunity were seen to be: coordinated programming, implementation and operation of technical standards on a regional basis, operational planning, tariff harmonization, and arrangement of finance for development and routing of traffic (*AMC Bulletin*, June 1975, p. 14; *Intermedia*, August 1975, p. 20).

Since the mid-1960s, utilization of satellites has been sought to ease the telecommunication problem. The United Nations itself and two of its specialized agencies are particularly involved with satellites, the UN dealing with peaceful uses of outer space, ITU with technical aspects and international coordination, and UNESCO with methods by which satellites can be used to promote the flow of cultural, educational, scientific, and informational materials (*UNESCO Chronicle* 1970). ITU and UNESCO have studied matters of immediate concern to Asian broadcasting systems.

At an ITU space communication meeting in 1971, particular attention was given to needs of developing nations and to reserving spectrum allocations for them when they have the technological capability to employ satellites. In its area of competence, UNESCO, beginning in 1963, issued reports on space communication and since 1965 conducted a series of meetings with government officials, space scientists, and broadcasting representatives (Gjesdal 1970, pp. 439–52). The 1965 meeting recommended that a pilot project be initiated in a large and heavily populated area to test satellite potentialities, particularly for educational purposes. As a result, India requested UNESCO to explore such possibilities within its boundaries. A resultant report, issued in 1968, was favorable, and the project proceeded with the aid of other UN agencies and the United States (see "Communications in Asia '75").

Of more immediate value to Asian broadcasters is the ABU Temporary Coordinating Centre for Satellite Transmissions. Supervised by NHK in Tokyo, the center assists those ABU members who can receive satellite transmissions and have television facilities. It operates on a cost-sharing principle, similar to EBU's Eurovision, whereby larger broadcasting organizations pay a greater share of the expenses, thus allowing participation by those smaller systems without substantial resources. The formula, based on the number of TV sets in each country, is used when three or more member states are sharing satellite facilities and is applied only to program costs related directly to satellite transmissions, including landline charges from the originating point to the ground station and the link from the ground stations to the satellite. Cost-sharing is not utilized in the down-link from the satellite to the receiving country and in charges for broadcasting rights. ABU members using the center also pay a proportionate share of its expenses, which, during the initial two years, were borne entirely by NHK. In the early 1970s, ABU, satisfied with the center's work, was studying means to make it a permanent operation (ABU 1972, pp. 1–4).

Finally, concerning the use of satellite communications, a new group, Working Group on Regional Satellite Systems of South East Asian Nations

(ASEAN) met in 1974 to study the feasibility of a satellite-based system of communications for Malaysia, Indonesia, Thailand, Singapore, and the Philippines (*Intermedia,* August 1975, p. 20).

7.1.3 Training Technical and Programming Personnel

Studies describing Asian mass media constantly emphasize the lack of qualified personnel as one of the most severe problems inhibiting the growth and quality of broadcast services. In response, many international agencies have established training schemes, such as training centers, seminars, visiting experts, and fellowships. Although providing some relief, these efforts cannot keep pace with the needs, especially as TV services are inaugurated and technology is broadened.

Broadcast training centers in Asia have been practically nonexistent, except in Japan. A 1967 UNESCO survey indicated that "the total range of what has been attempted (in broadcast training) so far, and its impact, have not been commensurate with the requirements" (Mullick and Bourke 1968, p. 10). This survey, as well as requests by ABU, eventually led UNESCO to support the National Broadcasting Training Centre in Kuala Lumpur, housed temporarily in the former facilities of Television Malaysia. Money for renovation and equipment was supplied by the British Special Aid Loan Fund and the Malaysian government (see also §7.2).

NBTC, immediately after its creation in 1971, started moving from a national to a regional format. For example, in 1972, UNESCO and UNDP sponsored regional courses at NBTC on educational production, film technique, and technical management and operations for television. More recent courses in which NBTC participated dealt with problems of rural broadcasters and broadcast engineers in Asia (*ABU Newsletter,* May 1975, pp. 21–22, and September 1974, pp. 9–12). At the same time, a UNESCO regional broadcasting training advisor, with the assistance and advice of ABU, visited Sri Lanka, Western Samoa, Fiji, Indonesia, and Nepal to give courses in educational broadcasting or radio production. Other visitations planned for 1973 included Afghanistan, Papua New Guinea, Cook Islands, and Tonga (McBain 1972, pp. 17–21).

Even with these initial efforts, it should not be assumed that the regional training institute will become a reality. Alan Hancock, then UNESCO regional training advisor responsible for developing the institute, indicated at a 1971 ABU meeting, that its success rested in the hands of Asian broadcasters and their governments. He explained that funding from international and bilateral agencies would depend on the types of priorities Asian governments attach to the institute, thus, broadcasters would have to convince their governments that the proposal is worth supporting (*ABU Newsletter* 1971c, p. 18). This financial uncertainty evidently still existed in 1973. Resolutions passed at an ABU meeting urged members to see to what extent they could contribute to the institute, asked UNESCO to make inquiries at the regional ministerial level, and "requested the (ABU) Secretary-General to solicit substantial financial support for the Institute from appropriate Foundations and international bodies" ("Resolutions" 1972, p. 2).

In 1975, an organization funded by UNESCO and meant to regionalize activities carried out by NBTC was sponsoring TV and training courses (*Malaysian Digest*, 15 September 1975, p. 7). The Asian Institute for Broadcasting Development, located in Kuala Lumpur and incorporating UNESCO's Asian Broadcasting Training Institute, was working in conjunction with ABU, NBTC, and the United Nations Development Program in the area of broadcasting training.

Some technical instruction related to broadcasting is provided at national telecommunication training centers located in Malaysia, Indonesia, Pakistan, Thailand, Afghanistan, and more recently, Singapore. Development of the centers was guided by ITU and funded by UNDP in conjunction with the respective governments (*Telecommunication Journal* 1972a). Since these centers are concerned with the general area of telecommunications, they deal only with such phases of broadcasting as transmission facilities and management and monitoring of frequency allocations. ITU also arranges for secondments of telecommunication experts for on-the-job training, as well as fellowships for trainees to visit developed countries. Additionally, ITU has three of its own experts assigned to Asia, stationed in Bangkok, where they are responsible for assisting countries in joint ITU/UNDP projects, including formulation of new training centers and telecommunication networks (*Telecommunication Journal* 1972b).

Despite such technical training and aid, there is not optimum utilization of spectrum resources in Asia. For example, a report to UNESCO's 1960 meeting on developing mass media in Asia indicated:

While there is an element of order in the medium frequency broadcasting bands for Region 3 (which covers a large portion of South East Asia), the same cannot be said for the tropical and high frequency broadcasting bands.

A very serious situation exists in South East Asia. It is serious enough for *international* high frequency broadcasting, because there is a reflected effect on the availability of international programmes to listeners. This is, of course, due to the harmful effects of mutual interference between different broadcasting stations operating on the same or adjacent frequencies.

However, if it is serious for the *international* service, it is doubly so for the *national* services of South East Asian countries since many of them rely upon high frequencies for national coverage. [UNESCO 1960, p. 91]

Expressing concern over this situation, the meeting suggested that a regional seminar be held to consider technical broadcasting matters.

This suggestion, however, was not acted upon until 1970, when ITU, with the collaboration of ABU and the Malaysian government, organized its first seminar for Asian programming engineers. Thirty-nine delegates from 25 nations attended and heard presentations on international regulations for frequency management in the broadcasting spectrum, radio-wave propagations, external and internal characteristics of antennas used in broadcasting, organization of a broadcasting transmission center, and recruitment and training of technical personnel. A second ITU seminar for technicians was arranged in conjunction with ABU in Jakarta during November 1973.

Other UN agencies collaborated with ABU on two occasions to provide training seminars on disseminating specialized content via broadcasting. As part of its program concerning young people, UNESCO participated in a 1972 seminar, also supported by the Prix Jeunesse Foundation of West Germany, which considered how broadcast media can best serve this age group (*ABU Newsletter*, November–December 1972, pp. 29–32). The Food and Agriculture Organization offered a farm broadcasting course for Asian nations in 1966, which was hosted by NHK.

With the limitation on national training opportunities in Asia, broadcasting organizations must send their staffs abroad or occasionally have foreign consultants seconded. Major contributors to such training are Australian Broadcating Commission, BBC, and NHK which, over 15 years, received 788 individuals from 17 Asian countries. Lasting from three to six months, these courses usually concern rural or educational broadcasting techniques, as well as engineering matters. Trainees living and travel expenses are generally borne under the Colombo Plan and technical assistance programs of host countries. A unique fellowship is also offered each year by the Federation of Australian Commercial Broadcasters (FACB), which selects one individual from an ABU member organization to study commercial techniques.

All such training programs and seminars are vital for the improvement of Asian broadcasting. Nevertheless, they do not fill current needs and there appears to be a widening gap. Responses by 15 nations to a UNESCO training survey reveal that 22,543 individuals were employed in their broadcasting activities in the late 1960s, and another 13,497 were expected to be added by 1972 or 1973 (Mullick and Bourke 1968, p. 25). Most of these personnel require training but cannot obtain it. Furthermore, serious questions are raised from time to time about training abroad, indicating it is frequently ineffectual.

7.1.4 Program Exchanges

ABU is apparently the only organization promoting a *regular* exchange of program materials among Asian broadcasting services. Its most successful exchange is the radio Folk Music Festival, organized annually since 1968. At least 18 nations are involved each year, participants sending one another approximately 30 minutes of recorded, indigenous music accompanied by background notes, on a common theme. On approximately the same date, each country presents selections of this music, crediting ABU as the organizer. The project is especially valuable for obtaining music from countries without extensive recording industries (see Sherman 1969, pp. 397–414). NHK planned a series of recordings based on the 1973 Folk Music Festival, which were to be issued in honor of ABU's tenth anniversary in 1974 (*ABU Newsletter*, September 1974, pp. 7–8). In addition to this exchange, NHK and ABC have produced special recordings, "Melodies of Asia" and "Popular Songs of the ABU Region," respectively, which are available to ABU members at cost, as well as to other interested parties (see *ABU Newsletter*, August 1973, pp. 14–15).

Since not all ABU members operate television services, exchanges in this field are more limited than radio. The only regular television exchange is the ABU magazine, originally initiated on a monthly basis; now, bimonthly. One- to four-minute filmed stories, depicting national events, are forwarded by participants, accompanied by an English-language script. The magazine is intended to be a complete presentation using the ABU signature and sound signal; larger Asian broadcasting organizations, however, do not abide by this format; instead, they use the pieces irregularly in their own programs. Apparently having limited value, this exchange is used primarily by smaller television services with minimal program and financial resources. Many participants also fail to send their contributions promptly, if at all, and frequently, materials from smaller services do not meet technical standards.

ABU members have coproduced a series of educational films, entitled "Neighbours," for· school and TV use. Underwritten by the Edward E. Ford Foundation of the United States, the initial six films were made during 1969 in Brunei, Malaysia, and Singapore, involving production personnel from those countries, as well as an ABC producer and director (*ABU Newsletter* 1969). Revenue from the first series was used to produce a second, concerning Iran and Afghanistan, with NHK assisting; still another is planned, on Fiji and New Zealand, with ABC participating again. As executed, the "Neighbours" project serves the purposes of supplying new program materials and having experienced producer-directors work with staffs from developing countries.

Other ABU attempts at arranging program exchanges have not met with much success, including those concerning farm broadcasts, dramatic scripts, and interlude films. In an effort to consolidate its program activities and to improve participation in the exchanges, the ninth ABU General Assembly passed resolutions stating:

that exchanges should be limited to those now being arranged which are proving successful;

that the assistance of the larger member organizations should continue to be sought in organising appropriate exchanges, thus enabling the small staff of the Secretariat to carry out its other pressing work more effectively;

that the exchanges involving drama scripts and interlude films, which have failed to elicit the interest of members, should be discontinued;

that, in order to make existing exchanges even more successful, members should be requested to consider the advisability of making the active participation of their programme staffs in such exchanges a matter of management policy, and

that, wherever possible, delegates attending meetings of the Programme

Committee should be staff actively engaged in the programme field. ["Resolutions 1972, p. 12]

Several reasons account for these ABU exchanges having achieved limited success, when compared with EBU and OIRT. Most important is the great diversity among ABU member nations, ranging from the sophisticated and large ABC and NHK to much smaller organizations in South Vietnam, Western Samoa, and Afghanistan. The difference in needs and resources of these services is vast, making it extremely difficult to develop program materials suited to each. A gap also exists in stations' technical standards and competence, and in national languages and cultures, all of which hamper exchanges. Most of these problems are minimized in EBU and OIRT because of a greater degree of homogeneity among members.

Another impediment is the lack of a regional telecommunication network, preventing permanent interconnection for programs of immediate interest and importance. Satellite transmissions occasionally fill this void and were used to televise portions of the Asian and Olympic Games and the last Apollo space missions. Nevertheless, participation in these exchanges is limited by a small number of earth stations operating in Asia, as well as the high rates charged by national post-telegraph-telephone administrations (PTT) for satellite utilization. Because of these factors, only such countries as Japan, Australia, Korea, and Indonesia participate frequently in satellite cost-sharing activities. To broaden participation, ABU passed several resolutions asking members to press their national PTT's for a reduction of satellite tariffs.

Asian broadcasters also obtain program materials either free or at low cost from, among other sources, foreign embassies and the UN and its agencies (see Thompson 1971). For example, UNESCO offers various coproduced television programs, including "Training for Tomorrow," concerning scientific and technological development in Pakistan, and "The Science Side," illustrating science teaching in New Delhi secondary schools (*UNESCO Chronicle* 1971). Many radio stations also broadcast news daily from either the ABC or BBC international services which are picked up off the air.

In 1974, the Hoso Bunka Foundation of Japan, affiliated with NHK to assist in the development of broadcasting, granted funds to ABU in conjunction with the annual ABU prize competitions. The prizes, designed to encourage better broadcast program production in Asia, are awarded for the best programs of folk or traditional music on radio, TV shows reflecting social or national development, radio programs supporting the objectives of International Women's Year, TV documentaries, and TV documentaries produced on a low budget (*ABU Newsletter*, August 1974, pp. 3–4, and June 1975, p. 7).

7.1.5 Research

Usually, internationally sponsored research concerning Asian mass media is contained in world-wide studies sponsored by such bodies as UNESCO and the

International Broadcast Institute. Few deal specifically with Asia.

Initial UNESCO studies focussed mainly on the status of media facilities and personnel in developing countries, seeking ways to improve their condition and encouraging governments to use them in the development process. While this descriptive research continues, especially regarding satellite communications, more attention is now given to socio-cultural influences of media. This approach was emphasized at a 1969 UNESCO "Meeting of Experts on Mass Communication and Society," which recommended more intensive research on media impact on social problems, transitional societies, values, attitudes, and world conflict (UNESCO 1970b, pp. 26–27). One of the more recent research projects of UNESCO concerning Asian mass media is in the area of professional standards. Meeting under UNESCO guidance in 1973, representatives of Asian print and electronic media organizations pledged to prepare draft guidelines to form "national codes for promoting the sense of responsibility which should accompany freedom of expression" (*AMC Bulletin,* December 1974, p. 19).

IBI, composed of broadcasters, social scientists, and journalists selected from throughout the world, conducts research and conferences that are congruent with UNESCO. It has considered the problems of news flow, influence of new communications technology, and broadcasting and national development.

There is still, however, a shortage of reliable data concerning Asian mass media, which led the Second International Conference on Mass Media in Asia, sponsored by Friedrich Ebert Stiftung (FES) in 1969, to recommend the founding in Singapore of the Asian Mass Communication Research and Information Centre (AMIC). The Singapore government and FES cosponsored AMIC, the latter providing initial financing until the center is self-supporting (*ABU Newsletter* 1969a). AMIC serves as a regional clearing house, collecting, cataloging, and disseminating information to individuals working in or studying Asian media. It promotes research through numerous seminars and by publishing *Media Asia,* numerous monographs and bibliographies and *Asian Mass Communication Bulletin;* AMIC, however, does not fund individual projects. A traveling seminar program is also arranged for educators to visit universities and institutes and discuss common research problems.

AMIC's region of interest is the eastern end of the Mediterranean Sea to the middle of the Pacific Ocean, the same area encompassed by ABU. Not to overextend its resources, however, in the early 1970s, AMIC was operating in an area bounded by Indonesia in the southeast, Korea in the northeast, and Afghanistan in the west. Membership is open to individuals connected with Asian mass media, subject to committee approval. AMIC also has a network of national correspondents who help provide information otherwise not widely available. In 1976, AMIC was "sold" to the Singapore government.

7.1.6 Discussion

It would be easy to criticize the international organizations for not doing enough regarding Asian broadcasting, but the needs are great and costly. In addition, international organization relationships, governmental or otherwise, are complex and affected by many considerations. For example, their aid programs are a result of compromise, attempting to reconcile the views and demands of national representatives. Frequently, projects are abandoned because they are considered not in a particular country's national interest. Even if aid is offered, national governments may reject it or use it in ways that were not originally intended. Finally, in still a few instances, broadcasting is not given a high priority by developing nations, whose governments will not support the work of the international organizations involved in the field.

An example of these nationalistic problems is provided by Lester Pearson, former Canadian Prime Minister and IBI chairman. Speaking on the political implications of satellite communications, he noted the roles played by ITU and UNESCO, stating, "The ITU has made efforts to discharge and develop its responsibilities in line with the changes that have taken place but, like UNESCO itself, its hands are too often tied by the governments and government-sponsored communications agencies which it represents" (Pearson 1972, p. 12). Similar problems afflict most international bodies, and their resolution requires unique tact and statesmanship.

Another serious problem is finding financial assistance, as exemplified by the Asian Broadcasting Training Institute. Often, projects are started on "soft" money and, once these funds are dissipated, the scale of the projects is drastically reduced or terminated — sometimes at a stage when they are beginning to produce desired benefits. This situation is frequently the fault of the national governments, which fail to continue projects after initial funding by an international body. Also, the amount of aid money available to international organizations might become more limited in the future, particularly for the UN agencies. For example, in 1971, UNDP began to reduce funds for certain programs, which had an adverse impact on the ITU. Because of this slash in funds, a number of ITU regional and interregional projects for Asia and Africa were placed in jeopardy, postponed or canceled completely (*Telecommunication Journal* 1972c).

Despite these problems, the international organizations have contributed greatly to Asian broadcasting growth, and it is evident that they intend, as much as resources and cooperation allow, to continue this important involvement in the years ahead. Without these efforts, the development of broadcasting in Asia could be seriously stunted.

7.2 UNESCO, *by Alan Hancock*

7.2.1 Integrative Philosophy

The United Nations Educational, Scientific, and Cultural Organization has been active in broadcasting — in Asia, as in other regions of the world — for over 20 years. While the "communication" did not appear in the organization's original title, communication development has been long recognized as an integral factor in the promotion of education, science, and culture, as in the promotion of development generally.

UNESCO's involvement in broadcasting rests on an assumption that, in modern societies, mass-media industries take up resources — human, financial, and material — which, in the context of their total operation, can be a most important part of a nation's economic and social infrastructure. For this reason, it is argued that all communication media need to be studied, analyzed, and planned together, not individually, sectorally, or on an *ad hoc* basis.

Such an integration concept has not always been clear, it frequently being argued that, in earlier decades, there was an exaggerated emphasis on technology and its products, and less attempt to deal with the more recalcitrant areas of materials development, utilization, and application. If this had been the case, it was partly so because of a feeling, current 15 years ago but no longer acceptable, that a machine technology might be developed to cope in a programmed format with all aspects of the learning process. This belief was compounded by the difficulty of facing up to the intellectual demands of producing and utilizing sophisticated materials for a rash of new technical devices. In the field of software design and instructional materials, external factors had to be accounted for — political, psychological, sectoral — which could only be approached outside the electronics laboratory.

Although true in both the developing and developed world, this situation has been even more marked in the context of development, where suitable infrastructures are not always available. It was to be expected therefore, that the earliest UNESCO ventures into the broadcasting arena were *ad hoc* and often on a very small scale; they included, in the 1950s, such characteristic activities as short-term training for radio operations and production personnel in Turkey. In the 1960s, however, greater international emphasis was placed on freedom of information as a fundamental human right. A report placed before ECOSOC (the UN Economic and Social Council) argued that 70% of the world's population was deprived of this basic freedom, and with the acceptance of the claim, development of mass media became more and more relevant as an aspect of economic development. In the decade which followed, UNESCO contributed to the planning and founding of such varied institutions as news agencies, journalism training programs, mass communication research centers, and a number of educational broadcasting projects.

7.2.2 Current Projects

A brief review of contemporary Asian activities of the Department of the Free Flow of Information and Development of Communication (the sector of

Alan Hancock holds a senior post with UNESCO in Paris. He was a former UNESCO regional broadcasting planning advisor for Asia and CETO advisor to the Singapore government from 1966-68, where he helped develop Educational Television Service. He was a BBC producer for many years and the author of about a half-dozen books on mass communication.

UNESCO most directly concerned with broadcasting) shows something of the present range. Broadcasting training projects are in progress, with UNESCO sponsorship, in India and Malaysia, and projected in the Pacific, on the premise that broadcasting media cannot be effectively harnessed to educational and social development unless professional techniques are also mastered effectively. The Indian project is a realistic adjunct to a massive expansion of television which is currently taking place, involving both the development of the terrestrial network and a satellite experiment for the direct transmission of TV programs to 5,000 isolated villages. The technology of such an expansion can be catered for, but the main effort now is to provide a sufficient cadre of trained personnel, in all fields, to handle the volume of programming and supporting structures necessary if technology is not to be wasted.

In Malaysia, the development of the National Broadcasting Training Centre is a practical offshoot of a move toward improved professional standards. It also derives from a belief that basic training is best given in a national environment, where surroundings, both technical and human, are familiar to the new trainee. A corollary of this position is that more experienced personnel may be trained regionally (since at the regional level, a greater economy of resources and instructional personnel is possible), with overseas and international training being reserved for more senior staff, who can gain most from an exposure to foreign practices and make the necessary transfer of experience so as to relate what they learn to their domestic problems.

NBTC works with some 100−150 full-time national trainees annually. At the same time, first steps have been taken toward the creation of a regional broadcasting training institute, eventually capable of providing advanced training each year for 300 senior personnel from countries spreading from Iran to the Pacific, as well as sending touring teams into member nations for more fundamental training exercises (also see §7.1.3). The initial NBTC program was being extended in 1973, to cover developmental and family-planning communication, as well as more traditional broadcasting skills. Meanwhile, work was beginning on the construction of a new training complex to cater to regional, as well as national, training. When completed in 1974, it was to offer two television studios with color capacity, three radio studios, and comprehensive film, engineering, laboratory, design, and lecturing facilities.

In the Philippines, in India, and more recently in Malaysia, UNESCO has been involved in undergraduate-level studies in mass communication, a little-known discipline in Asia until the late 1960s. The organization is also involved in the planning and extension of educational broadcasting, at both the in-school and out-of-school levels, in a number of countries ranging from Singapore and Malaysia to Thailand, Sri Lanka, India, and Afghanistan. In addition, particular attention is paid to specific applications of media, such as family planning and population education, in such nations as Thailand, Malaysia, and Indonesia.

The demands in such applied fields vary from year to year, following the pattern of priorities set by each country and by the prevailing attitude to development broadcasting. For this reason, regional advisors and touring teams are made available whenever possible to survey individual country situations, make project proposals, conduct training courses and workshops and monitor progress. These include advisors in broadcasting training, family-planning communication, and more recently, a team based in Bangkok which is developing the Asian Centre for Educational Innovation and Development, which includes in its broad educational framework interests of particular concern for mass media.

7.2.3 Planning Assistance

As an international agency, UNESCO is not equipped with large resources of its own. Even when it acts as executing agent for the UNDP or World Bank, mass-media development still remains at a restricted stage of growth. But UNESCO has always had one critical function to perform, that being the provision of planning assistance, at a formative stage, for the development of projects which may later be taken up by other agencies or governments themselves. This was true in the 1960s (as, for example, in the creation of Bernama, the Malaysian news agency), and holds currently, with studies in hand of communication in Indonesia and educational broadcasting in Thailand. The context of such studies, however, has changed radically.

The Department of the Free Flow of Information and Development of Communication in the early 1970s was reforming itself into three separate divisions of planning and research, development and applications, and free flow of information. The communication sector of UNESCO claims a wide range of interests: planning for communication growth in a systematic way, creating institutions and applying techniques to particular problem areas, and encouraging international exchanges of information and the consolidation of international agreements. These spheres of activity are not conceived as separate; rather, their relationship is essentially cyclic, proceeding from a general recognition that mass-communication channels, cutting as they do across whole populations, and even regions, cannot develop piecemeal if they are to be efficient and economical. The need is therefore to establish planning mechanisms which can be related, practically and nationally, to countries and regions as diverse as those of Asia.

In the first place, it is argued — and the claim was endorsed by a 1971 meeting of communication research specialists in Paris — that each country needs to develop a "communication policy," a set of norms designed to guide the behavior of communications institutions, expressed in realistic and practical terms. Such a policy is not visualized as a piece of legislative censorship; nor is it seen as a planning mechanism which can be applied to the public sector only. It is intended to be a pragmatic design, in which channels and media, under both public and private ownership, are taken into account, with no more attempt to impose an autocratic structure than the culture and tradition of the country endorses. The policy proceeds from two premises. First, it must be based upon a view of the communication process as a *total* process, looking at media in the widest possible economic, social, and political setting, and dealing with questions of utilization and response, as much as with production and distribution channels. Second, it must be based upon a complete review of the character and capacity of the country's communication networks. In the mass-communication field, too little information is available about the existing situation to allow for any effective forward planning. This is certainly true of many nations in the Asian region.

Such studies, in many cases, are novel, and some acknowledgment has to be made of their limitations. Most analyses of the media have been carried out, to date, in terms of channels, content analysis, and broad sociological trends, attempting to look at all media as a composite and interconnected whole, including radio, television, press, cinema, and all other associated media, mechanisms, and channels — from commercial advertising to distribution by satellites. Many analyses exist of society and of life styles of different societies, but few of these have been approached from a communication standpoint. As a result, the tools available to the communication planner are often crude, and there are few specialists who can look authoritatively at communication from a multidisciplinary viewpoint. Naturally, such multidisciplinary skills have to be taught, and training in communication planning is part of the current UNESCO program, drawing on experienced media personnel from all continents, including Asia.

7.2.4 Communication Policies

Development of communication policies at the national level was already initiated by the early 1970s. At a 1971 UNESCO meeting in Paris, it was proposed that in each country, a national communication policy council be formed, made up of opinion leaders in political, economic, media, and educational sectors, and that ultimately, communication planning units evolve, with the same broad terms of reference in their own sphere, as economic or educational planning units have elsewhere. This is a necessity, if the waste so frequent in modern communication networks is ever to be eliminated — waste which may mean that sound educational productions cannot be aired over national transmitters, or if aired, cannot be incorporated into educational and cultural systems. This situation is true of many developed nations, but in a developing region such as Asia, its solution is crucial. One of the major reasons why mass communication has been so disappointing as an agent of planned educational and social change is that media creations, though often individually ingenious and well-conceived, have rarely been systematized. Some countries are now, fortunately, acknowledging this situation and attempting to redress it; India and Malaysia are characteristic Asian examples.

The role of UNESCO in such a process cannot be large, but it can, nevertheless, be critical. Definitely, a need exists for some coordinating agent, free of political or commercial taint, at the planning and research level. One proposal has been to set up communication planning missions — interdisciplinary teams composed of media planners, educational technologists, sociologists, telecommunications engineers, and production and distribution specialists across a variety of media — which, while working within a country for a period of weeks or months, can evolve a basic set of guidelines for government use in its next development cycle. Such teams can begin by collecting and reviewing all basic communication data of the country, and from this base, proceed to develop practical proposals coordinating the work of different sectors and moving realistically toward new structures. An early attempt to practice this philosophy has taken place in Indonesia. Useful experience has also been derived from an international meeting of experts in a variety of media fields, including representatives of the Asian region, who met in Paris in 1972, to evolve some planning guidelines and undertook a simulation exercise to test the validity of their recommendations.

A supportive aspect of this practical exercise is the compilation of country profiles, based on inventories of national communication resources related to demographic data. Such profiles can be used to help devise the analytical tools of the communication trade, and to evolve new research and methodological procedures with general applications. Initially, such studies have been confined to four European nations, but will be extended to Asia within a few years. As a preliminary, a number of economic studies of communication have been commissioned to test draft guidelines for evaluation, and within Asia, Malaysia is currently undertaking such an exercise.

A further practical exercise lies in the strengthening of national institutions of merit, particularly by concentrating within them scarce expert resources, so that they can assume the role of centers of communication development. The broadcasting training project in Malaysia is one such example; here, resources consolidated at the national level can be offered regionally, to help spread the experience of the local project. In the National Broadcasting Training Centre, facilities and staff have been made available to a number of other institutions — the Educational Media Service, the universities, etc. — in an attempt to bring together communication interests. It is a guiding principle that regionalism follows coherent national growth.

In the past, regional experiments have often failed, because they have come about as a result of a vague commitment to the idea of regionalism, rather than out of a carefully formulated analysis of regional demands and possibilities. The first imperative is to create national institutions of significance: institutions which relate practically to other national centers, thus avoiding isolationism. A single expert working in the field of family planning cannot achieve much on his own account; if his efforts, however, are allied to those of others in parallel fields, and if he has production and experimental resources on which he can draw in support of his work, his contribution is likely to be far greater. It is likely that, in each country, a few centers will take on the role of coordinating agents; there is no set formula for what they should be — they may be universities, broadcasting services, training centers, or research bodies — but their roles are comparable.

7.2.5 Conclusion

Running through all this activity is a common set of objectives. The 1970s saw considerable advances in technology, and far more advances in the production of creative models than has been realized. Unfortunately, much of this development was random. There have been many examples of technical assistance in the communication field and many successful projects, but the interrelationships between them are rare. The activities now being urged by UNESCO are designed to help fill the vacuum. At the one level, of planning and analysis, there is a need to train competent planners and to provide them with adequate tools. At another level, in the field, there is a need for institutions which can draw together disparate threads of expertise, looking outwards at their total environment — first national, then when the time comes, regional. It is no accident that the problems of communication development are those of internationalism as a whole.

7.3 South Pacific Commission, *by Ian A. Johnstone*

7.3.1 Background

The South Pacific Commission (SPC), a regional consultative and advisory body to all the island territories of the South Pacific, is made up of the following nation members: Australia, Britain, Fiji, France, Nauru, New Zealand, United States, and Western Samoa. Yearly, delegates from every South Pacific island group meet at the South Pacific Conference, held either at Noumea or an island capital, to decide the work program and allocate the budget, which was over $1.7 million in 1973.

SPC work is divided into health, economic, and social development. Since its formation in 1947, the organization has provided technical help and encouraged regional action on common Pacific problems, such as the Rhinoceros Beetle (which attacks coconut crops), malnutrition, tuberculosis, language teaching, and youth work.

7.3.2 Cooperation Problems

It was not until 1970 that the concept of regional broadcasting cooperation and consultation was brought to the commission's attention. In that year, at an SPC training seminar on educational broadcasting, delegates defined needs for improved production facilities, better receiving sets in schools, and clear national policies on educational broadcasts. The seminar emphasized that broadcast

Ian A. Johnstone is Educational Broadcasts Officer for the South Pacific Commission Radio Bureau, Suva, Fiji. He has served in various TV, radio, and foreign-service posts in the Pacific, New Zealand, and Zambia, was an overseas civil service graduate, Oxford, and is the author of *The Right Channel.*

services must relate to the needs and conditions of Pacific people and recommended the appointment of an educational broadcasts officer to provide a tape exchange service, as well as to offer assistance and training for educational broadcast units in the region.

Regional cooperation in the South Pacific faces particular difficulties. The geography is not helpful. Fourteen island groups, scattered over 12 million square miles of ocean; only 3.75 million people, from three major ethnic groups — Micronesian, Polynesian, Melanesian — with various admixtures from Asian and European backgrounds; innumerable languages; a variety of government systems and traditions; uncoordinated communication networks; and the whole picture complicated by a range of economic resources, from the mineral wealth of Nauru and New Caledonia to the atoll poverty of the Gilberts or the Northern Cooks (see also §5.3).

And yet, as in any region, there are also factors which tend to hold the area together and thus help joint action. With the exception of Papua New Guinea, population sizes, land, products, and climate are all on a similar scale. The strengths of cultural pride, social unity, and openness apply generally, and most development problems — whether they be protein shortage, breadfruit disease, or rapid urbanization — are occurring in Pacific countries. Their diagnosis and treatment can profitably be considered regionally, which should not be difficult to arrange, given the readiness of Pacific peoples to talk out common problems and to work together to solve them.

SPC's broadcast tape exchange service took advantage of this cooperative tradition, though a first impression gained from a surface examination of broadcast systems within the region is of disparity and dissimilarity. Only Guam, American Samoa, French Polynesia, and New Caledonia have open television, run on United States and French technical standards, and transmitting a good deal of imported material from the parent countries. Radio systems also reflect approaches of metropolitan countries in these colonies or former colonies. In general, Fiji, the Solomons, and the Gilbert and Ellice Islands follow British practice; Papua New Guinea's service is an Australian offshoot; Western Samoa, the Cook Islands, and Niue are New Zealand oriented. American territories have a mixture of private and public stations, with American program approaches, while stations in French Polynesia and New Caledonia are run by ORTF, France's state broadcasting service.

7.3.3   Regional Broadcast Exchanges

Regional exchange possibilities, however, have emerged from this variegated assembly of approaches and organizations, notably, programs for schools, music, and background regional news and general interest material. A two-way flow of schools broadcast tapes functions; smaller islands are anxious to use programs produced in larger territories, while bigger schools' broadcast units are very interested in smaller-island material, such as short stories from the New Hebrides or legends from Niue, which give their schedules regional relevance.

Another major cooperative schools broadcast project was commencing in the early 1970s. At SPC's 1970 seminar, small production units said they were having difficulty with broadcasts supportive of teaching English as a second language. The result was that SPC and the Australian Broadcasting Commission, with considerable financial help from the Australian government, decided to work jointly on producing a pilot series of broadcasts to support the Tate English teaching course, which is used in most South Pacific countries. The series outline was to be drawn up by those teaching English in the 11 countries concerned; once the trial series had been evaluated, production of programs for five years of primary English teaching would commence.

Music being such a dynamic element in Pacific lives, it is no surprise that the exchange service constantly moves music tapes within and beyond the region. Through the generosity of the Fiji Broadcasting Commission, which made all its recordings available to the SPC library, SPC has an excellent collection of contemporary Pacific music.

The third area of common interest is the exchange of regional background news and feature material. The wide demand for this type of programming reflects the growing regional awareness of Pacific territories. Although metropolitan links still predominate in broadcast news and information services — making Pacific listeners better informed about American, Australian, or European events than developments of their own countries or region — this pattern is changing. By the early 1970s, broadcasting organizations were beefing up local news services and gradually assuming essential roles as communicators of ideas and information which must flow if change is to take place in the region. The SPC tape exchange service keeps news support material moving, and compiles and distributes to 17 Pacific countries a monthly backgrounder, "Pacific Magazine," a 15-minute radio program. Plans for 1973 called for increasing "Pacific Magazine's" frequency to twice monthly, working on a cooperative basis whereby each Pacific broadcasting outlet would contribute one program to the series yearly.

In line with its interests in broadcasting news and information, SPC was involved in the development of the Pacific Islands News Association (PICA) in June 1974. PICA is an organization of newspaper, broadcasting, and government information personnel dedicated to training journalists, developing an information exchange, and providing a clearing-house service for media (*ABU Newsletter,* August 1974, p. 14). Also in 1974, the SPC Radio Bureau organized a three-month experimental news-by-satellite scheme in which New Zealand, Fiji, Cook Islands, New Caledonia, Hawaii, Solomon Islands, and Papua New Guinea participated. News and information were exchanged via regular satellite schedules, and each country contributed to a weekly South Pacific round-up (Mackay 1975, p. 50; *PICN* 1975a).

As with all developing regions, the South Pacific is short of skilled communicators, a fact which has become extremely apparent as expatriates have withdrawn from civil services, and as broadcasters generally have come to realize the best broadcasts for Pacific people are those in their own languages. With help from organizations such as UNESCO and ABU, the commission operates regular training schemes — month-long general courses covering all basic production and presentation skills, and shorter in-service sessions where specific fields of announcing, script writing, or interviewing are studied under local staff at their own stations. Joint learning about the broadcasting business is going on continually at SPC's small studio in Suva, where SPC and broadcasters from schools, agriculture, and health departments often join forces to produce plays, try out new panel discussion approaches, assemble extension videotape programs, or compile sound tracks for films.

7.3.4 Television

To be sure, great extremes permeate Pacific broadcasting systems — from American Samoa's six educational television channels, to the small shipping transmitter through which, until recently, Radio Niue broadcast — therefore, it is dangerous to generalize about the region's broadcasting needs and the manner in which they will develop. But, as radio reaches larger sections of the island populations, there can be no doubt Pacific governments will turn increasingly to television.

The increased introduction of television will demand a great deal of thought and attention. A rapid, unplanned introduction of foreign television systems and approaches could damage valuable living societies. For example, there could be great wastage of the medium if open television is inaugurated quickly in Fiji, Papua New Guinea, Western Samoa, Tonga, New Hebrides, Solomons, Gilbert and Ellice, and Niue. For the most part, it would be urban-directed, expensive, English-language, and foreign-produced television in areas which need rural-oriented, inexpensive, vernacular and locally made fare.

One solution might be the use of small, closed-circuit TV units by government departments and agencies for training and classroom work, as well as local program production. Videotapes, made in rural areas, could be produced of village customs and events and then played back to villages in much the same way as mobile cinema units operate. If the islands can develop mobile units, capable of taking closed-circuit TV to villages and exchanging tapes among villages, islands, and countries, it would seem possible to improve rural communication and lessen migrations to the cities; prepare those who will come to live in towns for their moves; provide teachers and extension workers with a valuable tool; slowly build up a corps of local people knowledgeable about TV production; and start to use TV at a scale which fits locally.

Once closed-circuit television is in use in a number of South Pacific countries, regional plans can proceed for the introduction of open television in such a way as to minimize costs and maximize relevance. Some SPC officials are interested in developing television in this more modest but more universal fashion. Already, SPC has started a few pilot videotape programs in Fijian.

There is an exciting urgency about this common regional effort to extend broadcasting's effectiveness. In the past, and in common with most other government services, broadcasting was usually directed and controlled by foreign civil servants. Understandably, communication systems did not receive great attention from governments which had priorities to satisfy — demands for roads, schools, and hospitals — from quite restricted budgets.

In the 1970s, however, as Pacific Islanders gradually took more responsibility for their own affairs, and as the need grew for better communications within and between communities, South Pacific broadcasters began devising more effective ways of making and keeping contact with their society. As school curricula were being changed to relate more closely to local children's lives, and as projects for agricultural change in rice growing, cattle production, and the like were being introduced, broadcasters began to understand their roles as change agents.

7.4 British Broadcasting Corporation, *by Noel Harvey*

7.4.1 Background

British Broadcasting Corporation connections with broadcasting in Asia go back to the very beginning of radio services in that continent. They resulted partly because of the BBC position as a prototype of the national, public-service broadcasting organization, existing not for commercial gain, but for the provision of information, education, and entertainment, and partly because of the historical relationship between Britain and the Commonwealth, which associated BBC with the development of broadcasting services in many Commonwealth countries of Asia.

In the case of India, for example, the relationships developed when John Reith — later Lord Reith, first BBC director-general — in 1935, sent two of his staff to the subcontinent: Lionel Fielden to set up a radio service and G.W. Goyder to serve as chief engineer. Since partition, contact between the BBC and the broadcasting organizations in India, Pakistan, and Sri Lanka have remained close and constructive, with a two-way staff exchange existing, and with BBC making available its experience in the fields of production, management, and engineering. Likewise in Malaysia, where, after World War II, numbers of BBC or former BBC staff helped develop Radio Malaya (then located in Singapore) occupying posts in top management, news, general programs, educational, and engineering services. Additionally, large numbers of staff from what later became Radio Television Malaysia have trained with BBC in London.

BBC links, although beginning historically with the Commonwealth countries, now exist with broadcasting organizations all over Asia. BBC staff work in many Asian nations in a variety of capacities, including training and advising of broadcasters and engineers. For example, there are, or have been, BBC staff

Noel Harvey is head of Liaison, Overseas and Foreign Relations Department, BBC. For a decade he was district commissioner with Overseas Civil Service in Nyasaland.

working on secondment with stations in India, Pakistan, Sri Lanka, Nepal, Afghanistan, Japan, Thailand, Laos, Malaysia, and Singapore. This professional relationship is a two-way link, with many broadcasters from Asia working with BBC's External Services. The External Services either have or have had on their staff broadcasters from three Japanese networks, from Thai TV and the Public Relations Department of Thailand, and from Radio Television Malaysia, Radio Republik Indonesia, VTVN in Saigon, Radio Brunei, Radio Television Singapore, Radio Hong Kong. All India Radio, Pakistan Broadcasting Corporation, Sri Lanka Broadcasting Corporation, Radio Nepal, and Radio Afghanistan.

7.4.2 Examples of Assistance

The BBC connection with Radio Nepal arose out of a development plan prepared for the station in 1963 by a former BBC employee on behalf of the British government. A result of the plan was BBC's secondment of an engineer and a program expert to Radio Nepal between 1965 and 1969, to help with expansion of production and technical facilities. Simultaneously, a regular training relationship was established, continuing to this day, whereby a member of Radio Nepal attends the BBC general radio production course in London, following this with a period of attachment to BBC's Eastern Service. Also, other Radio Nepal staff have attended BBC engineering courses abroad, and in the early 1970s, BBC seconded one of its producers to Nepal. In addition, BBC regularly sends radio tapes to Radio Nepal for broadcasting in its vernacular service and has helped in a training course in Kathmandu.

Since 1966, an arrangement between Radio Afghanistan and BBC has allowed Afghan radio producers to attend production training courses in London and to follow this training with a period of attachment in BBC's Eastern Service. As with Radio Nepal, this system has benefited both organizations and has provided a steady flow of Kabul production staff to London. In the mid-1960s, BBC seconded a production specialist to advise Radio Afghanistan in program development, while on the technical side, technicians have been sent to BBC for training courses and attachments.

In addition, BBC supplies a regular service of radio tapes to the station, through the help of Radio Afghanistan producers who are seconded to BBC's External Services, after having attended the London radio production course.

Relations with radio-TV in Bangladesh grew out of BBC's former connections with East Pakistani broadcasting. For example, a BBC TV producer had spent a year in Dacca as program advisor up to the 1971 war, and various East Pakistan staff members had attended BBC courses over the years. After the setting up of Radio and TV Bangladesh, senior radio-TV staff members visited London, the result being two members of Bangladesh TV attended a BBC training course in 1972. Another result was an agreement whereby Radio Bangladesh sends its staff to the BBC Bengali section on working attachments.

No doubt training broadcasters in program production, engineering, or management has been a major factor in BBC's relations with Asia. Over the years, training offered by BBC has taken various forms, such as courses run in Great Britain, which have developed in variety and specialization and now provide for over 200 trainees annually; courses run in studios of sister broadcasting organizations seeking such training; or secondment of a BBC trainer to assist another training institute to operate its courses. BBC advisors on secondment usually help with in-service training, and where possible, BBC makes available some of its own program material to facilitate training.

One basic rule helps BBC avoid charges of "cultural imperialism": training is provided in response to specific requests. Through the Commonwealth Broadcasting Conference, BBC has publicly endorsed a policy of developing local or regional training centers throughout the world. It foresees future demands for its assistance in the field of specialized, rather than general, training and in the provision of help for local and regional training schemes as these develop. BBC training operations on behalf of other broadcasting organizations are not financed from domestic revenue but from scholarships and other financial underwriting, sometimes by the requesting broadcasting system, more often by British government development funds.

7.4.3 External Services

BBC External Services, however, provide the greatest link with Asia. In addition to the World Service in English, broadcasting 24 hours daily, BBC broadcasts to Asia in Japanese, Chinese (standard and Cantonese), Thai, Vietnamese, Bahasa Malaysian, Indonesian, Hindi, Bengali, Urdu, Persian, Burmese, Tamil, Sinhalese, and Nepali. BBC's non-English broadcasts faced the possibility of being severely restricted in 1974 because of expenditure cuts demanded by the British Treasury (see *Media*, May 1974, p. 23). About one-third of the entire budget of BBC's External Services goes for the maintenance of the Asia service (Spurr 1974b, p. 30). Quite apart from direct broadcasts in all these languages, Asian radio stations make widespread use of BBC programs in the form of relays and rebroadcasts and by transmitting specially prepared radio tapes sent from London. For example, news and commentary in Cantonese are relayed by Radio Hong Kong; news bulletins in English and Hindi are relayed on the Asia beam of Sri Lanka Broadcasting Corporation; programs in Thai are rebroadcast in Bangkok and on stations elsewhere in Thailand; and programs and radio tapes in other languages are rebroadcast in Malaysia, Singapore, Indonesia, Japan, Laos, Brunei, South Vietnam, Sri Lanka, Nepal, and Afghanistan (see also §6.1.7).

The kernel of all daily transmissions is news, with topical magazine programs providing background and analysis to current developments in Britain and the rest of the world. Science and technology also figure largely in programs, while the World Service includes a wide assortment of talk, sports, light entertainment, music, and drama shows.

These BBC broadcasts, rebroadcasts and relays are further supplemented by programs sold to Asian broadcasting stations by BBC Television Enterprises and Radio Transcription Service, and by the topical tapes distributed on a weekly basis to foreign subscribers, again covering world affairs, science, sports, agriculture, education, and the arts.

The BBC motto is "Nation shall speak peace unto Nation." As a founder member of the Commonwealth Broadcasting Conference and an associate ABU member, along with its London-to-Asia broadcasts, BBC has sought, over the past 40 years, to translate the words of this motto into action and cooperation with Asia and its broadcasters.

7.5 Regional Cooperation in South and Southeast Asian Radio, Television, and Educational Technology, *by Arthur Hungerford*

7.5.1 Introduction

Most broadcasting systems in Asia have a very strong educational component, based on educational systems that were derived from ancient cultures and modified by colonial powers such as the Dutch and English. In recent years, with a growing desire on the part of developing countries to modernize quickly, radio and television have been used increasingly to help achieve educational goals. For example, Pakistan now has a television system designed to run a limited evening commercial schedule, on the theory that commerce can underwrite the construction of facilities and night-time operations for entertainment purposes, while leaving the way clear to utilize the system for educational purposes during the day. Had not the educational purpose been in mind originally, it is most doubtful that the development of Pakistani television would have been permitted as early as it was.

One of the difficulties with educational broadcasting generally has been the problem of relating it directly to the central core of education. Usually radio programs have been supplemental, possibly because radio alone does have a limited potential in educational usage, simply because vision is missing. Yet, the use of television requires a much larger financial commitment, thus, if it is not used centrally in education, TV should be avoided in developing countries as being too expensive. But the prestige aspects of television, and the fact that entertainment can be distributed efficiently, practically guarantees that the medium will take hold, even in the poorest societies. So, with the tool at hand, it is only reasonable to develop for television, educational uses, even though this process tends to upset many apple carts in the educational establishment.

Essentially, two strategies can be followed with such expensive undertakings

Arthur Hungerford was Associate Professor of Speech and Radio-TV at Pennsylvania State University until his 1972 retirement. He has been a consultant in educational planning and technology in Honduras, Algeria, Philippines, Thailand, Malaysia, Singapore, and Pakistan. He is a member of the board of directors of NAEB and APBE. He was associated for 9 years with NBC during the experimental TV period.

as educational television. Projects can have a national base, and in larger countries such as India and the Philippines, this is a practical solution. But for small, poor countries as Nepal, Khmer Republic, and Laos, where the stakes are too high, a regional concept is the only practical choice. The United States, as the principal financial underwriter of development in Southeast Asia, opted for the regional idea during the Johnson administration. At that time, it was also decided that development of any regional projects would have to rely in increasing measure upon area resources and in decreasing amounts upon United States grants and other assistance.

The jury is still out as to the viability of regional projects (other than in the strictly economic sphere), but certainly there is a potential for optimism in the educational area. Economies in the utilization of innovative educational techniques and materials could be readily achieved by regional cooperation through projects such as INNOTECH — The Regional Centre for Educational Innovation and Technology, one of a number of projects of the Southeast Asian Ministers of Educational Organizations (SEAMEO). When fully operational, this facility will train nationals from Southeast Asia in, among other things, techniques for developing better instructional materials, including those related to radio and TV usage.

It is probably better that uses of radio and television for educational purposes arise from cooperative action in the broader field of education — such as SEAMEO and INNOTECH — than to have national broadcasters back into educational broadcasting. For example, in some Arab countries, educators fear cooperative efforts with regular broadcasters, reasoning that once information and broadcasting people get their fingers in the educational pie, they siphon off some of the limited educational budgets which educators guard tenaciously.

7.5.2 SEAMEO

Since educational broadcasting appeared in the initial planning of SEAMEO, it may be helpful to review this project in some detail. First, it must be acknowledged that regionalism is a relatively new concept in Southeast Asia, and where regional organizations begin to tap funds that otherwsie might be spent on a purely local basis, crucial decisions are faced; too often, regional projects take second priority. Yet the Asians felt that regionalism, so much indicated in the economic sphere (e.g., Mekong River project), should also be encouraged in the educational realm, hence SEAMEO, a regional organization to support and encourage cooperation in education.

The United States helped with the creation of SEAMEO. In November 1965, a special advisor to President Johnson met with education ministers of Laos, Malaysia/Singapore, Thailand, South Vietnam, and the Philippine UNESCO representative to consider the potential for regional cooperation in education. Substantial United States support was promised at this meeting, undoubtedly encouraging those who wished to pursue the ideal. An interim secretariat was installed in the educational planning office of the Thai Ministry of Education to initiate establishment of SEAMEO and development of its projects.

SEAMEO is organized into two units. The Southeast Asian Ministers of Education Council (SEAMEC) is the policy-making body, meeting annually to give staff direction and consider current problems and future plans, both regionally and nationally. The Southeast Asian Ministers of Education Secretariat (SEAMES) is the permanent secretariat which carries out the organization's work. Six regional centers, operated by SEAMEO, derive their legal status from the juridical personality of the organization and do not exist separately.

Among the principal responsibilities of SEAMEO are finding financial backing for its programs and allocating regional projects to willing host nations. Of course, hosting a project has meant supplying offices and other services which involve a considerable financial outlay on the part of the host country. Beyond this, some funds are available from the SEAMEO headquarters for project work.

The Ford Foundation has helped SEAMEO with a grant covering half of the secretariat's operational costs during its first three years and with the provision of consultants. Since expiration of the Ford grant, member countries themselves have been meeting these costs. Other donors have included the Netherlands, United Kingdom, Australia, and Japan, thus making this regional program a truly multilateral effort.

SEAMES began operations by collecting suggestions for projects grouped into ten areas: engineering, tropical medicine, agriculture, higher education, science, English, books, educational radio and television, instructional materials and manpower, and educational planning.

Soon after its establishment, proposals for tropical medicine, agriculture, science and mathematics, English, instructional materials and regional manpower assessment were approved for development and/or implementation. The latter two were approved only for seminars which would lead to further recommendations concerning implementation, whereas the engineering proposal was approved in principle, but with the understanding that it would be developed as a separate entity outside SEAMEO. Similarly, the higher education project was transferred to UNESCO for implementation. The book proposal and that for a regional institute of educational radio and television were referred back to the interim secretariat for further study. One of the difficulties concerning the radio-TV institute resulted when serious questioning arose as to whether national projects should not be given priority. Each country seemed to feel it would need all the resources it could muster to set up even a pilot project in educational television, let alone provide support for a regional one. Besides, they felt an instructional materials center could develop in such a way as to help educational broadcasting projects locally, and therefore, perhaps the two concepts — a center for regional radio-TV and a center for instructional materials — should be combined. This, in fact, was the action finally chosen: an integration of all instructional media projects into a single program, INNOTECH.

7.5.3 INNOTECH

INNOTECH, temporarily located in Singapore, originated from deliberations of a 1967 regional workshop on instructional materials held in Saigon, from a proposal to establish a regional textbook center, and from the educational television and radio proposal described above. Acting on consultants' advice and based on ideas proposed at the instructional materials workshop, South Vietnam prepared a composite proposal for a regional center for innovation and educational technology, which it was willing to host under auspices of SEAMEO. The project, approved in principle by SEAMEC in early 1968, was further refined at an educators' conference, held in Samoa in October of that year, at which delegates were afforded an opportunity to inspect the Samoan innovative project in elementary and secondary education, based heavily on the use of TV broadcasting. After a series of national and regional meetings, the final five-year development for INNOTECH was presented to SEAMEO for implementation at its January 1970 meeting (SEAMEO 1971).

The timing was not propitious for immediate operations in Saigon because of the disruptions caused by the 1968 Tet Offensive. Consequently, South Vietnam was amenable to an offer by Singapore to host INNOTECH on an interim basis. The first year's $250,000 budget resulted from an Agency for International Development grant.

INNOTECH's objectives include: creating and developing new approaches to education; supplying facilities and professional resources to facilitate testing and evaluation of innovation; attracting creative people in research and experimentation to the center; training key nationals so they can return to supply systems concepts to the solution of their countries' educational problems; providing library and informational services, and coordinating activities with other regional and national groups.

As with all SEAMEO projects, there is a regional governing board for INNOTECH, made up of a representative from each member nation and ex-officio representation of SEAMES and the project director. Three divisions exist under the director — administration, training and research, and library and information services. INNOTECH's budget over the first five years had been set at approximately $5.5 million, $3 million of which was for capital costs, $1.6 million for operating costs, and the remainder for scholarships and supporting funds. These costs, as may be mutually agreed upon, were shared between the United States and other donors. INNOTECH offers separate intern and key officials training schemes and a short-term course.

The center will carry out research using interns, trainees, and the resident staff as research teams. Hopefully, research will lead to development of prototype systems that can be taken back to member countries for refinement and adaptation by the trainees who helped develop them. Such prototype systems may include TV software and radio delivery systems (SEAMEO 1971, appendix A).

7.5.4   UNESCO

As indicated elsewhere (see §§7.1.3 and 7.2.2), UNESCO has been most useful to developing countries planning radio and television usage in education. For example, in 1966, UNESCO sponsored a meeting in Bangkok on "Broadcasting in the Service of Education and Development in Asia," attended by broadcasters and educators from 18 countries of the region, in addition to United Nations and non-Asian representatives. It has also prepared educational broadcasting plans for governments and educational establishments, as well as sent consultants to assist in the implementation of such plans.

UNESCO has stressed in-service training for veteran teachers in the use of television, at the same time indoctrinating new teachers in the medium's potential with courses in teacher-training colleges. Since poor instruction and too few teachers are chronic problems in Asia, this approach makes a great deal of sense. With teachers thoroughly familiar with radio and television utilization, it becomes much easier to make use of the media in schools for both direct and supplemental teaching. By the mid-1970s, UNESCO was inaugurating the Asian Centre for Educational Innovation and Development in Bangkok; one of the aims of ACEID will be the implementation of media in education.

7.5.5   British Council

One of the most important remnants of British control is the British Council, functioning to encourage English-language study and, in the case of the Commonwealth countries, to provide library and film services somewhat akin to the United States Information Service overseas. Since Asian languages have many completely different bases, the use of English as a second language is of great importance, especially in broadcasting. For example, it has been reported that in Indian broadcasting, scripts written in any native language are first translated into English and then dispatched to regional broadcasting centers throughout India, where they are translated into the local language. Also, English has been the medium of instruction in many Asian schools, particularly at the higher education level. The British Council has, as one of its principal missions, the encouragement of this practice, although it must contend with nationalistic objections nearly everywhere in Asia.

The British Council has been active in Asian broadcasting as well. In India, for example, it develops and produces programs which are broadcast to schools that teach English as a second language. Many of these programs do not use any language but English and are largely situational to enhance the assimilation of the English language. The British Council has also assisted INNOTECH by arranging for six weeks of educational technology lectures in Singapore, presented by a CEDO director.

7.5.6   National Radio/Television Projects

The Center for Educational Television in Manila, carefully developed to explore broadcast television, closed-circuit cable TV, and 2,500 mHz band transmissions, was, by the early 1970s, poised for expansion on a wider scale. A considerable inventory of televised courses and other instructional materials has been produced, and the center has conducted numerous seminars and training projects for principals from other Asian countries.

Still other national broadcasting projects in the education realm should be briefly mentioned. Experimental television programming in high school science was underway in Malaysia during the mid-1960s, with the national broadcasting agency cooperating with the education ministry in utilizing the services of United States Peace Corps volunteers. Also, an experimental program was set up in India in the early 1960s with support from the Ford Foundation; South Vietnam, which inherited a strong TV system installed by the United States, planned to utilize the facilities partly for educational purposes; and Hong Kong, anticipating long-term financing for a major effort, has expanded its educational broadcasting services. In addition, Thailand, which has an impressive record in educational radio, experimented with educational television as early as 1966; and TV Singapura had been telecasting schools programs produced in the teacher-training college for some time.

7.5.7 Satellites

Some countries, such as Indonesia with 3,000 islands and no terrestrial wide-band links, naturally look to satellite technology to make television usage practical in educational terms. Many countries already have access to internationally owned and operated satellite facilities (INTELSAT) for purposes of intercommunication. Utilization for more formal education purposes is simply a question of time. Although not yet on the SEAMEO agenda for the 1970s, use of satellites would seem to be a promising avenue for cooperative effort in the field of education.

Our novel project is already planned for the Asian area: the educational use of a NASA satellite to be stationed over India for a year's experimentation in 1973–74. With 14 major languages and countless dialects, it will be interesting to see if Indian educators can generate instructional materials stressing visual stimuli but supplemented by a variety of sound tracks, to be distributed by satellite to 5,000 villages. Under the original agreement between the United States and India, a 1,600-pound satellite of the ATS series was to be maneuvered into a parking orbit 22,300 miles above the Indian subcontinent. Its 30-foot-wide dish was to focus television signals of sufficient strength to be picked up by receivers utilizing special antennas ten feet in diameter. Ground equipment was to be powered by local electricity or, in its absence, by bicycle frame generators with which a man can pedal-generate 100 w. of electricity (Wilford 1969). Transmissions were to involve only the Hindi language at first, but once India was able to orbit its own satellite, narration in several languages would be practicable. It has been estimated that India can operate a three-channel satellite television system with complete coverage of the nation for about $6 million per year. The cost of building and operating terrestrial systems would be many times more.

7.5.8   Problems Ahead

There is the usual chicken-and-egg phenomenon in South and Southeast Asia with respect to using radio and television broadcasting for instructional purposes. Unless curricula are revised to be more relevant to the masses, there is not much sense in using mass media to distribute instruction. But most nations in the region are saddled with educational systems inherited from colonial overlords whose goals were very limited — just enough liberally educated young people to man lower-level civil service jobs; just enough technically trained personnel to exploit these nations' natural resources. Most colonial powers were not interested in industrializing these charges, preferring to ship raw materials to European factories. All of these South and Southeast Asian nations are now free in a political sense, although serious questions arise as to how free they are economically. All are prestige conscious and wish to have modern industrial plants, new communication systems, and a rising standard of living. All have a population explosion problem as modern medicine is introduced to reduce infant mortality and to extend old age. Most have a cultural system based upon the family, with the young taking care of the old. Few have any form of social security. Thus, a parent's only guarantee of old-age security is a passel of healthy sons. As a result, the population problem is compounded.

Many of the problems of these countries are amenable to partial solution by radio and television, if appropriate instructional goals are set and effective materials produced. Vernon Bronson, a United States authority on the utilization of television to educate developing societies, defines these goals as the acquisition of coping skills, including basic competence in language and science. For example, most children in Pakistan will not get beyond the fifth grade; actually, only one-half of all children even start school, and half of these drop out in the first year. One of the excuses given by parents relates to the uselessness of what is now being taught for the life these children will lead in their villages. What they need, of course, is knowledge about sanitation, water supplies, agriculture, child health, family planning, nutrition and homemaking. Television and other visual media are ideally suited to transmit this type of knowledge. Radio too can play a prominent role. But the fact remains that most educational institutions are still tied to traditional curricula, feeding just a few chosen elites to higher education.

There is another important factor at work in South and Southeast Asia. As industrialization proceeds, it must be labor intensive, not capital or machine intensive. For example, in 1968, the Dacca television station employed more than 150 people for an operation that would be handled by fewer than 50 employees in the United States. But, this was looked upon as a success in that poor country, for what else would the 100 people do if they did not work at the TV station. In Asia, the question is not substituting machines for manpower;

quite the contrary. So, the main educational problem remains that of practical coping skills to improve village and inner-city life. Even achieving this limited goal will be a slow process, but one to which radio and television can make unique contributions, particularly via satellites.

The prospect of having a series of satellites, each with multiple beams such that television and radio services can be fed both on national and regional patterns, is an exciting one. Educational materials with special accent on the visual aspects would have wide application, particularly if the materials were utilized and not fully organized into rigid patterns of courses and curricula. Rather, satellites could spray down upon earth nuggets of knowledge — materials which could be woven into a variety of educational patterns as befits the national systems of participating countries. Presumably each nation, and probably smaller units within the member states, would record the distributed materials on videotape for additional distribution by cable systems, and perhaps by 2,500 mHz television channels. Each nation would have at least one ground station capable of both sending and receiving, so that each could contribute to the whole process. In addition, there would be hundreds of receiver-only points, where better organized schools could make use of the instructional materials in the classrooms.

Countries of South and Southeast Asia are in a position to make efficient use of the newer technologies. It is just a question of whether the educational and cultural settings are such that the inherent flexibility and effectiveness of these newer media can be fully harnessed.

7.6 Centre for Educational Development Overseas, *by Alexander B. Edington*

7.6.1 Historical Perspective

The early to mid-1960s was a period of mushroom growth of national television services around the world. In Asia, this occurred in both newly independent nations and those which had controlled their own affairs for long periods of time. Such development, at least according to the politicans of the time, was to herald rapid and widespread increases of educational opportunity to large sectors of the population. It was hoped that it would bring about profound changes in both formal and nonformal systems of education. What it did in fact produce in its initial stages was a situation of intense need for aid on the part of those individuals and organizations operating these services.

At that time in Asia, or indeed to any significant extent elsewhere in the world, there was no source of advice, information training, or program material in the field of educational broadcasting. In response to these needs, the Centre for Educational Television Overseas (CETO) was set up in London in 1962. CETO was an independent, nonprofit organization sponsored by four founder

Alexander B. Edington is Director of Information and Research, Centre for Educational Development Overseas, London. For three years, he was education officer in northern Nigeria and educational broadcasting advisor to Ghana Broadcasting Corporation.

bodies: Nuffield Foundation, Independent Television Companies (acting as a group), British government (through the then Department of Technical Co-operation, and now the Overseas Development Administration of the Foreign and Commonwealth Office), and BBC. The Ford Foundation and Rockefeller Brothers Fund made funds available to CETO shortly after it had been developed.

In addition to establishing a service to collect, collate, and disseminate information about world developments in educational television, CETO became heavily involved in the provision of training and production of program material. Advisory and consultancy work leading to the establishment and development of educational services was also undertaken.

7.6.2 Training

The most urgent need was probably for assistance with the training of personnel. Training courses were run on a regular basis in London and conducted on request overseas. These course generally lasted 13 weeks, were practical in nature and intensive in method, and were essentially concerned with production training. No direct training was given in specialized aspects of television, such as engineering, graphics, or film-making, although individual secondments and attachments to the center were arranged on an *ad hoc* basis over the years, as subsequently at CETO's successor, the Centre for Educational Development Overseas.

After the pioneering, experimental efforts carried out by CETO in the 1960s, it was decided that CETO's work could best be continued and developed by amalgamation with two other London-based organizations, each concerned with a specialist field of educational innovation, to form the Centre for Educational Development Overseas. This new body came into being in 1970, with CETO forming the nucleus of its broadcasting division.

The instructional environment at both CETO and CEDO was devised to replicate the backgrounds to which trainees return after training. While not compromising high standards of maintenance and efficiency, training studios were designed to make use of the minimum professional equipment necessary for the production of programs to a broadcast standard.

During a course, each trainee writes, produces, and directs program exercises with immediate relevance to his own domestic educational situation. These begin with short, single-concept exercises and lead to a full-length program of the type that the trainee might expect to produce on his return home.

Although during the earliest courses, most emphasis was placed on the educational television production process; in recent times, more consideration has been given to the use of television as an educational resource. Problems of classroom utilization, relationship of the ETV service to the educational system in general and the curriculum unit of the education ministry in particular, and the relationship of television to other media are given due attention.

Training is only provided to individuals sponsored by their appropriate government department and who, theoretically, will then return to work in educational broadcasting. Most trainees have an educational background (inspectors, headmasters, ministry officials, and teachers), the remainder come from ministries of information, journalism, radio, or similar fields. A trainee must know English sufficiently well to be able to benefit from the training.

The experience of CETO and CEDO has been that all too frequently the official nominee is unsuitable, having been nominated for educational broadcasting training because he is "next in line" to receive one of the many and varied scholarships, fellowships, bursaries, or courses offered to his country from a wide range of donors. Without doubt, one of the most important elements in all training activities is the initial selection and recruitment of trainees. Very little thought, care, or attention has been paid to this problem universally, and educational broadcasting in Asia is no exception. Waste or nonutilization of training is a luxury that neither the trainee nor the trainers can afford.

The provision of these regularly scheduled courses in London has enabled a large number of Asian countries to send personnel for educational television training. For example, Hong Kong, India, Iran, Malaysia, Pakistan, Philippines, Singapore, South Vietnam, and Thailand have all been represented.

While it can be argued that at the Asian stations themselves first-level training can most effectively be given, the limited number of personnel in need of training from established services means that it is more cost-efficient to conduct courses centrally. To provide the individualized course schedules which have been a feature of CEDO training, the number of trainees must be limited to between 15 and 20 per course. Where considerable new developments or expansions have taken place in ETV services, it has proved more effective to send an officer or team out from London to conduct a training course on the spot. Courses of this type have taken place in Thailand, Singapore, India, Malaysia, and the Philippines.

A further type of training often associated with such expansion is in the utilization of educational broadcasts. These courses can only be carried out *in situ* because of the number of participants involved, the comparatively short duration of each course, and the dependence of the course on access to locally produced educational program material. Two courses of this type were conducted for the Ministry of Education in Malaysia prior to the 1972 opening of the national ETV service in Kuala Lumpur.

7.6.3 Program Material

Newly established educational television services found they could not produce sufficient programs to fill transmission schedules. Complete series of educational programs, however, produced in developed countries were not educationally viable in a developing nation, particularly at the primary and secondary levels of education which form the target audience of most ETV services in Asia.

To meet this need, CETO devised the concept of program kits. ETV program series — largely in subjects with a minimum of culture bias, e.g., science, mathematics, and English language — were produced in "do-it-yourself" kits, which contained full instructions for the producer and technical staff, scripts in English, and the visual material for a complete program. This visual material consisted of captions, photo captions, and 16-mm. mute film sequences, illustrating the key teaching points in the lessons. Also, there was descriptive material for the education authorities, specimen notes for teachers using the series, and, in some cases, samples of workbooks designed for duplication and distribution to the viewing audience.

CETO kits were designed for use in studios with the minimum of professional equipment (two cameras), staff, and facilities. The aim was to provide television material of high quality, adaptable to classroom needs of pupils and curricula of any country or region. The script could be translated or adapted, and local photographs or models substituted for those supplied. The material was not copyrighted, and broadcasting authorities were encouraged to modify and use the kit material any way they felt suited their purpose.

Series were produced in units of varying length on the following subjects: adult education, biology, geography, health education, heat, magnetism and electricity, optics, teacher training, and English language. Kits were used in such countries as Iran, India, Pakistan, Philippines, and Thailand.

Although the kits met an immediate programming need, it was felt they were not sufficiently relevant to local educational needs, in spite of adaptation. They did, however, provide a valuable in-service training device, enabling inexperienced producers to put out program material of an acceptable quality. One main disadvantage of the CETO kit was its very high cost of production to the center. This, combined with the evidence about its doubtful educational validity, led to cessation of production by the late 1960s.

CETO, and later CEDO, subsequently produced films on the techniques and methodologies of ETV production, which have been found to be of international value. Based on the training offered by CEDO in London, these films are used extensively by many agencies during both pre- and in-service training courses in developed and developing countries.

Prior to establishment of CEDO in 1970, British assistance in the field of Asian educational radio had been provided on a somewhat *ad hoc* basis by BBC. With the creation of CEDO, this situation was rationalized. The interrelationship of educational radio and educational television was recognized, and both were linked under the CEDO broadcasting division.

Experience gained by CETO in providing ETV training has been drawn on while establishing educational radio training programs. Intensive practical courses are run regularly in London, and considerable attention is paid to problems at the reception end — whether it be in the classroom or extension center. The courses are small in number, usually 12 participants being regarded as optimum. In the first three years of activity, trainees from Afghanistan, Iran, India, Indonesia, Malaysia, Pakistan, and the Philippines attended CEDO educational radio courses. There has also been a growth in training courses conducted *in situ,* such as in Sri Lanka.

7.6.4 Secondment

CEDO has involved itself in various cooperative training ventures by seconding staff members to conduct, or participate in, regional, subregional, or national courses arranged by international agencies, such as UNESCO. Participation in a 1972 regional course on "Educational Media Planning and Production," held in Kuala Lumpur, is typical of this kind of activity.

A feature of CETO's earlier activities, to some degree continued by CEDO, is the provision, on request, of personnel on long-term secondment. From 1966–69, a CEDO advisor assisted the ETV service of Singapore with its establishment, and the deputy director of CEDO's broadcasting division has been seconded to UNESCO for educational programming work in the Indian Television Training Institute. Long-term secondments have decreased of late, but short-term consultancy and advisory missions, undertaken by CEDO personnel, are on the upswing.

Reviewing the past ten years, it is possible to be critical of CETO's early response to demands. A more pointed criticism, however, may be made of the decisions leading to the introduction of educational broadcasting and the manner and form in which it was initiated in Asia.

Currently, as money is less available but educational problems more acute, consideration is again being given by most Asian countries to planned usage of media to solve their problems. This is a marked step forward from the earlier situation in which media were acquired before consideration was given to their use. CEDO is increasingly becoming involved in the identification of educational needs which can best be met by the application of the media.

7.7 Case Study: CEPTA-TV and Adult Education, *by Robert F. Bittner*

7.7.1 Assessment Period

The Centre for Production and Training for Adult Education Television (CEPTA Television), a regional mass-media venture designed to promote adult education in Southeast and East Asia, is financed by Friedrich Ebert Stiftung (FES) of West Germany and the Singapore government. FES also sponsors a radio project attached to station DYLA in Cebu City, Philippines.

CEPTA-TV was conceived as a service organization for television stations, education ministries, and institutions. Operating from premises in Singapore, CEPTA-TV produces programs and trains staff in the realm of adult education.

Robert F. Bittner is the former director of CEPTA Television in Singapore. He has been a part-time lecturer at Nanyang University, a TV correspondent in Paris and Southeast Asia, and a television producer in Germany. In 1965 he was managing director of a FES-TV project in Ghana and Lecturer at Legon University.

Main areas of production are motivational, informational, and instructional programs. The present infrastructure offers television as the most widely available means to reach the audience audiovisually, although it is realized that with the advent of video cassettes or video discs, TV's dominant role will diminish.

Originally, CEPTA-TV activities were to be mainly of an assessment and priority testing nature, as the organization awaited completion of the building, and thus, production facilities, it was to share with Singapore ETV services. For example, regional data on economic, manpower, and educational planning were collected, allowing for a definition of CEPTA-TV objectives, regional priorities, and available resources for implementation. The surveying approach was to find out specifically regional needs in programming, the project development of the region as specified in national plans, and adult educational planning for the next decade. Results were to serve as guidelines to identify needs and, at the same time, to avoid duplication of educational efforts. In addition, workshops were being organized throughout the region in 1972-73, to assess what key planners consider their aims and needs for audiovisual support. The assessment stage was to be concluded by mid-1973, at which time a CEPTA Association was to be formed, comprising agencies active in adult education. The association was designed to be a body dealing with program priorities and allocation of available training places at CEPTA-TV studios. Scripting was to begin immediately after the association was set up.

In November 1973, representatives from eight nations — Indonesia, Khmer Republic, South Korea, Laos, Philippines, Singapore, Thailand, and South Vietnam — signed the agreement forming CEPTA Association, an advisory group for CEPTA-TV. With primary purposes of producing media support for adult-education agencies and of training regional personnel, CEPTA-TV immediately started functioning. By 1974, film production commenced and the first training course, in media production organization, was held (*AMC Bulletin,* September 1974, p. 5). At the second annual meeting of CEPTA-TV in late 1974, the organization could boast of having built up two production teams capable of undertaking production overseas simultaneously, developed an operational procedure, established a working relationship with participant nations, and produced 21 color films. Six TV programs had been completed, and 11 others were being prepared (*CEPTA Circuit* 1975, p. 2).

7.7.2 Modular Stages

The actual programming and production stage will identify common denominators of CEPTA-TV partner nations. Production methods will be utilized on a modular basis, consisting of the presenter's part recorded in the studio, and the visual part comprised of film, animation, photographs, or graphics. The visual part is made up of modules, corresponding to the conventional term, sequence of shots. Visuals will be the only common feature in all programs, the presenter changing from program to program. The advantage of this method is that the presenter, an expert in the program topic, will bring to the show his ethnic features, language, and most important of all, a knowledge of the audience's level of understanding in his country. Thus, a program for a Singapore audience would necessarily differ from a Thai, Korean, or Indonesian version. The individual countries, therefore, use CEPTA-TV equipment, manpower, and funds to produce a program with direct relevance to its own audience.

An alternative approach that was being considered in 1973 is also based on the modular system. Here, all programs will, as far as possible, be treated as one, made up of script modules, written before actual production commences. The vast number of modules contained in programs in this phase, all having more or less similar topics, will result in the possibility of multiple use of modules. Examples would include modules showing plowing by oxen and by tractors; washing one's hands and a microscopic view of the impurities of the water used; paying taxes at a counter and the construction of a road. These are modules, in other words, which can be used in different contexts to illustrate a point about old and new concepts of man's relationship with his surroundings. A single module will be composed of a number of shots, thus allowing a producer who may want to use the modules again for a new program to select from the various single shots to form a new module suitable for his purpose.

Descriptions of these modules, existing in the script, will be fed into a computer which, in turn, will sort out identical or similar modules. Finally, film crews will be sent throughout Southeast Asia shooting material and indicating on clapper boards programs which will be able to use this raw material to edit into modules.

The second stage of the modular production process will involve classifying the actual modules of finished programs for computer storage. This will be necessary because script modules, for example, will differ from film modules, due to circumstances on location which will not be foreseen by the scriptwriter. Thus, a computer retrieval archive will develop at CEPTA-TV. Both identification of similar script modules and classification of the actual film archive will depend on CEPTA's access to a computer system and funding of ancillary costs. In 1973, however, chances were good that these obstacles would be overcome.

7.7.3 Conclusion

CEPTA-TV's aim to assist in adult education embraces not only nonformal education activities, but also lifelong learning. The latter is probably more important to CEPTA-TV because, although there are satisfactory primary school enrollments and substantial increases in those on secondary and tertiary levels, there also exists stagnation in vocational school enrollments and little progress in adult education. This clearly identifies vocational training and adult education as priority areas.

CEPTA-TV has also recognized the importance of mass-media support by patterning programs in such ways that presentation can be via television, 16-mm or 8-mm projector or videotape, either on cassettes or discs. This necessitates certain compromises as each medium has its particular characteristics. But it is expected that upon completion of the first production phase in 1976 the technological basis for audiovisual presentation of learning material will have advanced so much that the distribution infrastructure can be narrowed to a few identifiable devices. Even by the time the proposed studio complex was completed in mid-1974, CEPTA-TV should have had a good idea which media device, cassettes and/or discs, will dominate the future. The project's second long-term phase, envisaged to begin in 1977, would then be able to adjust to the medium's peculiarities.

Bibliography

This bibliography lists primarily sources cited in the text. A partial list of interviews and correspondence appears in the Acknowledgments. For more comprehensive references on Asian broadcasting see John A. Lent, *Asian Mass Communications: A Comprehensive Bibliography* (Philadelphia: Temple University, 1975), which contains over 15,000 items, many relating to broadcasting.

Abas, Sam. 1974. "Sabah: The Wrong Waveband." *Far Eastern Economic Review* (Hong Kong), 4 March, p. 18.

ABC (Australian Broadcasting Commission). 1970-71. *Thirty-Ninth Annual Report.* Sydney: ABC.

ABCB (Australian Broadcasting Control Board). 1967. *Broadcasting Program Standards.* Canberra: Commonwealth Government Printing Office.

_____. 1970. *Attitudes to Television, 1968, 1969.* Melbourne: Australian Broadcasting Control Board.

_____. 1972. *Twenty-Fourth Annual Report.* Canberra: Australian Government Publishing Service.

ABU (Asian Broadcasting Union). 1972. "Report of Study Group 8." Report SGA/S. Sydney: ABU.

ABU Newsletter (Sydney). 1969a. *"Friedrich Ebert Stiftung Conference in Singapore."* April, pp. 3-7.

_____. 1969b. "Work Begins on ABU Film Project." May, p. 26.

_____. 1970. "Towards an Asian Telecommunity." June, pp. 25-27.

_____. 1971a. "EBU and ABU News Experts Meet in Delhi." January, p. 8.

_____. 1971b. "Public Service Broadcasting in the Philippines." February, pp. 14-17.

_____. 1971c. "Regional Broadcasting Training Institute." November-December, p. 18.

_____. 1972. "ECAFE Moves for an Asian Telecommunication Network." November-December, pp. 45-46.

_____. 1973a. "Educational Broadcasting Seminar in Afghanistan." August, pp. 12-13.

_____. 1973b. "Many Sharing in CEPTA TV's Pacific Project." August, p. 27.

_____. 1973c. "News in Indonesian TV and Its Problems." August, pp. 16-17.

_____. 1973d. "Changes in Fiji." September, pp. 34-35.

_____. 1974a. "TV Proposed for Tonga." July, p. 12.

_____. 1974b. "Broadcasting-Niue Style." September, pp. 23-24.

_____. 1974c. "Preserving the Songs of the Common People." September, p. 29.

ABU. 1972. "Report of Study Group 8." Report No. SGA/S. Sydney: *ABU.*

Adam, Kenneth. 1974. "The Broadcasting Future for New Zealand." *Gazette* (Deventer) 20 (Fall): 162–70.

Administration Report, Ceylon Broadcasting Corporation. 1967–70. Colombo: Ceylon Broadcasting Corporation.

Administration Report of the Director-General of Broadcasting. 1950–66. Colombo: Ceylon Government Press.

Agassi, Judith. 1969. "Mass Media in Indonesia." Mimeographed. Cambridge: Center for International Studies, Massachusetts Institute of Technology.

Almario, Simoun O. 1972. "Broadcasting in the Philippines." Paper prepared for Broadcasting in Pacific Nations Symposium, San Francisco.

AMC (Asian Mass Communication Research and Information Center) *Bulletin* (Singapore). 1973a. "Korean Broadcasting System Goes Public." June, p. 13.

––––––––––. 1973b. "Low Cost TV Sets for Korean Rural Folk." September, p. 14.

––––––––––. 1973c. "CEPTA Association Is Set Up." December, p. 18.

––––––––––. 1974. "Colour TV in China." September, p. 17.

Apia Advertiser (Western Samoa). 1967. "Politicians Ban 2AP News." 6 December, p. 1.

Area Handbook for Burma. 1968. American University Foreign Area Studies. Washington, D.C.: Government Printing Office.

Area Handbook for India. 1970. American University Foreign Area Studies, DA Pam. 550–21. Washington, D.C.: Government Printing Office.

Area Handbook for the People's Republic of China. 1972. Washington, D.C.: Government Printing Office.

The Asian (Hong Kong). 1972. "Colour TV Divides Seoul." 1–7 October.

Asian Press. Annual. Seoul: Readership Research Center, Press Foundation of Asia.

Asia Yearbook, **Annual.** Hong Kong: Far Eastern Economic Review.

Austin, William. 1972. "Television Drama in New Zealand." *COMBROAD* (London) July–September, p. 15.

Australian Financial Review. 1971. "NZ Color TV." 21 December.

Avellana, Lamberto. 1963. "The Cinema in the Philippines." *Unitas* (Manila), September, pp. 382–86.

Awasthy, G.C. 1965. *Broadcasting in India.* Bombay: Allied Publishers Pvt., Ltd.

Baji, A.R. 1974. "News and Current Affairs in All India Radio." *COMBROAD* (London), March–April, pp. 15–17.

Balakrishnan, R. 1974. "Training for Broadcasting: the Malaysian Experience." *Media Asia* (Singapore) 1, no. 3:22–24.

Barlow, David. 1971. "Educational Broadcasting in Ceylon: A New Phase." *ABU Newsletter* (Sydney), October, pp. 3–5.

Barney, Ralph D. 1971. "The Mass Media: Their Environment and Prospects in Western Polynesia." Ph.D. dissertation, University of Missouri.

Bas, Rene Q. 1974. "Philippines: Are Agencies 'Mass Media'?" *Media for Asia's Communications Industry* (Hong Kong), November, pp. 10–12.

Basic Facts. 1970. Karachi: Pakistan Television Corporation.

Bayliss, Ovid L. 1969. "The American Forces Vietnam Network." *Journal of Broadcasting* (Philadelphia) 13 (Spring): 145–51.

BBC (British Broadcasting Corporation). Annual. *BBC Handbook.* London: BBC.

BBC Record. 1971. "Boosting Exports." May, p. 7.

Bednall, Colin. 1975. "Concern over Media Control." *The Times* (London), 7 July, p. viii.

Bennett, Nicholas. 1974. "Planning for the Development of Educational Media in Thailand." *Educational Broadcasting International* (London), December, pp. 176–79.

Bick, Gordon. 1968. *The Compass File.* Christchurch (New Zealand): Caxton Press.

Bittner, Robert. 1973. "Producing for Multi-National Transmission." *ABU Newsletter* (Sydney), September, pp. 11–13.

Blackburn, Paul. 1971. "Communication and National Development in Burma, Malaysia and Thailand: A Comparative Systematic Analysis." Ph.D. dissertation, American University.

Bloch, Peter. 1974. "Australia Backs Alternative Television." *Intermedia* (London) 2, no. 3: 20–21.

Breen, Patricia. 1972. "Interview with Subha Malakul." *Impact,* 8 April, p. 5.

Broadcasting (Washington, D.C.). 1966a. "Vietnam to Get Airborne TV." 6 January.

————. 1966b. "Hollywood Talent to Open New Vietnam TV." 10 January.

————. 1966c. "Radio Stateside Producers Unknown." 31 January.

————. 1966d. "New Start Set for Vietnam TV." 7 February.

————. 1966e. "Radio Stateside Voice Is Identified in L.A." 14 February.

————. 1972. "Never on a Sunday." 31 July, p. 24.

Broadcasting Corporation of China. 1972. *Challenge Statement by BCC.* Taipei: BCC.

Broadcasting in Malaysia. 1971. Kuala Lumpur: Government Press.

Brooks, D.E. 1969–70. *Annual Departmental Report.* Director of Broadcasting, Code no. 0346470. Hong Kong: Radio Hong Kong.

————. 1970–71. *Annual Departmental Report.* Director of Broadcasting, Code no. 0346471. Hong Kong: Radio Hong Kong.

Brown, Marion, and Kearl, Bryant. 1967. "Communicacion y Desarrollo: El Problema de la Relevancia Local y Funcional." Mimeographed. Madison: Land Tenure Center, University of Wisconsin.

Borwne, Donald R. 1971. "The World in the Pentagon's Shadow." *Educational Broadcasting Review* 5, no. 3 (April): 31–48.

Budget 1971–72. Ministry of Information and National Affairs. 1971. Islamabad: Printing Corporation of Pakistan.

Burns, John. 1975. "A Night of TV in China." *Christian Science Monitor* (Boston), 21 January.

Butterfield, Fox. 1975. "Clues to China's Political Life Sought below Surface Tranquility." *New York Times,* 4 November, p. c–4.

Caroe, Olaf Kirkpatrick. 1958. *The Pathans.* New York: St. Martins Press.

Carroll, John J. 1970. *Philippine Institutions.* Manila: Solidaridad.

CBA (Commonwealth Broadcasting Association). 1974. *Commonwealth Broadcasting Association 1974.* London: CBA.

Central Yearbook. Annual. Pyongyang: Korean Central News Agency.

CEPTA Circuit (Singapore). 1974. "Eight Nations Form CEPTA TV Association." 1, no. 1; 1–10.

————. 1975. "CEPTA Council Meets in Bangkok." 2 (February): 1–3, 6.

Ceylon Daily News. 1972. 7 August.

Chanda, Nayan. 1975. "Requiem for an Old Order." *Far Eastern Economic Review* (Hong Kong), 6 June, pp. 12–14.

Chander, Romesh. 1973. "Television in India." *COMBROAD* (London), April–June, pp. 16–19.

————. 1974a. "Getting Ready for SITE." *Vidura* (New Delhi), April, pp. 545–46.

————. 1974b. "Programming for the Satellite Instructional Television Experiment in India." *Educational Broadcasting International* (London), June, pp. 80–84.

————. 1975. "Satellite Television in India." *COMBROAD* (London), January–March, pp. 21–22.

Chandiram, Gita. 1974. "Social Education through Teleclubs: Success or Failure?" *Vidura* (New Delhi), August, pp. 730–31.

Chandra-Sekkar, Sritati. 1961. *Red China: An Asian View.* New York: Frederick A. Praeger.

Chang, Shu-hua Samuel. 1973. "Challenge of Press Freedom and Commercial Television in Taiwan." Masters thesis, University of Missouri.

Chang Kuo-sin. 1975. "Radio Hongkong Finds Its Own Voice . . . Well, Almost." *IPI Report* (Zurich), April–May, pp. 15–16.

Chatterji, P.C. 1974. "AIR: Programme Planning for a Countrywide Network." *Indian Press* (New Delhi), May, pp. 35–9.

Chen, Jerome. 1970. *Mao Papers: Anthology and Bibliography.* New York: Oxford University Press.

Cheng Chia. 1959. "Broadcasting – An Outstanding Instrument of Child Education." *Hsin-wen Chan-hsien* (News Front), no. 8, pp. 13–16.

Cheong Mei Sui. 1973. "Changes for Radio and TV." *Straits Times* (Kuala Lumpur), 29 August.

Cherry, Colin. 1971. *World Communication: Threat or Promise?* New York: John Wiley and Sons.

China Topics (Hong Kong) 1968. "The Sino-Soviet Radio War." 29 January, p. 8.

China Yearbook. Annual. Taipei: China Publishing Co.

Chong Seck Chin. 1974. "ETV in Malaysia – A Personal Assessment." *Educational Broadcasting International* (London), December, pp. 184–87.

Chou Hsin-wu. 1959. "China's Broadcast Affairs during the Great Leap Forward." *Hsin-wen Chan-hsien* (News Front) 18 (24 September): 5.

Christian Science Monitor (Boston). 1972a. "China 'Children's Palaces' – Recreation, Indoctrination." 8 August.

————. 1972b. "Shanghai English Craze Follows Language Broadcasts." 16 August.

————. 1972c. "Chinese Look to Europe for Color-TV Technology." 4 December.

Chu, Godwin, and Chi, G.Y. 1965. *Functions of Mass Communication in the Government Public Relations.* Taipei: National Chengchi University. In Chinese.

Chu, James, and Fang, William. 1972. "The Training of Journalists in Communist China." *Journalism Quarterly*, 49, no. 3:489–97.

Chu, Tull. 1967. *Political Attitudes of the Overseas Chinese in Japan.* Hong Kong: Union Research Institute.

Chu Ching-kwei. 1959. "Development of China's Minority Broadcasting Work." *Hsin-wen Chan-hsien* (News Front), no. 11, p. 25.

Coats, Howard. 1975. "Broadcasting: Voicing the Grand Development Design." *Media for Asia's Communications Industry* (Hong Kong), May, pp. 14–15.

Cole, Barry. 1966. "The Australian Broadcasting Control Board and the Regulation of Commercial Radio in Australia Since 1948." Ph.D. dissertation, Northwestern University.

Coller, Richard. 1961. "Social Aspects of Donated Radios on Barrio Life." Mimeographed. Quezon City: Community Development Research Council, University of the Philippines.

COMBROAD (London). 1971. "NZBC and Government." July–September, p. 6.

————. 1974a. "Radio and Television Malaysia." April–June, pp. 62–63.

————. 1974b. "Australia's TV Coverage." July–September, p. 51.

————. 1974c. "Australian Broadcasting Commission: Annual Report." October–December, pp. 61–62.

————. 1974d. "Radio and Television Singapore." October–December, p. 58.

————. 1974e. "Radio Bangladesh." October–December, pp. 65–66.

————. 1975a. "ABC: Shattered Darwin's Lifeline." January–March, pp. 59–60.

————. 1975b. "Broadcasting Restructure in New Zealand." January–March, pp. 4–7.

————. 1975c. "Radio Bangladesh." January–March, pp. 65–66.

————. 1975d. "New Zealand's New Television Complex." April–June, pp. 21–24.

Committee on Broadcasting. 1973. *The Broadcasting Future for New Zealand.* Wellington: Government Printer.

"Communications in Asia '75." *Far Eastern Economic Review* (Hong Kong), 7 March, pp. 1–18.

Conley, Michael Charles. 1966. *The Communist Insurgent Infrastructure in South Vietnam: A Study of Organization and Strategy.* Washington, D.C.: Government Printing Office.

Crawford, Robert H. 1967. "The Daily Indonesian-Language Press of Djakarta: Analysis of

Two Recent Critical Periods." Ph.D. dissertation, Syracuse University.

Daily Report, Communist China (Washington, D.C.). 1968. 28 August, p. A-1; 9 September, p. E-8; 10 September, p. C-4.

Das, Gopal. 1974. "People Playing Their Part in AIR's Programmes." *ABU Newsletter* (Sydney), July, pp. 14–16.

Data for Decision (Manila), 1974a. "Australia: Restrictions on Foreign-Language Broadcasts Lifted." 28 January–3 February, p. 1526.

————. 1974b. "Homes with TV Sets Increase 100 Per Cent in 1972." 8–14 April, p. 1746.

————. 1974c. "Pakistan: Growth of Broadcasting." 22–28 April, pp. 1802–3.

————. 1974d. "RTV English Channels Open." 22–28 April, p. 1790.

————. 1974e. "400,000 Elementary Students Covered by ETV." 28 October–3 November, p. 2370.

————. 1974f. "Radio Staff (Laos) Strike Ends." 9–15 December, p. 2473.

Davies, Derek. 1973. "Traveller's Tales." *Far Eastern Economic Review* (Hong Kong), 14 May, p. 17.

————. 1975. "Traveller's Tales." *Far Eastern Economic Review* (Hong Kong), 28 March, p. 21.

Dawn (Karachi). 1974. "Pakistan Television 10th Anniversary Special Report." 26 November, p. 1.

Den, Hideo. 1971. *Joho Kakumei no Shinwa to Genjitsu* [The myths and facts of information revolution]. Tokyo: Bronzu-sha.

Developments in Broadcasting. 1971. Wellington: Office of the Minister of Broadcasting.

De Vera, Jose M. 1967. *Educational Television in Japan.* Rutland, Vt.: Charles Tuttle Co.

De Young, John. 1957. *A Study of Communications Problems on Barrio Level.* Quezon City: University of the Philippines.

Dhawan, B.D. 1974. "SITE Is of Little Relevance." *Vidura* (New Delhi), April, p. 547.

Djajanto, Warief. 1975. "Indonesia Moves into the Satellite Set." *Media for Asia's Communications Industry* (Hong Kong), March, p. 25.

Dock, Marie-Claude. 1972. "The Revised Universal Copyright Convention." *UNESCO Chronicle* 18, no. 5 (May): 175–85.

Dominion. 1972. "Five Year Target Set for Schools' TV Broadcasts." 18 July.

————. 1973. "Four to Control Broadcasting." 3 February.

Donchin, Gwyneth G. 1971. "Suggestions for Inclusion in a Joint Senate/House Bill for the Congress of Micronesia to Authorize 'A Commission to Study the Establishment of an Independent Micronesian Broadcasting System." Mimeographed.

————. 1972. "Broadcasting at the Birth of a New State – Micronesia." Paper prepared for Broadcasting in Pacific Nations Symposium, San Francisco.

Dong-A Yearbook. 1971. Seoul: Dong-A Daily News. In Korean.

Dubbelt, D.G. 1975a. "2nd Tver in the New Zealand; First's First-Night a Comedy of Errors." *Variety* (New York), 25 June, pp. 44, 56.

————. 1975b. "New Zealand Banks on US-UK Shows as 2nd TVer Bows Quietly." *Variety* (New York), 16 July, pp. 41. 46.

Duckmanton, T.S. 1970. "The Philosophy of Communications." Speech prepared for Australian Broadcasting Commission, 21 August.

————. 1971. "Some Thoughts on Broadcasting in the '70s." Speech prepared for Australian Broadcasting Commission, 10 March.

Dupree, Louis. 1971. "Parliament Versus the Executive in Afghanistan 1969–71." *American Universities Field Staff Reports,* South Asian Series. 15:5.

Dyer, Frances. 1974. "Broadcasting." *Leader: Malaysian Journalism Review* (Kuala Lumpur) 3, no.1:19–21.

Eapen, K.E. 1974. "Communication – Indonesian Style." *Media Asia* (Singapore) 1, no. 2; 35–44.

Educational Broadcasting International (London). 1974. "The Center for Educational Television, Philippines: Growth, Development, Decline." September, pp. 121–26.

Edwards, Brian. 1971. *The Public Eye.* Wellington: A.H. and A.W. Reed.

Elegant, Robert S. 1971. *Mao's Great Revolution.* New York: World Publishing Co.

Emerson, Gloria. 1970. "Soap Operas Hold Vietnam's TV Together." *Wisconsin State Journal,* 5 April.

Emery, Walter. 1969. *National and International Systems of Broadcasting.* East Lansing: Michigan State University Press.

Eschenbach, Josef. 1970. "Farm Broadcasting in Indonesia." Prepared for Rural Broadcasting Workshop, Lusaka, Zambia.

————. 1971. "Rural Broadcasting in Indonesia: Report after Two Years of Experience." Mimeographed, Jakarta: Directorate of Agricultural Extension.

Esper, George. 1975. "A Portrait of Saigon in Change." *New York Times,* 1 June, p. 6.

Essai, Brian. 1961. *Papua and New Guinea: A Contemporary Survey.* Melbourne: Oxford University Press.

FACTS (Federation of Australian Commercial Television Stations). 1970–71. *Annual Report.* Sydney: FACTS.

Fagen, Richard R. 1962. "Politics and Communication in the New States: Burma and Ghana." Ph.D. dissertation, Stanford University.

Fan Chih-lung. 1961. "College Course by Television." *China Reconstructs* (Hong Kong), April, pp. 10–11.

Faragler, Neil. 1971. "Television Reaches into Two-Thirds of Australia's Schools." *Educational Television,* April.

FBIS (Foreign Broadcasting Information Service). 1971 and 1975. *Broadcasting Stations of the World.* 4 vol. Washington, D.C.: Government Printing Office.

FEER (Far Eastern Economic Review) (Hong Kong). 1973. "Hatch and Dispatch." 5 March, p. 22.

————. 1974. "Exporting Colour." 9 August, p. 38.

————. 1975. "Communications in Asia '75." 7 March, pp. 1–18.

Feliciano, Gloria D. 1966. *Philippine Mass Media in Perspective.* Manila: University of the Philippines.

Fenton, James. 1975a. "New Shows in Saigon." *Washington Post,* 28 May, p. A-21.

————. 1975b. "The New Censors Assure S. Vietnam a Good Press." *International Herald Tribune,* 18 August.

Fernando, C.S., et al. 1968. *Thailand Yearbook.* Bangkok: Temple University Services.

Fiefia, Sione N. 1968. *Report on the Results of the 1966 Census.* Nukualofa, Tonga: R.S. Wallbank, Government Printer.

Fiji Times. 1972. 1 August.

Fitzgerald, Stephen. 1969. "Overseas Chinese Affairs and the Cultural Revolution." *China Quarterly.* October–December, pp. 103–26.

Foster, Des. 1975. "Guerrilla Tactics in Absence of Master Broadcasting Plan." *IPI Report* (Zurich), July, pp. 10–12.

Fraser-Tytler, William Kerr. 1967. *Afghanistan: A Study of Political Development in Central and Southern Asia.* 3rd ed., revised by M.C. Gillett. New York and London: Oxford University Press.

Free China Review (Taipei). 1975. "Police Radio Serves People of Taiwan." May, p. 51.

Free China Weekly (Taipei). 1975a. "Ding Reports on ROC Television." 29 June, p. 2.

————. 1975b. "Pres. Yen Urges TV Upgrading." 29 June, pp. 1–2.

Given, John. 1975. "Nudity Programs Wow Japan's Audience." *Evening Bulletin* (Philadelphia). 18 February, p. 26–A.

Gjesdal, Tor. 1970. "UNESCO's Programme in Space Communication." *UNESCO Chronicle* 16, no. 11 (November): 439–52.

Glattbach, Jack, and Anderson, Mike. 1971. "Print and Broadcasting Media in Malaysia."

Mimeographed. Kuala Lumpur: South East Asia Press Centre.

Glunt, E. Merle, and Stelzenmuller, George V. 1966. *Radio Frequency Management in Thailand.* Bangkok: USOM/Thailand.

Goodman, C.R. 1968. "Education by Radio in Papua and New Guinea." *EBU Review* (Brussels and Geneva), 112b (November).

Goodship, F.L. 1967 "Ceylon: Establishment of Television." Serial no. 268. Paris: UNESCO.

Gorrick, Eric. 1971. "Australian TV Now 15 Years of Age: Commercial Stations 85% of Audience." *Variety* (New York), 5 May, p. 48.

Gozo, Danny. 1975. "A New Order Takes Over the Old Spiders' Webs." *Media,* August, pp. 9, 11.

Green, Timothy. 1972. *The Universal Eye.* New York: Stein and Day.

Guardian (Rangoon). 1971. 15 February, p. 1.

Guide to Television Advertising in Pakistan. 1970. Karachi: Pakistan Television Corporation Ltd.

Gunaratne, Shelton. 1970. "Government-Press Conflict in Ceylon: Freedom Versus Responsibility." *Journalism Quarterly* 47, no. 3: 530–43, 552.

Gupta, R.N. 1974. "SITE Needs a TV Research Bureau." *Vidura* (New Delhi), April, pp. 537–39.

Hancock, Alan. 1972. "Asian Broadcasting Training Institute: A Supplementary Report." Serial no. COM/WS/263. Paris: UNESCO.

▬▬▬. 1974. "Mass Media and National Development." *Educational Broadcasting International* (London), June, pp. 58–68.

Hangen, Wells. 1970. "Saturday Night at the Maos." *TV Guide,* 31 January, p. 9.

Harvey, Steve. 1971. "East or West – Rock Music Just Won't Be Suppressed." *Capitol Times* (Madison, Wisconsin), 8 February.

Hawthorne, James. 1974. "On Government Radio and TV, Canned Imported Programmes." *Media for Asia's Communications Industry* (Hong Kong), June, p. 7.

Henderson, John W., et al. 1971. *Area Handbook for Oceania.* American University Foreign Area Studies. Washington, D.C.: Government Printing Office.

Hilbrink, Albert, and Lohmann, Manfred. 1974. "Are Rural Radio Forums Dying in Indonesia?" *Media Asia* (Singapore) 1, no. 3: 37–40.

Hiner, Richard. 1975. "NHK: Japan's Other Miracle." *Public Telecommunications Review* (Washington, D.C.), May–June, pp. 22–31.

History of Broadcasting in Japan. 1967. Tokyo: Nippon Hoso Kyokai.

Ho Chia-chu. 1971. "The Impact of TV's Rise on Radio in Taiwan." Masters thesis, National Chengchi University (Taipei). In Chinese.

Hoffer, Thomas William. 1972. "Broadcasting in an Insurgency Environment: USIA in Vietnam, 1965–70." Ph.D. dissertation, University of Wisconsin.

▬▬▬. 1974. "Nguyen Van Be as Propaganda Hero of the North and South Vietnamese Governments: A Case Study of Mass Media Conflict." *Southern Speech Communication Journal,* Fall, pp. 63–80.

Horley, A., and Sanfridsson; A. 1973. "Indonesia: Communication Policies and Planning." Serial no. 2888/RMO. RD/FDC. Paris: UNESCO.

Horne, Donald. 1968. *The Lucky Country.* Baltimore: Penguin Books.

Hotchkiss, David. 1964. "New Zealand: You Can Be Too Careful." *Contrast* 3, no. 4: 235.

Houn, Franklin W. 1961. *To Change a Nation: Propaganda and Indoctrination in Communist China.* New York: The Free Press.

Hsin-wen Chan-hsien (News Front). 1959a. "Preliminary Report of Hopei Broadcasting Station's Manure Accumulating Drive." No. 4, pp. 20–21.

▬▬▬. 1959b. "Our Specialized Musical Programs." no. 5, p. 26.

▬▬▬. 1959c. "The Bureau of Broadcasting Affairs Convened the Sixth National Conference on Broadcasting." No. 6, p. 2.

————. 1959d. "Broadcasting Must Serve the Continuing Leap Forward of the Industrial and Agricultural Production." No. 22, p. 10.

Hsu, James C. 1974. "Utilization of Satellites for Television, Republic of China." In *Pacific Nations Broadcasting II,* ed. Benjamin Draper, pp. 37–38. San Francisco: San Francisco State College.

Hull, Ronald E. 1970. "A Critical Analysis of the Development of Television for Vietnam." Ed.D. dissertation, University of Nebraska.

Hull, William H.N. 1962. "Public Control of Broadcasting: The Canadian and Australian Experiences." *Canadian Journal of Economics and Political Science* 28 (February): 118.

————. 1970. "A Comprehensive Study of the Problems of Ministerial Responsibility in Australian and Canadian Broadcasting." Ph.D. dissertation, Duke University.

Hur Kyoon. 1974. "Satellite Use in Korea." In *Pacific Nations Broadcasting II,* ed. Benjamin Draper, pp. 42–45. San Francisco: San Francisco State College.

Inkeles, Alex. 1958. *Public Opinion in Soviet Russia: A Study in Mass Persuasion.* Cambridge: Harvard University Press.

Intermedia (London). 1973. "Community TV Backed by Japanese Government." March–April, pp. 15–17.

————. 1974a. "Educational Television: Four Asian Experiences." 2, no. 1: 14–15.

————. 1974b. "Indonesia: Where Satellites Make Communications Cheaper and Quicker." 2, no. 3: 22–23.

————. 1975a. "Asians Expand News Exchange." March, pp. 18–19.

————. 1975b. "End of NZBC." March, p. 23.

Inventory of Family Planning Research in Pakistan. 1969. Karachi: National Research Institute of Family Planning.

Jacobs, Milton; Rice, Charles E.; and Szalay, Lorand. 1964. *The Study of Communication in Thailand.* Washington, D.C.: Special Operations Research Office, American University.

Jameson, Sam. 1975. "Newspaper Wins Allies in Fight with Park." *Philadelphia Inquirer,* 1 March, p. 5-A.

Jan, George P. 1967. "Radio Propaganda in Chinese Villages." *Asian Survey,* May, pp. 305–15.

Japanese Press. Annual. Tokyo: Nihon Shinbun Kyokai.

Jareunsak, Sirirat. 1970. "Upper Secondary School Students' Interest in Television Programmes." Masters thesis, Chulalongkorn University (Bangkok).

Jayaweera, Neville. 1967. "Role of Radio in a Developing Country." *Ceylon Daily News,* 5 January, CBC advertising supplement.

————. 1970. "Mass Media and Development." *International Broadcasting Institute Newsletter,* no. 2.

Jeffery, Peter. 1971. "Radio and Loudspeaker Combination for Schools in Papua New Guinea." *Educational Broadcasting International* (London) 5, no. 4 (December).

Jen-min Jih-pao, (Peking). 1955. "Editorial." 12 December.

————. 1960a. "Party Control of Communication Media." 11 June.

————. 1960b. "New Development in Running the Press by the Whole Party." 11 June.

————. 1962. 12 August.

Juang-ming Jih-pao (Peking). 1968. "Socialist Journalism Is an Instrument of Proletarian Dictatorship – China's Khruschev's Counter-Revolutionary Revisionist Viewpoint on Journalism Thoroughly Repudiated." 4 September.

JUSPAO (Joint United States Public Affairs Office). 1970. *Media Survey in Urban Vietnam.* Parts I-III. Saigon: JUSPAO.

Kale, Pramod. 1974. "Are SITE's Premises Correct?" *Vidura* (New Delhi), April, pp. 533–35.

Kalimullah, A.F. 1975. "Information Imbalance in Asia." *Indian Press,* August, pp. 7–11.

Kamath, M.G. 1974. "Problems SITE Will Have to Solve." *Vidura* (New Delhi), April, pp.

555, 560.

Kamm, Henry. 1970. "Lon Nol Reads No Newspaper and Never Uses a Telephone." *New York Times Magazine,* 13 December, p. 28.

Kanabayashi, Masayoshi. 1974. "Television: Japan's New Strategy." *Far Eastern Economic Review* (Hong Kong), 20 May, pp. 62–63.

Karamchandani, Lal. 1974. "TV – A Challenge and an Opportunity: India's Satellite Experiment Should Answer Many Questions." *Media Asia* (Singapore) 1, no. 2: 21–25.

Katz, Elihu. 1972. "Television as a Horseless Carriage." Prepared for International Symposium on Communication, Philadelphia.

Kaviya, Somkuan, ed. 1971. *Directory of Mass Communication Resources in Thailand.* Bangkok: School of Journalism, Thammasat University. In Thai and English.

Keesing, Felix M., and Keesing, Marie M. 1956. *Elite Communication in Samoa: A Study of Leadership.* Stanford, Ca.: Stanford University Press.

Kim Chong Chul. 1975. "The Committee for the Struggle to Protect Freedom of the Speech in the Dong-A." Unpublished paper.

Kimberley, John. 1969. "This is Radio Peking." *Popular Electronics,* April, pp. 59–61.

Koch, C. 1968. "Indonesia: Educational Broadcasting." Serial no. 919/BMS. RD/MC. Paris: UNESCO.

Koh, Edgar. 1975a. "TV in a Developing Nation: Singapore's U.K.-U.S. Yen." *Variety* (New York), 9 July, p. 58.

——————. 1975b. "Singapore TV Using Plenty of U.S. Series: Lotsa Repeats." *Variety* (New York), 22 October, p. 115.

Kolodin, Irving. 1971: "How Australians Learn Their ABCs." *Saturday Review* (New York), 24 July, p. 48.

Ko Youngbok. 1972. "The Backwardness and the Task of the Rural Culture." *Shin Dong-A* (Seoul), March, pp. 96–107. In Korean.

Krishnamoorthy, P.V. 1975. "Satellite Broadcasting." *Communicator* (New Delhi), July, pp. 19–24.

Lamb, David. 1974. "Television Teaching Fails to Pass Test in Pago Pago." *Los Angeles Times,* 16 October, p. 4-A.

Larsen, A.A. 1974. "Malaysia: More Insertions for the Bumiputras." *Media for Asia's Communications Industry* (Hong Kong), November, pp. 21–22.

Leader: Malaysian Journalism Review (Kuala Lumpur). 1974. "Broadcasting." 3, no. 1: 19–21.

Lee Dukgun. 1969. "Study of the Opinion Function of Broadcasting and the Surrounding Circumstances of the Function in Korea." *Journalism Study* (Seoul), no. 2, pp. 59–71. In Korean.

Lee Younghi. 1972. "The Bias and Anti-Intellectualism of TV." *Shin Dong-A* (Seoul), March, pp. 226–31.. In Korean.

Lelyveld, Joseph. 1975. "Wealthy Family Loses Power in Bitter Feud with Marcos." *New York Times,* 22 April, p. 2.

Lent, John A. 1970. "Philippine Media and Nation-Building: An Overview." *Gazette* (Deventer) 16 (Spring): 2–12.

——————. 1971. *Philippine Mass Communications: Before 1811, After 1966.* Manila: Philippine Press Institute.

——————. 1974a. "The Philippine Press under Martial Law." *Index on Censorship* (London) 3 (Spring): 47–59.

——————. 1974b. "Malaysia's Guided Media." *Index on Censorship* (London), Winter, pp. 65–75.

——————. 1974c. "Mass Media in Laos." *Gazette* (Deventer) 20: 170–79.

——————. 1975a. "Lee Kuan Yew and the Singapore Media." *Index on Censorship* (London) 4 (Fall): 7–16.

——————. 1975b. "Bangladesh: an About Face Followed by New Uncertainty." *IPI*

Report (Zurich), October, pp. 8–10.

Lieber, Leslie. 1966. "Hanoi Hannah." *This Week,* 13 February.

Liew, Maureen Eng Neo. 1975. "Radio and Population Control in Singapore." *COMBROAD* (London), April–June, pp. 37–39.

Liu, Alan P.L. 1964a. "Growth and Modernizing Function of Rural Radio in Communist China." *Journalism Quarterly* 44, no. 4: 573–74.

—————. 1964b. "Radio Broadcasting in Communist China." Mimeographed. Cambridge: Center for International Studies, Massachusetts Institute of Technology.

—————. 1971. *Communications and National Integration in Communist China.* Berkeley: University of California Press.

Los Anglees Times. 1964. "Nine Newspapers Shut Down by Saigon Regime." 19 January.

—————. 1966a. "Four-Station TV Networks Set for South Vietnam." 4 July.

—————. 1966b. "G.I.s Forget Fighting by Watching 'Combat.' " 7 December.

—————. 1967. " 'Hanoi Hannah' Better than Nothing to G.I.s." 23 August.

Löser, Horst. 1972. "Der Politische Geheimsender." In *Handbuch 1972,* p. 36. Cologne: Deutsche Welle.

Lucas, Peter. 1975. "ABC Converts to Colour." *COMBROAD* (London), April–June, pp. 3–6.

Maast, Benjamin V. 1958. "A Study of the Rise of Television and Its Impact on the Broadcasting Control Mechanism of the English Speaking Commonwealth Countries." Masters thesis, University of North Carolina.

McBain, Norman. 1972. "Extensive Training for Asian Broadcasters." *ABU Newsletter* (Sydney), October, pp. 17–21.

Mackay, Ian K. 1953. *Broadcasting in New Zealand.* Wellington: A.H. and A.W. Reed.

—————. 1957. *Broadcasting in Australia.* Melbourne: Melbourne University.

—————. 1969. "Broadcasting in Papua and New Guinea." *Gazette* (Deventer) 15, no. 4: 241–48.

—————. 1974. "Upgrading News in Papua New Guinea." *COMBROAD* (London), October–December, p. 59.

—————. 1975. "First Anniversary of NBC in Papua New Guinea." *COMBROAD* (London), January–March, pp. 49–50.

Mackerras, Colin, and Hunter, Neale. 1967. *China Observed.* Australia: Thomas Nelson Ltd.

Madgwick, Sir Robert. 1972. "Forty Years of the Australian Broadcasting Commission." *EBU Review* (Geneva) 23, no. 5 (September): 24.

Maheu, Rene. 1948. "The Work of UNESCO in the Field of Mass Communications." *Journalism Quarterly* 25 (Summer): 157–62.

Malay Mail (Kuala Lumpur). 1972a. "What's Wrong with TV?" 15 October.

—————. 1972b. "TV – The Other Side of the Story." 22 October.

—————. 1972c. "TV – The New Formula." 29 October.

Malaysian Digest. 1975. "Educational TV for Sarawak Next Year." 15 August, p. 3.

Mao Tse Tung. 1967. *Selected Works of Mao Tse Tung.* Peking: Foreign Language Press.

Marshall, Cooper. 1966. "Broadcasting and Television." In *An Encyclopedia of New Zealand,* ed. A.H. McLintock. Wellington: Government Printer.

Masani, Mehra. 1974. "Second Thoughts on Satellites." *Indian Press* (New Delhi), November, pp. 15–16.

—————. 1975. "The Satellite Experiment in India – A Word of Caution." *COMBROAD* (London), April–June, pp. 25–27.

Media Advisory Council, Philippines. 1973. "Policies, Objectives, Organizational Setup, Code of Ethical Conduct, Guidelines, Rules and Regulations for Mass Media." Mimeographed. Manila: MAC.

Media Asia (Singapore). 1974. "TV's Prickly Role in Hong Kong" 1, no. 3: 8.

Media for Asia's Communications Industry (Hong Kong). 1974a. "Bangla Spares Shortage." January, p. 22.

————— . 1974b. "Student Revolt Frees Thai Press?" January, pp. 3–4.

————— . 1974c. "China Will Join the ABU." February, p. 3.

————— . 1974d. "Sir Charles Moses on Broadcasting, Development and the ABU." February, p. 5.

————— . 1974e. "TV 'Cleansed.' " February, p. 20.

————— . 1974f. "BBC Link Closing." March, p. 20.

————— . 1974g. "Macau May Beam TV to Hong Kong." May, pp. 22–23.

————— . 1974h. "New HK Studios." May, p. 19.

————— . 1974i. "RHTV Keeps the Needle." May, p. 23.

————— . 1974j. "New TV Code in Force." July, p. 3.

————— . 1974k. "HK-ETV Go to Color." September, p. 26.

————— . 1974m. "Debate: Wrong Time for the Right SITE?" October, pp. 9–11.

————— . 1974n. "New Set-Up for Indian Television?" October, p. 23.

————— . 1975a. "Singapore Favourite Site for New BBC Station'" January, p. 23.

————— . 1975b. "The Leaning Tower of . . . " March, p. 4.

————— . 1975c. "32 Per Cent Rise in HK Billings." April, p. 21.

————— . 1975d. "ABC's All Rock Station Wows Sydney." May, pp. 6–7.

Meenpradit, Ranjuan. 1970. "The Influence of Television Programming on Upper Elementary School Students from Families of Different Social Status." Masters thesis, Chulalongkorn University (Bangkok).

Mei Yi. 1950. "People's Broadcasting in China." *Jen-min Jih-pao* (Peking), 25 April.

Meyer, Richard J. 1971. "Educational Broadcasting in Thailand: A Microcosm of Asia." *Educational Broadcasting Review* 5 (February): 30–34.

Milne, R.S., ed. 1957. *Bureaucracy in New Zealand.* Wellington: New Zealand Institute of Public Administration.

Milwaukee Journal. 1971. 31 October.

Mohan, Lalit. 1974. "Where Amritsar TV Beats Lahore." *Vidura* (New Delhi), April, p. 579.

Moody, Randall J. 1970. "The Armed Forces Broadcast News System: Vietnam Version." *Journalism Quarterly* 47 (Spring): 27–30.

Moore, Charles B. 1971. "Censorship of AFVN News in Vietnam." *Journal of Broadcasting* (Philadelphia) 15 (Fall): 387–95.

Mosel, James N. 1963. "Communication Patterns and Political Socialization in Transitional Thailand." In *Communications and Political Development,* ed. Lucian Pye, pp. 184–228. Princeton: Princeton University Press.

Moses, Sir Charles. 1974a. "Broadcasting in Asia and the Pacific – An Overview." *Media Asia* (Singapore) 1, no. 3: 9–13.

————— . 1974b. "The Challenges Facing Asian Broadcasting." In *The 1974 Asian Press and Media Directory,* pp. 9–11. Manila: Press Foundation of Asia.

Muir, T. 1963. "Radio Cook Islands." *South Pacific Bulletin* 13 (July): 34–36.

Mujahid, Sharif al. 1952. "Media of Mass Communication in Pakistan." Masters thesis, Stanford University.

Mulay, Vijaya. 1974. "Will SITE Be Rural Enough?" *Vidura* (New Delhi), April, pp. 551–54.

Mullick, K.S., and Bourke, T.K. 1968. "Asia – Training Resources and Needs in Radio and Television." Serial no. 502/BMS. RD/COM. Paris: UNESCO.

Mun Shi Hyung. 1972. "Radio and Television Services in Korea." *ABU Newsletter* (Sydney), no. 80 (January): 24–26.

Munson, Frederick P. 1968. *Area Handbook for Cambodia.* American University Foreign Area Studies. Washington, D.C.: Government Printing Office.

Munster, G.J. 1960. "Television in Australia." *NAEB Journal* (Washington, D.C.) no. 19 (July–August).

Nakajima, Iwao. 1974. "Social Climate and Television in Pakistan and Burma." In *Studies of Broadcasting,* pp. 99–113. Tokyo: NHK.

The Nation. 1967. "The VOA Technique." 5 June, p. 709.

National Statistics Office, Thailand. 1970. "Report of the Radio and Television Survey: Radio Listening – Whole Kingdom Survey, 1968–69." Bangkok: Office of the Prime Minister.

Naylor, Malcolm. 1973. "The ABC in Papua New Guinea.." *ABU Newsletter* (Sydney), August, pp. 19–21.

Nelson, Lyle. 1974. "Keeping SITE on the Right Lines." *Vidura* (New Delhi), December, pp. 907–10.

Neuhauser, Charles. 1968. "The Impact of the Cultural Revolution on the Chinese Communist Party Machine." *Asian Survey,* June, p. 467.

New China News Agency (Peking). 1956. Dispatch. 24 December.

——————. 1969. Dispatch. 27 October.

——————. 1971. Dispatch. 21 September.

Newsweek. 1966. "Hanoi Harry." 14 February.

New York Post. 1966. 23 February.

New York Times. 1968. "Saigon Sentences UPI Photographer." 26 May.

——————. 1972. "Thieu Announces Harsh New Rules for Newspapers." 6 August.

——————. 1975. "Saigon Will Base Local Government on Family Groups." 29 May.

NHK Handbook. Annual. Tokyo: Nippon Hoso Kyokai.

Nickelson, Richard L. 1974. "What U.N. Has Done for SITE." *Vidura* (New Delhi), June, pp. 647–50.

Nishimoto, Mitoji. 1969. *The Development of Educational Broadcasting in Japan.* Rutland, Vt.: Charles Tuttle Co.

Noah, Lynn. 1969. "Mass Media in Phon Thong Country." Mimeographed. Washington, D.C.: United States Information Agency.

Noorani, Hafeez. 1975. "Bombay TV: The Darshak's View." *Hindustan Times,* 9 March.

North Korean Fact Book. 1971. Seoul: Research Institute on the Communist Affairs.

NZBC (New Zealand Broadcasting Corporation). 1970–71. *Annual Report.* Wellington: NZBC.

——————. 1971. *Annual Report.* Wellington: NZBC.

Okada, Naoyuki. 1970. "Criticism to the Planned Governmental Monitoring Systems." In *Chosa Joho* (Information from Research). Tokyo: Tokyo Broadcasting Station. In Japanese.

Olson, Kenneth E., and Eirabi, Abdul G. 1954. "Radio Pakistan: Voice of a New Nation." *Journalism Quarterly* 31: 73–79.

Ono, Kichiro. 1974a. "How Research Can Help Broadcasters." *Media Asia* (Singapore) 1, no. 3: 17–21.

——————. 1974b. "The Birth of the ABU." *ABU Newsletter* (Sydney), July, pp 5–18.

Pacific Islands Monthly (Sydney). 1961. "Tonga Radio Has 'Excellent' Cover." 31, no. 9 (April): 65.

——————. 1969. "Fiji Should Have Television (But Not the Commercial Kind)." 40, no. 1 (January): 31.

Padilla, Charles E. 1975. "Television Has Come to Tiny Easter Island." *Philadelphia Inquirer,* 11 May, p. 10–L.

Pakistan Year Book. Annual. Karachi: National Publishing House Ltd.

Papua New Guinea *Post Courier.* 1973. 7 February; 14 February.

Parajuli, Mukunda. 1972. "Nepal Experiences in Developmental Communications." Mimeographed. Honolulu: Communication Institute, East-West Center.

Parliamentary Debates, Ceylon House of Representatives. 1966. Official Report, vol. 70 (8 October), columns 1055–56.

Pearson, Lester. 1972. "Communication: Its Real Meaning." *ABU Newsletter* (Sydney), May, p. 12.

Peking Review. 1971. 1 January, p. 15.

_____. 1972. 2 June, p. 23.

Peng Yao. 1971. "The Historical Development of the Chinese Press." In *Press Milestones of the Republic of China*, p. 11. Taipei: Taipei Journalists Association. In Chinese.

Penniman, Howard R. 1972. "Press Freedom in South Vietnam." In *Elections in South Vietnam*, pp. 153–65. Washington, D.C.: American Enterprise Institute for Public Policy Research.

Petersen, Neville. 1972. "ABU's Part in the EBU Working Party for TV News." *ABU Newsletter* (Sydney), January, p. 8.

PFA (Press Foundation of Asia). Annual. *The Asian Press and Media Directory*. Manila: PFA.

Philadelphia Inquirer. 1975. "Sabotage Suspected in Delhi Fire." 29 June, p. 3-A.

Philippine Times (Chicago). 1974. "New Media Watchdogs: Hans and Ted." 16–30 November, pp. 4, 8.

_____. 1975. "Opposing Views by Mijares, Mutuc." 1–15 July, pp. 8, 18, 21.

Phillips, Herbert P. 1965. *Thai Peasant Personality: The Patterning of Interpersonal Behavior in the Village of Bang Chan*. Berkeley: University of California Press.

_____ and Wilson, David A. 1964. "Certain Effects of Culture and Organization on Internal Security in Thailand." Memorandum RM3786 ARPA. Santa Monica: Rand Corporation.

PICN (Pacific Islands Communication Newsletter) (Honolulu). 1975a. "Satellite News Exchange Report." February, pp. 3–5.

_____. 1975b. "TV Controversy in American Samoa." February, pp. 10–11.

_____. 1975c. "Year of Change for PNG Broadcasting." February, pp. 16–17.

Pike, Douglas. 1966. *Viet Cong: The Organization and Techniques of the National Liberation Front of South Vietnam*. Cambridge: Massachusetts Institute of Technology Press.

Pines, Aaron. 1974a. "The Philippines at Noon." *Variety* (New York), 2 January, p. 30.

_____. 1974b. "Philippines under Martial Law: the Word in TV Is Uptrend." *Variety* (New York), 24 April, p. 47.

_____. 1975. "Broadcasting in the Philippines Subject to Emerging 'New Order.' " *Variety* (New York), 21 May, p. 38.

Pitman, Jack. 1972. "World's Most Permissive Medium or Not." *Variety* (New York), 29 August.

Polaschek, R.J. 1958. *Government Administration in New Zealand*. Wellington: New Zealand Institute of Public Administration.

"Quick TV Facts of the Republic of China." 1975. Taipei: Television Academy of Arts and Sciences.

"Radio Afghanistan." 1967 Kabul: Ministry of Information and Culture.

Radio and Television of the World. 1972. Tokyo: Nippon Hoso Kyokai. In Japanese.

Radio and Television Yearbook 1971. Seoul: Korean Broadcasting Association. In Korean.

Radio Ceylon. 1960. Colombo: Government Information Department.

Ragsdale, Wilmott. 1960. "A Program for Developing the Media of Southeast Asia." *Journalism Quarterly* 37 (Spring): 275–79.

Rana, Narendra. 1974. "Wanted: Mass Based Software." *Vidura* (New Delhi), April, pp. 557–60.

Rao, B.S.S. 1974, "All India Radio and Its Consumers." *Indian Press* (New Delhi), November, pp. 17–21.

Rao, N. Bhaskara. 1974. "How to Make SITE Effective." *Vidura* (New Delhi), April, pp. 549–50.

Rao, Y.V. Lakshmana, and Sinha, P.R.R. 1974. "Is the Asian Broadcaster Serving Two Masters or One?" *Media Asia* (Singapore) 1, no. 4: 33–37.

Reid, Thomas R. 1974. "Where the Singer May Be Slender, Pretty and Nude." *TV Guide*, 6 July, pp. 10–12.

Report of the Broadcasting Review Committee, 1969–70, together with a Report on the

Fiji Radio Audience Survey, June–September 1969. 1970. Suva: Government Printer.

Report of the Commission of Inquiry on the Ceylon Broadcasting Corporation 1970. 1972. Sessional Paper X. Colombo: Department of Government Printing.

Report of the Commission on Broadcasting 1953. 1955. Sessional Paper XX. Colombo. Ceyon Government Press.

Report of the Commission on Broadcasting and Information 1965. 1966. Sessional Paper XII. Colombo: Ceylon Government Press.

"Request for Assistance in Undertaking a Preinvestment Study of the Use of Educational Television for Improving the Quality of Education, and Also for Preparing Detailed Projects for Such a Scheme and for the Development of Educational Radio." 1972. Bangkok: Ministry of Education.

"Resolutions of the 9th ABU General Assembly, October 9–14, 1972." 1972. Sydney: Asian Broadcasting Union.

Roberts, T.D., et al. 1967. *Area Handbook for Laos.* American University Foreign Area Studies. Washington, D.C.: Government Printing Office.

Robinson, Douglas. 1968. " 'Nose for News' of Censorship Enrage Saigon Editors." *New York Times,* 26 May.

Rosario, Florangel Z. 1964. "An Analysis of Broadcasting Practices in the Philippines." Prepared for SEATO Expert Group in Radio Broadcasting, Manila.

Rowe, James W., and Rowe, Margaret A. 1968. *New Zealand.* New York: Frederick A. Praeger.

Rowland, G.F. 1973. "Thailand: Educational Broadcasting, Thammasat University." Serial no. 2879/RMO. RD/MC. Paris: UNESCO.

Salazar, Ruben. 1966a "Villagers More Interested in Watching 'Watchers' than Tube." *Los Angeles Times,* 6 February.

——————. 1966b. "U.S. Hopes TV Will Aid in Whipping Viet Cong." *Los Angeles Times,* 10 February.

Schramm, Wilbur, ed. 1960. *Mass Communications.* Urbana: University of Illinois Press.

Schroder, J.H.E. 1961. "Development of a Commercial Service." *EBU Review* (Geneva) 67B (May): 22.

Schuman, Julian. 1972. "Serving the Revolution with Words." *Far Eastern Economic Review* (Hong Kong), 22 January, pp. 18–19.

SEAMEO (Southeast Asia Ministers of Education Organization). 1971. *SEAMEO Regional Center for Education Innovation and Technology – Final Report – 4th Meeting of Governing Board. Saigon, 13–16 July 1971.*

Second Five Year Plan (1960–65). 1960. Karachi: Planning Commission, Government of Pakistan.

Sengupta, Utpal. 1975. "Television in Calcutta." *Vidura* (New Delhi), February, p. 53.

Seow, Peter. 1974. "Singapore ETV Has Wide Reach." *Media Asia* (Singapore) 1, no. 1: 29–30.

Shaplen, Robert. 1971. *The Road from War: Vietnam, 1965–70.* New York: Harper and Row.

Sharuprapai, Ananda. 1972. "Telecommunications in Thailand." *The Nation,* 22 September.

Sheridan, Mary. 1968. "The Emulation of Heroes." *The China Quarterly,* no. 33, pp. 51, 62.

Sherman, Charles E. 1969. "The Asian Broadcasting Union." *Journal of Broadcasting* (Philadelphia) 13 (Fall): 397–412.

Shih Chang-yao. 1972. "A Study of Sources of Public Affairs News for Taiwan's Peasants." Masters thesis, National Chengchi University (Taipei). In Chinese.

Shin Dong-A (Seoul). 1972. "News and Topics: Mass Communication." February, p. 347. In Korean.

Shinn, Rinn-Sup, et al. 1969. *Area Handbook for North Korea.* American University Foreign Area Studies. Washington, D.C.: Government Printing Office.

Simpson, E.C. 1961. *A Survey of the Arts in New Zealand.* Wellington: New Zealand

Chamber Music Society.

Simulmatics Corporation. 1967. "Research Reports on Communications in South Vietnamese Villages, No. 1–68." Cambridge: Massachusetts Institute of Technology.

Singapore, Ministry of Health and Home Affairs. 1974. "Report of the Committee on Crime and Delinquency." Singapore: Ministry of Health and Home Affairs.

Singapore Facts and Figures. 1970. Singapore: Ministry of Culture.

Singh, Kedar Man. 1975. "Nepal: Transistor Bonanza No More." *Far Eastern Economic Review* (Hong Kong), 28 March, p. 29.

Singh, Samar Bahadur. 1974. "Commercial Broadcasting in India." *Indian Press* (New Delhi), October, pp. 7–8, 11.

Sixth Year Pakistan 1953. 1953. Karachi: Pakistan Publications.

Smith, Anthony. 1973. *The Shadow in the Cave*. Urbana: University of Illinois Press.

Smith, Charles. 1972. "China's TV Is Still in Its Infancy." *The Star* (Penang, Malaysia), 24 November.

Smith, Harvey H., et al. 1962. *Area Handbook for North Vietnam*. American University Foreign Area Studies. Washington, D.C.: Government Printing Office.

Snare, Austin. 1962–63. "The Development and Problems of Australian Broadcast Services." *Journal of Broadcasting* (Philadelphia) 7 (Winter): 23–34.

Snider, Paul B. 1968. "International News Exposure in Afghanistan." Prepared for Association for Education in Journalism, Lawrence, Kansas.

Solley, Alan. 1975. "Communication: Brunei on the Air in Record Time." *Far Eastern Economic Review* (Hong Kong), 7 February, p. 46.

So Woon. 1971a. "Khmer Republic." In *Asian Press, 1971*, ed. Kim Kyu-whan, pp. 108–10. Seoul: Readership Research Center, Press Foundation of Asia.

————. 1971b. "Laos." In *Asian Press, 1971*, ed. Kim Kyu-whan, pp. 118–19. Seoul: Readership Research Center, Press Foundation of Asia.

Spackman, Jack. 1974. "Hongkong TV Fights for $40M Ads." *Media for Asia's Communications Industry* (Hong Kong), January, p. 22.

Spurr, Russell. 1974a. "North Korea: A Monument Called Pyongyang." *Far Eastern Economic Review* (Hong Kong), 15 July, pp. 27–28.

————. 1974b. "Media: The Beeb Is Looking for a New Home." *Far Eastern Economic Review* (Hong Kong), 15 November, p. 30.

Sripraphai, Somsiri. 1970. "The Influence of Mass Media on Studying Science among Bangkok and Dhonburi Secondary School Students." Masters thesis, Chulalongkorn University (Bangkok).

Srisamt, Sriyon, et al. 1973. "Review of Radio and Television Work in Southern Thailand and Malaysia." Prepared for Public Relations in Management Seminar, Bangkok.

Star (Penang, Malaysia). 1973a. "Nostalgic Goodbyes from U.S. Armed Forces Radio and TV." 23 March.

————. 1973b. "No Radio Time for Opposition." 3 May.

Star-Bulletin (Honolulu). 1970. "Television Teaching Called a Failure on Samoa." 4 March, p. C-2.

Steinle, Peggy. 1970. "You Like It Raw, We Like It Cooked." *New York Times*, 16 August.

Story, John. 1971. "A Target Audience – The Hill Tribes of Northern Thailand." Prepared for Annual Meeting, International Communication Association, Phoenix, Arizona.

Straits Times (Kuala Lumpur). 1972. "Colour TV for You by 1975." 21 December.

————. 1973a. "Colour TV Next Year in Singapore." 15 March.

————. 1973b. "Two Singapore Companies May Assemble Colour TV Sets." 27 March.

————. 1973c. "Dialects May Be Used for Regional Broadcasts." 29 March.

————. 1973d. "Rediffusion Folds Up." 3 December.

————. 1973e. "Singapore Chops Radio Broadcast Time." 31 December.

Stringer, Gilbert. 1964. "The New Zealand Broadcasting Corporation." *EBU Review*

(Geneva) 83B (January): 18.

—————. 1966. "The Establishment of Private TV Translators in New Zealand." *EBU Review* (Geneva) 96B (March): 24.

Studies of Broadcasting. Annual. Tokyo: Radio and TV Culture Research Institute, Nippon Hoso Kyokai.

Suh Young-nee. 1968. "History of Korean Broadcasting System Television Station (KBS-TV)." Masters thesis, University of Missouri.

Sumadi, M. Ec. 1971. "Television and National Development: The Indonesian Experience." Prepared for WHO Workshop on Development of Health Education Media, New Delhi.

Sunday Star-Bulletin and Advertiser (Honolulu). 1969. "Aspinall Issue Fraught with Dynamite." 9 March, p. A-3.

—————. 1970. "American Samoa Governor Fired Education Director." 5 July, p. A-5.

"Survey of Radio Industry in Pakistan." 1965. Report no. K-192-P. Karachi: Investment Advisory Centre of Pakistan.

Sutherland, Daniel. 1975. "How Saigon's New Regime Profits from Past Injustice." *Christian Science Monitor* (Boston), 5 May, p. 1.

Su Tung-feng. 1969. "Development of the Chinese Communist Rural Wired Broadcasting Networks." *Chinese Communist Affairs Monthly* (Taipei) 12, no. 4 (June): 53.

Tadao, Uryu. 1967. *Hoso Sangyo* [Broadcasting industry]. Tokyo: Hosei University Press. In Japanese.

Tamrongshod, Suda. 1966. "The Influence of Mass Media on Social Studies Learning in Vocational Schools in Bangkok." Masters thesis, Chulalongkorn University (Bangkok).

Tan, Sebastian Chiaw Hock. 1974. "Colour Television in Singapore." *COMBROAD* (London), October–December, pp. 37–39.

Taw Daw Shin (Rangoon). 1971. "25 Years Journey of the Burma Broadcasting Service." February, pp. 2–8.

Telecommunication Journal (Geneva). 1972a. "Technical Co-operation in Telecommunications in 1970." February, pp. 75–84.

—————. 1972b. "Activities of the ITU Regional Experts under the UNDP Technical Assistance Component in 1971." November, pp. 651–58.

—————. 1972c. "Editorial: The Regional Offices and the New Procedures of UNDP." December, pp. 705–06.

Television Factbook. Annual. Washington, D.C.: Television Digest Incorporated.

Television/Radio Age. 1973. "TV Facilities of 'Developing' Nations Just Scratch Surface." 29 October, pp. 36, 63.

Teo, Peter. 1973. "Getting Ready for Colour TV in Singapore." *Sunday Mail* (Kuala Lumpur), 10 June, p. 12.

Thai, Nguyen. 1963. " 'News' in Vietnam a Case of Underdeveloped Freedom to Know." *Nieman Reports* 16 (March): 19–21.

Thien, Nghiem Xuan. 1970. "Observations on the Press of South Vietnam and Its New Press Regulations." Prepared for International Journalism Seminar, Southern Illinois University, Carbondale.

This Is NHK. 1972. Tokyo: Nippon Hoso Kyokai.

Thompson, J.G. 1975. "Thai Broadcasting." *Far Eastern Economic Review* (Hong Kong), 28 March, p. 6.

Thompson, Marion E. 1971. "A Study of International Television Programming within the Structure of Global Communications." Ph.D. dissertation, University of Wisconsin.

Thomson, George G. 1974. "Communication's Tasks in a City State: Singapore's Unique Experience." *Media Asia* (Singapore) 1, no. 1: 23–30.

Three Years of Radio Pakistan 1947–50. 1950. Karachi: Radio Pakistan.

Tobias, Mel C. 1975. "In Hong Kong, Reshuffle at RTV and Government Investigation of TVB." *Variety* (New York), 9 July, p. 47.

Toeplitz, Jerzy. 1975. "A Film School: Not Least in Australia's Screen Planning." *Variety* (New York), 1 January.

Toogood, Alexander. 1968. "The Development, Structure, and Function of Television Broadcasting in New Zealand: The First Seven Years of a Government's Monopolistic System." Masters thesis, University of North Carolina.

——————. 1969–70. "New Zealand Broadcasting: A Monopoly in Action." *Journal of Broadcasting* (Philadelphia) 14 (Winter): 13–24.

Topuz, Hifzi. 1968. "UNESCO and the Training of Journalists." *UNESCO Chronicle*, November, pp. 419–24.

——————. 1970. "UNESCO and the News Agencies." *UNESCO Chronicle*, December, pp. 501–54.

Tudor, Judy, ed. 1966. *The Handbook of Papua and New Guinea.* 5th ed. Sydney: Pacific Publications Ltd.

——————. 1968. *Pacific Islands Yearbook and Who's Who.* Sydney: Pacific Publications Ltd.

TV Advertising: Standards and Practices. 1971. Karachi: Pakistan Television Corporation Ltd.

TV Guide. 1967. "Television on the Wing." 11 February.

25 Years of Pakistan in Statistics 1947–72. 1972. Karachi: Manager of Publications, Government of Pakistan.

Twenty Years of Pakistan 1947–67. 1967. *Karachi: Pakistan Publications.*

UNESCO (United Nations Educational, Scientific and Cultural Organization). Annual. *Statistical Yearbook.* Paris: UNESCO.

——————. 1960. *Developing Mass Media in Asia.* Report no. 30. Paris: UNESCO.

——————. 1961. *Mass Media in the Developing Countries.* Report no. 3. Paris: UNESCO.

——————. 1964. *World Communications: Press, Radio, Television, Film.* Paris: UNESCO.

——————. 1967a. *New Educational Media in Action: Case Studies for Planners.* 3 vols. Paris: UNESCO.

——————. 1967b. *Radio and Television in the Service of Education and Development in Asia.* Report no. 49. Paris: UNESCO.

——————. 1969. "Seminar on Mass Media and National Family Planning Programmes." Mimeographed. Paris: UNESCO.

——————. 1970a. "Educational Broadcasting in Indonesia." Serial no. MC/3200/2408. Paris: UNESCO.

——————. 1970b. *Mass Media in Society: The Need for Research.* Report no. 59. Paris: UNESCO.

——————. 1975. *World Communications: A 200 Country Survey of Press, Radio, Television, Film.* New York: Unipub.

UNESCO Chronicle. 1970. "Satellite to Serve World Communication Needs." 16, no. 2 (February): 53–59.

· ——————. 1971. "Television Co-Productions." 17, no. 2 (February): 70.

Union of Burma, Revolutionary Council. 1966. *Report to the People by the Union of Burma Revolutionary Council on the Revolutionary Government's Budget Estimates for 1966–67.* Rangoon: Revolutionary Council.

Union of Korean Journalists. 1971. "The 25th Anniversary of the Union of Korean Journalists." *The Democratic Journalist* (Prague), no. 5.

USIA (United States Information Agency). 1960a. "Basic Communication Habits of Thai Students." Mimeographed. Bangkok: USIS.

——————. 1960b. *Radio Listening and Media Habits in Burma.* Bangkok: USIS.

——————. 1961. "Basic Communication Habits: Government Officials." Mimeographed. Bangkok: USIS.

_____. 1966. "Communication Fact Book: Burma." Mimeographed. Washington, D.C.: USIA.

_____. 1970. "U.S. Senate Sub-Committee on Foreign Relations Briefing Books and Documents." Mimeographed. Saigon and Washington, D.C.: USIA, Southeast Asia and Pacific Area.

_____. Voice of America. 1970a. "International Broadcasting in VOA Languages." Mimeographed. Washington, D.C.: USIA, VOA.

_____. 1970b. "Summary of Activities." Mimeographed. Washington, D.C.: USIA, VOA.

Variety (New York). 1966. "Need Nielsen to Count Vietcong Eavesdropper on Ky's ETV Weapon." 14 December.

_____. 1974a. "Aussie Cabinet Nixes Plan for Government Pool on TV Program Buys." 2 January, p. 30.

_____. 1974b. "TV 13, Prod. Center a Merger in Manila." 2 January, p. 30.

_____. 1975a. "Aussie's Channel 9 to Spend Record Budget on Major Shows." 29 January, p. 55.

_____. 1975b. "Japanese TV Cuts Back Features as Oil Crisis Reduces Airtime." 5 February, p. 62.

_____. 1975c. "Philippine Film Industry Heartened as TV Slows." 12 February, p. 47.

_____. 1975d. "TV Cutback Fever in the Philippines." 12 February, p. 58.

_____. 1975e. "TV in Japan Overcomes That Oriental Reticence When It Comes to Sex." 12 February, p. 56.

_____. 1975f. "Pakistan TV Raising License Fees to Cover Three Stations' Costs." 2 April, p. 52.

_____. 1975g. "Saleless Aussies Urge Curb on U.S., U.K. Shows." 7 May, p. 326.

_____. 1975h. "Show Business in the Far East: Broadcasting." 14 May, pp. 110–16.

_____. 1975i. "Propose Killing of License Fees on Cheap Radio Sets as Aid to Rurals in India." 25 June.

_____. 1975j. "India's AIR Looks Like All-Indira Radio." 2 July, p. 45.

_____. 1975k. "Newsmen of TV Webs Pull Ruse on India to Beat Censor Rap." 16 July, p. 1.

_____. 1975m. "Philippines See Domsat by 1976." 8 October, p. 44.

Vidura (New Delhi). 1974a. "SITE's Target Areas." April, pp. 540–44.

_____. 1974b. "Will SITE Be of Real Use?" April, p. 526.

_____. 1974c. "SITE: Whistling in the Dark." August, p. 675.

Wall Street Journal. 1964. "South Vietnam Studies Plan for TV Network to Help Unify Nation." 9 June.

_____. 1966. "NBC Agrees to Help South Vietnam Build a Television Network." 1 July.

Wang, Steve Hwa-Kai. 1971. "Development of Broadcasting in Taiwan (1949–70)." Masters thesis, Brigham Young University.

Washingtin Post Service. 1972. "The Ripples Reach North Korea." 2 April.

Watts, Frank. 1970. "Australia's 'School of the Air.'" *EBU Review* (Geneva) 121B (May): 32.

Watts, Kenneth. 1974. "Analysis of the Success of 'A Big Country.'" *COMBROAD* (London), October–December, pp. 40–41.

Wavell, Stewart. 1969. *The Art of Radio, A CBC Training Manual.* Colombo: Ceylon Broadcasting Corporation.

Wederell, Denis. 1973. "New Zealand: Media Mishap." *Far Eastern Economic Review* (Hong Kong), 22 October.

_____. 1974a. "New Zealand: Kirk and the Media: An Encore." *Far Eastern*

Economic Review (Hong Kong), 8 July, p. 23.

————. 1974b. "New Zealand's Year of Poor Reception." *Far Eastern Economic Review* (Hong Kong), 29 November.

Weinrab, Bernard. 1967. "Music Censorship." *New York Times,* 27 August.

Wen Chi-tse. 1950. "A Survey of the People's Broadcasting Affairs in China." *Jen-min Jih-pao* (Peking), 1 February.

————. 1955. "People's Broadcasting during the Past Ten Years." *Hsin-hua Yueh-pao* (New China Monthly), no. 72 (October): 232–33.

Wentz, James E. 1969. "American Forces Vietnam Network, Audience Opinion Research and Analysis." Saigon, January.

White, Graham. 1972. "Rural Broadcasting in Australia." *EBU Review* (Geneva) 23, no. 3 (May): 19.

White, Peter T. 1971. "Mosaic of Cultures." *National Geographic,* March, p. 329.

Whiting, Gordon C. 1971. "The Development Role of Mass Media in Afghanistan." Prepared for Annual Convention, Association for Education in Journalism, Columbia, South Carolina.

Whymant, Robert. 1975. "Japanese Complain about Programs, Pay TV Fees without a Murmur." *Philadelphia Inquirer,* 5 April, p. 19–B.

Wilford, J.N. 1969. "For India's Villages, Education by TV." *New York Times,* 28 September, science section.

Wilson, David. 1962. *Politics in Thailand.* Ithaca, N.Y.: Cornell University Press.

————. 1967. "China, Thailand and the Spirit of Bandung." *China Quarterly,* April–June, pp. 103–5.

Wilson, Michael. 1972. "Annual Report, Educational Broadcasting: Period of Report 15 November 1971–31 December 1972." Mimeographed. Kabul: UNESCO.

————. 1973. "Semi-Annual Report Educational Broadcasting: Period of Report 1 January 1973–30 June 1973." Mimeographed. Kabul: UNESCO.

Wingomint, Porntip. 1970. "The Influence of Entertainment Films on Vocational Students' Behavior." Masters thesis, Chulalongkorn University (Bangkok).

Wisconsin State Journal. 1966. "Passport Is Cancelled on Yank Broadcaster." 9 March.

————. 1968. "Saigon Bill Aimed at Newsmen." 18 May.

————. 1973. "North Viet Radio Station Says Bombs Halt Broadcast." 22 January.

Wood, Richard. 1969. *Shortwave Voices of the World.* Park Ridge, N.J.: Gilfer Associates.

Woon, Doris. 1974. "Language Learning and ETV in Singapore." *Educational Broadcasting International* (London), March, pp. 17–21.

Working People's Daily (Rangoon). 1966. 21 August, p. 1.

————. 1969. 17 May, p. 1.

————. 1970a. 26 April, p. 1.

————. 1970b. 27 June, p. 1.

————. 1970c. 20 August, p. 1.

WRTH (World Radio & TV Handbook). Annual. Ed. J.M. Frost. New York: Billboard Publications.

Yamaguchi, Hideo, and Ishizaka, Kyu. 1972. "A History of Broadcasting in Okinawa." *The NHK Report on Broadcasting Research* (Tokyo), April, pp. 37–44.

Yang Chao-lin. 1959a. "Live Broadcast of Athletic Events." *Hsin-wen Chan-hsien* (News Front), no. 6, pp. 8–11.

————. 1959b. "Study of the Problem of Improving the Style of Broadcasts." *Hsin-wen Chan-hsien* (News Front) 20 (October): 22.

Yearbook on Chinese Communism. Annual. Taipei: Institute for the Study of Chinese Communist Affairs.

Yeh Hui. 1966. "A Television Cameraman in South Vietnam." *China Reconstructs* (Hong Kong), June, pp. 8–11.

Yeh Kuang-chien. 1967 "The Confusion of the Provincial Radio Broadcasting Stations."

China Monthly (Hong Kong) 35 (February): 58.

Yu, Frederick. 1964. *Mass Persuasion in Communist China.* New York: Frederick A. Praeger.

——————. 1970. "Persuasive Communications during the Cultural Revolution (I)." *Gazette* (Deventer) 16, no. 2.

Yung I. 1959. "The Peking Broadcast College; A New Base for the Training of Broadcast Cadre." *Hsin-wen Chan-hsien* (News Front), no. 21, pp. 28–29.

Yung Shen. 1969. "Development of the Chinese Communist Wired Broadcasting System in Rural Areas." *Studies on Chinese Communism* (Taipei) 3, no. 6 (June): 74.

Yu Shiu. 1959. "Broadcasting Must Serve the Continuing Leap Forward of the Industrial and Agricultural Production." *Hsin-wen Chan-hsien* (News Front), no. 22, p. 10.

Yu Yu-hsiu. 1963. "Radio in the Villages." *China Reconstructs* (Hong Kong), April, pp. 11–13.

Zaidi, Wiqar H. 1969. "Effectiveness of Communication Strategy for Family Planning Information in West Pakistan." *Pakistan Journal of Family Planning,* January, pp. 35–44.

Zaman, Rafe-uz. 1974. "Developing ETV for Social Education in Pakistan." *Educational Broadcasting International* (London), June, pp. 69–72.

Index